ASP.NET Cookbook™

Other Microsoft .NET resources from O'Reilly

Related titles
Programming ASP.NET
ASP.NET in a Nutshell
Programming .NET Web
   Services
.NET Framework Essentials
.NET and XML

C# Language Pocket
   Reference
Programming C#
C# in a Nutshell
C# Cookbook
Learning C#
C# Essentials

**.NET Books
Resource Center**
dotnet.oreilly.com is a complete catalog of O'Reilly's books on .NET and related technologies, including sample chapters and code examples.

ONDotnet.com provides independent coverage of fundamental, interoperable, and emerging Microsoft .NET programming and web services technologies.

Conferences
O'Reilly brings diverse innovators together to nurture the ideas that spark revolutionary industries. We specialize in documenting the latest tools and systems, translating the innovator's knowledge into useful skills for those in the trenches. Visit *conferences.oreilly.com* for our upcoming events.

Safari Bookshelf (*safari.oreilly.com*) is the premier online reference library for programmers and IT professionals. Conduct searches across more than 1,000 books. Subscribers can zero in on answers to time-critical questions in a matter of seconds. Read the books on your Bookshelf from cover to cover or simply flip to the page you need. Try it today with a free trial.

ASP.NET Cookbook™

Michael A. Kittel and Geoffrey T. LeBlond

O'REILLY®

Beijing · Cambridge · Farnham · Köln · Paris · Sebastopol · Taipei · Tokyo

ASP.NET Cookbook™
by Michael A. Kittel and Geoffrey T. LeBlond

Copyright © 2004 O'Reilly Media, Inc. All rights reserved.
Printed in the United States of America.

Published by O'Reilly Media, Inc., 1005 Gravenstein Highway North, Sebastopol, CA 95472.

O'Reilly books may be purchased for educational, business, or sales promotional use. Online editions are also available for most titles (*safari.oreilly.com*). For more information, contact our corporate/institutional sales department: (800) 998-9938 or *corporate@oreilly.com*.

Editor:	John Osborn
Production Editor:	Genevieve d'Entremont
Cover Designer:	Emma Colby
Interior Designer:	Melanie Wang

Printing History:

August 2004:	First Edition.

Nutshell Handbook, the Nutshell Handbook logo, and the O'Reilly logo are registered trademarks of O'Reilly Media, Inc. The *Cookbook* series designations, *ASP.NET Cookbook*, the image of a thorny woodcock, and related trade dress are trademarks of O'Reilly Media, Inc.

Intellisense, ActiveX, JScript, Microsoft, Visual Basic, Visual C++, Visual Studio, Windows, and Windows NT are registered trademarks, and Visual C# is a trademark of Microsoft Corporation. Java™ and all Java-based trademarks and logos are trademarks or registered trademarks of Sun Microsystems, Inc., in the United States and other countries. Many of the designations used by manufacturers and sellers to distinguish their products are claimed as trademarks. Where those designations appear in this book, and O'Reilly Media, Inc. was aware of a trademark claim, the designations have been printed in caps or initial caps.

While every precaution has been taken in the preparation of this book, the publisher and authors assume no responsibility for errors or omissions, or for damages resulting from the use of the information contained herein.

 This book uses RepKover™, a durable and flexible lay-flat binding.

ISBN: 0-596-00378-1
[M]

Table of Contents

Preface ix

1. **Tabular Data** 1
   1.1 Selecting the Right Tabular Control   1
   1.2 Generating a Quick-and-Dirty Tabular Display   3
   1.3 Enhancing the Output of a Tabular Display   9
   1.4 Displaying Data from an XML File   16
   1.5 Displaying an Array as a Group of Checkboxes   23
   1.6 Displaying Data from a Hashtable   28
   1.7 Adding Next/Previous Navigation to a DataGrid   33
   1.8 Adding First/Last Navigation to a DataGrid   42
   1.9 Adding Direct Page Navigation to a DataGrid   52
   1.10 Paging Through a Record-Heavy DataGrid   61
   1.11 Sorting Data Within a DataGrid   75
   1.12 Sorting Data in Ascending/Descending Order Within a DataGrid   85
   1.13 Combining Sorting and Paging in a DataGrid   97
   1.14 Editing Data Within a DataGrid   108
   1.15 Formatting Columnar Data in a DataGrid   121
   1.16 Allowing Selection Anywhere Within a DataGrid Row   129
   1.17 Adding a Delete Confirmation Pop Up   141
   1.18 Displaying a Pop-Up Details Window   152
   1.19 Adding a Totals Row to a DataGrid   167

2. **Validation** 179
   2.1 Requiring that Data be Entered in a Field   180
   2.2 Requiring Data to Be In a Range   188
   2.3 Requiring that Two Data Input Fields Match   195

2.4 Requiring that Data Matches a Predefined Pattern   200

2.5 Requiring that a Drop-Down List Selection Be Made   206

2.6 Requiring Data to Match a Database Entry   218

3. Forms **227**

3.1 Using the Enter Key to Submit a Form   227

3.2 Using the Enter Key to Submit a Form After Validation   238

3.3 Submitting a Form to a Different Page   248

3.4 Simulating Multipage Forms   259

3.5 Setting the Initial Focus to a Specific Control   269

3.6 Setting the Focus to a Control with a Validation Error   278

4. User Controls **281**

4.1 Sharing a Page Header on Multiple Pages   281

4.2 Creating a Customizable Navigation Bar   290

4.3 Reusing Code-Behind Classes   302

4.4 Communicating Between User Controls   303

4.5 Adding User Controls Dynamically   314

5. Custom Controls **322**

5.1 Combining HTML Controls in a Single Custom Control   323

5.2 Creating a Custom Control with Attributes   329

5.3 Creating a Custom Control with State   337

5.4 Customizing an ASP.NET TextBox Server Control   358

6. Maintaining State **366**

6.1 Maintaining Information Needed by All Users of an Application   367

6.2 Maintaining Information about a User Throughout a Session   376

6.3 Preserving Information Between Postbacks   388

6.4 Preserving Information Across Multiple Requests for a Page   395

7. Error Handling **416**

7.1 Handling Errors at the Method Level   417

7.2 Handling Errors at the Page Level   423

7.3 Handling Errors at the Application Level   427

7.4 Displaying User-Friendly Error Messages   434

8. Security **442**

8.1 Restricting Access to All Application Pages   443

8.2 Restricting Access to Selected Application Pages   455

8.3 Restricting Access to Application Pages by Role   459

8.4 Using Windows Authentication   474

9. Configuration **483**

9.1 Overriding Default HTTP Runtime Parameters in web.config   485

9.2 Adding Custom Application Settings in web.config   487

9.3 Displaying Custom Error Messages   491

9.4 Maintaining Session State Across Multiple Web Servers   493

9.5 Accessing Other web.config Configuration Elements   498

9.6 Adding Your Own Configuration Elements to web.config   504

10. Tracing and Debugging **520**

10.1 Uncovering Page-Level Problems   521

10.2 Uncovering Problems Application Wide   526

10.3 Pinpointing the Cause of an Exception   528

10.4 Uncovering Problems Within Web Application Components   534

10.5 Uncovering Problems Within Dual-Use Components   542

10.6 Writing Trace Data to the Event Log with Controllable Levels   552

10.7 Using a Breakpoint to Stop Execution of an Application When a Condition Is Met   559

10.8 Stress Testing a Web Application or Service   561

11. Web Services **564**

11.1 Creating a Web Service   564

11.2 Consuming a Web Service   572

11.3 Creating a Web Service That Returns a Custom Object   579

11.4 Setting the URL of a Web Service at Runtime   601

12. Dynamic Images **605**

12.1 Drawing Button Images on the Fly   605

12.2 Creating Bar Charts on the Fly   618

12.3 Displaying Images Stored in a Database   625

12.4 Displaying Thumbnail Images   636

13. Caching **648**

13.1 Caching Pages   648

13.2 Caching Pages Based on Query String Parameter Values   650

13.3 Caching Pages Based on Browser Type and Version   651

13.4 Caching Pages Based on Developer-Defined Custom Strings   653

13.5 Caching User Controls   655

13.6 Caching Application Data   656

14. Internationalization **663**

14.1 Localizing Request/Response Encoding   663

14.2 Providing Multiple Language Support   665

14.3 Overriding Currency Formatting   675

15. File Operations **677**

15.1 Downloading a File from the Web Server   677

15.2 Uploading a File to the Web Server   685

15.3 Processing an Uploaded File Without Storing It on the Filesystem   692

15.4 Storing the Contents of an Uploaded File in a Database   700

16. Performance **704**

16.1 Reducing Page Size by Selectively Disabling the ViewState   705

16.2 Speeding up String Concatenation with a StringBuilder   719

16.3 Speeding Up Read-Only Data Access   724

16.4 Speeding Up Data Access to a SQL Server Database Using the SQL Provider   733

17. HTTP Handlers **739**

17.1 Creating a Reusable Image Handler   740

17.2 Creating a File Download Handler   754

18. Assorted Tips **763**

18.1 Accessing HTTP-Specific Information from Within a Class   763

18.2 Executing External Applications   766

18.3 Transforming XML to HTML   768

18.4 Determining the User's Browser Type   775

18.5 Dynamically Creating Browser-Specific Stylesheets   780

18.6 Saving and Reusing HTML Output   790

18.7 Sending Mail   795

18.8 Creating and Using Page Templates   801

Index **817**

Preface

What This Book Is About

This book is a collection of ASP.NET recipes that aims to help you quickly and efficiently solve many of the day-to-day problems you face developing web applications with the .NET platform. Our recipes run the gamut from simple coding techniques to more comprehensive development strategies that even the most experienced ASP. NET programmers will savor.

More than a compilation of tips and tricks, the *ASP.NET Cookbook* solves real-world programming problems and is rooted in our experience as professional programmers who have designed and built richly functional web-based projects for a variety of corporate clients. We think we know the kinds of problems that you face, and we aim to help you solve them.

The *ASP.NET Cookbook* also contains dozens of code examples ranging from relatively simple 10-liners to comprehensive multipage solutions. Without solid and complete working examples, it's difficult to make an informed decision about whether an approach is the right one, or whether you should be looking elsewhere. We are convinced that reading good example code is the best path to understanding any development platform, so we've included lots of it and commented our listings generously to help you follow the logic.

The *ASP.NET Cookbook* is written in classic O'Reilly cookbook style to focus directly on problems you face today or are likely to face in the future. Using a problem-and-solution format, we make it easy for you to skim for a near match to your particular problem. We have pared down the headings to a bare minimum so you can quickly assess whether a recipe is pertinent.

Many of us occasionally browse through cookbooks looking for new recipe ideas or exploring the nuances of a culinary style. Similarly, we hope you find this book sufficiently interesting to browse, because in many respects it is as much about software techniques and methodology as it is about ASP.NET. For example, we offer a full course of error-handling recipes because we believe the topic is important to our audience and there just isn't enough information about it in general circulation. We could have restricted our discussion to page-level error handling, but that seems inadequate to us. Instead, we prefer to help you deal with error handling at the application level, a more difficult subject but ultimately more useful to serious developers. We have already done the heavy lifting on this and many other important subjects so that you don't have to.

From our point of view, the complexity of web-based development projects is now equal to that of traditional large-scale software development where teams of specialists—architects, developers, project managers, designers, and the like—carry out a thoroughgoing development process. This is certainly not news to the many professional developers and others who have been working on Internet team development projects since early DARPA-NET days. What is new is that ASP.NET (and .NET in general) raises the bar for those in the Microsoft camp who consider themselves professional Internet developers but have yet to suffer the slings and arrows of improperly checked-in code, lack of coordination between designers and programmers, drifting project focus, mismanaged risks, and the host of other distractions that team development can bring.

The increased complexity of web projects has direct ramifications in our ASP.NET coding techniques and the organization of this book, and leads directly to some of the recommendations we make. For instance, we believe strongly in using the code-behind feature of ASP.NET to separate server-side code from the user presentation (HTML and content), because this approach allows developers, web designers, and information architects to work independently and concentrate on what each does best. Thus, every recipe we offer consistently splits the code and UI into separate files. There's a small price to pay for the reader who is attempting to decipher the relationship between the two and might prefer to see them bunched together for sake of readability, but we think their separation is worth the price. This approach also supports team development, where the separation of code and content is absolutely essential to good development practice.

Code reuse is another practice that we hold near and dear, and we've gone to some lengths to illustrate its application in ASP.NET. For example, Chapter 4, *User Controls*, includes a recipe that shows how to reuse a code-behind class with another *.aspx* file to provide a different user interface. This is done without any additional coding. As another example, Chapter 3, *Forms*, includes a recipe that sets the focus to a specific control when a page is first loaded, something that could easily have been accomplished by including some simple JavaScript in the page's HTML. However, we take a different tack by programmatically generating JavaScript client-side code. The reason stems from the type of development work we do, where we are constantly under the gun to quickly generate high-quality code, the ultimate in "short-order cooking." As such, we are constantly looking for ways to reuse code. By creating a forms library, complete with custom classes that can programmatically generate JavaScript, we are able to build custom forms with a few calls to the library. It's an approach that has proven highly successful for us, and we felt it was important to provide you a glimpse of it. This is just one of many "reuse-oriented" approaches that you'll find in this book.

Who This Book Is For

This book is for journeyman programmers who already know the basics of ASP. That said, we're confident that novice ASP.NET programmers also will find a home here, provided you have done some ASP and VB or C# programming and are willing to invest time in closely studying our code.

Because this book is not a complete reference for ASP.NET, it is unlikely to appeal to you if you have merely dabbled in ASP.NET up to this point. You will be better served by first reading a general introduction to ASP.NET programming, such as *ASP.NET in a Nutshell*, by G. Andrew Duthie and Matthew MacDonald (O'Reilly), or *Programming ASP.NET*, by Jesse Liberty and Dan Hurwitz (O'Reilly), where topics are dosed out in measured spoonfuls. After you have mastered the basics, you'll be ready to read this book. We encourage you to look to a general reference or to the MSDN Library when you have routine questions about ASP.NET.

How This Book Is Organized

This book is organized into 18 chapters, each of which focuses on a distinct ASP.NET topic area.

Chapter 1, *Tabular Data*
> In its simplest form, displaying tabular data is easy in ASP.NET. Drop in an ASP.NET grid control, connect to the database, and bind it to the control—simple enough. But it doesn't take long before you realize that the default appearance and behavior of the control is lacking. Indeed, you may even find that the control you've chosen is too bulky, too slow, or just plain confusing when it comes to adding to or modifying its behavior. This chapter will help you make a well-informed decision about which control to use, and then provides you with some recipes to solve common development problems as you adapt it to your liking.

Chapter 2, *Validation*
> This chapter provides recipes that perform a number of data validation tasks, such as ensuring that the data a user enters is within a defined range or conforms to a specific data type. Other validation recipes show how to ensure that the data entered by the user matches a specific pattern or an entry in a database. You'll also learn how to ensure that the user selects an entry in a drop-down list.

Chapter 3, *Forms*
> The solutions in this chapter provide a series of non-obvious solutions for working with forms. For example, rather than requiring that the user always click a Submit button in order to send the information on a form to the server, you'll learn how to support the Enter key as well. Another recipe shows how to submit a form to a page that is different than the current page, which is handy when you want to, for example, have one page that collects form data and a second page

that processes it. Still another shows how to create what appears from the users' perspective as a multipage form but which is actually a series of panels that simulate "virtual" pages, a useful technique when you want to keep all of your code in one cohesive unit. Finally, you'll learn how to set the focus to a specific control when a page is first loaded, an easy solution for JavaScript but one that is slightly more complicated (and ultimately more useful) when you focus on code reuse.

Chapter 4, *User Controls*

User controls are a way of encapsulating other controls and code into reusable packages. This chapter shows some ways to use these extraordinary time- and work-savers to share the same header across multiple pages, display a navigation bar that appears "customized" on each page simply by setting properties, and reuse identical code-behind classes within different pages while changing the user presentation in the process. Still another recipe shows how to communicate between user controls using event delegates, a technique that is handy, for example, when you want an action taken with one control to affect multiple other controls. The final recipe in this chapter shows how to programmatically load a user control at runtime, which allows you to customize web page content based on a user's selection.

Chapter 5, *Custom Controls*

The recipes in this chapter center on custom controls, for which you can build your own user interface and add your own backend functionality through the methods, properties, and events that you implement for the controls. For instance, one recipe shows how to combine two or more controls into a single custom control. Another recipe shows how to create a custom control that has HTML-style attributes, which can be handy for customizing the control when it is used in a page. There's also a recipe for creating a custom control that maintains state between postbacks, like the server controls in ASP.NET. Still another recipe shows how to customize an ASP.NET TextBox server control to allow only numeric input.

Chapter 6, *Maintaining State*

The recipes in this chapter are all about maintaining state at the application, session, and page levels, all for the purpose of improving the user's experience. For instance, one recipe shows you how to maintain information needed by all users of an application by placing it in the Application object. Another shows how to maintain information about a user throughout a session, the advantage here being that you avoid accessing the database each time the data is needed. Another recipe shows how to preserve small amounts of information on a page between postbacks, which is useful when a page has multiple states and it needs to remember the current state value between postbacks to display properly. Still another recipe shows you how to persist complex object information between requests for a page, a useful technique when the page itself is complex and you don't want to use a database to preserve the information.

Chapter 7, *Error Handling*

This chapter covers error handling at different levels of granularity. For example, one recipe shows how to provide robust error handling in methods by taking best advantage of .NET structured exception handling for dealing with errors. A page-level error-handling recipe shows you how to trap any error that occurs on a page and then, using a page-level event handler, redirect the user to another page that displays information about the problem. Yet another recipe shows how to handle errors at the application level to log the error information and perform a redirect to a common error page. The final recipe shows how to log detailed messages for debugging but display friendly messages to the user.

Chapter 8, *Security*

Security can be handled in many different ways and at many different levels in ASP.NET, and this chapter provides recipes that delve into some of the most common solutions. For instance, the first two recipes show you how to use Forms authentication to restrict access to all or only some pages of an application. Another recipe shows you how to restrict access to pages by the user's role. There is also a recipe that shows you how to use Windows authentication, which is useful when all users have accounts on your LAN.

Chapter 9, *Configuration*

The recipes in this chapter deal with how to configure your applications. For instance, one recipe shows you how to change the default HTTP runtime settings in *web.config* as a way to familiarize yourself with this file, its contents, and its purpose. Another recipe shows you how to add your own custom application settings to *web.config* (by adding an <appSettings> element). Still another shows you how to display custom error messages by adding a <customErrors> element to *web.config*. Configuring your application to maintain session state across multiple web servers is the focus of another recipe; this is useful because it shows how to activate the ASP.NET State Service and make the attendant modifications to the *web.config* file. Another recipe shows you how to read configuration data from something other than the <appSettings> element of *web.config* (by reading the contents of *web.config* into an XmlDocument object), a technique that is enormously useful when you need it but, surprisingly, is not covered anywhere in the ASP.NET documentation. The chapter's final recipe covers how to add your own configuration elements to *web.config*, which is valuable when the predefined configuration elements provided by ASP.NET are not enough.

Chapter 10, *Tracing and Debugging*

The recipes in this chapter will help you make sure that your applications work as anticipated in their first release. For example, one recipe shows you how to identify the source of page-level problems, such as a slowly performing page. Another shows you how to use tracing to identify problems application-wide without having to modify every page or disrupt output. Still another shows you how to dynamically turn on page tracing to pinpoint the cause of an exception error. Identifying problems within web application components is addressed by another recipe. A follow-on recipe shows you how to identify problems within dual use (non-web-specific) components, which requires a slightly different approach to avoid breaking the component when it is used outside ASP.NET applications. The final few recipes deal with writing trace data to the event log, using a breakpoint to peer into an application when a condition is met, and stress testing a web application.

Chapter 11, *Web Services*

XML web services are *the* marquee feature of .NET, and the recipes in this chapter will help you create and consume them. You will also find a recipe for creating a web service that returns a custom object, a handy approach when none of the .NET data types meets your needs. Still another recipe shows you how to control the URL of a web service at runtime.

Chapter 12, *Dynamic Images*

When working with a creative design team, you may run into the situation where a design uses images for buttons but the button labels need to be dynamic. A recipe in this chapter will show you how to deal with this situation with aplomb by drawing button images on the fly. Another recipe shows you how to create bar charts on the fly from dynamic data. Displaying images stored in a database is the focus of another recipe; it shows you how to read an image from the database, and then stream it to the browser. The final recipe in the chapter shows you how to display a page of images in thumbnail format.

Chapter 13, *Caching*

ASP.NET provides the ability to cache the output of pages or portions of pages in memory, to reduce latency and make your applications more responsive. If pages are completely static, it's a simple decision to cache them. But if the pages change as a function of query string values or are dynamically created from a database, the decision to cache is not so straightforward. The recipes in this chapter will help you sort through these issues. An additional recipe delves into caching pages based on the browser type and version. A follow-on recipe discusses how to cache pages based on your own custom strings, which gives you, for example, the ability to cache a page based on the browser type, the major version (integer portion of the version number), and the minor version (the decimal portion of the version number). The last two recipes show you how to cache user controls and application data.

Chapter 14, *Internationalization*

The recipes in this chapter show you the basics of how to internationalize your applications. For instance, the first recipe shows you the necessary *web.config* settings to inform the browser of the character set to use when rendering the application's pages. Another recipe shows you how to support multiple languages in an application without having to develop multiple versions of pages. The final recipe shows you how to override currency formatting, which can be handy, for example, when you want all the text displayed in the user's language but currency values displayed in a specific format, such as U.S. dollars.

Chapter 15, *File Operations*

The recipes in this chapter focus on how to download files from and upload files to the web server. There's also a recipe that shows you how to immediately process an uploaded file without storing it on the filesystem, which is handy when you want to avoid the potential pitfalls of uploaded files having the same name or filling the hard drive, or when dealing with the security aspects of allowing ASP.NET write privileges on the local filesystem. The final recipe in the chapter shows you how to store the contents of an uploaded file in a database, which is a useful approach when you want to upload a file to the web server but process it later.

Chapter 16, *Performance*

You will find that performance is a running theme throughout the course of this book. Nevertheless, there are a handful of topics in ASP.NET for which performance bears explicit mention. For instance, as discussed in one recipe, you can often reduce a page's size (and improve a page's performance) by disabling the ViewState for the page or for a set of controls on the page. Another recipe deals with the oft-mentioned topic of using a StringBuilder object instead of the classic string concatenation operators ("&" or "+") to speed up string concatenation. The difference in this recipe is that we give you some tangible measures that will help you understand just how important this approach is and when you can do without it. Another recipe illustrates how to get the best performance out of your application when you are using read-only data access. Still another recipe shows you how to use SQL Server Managed Provider to get the best performance when accessing SQL Server data. Here, again, we give you some tangible measures, and the results are eye-opening.

Chapter 17, *HTTP Handlers*

An HTTP handler is a class that handles requests for a given resource or resource type. For instance, ASP.NET has built-in HTTP handlers that process requests for *.aspx*, *.asmx*, *.ascx*, *.cs*, *.vb*, and other file types. This chapter provides recipes for creating your own custom HTTP handler, which is a useful approach any time you want to handle an HTTP request for a resource on your own. For example, there's a recipe that retrieves image data from a database and sends the image data to a browser. A second recipe shows how to create a file download handler.

Chapter 18, *Assorted Tips*

This chapter contains a handful of assorted recipes that do not fit conveniently into other chapters of the book. There are, for instance, recipes for accessing HTTP-specific information in classes, executing external applications, transforming XML to HTML, determining the user's browser type, dynamically creating browser-specific stylesheets, capturing rendered HTML output, sending mail, and using page templates.

Topics Not Covered

Although *ASP.NET Cookbook*'s coverage is wide-ranging, there are many topics that we do not cover. For instance, we won't teach you the basics of XML. (There are many other books that do a fine job of it, including O'Reilly's *XML in a Nutshell*.) Rather, we assume that you already know the basics of XML, because we use it in many examples throughout the book. Likewise, we apply a similar standard when discussing the fundamentals of object-oriented development and other base-level programming topics.

In a similar vein, we deliberately avoid topics that are interesting but not all that useful in solving day-to-day development problems. For example, Passport authentication is a topic we left out. Although interesting, the use of Passport authentication is not yet widespread, something that will possibly change in the months ahead. Indeed, we have cast away more ideas than we can name, because they seemed somehow "off target" for our audience.

It should also be mentioned that there are many .NET-related topics that are interesting from a programmer's point of view but simply not pertinent to ASP.NET. For instance, working with the .NET process model is a career topic, but a programmer's ability to control it through ASP.NET is limited. As a practical matter, topics of this kind didn't make the cut.

Sample Source Code

The full source code for the recipes in this book can be found at *http://www. dominiondigital.com/AspNetCookbook/*. Samples are provided in VB.NET and C# along with working versions of all the recipes that involve code. The web site will give you all the details on how to download the source code.

Sample Database, Scripts, and Connection Strings

As for the database that is used in the samples, it also can be found at *http://www. dominiondigital.com/AspNetCookbook/*. The database used for all samples is a SQL Server 2000 database.

As you browse the different sample programs throughout the book, you will see that our preferred method of data access is OLE DB. From our experience writing applications for corporate clients, we have learned that many projects start out using SQL Server but migrate to other database servers, such as Oracle or DB2, during the life of the project. By using OLE DB for data access, we gain the necessary layer of abstraction to easily switch database platforms when and if we need to without having to change the underlying source code. Nevertheless, when you know that SQL Server will be your database platform for the long run, you will undoubtedly want to use SQL Provider to improve its performance, and Recipe 16.4 will show you how.

The connection string used in the samples throughout the book is shown next. It designates the server as `localhost`, the database as `ASPNetCookbook`, the database user as `ASPNetCookbook_User`, and the password for the user as `wOrk`. You will need to change these parameters to conform to your database installation.

```
Provider=SQLOLEDB;Data Source=localhost;
Initial Catalog=ASPNetCookbook;
UID=ASPNetCookbook_User;
PWD=wOrk"
```

Do I Need Visual Studio .NET?

You can use any text editor you like when writing ASP.NET applications, and the same applies to the recipes in this book. However, as professional developers, we prefer to use Visual Studio .NET, mainly because it offers a rich design environment and Intellisense. Other advantages include drag-and-drop server controls, integrated debugging, and automatic deployment. To our way of thinking, these advantages make a strong case for using Visual Studio for all your ASP.NET development.

For these reasons, all the recipes in this book have been set up for use with Visual Studio .NET. That said, you can still make use of the code in this book even if you don't have a copy of Visual Studio .NET. (The one exception is in Chapter 11, *Web Services*, where using Visual Studio saves so much time and effort that we elected to gear all of the recipes for this platform.)

The most tangible effect of our gearing the code to Visual Studio .NET is that all the @ Page directives in all the *.aspx* pages in this book have a CodeBehind attribute to identify the source file for the code-behind page, something that Visual Studio does automatically when you create an ASP.NET project. If you are not using Visual Studio .NET, you'll need to substitute an Src attribute for the CodeBehind attribute in each recipe.

For instance, here is a sample of the kind of @ Page directive you'll find in this book:

```
<%@ Page Language="vb" AutoEventWireup="false"
        CodeBehind="QuickAndDirtyDatagridVB.aspx.vb"
        Inherits="QuickAndDirtyDatagridVB"%>
```

And here is how you would modify it when not using Visual Studio .NET:

```
<%@ Page Language="vb" AutoEventWireup="false"
        Src="QuickAndDirtyDatagridVB.aspx.vb"
        Inherits="QuickAndDirtyDatagridVB"%>
```

Web Resources

This section lists web sites and newsgroups that we have found highly useful.

Web Sites

These web sites provide interesting insights into ASP.NET and/or sample code:

- *http://www.4guysfromrolla.com*
- *http://www.andymcm.com/dotnetfaq.htm*
- *http://www.asp.net*
- *http://www.aspalliance.com*
- *http://www.dotnetjunkies.com*
- *http://www.gotdotnet.com*
- *http://www.ibuyspy.com*

Newsgroups

These are some of the newsgroups that we monitor regularly:

- Microsoft DOTNET newsgroups
- *http://discuss.develop.com/advanced-dotnet.html*
- *http://www.aspmessageboard.com*
- *http://www.asplists.com/aspngfreeforall*

 An especially convenient way to see in one view all the messages posted to the Microsoft DOTNET newsgroups is to go to Google Groups (*http://groups.google.com*), choose its Advanced Groups Search feature, and enter "Microsoft.public.dotnet.*" in the Newsgroup text box along with the desired search terms.

Conventions Used in This Book

Throughout this book, we've used the following typographic conventions:

Italic
> This character style is used for emphasis as well as for online items and email addresses. It also indicates the following elements: commands, file extensions, filenames, directory or folder names, and UNC pathnames.

`Constant width`
> Constant width in body text indicates a language construct, such as the names of keywords, constants, variables, attributes, objects, methods, events, controls, and HTML and XML tags.

`Constant width bold`
> This character style is used to call your attention to lines of source code that are especially pertinent in a recipe.

Constant width italic

This character style indicates replaceable variables in examples. The variable that appears in this style is a signal to you that the variable needs to be replaced by contents of your own choosing.

VB Indicates a VB code snippet.

C# Indicates a C# code snippet.

 This icon signifies a tip, suggestion, or general note.

 This icon indicates a warning or caution.

Using Code Examples

This book is here to help you get your job done. In general, you may use the code in this book in your programs and documentation. You do not need to contact us for permission unless you're reproducing a significant portion of the code. For example, writing a program that uses several chunks of code from this book does not require permission. Selling or distributing a CD-ROM of examples from O'Reilly books *does* require permission. Answering a question by citing this book and quoting example code does not require permission. Incorporating a significant amount of example code from this book into your product's documentation *does* require permission.

We appreciate, but do not require, attribution. An attribution usually includes the title, author, publisher, and ISBN. For example: "*ASP.NET Cookbook*, by Michael A. Kittel and Geoffrey T. LeBlond. Copyright 2004 O'Reilly Media, Inc., 0-596-00378-1."

If you feel your use of code examples falls outside fair use or the permission given here, feel free to contact us at *permissions@oreilly.com*.

Comments and Questions

Please address comments and questions concerning this book to the publisher:

O'Reilly Media, Inc.
1005 Gravenstein Highway North
Sebastopol, CA 95472
(800) 998-9938 (in the United States or Canada)
(707) 829-0515 (international/local)
(707) 829-0104 (fax)

There is a web page for this book, which lists errata, examples, or any additional information. You can access this page at:

http://www.dominiondigital.com/AspNetCookbook/Errata.aspx

To comment or ask technical questions about this book, send email to:

bookquestions@oreilly.com

For more information about books, conferences, Resource Centers, and the O'Reilly Network, see the O'Reilly web site at:

http://www.oreilly.com

Acknowledgments

The authors would like to acknowledge our editors at O'Reilly. First, our profound thanks to Ron Petrusha who took us through the early stages of the project, helping us mold the book into the form you see today. But even more to the point, we appreciate Ron's willingness to give us the opportunity to write this book—it simply would not have happened without him. We'd also like to thank John Osborn for shepherding the manuscript through the final stages, giving focus to our often garbled message, reminding us of important details, insisting that we cite examples that would make the connection for the reader, adding things that we'd overlooked, and being a tireless advocate for the O'Reilly cookbook format. John's command of the language is extraordinary, and we now know what it is like to be in the hands of a master editor.

The authors would also like to thank our technical editors: Doug Reilly, Rob Howard, and Bill Hamilton.

The authors would also like to acknowledge the management team at Dominion Digital, Inc. for their consistent support, and their willingness to host the web site for the book.

Finally, and most importantly, we would like to acknowledge the patience and forbearance of our families who spent countless hours without us as we toiled over these pages these many months.

CHAPTER 1

Tabular Data

1.0 Introduction

When it comes to displaying tabular data, ASP.NET can save you a lot of time, provided you play your cards right. If you want to display data from a database in a table and you're not concerned about performance or your ability to control the arrangement of the data items within the display, you can whip up something with the DataGrid control in mere minutes using relatively few lines of code. Alternatively, if you're more inclined to control nearly every aspect of the tabular display, you can shape and mold the template-driven Repeater and DataList controls nearly beyond recognition, and still not step very far outside a well-trodden path. But like everything else in ASP.NET, you have to know where to start and what the trade-offs are. For instance, it's helpful to know how and when the DataGrid control begins to fall short of the mark. That knowledge will save you having to retrace your steps later to implement another tabular control altogether, something we've had to do ourselves at an inopportune moment during a hot project. The recipes in this chapter ought to get you well down the curve with displaying your tabular data and prevent you having to revisit some of our same mistakes.

1.1 Selecting the Right Tabular Control

Problem

You want to use an ASP.NET control to display some data in a tabular format.

Solution

Use a Repeater, DataList, or DataGrid control. Always choose the smallest and fastest control that meets your needs, which invariably will be influenced by other criteria. For example:

If you need a quick and easy solution
    Use a DataGrid.

If you need a lightweight read-only tabular display
> Use a Repeater.

If you need your solution to be small and fast
> Use a Repeater (lightest) or DataList (lighter).

If you want to use a template to customize the appearance of the display
> Choose a Repeater or DataList.

If you want to select rows or edit the contents of a data table
> Choose a DataList or a DataGrid.

If you want built-in support to sort your data by column or paginate its display
> Choose a DataGrid.

Discussion

ASP.NET provides three excellent options for displaying tabular data—Repeater, DataList, and DataGrid—but each comes with trade-offs. For instance, the DataGrid control is particularly versatile, but you can pay a heavy price in terms of performance. On the flip side, the Repeater control is lighter weight, but is for read-only display; if you later decide you need to edit your data, you must rework your code to use the DataList or DataGrid control instead (unless, of course, you want to embark on your own custom coding odyssey).

The impact on performance is due to the fact that ASP.NET creates an actual control for every element of a DataGrid control, even whitespace, which is built as a Literal control. Each of these controls is then responsible for rendering the appropriate HTML output. The DataGrid is, therefore, the heavyweight of the grid control group, because of the server processing required to build the applicable output. The DataList is lighter and the Repeater lighter still.

Table 1-1 summarizes the built-in features supported by the tabular controls and only includes controls that support data binding. (A standard Table control is not included because it does not inherently support data binding, even though individual controls placed in a table can be data bound.) With custom code, there are virtually no limits to what you can do to modify the behavior of these controls.

Table 1-1. Comparative summary of native tabular control features

Feature	Repeater control	DataList control	DataGrid control
Default appearance	None (template driven)	Table	Table
Automatically generates columns from the data source	No	No	Yes
Header can be customized	Yes	Yes	Yes
Data row can be customized	Yes	Yes	Yes
Supports alternating row customization	Yes	Yes	Yes
Supports customizable row separator	Yes	Yes	No

Feature	Repeater control	DataList control	DataGrid control
Footer can be customized	Yes	Yes	Yes
Supports pagination	No	No	Yes
Supports sorting	No	No	Yes
Supports editing contents	No	Yes	Yes
Supports selecting a single row	No	Yes	Yes
Supports selecting multiple rows	No	No	No
Supports arranging data items horizontally or vertically (from left-to-right or top-to-bottom)	No	Yes	No

Performance issues aside, there are some other aspects to consider when choosing a tabular control. As a general rule, the DataGrid works extraordinarily well for a quick-and-dirty tabular display (see Recipe 1.2) and for other situations in which you think you'll be reasonably satisfied with its default appearance and behavior. Indeed, because the DataGrid is so versatile, this chapter provides many recipes for modifying and adapting it. However, if you anticipate needing a lot of flexibility in controlling the organization and layout of the tabular display or you do not need to edit or paginate the data, you may want to consider using the DataList or Repeater instead. For example, Recipe 1.3 shows how you can use templates to organize and enhance the output of a tabular display. Take a look at that recipe's output (Figure 1-2) to see what we're driving at. Some up-front planning in this respect can save you considerable time and effort down the road.

1.2 Generating a Quick-and-Dirty Tabular Display

Problem

You want to display data from a database in a table, and you're not overly concerned about performance or your ability to control the arrangement of the data items within the display.

Solution

Use a DataGrid control and bind the data to it.

In the *.aspx* file, add the DataGrid control responsible for displaying the data.

In the code-behind class for the page, use the .NET language of your choice to:

1. Open a connection to the database.
2. Build a query string, and read the desired data from the database.
3. Assign the data source to the DataGrid control and bind it.

Figure 1-1 shows the appearance of a typical DataGrid in a browser. Examples 1-1 through 1-3 show the *.aspx* and VB and C# code-behind files for the application that produces this result.

ASP.NET Cookbook
The Ultimate ASP.NET Code Sourcebook

Quick and Dirty DataGrid With Data From Database (VB)

Title	ISBN	Publisher
.Net Framework Essentials	0-596-00302-1	O'Reilly
Access Cookbook	0-596-00084-7	O'Reilly
ADO: ActiveX Data Objects	1-565-92415-0	O'Reilly
ASP.NET in a Nutshell	0-596-00116-9	O'Reilly
C# Essentials	0-596-00315-3	O'Reilly
C# in a Nutshell	0-596-00181-9	O'Reilly
COM and .Net Component Services	0-596-00103-7	O'Reilly
COM+ Programming with Visual Basic	1-565-92840-7	O'Reilly
Developing ASP Components	1-565-92750-8	O'Reilly
HTML & XHTML: The Definitive Guide	0-596-00026-X	O'Reilly

Figure 1-1. Quick-and-dirty DataGrid output

Discussion

Implementing a simple DataGrid requires very little coding. You must first add a DataGrid tag to the *.aspx* file for your application and set a few of its attributes, as shown in Example 1-1. The DataGrid tag has many attributes you can use to control the creation of a DataGrid object, but only three are required: the id, runat, and AutoGenerateColumns attributes. The id and runat attributes are required by all server controls. When the AutoGenerateColumns attribute is set to True, it causes the DataGrid to automatically create the required columns along with their headings from the data source.

The code required to read the data and bind it to the DataGrid goes into the code-behind class associated with the *.aspx* file, as shown in Example 1-2 (VB) and Example 1-3 (C#). In our example, this code is placed in the Page_Load method, for convenience of illustration. It opens a connection to the database, reads the data from the database using an OleDbCommand and an OleDbDataReader, binds the data reader to the DataGrid control, and then performs the necessary cleanup.

 When using the data reader objects, be sure to close the connection to the database. Failing to close the connection will tie up system resources, because the garbage collector will not close database connections. In addition, be aware that while the data reader is using the database connection, no other operations can be performed with the data connection, other than closing it.

Setting the `AutoGenerateColumns` attribute of a `DataGrid` to `True` is a simple way to format your data, but it has a couple of drawbacks. First, using the attribute causes a column to be created for every column specified in the `Select` statement, so you should be careful to include in the statement only the data you want to see in the `DataGrid`. In other words, use the `SELECT *` statement with caution. Second, the columns you `SELECT` will be given the same names as the columns in the database. You can get around this problem by using the `AS` clause in your `SELECT` statement to rename the columns when the data is read into the data reader.

See Also

For more information on the `DataGrid` control, see *ASP.NET in a Nutshell* and *Programming ASP.NET* (O'Reilly); search for `OleDBCommand` and `OleDbDataReader:` on the MSDN Library; other sources for ADO.NET-specific information are *ADO.NET in a Nutshell* and *ADO.NET Cookbook* (O'Reilly).

Example 1-1. Quick-and-dirty DataGrid (.aspx)

```
<%@ Page Language="vb" AutoEventWireup="false"
        Codebehind="CH01QuickAndDirtyDatagridVB.aspx.vb"
        Inherits="ASPNetCookbook.VBExamples.CH01QuickAndDirtyDatagridVB" %>
<!DOCTYPE HTML PUBLIC "-//W3C//DTD HTML 4.0 Transitional//EN">
<html>
  <head>
    <title>Quick and Dirty Datagrid</title>
    <link rel="stylesheet" href="css/ASPNetCookbook.css">
  </head>
  <body leftmargin="0" marginheight="0" marginwidth="0" topmargin="0">
    <form id="frmData" method="post" runat="server">
      <table width="100%" cellpadding="0" cellspacing="0" border="0">
        <tr>
          <td align="center">
            <img src="images/ASPNETCookbookHeading_blue.gif">
          </td>
        </tr>
        <tr>
          <td class="dividerLine">
            <img src="images/spacer.gif" height="6" border="0"></td>
        </tr>
      </table>
      <table width="90%" align="center" border="0">
        <tr>
          <td><img src="images/spacer.gif" height="10" border="0"></td>
        </tr>
        <tr>
          <td align="center" class="PageHeading">
              Quick and Dirty DataGrid With Data From Database (VB)</td>
        </tr>
        <tr>
          <td><img src="images/spacer.gif" height="10" border="0"></td>
        </tr>
```

Example 1-1. Quick-and-dirty DataGrid (.aspx) (continued)

```
       <tr>
         <td align="center">
           <!-- Minimal datagrid -->
           <asp:DataGrid id="dgQuick"
                         runat="server"
                         BorderColor="000080"
                         BorderWidth="2px"
                         AutoGenerateColumns="True"
                         width="100%" />
         </td>
       </tr>
     </table>
   </form>
 </body>
</html>
```

Example 1-2. Quick-and-dirty DataGrid code-behind (.vb)

```
Option Explicit On
Option Strict On
'-----------------------------------------------------------------------------
'
'   Module Name: CH01QuickAndDirtyDatagridVB.aspx.vb
'
'   Description: This class provides the code behind for
'                CH01QuickAndDirtyDatagridVB.aspx
'
'*****************************************************************************
Imports Microsoft.VisualBasic
Imports System.Configuration
Imports System.Data
Imports System.Data.OleDb

Namespace ASPNetCookbook.VBExamples
  Public Class CH01QuickAndDirtyDatagridVB
    Inherits System.Web.UI.Page

    'controls on form
    Protected dgQuick As System.Web.UI.WebControls.DataGrid

    '*****************************************************************************
    '
    '   ROUTINE: Page_Load
    '
    '   DESCRIPTION: This routine provides the event handler for the page load
    '                event.  It is responsible for initializing the controls
    '                on the page.
    '
    '-----------------------------------------------------------------------------
    Private Sub Page_Load(ByVal sender As System.Object, _
                    ByVal e As System.EventArgs) _
```

Example 1-2. Quick-and-dirty DataGrid code-behind (.vb) (continued)

```
            Handles MyBase.Load
    Dim dbConn As OleDbConnection
    Dim dCmd As OleDbCommand
    Dim dReader As OleDbDataReader
    Dim strConnection As String
    Dim strSQL As String

    If (Not Page.IsPostBack) Then
      Try
        'get the connection string from web.config and open a connection
        'to the database
        strConnection = _
            ConfigurationSettings.AppSettings("dbConnectionString")
        dbConn = New OleDb.OleDbConnection(strConnection)
        dbConn.Open()

        'build the query string and get the data from the database
        strSQL = "SELECT Title, ISBN, Publisher " & _
                "FROM Book " & _
                "ORDER BY Title"
        dCmd = New OleDbCommand(strSQL, dbConn)
        dReader = dCmd.ExecuteReader()

        'set the source of the data for the datagrid control and bind it
        dgQuick.DataSource = dReader
        dgQuick.DataBind()

      Finally
        'cleanup
        If (Not IsNothing(dReader)) Then
          dReader.Close()
        End If

        If (Not IsNothing(dbConn)) Then
          dbConn.Close()
        End If
      End Try
    End If
  End Sub  'Page_Load
  End Class  'CH01QuickAndDirtyDatagridVB
End Namespace
```

Example 1-3. Quick-and-dirty DataGrid code-behind (.cs)

```
//-----------------------------------------------------------------------
//
//   Module Name: CH01QuickAndDirtyDatagridCS.aspx.cs
//
//   Description: This class provides the code behind for
//                CH01QuickAndDirtyDatagridCS.aspx
//
```

Example 1-3. Quick-and-dirty DataGrid code-behind (.cs) (continued)

```
//****************************************************************************
using System;
using System.Configuration;
using System.Data;
using System.Data.OleDb;

namespace ASPNetCookbook.CSExamples
{
  public class CH01QuickAndDirtyDatagridCS : System.Web.UI.Page
  {
    // controls on form
    protected System.Web.UI.WebControls.DataGrid dgQuick;

    //****************************************************************************
    //
    //    ROUTINE: Page_Load
    //
    //    DESCRIPTION: This routine provides the event handler for the page
    //                 load event.  It is responsible for initializing the
    //                 controls on the page.
    //
    //----------------------------------------------------------------------------
    private void Page_Load(object sender, System.EventArgs e)
    {
      OleDbConnection dbConn = null;
      OleDbCommand dCmd = null;
      OleDbDataReader dReader = null;
      String strConnection = null;
      String strSQL = null;

      if (!Page.IsPostBack)
      {
        try
        {
          // get the connection string from web.config and open a connection
          // to the database
          strConnection =
              ConfigurationSettings.AppSettings["dbConnectionString"];
          dbConn = new OleDbConnection(strConnection);
          dbConn.Open();

          // build the query string and get the data from the database
          strSQL = "SELECT Title, ISBN, Publisher " +
                   "FROM Book " +
                   "ORDER BY Title";
          dCmd = new OleDbCommand(strSQL, dbConn);
          dReader = dCmd.ExecuteReader();

          // set the source of the data for the datagrid control and bind it
          dgQuick.DataSource = dReader;
          dgQuick.DataBind();
```

Example 1-3. Quick-and-dirty DataGrid code-behind (.cs) (continued)

```
    }  // try

    finally
    {
      // cleanup
      if (dReader != null)
      {
        dReader.Close();
      }

      if (dbConn != null)
      {
        dbConn.Close();
      }
    }  // finally
  }
} // Page_Load
} // CH01QuickAndDirtyDatagridCS
}
```

1.3   Enhancing the Output of a Tabular Display

Problem

You need to display data from a database in a way that lets you organize and enhance the output beyond the confines of the DataGrid control's default tabular display. Selecting and editing the data are not important, nor is navigating through the data.

Solution

Use a Repeater control with templates and then bind the data to the control.

In the *.aspx* file, add a Repeater control and the associated templates for displaying the data.

In the code-behind class for the page, use the .NET language of your choice to:

1. Open a connection to the database.
2. Build a query string, and read the desired data from the database using an OleDbCommand and OleDbDataReader.
3. Assign the data source to the Repeater control and bind it.

Figure 1-2 shows the appearance of a typical Repeater in a browser. Examples 1-4 through 1-6 show the *.aspx* and code-behind files for an application that produces this result.

ASP.NET Cookbook
The Ultimate ASP.NET Code Sourcebook

Templates With Repeater (VB)

Title	ISBN	Publisher
.Net Framework Essentials	0-596-00302-1	O'Reilly
Access Cookbook	0-596-00004-7	O'Reilly
ADO: ActiveX Data Objects	1-565-92415-0	O'Reilly
ASP.NET in a Nutshell	0-596-00116-9	O'Reilly
C# Essentials	0-596-00315-3	O'Reilly
C# in a Nutshell	0-596-00181-9	O'Reilly
COM and .Net Component Services	0-596-00103-7	O'Reilly
COM+ Programming with Visual Basic	1-565-92840-7	O'Reilly
Developing ASP Components	1-565-92750-8	O'Reilly
HTML & XHTML: The Definitive Guide	0-596-00026-X	O'Reilly

Figure 1-2. Using templates with Repeater control display output

Discussion

When your primary aim is to organize and enhance the output beyond the confines of the DataGrid control's default tabular display, the Repeater control is a good choice because, unlike a DataGrid, it has associated templates that allow you to use virtually any HTML to format the displayed data. It also has the advantage of being relatively lightweight and easy to use. When using Repeater, however, there are a handful of nuances you should know about that can make life easier and, in one instance, enhance performance.

Example 1-4 shows one of the most common approaches to using the Repeater control, which is to place the asp:Repeater element in a table and use its HeaderTemplate, ItemTemplate, and AlternatingItemTemplate attributes to format the displayed data as rows in the table.

A HeaderTemplate is used to define the header row of the table. In this example, the header is straight HTML with a single table row and three columns.

An ItemTemplate formats the even-numbered rows of data, while an AlternatingItemTemplate formats the odd-numbered rows. For both templates, a single row in the table is defined with the same three columns defined in the header template. In each of the three columns, data-binding statements (described later) define the data to be placed in each of the columns. The only differences between ItemTemplate and AlternatingItemTemplate are the color schemes and stylesheet classes used to output the rows. If you do not need to output the data using alternating styles, then omit the AlternatingItemTemplate attribute.

The data from the database is bound to the cells in the templates using the DataBinder.Eval method. The Title field is placed in the first column, the ISBN field is placed in the second column, and the Publisher field is placed in the third column:

```
DataBinder.Eval(Container.DataItem, "Title")
DataBinder.Eval(Container.DataItem, "ISBN")
DataBinder.Eval(Container.DataItem, "Publisher")
```

If the header is pure HTML with no data binding required, it is more efficient to remove the HeaderTemplate attribute and place the header HTML before the asp:Repeater tag. By moving the header outside of the asp:Repeater tag, the creation of several server-side controls is eliminated, which reduces the time required to render the page and improves performance.

```
<table width="100%" border="2" bordercolor="#000080"
       bgcolor="#FFFFE0"
       style="border-style:solid;
       border-collapse:collapse;">
    <thead bgcolor="#000080" class="TableHeader">
      <tr>
        <th align="center">Title</th>
        <th align="center">ISBN</th>
        <th align="center">Publisher</th>
      </tr>
    </thead>
    <asp:Repeater id=repBooks runat="server">
        ...
    </asp:Repeater>
</table>
```

The Page_Load method in the code-behind, shown in Example 1-5 (VB) and Example 1-6 (C#), opens a connection to the database, reads the data from the database using an OleDbCommand and an OleDbDataReader object, binds the data reader to the Repeater control, and then performs the necessary cleanup.

See Also

Recipe 1.6 for another example of using a template with a tabular control

---

More About the DataBinder.Eval Method

Recipe 1.3 uses the DataBinder.Eval method to bind data from the database to cells in the templates, as in:

```
<%# DataBinder.Eval(Container.DataItem, "Title") %>
```

The advantage of this approach is its relatively simple syntax. However, because the DataBinder.Eval method uses late-bound reflection to parse and evaluate a data-binding expression (in this case it's a simple string), there's a performance penalty associated with it.

If performance is your prime concern, you could use the following syntax instead:

```
<%# ((DbDataRecord)Container.DataItem)["Title"] %>
```

In order for this syntax to work, explicit casting is required. Also, when casting to DbDataRecord, make sure to add the following page-level directive to the beginning of your *.aspx* file:

```
<%@ Import namespace="System.Data.Common" %>
```

Example 1-4. Templates with Repeater control (.aspx)

```
<%@ Page Language="vb" AutoEventWireup="false"
        Codebehind="CH01TemplatesWithRepeaterVB.aspx.vb"
        Inherits="ASPNetCookbook.VBExamples.CH01TemplatesWithRepeaterVB" %>
<!DOCTYPE HTML PUBLIC "-//W3C//DTD HTML 4.0 Transitional//EN">
<html>
  <head>
    <title>Templates with Repeater</title>
    <link rel="stylesheet" href="css/ASPNetCookbook.css">
  </head>
  <body leftmargin="0" marginheight="0" marginwidth="0" topmargin="0">
    <form id="frmData" method="post" runat="server">
      <table width="100%" cellpadding="0" cellspacing="0" border="0">
        <tr>
          <td align="center">
            <img src="images/ASPNETCookbookHeading_blue.gif">
          </td>
        </tr>
        <tr>
          <td class="dividerLine">
            <img src="images/spacer.gif" height="6" border="0"></td>
        </tr>
      </table>
      <table width="90%" align="center" border="0">
        <tr>
          <td><img src="images/spacer.gif" height="10" border="0"></td>
        </tr>
        <tr>
          <td align="center" class="PageHeading">
              Templates With Repeater (VB)</td>
        </tr>
        <tr>
          <td><img src="images/spacer.gif" height="10" border="0"></td>
        </tr>
        <tr>
          <td align="center">
            <!-- Create a table within the cell to provide localized
                 customization for the book list -->
            <table width="100%" border="2" bordercolor="#000080"
                   bgcolor="#FFFFE0"
                   style="border-style:solid;border-collapse:collapse;">
              <asp:Repeater id=repBooks runat="server">
                <HeaderTemplate>
                  <thead bgcolor="#000080" class="TableHeader">
                    <tr>
                      <th align="center">Title</th>
                      <th align="center">ISBN</th>
                      <th align="center">Publisher</th>
                    </tr>
                  </thead>
                </HeaderTemplate>
                <ItemTemplate>
                  <tr bordercolor="#000080" class="TableCellNormal">
                    <td><%# DataBinder.Eval(Container.DataItem, "Title") %>
                    </td>
```

Example 1-4. Templates with Repeater control (.aspx) (continued)

```
                        <td align="center">
                          <%# DataBinder.Eval(Container.DataItem, "ISBN") %>
                        </td>
                        <td align="center">
                          <%# DataBinder.Eval(Container.DataItem, "Publisher") %>
                        </td>
                      </tr>
                    </ItemTemplate>
                    <AlternatingItemTemplate>
                      <tr bordercolor="#000080" bgcolor="#FFFFFF"
                          class="TableCellAlternating">
                        <td><%# DataBinder.Eval(Container.DataItem, "Title") %>
                        </td>
                        <td align="center">
                          <%# DataBinder.Eval(Container.DataItem, "ISBN") %>
                        </td>
                        <td align="center">
                          <%# DataBinder.Eval(Container.DataItem, "Publisher") %>
                        </td>
                      </tr>
                    </AlternatingItemTemplate>
                  </asp:Repeater>
                </table>
              </td>
            </tr>
          </table>
        </form>
      </body>
    </html>
```

Example 1-5. Templates with Repeater control code-behind (.vb)

```
Option Explicit On
Option Strict On
'----------------------------------------------------------------------------
'
'   Module Name: CH01TemplatesWithRepeaterVB.aspx.vb
'
'   Description: This class provides the code behind for
'                CH01TemplatesWithRepeaterVB.aspx
'
'****************************************************************************
Imports Microsoft.VisualBasic
Imports System.Configuration
Imports System.Data
Imports System.Data.OleDb

Namespace ASPNetCookbook.VBExamples
  Public Class CH01TemplatesWithRepeaterVB
    Inherits System.Web.UI.Page

    'controls on form
    Protected repBooks As System.Web.UI.WebControls.Repeater
```

Example 1-5. Templates with Repeater control code-behind (.vb) (continued)

```
'***************************************************************************
'
'    ROUTINE: Page_Load
'
'    DESCRIPTION: This routine provides the event handler for the page load
'                 event.  It is responsible for initializing the controls
'                 on the page.
'
'---------------------------------------------------------------------------
Private Sub Page_Load(ByVal sender As System.Object, _
                      ByVal e As System.EventArgs) _
           Handles MyBase.Load
  Dim dbConn As OleDbConnection
  Dim dCmd As OleDbCommand
  Dim dReader As OleDbDataReader
  Dim strConnection As String
  Dim strSQL As String

  If (Not Page.IsPostBack) Then
    Try
      'get the connection string from web.config and open a connection
      'to the database
      strConnection = _
          ConfigurationSettings.AppSettings("dbConnectionString")
      dbConn = New OleDbConnection(strConnection)
      dbConn.Open()

      'build the query string and get the data from the database
      strSQL = "SELECT Title, ISBN, Publisher " & _
               "FROM Book " & _
               "ORDER BY Title"
      dCmd = New OleDbCommand(strSQL, dbConn)
      dReader = dCmd.ExecuteReader()

      'set the source of the data for the repeater control and bind it
      repBooks.DataSource = dReader
      repBooks.DataBind()

    Finally
      'cleanup
      If (Not IsNothing(dReader)) Then
        dReader.Close()
      End If

      If (Not IsNothing(dbConn)) Then
        dbConn.Close()
      End If
    End Try
  End If
End Sub   'Page_Load
End Class   'CH01TemplatesWithRepeaterVB
End Namespace
```

Example 1-6. Templates with Repeater control code-behind (.cs)

```csharp
//-----------------------------------------------------------------------------
//
//    Module Name: CH01TemplatesWithRepeaterCS.aspx.cs
//
//    Description: This class provides the code behind for
//                 CH01TemplatesWithRepeaterCS.aspx
//
//*****************************************************************************
using System;
using System.Configuration;
using System.Data;
using System.Data.OleDb;

namespace ASPNetCookbook.CSExamples
{
  public class CH01TemplatesWithRepeaterCS : System.Web.UI.Page
  {
    // controls on form
    protected System.Web.UI.WebControls.Repeater repBooks;

    //*****************************************************************************
    //
    //    ROUTINE: Page_Load
    //
    //    DESCRIPTION: This routine provides the event handler for the page
    //                 load event.  It is responsible for initializing the
    //                 controls on the page.
    //
    //-----------------------------------------------------------------------------
    private void Page_Load(object sender, System.EventArgs e)
    {
      OleDbConnection dbConn = null;
      OleDbCommand dCmd = null;
      OleDbDataReader dReader = null;
      String strConnection = null;
      String strSQL = null;

      if (!Page.IsPostBack)
      {
        try
        {
          // get the connection string from web.config and open a connection
          // to the database
          strConnection =
              ConfigurationSettings.AppSettings["dbConnectionString"];
          dbConn = new OleDbConnection(strConnection);
          dbConn.Open();

          // build the query string and get the data from the database
          strSQL = "SELECT Title, ISBN, Publisher " +
                   "FROM Book " +
                   "ORDER BY Title";
```

Example 1-6. Templates with Repeater control code-behind (.cs) (continued)

```
        dCmd = new OleDbCommand(strSQL, dbConn);
        dReader = dCmd.ExecuteReader();

        // set the source of the data for the repeater control and bind it
        repBooks.DataSource = dReader;
        repBooks.DataBind();
    }

    finally
    {
        // cleanup
        if (dReader != null)
        {
            dReader.Close();
        }

        if (dbConn != null)
        {
            dbConn.Close();
        }
    }  // finally
    }
    }  // Page_Load
    }  // CHO1TemplatesWithRepeaterCS
}
```

1.4   Displaying Data from an XML File

Problem

You want a quick and convenient way to display data from an XML file.

Solution

Use a DataGrid control and the ReadXml method of the DataSet class.

In the *.aspx* file, add a DataGrid control for displaying the data.

In the code-behind class for the page, use the .NET language of your choice to:

1. Read the data from the XML file using the ReadXml method of the DataSet class.

2. Bind the DataSet to the DataGrid control.

Figure 1-3 shows the appearance of a typical DataGrid in a browser. Example 1-7 shows the XML used for the recipe. Examples 1-8 through 1-10 show the *.aspx* and code-behind files for an application that produces this result.

Discussion

The Page_Load method in the code-behind, shown in Example 1-9 (VB) and Example 1-10 (C#), reads the data from the XML file using the ReadXml method of

Title	ISBN	Publisher
Access Cookbook	0-596-00084-7	O'Reilly
Perl Cookbook	1-565-92243-3	O'Reilly
Java Cookbook	0-596-00170-3	O'Reilly
JavaScript Application Cookbook	1-565-92577-7	O'Reilly
VB .Net Language in a Nutshell	0-596-00092-8	O'Reilly
Programming Visual Basic .Net	0-596-00093-6	O'Reilly
Programming C#	0-596-00117-7	O'Reilly
.Net Framework Essentials	0-596-00165-7	O'Reilly
COM and .Net Component Services	0-596-00103-7	O'Reilly

Figure 1-3. DataGrid with XML data output

the DataSet class, binds the DataSet to the DataGrid control, and then performs the necessary cleanup.

Datasets are designed to support hierarchical data and can contain multiple tables of data. Because of this support, when data is loaded into the dataset, it is loaded into a Tables collection. In this example, there is a single node in the XML called Book. The DataSet will automatically load the XML data into a table named Book. When binding the data to the DataGrid, you must reference the desired table if the DataSet contains more than one table. It is always best to reference the table by name instead of by index because the index value can change if the structure of the data changes.

It's no secret that the DataGrid control is one of the most flexible controls provided with ASP.NET. It outputs a complete HTML table with the bound data displayed in its cells. When used with a rich data source, such as a data reader, a DataTable, or a DataSet, the DataGrid can automatically generate columns for the data, complete with column headers (see Recipe 1.2). Unfortunately, its default appearance and automatic behavior rarely meet the needs of a project. In this section we discuss some ways to make changing the default appearance and behavior a little easier, especially as it relates to displaying XML data.

First, provide more flexibility for your graphical design team to achieve the desired appearance by defining an asp:DataGrid with HeaderStyle, ItemStyle, AlternatingItemStyle, and Columns elements, as shown in Example 1-8.

In this example, we use the BorderColor and the BorderWidth attributes of the asp: DataGrid element to define the color and width of the border around the table generated by the DataGrid. The AutoGenerateColumns attribute is set to False to allow us to define the columns that will be displayed in the grid. If this attribute is set to True, the DataGrid will automatically generate columns as a function of the data bound to the grid.

The HeaderStyle element and its attributes are used to define the appearance of the grid header. The ItemStyle element and its attributes are used to define the appearance of the even-numbered rows in the grid. The AlternatingItemStyle element and its attributes are used to define the appearance of the odd-numbered rows in the grid. If you do not need to output the data using alternating styles, then omit the AlternatingItemStyle element.

The Columns element is used to define the columns in the grid, their headings, and the data fields that are bound to each of the columns. For each column that is to appear in the grid, an asp:BoundColumn element must be included. At a minimum, each asp:BoundColumn element must define the HeaderTitle attribute and the DataField attribute. The HeaderTitle attribute is set to the label for the column. The DataField attribute is set to the name of the data field in the dataset whose data is to be bound to the column. In addition, many other attributes can be included to define alignment, fonts, stylesheet classes, and the like as required to achieve the desired appearance.

Example 1-7. XML data used for example

```
<Root>
  <Book>
    <BookID>1</BookID>
    <Title>Access Cookbook</Title>
    <ISBN>0-596-00084-7</ISBN>
    <Publisher>O'Reilly</Publisher>
  </Book>
  <Book>
    <BookID>2</BookID>
    <Title>Perl Cookbook</Title>
    <ISBN>1-565-92243-3</ISBN>
    <Publisher>O'Reilly</Publisher>
  </Book>
  <Book>
    <BookID>3</BookID>
    <Title>Java Cookbook</Title>
    <ISBN>0-596-00170-3</ISBN>
    <Publisher>O'Reilly</Publisher>
  </Book>
  <Book>
    <BookID>4</BookID>
    <Title>JavaScript Application Cookbook</Title>
    <ISBN>1-565-92577-7</ISBN>
    <Publisher>O'Reilly</Publisher>
  </Book>
  <Book>
    <BookID>5</BookID>
    <Title>VB .Net Language in a Nutshell</Title>
    <ISBN>0-596-00092-8</ISBN>
    <Publisher>O'Reilly</Publisher>
  </Book>
  <Book>
    <BookID>6</BookID>
    <Title>Programming Visual Basic .Net</Title>
```

Example 1-7. XML data used for example (continued)

```
      <ISBN>0-596-00093-6</ISBN>
      <Publisher>O'Reilly</Publisher>
    </Book>
    <Book>
      <BookID>7</BookID>
      <Title>Programming C#</Title>
      <ISBN>0-596-00117-7</ISBN>
      <Publisher>O'Reilly</Publisher>
    </Book>
    <Book>
      <BookID>8</BookID>
      <Title>.Net Framework Essentials</Title>
      <ISBN>0-596-00165-7</ISBN>
      <Publisher>O'Reilly</Publisher>
    </Book>
    <Book>
      <BookID>9</BookID>
      <Title>COM and .Net Component Services</Title>
      <ISBN>0-596-00103-7</ISBN>
      <Publisher>O'Reilly</Publisher>
    </Book>
  </Root>
```

Example 1-8. DataGrid with XML data (.aspx)

```
<%@ Page Language="vb" AutoEventWireup="false"
        Codebehind="CH01DataGridWithXMLVB.aspx.vb"
        Inherits="ASPNetCookbook.VBExamples.CH01DataGridWithXMLVB" %>
<!DOCTYPE HTML PUBLIC "-//W3C//DTD HTML 4.0 Transitional//EN">
<html>
  <head>
    <title>Datagrid With XML VB</title>
    <link rel="stylesheet" href="css/ASPNetCookbook.css">
  </head>
  <body leftmargin="0" marginheight="0" marginwidth="0" topmargin="0">
    <form id="frmDatagrid" method="post" runat="server">
      <table width="100%" cellpadding="0" cellspacing="0" border="0">
        <tr>
          <td align="center">
            <img src="images/ASPNETCookbookHeading_blue.gif">
          </td>
        </tr>
        <tr>
          <td class="dividerLine">
            <img src="images/spacer.gif" height="6" border="0"></td>
        </tr>
      </table>
      <table width="90%" align="center" border="0">
        <tr>
          <td><img src="images/spacer.gif" height="10" border="0"></td>
        </tr>
        <tr>
```

Example 1-8. DataGrid with XML data (.aspx) (continued)

```
          <td align="center" class="PageHeading">
              DataGrid Using Data From XML (VB)</td>
      </tr>
      <tr>
        <td><img src="images/spacer.gif" height="10" border="0"></td>
      </tr>
      <tr>
        <td align="center">
          <asp:DataGrid
            id="dgBooks"
            runat="server"
            BorderColor="000080"
            BorderWidth="2px"
            AutoGenerateColumns="False"
            width="100%">

            <HeaderStyle
              HorizontalAlign="Center"
              ForeColor="#FFFFFF"
              BackColor="#000080"
              Font-Bold=true
              CssClass="TableHeader" />

            <ItemStyle
              BackColor="#FFFFE0"
              cssClass="TableCellNormal" />

            <AlternatingItemStyle
              BackColor="#FFFFFF"
              cssClass="TableCellAlternating" />

            <Columns>
              <asp:BoundColumn HeaderText="Title" DataField="Title" />
              <asp:BoundColumn HeaderText="ISBN" DataField="ISBN"
                               ItemStyle-HorizontalAlign="Center" />
              <asp:BoundColumn HeaderText="Publisher" DataField="Publisher"
                               ItemStyle-HorizontalAlign="Center" />

            </Columns>
          </asp:DataGrid>
        </td>
      </tr>
    </table>
  </form>
</body>
</html>
```

Example 1-9. DataGrid with XML data code-behind (.vb)

```
Option Explicit On
Option Strict On
'-------------------------------------------------------------------------
'
'   Module Name: CH01DataGridWithXMLVB.aspx.vb
```

Example 1-9. DataGrid with XML data code-behind (.vb) (continued)

```vb
'
'   Description: This class provides the code behind for
'                CH01DataGridWithXMLVB.aspx
'
'***************************************************************************
Imports Microsoft.VisualBasic
Imports System
Imports System.Configuration
Imports System.Data
Imports System.Data.OleDb

Namespace ASPNetCookbook.VBExamples
  Public Class CH01DataGridWithXMLVB
    Inherits System.Web.UI.Page

    'controls on form
    Protected dgBooks As System.Web.UI.WebControls.DataGrid

    '***************************************************************************
    '
    '   ROUTINE: Page_Load
    '
    '   DESCRIPTION: This routine provides the event handler for the page load
    '                event.  It is responsible for initializing the controls
    '                on the page.
    '
    '--------------------------------------------------------------------------
    Private Sub Page_Load(ByVal sender As System.Object, _
                          ByVal e As System.EventArgs) _
           Handles MyBase.Load
      Const BOOK_TABLE As String = "Book"

      Dim dSet As DataSet
      Dim xmlFilename As String

      If (Not Page.IsPostBack) Then
        Try
          'get fully qualified path to the "books" xml document located
          'in the xml directory
          xmlFilename = Server.MapPath("xml") & "\books.xml"

          'create a dataset and load the books xml document into it
          dSet = New DataSet
          dSet.ReadXml(xmlFilename)

          'bind the dataset to the datagrid
          dgBooks.DataSource = dSet.Tables(BOOK_TABLE)
          dgBooks.DataBind()

        Finally
          'cleanup
          If (Not IsNothing(dSet)) Then
```

Example 1-9. DataGrid with XML data code-behind (.vb) (continued)

```
            dSet.Dispose( )
          End If
        End Try
      End If
    End Sub   'Page_Load
  End Class   'CH01DataGridWithXMLVB
End Namespace
```

Example 1-10. DataGrid with XML data code-behind (.cs)

```
//-----------------------------------------------------------------------------
//
//   Module Name: CH01DataGridWithXMLCS.aspx.cs
//
//   Description: This class provides the code behind for
//                CH01DataGridWithXMLCS.aspx
//
//*****************************************************************************
using System;
using System.Configuration;
using System.Data;
using System.Data.OleDb;

namespace ASPNetCookbook.CSExamples
{
  public class CH01DataGridWithXMLCS : System.Web.UI.Page
  {
    // controls on form
    protected System.Web.UI.WebControls.DataGrid dgBooks;

    //*************************************************************************
    //
    //   ROUTINE: Page_Load
    //
    //   DESCRIPTION: This routine provides the event handler for the page
    //                load event.  It is responsible for initializing the
    //                controls on the page.
    //
    //-------------------------------------------------------------------------
    private void Page_Load(object sender, System.EventArgs e)
    {
      const String BOOK_TABLE = "Book";

      DataSet dSet = null;
      String xmlFilename = null;

      if (!Page.IsPostBack)
      {
        try
        {
          // get fully qualified path to the "books" xml document located
          // in the xml directory
          xmlFilename = Server.MapPath("xml") + "\\books.xml";
```

Example 1-10. DataGrid with XML data code-behind (.cs) (continued)

```
        // create a dataset and load the books xml document into it
        dSet = new DataSet( );
        dSet.ReadXml(xmlFilename);

        // bind the dataset to the datagrid
        dgBooks.DataSource = dSet.Tables[BOOK_TABLE];
        dgBooks.DataBind( );
      }  // try

      finally
      {
        // cleanup
        if (dSet != null)
        {
          dSet.Dispose( );
        }
      }  // finally
    }
  }  // Page_Load
  }  // CH01DataGridWithXMLCS
}
```

1.5   Displaying an Array as a Group of Checkboxes

Problem

You have data in an array that needs to be displayed as a group of checkboxes.

Solution

Use a CheckBoxList control and bind the array to it.

Add a CheckBoxList control to the *.aspx* file.

In the code-behind class for the page, bind the array to the CheckBoxList control.

Figure 1-4 shows the appearance of a typical CheckBoxList in a browser, with a couple of checkboxes preselected. Examples 1-11 through 1-13 show the *.aspx* and code-behind files for an application that produces this result.

Discussion

The CheckBoxList control makes the job of generating a list of checkboxes extremely easy. Here's a rundown of some of the attributes that control the checkbox display. In the example that we developed for this recipe, we have placed a CheckBoxList control in a Table cell to control its position on the form, as shown in Example 1-11.

The RepeatColumns attribute of the CheckBoxList control is used to set the number of columns in which the checkboxes are to be displayed.

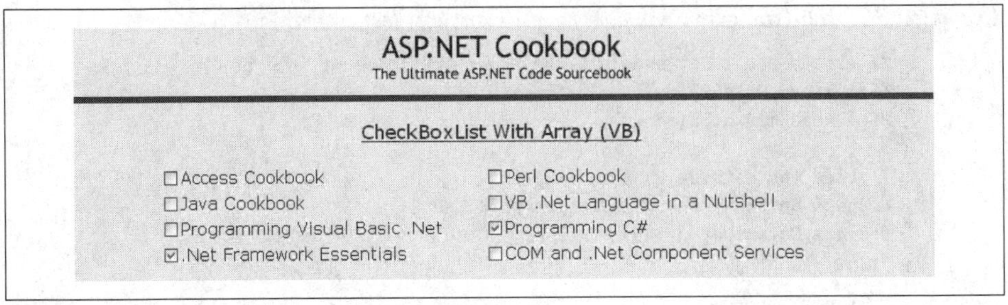

Figure 1-4. CheckBoxList with array data output

The RepeatDirection attribute is set to Horizontal, which displays the checkboxes in rows from left-to-right and then top-to-bottom. This attribute can also be set to Vertical to display the checkboxes in columns from top-to-bottom and then left-to-right.

The RepeatLayout attribute is set to Table, which causes the CheckBoxList control to output an HTML table that contains the checkboxes. Using Table ensures the checkboxes are aligned vertically. This attribute can also be set to Flow, which causes the CheckBoxList control to output a <span> element for the checkboxes with <br> elements, thus placing the checkboxes in rows. In this case, unless all of your data is the same size, the checkboxes will not be aligned vertically.

The CssClass attribute controls the format of the text displayed with the checkboxes, and the width attribute sets the width of the HTML table that is generated.

The styles attribute can be used to format the data in any manner supported by inline HTML styles. If you're considering using inline styles, though, it is important to remember that some older browsers do not fully support them.

If you need a list of radio buttons instead of checkboxes, substitute RadioButtonList for CheckBoxList in both the *.aspx* file and the code-behind.

The Page_Load method in the code-behind, shown in Example 1-12 (VB) and Example 1-13 (C#), builds the array of data by declaring an ArrayList and adding the text for the checkboxes to the ArrayList. It then sets the source of the data to the ArrayList and performs a data bind.

The ArrayList class provides a convenient, lightweight container for data that is to be bound to list controls. An ArrayList is virtually identical to the built-in Array type but adds automatic size management that makes it a bit easier to use.

To preselect a single checkbox, set the SelectedIndex property of the CheckBoxList control to the index of the item that is to be preselected. If multiple checkboxes need to be preselected, use the FindByText (or FindByValue) method of the Items collection in the CheckBoxList control to find the appropriate item(s), and then set the Selected property to True, as shown in the code-behind.

Example 1-11. CheckBoxList with array data (.aspx)

```
<%@ Page Language="vb" AutoEventWireup="false"
         Codebehind="CH01CheckboxListWithArrayVB.aspx.vb"
         Inherits="ASPNetCookbook.VBExamples.CH01CheckboxListWithArrayVB" %>
<!DOCTYPE HTML PUBLIC "-//W3C//DTD HTML 4.0 Transitional//EN">
<html>
  <head>
    <title>Checkbox List With Array</title>
    <link rel="stylesheet" href="css/ASPNetCookbook.css">
  </head>
  <body leftmargin="0" marginheight="0" marginwidth="0" topmargin="0">
    <form id="frmData" method="post" runat="server">
      <table width="100%" cellpadding="0" cellspacing="0" border="0">
        <tr>
          <td align="center">
            <img src="images/ASPNETCookbookHeading_blue.gif">
          </td>
        </tr>
        <tr>
          <td class="dividerLine">
            <img src="images/spacer.gif" height="6" border="0"></td>
        </tr>
      </table>
      <table width="90%" align="center" border="0">
        <tr>
          <td><img src="images/spacer.gif" height="10" border="0"></td>
        </tr>
        <tr>
          <td align="center" class="PageHeading">
            CheckBoxList With Array (VB)</td>
        </tr>
        <tr>
          <td><img src="images/spacer.gif" height="10" border="0"></td>
        </tr>
        <tr>
          <td align="center">
            <asp:CheckBoxList id="cbBooks" runat="server"
                        RepeatColumns="2"
                        RepeatDirection="Horizontal"
                        RepeatLayout="Table"
                        CssClass="MenuItem"
                        width="90%" />
          </td>
        </tr>
      </table>
    </form>
  </body>
</html>
```

Example 1-12. CheckBoxList with array data code-behind (.vb)

```vb
Option Explicit On
Option Strict On
'-------------------------------------------------------------------------------
'
'   Module Name: CH01CheckboxListWithArrayVB.aspx.vb
'
'   Description: This class provides the code behind for
'                CH01CheckboxListWithArrayVB.aspx
'
'*******************************************************************************
Imports System.Collections

Namespace ASPNetCookbook.VBExamples
  Public Class CH01CheckboxListWithArrayVB
    Inherits System.Web.UI.Page

    'controls on form
    Protected cbBooks As System.Web.UI.WebControls.CheckBoxList

    '*******************************************************************************
    '
    '   ROUTINE: Page_Load
    '
    '   DESCRIPTION: This routine provides the event handler for the page load
    '                event.  It is responsible for initializing the controls
    '                on the page.
    '
    '-------------------------------------------------------------------------------
    Private Sub Page_Load(ByVal sender As System.Object, _
                          ByVal e As System.EventArgs) _
              Handles MyBase.Load
      Dim values As ArrayList

      If (Not Page.IsPostBack) Then
        'build array of data to bind to checkboxlist
        values = New ArrayList
        values.Add("Access Cookbook")
        values.Add("Perl Cookbook")
        values.Add("Java Cookbook")
        values.Add("VB .Net Language in a Nutshell")
        values.Add("Programming Visual Basic .Net")
        values.Add("Programming C#")
        values.Add(".Net Framework Essentials")
        values.Add("COM and .Net Component Services")

        'bind the data to the checkboxlist
        cbBooks.DataSource = values
        cbBooks.DataBind()

        'preselect several books
        cbBooks.Items.FindByText("Programming C#").Selected = True
        cbBooks.Items.FindByText(".Net Framework Essentials").Selected = True
```

Example 1-12. CheckBoxList with array data code-behind (.vb) (continued)

```
        End If
    End Sub  'Page_Load
  End Class  'CH01CheckboxListWithArrayVB
End Namespace
```

Example 1-13. CheckBoxList with array data code-behind (.cs)

```
//---------------------------------------------------------------------------
//
//   Module Name: CH01DataGridWithXMLCS.aspx.cs
//
//   Description: This class provides the code behind for
//                CH01DataGridWithXMLCS.aspx
//
//***************************************************************************
using System;
using System.Collections;

namespace ASPNetCookbook.CSExamples
{
  public class CH01CheckboxListWithArrayCS : System.Web.UI.Page
  {
    // controls on form
    protected System.Web.UI.WebControls.CheckBoxList cbBooks;

    //***********************************************************************
    //
    //   ROUTINE: Page_Load
    //
    //   DESCRIPTION: This routine provides the event handler for the page
    //                load event.  It is responsible for initializing the
    //                controls on the page.
    //
    //-----------------------------------------------------------------------
    private void Page_Load(object sender, System.EventArgs e)
    {
      if (!Page.IsPostBack)
      {
        ArrayList values = new ArrayList();

        // build array of data to bind to checkboxlist
        values.Add("Access Cookbook");
        values.Add("Perl Cookbook");
        values.Add("Java Cookbook");
        values.Add("VB .Net Language in a Nutshell");
        values.Add("Programming Visual Basic .Net");
        values.Add("Programming C#");
        values.Add(".Net Framework Essentials");
        values.Add("COM and .Net Component Services");

        // bind the data to the checkboxlist
        cbBooks.DataSource = values;
        cbBooks.DataBind();
```

Example 1-13. CheckBoxList with array data code-behind (.cs) (continued)

```
        // preselect several books
        cbBooks.Items.FindByText("Programming C#").Selected = true;
        cbBooks.Items.FindByText(".Net Framework Essentials").Selected = true;
      }
    } // Page_Load
  } // CH01CheckboxListWithArrayCS
}
```

1.6   Displaying Data from a Hashtable

Problem

You have data in a Hashtable, a class that provides the ability to store a collection of key/value pairs, and you want to display the data in a columnar table.

Solution

Use a DataList control and bind the Hashtable to it.

Add a DataList control to the *.aspx* file, being careful to place it in a Table cell in order to control its position on the form.

In the code-behind class for the page, use the .NET language of your choice to:

1. Define the Hashtable as the data source for the DataList control.

2. Set the control's key and value.

3. Bind the Hashtable to the DataList control.

Figure 1-5 shows the appearance of a typical DataList within a browser that has been bound to a Hashtable filled with, in our case, book data. Examples 1-14 through 1-16 show the *.aspx* and code-behind files for an application that produces this result.

Discussion

The DataList control can display almost any type of data in a variety of ways using its available templates and styles. Templates are available for the header, footer, items, alternating items, separators, selected items, and edit items to define and organize the data to output. Styles are available for each of the templates to define how the content appears.

In this example, an asp:DataList tag is placed in a Table cell to control its position on the form, as shown in Example 1-14. The RepeatColumns attribute of the control defines the number of columns that should be output, which in this case is 4. The RepeatDirection attribute indicates that the data should be output horizontally, which displays the data in rows from left-to-right and then top-to-bottom. The RepeatLayout attribute indicates that the data should be output in an HTML table, which provides the greatest flexibility in arranging the data items.

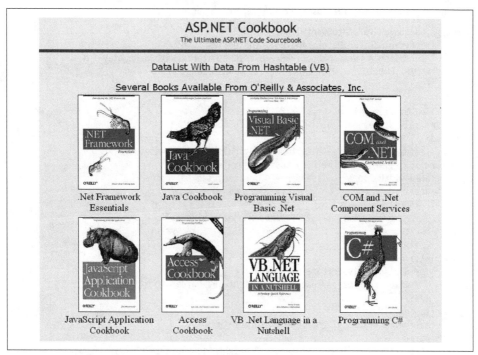

Figure 1-5. DataList with Hashtable data output

The HeaderTemplate element defines a simple line of text to be used as a header for the data list. The HeaderTemplate can also contain any HTML and ASP controls.

The HeaderStyle element defines the positioning of the header as well as the stylesheet class used to define the text formatting. A large number of style attributes are available to format the header data.

The ItemTemplate element defines an HTML table that contains an image and text describing the image. A table controls the positioning of the data items.

The ItemStyle element defines the positioning of the items output using the ItemTemplate. In this example only horizontal and vertical positioning are defined, but there are many styles available.

The Page_Load method of the code-behind, shown in Example 1-15 (VB) and Example 1-16 (C#), uses a Hashtable as the container for the data to bind to the DataList. A Hashtable provides the ability to store a collection of key/value pairs. This is the equivalent of a two-column table, which provides a lightweight container for data when only two items are required per row, such as in this example.

This example builds the Hashtable of data by declaring a Hashtable object and adding the key/value pairs to the Hashtable. It then sets the source of the data to the Hashtable object, defines the key field (the key in the Hashtable) and the data member (the value in the Hashtable), and performs a data bind.

Example 1-14. DataList with Hashtable data (.aspx)

```
<%@ Page Language="vb" AutoEventWireup="false"
        Codebehind="CH01DataListWithHashtableVB.aspx.vb"
        Inherits="ASPNetCookbook.VBExamples.CH01DataListWithHashtableVB" %>
<!DOCTYPE HTML PUBLIC "-//W3C//DTD HTML 4.0 Transitional//EN">
<html>
  <head>
    <title>DataList With Hashtable</title>
    <link rel="stylesheet" href="css/ASPNetCookbook.css">
  </head>
  <body leftmargin="0" marginheight="0" marginwidth="0" topmargin="0">
    <form id="frmRepeater" method="post" runat="server">
      <table width="100%" cellpadding="0" cellspacing="0" border="0">
        <tr>
          <td align="center">
            <img src="images/ASPNETCookbookHeading_blue.gif">
          </td>
        </tr>
        <tr>
          <td class="dividerLine">
            <img src="images/spacer.gif" height="6" border="0"></td>
        </tr>
      </table>
      <table width="90%" align="center" border="0">
        <tr>
          <td><img src="images/spacer.gif" height="10" border="0"></td>
        </tr>
        <tr>
          <td align="center" class="PageHeading">
            DataList With Data From Hashtable (VB)</td>
        </tr>
        <tr>
          <td><img src="images/spacer.gif" height="10" border="0"></td>
        </tr>
        <tr>
          <td align="center">
            <asp:DataList id="dlBooks" runat="server"
                          RepeatColumns="4"
                          RepeatDirection="Horizontal"
                          RepeatLayout="Table" >
          <HeaderTemplate>
            Several Books Available From O'Reilly & Associates, Inc.
          </HeaderTemplate>
          <HeaderStyle HorizontalAlign="Center"
                       CssClass="BlackPageHeading" />
          <ItemTemplate>
            <table align="center">
              <tr>
                <td align="center">
                  <img src="<%# DataBinder.Eval(Container.DataItem, _
                                                "Value") %>"
                       height="190" width="127"></td>
              </tr>
```

Example 1-14. DataList with Hashtable data (.aspx) (continued)

```
            <tr>
              <td align="center">
                <%# DataBinder.Eval(Container.DataItem, "Key") %></td>
              </tr>
            </table>
          </ItemTemplate>
          <ItemStyle HorizontalAlign="Center" VerticalAlign="Top" />
        </asp:DataList>
      </td>
    </tr>
  </table>
  </form>
  </body>
</html>
```

Example 1-15. DataList with Hashtable data code-behind (.vb)

```
Option Explicit On
Option Strict On
'-----------------------------------------------------------------------------
'
'   Module Name: CH01DataListWithHashtableVB.aspx.vb
'
'   Description: This class provides the code behind for the
'                CH01DataListWithHashtableVB.aspx page
'
'*****************************************************************************
Imports System.Collections

Namespace ASPNetCookbook.VBExamples
  Public Class CH01DataListWithHashtableVB
    Inherits System.Web.UI.Page

    'controls on form
    Protected dlBooks As System.Web.UI.WebControls.DataList

    '*****************************************************************************
    '
    '   ROUTINE: Page_Load
    '
    '   DESCRIPTION: This routine provides the event handler for the page load
    '                event.  It is responsible for initializing the controls
    '                on the page.
    '
    '-------------------------------------------------------------------------
    Private Sub Page_Load(ByVal sender As System.Object, _
                        ByVal e As System.EventArgs) _
               Handles MyBase.Load
      Dim values As Hashtable

      If (Not Page.IsPostBack) Then
        'build HashTable with the names of the books as the key and the
        'relative path to the cover image as the value
```

Example 1-15. DataList with Hashtable data code-behind (.vb) (continued)

```vb
        values = New Hashtable
        values.Add(".Net Framework Essentials", _
                   "images/books/DotNetFrameworkEssentials.gif")
        values.Add("Access Cookbook", _
                   "images/books/AccessCookbook.gif")
        values.Add("COM and .Net Component Services", _
                   "images/books/ComAndDotNet.gif")
        values.Add("Java Cookbook", _
                   "images/books/JavaCookbook.gif")
        values.Add("JavaScript Application Cookbook", _
                   "images/books/JavaScriptCookbook.gif")
        values.Add("Programming C#", _
                   "images/books/ProgrammingCSharp.gif")
        values.Add("Programming Visual Basic .Net", _
                   "images/books/ProgrammingVBDotNet.gif")
        values.Add("VB .Net Language in a Nutshell", _
                   "images/books/VBDotNetInANutshell.gif")

        'define the data source, key, value, and bind to the Hashtable
        dlBooks.DataSource = values
        dlBooks.DataKeyField = "Key"
        dlBooks.DataMember = "Value"
        dlBooks.DataBind( )
      End If
    End Sub  'Page_Load
  End Class  'CH01DataListWithHashtableVB
End Namespace
```

Example 1-16. DataList with Hashtable data code-behind (.cs)

```cs
//----------------------------------------------------------------------------
//
//     Module Name: CH01DataListWithHashtableCS.aspx.cs
//
//     Description: This class provides the code behind for
//                  CH01DataListWithHashtableCS.aspx
//
//****************************************************************************
using System;
using System.Collections;

namespace ASPNetCookbook.CSExamples
{
  public class CH01DataListWithHashtableCS : System.Web.UI.Page
  {
    // controls on form
    protected System.Web.UI.WebControls.DataList dlBooks;

    //************************************************************************
    //
    //     ROUTINE: Page_Load
    //
    //     DESCRIPTION: This routine provides the event handler for the page
```

Example 1-16. DataList with Hashtable data code-behind (.cs) (continued)

```
//                   load event.  It is responsible for initializing the
//                   controls on the page.
//
//-------------------------------------------------------------------------
private void Page_Load(object sender, System.EventArgs e)
{
    Hashtable values = new Hashtable( );

    // build HashTable with the names of the books as the key and the
    // relative path to the cover image as the value
    values = new Hashtable( );
    values.Add(".Net Framework Essentials",
               "images/books/DotNetFrameworkEssentials.gif");
    values.Add("Access Cookbook",
               "images/books/AccessCookbook.gif");
    values.Add("COM and .Net Component Services",
               "images/books/ComAndDotNet.gif");
    values.Add("Java Cookbook",
               "images/books/JavaCookbook.gif");
    values.Add("JavaScript Application Cookbook",
               "images/books/JavaScriptCookbook.gif");
    values.Add("Programming C#",
               "images/books/ProgrammingCSharp.gif");
    values.Add("Programming Visual Basic .Net",
               "images/books/ProgrammingVBDotNet.gif");
    values.Add("VB .Net Language in a Nutshell",
               "images/books/VBDotNetInANutshell.gif");

    // define the data source, key, value, and bind to the Hashtable
    dlBooks.DataSource = values;
    dlBooks.DataKeyField = "Key";
    dlBooks.DataMember = "Value";
    dlBooks.DataBind( );
    } // Page_Load
  } // CH01DataListWithHashtableCS
}
```

1.7   Adding Next/Previous Navigation to a DataGrid

Problem

You need to display data from a database in a table, but the database has more rows than can fit on a single page so you want to use next/previous buttons for navigation.

Solution

Use a DataGrid control, enable its built-in pagination features, and then bind the data to it.

Add a `DataGrid` control to the *.aspx* file, and use its `AllowPaging` and other related attributes to enable pagination.

In the code-behind class for the page, use the .NET language of your choice to:

1. Create a routine that binds a `DataSet` to the `DataGrid` in the usual fashion.

2. Create an event handler that performs the page navigation—for example, one that handles the `PageIndexChanged` event for the `DataGrid`—and rebinds the data.

Figure 1-6 shows the appearance of a typical `DataGrid` within a browser with next/previous navigation. Examples 1-17 through 1-19 show the *.aspx* and code-behind files for an application that produces this result.

ASP.NET Cookbook
The Ultimate ASP.NET Code Sourcebook

DataGrid Using Text For Next/Previous Navigation (VB)

Title	ISBN	Publisher
.Net Framework Essentials	0-596-00302-1	O'Reilly
Access Cookbook	0-596-00084-7	O'Reilly
ADO: ActiveX Data Objects	1-565-92415-0	O'Reilly
ASP.NET in a Nutshell	0-596-00116-9	O'Reilly
C# Essentials	0-596-00315-3	O'Reilly
Prev Next		

Figure 1-6. DataGrid with next/previous navigation output

Discussion

The `DataGrid` control includes the ability to perform pagination of the data that is displayed in the grid, and using the built-in pagination requires very little code. Pagination is enabled and configured by the attributes of the `DataGrid` element:

```
AllowPaging="True"
PageSize="5"
PagerStyle-Mode="NextPrev"
PagerStyle-Position="Bottom"
PagerStyle-HorizontalAlign="Center"
PagerStyle-NextPageText="Next"
PagerStyle-PrevPageText="Prev">
```

Setting the `AllowPaging` attribute to `True` enables paging for the `DataGrid`, and the `PageSize` attribute defines the number of rows that will be displayed in a single page. Setting the `PageStyle-Mode` attribute to `NextPrev` enables the output of the Next/Prev controls (see Recipe 1.9 for other uses of this attribute).

The remaining attributes define how the pagination controls look. `PageStyle-Position` defines the location of the Next/Prev controls. Valid values include `Bottom`, `Top`, and `TopAndBottom`. `PagerStyle-HorizontalAlign` defines the horizontal positioning of the Next/Prev controls. Valid values include `Left`, `Center`, `Right`, and `NotSet`. `NotSet` is effectively the same as `Left` because `Left` is the default.

`PagerStyle-NextPageText` defines the text to output for the next page navigation control, and `PagerStyle-PrevPageText` defines the text to output for the previous page navigation.

 The `PagerStyle-NextPageText` and `PagerStyle-PrevPageText` attribute values can include HTML to format the text of the controls. Virtually any HTML can be used, including image tags. If you change the values of the two text attributes, the Next/Prev controls will be output, as shown in Figure 1-7.

```
PagerStyle-NextPageText=
    "<img src='images/buttons/button_next.gif'
        border='0'>"
PagerStyle-PrevPageText=
    "<img src='images/buttons/button_prev.gif'
        border='0'>">
```

ASP.NET Cookbook
The Ultimate ASP.NET Code Sourcebook

DataGrid Using Images For Next/Previous Navigation (VB)

Title	ISBN	Publisher
.Net Framework Essentials	0-596-00302-1	O'Reilly
Access Cookbook	0-596-00084-7	O'Reilly
ADO: ActiveX Data Objects	1-565-92415-0	O'Reilly
ASP.NET in a Nutshell	0-596-00116-9	O'Reilly
C# Essentials	0-596-00315-3	O'Reilly

Prev Next

Figure 1-7. DataGrid output using image tags for next/previous controls

The `bindData` routine, shown in the code-behind in Example 1-18 (VB) and Example 1-19 (C#), performs the data binding. This routine provides the typical binding of a dataset to the `DataGrid`. No additional code is required in this routine to support the default pagination.

The `dgBooks_PageIndexChanged` event handler provides the code required to perform the page navigation. The new page number to display is passed in the event arguments (e). The `CurrentPageIndex` property of the `DataGrid` must be set to the passed value, and the data must be rebound to the `DataGrid`.

 The default pagination code shown in this recipe can be very inefficient when used with data containing a large number of rows. By default, all of the data for a query is returned and used to populate the DataSet. When the query returns a relatively small set of data (less than 100 rows and a small number of columns), the pagination shown in this recipe is adequate for most applications. If your query returns a million rows, the performance of your application will be unacceptable. See Recipe 1.10 for a more efficient approach to the pagination of large datasets.

See Also

Recipes 1.8, 1.9, and 1.10 for other examples of pagination

Event Handlers

VB and C# connect event handlers to events in very different ways. VB requires two additions to your code to handle an event. First, the control that has events to handle must be declared in the code-behind class using the WithEvents keyword, as shown here:

```
Protected WithEvents dgBooks As DataGrid
```

Second, the method that will be used to handle an event must have the Handles keyword added to the end of the method and include the control and event to be handled. This informs the compiler to add the code required to "wire" the event to the method.

```
Private Sub dgBooks_PageIndexChanged(ByVal source As Object, _
        ByVal e As DataGridPageChangedEventArgs) _
        Handles dgBooks.PageIndexChanged
```

In C#, events are connected to methods by explicitly creating a new event handler of the required type and "wiring" it to the desired control's event:

```
this.dgBooks.PageIndexChanged +=
    new DataGridPageChangedEventHandler
        (this.dgBooks_PageIndexChanged);
```

In both VB and C# one method can be used to handle multiple events. This is useful when a page contains multiple buttons for the same action, such as a set of next/previous buttons at the top and bottom of a grid. This is accomplished in VB by listing the events that are to be handled after the Handles keyword:

```
Private Sub btnNext_ServerClick(ByVal sender As Object, _
        ByVal e As ImageClickEventArgs) _
        Handles btnNext1.ServerClick, btnNext2.ServerClick
```

In C#, using a single method to handle two events is done as shown here:

```
this.btnNext.ServerClick +=
    new ImageClickEventHandler(this.btnNext1_ServerClick);
this.btnNext.ServerClick +=
    new ImageClickEventHandler(this.btnNext2_ServerClick);
```

Example 1-17. DataGrid with next/previous navigation (.aspx)

```
<%@ Page Language="vb" AutoEventWireup="false"
        Codebehind="CH01DatagridWithNextPrevNavVB1.aspx.vb"
        Inherits="ASPNetCookbook.VBExamples.CH01DatagridWithNextPrevNavVB1" %>
<!DOCTYPE HTML PUBLIC "-//W3C//DTD HTML 4.0 Transitional//EN">
<html>
  <head>
    <title>Datagrid With Text For Next/Prev Navigation</title>
    <link rel="stylesheet" href="css/ASPNetCookbook.css">
  </head>
```

Example 1-17. DataGrid with next/previous navigation (.aspx) (continued)

```
<body leftmargin="0" marginheight="0" marginwidth="0" topmargin="0">
  <form id="frmData" method="post" runat="server">
    <table width="100%" cellpadding="0" cellspacing="0" border="0">
      <tr>
        <td align="center">
          <img src="images/ASPNETCookbookHeading_blue.gif">
        </td>
      </tr>
      <tr>
        <td class="dividerLine">
          <img src="images/spacer.gif" height="6" border="0"></td>
      </tr>
    </table>
    <table width="90%" align="center" border="0">
      <tr>
        <td><img src="images/spacer.gif" height="10" border="0"></td>
      </tr>
      <tr>
        <td align="center" class="PageHeading">
          DataGrid Using Text For Next/Previous Navigation (VB)
        </td>
      </tr>
      <tr>
        <td><img src="images/spacer.gif" height="10" border="0"></td>
      </tr>
      <tr>
        <td align="center">
          <asp:DataGrid
            id="dgBooks"
            runat="server"
            BorderColor="000080"
            BorderWidth="2px"
            AutoGenerateColumns="False"
            width="100%"
            AllowPaging="True"
            PageSize="5"
            PagerStyle-Mode="NextPrev"
            PagerStyle-Position="Bottom"
            PagerStyle-HorizontalAlign="Center"
            PagerStyle-NextPageText="Next"
            PagerStyle-PrevPageText="Prev">

            <HeaderStyle HorizontalAlign="Center"
                         ForeColor="#FFFFFF"
                         BackColor="#000080"
                         Font-Bold=true
                         CssClass="TableHeader" />

            <ItemStyle BackColor="#FFFFE0"
                       cssClass="TableCellNormal" />

            <AlternatingItemStyle BackColor="#FFFFFF"
                                  cssClass="TableCellAlternating" />
```

Example 1-17. DataGrid with next/previous navigation (.aspx) (continued)

```
            <Columns>
                <asp:BoundColumn HeaderText="Title" DataField="Title" />
                <asp:BoundColumn HeaderText="ISBN" DataField="ISBN"
                            ItemStyle-HorizontalAlign="Center" />
                <asp:BoundColumn HeaderText="Publisher" DataField="Publisher"
                            ItemStyle-HorizontalAlign="Center" />
            </Columns>
          </asp:DataGrid>
        </td>
      </tr>
    </table>
  </form>
 </body>
</html>
```

Example 1-18. DataGrid with next/previous navigation code-behind (.vb)

```
Option Explicit On
Option Strict On
'-----------------------------------------------------------------------------
'
'   Module Name: CH01DatagridWithNextPrevNavVB1.aspx.vb
'
'   Description: This class provides the code behind for
'                CH01DatagridWithNextPrevNavVB1.aspx
'
'*****************************************************************************
Imports Microsoft.VisualBasic
Imports System.Configuration
Imports System.Data
Imports System.Data.OleDb

Namespace ASPNetCookbook.VBExamples
  Public Class CH01DatagridWithNextPrevNavVB1
    Inherits System.Web.UI.Page

    'controls on form
    Protected WithEvents dgBooks As System.Web.UI.WebControls.DataGrid

    '*****************************************************************************
    '
    '   ROUTINE: Page_Load
    '
    '   DESCRIPTION: This routine provides the event handler for the page load
    '                event.  It is responsible for initializing the controls
    '                on the page.
    '-----------------------------------------------------------------------------
    Private Sub Page_Load(ByVal sender As System.Object, _
                    ByVal e As System.EventArgs) _
          Handles MyBase.Load

      If (Not Page.IsPostBack) Then
        bindData()
      End If
```

Example 1-18. DataGrid with next/previous navigation code-behind (.vb) (continued)

```vb
End Sub   'Page_Load

'************************************************************************
'
'   ROUTINE: dgCustomers_PageIndexChanged
'
'   DESCRIPTION: This routine provides the event handler for the page
'                index changed event of the datagrid.  It is responsible
'                for setting the page index from the passed arguments and
'                rebinding the data.
'------------------------------------------------------------------------
Private Sub dgBooks_PageIndexChanged(ByVal source As Object, _
      ByVal e As System.Web.UI.WebControls.DataGridPageChangedEventArgs) _
      Handles dgBooks.PageIndexChanged

   'set new page index and rebind the data
   dgBooks.CurrentPageIndex = e.NewPageIndex
   bindData( )
End Sub   'dgCustomers_PageIndexChanged

'************************************************************************
'
'   ROUTINE: bindData
'
'   DESCRIPTION: This routine queries the database for the data to
'                displayed and binds it to the datagrid
'------------------------------------------------------------------------
Private Sub bindData( )
  Dim dbConn As OleDbConnection
  Dim da As OleDbDataAdapter
  Dim dSet As DataSet
  Dim strConnection As String
  Dim strSQL As String

  Try
    'get the connection string from web.config and open a connection
    'to the database
    strConnection = _
        ConfigurationSettings.AppSettings("dbConnectionString")
    dbConn = New OleDb.OleDbConnection(strConnection)
    dbConn.Open( )

    'build the query string and get the data from the database
    strSQL = "SELECT Title, ISBN, Publisher " & _
             "FROM Book " & _
             "ORDER BY Title"
    da = New OleDbDataAdapter(strSQL, dbConn)
    dSet = New DataSet
    da.Fill(dSet)

    'set the source of the data for the datagrid control and bind it
    dgBooks.DataSource = dSet
    dgBooks.DataBind( )
```

Example 1-18. DataGrid with next/previous navigation code-behind (.vb) (continued)

```
      Finally
        'cleanup
        If (Not IsNothing(dbConn)) Then
          dbConn.Close()
        End If
      End Try
    End Sub  'bindData
  End Class  'CH01DatagridWithNextPrevNavVB1
End Namespace
```

Example 1-19. DataGrid with next/previous navigation code-behind (.cs)

```
//----------------------------------------------------------------------------
//
//   Module Name: CH01DatagridWithNextPrevNavCS1.aspx.cs
//
//   Description: This class provides the code behind for
//                CH01DatagridWithNextPrevNavCS1.aspx
//
//****************************************************************************
using System;
using System.Configuration;
using System.Data;
using System.Data.OleDb;
using System.Web.UI.WebControls;

namespace ASPNetCookbook.CSExamples
{
  public class CH01DatagridWithNextPrevNavCS1 : System.Web.UI.Page
  {
    // controls on form
    protected System.Web.UI.WebControls.DataGrid dgBooks;

    //****************************************************************************
    //
    //   ROUTINE: Page_Load
    //
    //   DESCRIPTION: This routine provides the event handler for the page
    //                load event.  It is responsible for initializing the
    //                controls on the page.
    //
    //----------------------------------------------------------------------------
    private void Page_Load(object sender, System.EventArgs e)
    {
      // wire in the page index changed event
      this.dgBooks.PageIndexChanged +=
        new DataGridPageChangedEventHandler(this.dgBooks_PageIndexChanged);

      if (!Page.IsPostBack)
      {
        bindData();
      }
    }  // Page_Load
```

Example 1-19. DataGrid with next/previous navigation code-behind (.cs) (continued)

```
//****************************************************************************
//
//    ROUTINE: dgCustomers_PageIndexChanged
//
//    DESCRIPTION: This routine provides the event handler for the page
//                 index changed event of the datagrid.  It is responsible
//                 for setting the page index from the passed arguments
//                 and rebinding the data.
//
//----------------------------------------------------------------------------
private void dgBooks_PageIndexChanged(Object source,
  System.Web.UI.WebControls.DataGridPageChangedEventArgs e)
{
  // set new page index and rebind the data
  dgBooks.CurrentPageIndex = e.NewPageIndex;
  bindData();
} // dgCustomers_PageIndexChanged

//****************************************************************************
//
//    ROUTINE: bindData
//
//    DESCRIPTION: This routine queries the database for the data to
//                 displayed and binds it to the repeater
//
//----------------------------------------------------------------------------
private void bindData()
{
  OleDbConnection dbConn = null;
  OleDbDataAdapter da = null;
  DataSet dSet = null;
  String strConnection = null;
  String strSQL =null;

  try
  {
    // get the connection string from web.config and open a connection
    // to the database
    strConnection =
        ConfigurationSettings.AppSettings["dbConnectionString"];
    dbConn = new OleDbConnection(strConnection);
    dbConn.Open();

    // build the query string and get the data from the database
    strSQL = "SELECT Title, ISBN, Publisher " +
            "FROM Book " +
            "ORDER BY Title";
    da = new OleDbDataAdapter(strSQL, dbConn);
    dSet = new DataSet();
    da.Fill(dSet, "Table");

    // set the source of the data for the datagrid control and bind it
    dgBooks.DataSource = dSet;
```

```
      dgBooks.DataBind( );
   }  // try

   finally
   {
      //clean up
      if (dbConn != null)
      {
         dbConn.Close( );
      }
   }  // finally
  }  // bindData
 }  // CH01DatagridWithNextPrevNavCS1
}
```

1.8   Adding First/Last Navigation to a DataGrid

Problem

You need to display data from a database in a table, but the database has more rows than will fit on a single page, and you want to use first/last buttons along with next/previous buttons for navigation.

Solution

Use a DataGrid control, add first/last and next/previous buttons (with event handlers for each one), and then bind the data to it.

In the *.aspx* file:

1. Add a DataGrid control to the *.aspx* file.

2. Add a row below the DataGrid with first/last and next/previous buttons for navigation.

In the code-behind class for the page, use the .NET language of your choice to:

1. Create a routine that binds a dataset to the DataGrid in the usual fashion.

2. For each of the four buttons, create an event handler to handle the button's click event, perform the requisite page navigation, and rebind the data.

Figure 1-8 shows the appearance of a typical DataGrid within a browser with first/last and next/previous buttons for navigation. Examples 1-20 through 1-22 show the *.aspx* and code-behind files for an application that produces this result.

Discussion

The main theme of this recipe is to provide an alternative to the DataGrid control's default pagination controls and, at the same time, handle the custom paging. Setting the PagerStyle-Visible attribute to False makes the pager invisible in a DataGrid

ASP.NET Cookbook
The Ultimate ASP.NET Code Sourcebook

DataGrid With First/Last and Next/Previous Navigation (VB)		
Title	ISBN	Publisher
.Net Framework Essentials	0-596-00302-1	O'Reilly
Access Cookbook	0-596-00084-7	O'Reilly
ADO: ActiveX Data Objects	1-565-92415-0	O'Reilly
ASP.NET in a Nutshell	0-596-00116-9	O'Reilly
C# Essentials	0-596-00315-3	O'Reilly

First   Prev   Next   Last

Figure 1-8. DataGrid with first/last and next/previous navigation output

control, allowing you to implement your own user interface for the pagination controls. (The *pager* is the element on the DataGrid control that allows you to link to other pages when paging is enabled.) When the pager is invisible, some appearance-related attributes for the pager are not required and can therefore be eliminated, specifically PagerStyle-Position, PagerStyle-HorizontalAlign, PagerStyle-NextPageText, and PagerStyle-PrevPageText. Adding a row below the DataGrid to hold the four navigation buttons (Next, Prev, First, and Last) is also a key ingredient.

In the application we have developed for this recipe, we added four event handler routines to the code-behind to handle the click events for the four buttons, a strategy you might find handy for your application as well. The event handlers simply alter the current page index for the grid (CurrentPageIndex), as appropriate, and rebind the data.

> To improve performance, the event handlers check to see if the page really needs changing and rebinding prior to changing the current page index value. For example, the btnPrev_ServerClick handler checks to see if CurrentPageIndex is greater than zero before subtracting one from it.
>
> To improve performance still further, you could add the following code to the end of the bindData method to disable the appropriate buttons when no action would be taken on the server call—for example, disabling the First and Prev buttons when the first page is displayed. This would avoid an unnecessary trip to the server.
>
> ```
> Dim pageIndex as Integer = dgBooks.CurrentPageIndex
> If (pageIndex = 0) Then
>   btnFirst.Disabled = True
> Else
>   btnFirst.Disabled = False
> End If
>
> If (pageIndex = dgBooks.PageCount - 1) then
>   btnLast.Disabled = True
> Else
>   btnLast.Disabled = False
> End If
> ```

See Also

The sidebar "Event Handlers" in Recipe 1.7

Example 1-20. DataGrid with first/last navigation (.aspx)

```
<%@ Page Language="vb" AutoEventWireup="false"
        Codebehind="CH01DatagridWithFirstLastNavVB.aspx.vb"
        Inherits="ASPNetCookbook.VBExamples.CH01DatagridWithFirstLastNavVB" %>
<!DOCTYPE HTML PUBLIC "-//W3C//DTD HTML 4.0 Transitional//EN">
<html>
  <head>
    <title>Datagrid With First/Last Navigation</title>
    <link rel="stylesheet" href="css/ASPNetCookbook.css">
  </head>
  <body leftmargin="0" marginheight="0" marginwidth="0" topmargin="0">
    <form id="frmDatagrid" method="post" runat="server">
      <table width="100%" cellpadding="0" cellspacing="0" border="0">
        <tr>
          <td align="center">
            <img src="images/ASPNETCookbookHeading_blue.gif">
          </td>
        </tr>
        <tr>
          <td class="dividerLine">
            <img src="images/spacer.gif" height="6" border="0"></td>
        </tr>
      </table>
      <table width="90%" align="center" border="0">
        <tr>
          <td><img src="images/spacer.gif" height="10" border="0"></td>
        </tr>
        <tr>
          <td align="center" class="PageHeading">
            DataGrid With First/Last and Next/Previous Navigation (VB)
          </td>
        </tr>
        <tr>
          <td><img src="images/spacer.gif" height="10" border="0"></td>
        </tr>
        <tr>
          <td align="center">
            <asp:DataGrid
              id="dgBooks"
              runat="server"
              BorderColor="000080"
              BorderWidth="2px"
              AutoGenerateColumns="False"
              width="100%"
              AllowPaging="True"
              PageSize="5"
              PagerStyle-Visible="False">
```

Example 1-20. DataGrid with first/last navigation (.aspx) (continued)

```
            <HeaderStyle
              HorizontalAlign="Center"
              ForeColor="#FFFFFF"
              BackColor="#000080"
              Font-Bold=true
              CssClass="TableHeader" />

            <ItemStyle
              BackColor="#FFFFE0"
              cssClass="TableCellNormal" />

            <AlternatingItemStyle
              BackColor="#FFFFFF"
              cssClass="TableCellAlternating" />

            <Columns>
              <asp:BoundColumn HeaderText="Title" DataField="Title" />
              <asp:BoundColumn HeaderText="ISBN" DataField="ISBN"
                              ItemStyle-HorizontalAlign="Center" />
              <asp:BoundColumn HeaderText="Publisher" DataField="Publisher"
                              ItemStyle-HorizontalAlign="Center" />
            </Columns>
          </asp:DataGrid>
        </td>
      </tr>
      <tr>
        <td align="center">
          <table width="40%" border="0">
            <tr>
              <td align="center">
                <input id="btnFirst" runat="server" type="image"
                       src="images/buttons/button_first.gif">
              </td>
              <td align="center">
                <input id="btnPrev" runat="server" type="image"
                       src="images/buttons/button_prev.gif">
              </td>
              <td align="center">
                <input id="btnNext" runat="server" type="image"
                       src="images/buttons/button_next.gif">
              </td>
              <td align="center">
                <input id="btnLast" runat="server" type="image"
                       src="images/buttons/button_last.gif">
              </td>
            </tr>
          </table>
        </td>
      </tr>
    </table>
  </form>
 </body>
</html>
```

Example 1-21. DataGrid with first/last navigation code-behind (.vb)

```vb
Option Explicit On
Option Strict On
'-------------------------------------------------------------------------
'
'   Module Name: CH01DatagridWithFirstLastNavVB.aspx.vb
'
'   Description: This class provides the code behind for
'                CH01DatagridWithFirstLastNavVB.aspx
'
'*************************************************************************
Imports Microsoft.VisualBasic
Imports System.Configuration
Imports System.Data
Imports System.Data.OleDb

Namespace ASPNetCookbook.VBExamples
  Public Class CH01DatagridWithFirstLastNavVB
    Inherits System.Web.UI.Page

    'controls on form
    Protected WithEvents dgBooks As System.Web.UI.WebControls.DataGrid
    Protected WithEvents btnFirst As System.Web.UI.HtmlControls.HtmlInputImage
    Protected WithEvents btnPrev As System.Web.UI.HtmlControls.HtmlInputImage
    Protected WithEvents btnNext As System.Web.UI.HtmlControls.HtmlInputImage
    Protected WithEvents btnLast As System.Web.UI.HtmlControls.HtmlInputImage


    '*************************************************************************
    '
    '   ROUTINE: Page_Load
    '
    '   DESCRIPTION: This routine provides the event handler for the page load
    '                event.  It is responsible for initializing the controls
    '                on the page.
    '-------------------------------------------------------------------------
    Private Sub Page_Load(ByVal sender As System.Object, _
                        ByVal e As System.EventArgs) _
            Handles MyBase.Load

      If (Not Page.IsPostBack) Then
        bindData()
      End If
    End Sub   'Page_Load


    '*************************************************************************
    '
    '   ROUTINE: btnFirst_ServerClick
    '
    '   DESCRIPTION: This routine provides the event handler for the first
    '                button click event.  It is responsible for setting the
    '                page index to the first page and rebinding the data.
    '-------------------------------------------------------------------------
    Private Sub btnFirst_ServerClick(ByVal sender As Object, _
            ByVal e As System.Web.UI.ImageClickEventArgs) _
```

```vb
            Handles btnFirst.ServerClick

   'set new page index and rebind the data
   If (dgBooks.CurrentPageIndex > 0) Then
     dgBooks.CurrentPageIndex = 0
     bindData( )
   End If
End Sub   'btnFirst_ServerClick

'*************************************************************************
'
'   ROUTINE: btnPrev_ServerClick
'
'   DESCRIPTION: This routine provides the event handler for the previous
'               button click event.  It is responsible for setting the
'               page index to the previous page and rebinding the data.
'-------------------------------------------------------------------------
Private Sub btnPrev_ServerClick(ByVal sender As Object, _
            ByVal e As System.Web.UI.ImageClickEventArgs) _
            Handles btnPrev.ServerClick

   'set new page index and rebind the data
   If (dgBooks.CurrentPageIndex > 0) Then
     dgBooks.CurrentPageIndex -= 1
     bindData( )
   End If
End Sub   'btnPrev_ServerClick

'*************************************************************************
'
'   ROUTINE: btnNext_ServerClick
'
'   DESCRIPTION: This routine provides the event handler for the next
'               button click event.  It is responsible for setting the
'               page index to the next page and rebinding the data.
'-------------------------------------------------------------------------
Private Sub btnNext_ServerClick(ByVal sender As Object, _
            ByVal e As System.Web.UI.ImageClickEventArgs) _
            Handles btnNext.ServerClick

   'set new page index and rebind the data
   If (dgBooks.CurrentPageIndex < dgBooks.PageCount - 1) Then
     dgBooks.CurrentPageIndex += 1
     bindData( )
   End If
End Sub   'btnNext_ServerClick

'*************************************************************************
'
'   ROUTINE: btnLast_ServerClick
'
'   DESCRIPTION: This routine provides the event handler for the last
'               button click event.  It is responsible for setting the
```

Example 1-21. DataGrid with first/last navigation code-behind (.vb) (continued)

```
'                 page index to the last page and rebinding the data.
'-------------------------------------------------------------------------
Private Sub btnLast_ServerClick(ByVal sender As Object, _
        ByVal e As System.Web.UI.ImageClickEventArgs) _
        Handles btnLast.ServerClick

  'set new page index and rebind the data
  If (dgBooks.CurrentPageIndex < dgBooks.PageCount - 1) Then
    dgBooks.CurrentPageIndex = dgBooks.PageCount - 1
    bindData( )
  End If
End Sub   'btnLast_ServerClick

'*************************************************************************
'
'   ROUTINE: bindData
'
'   DESCRIPTION: This routine queries the database for the data to
'                 displayed and binds it to the datagrid
'-------------------------------------------------------------------------
Private Sub bindData( )
  Dim dbConn As OleDbConnection
  Dim da As OleDbDataAdapter
  Dim dSet As DataSet
  Dim strConnection As String
  Dim strSQL As String

  Try
    'get the connection string from web.config and open a connection
    'to the database
    strConnection = _
        ConfigurationSettings.AppSettings("dbConnectionString")
    dbConn = New OleDbConnection(strConnection)
    dbConn.Open( )

    'build the query string and get the data from the database
    strSQL = "SELECT Title, ISBN, Publisher " & _
            "FROM Book " & _
            "ORDER BY Title"
    da = New OleDbDataAdapter(strSQL, dbConn)
    dSet = New DataSet
    da.Fill(dSet)

    'set the source of the data for the datagrid control and bind it
    dgBooks.DataSource = dSet
    dgBooks.DataBind( )

  Finally
    'cleanup
    If (Not IsNothing(dbConn)) Then
      dbConn.Close( )
    End If
```

Example 1-21. DataGrid with first/last navigation code-behind (.vb) (continued)

```
      End Try
    End Sub    'bindData
  End Class    'CH01DatagridWithFirstLastNavVB
End Namespace
```

Example 1-22. DataGrid with first/last navigation code-behind (.cs)

```csharp
//---------------------------------------------------------------------------
//
//    Module Name: CH01DatagridWithFirstLastNavCS.aspx.cs
//
//    Description: This class provides the code behind for
//                 CH01DatagridWithFirstLastNavCS.aspx
//
//***************************************************************************
using System;
using System.Configuration;
using System.Data;
using System.Data.OleDb;

namespace ASPNetCookbook.CSExamples
{
  public class CH01DatagridWithFirstLastNavCS : System.Web.UI.Page
  {
    protected System.Web.UI.HtmlControls.HtmlInputImage btnFirst;
    protected System.Web.UI.HtmlControls.HtmlInputImage btnPrev;
    protected System.Web.UI.HtmlControls.HtmlInputImage btnNext;
    protected System.Web.UI.HtmlControls.HtmlInputImage btnLast;
    protected System.Web.UI.WebControls.DataGrid dgBooks;

    //***************************************************************************
    //
    //    ROUTINE: Page_Load
    //
    //    DESCRIPTION: This routine provides the event handler for the page
    //                 load event.  It is responsible for initializing the
    //                 controls on the page.
    //---------------------------------------------------------------------------
    private void Page_Load(object sender, System.EventArgs e)
    {
      // wire in the button click events
      this.btnFirst.ServerClick +=
        new System.Web.UI.ImageClickEventHandler(this.btnFirst_ServerClick);
      this.btnPrev.ServerClick +=
        new System.Web.UI.ImageClickEventHandler(this.btnPrev_ServerClick);
      this.btnNext.ServerClick +=
        new System.Web.UI.ImageClickEventHandler(this.btnNext_ServerClick);
      this.btnLast.ServerClick +=
        new System.Web.UI.ImageClickEventHandler(this.btnLast_ServerClick);

      if (!Page.IsPostBack)
      {
        bindData();
```

Example 1-22. DataGrid with first/last navigation code-behind (.cs) (continued)

```csharp
  }
} // Page_Load

//**********************************************************************
//
//    ROUTINE: btnFirst_ServerClick
//
//    DESCRIPTION: This routine provides the event handler for the first
//                 button click event.  It is responsible for setting the
//                 page index to the first page and rebinding the data.
//----------------------------------------------------------------------
private void btnFirst_ServerClick(Object sender,
                                  System.Web.UI.ImageClickEventArgs e)
{
  // set new page index and rebind the data
  if (dgBooks.CurrentPageIndex > 0)
  {
    dgBooks.CurrentPageIndex = 0;
    bindData();
  }
} //btnFirst_ServerClick


//**********************************************************************
//
//    ROUTINE: btnPrev_ServerClick
//
//    DESCRIPTION: This routine provides the event handler for the previous
//                 button click event.  It is responsible for setting the
//                 page index to the previous page and rebinding the data.
//----------------------------------------------------------------------
private void btnPrev_ServerClick(Object sender,
                                 System.Web.UI.ImageClickEventArgs e)
{
  // set new page index and rebind the data
  if (dgBooks.CurrentPageIndex > 0)
  {
    dgBooks.CurrentPageIndex -= 1;
    bindData();
  }
} //btnPrev_ServerClick


//**********************************************************************
//
//    ROUTINE: btnNext_ServerClick
//
//    DESCRIPTION: This routine provides the event handler for the next
//                 button click event.  It is responsible for setting the
//                 page index to the next page and rebinding the data.
//----------------------------------------------------------------------
private void btnNext_ServerClick(Object sender,
                                 System.Web.UI.ImageClickEventArgs e)
{
```

```
      // set new page index and rebind the data
      if (dgBooks.CurrentPageIndex < dgBooks.PageCount - 1)
      {
        dgBooks.CurrentPageIndex += 1;
        bindData( );
      }
    } //btnNext_ServerClick

    //***********************************************************************
    //
    //   ROUTINE: btnLast_ServerClick
    //
    //   DESCRIPTION: This routine provides the event handler for the last
    //                button click event.  It is responsible for setting the
    //                page index to the last page and rebinding the data.
    //-----------------------------------------------------------------------
    private void btnLast_ServerClick(Object sender,
                                     System.Web.UI.ImageClickEventArgs e)
    {
      // set new page index and rebind the data
      if (dgBooks.CurrentPageIndex < dgBooks.PageCount - 1)
      {
        dgBooks.CurrentPageIndex = dgBooks.PageCount - 1;
        bindData( );
      }
    } //btnLast_ServerClick

    //***********************************************************************
    //
    //   ROUTINE: bindData
    //
    //   DESCRIPTION: This routine queries the database for the data to
    //                displayed and binds it to the repeater
    //-----------------------------------------------------------------------
    private void bindData( )
    {
      OleDbConnection dbConn = null;
      OleDbDataAdapter da = null;
      DataSet dSet = null;
      String strConnection = null;
      String strSQL =null;

      try
      {
        // get the connection string from web.config and open a connection
        // to the database
        strConnection =
            ConfigurationSettings.AppSettings["dbConnectionString"];
        dbConn = new OleDbConnection(strConnection);
        dbConn.Open( );
```

```
    // build the query string and get the data from the database
    strSQL = "SELECT Title, ISBN, Publisher " +
             "FROM Book " +
             "ORDER BY Title";
    da = new OleDbDataAdapter(strSQL, dbConn);
    dSet = new DataSet();
    da.Fill(dSet);

    // set the source of the data for the datagrid control and bind it
    dgBooks.DataSource = dSet;
    dgBooks.DataBind();
  }  // try

  finally
  {
    //clean up
    if (dbConn != null)
    {
      dbConn.Close();
    }
  }  // finally
  }  // bindData
  }  // CH01DatagridWithFirstLastNavCS
}
```

1.9   Adding Direct Page Navigation to a DataGrid

Problem

You need to display data in a table, but the database that stores it has more rows than can fit on a single page, and you want to allow the user to select the page to display.

Solution

The simplest solution is to use a DataGrid control and its PagerStyle-Mode and PagerStyle-PageButton attributes to enable page selection. This approach produces output like that shown in Figure 1-9. To create an application that employs this approach, start by implementing Recipe 1.7 with the changes to the DataGrid tag shown here:

```
PagerStyle-Mode="NumericPages"
PagerStyle-PageButtonCount="5"
```

A more flexible solution is to hide the pager provided by the DataGrid control and implement your own user interface for the pagination controls. This approach allows the user to, for example, input a page number in a text box and then click a button to display the data, as shown in Figure 1-10. Examples 1-23 through 1-25 show the *.aspx* and code-behind files for an application that produces this result.

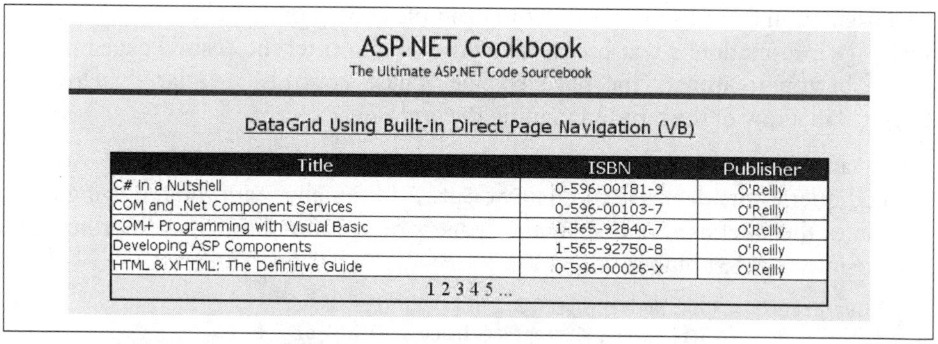

ASP.NET Cookbook
The Ultimate ASP.NET Code Sourcebook

DataGrid Using Built-in Direct Page Navigation (VB)

Title	ISBN	Publisher
C# in a Nutshell	0-596-00181-9	O'Reilly
COM and .Net Component Services	0-596-00103-7	O'Reilly
COM+ Programming with Visual Basic	1-565-92840-7	O'Reilly
Developing ASP Components	1-565-92750-8	O'Reilly
HTML & XHTML: The Definitive Guide	0-596-00026-X	O'Reilly

1 2 3 4 5 ...

Figure 1-9. Output of simple solution to DataGrid direct paging

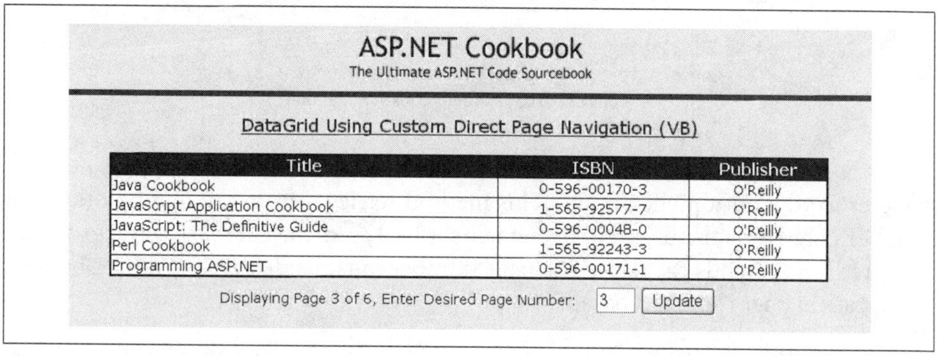

ASP.NET Cookbook
The Ultimate ASP.NET Code Sourcebook

DataGrid Using Custom Direct Page Navigation (VB)

Title	ISBN	Publisher
Java Cookbook	0-596-00170-3	O'Reilly
JavaScript Application Cookbook	1-565-92577-7	O'Reilly
JavaScript: The Definitive Guide	0-596-00048-0	O'Reilly
Perl Cookbook	1-565-92243-3	O'Reilly
Programming ASP.NET	0-596-00171-1	O'Reilly

Displaying Page 3 of 6, Enter Desired Page Number: 3 [Update]

Figure 1-10. Custom direct page navigation with a DataGrid output

Discussion

In the simple solution, setting the PagerStyle-Mode attribute to NumericPages causes the DataGrid to be rendered with page number buttons for navigating through the grid. The PagerStyle-ButtonCount attribute defines the number of "page buttons" that are output. If more pages are available than can be displayed, an ellipsis (...) is displayed at the end(s) of the page buttons containing additional pages. As shown in Figure 1-9, additional pages of data are available beyond page 5. Clicking on the ellipsis will update the data in the DataGrid and display the next block of available pages for navigation. In our example, clicking on the ellipsis will cause page 6 to be displayed in the DataGrid and pages 6–10 will be available for direct navigation.

The more flexible solution enables paging in the grid but, with the code shown next, hides the pager provided by the DataGrid. Enabling pagination is required in order to have the DataGrid provide the infrastructure needed to perform the paging. Hiding the pager provides you with the ability to implement your own user interface for the pagination controls.

```
AllowPaging="True"
PageSize="5"
PagerStyle-Visible="False">
```

The pagination controls provided in our example consist of a label to display the current page information, a text box to allow the user to enter the desired page number, and a button to initiate the page change. These controls are placed below the DataGrid in a row of the table containing the grid.

Like many of the previous examples in this chapter, the code-behind's bindData method queries the database to fill a DataSet. Additionally, with the following code, it updates the label used to display the "page x of y" information and to prompt the user to enter a page number.

VB
```
lblPager.Text = "Displaying Page " & _
                CStr(dgBooks.CurrentPageIndex + 1) & " of " & _
                CStr(dgBooks.PageCount) & _
                ", Enter Desired Page Number:"
```

C#
```
lblPager.Text = "Displaying Page " +
                Convert.ToString(dgBooks.CurrentPageIndex + 1) +
                " of " + Convert.ToString(dgBooks.PageCount) +
                ", Enter Desired Page Number:";
```

The btnDisplayPage_Click method in the code-behind provides the server-side event handler for the button click event. This method retrieves from the text box the page number entered by the user and decrements it by 1, sets the CurrentPageIndex for the DataGrid, and rebinds the data. The page number must be decremented by 1 because the DataGrid pages are zero-based.

The pagination controls we provide here are relatively simple. But, as you can imagine, virtually any user interface can be constructed using HTML and tied into the DataGrid pagination functionality.

 Production code should include validation of the page number entered by the user. This can be implemented using a RangeValidator control as described in Recipe 2.2.

See Also

Recipes 1.7 and 1.8 for implementing first/last and next/previous page navigation

Example 1-23. Custom direct page navigation with a DataGrid (.aspx)

```
<%@ Page Language="vb" AutoEventWireup="false"
        Codebehind="CH01DatagridWithDirectPageNavVB2.aspx.vb"
        Inherits="ASPNetCookbook.VBExamples.CH01DatagridWithDirectPageNavVB2" %>
<!DOCTYPE HTML PUBLIC "-//W3C//DTD HTML 4.0 Transitional//EN">
<html>
  <head>
    <title>DataGrid With Direct Page Navigation 2</title>
    <link rel="stylesheet" href="css/ASPNetCookbook.css">
  </head>
  <body leftmargin="0" marginheight="0" marginwidth="0" topmargin="0">
    <form id="frmData" method="post" runat="server">
```

Example 1-23. Custom direct page navigation with a DataGrid (.aspx) (continued)

```
<table width="100%" cellpadding="0" cellspacing="0" border="0">
  <tr>
    <td align="center">
      <img src="images/ASPNETCookbookHeading_blue.gif">
    </td>
  </tr>
  <tr>
    <td class="dividerLine">
      <img src="images/spacer.gif" height="6" border="0"></td>
  </tr>
</table>
<table width="90%" align="center" border="0">
  <tr>
    <td><img src="images/spacer.gif" height="10" border="0"></td>
  </tr>
  <tr>
    <td align="center" class="PageHeading">
      DataGrid Using Custom Direct Page Navigation (VB)
    </td>
  </tr>
  <tr>
    <td><img src="images/spacer.gif" height="10" border="0"></td>
  </tr>
  <tr>
    <td align="center">
      <asp:DataGrid
        id="dgBooks"
        runat="server"
        BorderColor="000080"
        BorderWidth="2px"
        AutoGenerateColumns="False"
        width="100%"
        AllowPaging="True"
        PageSize="5"
        PagerStyle-Visible="False">

        <HeaderStyle
          HorizontalAlign="Center"
          ForeColor="#FFFFFF"
          BackColor="#000080"
          Font-Bold=true
          CssClass="TableHeader" />

        <ItemStyle
          BackColor="#FFFFE0"
          cssClass="TableCellNormal" />

        <AlternatingItemStyle
          BackColor="#FFFFFF"
          cssClass="TableCellAlternating" />

        <Columns>
          <asp:BoundColumn HeaderText="Title" DataField="Title" />
```

Example 1-23. Custom direct page navigation with a DataGrid (.aspx) (continued)

```
                    <asp:BoundColumn HeaderText="ISBN" DataField="ISBN"
                                     ItemStyle-HorizontalAlign="Center" />
                    <asp:BoundColumn HeaderText="Publisher" DataField="Publisher"
                                     ItemStyle-HorizontalAlign="Center" />
                </Columns>
            </asp:DataGrid>
          </td>
        </tr>
        <tr>
          <td align="center">
            <table width="70%" border="0">
              <tr>
                <td><asp:Label id="lblPager" runat="server"
                               CssClass="PagerText" /></td>
                <td><asp:TextBox id="txtNewPageNumber" runat="server"
                                 Width="40" /></td>
                <td><asp:Button id="btnDisplayPage" runat="server"
                                Text="Update" /></td>
              </tr>
            </table>
          </td>
        </tr>
      </table>
    </form>
  </body>
</html>
```

Example 1-24. Custom direct page navigation with a DataGrid code-behind (.vb)

```
Option Explicit On
Option Strict On
'----------------------------------------------------------------------------
'
'   Module Name: CH01DatagridWithDirectPageNavVB2.aspx.vb
'
'   Description: This class provides the code behind for
'                CH01DatagridWithDirectPageNavVB2.aspx
'
'****************************************************************************
Imports Microsoft.VisualBasic
Imports System.Configuration
Imports System.Data
Imports System.Data.OleDb

Namespace ASPNetCookbook.VBExamples
  Public Class CH01DatagridWithDirectPageNavVB2
    Inherits System.Web.UI.Page

    'controls on form
    Protected WithEvents dgBooks As System.Web.UI.WebControls.DataGrid
    Protected lblPager As System.Web.UI.WebControls.Label
    Protected txtNewPageNumber As System.Web.UI.WebControls.TextBox
    Protected WithEvents btnDisplayPage As System.Web.UI.WebControls.Button
```

Example 1-24. Custom direct page navigation with a DataGrid code-behind (.vb) (continued)

```vb
'*************************************************************************
'
'    ROUTINE: Page_Load
'
'    DESCRIPTION: This routine provides the event handler for the page load
'                 event.  It is responsible for initializing the controls
'                 on the page.
'-------------------------------------------------------------------------
Private Sub Page_Load(ByVal sender As System.Object, _
                      ByVal e As System.EventArgs) _
        Handles MyBase.Load

  If (Not Page.IsPostBack) Then
    bindData( )
  End If
End Sub   'Page_Load


'*************************************************************************
'
'    ROUTINE: btnDisplayPage_Click
'
'    DESCRIPTION: This routine provides the event handler for the display
'                 page button click event of the datagrid.  It is
'                 responsible for setting the page index to the entered
'                 page and rebinding the data.
'-------------------------------------------------------------------------
Private Sub btnDisplayPage_Click(ByVal sender As Object, _
                                 ByVal e As System.EventArgs) _
        Handles btnDisplayPage.Click

  'set new page index and rebind the data
  'NOTE: The page numbers used by the datagrid control are 0 based
  '      so adjust the user enter page number to be 0 based
  dgBooks.CurrentPageIndex = CInt(txtNewPageNumber.Text) - 1
  bindData( )
End Sub   'btnDisplayPage_Click


'*************************************************************************
'
'    ROUTINE: bindData
'
'    DESCRIPTION: This routine queries the database for the data to
'                 displayed and binds it to the datagrid
'-------------------------------------------------------------------------
Private Sub bindData( )
  Dim dbConn As OleDbConnection
  Dim da As OleDbDataAdapter
  Dim dSet As DataSet
  Dim strConnection As String
  Dim strSQL As String
```

Example 1-24. Custom direct page navigation with a DataGrid code-behind (.vb) (continued)

```
    Try
      'get the connection string from web.config and open a connection
      'to the database
      strConnection = _
          ConfigurationSettings.AppSettings("dbConnectionString")
      dbConn = New OleDb.OleDbConnection(strConnection)
      dbConn.Open()

      'build the query string and get the data from the database
      strSQL = "SELECT Title, ISBN, Publisher " & _
              "FROM Book " & _
              "ORDER BY Title"
      da = New OleDbDataAdapter(strSQL, dbConn)
      dSet = New DataSet
      da.Fill(dSet)

      'set the source of the data for the datagrid control and bind it
      dgBooks.DataSource = dSet
      dgBooks.DataBind()

      'update label on custom pager to show current page and total pages
      lblPager.Text = "Displaying Page " & _
                      CStr(dgBooks.CurrentPageIndex + 1) & " of " & _
                      CStr(dgBooks.PageCount) & _
                      ", Enter Desired Page Number:"

    Finally
      'cleanup
      If (Not IsNothing(dbConn)) Then
        dbConn.Close()
      End If
    End Try
  End Sub   'bindData

  End Class   'CH01DatagridWithDirectPageNavVB2
End Namespace
```

Example 1-25. Custom direct page navigation with a DataGrid code-behind (.cs)

```
//-------------------------------------------------------------------------
//
//   Module Name: CH01DatagridWithDirectPageNavCS2.aspx.cs
//
//   Description: This class provides the code behind for
//                CH01DatagridWithDirectPageNavCS2.aspx
//
//*************************************************************************
using System;
using System.Configuration;
using System.Data;
using System.Data.OleDb;
using System.Web.UI.WebControls;
```

Example 1-25. Custom direct page navigation with a DataGrid code-behind (.cs) (continued)

```csharp
namespace ASPNetCookbook.CSExamples
{
  public class CH01DatagridWithDirectPageNavCS2 : System.Web.UI.Page
  {
    // controls on form
    protected System.Web.UI.WebControls.DataGrid dgBooks;
    protected System.Web.UI.WebControls.Label lblPager;
    protected System.Web.UI.WebControls.TextBox txtNewPageNumber;
    protected System.Web.UI.WebControls.Button btnDisplayPage;

    //*********************************************************************
    //
    //   ROUTINE: Page_Load
    //
    //   DESCRIPTION: This routine provides the event handler for the page
    //                load event.  It is responsible for initializing the
    //                controls on the page.
    //---------------------------------------------------------------------
    private void Page_Load(object sender, System.EventArgs e)
    {
      // wire in the display page click event
      this.btnDisplayPage.Click +=
        new System.EventHandler(this.btnDisplayPage_Click);

      if (!Page.IsPostBack)
      {
        bindData();
      }
    }  // Page_Load

    //*********************************************************************
    //
    //   ROUTINE: btnDisplayPage_Click
    //
    //   DESCRIPTION: This routine provides the event handler for the display
    //                page button click event of the datagrid.  It is
    //                responsible for setting the page index to the entered
    //                page and rebinding the data.
    //---------------------------------------------------------------------
    private void btnDisplayPage_Click(Object sender,
      System.EventArgs e)
    {
      //set new page index and rebind the data
      //NOTE: The page numbers used by the datagrid control are 0 based
      //      so adjust the user enter page number to be 0 based
      dgBooks.CurrentPageIndex = Convert.ToInt32(txtNewPageNumber.Text) - 1;
      bindData();
    }  //btnDisplayPage_Click

    //*********************************************************************
    //
```

Example 1-25. Custom direct page navigation with a DataGrid code-behind (.cs) (continued)

```csharp
//   ROUTINE: bindData
//
//   DESCRIPTION: This routine queries the database for the data to
//                displayed and binds it to the repeater
//------------------------------------------------------------------------
private void bindData()
{
  OleDbConnection dbConn = null;
  OleDbDataAdapter da = null;
  DataSet dSet = null;
  String strConnection = null;
  String strSQL =null;

  try
  {
    // get the connection string from web.config and open a connection
    // to the database
    strConnection =
        ConfigurationSettings.AppSettings["dbConnectionString"];
    dbConn = new OleDbConnection(strConnection);
    dbConn.Open();

    // build the query string and get the data from the database
    strSQL = "SELECT Title, ISBN, Publisher " +
             "FROM Book " +
             "ORDER BY Title";
    da = new OleDbDataAdapter(strSQL, dbConn);
    dSet = new DataSet();
    da.Fill(dSet, "Table");

    // set the source of the data for the datagrid control and bind it
    dgBooks.DataSource = dSet;
    dgBooks.DataBind();

    //update label on custom pager to show current page and total pages
    lblPager.Text = "Displaying Page " +
                    Convert.ToString(dgBooks.CurrentPageIndex + 1) +
                    " of " + Convert.ToString(dgBooks.PageCount) +
                    ", Enter Desired Page Number:";
  }  // try

  finally
  {
    //clean up
    if (dbConn != null)
    {
      dbConn.Close();
    }
  } // finally
} // bindData
} // CH01DatagridWithDirectPageNavCS2
}
```

1.10 Paging Through a Record-Heavy DataGrid

Problem

You need to display a very large set of data in a DataGrid, yet the user must be able to page through it quickly. This approach is beneficial anytime you have to navigate through thousands of records.

Solution

Use custom paging with a DataGrid and, using a stored procedure, read from the database only the data that is needed for a given page. An example of the output that can be achieved with this approach is shown in Figure 1-11. Examples 1-27 through 1-29 show the *.aspx* and code-behind files for an application that illustrates this approach; the application uses the stored procedure shown in Example 1-26 to retrieve the data to display.

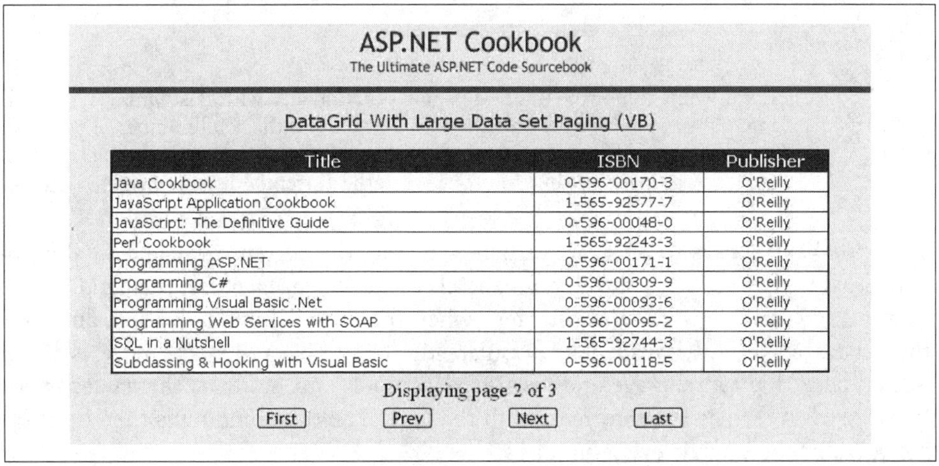

Figure 1-11. Paging through a record-heavy DataGrid output

Discussion

The solution we advocate for the problem of paging through large datasets requires a somewhat different approach to both custom paging and managing the labels used to display the current and total pages.

To enable paging and to allow you to control movement within the dataset when data binding, the DataGrid's AllowPaging and AllowCustomPaging attributes must be set to True. When AllowCustomPaging is set to False (the default), the DataGrid assumes that all of the data that can be displayed in all pages is present in the data source, and it calculates the group of records to display from the CurrentPageIndex and PageSize attributes. When AllowCustomPaging is set to True, the DataGrid expects only one page (as defined by the PageSize attribute) to be present in the data source and you are responsible for filling the data source with the proper page of data.

```
<asp:DataGrid
    id="dgBooks"
    runat="server"
    BorderColor="000080"
    BorderWidth="2px"
    AutoGenerateColumns="False"
    width="100%"
    AllowPaging="True"
    AllowCustomPaging="True"
    PageSize ="10"
    PagerStyle-Visible="False" >
```

For this example, the internal paging controls of the DataGrid are not used, so the PagerStyle-Visible attribute is set False to hide the DataGrid's pager control.

A pair of labels is used to display the current page and total number of pages available. In addition, four buttons are used to provide navigation (First, Prev, Next, and Last).

 If you want to use the internal paging functionality with custom paging, the VirtualItemCount attribute must be set to the total number of items that can be displayed in the DataGrid (all pages). In addition, the CurrentPageIndex attribute must be set to the currently displayed page.

The code-behind uses two private variables to store the current page and total number of pages that are used throughout the class. In the Page_Load event handler, the currentPage variable is initialized to zero when the page is initially loaded, and then the bindData method is called to populate the DataGrid. When the page is being posted back, the currentPage and totalPages variables are set from the values in the labels used to display the information to the user. The data binding is then done, as required, by the specific event handlers.

Four event handler routines are included in the code-behind to handle the click events for the four buttons. The event handlers alter the currentPage variable as appropriate and rebind the data. Note that, to improve performance, the event handlers first check to see if the page really needs changing and rebinding.

With standard paging, all of the data is returned, even if there are thousands of rows, and the DataGrid determines which ones are displayed. In this case, however, the bindData method uses the stored procedure shown in Example 1-26 to retrieve only the data to be displayed for the required page.

The stored procedure uses three parameters: pageNumber, pageSize, and totalRecords. The pageNumber is an input parameter that defines the page to be displayed. The pageSize is an input parameter that defines the number of rows to be displayed per page; this must be the same as the DataGrid's PageSize property. totalRecords is an output parameter used to obtain the total number of rows of data available for display.

The stored procedure first calculates the index of the first record and the last record to display in the requested page, as shown here:

```
SELECT @firstRecordInPage = @pageNumber * @pageSize + 1
SELECT @lastRecordInPage = @firstRecordInPage + @pageSize
```

A temporary table is then created to store the data from the Book table in the desired order. This table contains an Identity column that is set up to number the records from 1 to the total number of records added to the table. This provides the ability to select only the specific rows needed for the requested page number.

```
CREATE TABLE #Book
(
[ID] [int] IDENTITY (1, 1) NOT NULL ,
[BookID] [int] NOT NULL ,
[Title] [nvarchar] (100) NOT NULL ,
[ISBN] [nvarchar] (50) NOT NULL ,
[Publisher] [nvarchar] (50) NOT NULL
)
```

Next, the data from the Book table is copied into the temporary table and ordered by the book title. Now you have an ordered list of the books with the ID column set to 1 for the first book and N for the last book.

```
INSERT INTO #Book
(BookID, Title, ISBN, Publisher)
SELECT BookID, Title, ISBN, Publisher FROM Book ORDER BY Title
```

The next step is to query the temporary table for only the rows required for the page being displayed. This is done by qualifying the query based on the ID being within the range of the first and last records to display.

```
SELECT * FROM #Book
WHERE ID >= @firstRecordInPage
AND ID < @lastRecordInPage
```

Finally, you query the Book table for the total number of books and set the totalRecords output parameter to the count:

```
SELECT @totalRecords = COUNT(*) FROM Book
```

 The stored procedure used here was kept simple to illustrate the concept of returning only the required data. One negative of the example code is that all of the data from the Book table is copied to the temporary table, unnecessarily bloating the table. One way to reduce the amount of data copied is to copy rows only up to the last row required, a modification you will want to consider when adapting this code to your unique environment.

The bindData method first opens a connection to the database. A command is then created to execute the stored procedure, and the three parameters required for the stored procedure are added to it. The command is then executed using the ExecuteReader method and the returned data reader is set as the data source for the DataGrid.

 The returned DataReader must be closed to retrieve the output parameter from the stored procedure. Attempting to access the output parameter before the DataReader is closed will return null.

Finally, the total number of records is retrieved from the parameter collection, and the labels on the form that are used to inform the user of the current page and total number of pages are initialized.

Example 1-26. Stored procedure for record-heavy DataGrid

```
CREATE PROCEDURE getPageData
@pageNumber INT,
@pageSize INT,
@totalRecords INT OUTPUT
AS
DECLARE @firstRecordInPage INT
DECLARE @lastRecordInPage INT

-- Calculate the number of rows needed to get to the current page
SELECT @firstRecordInPage = @pageNumber * @pageSize + 1
SELECT @lastRecordInPage = @firstRecordInPage + @pageSize

-- Create a temporary table to copy the book data into.
-- Include only the columns needed with an additional ID
-- column that is the primary key of the temporary table.
-- In addition, it is an identity that will number the
-- records copied into the table starting with 1 thus allowing
-- us to query only for the specific records needed for the
-- requested page.
CREATE TABLE #Book
(
[ID] [int] IDENTITY (1, 1) NOT NULL ,
[BookID] [int] NOT NULL ,
[Title] [nvarchar] (100) NOT NULL ,
[ISBN] [nvarchar] (50) NOT NULL ,
[Publisher] [nvarchar] (50) NOT NULL
)

-- Copy the data from the book table into the temp table
INSERT INTO #Book
(BookID, Title, ISBN, Publisher)
SELECT BookID, Title, ISBN, Publisher FROM Book ORDER BY Title

-- Get the rows required for the passed page
SELECT * FROM #Book
```

Example 1-26. Stored procedure for record-heavy DataGrid (continued)

```
WHERE ID >= @firstRecordInPage
AND ID < @lastRecordInPage

-- Get the total number of records in the table
SELECT @totalRecords = COUNT(*) FROM Book

GO
```

Example 1-27. Paging through a record-heavy DataGrid (.aspx)

```
<%@ Page Language="vb" AutoEventWireup="false"
        Codebehind="CH01LargeDatasetPagingVB.aspx.vb"
        Inherits="ASPNetCookbook.VBExamples.CH01LargeDatasetPagingVB" %>
<!DOCTYPE HTML PUBLIC "-//W3C//DTD HTML 4.0 Transitional//EN">
<html>
  <head>
    <title>DataGrid With Large Data Set Paging</title>
    <link rel="stylesheet" href="css/ASPNetCookbook.css">
  </head>
  <body leftmargin="0" marginheight="0" marginwidth="0" topmargin="0">
    <form id="frmData" method="post" runat="server">
      <table width="100%" cellpadding="0" cellspacing="0" border="0">
        <tr>
          <td align="center">
            <img src="images/ASPNETCookbookHeading_blue.gif">
          </td>
        </tr>
        <tr>
          <td class="dividerLine">
            <img src="images/spacer.gif" height="6" border="0"></td>
        </tr>
      </table>
      <table width="90%" align="center" border="0">
        <tr>
          <td><img src="images/spacer.gif" height="10" border="0"></td>
        </tr>
        <tr>
          <td align="center" class="PageHeading">
            DataGrid With Large Data Set Paging (VB)
          </td>
        </tr>
        <tr>
          <td><img src="images/spacer.gif" height="10" border="0"></td>
        </tr>
        <tr>
          <td align="center">
            <asp:DataGrid
              id="dgBooks"
              runat="server"
              BorderColor="000080"
              BorderWidth="2px"
              AutoGenerateColumns="False"
              width="100%"
```

Example 1-27. Paging through a record-heavy DataGrid (.aspx) (continued)

```
        AllowPaging="True"
        AllowCustomPaging="True"
        PageSize ="10"
        PagerStyle-Visible="False" >

        <HeaderStyle
          HorizontalAlign="Center"
          ForeColor="#FFFFFF"
          BackColor="#000080"
          Font-Bold=true
          CssClass="TableHeader" />

        <ItemStyle
          BackColor="#FFFFE0"
          cssClass="TableCellNormal" />

        <AlternatingItemStyle
          BackColor="#FFFFFF"
          cssClass="TableCellAlternating" />

        <Columns>
          <asp:BoundColumn HeaderText="Title" DataField="Title" />
          <asp:BoundColumn HeaderText="ISBN" DataField="ISBN"
                          ItemStyle-HorizontalAlign="Center" />
          <asp:BoundColumn HeaderText="Publisher" DataField="Publisher"
                          ItemStyle-HorizontalAlign="Center" />
        </Columns>
      </asp:DataGrid>
    </td>
  </tr>
  <tr>
    <td align="center">
      <table width="70%" border="0">
        <tr>
          <td colspan="4" align="center">
            Displaying page
            <asp:Literal id="labCurrentPage" runat="server" /> of
            <asp:Literal id="labTotalPages" runat="server" /></td>
        </tr>
        <tr>
          <td align="center">
            <input type="image" id="btnFirst" runat="server"
                   src="images/buttons/button_first.gif"></td>
          <td align="center">
            <input type="image" id="btnPrev" runat="server"
                   src="images/buttons/button_prev.gif"></td>
          <td align="center">
            <input type="image" id="btnNext" runat="server"
                   src="images/buttons/button_next.gif"></td>
          <td align="center">
            <input type="image" id="btnLast" runat="server"
                   src="images/buttons/button_last.gif"></td>
        </tr>
```

Example 1-27. Paging through a record-heavy DataGrid (.aspx) (continued)

```
            </table>
          </td>
        </tr>
      </table>
    </form>
  </body>
</html>
```

Example 1-28. Paging through a record-heavy DataGrid (.vb)

```vb
Option Explicit On
Option Strict On
'----------------------------------------------------------------------------
'
'   Module Name: CH01LargeDatasetPagingVB.aspx.vb
'
'   Description: This class provides the code behind for
'                CH01LargeDatasetPagingVB.aspx
'
'****************************************************************************
Imports Microsoft.VisualBasic
Imports System
Imports System.Configuration
Imports System.Data
Imports System.Data.OleDb

Namespace ASPNetCookbook.VBExamples
  Public Class CH01LargeDatasetPagingVB
    Inherits System.Web.UI.Page

    'controls on form
    Protected dgBooks As System.Web.UI.WebControls.DataGrid
    Protected labCurrentPage As System.Web.UI.WebControls.Literal
    Protected labTotalPages As System.Web.UI.WebControls.Literal
    Protected WithEvents btnPrev As System.Web.UI.HtmlControls.HtmlInputImage
    Protected WithEvents btnNext As System.Web.UI.HtmlControls.HtmlInputImage
    Protected WithEvents btnLast As System.Web.UI.HtmlControls.HtmlInputImage
    Protected WithEvents btnFirst As System.Web.UI.HtmlControls.HtmlInputImage

    'private variables used to store the current page and total number of
    'pages.  This is required since the CurrentPageIndex and PageCount
    'properties of the datagrid cannot be used with custom paging
    Private currentPage As Integer
    Private totalPages As Integer

    '****************************************************************************
    '
    '   ROUTINE: Page_Load
    '
    '   DESCRIPTION: This routine provides the event handler for the page load
    '                event.  It is responsible for initializing the controls
    '                on the page.
    '----------------------------------------------------------------------------
```

Example 1-28. Paging through a record-heavy DataGrid (.vb) (continued)

```
Private Sub Page_Load(ByVal sender As System.Object, _
                      ByVal e As System.EventArgs) _
        Handles MyBase.Load

    If (Page.IsPostBack) Then
      'This is a post back so initialize the current and total page variables
      'with the values currently being displayed
      currentPage = CInt(labCurrentPage.Text) - 1   'zero based page numbers
      totalPages = CInt(labTotalPages.Text)
    Else
      'This is the first rendering of the form so set the current page to the
      'first page and bind the data
      currentPage = 0
      bindData()
    End If
End Sub   'Page_Load

'*************************************************************************
'
'    ROUTINE: btnFirst_ServerClick
'
'    DESCRIPTION: This routine provides the event handler for the first
'                 button click event.  It is responsible for setting the
'                 page index to the first page and rebinding the data.
'-------------------------------------------------------------------------
Private Sub btnFirst_ServerClick(ByVal sender As Object, _
            ByVal e As System.Web.UI.ImageClickEventArgs) _
            Handles btnFirst.ServerClick

    'set new page index and rebind the data
    If (currentPage > 0) Then
      currentPage = 0
      bindData()
    End If
End Sub   'btnFirst_ServerClick

'*************************************************************************
'
'    ROUTINE: btnPrev_ServerClick
'
'    DESCRIPTION: This routine provides the event handler for the previous
'                 button click event.  It is responsible for setting the
'                 page index to the previous page and rebinding the data.
'-------------------------------------------------------------------------
Private Sub btnPrev_ServerClick(ByVal sender As Object, _
            ByVal e As System.Web.UI.ImageClickEventArgs) _
            Handles btnPrev.ServerClick

    'set new page index and rebind the data
    If (currentPage > 0) Then
      currentPage -= 1
      bindData()
```

Example 1-28. Paging through a record-heavy DataGrid (.vb) (continued)

```vb
    End If
End Sub   'btnPrev_ServerClick


'************************************************************************
'
'   ROUTINE: btnNext_ServerClick
'
'   DESCRIPTION: This routine provides the event handler for the next
'                button click event.  It is responsible for setting the
'                page index to the next page and rebinding the data.
'-----------------------------------------------------------------------
Private Sub btnNext_ServerClick(ByVal sender As Object, _
          ByVal e As System.Web.UI.ImageClickEventArgs) _
          Handles btnNext.ServerClick

    'set new page index and rebind the data
    If (currentPage < totalPages - 1) Then
      currentPage += 1
      bindData( )
    End If
End Sub   'btnNext_ServerClick


'************************************************************************
'
'   ROUTINE: btnLast_ServerClick
'
'   DESCRIPTION: This routine provides the event handler for the last
'                button click event.  It is responsible for setting the
'                page index to the last page and rebinding the data.
'-----------------------------------------------------------------------
Private Sub btnLast_ServerClick(ByVal sender As Object, _
        ByVal e As System.Web.UI.ImageClickEventArgs) _
        Handles btnLast.ServerClick

    'set new page index and rebind the data
    If (currentPage < totalPages - 1) Then
      currentPage = totalPages - 1
      bindData( )
    End If
End Sub   'btnLast_ServerClick


'************************************************************************
'
'   ROUTINE: bindData
'
'   DESCRIPTION: This routine queries the database for the data to
'                displayed and binds it to the datagrid
'-----------------------------------------------------------------------
Private Sub bindData( )
  Dim dbConn As OleDbConnection
  Dim dCmd As OleDbCommand
  Dim dReader As OleDbDataReader
```

Example 1-28. Paging through a record-heavy DataGrid (.vb) (continued)

```vb
Dim param As OleDbParameter
Dim strConnection As String
Dim strSQL As String
Dim totalRecords As Integer

Try
  'get the connection string from web.config and open a connection
  'to the database
  strConnection = _
      ConfigurationSettings.AppSettings("dbConnectionString")
  dbConn = New OleDb.OleDbConnection(strConnection)
  dbConn.Open()

  'create command to execute the stored procedure along with the
  'parameters required in and out of the procedure
  strSQL = "getPageData"      'name of stored procedure
  dCmd = New OleDbCommand(strSQL, dbConn)
  dCmd.CommandType = CommandType.StoredProcedure

  param = dCmd.Parameters.Add("pageNumber", OleDbType.Integer)
  param.Direction = ParameterDirection.Input
  param.Value = currentPage

  param = dCmd.Parameters.Add("pageSize", OleDbType.Integer)
  param.Direction = ParameterDirection.Input
  param.Value = dgBooks.PageSize

  param = dCmd.Parameters.Add("totalRecords", OleDbType.Integer)
  param.Direction = ParameterDirection.Output

  'execute the stored procedure and set the datasource for the datagrid
  dReader = dCmd.ExecuteReader()
  dgBooks.DataSource = dReader
  dgBooks.DataBind()

  'close the dataReader to make the output parameter available
  dReader.Close()

  'output information about the current page and total number of pages
  totalRecords = CInt(dCmd.Parameters.Item("totalRecords").Value)
  totalPages = CInt(Math.Ceiling(totalRecords / dgBooks.PageSize))
  labTotalPages.Text = totalPages.ToString()
  labCurrentPage.Text = (currentPage + 1).ToString()

Finally
  'cleanup
  If (Not IsNothing(dReader)) Then
    dReader.Close()
  End If

  If (Not IsNothing(dbConn)) Then
    dbConn.Close()
```

Example 1-28. Paging through a record-heavy DataGrid (.vb) (continued)

```
        End If
      End Try
    End Sub  'bindData
  End Class  'CH01LargeDatasetPagingVB
End Namespace
```

Example 1-29. Paging through a record-heavy DataGrid (.cs)

```
//-----------------------------------------------------------------------------
//
//    Module Name: CH01LargeDatasetPagingCS.aspx.cs
//
//    Description: This class provides the code behind for
//                 CH01LargeDatasetPagingCS.aspx
//
//*****************************************************************************
using System;
using System.Configuration;
using System.Data;
using System.Data.OleDb;

namespace ASPNetCookbook.CSExamples
{
  public class CH01LargeDatasetPagingCS : System.Web.UI.Page
  {
    // controls on form
    protected System.Web.UI.HtmlControls.HtmlInputImage btnFirst;
    protected System.Web.UI.HtmlControls.HtmlInputImage btnPrev;
    protected System.Web.UI.HtmlControls.HtmlInputImage btnNext;
    protected System.Web.UI.HtmlControls.HtmlInputImage btnLast;
    protected System.Web.UI.WebControls.DataGrid dgBooks;
    protected System.Web.UI.WebControls.Literal labCurrentPage;
    protected System.Web.UI.WebControls.Literal labTotalPages;

    // private variables used to store the current page and total number of
    // pages.  This is required since the CurrentPageIndex and PageCount
    // properties of the datagrid cannot be used with custom paging
    private int currentPage;
    private int totalPages;

    //*****************************************************************************
    //
    //    ROUTINE: Page_Load
    //
    //    DESCRIPTION: This routine provides the event handler for the page
    //                 load event.  It is responsible for initializing the
    //                 controls on page.
    //-----------------------------------------------------------------------------
    private void Page_Load(object sender, System.EventArgs e)
    {
      // wire in the button click events
      this.btnFirst.ServerClick +=
        new System.Web.UI.ImageClickEventHandler(this.btnFirst_ServerClick);
```

Example 1-29. Paging through a record-heavy DataGrid (.cs) (continued)

```csharp
      this.btnPrev.ServerClick +=
        new System.Web.UI.ImageClickEventHandler(this.btnPrev_ServerClick);
      this.btnNext.ServerClick +=
        new System.Web.UI.ImageClickEventHandler(this.btnNext_ServerClick);
      this.btnLast.ServerClick +=
        new System.Web.UI.ImageClickEventHandler(this.btnLast_ServerClick);

      if (Page.IsPostBack)
      {
        // This is a post back so initialize the current and total page
        // variables with the values currently being displayed
        currentPage = Convert.ToInt32(labCurrentPage.Text) - 1;
        totalPages = Convert.ToInt32(labTotalPages.Text);
      }
      else
      {
        // This is the first rendering of the form so set the current page to
        // the first page and bind the data
        currentPage = 0;
        bindData( );
      }
    }  //Page_Load

    //*************************************************************************
    //
    //    ROUTINE: btnFirst_ServerClick
    //
    //    DESCRIPTION: This routine provides the event handler for the first
    //                 button click event.  It is responsible for setting the
    //                 page index to the first page and rebinding the data.
    //-------------------------------------------------------------------------
    private void btnFirst_ServerClick(Object sender,
      System.Web.UI.ImageClickEventArgs e)
    {
      // set new page index and rebind the data
      if (currentPage > 0)
      {
        currentPage = 0;
        bindData( );
      }
    }  //btnFirst_ServerClick

    //*************************************************************************
    //
    //    ROUTINE: btnPrev_ServerClick
    //
    //    DESCRIPTION: This routine provides the event handler for the previous
    //                 button click event.  It is responsible for setting the
    //                 page index to the previous page and rebinding the data.
    //-------------------------------------------------------------------------
    private void btnPrev_ServerClick(Object sender,
      System.Web.UI.ImageClickEventArgs e)
    {
```

Example 1-29. Paging through a record-heavy DataGrid (.cs) (continued)

```
    // set new page index and rebind the data
    if (currentPage > 0)
    {
      currentPage -= 1;
      bindData( );
    }
} //btnPrev_ServerClick


//*************************************************************************
//
//    ROUTINE: btnNext_ServerClick
//
//    DESCRIPTION: This routine provides the event handler for the next
//                 button click event.  It is responsible for setting the
//                 page index to the next page and rebinding the data.
//-------------------------------------------------------------------------
private void btnNext_ServerClick(Object sender,
  System.Web.UI.ImageClickEventArgs e)
{
    // set new page index and rebind the data
    if (currentPage < totalPages - 1)
    {
      currentPage += 1;
      bindData( );
    }
} //btnNext_ServerClick


//*************************************************************************
//
//    ROUTINE: btnLast_ServerClick
//
//    DESCRIPTION: This routine provides the event handler for the last
//                 button click event.  It is responsible for setting the
//                 page index to the last page and rebinding the data.
//-------------------------------------------------------------------------
private void btnLast_ServerClick(Object sender,
  System.Web.UI.ImageClickEventArgs e)
{
    // set new page index and rebind the data
    if (currentPage < totalPages - 1)
    {
      currentPage = totalPages - 1;
      bindData( );
    }
} //btnLast_ServerClick


//*************************************************************************
//
//    ROUTINE: bindData
//
//    DESCRIPTION: This routine queries the database for the data to
//                 displayed and binds it to the repeater
//-------------------------------------------------------------------------
```

Example 1-29. Paging through a record-heavy DataGrid (.cs) (continued)

```csharp
private void bindData()
{
  OleDbConnection dbConn = null;
  OleDbCommand dCmd = null;
  OleDbDataReader dReader = null;
  OleDbParameter param = null;
  String strConnection = null;
  String strSQL = null;
  int totalRecords = 0;

  try
  {
    // get the connection string from web.config and open a connection
    // to the database
    strConnection =
      ConfigurationSettings.AppSettings["dbConnectionString"];
    dbConn = new OleDbConnection(strConnection);
    dbConn.Open();

    // create command to execute the stored procedure along with the
    // parameters required in/out of the procedure
    strSQL = "getPageData";     // name of stored procedure
    dCmd = new OleDbCommand(strSQL, dbConn);
    dCmd.CommandType = CommandType.StoredProcedure;

    param = dCmd.Parameters.Add("pageNumber", OleDbType.Integer);
    param.Direction = ParameterDirection.Input;
    param.Value = currentPage;

    param = dCmd.Parameters.Add("pageSize", OleDbType.Integer);
    param.Direction = ParameterDirection.Input;
    param.Value = dgBooks.PageSize;

    param = dCmd.Parameters.Add("totalRecords", OleDbType.Integer);
    param.Direction = ParameterDirection.Output;

    //execute the stored procedure and set the datasource for the datagrid
    dReader = dCmd.ExecuteReader();
    dgBooks.DataSource = dReader;
    dgBooks.DataBind();

    // close the dataReader to make the output parameter available
    dReader.Close();

    // output information about the current page and total number of pages
    totalRecords = Convert.ToInt32(dCmd.Parameters["totalRecords"].Value);
    totalPages = Convert.ToInt32(Math.Ceiling(Convert.ToDouble(totalRecords) /
                 dgBooks.PageSize));
    labTotalPages.Text = totalPages.ToString();
    labCurrentPage.Text = (currentPage + 1).ToString();
```

Example 1-29. Paging through a record-heavy DataGrid (.cs) (continued)

```
    }  // try

    finally
    {
      //clean up
      if (dReader != null)
      {
        dReader.Close();
      }

      if (dbConn != null)
      {
        dbConn.Close();
      }
    }  // finally
  }  // bindData
}  // CH01LargeDatasetPagingCS
}
```

1.11   Sorting Data Within a DataGrid

Problem

You are displaying a table of data and you want to let the user sort the data in a DataGrid by clicking on its column headers.

Solution

Enable the DataGrid control's sorting features, and create a routine that binds the appropriate data to the control when it is initially displayed and whenever the user clicks a column header.

In the *.aspx* file, enable the DataGrid control's sorting features.

In the code-behind class for the page, use the .NET language of your choice to:

1. Create a data-binding method (bindData in our example) that performs the actual sorting based on the value of a sortExpression parameter and binds a dataset to the DataGrid (this parameter is used in the ORDER BY clause of the SQL statement).

2. Call the data-binding method from the Page_Load method (to support the initial display of the grid) and from the event that is fired when the user clicks on a column header (the dgBooks_SortCommand event in our example).

Figure 1-12 shows the appearance of a typical DataGrid sorted by title, the information in the first column. Examples 1-30 through 1-32 show the *.aspx* and code-behind files for an example application that produces this result.

ASP.NET Cookbook
The Ultimate ASP.NET Code Sourcebook

DataGrid With Column Sorting (VB)

Title	ISBN	Publisher
.Net Framework Essentials	0-596-00302-1	O'Reilly
Access Cookbook	0-596-00084-7	O'Reilly
ADO: ActiveX Data Objects	1-565-92415-0	O'Reilly
ASP.NET in a Nutshell	0-596-00116-9	O'Reilly
C# Essentials	0-596-00315-3	O'Reilly
C# in a Nutshell	0-596-00181-9	O'Reilly
COM and .Net Component Services	0-596-00103-7	O'Reilly
COM+ Programming with Visual Basic	1-565-92840-7	O'Reilly
Developing ASP Components	1-565-92750-8	O'Reilly
HTML & XHTML: The Definitive Guide	0-596-00026-X	O'Reilly
Java Cookbook	0-596-00170-3	O'Reilly
JavaScript Application Cookbook	1-565-92577-7	O'Reilly
JavaScript: The Definitive Guide	0-596-00048-0	O'Reilly
Perl Cookbook	1-565-92243-3	O'Reilly
Programming ASP.NET	0-596-00171-1	O'Reilly
Programming C#	0-596-00309-9	O'Reilly
Programming Visual Basic .Net	0-596-00093-6	O'Reilly
Programming Web Services with SOAP	0-596-00095-2	O'Reilly
SQL in a Nutshell	1-565-92744-3	O'Reilly
Subclassing & Hooking with Visual Basic	0-596-00118-5	O'Reilly
Transact-SQL Cookbook	1-565-92756-7	O'Reilly
Transact-SQL Programming	1-565-92401-0	O'Reilly
VB .Net Language in a Nutshell	0-596-00092-8	O'Reilly
Web Services Essentials	0-596-00224-6	O'Reilly
XML in a Nutshell	0-596-00058-8	O'Reilly
XSLT	0-596-00053-7	O'Reilly

Figure 1-12. DataGrid with column sorting output

Discussion

The DataGrid control provides the basic plumbing required to support sorting. It will generate the links for the column headers that will raise the SortCommand server-side event when a column header is clicked. The DataGrid does not provide the code required to perform the actual sorting, but very little code is required to complete that job.

To enable sorting, the AllowSorting attribute of the DataGrid element must be set to True. In addition, the SortExpression attribute of the BoundColumn element must be set to the expression that will be used in your code to perform the sorting. This would normally be set to the name of the database column displayed in the DataGrid column; however, it can be set to any value required by your code to perform the sorting.

Your code will need to perform the actual sorting. For example, the application that we developed for this recipe supports sorting in a centralized manner by using a sortExpression parameter with its bindData method. This parameter is used in the ORDER BY clause of the SQL statement.

The bindData method is called from two places:

- In the Page_Load method to support the initial display of the grid. The value "Title" is passed to provide the default sorting by title.
- From the dgBooks_SortCommand method. This method is called when the user clicks on a column header. The e argument contains the SortExpression value for the clicked column that was set in the BoundColumn element. This value is passed to the bindData method where it is used in the SQL statement to perform the sorting by the selected column.

Our solution is quick and easy but lacks polish, in that it does not identify the current sort column. With the addition of a few lines of code to the bindData method, the sort column can be highlighted, as shown in Figure 1-13 (sort column is shown in yellow when displayed on the screen). The code added to the bindData method is shown next. It loops through the columns in the DataGrid, comparing the SortExpression for the column to the sortExpression passed to the bindData method. If the values match, the foreground color of the HeaderStyle for the color is set to yellow to highlight the column. Otherwise, the color is set to white.

 When working with this recipe's sample application, be aware that the following code must be placed *before* the DataBind statement. As a general rule, changes of this sort made to a DataGrid control that are placed after data binding may not be displayed as intended.

VB

```
Dim col As DataGridColumn

    ...

For Each col In dgBooks.Columns
  If (col.SortExpression = sortExpression) Then
    'this is the sort column so highlight it
    col.HeaderStyle.ForeColor = Color.Yellow
  Else
    'this is not the sort column so use the normal coloring
    col.HeaderStyle.ForeColor = Color.White
  End If
Next col
```

C#

```
foreach (DataGridColumn col in dgBooks.Columns)
  {
  if (col.SortExpression == sortExpression)
  { //this is the sort column so highlight it
    col.HeaderStyle.ForeColor = Color.Yellow;
  }
  else
  { //this is not the sort column so use the normal coloring
    col.HeaderStyle.ForeColor = Color.White;
  }
  } // foreach
```

ASP.NET Cookbook
The Ultimate ASP.NET Code Sourcebook

DataGrid With Column Sorting And Highlighted Column (VB)

Title	ISBN	Publisher
.Net Framework Essentials	0-596-00302-1	O'Reilly
Access Cookbook	0-596-00084-7	O'Reilly
ADO: ActiveX Data Objects	1-565-92415-0	O'Reilly
ASP.NET in a Nutshell	0-596-00116-9	O'Reilly
C# Essentials	0-596-00315-3	O'Reilly
C# in a Nutshell	0-596-00181-9	O'Reilly
COM and .Net Component Services	0-596-00103-7	O'Reilly
COM+ Programming with Visual Basic	1-565-92840-7	O'Reilly
Developing ASP Components	1-565-92750-8	O'Reilly
HTML & XHTML: The Definitive Guide	0-596-00026-X	O'Reilly
Java Cookbook	0-596-00170-3	O'Reilly
JavaScript Application Cookbook	1-565-92577-7	O'Reilly
JavaScript: The Definitive Guide	0-596-00048-0	O'Reilly
Perl Cookbook	1-565-92243-3	O'Reilly
Programming ASP.NET	0-596-00171-1	O'Reilly
Programming C#	0-596-00309-9	O'Reilly
Programming Visual Basic .Net	0-596-00093-6	O'Reilly
Programming Web Services with SOAP	0-596-00095-2	O'Reilly
SQL in a Nutshell	1-565-92744-3	O'Reilly
Subclassing & Hooking with Visual Basic	0-596-00118-5	O'Reilly
Transact-SQL Cookbook	1-565-92756-7	O'Reilly
Transact-SQL Programming	1-565-92401-0	O'Reilly
VB .Net Language in a Nutshell	0-596-00092-8	O'Reilly
Web Services Essentials	0-596-00224-6	O'Reilly
XML in a Nutshell	0-596-00058-8	O'Reilly
XSLT	0-596-00053-7	O'Reilly

Figure 1-13. DataGrid with highlighted sort column output

Another possibility for highlighting the sort column is to place an image beside the header title of the current sort column. In our application, this is accomplished by changing two lines of code (and the associated comments) in the highlighting solution. The code changes are shown here:

VB

```
For Each col In dgBooks.Columns
  If (col.SortExpression = sortExpression) Then
    'this is the sort column so add an image to mark it
    col.HeaderText = col.SortExpression & _
                 " <img src='images/asterisk.gif' border='0'>"
  Else
    'this is not the sort column so just display the title
    col.HeaderText = col.SortExpression
  End If
Next col
```

C#

```
foreach (DataGridColumn col in dgBooks.Columns)
{
  if (col.SortExpression == sortExpression)
  { //this is the sort column so add an image to mark it
    col.HeaderText = col.SortExpression +
                 " <img src='images/asterisk.gif' border='0'>";
  }
```

```
      else
      { //this is not the sort column so just display the title
        col.HeaderText = col.SortExpression;
      }
    } // foreach
```

The DataGrid header is rendered as a table row, with each column header appearing as a cell in the row. When sorting is enabled, the header text is rendered within an anchor tag, as shown in Figure 1-14. Placing the HTML for an image tag in the header text simply places the image within an anchor tag, which is a common way to make an image a link in a standard HTML page.

ASP.NET Cookbook
The Ultimate ASP.NET Code Sourcebook

DataGrid With Column Sorting And Highlighted Column (VB)

Title *	ISBN	Publisher
.Net Framework Essentials	0-596-00302-1	O'Reilly
Access Cookbook	0-596-00084-7	O'Reilly
ADO: ActiveX Data Objects	1-565-92415-0	O'Reilly
ASP.NET in a Nutshell	0-596-00116-9	O'Reilly
C# Essentials	0-596-00315-3	O'Reilly
C# in a Nutshell	0-596-00181-9	O'Reilly
COM and .Net Component Services	0-596-00103-7	O'Reilly
COM+ Programming with Visual Basic	1-565-92840-7	O'Reilly
Developing ASP Components	1-565-92750-8	O'Reilly
HTML & XHTML: The Definitive Guide	0-596-00026-X	O'Reilly
Java Cookbook	0-596-00170-3	O'Reilly
JavaScript Application Cookbook	1-565-92577-7	O'Reilly
JavaScript: The Definitive Guide	0-596-00048-0	O'Reilly
Perl Cookbook	1-565-92243-3	O'Reilly
Programming ASP.NET	0-596-00171-1	O'Reilly
Programming C#	0-596-00309-9	O'Reilly
Programming Visual Basic .Net	0-596-00093-6	O'Reilly
Programming Web Services with SOAP	0-596-00095-2	O'Reilly
SQL in a Nutshell	1-565-92744-3	O'Reilly
Subclassing & Hooking with Visual Basic	0-596-00118-5	O'Reilly
Transact-SQL Cookbook	1-565-92756-7	O'Reilly
Transact-SQL Programming	1-565-92401-0	O'Reilly
VB .Net Language in a Nutshell	0-596-00092-8	O'Reilly
Web Services Essentials	0-596-00224-6	O'Reilly
XML in a Nutshell	0-596-00058-8	O'Reilly
XSLT	0-596-00053-7	O'Reilly

Figure 1-14. DataGrid with sort column highlighted with an image (in this case, an asterisk)

Example 1-30. DataGrid with column sorting (.aspx)

```
<%@ Page Language="vb" AutoEventWireup="false"
        Codebehind="CH01DatagridSortingVB1.aspx.vb"
        Inherits="ASPNetCookbook.VBExamples.CH01DatagridSortingVB1" %>
<!DOCTYPE HTML PUBLIC "-//W3C//DTD HTML 4.0 Transitional//EN">
<html>
  <head>
    <title>DataGrid With Sorting</title>
    <link rel="stylesheet" href="css/ASPNetCookbook.css">
  </head>
  <body leftmargin="0" marginheight="0" marginwidth="0" topmargin="0">
```

Example 1-30. DataGrid with column sorting (.aspx) (continued)

```
<form id="frmDatagrid" method="post" runat="server">
  <table width="100%" cellpadding="0" cellspacing="0" border="0">
    <tr>
      <td align="center">
        <img src="images/ASPNETCookbookHeading_blue.gif">
      </td>
    </tr>
    <tr>
      <td class="dividerLine">
        <img src="images/spacer.gif" height="6" border="0"></td>
    </tr>
  </table>
  <table width="90%" align="center" border="0">
    <tr>
      <td><img src="images/spacer.gif" height="10" border="0"></td>
    </tr>
    <tr>
      <td align="center" class="PageHeading">
        DataGrid With Column Sorting (VB)
      </td>
    </tr>
    <tr>
      <td><img src="images/spacer.gif" height="10" border="0"></td>
    </tr>
    <tr>
      <td align="center">
        <asp:DataGrid
          id="dgBooks"
          runat="server"
          BorderColor="000080"
          BorderWidth="2px"
          AutoGenerateColumns="False"
          width="100%"
          AllowSorting="True">

          <HeaderStyle
            HorizontalAlign="Center"
            ForeColor="#FFFFFF"
            BackColor="#000080"
            Font-Bold=true
            CssClass="TableHeader" />

          <ItemStyle
            BackColor="#FFFFE0"
            cssClass="TableCellNormal" />

          <AlternatingItemStyle
            BackColor="#FFFFFF"
            cssClass="TableCellAlternating" />

          <Columns>
            <asp:BoundColumn HeaderText="Title" DataField="Title"
                             SortExpression="Title" />
```

Example 1-30. DataGrid with column sorting (.aspx) (continued)

```
                    <asp:BoundColumn HeaderText="ISBN" DataField="ISBN"
                                     ItemStyle-HorizontalAlign="Center"
                                     SortExpression="ISBN" />
                    <asp:BoundColumn HeaderText="Publisher" DataField="Publisher"
                                     ItemStyle-HorizontalAlign="Center"
                                     SortExpression="Publisher" />
                </Columns>
              </asp:DataGrid>
            </td>
          </tr>
        </table>
      </form>
    </body>
</html>
```

Example 1-31. DataGrid with column sorting code-behind (.vb)

```
Option Explicit On
Option Strict On
'-----------------------------------------------------------------------------
'
'   Module Name: CH01DatagridSortingVB1.aspx.vb
'
'   Description: This class provides the code behind for
'                CH01DatagridSortingVB1.aspx
'
'*****************************************************************************
Imports Microsoft.VisualBasic
Imports System.Configuration
Imports System.Data
Imports System.Data.OleDb
Imports System.Web.UI.WebControls

Namespace ASPNetCookbook.VBExamples
  Public Class CH01DatagridSortingVB1
    Inherits System.Web.UI.Page

    'controls on form
    Protected WithEvents dgBooks As System.Web.UI.WebControls.DataGrid

    '*****************************************************************************
    '
    '   ROUTINE: Page_Load
    '
    '   DESCRIPTION: This routine provides the event handler for the page load
    '                event.  It is responsible for initializing the controls
    '                on the page.
    '-------------------------------------------------------------------------
    Private Sub Page_Load(ByVal sender As System.Object, _
                          ByVal e As System.EventArgs) _
            Handles MyBase.Load

      If (Not Page.IsPostBack) Then
```

Example 1-31. DataGrid with column sorting code-behind (.vb) (continued)

```vb
      'sort by title and bind data to DataGrid
      bindData("Title")
   End If
End Sub   'Page_Load

'****************************************************************************
'
'    ROUTINE: dgBooks_SortCommand
'
'    DESCRIPTION: This routine provides the event handler for the datagrid
'                 sort event.  It is responsible re-binding the data to the
'                 datagrid by the selected column.
'----------------------------------------------------------------------------
Private Sub dgBooks_SortCommand(ByVal source As Object, _
                                ByVal e As DataGridSortCommandEventArgs) _
      Handles dgBooks.SortCommand

   'sort the data by the selected column and re-bind the data
   bindData(e.SortExpression)
End Sub   'dgBooks_SortCommand

'****************************************************************************
'
'    ROUTINE: bindData
'
'    DESCRIPTION: This routine queries the database for the data to
'                 displayed and binds it to the datagrid
'----------------------------------------------------------------------------
Private Sub bindData(ByVal sortExpression As String)
   Dim dbConn As OleDbConnection
   Dim da As OleDbDataAdapter
   Dim ds As DataSet
   Dim strConnection As String
   Dim strSQL As String

   Try
     'get the connection string from web.config and open a connection
     'to the database
     strConnection = _
         ConfigurationSettings.AppSettings("dbConnectionString")
     dbConn = New OleDbConnection(strConnection)
     dbConn.Open( )

     'build the query string and get the data from the database
     strSQL = "SELECT Title, ISBN, Publisher " & _
              "FROM Book " & _
              "ORDER BY " & sortExpression

     da = New OleDbDataAdapter(strSQL, dbConn)
     ds = New DataSet
     da.Fill(ds)
```

Example 1-31. DataGrid with column sorting code-behind (.vb) (continued)

```
        'set the source of the data for the datagrid control and bind it
        dgBooks.DataSource = ds
        dgBooks.DataBind( )

      Finally
        'cleanup
        If (Not IsNothing(dbConn)) Then
          dbConn.Close( )
        End If
      End Try
    End Sub   'bindData
  End Class   'CH01DatagridSortingVB1
End Namespace
```

Example 1-32. DataGrid with column sorting code-behind (.cs)

```csharp
//----------------------------------------------------------------------
//
//   Module Name: CH01DatagridSortingCS1.aspx.cs
//
//   Description: This class provides the code behind for
//                CH01DatagridSortingCS1.aspx
//
//*********************************************************************
using System;
using System.Configuration;
using System.Data;
using System.Data.OleDb;
using System.Web.UI.WebControls;

namespace ASPNetCookbook.CSExamples
{
  public class CH01DatagridSortingCS1 : System.Web.UI.Page
  {
    // controls on form
    protected System.Web.UI.WebControls.DataGrid dgBooks;

    //*********************************************************************
    //
    //   ROUTINE: Page_Load
    //
    //   DESCRIPTION: This routine provides the event handler for the page
    //                load event.  It is responsible for initializing the
    //                controls on the page.
    //----------------------------------------------------------------------
    private void Page_Load(object sender, System.EventArgs e)
    {
      // wire the event handler for the sort command
      this.dgBooks.SortCommand +=
        new DataGridSortCommandEventHandler(this.dgBooks_SortCommand);

      if (!Page.IsPostBack)
      {
```

Example 1-32. DataGrid with column sorting code-behind (.cs) (continued)

```csharp
      // sort by title and bind data to DataGrid
      bindData("Title");
   }
}  // Page_Load


//*************************************************************************
//
//    ROUTINE: dgBooks_SortCommand
//
//    DESCRIPTION: This routine provides the event handler for the
//                 datagrid sort event.  It is responsible re-binding
//                 the data to the datagrid by the selected column.
//-------------------------------------------------------------------------
private void dgBooks_SortCommand(Object source,
   System.Web.UI.WebControls.DataGridSortCommandEventArgs e)
{
   // sort the data by the selected column and re-bind the data
   bindData(e.SortExpression);
}  // dgBooks_SortCommand


//*************************************************************************
//
//    ROUTINE: bindData
//
//    DESCRIPTION: This routine queries the database for the data to
//                 displayed and binds it to the repeater
//-------------------------------------------------------------------------
private void bindData(String sortExpression)
{
   OleDbConnection dbConn = null;
   OleDbDataAdapter da = null;
   DataSet ds = null;
   String strConnection = null;
   String strSQL =null;

   try
   {
     // get the connection string from web.config and open a connection
     // to the database
     strConnection =
       ConfigurationSettings.AppSettings["dbConnectionString"];
     dbConn = new OleDbConnection(strConnection);
     dbConn.Open();

     // build the query string and get the data from the database
     strSQL = "SELECT Title, ISBN, Publisher " +
              "FROM Book " +
              "ORDER BY " + sortExpression;

     da = new OleDbDataAdapter(strSQL, dbConn);
     ds = new DataSet();
     da.Fill(ds);
```

Example 1-32. DataGrid with column sorting code-behind (.cs) (continued)

```
      // set the source of the data for the datagrid control and bind it
      dgBooks.DataSource = ds;
      dgBooks.DataBind( );
    } // try

    finally
    {
      //clean up
      if (dbConn != null)
      {
        dbConn.Close( );
      }
    } // finally
  } // bindData
} // CH01DatagridSortingCS1
}
```

1.12 Sorting Data in Ascending/Descending Order Within a DataGrid

Problem

You are displaying a table of data in a DataGrid, and you want to let the user sort the data and change the sort order by clicking on the column headers.

Solution

Enable the sorting features of the DataGrid control and add custom coding to support the sorting along with an indication of the current sort column and order. An example of the output that is possible with this approach is shown in Figure 1-15. Examples 1-33 through 1-35 show the *.aspx* file and code-behind files for an application that produces this output.

Discussion

To add sorting to a DataGrid control, you must first enable its sorting features by setting the AllowSorting attribute of the DataGrid element to True. In addition, set the SortExpression attribute of the asp:BoundColumn element to the expression that will be used in your code to perform the sorting. See Recipe 1.11 for details on these steps.

Next, remove the HeadingText attribute in the asp:BoundColumn element. You will want to set the heading text in the code-behind, so it is not needed in the *.aspx* file.

To support sorting in both ascending and descending order as well as visually indicating the sort order requires a bit more code in the code-behind class. This is driven by needing to know the current sort column and the current sort order to determine

ASP.NET Cookbook

The Ultimate ASP.NET Code Sourcebook

DataGrid With Ascend/Descend Sorting (VB)

Title	ISBN ▲	Publisher
HTML & XHTML: The Definitive Guide	0-596-00026-X	O'Reilly
JavaScript: The Definitive Guide	0-596-00048-0	O'Reilly
XSLT	0-596-00053-7	O'Reilly
XML in a Nutshell	0-596-00058-8	O'Reilly
Access Cookbook	0-596-00084-7	O'Reilly
VB .Net Language in a Nutshell	0-596-00092-8	O'Reilly
Programming Visual Basic .Net	0-596-00093-6	O'Reilly
Programming Web Services with SOAP	0-596-00095-2	O'Reilly
COM and .Net Component Services	0-596-00103-7	O'Reilly
ASP.NET in a Nutshell	0-596-00116-9	O'Reilly
Subclassing & Hooking with Visual Basic	0-596-00118-5	O'Reilly
Java Cookbook	0-596-00170-3	O'Reilly
Programming ASP.NET	0-596-00171-1	O'Reilly
C# in a Nutshell	0-596-00181-9	O'Reilly
Web Services Essentials	0-596-00224-6	O'Reilly
.Net Framework Essentials	0-596-00302-1	O'Reilly
Programming C#	0-596-00309-9	O'Reilly
C# Essentials	0-596-00315-3	O'Reilly
Perl Cookbook	1-565-92243-3	O'Reilly
Transact-SQL Programming	1-565-92401-0	O'Reilly
ADO: ActiveX Data Objects	1-565-92415-0	O'Reilly
JavaScript Application Cookbook	1-565-92577-7	O'Reilly
SQL in a Nutshell	1-565-92744-3	O'Reilly
Developing ASP Components	1-565-92750-8	O'Reilly
Transact-SQL Cookbook	1-565-92756-7	O'Reilly
COM+ Programming with Visual Basic	1-565-92840-7	O'Reilly

Figure 1-15. DataGrid with ascending/descending sorting output

what needs to be done when the user clicks a column header. From here on, it's useful to examine our example application to see how we've juggled these needs.

We've added an enumeration and several constants to the top of the code-behind class shown in Example 1-34 (VB) and Example 1-35 (C#). The enuSortOrder enumeration defines the available sort orders that are used to store and compare sort order data. The sortExpression and columnTitle arrays are used to define the sort expression and column title for each column in the DataGrid. As their names imply, the VS_CURRENT_SORT_EXPRESSION and VS_CURRENT_SORT_ORDER constants define the names of variables stored in the ViewState to track the current sort expression and order between page submittals.

In our example application, the Page_Load method performs two operations. First, the view state variables used to store the current sort expression and sort order (VS_CURRENT_SORT_EXPRESSION and VS_CURRENT_SORT_ORDER) are set to their default values. For this example, the title column is sorted in ascending order by default. Second, the bindData method is called to pass the current sort expression and sort order.

Two features of the bindData method are worth special note. First, the SQL statement used to query the database includes an ORDER BY clause that reflects the current sort order.

Second, the `bindData` method also loops through each column in the grid, determines which column is the sort column, and marks the sort order for the column. The sort column is determined by comparing the current sort expression passed to the `bindData` method with the sort expression for each of the columns. The sort expression for the one column that matches the current sort expression is the sort column. After finding the sort column, the sort order is checked to determine whether the ascending or descending image should be output in the header for the sort column. Finally, the header text is set to the title for the column and, when relevant, the HTML image tag used to indicate the sort order is also set. For columns that are not the current sort column, the image-related HTML is simply set to an empty string.

When the user clicks a column header in the grid, the `dgBooks_SortCommand` method is called and determines the changes that need to be made prior to rebinding the data. The first step is to get the current sort expression and sort order from the view state, as shown here:

VB
```
currentSortExpression = CStr(viewstate(VS_CURRENT_SORT_EXPRESSION))
currentSortOrder = CType(viewstate(VS_CURRENT_SORT_ORDER), enuSortOrder)
```

C#
```
currentSortExpression = (String)(this.ViewState[VS_CURRENT_SORT_EXPRESSION]);
currentSortOrder = (enuSortOrder)(this.ViewState[VS_CURRENT_SORT_ORDER]);
```

After getting the current information, we determine if a column other than the current sort column has been clicked. If so, the clicked column is set as the new sort column and the sort order is set to ascending. If not, we need to change the sort order of the original column.

After determining the sort expression and sort order, the view state is updated to reflect what will be the current information once the page is rendered.

Finally, the data is rebound to the grid by calling the `bindData` method with the new sort information.

See Also

Recipe 1.11

Example 1-33. DataGrid with ascending/descending sorting (.aspx)

```
<%@ Page Language="vb" AutoEventWireup="false"
        Codebehind="CH01DatagridAscDescSortingVB.aspx.vb"
        Inherits="ASPNetCookbook.VBExamples.CH01DatagridAscDescSortingVB" %>
<!DOCTYPE HTML PUBLIC "-//W3C//DTD HTML 4.0 Transitional//EN">
<html>
  <head>
    <title>DataGrid With Ascend/Descend Sorting </title>
    <link rel="stylesheet" href="css/ASPNetCookbook.css">
  </head>
  <body leftmargin="0" marginheight="0" marginwidth="0" topmargin="0">
    <form id="frmDatagrid" method="post" runat="server">
```

Example 1-33. DataGrid with ascending/descending sorting (.aspx) (continued)

```
<table width="100%" cellpadding="0" cellspacing="0" border="0">
  <tr>
    <td align="center">
      <img src="images/ASPNETCookbookHeading_blue.gif">
    </td>
  </tr>
  <tr>
    <td class="dividerLine">
      <img src="images/spacer.gif" height="6" border="0"></td>
  </tr>
</table>
<table width="90%" align="center" border="0">
  <tr>
    <td><img src="images/spacer.gif" height="10" border="0"></td>
  </tr>
  <tr>
    <td align="center" class="PageHeading">
      DataGrid With Ascend/Descend Sorting (VB)
    </td>
  </tr>
  <tr>
    <td><img src="images/spacer.gif" height="10" border="0"></td>
  </tr>
  <tr>
    <td align="center">
      <asp:DataGrid
        id="dgBooks"
        runat="server"
        BorderColor="000080"
        BorderWidth="2px"
        AutoGenerateColumns="False"
        width="100%"
        AllowSorting="True">

        <HeaderStyle
          HorizontalAlign="Center"
          ForeColor="#FFFFFF"
          BackColor="#000080"
          Font-Bold=true
          CssClass="TableHeader" />

        <ItemStyle
          BackColor="#FFFFE0"
          cssClass="TableCellNormal" />

        <AlternatingItemStyle
          BackColor="#FFFFFF"
          cssClass="TableCellAlternating" />

        <Columns>
          <asp:BoundColumn DataField="Title"
                           SortExpression="Title" />
```

Example 1-33. DataGrid with ascending/descending sorting (.aspx) (continued)

```
                <asp:BoundColumn DataField="ISBN"
                                 ItemStyle-HorizontalAlign="Center"
                                 SortExpression="ISBN" />
                <asp:BoundColumn DataField="Publisher"
                                 ItemStyle-HorizontalAlign="Center"
                                 SortExpression="Publisher" />
            </Columns>
          </asp:DataGrid>
        </td>
      </tr>
    </table>
  </form>
 </body>
</html>
```

Example 1-34. DataGrid with ascending/descending sorting code-behind (.vb)

```
Option Explicit On
Option Strict On
'-----------------------------------------------------------------------------
'
'   Module Name: CH01DatagridAscDescSortingVB.aspx.vb
'
'   Description: This class provides the code behind for
'                CH01DatagridAscDescSortingVB.aspx
'
'*****************************************************************************
Imports Microsoft.VisualBasic
Imports System.Configuration
Imports System.Data
Imports System.Data.OleDb
Imports System.Web.UI.WebControls

Namespace ASPNetCookbook.VBExamples
  Public Class CH01DatagridAscDescSortingVB
    Inherits System.Web.UI.Page

    'controls on form
    Protected WithEvents dgBooks As System.Web.UI.WebControls.DataGrid

    'the following enumeration is used to define the sort orders
    Private Enum enuSortOrder
      soAscending = 0
      soDescending = 1
    End Enum

    'strings to use for the sort expressions and column title
    'separate arrays are used to support the sort expression and titles
    'being different
    Private ReadOnly sortExpression() As String = {"Title", "ISBN", "Publisher"}
    Private ReadOnly columnTitle() As String = {"Title", "ISBN", "Publisher"}
```

Example 1-34. DataGrid with ascending/descending sorting code-behind (.vb) (continued)

```
'the names of the variables placed in the viewstate
Private Const VS_CURRENT_SORT_EXPRESSION As String = "currentSortExpression"
Private Const VS_CURRENT_SORT_ORDER As String = "currentSortOrder"

'************************************************************************
'
'   ROUTINE: Page_Load
'
'   DESCRIPTION: This routine provides the event handler for the page load
'                event.  It is responsible for initializing the controls
'                on the page.
'------------------------------------------------------------------------
Private Sub Page_Load(ByVal sender As System.Object, _
                      ByVal e As System.EventArgs) _
        Handles MyBase.Load

  Dim defaultSortExpression As String
  Dim defaultSortOrder As enuSortOrder

  If (Not Page.IsPostBack) Then
    'sort by title, ascending as the default
    defaultSortExpression = sortExpression(0)
    defaultSortOrder = enuSortOrder.soAscending

    'store current sort expression and order in the viewstate then
    'bind data to the DataGrid
    viewstate(VS_CURRENT_SORT_EXPRESSION) = defaultSortExpression
    viewState(VS_CURRENT_SORT_ORDER) = defaultSortOrder
    bindData(defaultSortExpression, _
             defaultSortOrder)
  End If
End Sub  'Page_Load

'************************************************************************
'
'   ROUTINE: dgBooks_SortCommand
'
'   DESCRIPTION: This routine provides the event handler for the datagrid
'                sort event.  It is responsible re-binding the data to the
'                datagrid by the selected column.
'------------------------------------------------------------------------
Private Sub dgBooks_SortCommand(ByVal source As Object, _
                              ByVal e As DataGridSortCommandEventArgs) _
        Handles dgBooks.SortCommand

  Dim newSortExpression As String
  Dim currentSortExpression As String
  Dim currentSortOrder As enuSortOrder

  'get the current sort expression and order from the viewstate
  currentSortExpression = CStr(viewstate(VS_CURRENT_SORT_EXPRESSION))
  currentSortOrder = CType(viewstate(VS_CURRENT_SORT_ORDER), enuSortOrder)
```

```vb
        'check to see if this is a new column or the sort order
        'of the current column needs to be changed.
        newSortExpression = e.SortExpression
        If (newSortExpression = currentSortExpression) Then
          'sort column is the same so change the sort order
          If (currentSortOrder = enuSortOrder.soAscending) Then
            currentSortOrder = enuSortOrder.soDescending
          Else
            currentSortOrder = enuSortOrder.soAscending
          End If
        Else
          'sort column is different so set the new column with ascending
          'sort order
          currentSortExpression = newSortExpression
          currentSortOrder = enuSortOrder.soAscending
        End If

        'update the view state with the new sort information
        viewstate(VS_CURRENT_SORT_EXPRESSION) = currentSortExpression
        viewstate(VS_CURRENT_SORT_ORDER) = currentSortOrder

        'rebind the data in the datagrid
        bindData(currentSortExpression, _
                 currentSortOrder)
    End Sub   'dgBooks_SortCommand

    '*************************************************************************
    '
    '   ROUTINE: bindData
    '
    '   DESCRIPTION: This routine queries the database for the data to
    '                displayed and binds it to the datagrid
    '-------------------------------------------------------------------------
    Private Sub bindData(ByVal sortExpression As String, _
                         ByVal sortOrder As enuSortOrder)
      Dim dbConn As OleDbConnection
      Dim da As OleDbDataAdapter
      Dim ds As DataSet
      Dim strConnection As String
      Dim strSQL As String
      Dim index As Integer
      Dim col As DataGridColumn
      Dim colImage As String
      Dim strSortOrder As String

      Try
        'get the connection string from web.config and open a connection
        'to the database
        strConnection = _
            ConfigurationSettings.AppSettings("dbConnectionString")
        dbConn = New OleDbConnection(strConnection)
        dbConn.Open( )
```

Example 1-34. DataGrid with ascending/descending sorting code-behind (.vb) (continued)

```
        'build the query string and get the data from the database
        If (sortOrder = enuSortOrder.soAscending) Then
          strSortOrder = " ASC"
        Else
          strSortOrder = " DESC"
        End If

        strSQL = "SELECT Title, ISBN, Publisher " & _
                 "FROM Book " & _
                 "ORDER BY " & sortExpression & _
                 strSortOrder

      da = New OleDbDataAdapter(strSQL, dbConn)
      ds = New DataSet
      da.Fill(ds)

        'loop through the columns in the datagrid updating the heading to
        'mark which column is the sort column and the sort order
        For index = 0 To dgBooks.Columns.Count - 1
          col = dgBooks.Columns(index)

          'check to see if this is the sort column
          If (col.SortExpression = sortExpression) Then
            'this is the sort column so determine whether the ascending or
            'descending image needs to be included
            If (sortOrder = enuSortOrder.soAscending) Then
              colImage = " <img src='images/sort_ascending.gif' border='0'>"
            Else
              colImage = " <img src='images/sort_descending.gif' border='0'>"
            End If
          Else
            'This is not the sort column so include no image html
            colImage = ""
          End If  'If (col.SortExpression = sortExpression)

          'set the title for the column
          col.HeaderText = columnTitle(index) & colImage
        Next index

      'set the source of the data for the datagrid control and bind it
      dgBooks.DataSource = ds
      dgBooks.DataBind( )

    Finally
      'cleanup
      If (Not IsNothing(dbConn)) Then
        dbConn.Close( )
      End If
    End Try
  End Sub  'bindData
  End Class  'CH01DatagridAscDescSortingVB
End Namespace
```

Example 1-35. DataGrid with ascending/descending sorting code-behind (.cs)

```
//----------------------------------------------------------------------------
//
//   Module Name: CH01DatagridAscDescSortingCS.aspx.cs
//
//   Description: This class provides the code behind for
//                CH01DatagridAscDescSortingCS.aspx
//
//****************************************************************************
using System;
using System.Configuration;
using System.Data;
using System.Data.OleDb;
using System.Web.UI.WebControls;

namespace ASPNetCookbook.CSExamples
{
  public class CH01DatagridAscDescSortingCS : System.Web.UI.Page
  {
    // controls on form
    protected System.Web.UI.WebControls.DataGrid dgBooks;

    // the following enumeration is used to define the sort orders
    private enum enuSortOrder : int
    {
      soAscending = 0,
      soDescending = 1
    }

    // strings to use for the sort expressions and column title
    // separate arrays are used to support the sort expression and titles
    // being different
    static readonly String [] sortExpression =
                              new String [] {"Title", "ISBN", "Publisher"};
    static readonly String[] columnTitle =
                              new String [] {"Title", "ISBN", "Publisher"};

    // the names of the variables placed in the viewstate
    static readonly String VS_CURRENT_SORT_EXPRESSION =
                              "currentSortExpression";
    static readonly String VS_CURRENT_SORT_ORDER = "currentSortOrder";

    //****************************************************************************
    //
    //   ROUTINE: Page_Load
    //
    //   DESCRIPTION: This routine provides the event handler for the page
    //                load event.  It is responsible for initializing the
    //                controls on the page.
    //----------------------------------------------------------------------------
    private void Page_Load(object sender, System.EventArgs e)
    {
      String defaultSortExpression;
      enuSortOrder defaultSortOrder;
```

Example 1-35. DataGrid with ascending/descending sorting code-behind (.cs) (continued)

```
    // wire the event handler for the sort command
    this.dgBooks.SortCommand +=
        new DataGridSortCommandEventHandler(this.dgBooks_SortCommand);

    if (!Page.IsPostBack)
    {
        // sort by title, ascending as the default
        defaultSortExpression = sortExpression[0];
        defaultSortOrder = enuSortOrder.soAscending;

        // bind data to the DataGrid
        this.ViewState.Add(VS_CURRENT_SORT_EXPRESSION, defaultSortExpression);
        this.ViewState.Add(VS_CURRENT_SORT_ORDER, defaultSortOrder);
        bindData(defaultSortExpression,
                defaultSortOrder);
    }
}  // Page_Load

//*************************************************************************
//
//    ROUTINE: dgBooks_SortCommand
//
//    DESCRIPTION: This routine provides the event handler for the
//                datagrid sort event.  It is responsible re-binding
//                the data to the datagrid by the selected column.
//-------------------------------------------------------------------------
private void dgBooks_SortCommand(Object source,
                System.Web.UI.WebControls.DataGridSortCommandEventArgs e)
{
    String newSortExpression = null;
    String currentSortExpression = null;
    enuSortOrder currentSortOrder;

    // get the current sort expression and order from the viewstate
    currentSortExpression =
                    (String)(this.ViewState[VS_CURRENT_SORT_EXPRESSION]);
    currentSortOrder =
                    (enuSortOrder)(this.ViewState[VS_CURRENT_SORT_ORDER]);

    // check to see if this is a new column or the sort order
    // of the current column needs to be changed.
    newSortExpression = e.SortExpression;
    if (newSortExpression == currentSortExpression)
    {
        // sort column is the same so change the sort order
        if (currentSortOrder == enuSortOrder.soAscending)
        {
            currentSortOrder = enuSortOrder.soDescending;
        }
        else
        {
            currentSortOrder = enuSortOrder.soAscending;
        }
```

```
    }
    else
    {
      // sort column is different so set the new column with ascending
      // sort order
      currentSortExpression = newSortExpression;
      currentSortOrder = enuSortOrder.soAscending;
    }

    // update the view state with the new sort information
    this.ViewState.Add(VS_CURRENT_SORT_EXPRESSION, currentSortExpression);
    this.ViewState.Add(VS_CURRENT_SORT_ORDER, currentSortOrder);

    // rebind the data in the datagrid
    bindData(currentSortExpression,
             currentSortOrder);
  } // dgBooks_SortCommand

  //*************************************************************************
  //
  //   ROUTINE: bindData
  //
  //   DESCRIPTION: This routine queries the database for the data to
  //                displayed and binds it to the repeater
  //-------------------------------------------------------------------------
  private void bindData(String sortExpression,
                        enuSortOrder sortOrder)
  {
    OleDbConnection dbConn = null;
    OleDbDataAdapter da = null;
    DataSet ds = null;
    String strConnection = null;
    String strSQL =null;
    int index = 0;
    DataGridColumn col = null;
    String colImage = null;
    String strSortOrder = null;

    try
    {
      // get the connection string from web.config and open a connection
      // to the database
      strConnection =
        ConfigurationSettings.AppSettings["dbConnectionString"];
      dbConn = new OleDbConnection(strConnection);
      dbConn.Open( );

      // build the query string and get the data from the database
      if (sortOrder == enuSortOrder.soAscending)
      {
        strSortOrder = " ASC";
      }
      else
```

```
      {
        strSortOrder = " DESC";
      }

      strSQL = "SELECT Title, ISBN, Publisher " +
               "FROM Book " +
               "ORDER BY " + sortExpression +
               strSortOrder;

  da = new OleDbDataAdapter(strSQL, dbConn);
  ds = new DataSet();
  da.Fill(ds, "Table");


  // loop through the columns in the datagrid updating the heading to
  // mark which column is the sort column and the sort order
  for (index = 0; index < dgBooks.Columns.Count; index++)
  {
    col = dgBooks.Columns[index];
    // check to see if this is the sort column
    if (col.SortExpression == sortExpression)
    {
      // this is the sort column so determine whether the ascending or
      // descending image needs to be included
      if (sortOrder == enuSortOrder.soAscending)
      {
        colImage = " <img src='images/sort_ascending.gif' border='0'>";
      }
      else
      {
        colImage = " <img src='images/sort_descending.gif' border='0'>";
      }
    }
    else
    {
      // This is not the sort column so include no image html
      colImage = "";
    }  // if (col.SortExpression == sortExpression)

    // set the title for the column
    col.HeaderText = columnTitle[index] + colImage;
  }  // for index

  // set the source of the data for the datagrid control and bind it
  dgBooks.DataSource = ds;
  dgBooks.DataBind();
}  // try

finally
{
  //clean up
  if (dbConn != null)
  {
```

Example 1-35. DataGrid with ascending/descending sorting code-behind (.cs) (continued)

```
            dbConn.Close();
        }
    } // finally
  } // bindData
} // CH01DatagridAscDescSortingCS
}
```

1.13 Combining Sorting and Paging in a DataGrid

Problem

You are implementing a DataGrid with both sorting and pagination, and you are having trouble making the two features work together.

Solution

Enable the sorting features of the DataGrid control, and add custom code to support the sorting along with an indication of the current sort column and order (see Recipe 1.12 for details). Next, with pagination enabled, add a small amount of custom code to track the sort column and sort order so that they can be maintained between client round trips and used any time rebinding is required. Figure 1-16 shows a typical DataGrid with this solution implemented. Examples 1-36 through 1-38 show the *.aspx* file and code-behind files for an application that produces this output.

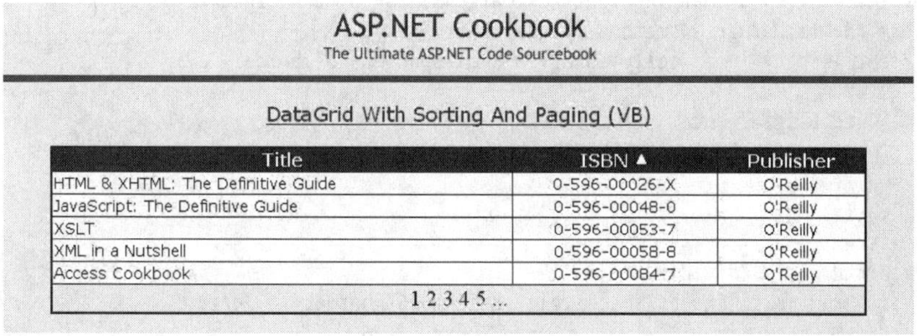

Figure 1-16. Combining sorting and paging in a DataGrid output

Discussion

Getting both sorting and paging to work at the same time is a notorious problem with a DataGrid. The key to making it all work is to track the sort column and sort order so that they can be used any time rebinding is required, whether because of a page change or a sort command. Likewise, it is useful to put the sort column and sort order data in the view state so that they are properly maintained between client round trips.

The DataGrid provides the basic plumbing for sorting and paging the data displayed in the grid. The DataGrid also provides a property (CurrentPageIndex) that is always available to indicate which page is to be displayed. Unfortunately, the DataGrid provides no information regarding the sort column or the sort order, forcing you, as a programmer, to track this information outside of the DataGrid so it will be available when performing pagination operations.

The application we've developed for this recipe should give you a good idea of how to handle sorting and paging simultaneously. It tracks the sort column and the sort order so that the proper data can be bound to the DataGrid any time rebinding is required—for example, when the user clicks on a row header to resort a column or selects a page from the DataGrid control's built-in navigation control. Refer to Recipes 1.9 and 1.12 for more detailed discussions of the various nuances of this recipe.

See Also

Recipe 1.9; Recipe 1.12

Example 1-36. Combining sorting and paging in a DataGrid (.aspx)

```
<%@ Page Language="vb" AutoEventWireup="false"
    Codebehind="CH01DatagridWithSortingAndPagingVB.aspx.vb"
    Inherits="ASPNetCookbook.VBExamples.CH01DatagridWithSortingAndPagingVB" %>
<!DOCTYPE HTML PUBLIC "-//W3C//DTD HTML 4.0 Transitional//EN">
<html>
  <head>
    <title>DataGrid With Sorting And Paging</title>
    <link rel="stylesheet" href="css/ASPNetCookbook.css">
  </head>
  <body leftmargin="0" marginheight="0" marginwidth="0" topmargin="0">
    <form id="frmDatagrid" method="post" runat="server">
      <table width="100%" cellpadding="0" cellspacing="0" border="0">
        <tr>
          <td align="center">
            <img src="images/ASPNETCookbookHeading_blue.gif">
          </td>
        </tr>
        <tr>
          <td class="dividerLine">
            <img src="images/spacer.gif" height="6" border="0"></td>
        </tr>
      </table>
      <table width="90%" align="center" border="0">
        <tr>
          <td><img src="images/spacer.gif" height="10" border="0"></td>
        </tr>
        <tr>
          <td align="center" class="PageHeading">
            DataGrid With Sorting And Paging (VB)
          </td>
        </tr>
        <tr>
```

```
        <td><img src="images/spacer.gif" height="10" border="0"></td>
      </tr>
      <tr>
        <td align="center">
          <asp:DataGrid
            id="dgBooks"
            runat="server"
            BorderColor="000080"
            BorderWidth="2px"
            AutoGenerateColumns="False"
            width="100%"
            AllowSorting="True"
            AllowPaging="True"
            PageSize="5"
            PagerStyle-Mode="NumericPages"
            PagerStyle-PageButtonCount="5"
            PagerStyle-Position="Bottom"
            PagerStyle-HorizontalAlign="Center"
            PagerStyle-NextPageText="Next"
            PagerStyle-PrevPageText="Prev">

            <HeaderStyle
              HorizontalAlign="Center"
              ForeColor="#FFFFFF"
              BackColor="#000080"
              Font-Bold=true
              CssClass="TableHeader" />

            <ItemStyle
              BackColor="#FFFFE0"
              cssClass="TableCellNormal" />

            <AlternatingItemStyle
              BackColor="#FFFFFF"
              cssClass="TableCellAlternating" />

            <Columns>
              <asp:BoundColumn DataField="Title"
                               SortExpression="Title" />
              <asp:BoundColumn DataField="ISBN"
                               ItemStyle-HorizontalAlign="Center"
                               SortExpression="ISBN" />
              <asp:BoundColumn DataField="Publisher"
                               ItemStyle-HorizontalAlign="Center"
                               SortExpression="Publisher" />
            </Columns>
          </asp:DataGrid>
        </td>
      </tr>
    </table>
  </form>
 </body>
</html>
```

Example 1-37. Combining sorting and paging in a DataGrid code-behind (.vb)

```vb
Option Explicit On
Option Strict On
'----------------------------------------------------------------------------
'
'   Module Name: CH01DatagridWithSortingAndPagingVB.aspx.vb
'
'   Description: This class provides the code behind for
'               CH01DatagridWithSortingAndPagingVB.aspx
'
'****************************************************************************
Imports Microsoft.VisualBasic
Imports System.Configuration
Imports System.Data
Imports System.Data.OleDb
Imports System.Web.UI.WebControls

Namespace ASPNetCookbook.VBExamples
  Public Class CH01DatagridWithSortingAndPagingVB
    Inherits System.Web.UI.Page

    'controls on form
    Protected WithEvents dgBooks As System.Web.UI.WebControls.DataGrid

    'the following enumeration is used to define the sort orders
    Private Enum enuSortOrder
      soAscending = 0
      soDescending = 1
    End Enum

    'strings to use for the sort expressions and column title
    'separate arrays are used to support the sort expression and titles
    'being different
    Private ReadOnly sortExpression() As String = {"Title", "ISBN", "Publisher"}
    Private ReadOnly columnTitle() As String = {"Title", "ISBN", "Publisher"}

    'the names of the variables placed in the viewstate
    Private Const VS_CURRENT_SORT_EXPRESSION As String = "currentSortExpression"
    Private Const VS_CURRENT_SORT_ORDER As String = "currentSortOrder"

    '****************************************************************************
    '
    '   ROUTINE: Page_Load
    '
    '   DESCRIPTION: This routine provides the event handler for the page load
    '               event.  It is responsible for initializing the controls
    '               on the page.
    '----------------------------------------------------------------------------
    Private Sub Page_Load(ByVal sender As System.Object, _
                          ByVal e As System.EventArgs) _
            Handles MyBase.Load

      Dim defaultSortExpression As String
      Dim defaultSortOrder As enuSortOrder
```

```vb
    If (Not Page.IsPostBack) Then
      'sort by title, ascending as the default
      defaultSortExpression = sortExpression(0)
      defaultSortOrder = enuSortOrder.soAscending

      'store current sort expression and order in the viewstate then
      'bind data to the DataGrid
      viewstate(VS_CURRENT_SORT_EXPRESSION) = defaultSortExpression
      viewState(VS_CURRENT_SORT_ORDER) = defaultSortOrder
      bindData(defaultSortExpression, _
               defaultSortOrder)
    End If
  End Sub  'Page_Load

  '*************************************************************************
  '
  '   ROUTINE: dgBooks_SortCommand
  '
  '   DESCRIPTION: This routine provides the event handler for the datagrid
  '                sort event.  It is responsible re-binding the data to the
  '                datagrid by the selected column.
  '-------------------------------------------------------------------------
  Private Sub dgBooks_SortCommand(ByVal source As Object, _
                                  ByVal e As DataGridSortCommandEventArgs) _
        Handles dgBooks.SortCommand

    Dim newSortExpression As String
    Dim currentSortExpression As String
    Dim currentSortOrder As enuSortOrder

    'get the current sort expression and order from the viewstate
    currentSortExpression = CStr(viewstate(VS_CURRENT_SORT_EXPRESSION))
    currentSortOrder = CType(viewstate(VS_CURRENT_SORT_ORDER), enuSortOrder)

    'check to see if this is a new column or the sort oder
    'of the current column needs to be changed.
    newSortExpression = e.SortExpression
    If (newSortExpression = currentSortExpression) Then
      'sort column is the same so change the sort order
      If (currentSortOrder = enuSortOrder.soAscending) Then
        currentSortOrder = enuSortOrder.soDescending
      Else
        currentSortOrder = enuSortOrder.soAscending
      End If
    Else
      'sort column is different so set the new column with ascending
      'sort order
      currentSortExpression = newSortExpression
      currentSortOrder = enuSortOrder.soAscending
    End If

    'update the view state with the new sort information
    viewstate(VS_CURRENT_SORT_EXPRESSION) = currentSortExpression
```

```
      viewstate(VS_CURRENT_SORT_ORDER) = currentSortOrder

    'rebind the data in the datagrid
    bindData(currentSortExpression, _
             currentSortOrder)
  End Sub    'dgBooks_SortCommand

  '**************************************************************************
  '
  '    ROUTINE: dgBooks_PageIndexChanged
  '
  '    DESCRIPTION: This routine provides the event handler for the page index
  '                 changed event of the datagrid.  It is responsible for
  '                 setting the page index from the passed arguments and
  '                 rebinding the data.
  '-------------------------------------------------------------------------
  Private Sub dgBooks_PageIndexChanged(ByVal source As Object, _
       ByVal e As System.Web.UI.WebControls.DataGridPageChangedEventArgs) _
       Handles dgBooks.PageIndexChanged

    Dim currentSortExpression As String
    Dim currentSortOrder As enuSortOrder

    'set new page index and rebind the data
    dgBooks.CurrentPageIndex = e.NewPageIndex

    'get the current sort expression and order from the viewstate
    currentSortExpression = CStr(viewstate(VS_CURRENT_SORT_EXPRESSION))
    currentSortOrder = CType(viewstate(VS_CURRENT_SORT_ORDER), enuSortOrder)

    'rebind the data in the datagrid
    bindData(currentSortExpression, _
             currentSortOrder)
  End Sub    'dgBooks_PageIndexChanged

  '**************************************************************************
  '
  '    ROUTINE: bindData
  '
  '    DESCRIPTION: This routine queries the database for the data to
  '                 displayed and binds it to the datagrid
  '-------------------------------------------------------------------------
  Private Sub bindData(ByVal sortExpression As String, _
                       ByVal sortOrder As enuSortOrder)
    Dim dbConn As OleDbConnection
    Dim da As OleDbDataAdapter
    Dim ds As DataSet
    Dim strConnection As String
    Dim strSQL As String
    Dim index As Integer
    Dim col As DataGridColumn
    Dim colImage As String
```

```vb
Dim strSortOrder As String

Try
    'get the connection string from web.config and open a connection
    'to the database
    strConnection = _
        ConfigurationSettings.AppSettings("dbConnectionString")
    dbConn = New OleDbConnection(strConnection)
    dbConn.Open( )

    'build the query string and get the data from the database
    If (sortOrder = enuSortOrder.soAscending) Then
        strSortOrder = " ASC"
    Else
        strSortOrder = " DESC"
    End If

    strSQL = "SELECT Title, ISBN, Publisher " & _
             "FROM Book " & _
             "ORDER BY " & sortExpression & _
             strSortOrder

    da = New OleDbDataAdapter(strSQL, dbConn)
    ds = New DataSet
    da.Fill(ds)

    'loop through the columns in the datagrid updating the heading to
    'mark which column is the sort column and the sort order
    For index = 0 To dgBooks.Columns.Count - 1
        col = dgBooks.Columns(index)

        'check to see if this is the sort column
        If (col.SortExpression = sortExpression) Then
            'this is the sort column so determine whether the ascending or
            'descending image needs to be included
            If (sortOrder = enuSortOrder.soAscending) Then
                colImage = " <img src='images/sort_ascending.gif' border='0'>"
            Else
                colImage = " <img src='images/sort_descending.gif' border='0'>"
            End If
        Else
            'This is not the sort column so include no image html
            colImage = ""
        End If  'If (col.SortExpression = sortExpression)

        'set the title for the column
        col.HeaderText = columnTitle(index) & colImage
    Next index

    'set the source of the data for the datagrid control and bind it
    dgBooks.DataSource = ds
    dgBooks.DataBind( )
```

Example 1-37. Combining sorting and paging in a DataGrid code-behind (.vb) (continued)

```vb
      Finally
        'cleanup
        If (Not IsNothing(dbConn)) Then
          dbConn.Close()
        End If
      End Try
    End Sub  'bindData

  End Class  'CH01DatagridWithSortingAndPagingVB
End Namespace
```

Example 1-38. Combining sorting and paging in a DataGrid code-behind (.cs)

```cs
//-----------------------------------------------------------------------------
//
//    Module Name: CH01DatagridWithSortingAndPagingCS.aspx.cs
//
//    Description: This class provides the code behind for
//                 CH01DatagridWithSortingAndPagingCS.aspx
//
//*****************************************************************************
using System;
using System.Configuration;
using System.Data;
using System.Data.OleDb;
using System.Web.UI.WebControls;

namespace ASPNetCookbook.CSExamples
{
  public class CH01DatagridWithSortingAndPagingCS : System.Web.UI.Page
  {
    // controls on form
    protected System.Web.UI.WebControls.DataGrid dgBooks;

    // the following enumeration is used to define the sort orders
    private enum enuSortOrder : int
    {
      soAscending = 0,
      soDescending = 1
    }

    // strings to use for the sort expressions and column title
    // separate arrays are used to support the sort expression and titles
    // being different
    static readonly String [] sortExpression =
                              new String [] {"Title", "ISBN", "Publisher"};
    static readonly String[] columnTitle =
                              new String [] {"Title", "ISBN", "Publisher"};

    // the names of the variables placed in the viewstate
    static readonly String VS_CURRENT_SORT_EXPRESSION =
                                            "currentSortExpression";
    static readonly String VS_CURRENT_SORT_ORDER = "currentSortOrder";
```

Example 1-38. Combining sorting and paging in a DataGrid code-behind (.cs) (continued)

```
//**************************************************************************
//
//   ROUTINE: Page_Load
//
//   DESCRIPTION: This routine provides the event handler for the page
//                load event.  It is responsible for initializing the
//                controls on the page.
//--------------------------------------------------------------------------
private void Page_Load(object sender, System.EventArgs e)
{
  String defaultSortExpression;
  enuSortOrder defaultSortOrder;

  // wire the event handlers
  this.dgBooks.PageIndexChanged +=
    new DataGridPageChangedEventHandler(this.dgBooks_PageIndexChanged);
  this.dgBooks.SortCommand +=
    new DataGridSortCommandEventHandler(this.dgBooks_SortCommand);

  if (!Page.IsPostBack)
  {
    // sort by title, ascending as the default
    defaultSortExpression = sortExpression[0];
    defaultSortOrder = enuSortOrder.soAscending;

    // bind data to the DataGrid
    this.ViewState.Add(VS_CURRENT_SORT_EXPRESSION, defaultSortExpression);
    this.ViewState.Add(VS_CURRENT_SORT_ORDER, defaultSortOrder);
    bindData(defaultSortExpression,
             defaultSortOrder);
  }
} // Page_Load

//**************************************************************************
//
//   ROUTINE: dgBooks_SortCommand
//
//   DESCRIPTION: This routine provides the event handler for the
//                datagrid sort event.  It is responsible re-binding
//                the data to the datagrid by the selected column.
//--------------------------------------------------------------------------
private void dgBooks_SortCommand(Object source,
  System.Web.UI.WebControls.DataGridSortCommandEventArgs e)
{
  String newSortExpression = null;
  String currentSortExpression = null;
  enuSortOrder currentSortOrder;

  // get the current sort expression and order from the viewstate
  currentSortExpression =
    (String)(this.ViewState[VS_CURRENT_SORT_EXPRESSION]);
  currentSortOrder =
    (enuSortOrder)(this.ViewState[VS_CURRENT_SORT_ORDER]);
```

```
// check to see if this is a new column or the sort oder
// of the current column needs to be changed.
newSortExpression = e.SortExpression;
if (newSortExpression == currentSortExpression)
{
  // sort column is the same so change the sort order
  if (currentSortOrder == enuSortOrder.soAscending)
  {
    currentSortOrder = enuSortOrder.soDescending;
  }
  else
  {
    currentSortOrder = enuSortOrder.soAscending;
  }
}
else
{
  // sort column is different so set the new column with ascending
  //sort order
  currentSortExpression = newSortExpression;
  currentSortOrder = enuSortOrder.soAscending;
}

// update the view state with the new sort information
this.ViewState.Add(VS_CURRENT_SORT_EXPRESSION, currentSortExpression);
this.ViewState.Add(VS_CURRENT_SORT_ORDER, currentSortOrder);

// rebind the data in the datagrid
bindData(currentSortExpression,
         currentSortOrder);
}  // dgBooks_SortCommand

//**************************************************************************
//
//    ROUTINE: dgBooks_PageIndexChanged
//
//    DESCRIPTION: This routine provides the event handler for the page
//                 index changed event of the datagrid.  It is responsible
//                 for setting the page index from the passed arguments
//                 and rebinding the data.
//--------------------------------------------------------------------------
private void dgBooks_PageIndexChanged(Object source,
  System.Web.UI.WebControls.DataGridPageChangedEventArgs e)
{
  String currentSortExpression;
  enuSortOrder currentSortOrder;

  // set new page index and rebind the data
  dgBooks.CurrentPageIndex = e.NewPageIndex;

  // get the current sort expression and order from the viewstate
  currentSortExpression = (String)(ViewState[VS_CURRENT_SORT_EXPRESSION]);
  currentSortOrder = (enuSortOrder)(ViewState[VS_CURRENT_SORT_ORDER]);
```

Example 1-38. Combining sorting and paging in a DataGrid code-behind (.cs) (continued)

```
      // rebind the data in the datagrid
      bindData(currentSortExpression,
               currentSortOrder);
  }  // dgBooks_PageIndexChanged

  //*************************************************************************
  //
  //    ROUTINE: bindData
  //
  //    DESCRIPTION: This routine queries the database for the data to
  //                 displayed and binds it to the repeater
  //-------------------------------------------------------------------------
  private void bindData(String sortExpression,
    enuSortOrder sortOrder)
  {
    OleDbConnection dbConn = null;
    OleDbDataAdapter da = null;
    DataSet ds = null;
    String strConnection = null;
    String strSQL =null;
    int index = 0;
    DataGridColumn col = null;
    String colImage = null;
    String strSortOrder = null;

    try
    {
      // get the connection string from web.config and open a connection
      // to the database
      strConnection =
        ConfigurationSettings.AppSettings["dbConnectionString"];
      dbConn = new OleDbConnection(strConnection);
      dbConn.Open( );

      // build the query string and get the data from the database
      if (sortOrder == enuSortOrder.soAscending)
      {
        strSortOrder = " ASC";
      }
      else
      {
        strSortOrder = " DESC";
      }

      strSQL = "SELECT Title, ISBN, Publisher " +
               "FROM Book " +
               "ORDER BY " + sortExpression +
               strSortOrder;

      da = new OleDbDataAdapter(strSQL, dbConn);
      ds = new DataSet( );
      da.Fill(ds);
```

```
            // loop through the columns in the datagrid updating the heading to
            // mark which column is the sort column and the sort order
            for (index = 0; index < dgBooks.Columns.Count; index++)
            {
              col = dgBooks.Columns[index];
              // check to see if this is the sort column
              if (col.SortExpression == sortExpression)
              {
                // this is the sort column so determine whether the ascending or
                // descending image needs to be included
                if (sortOrder == enuSortOrder.soAscending)
                {
                  colImage = " <img src='images/sort_ascending.gif' border='0'>";
                }
                else
                {
                  colImage = " <img src='images/sort_descending.gif' border='0'>";
                }
              }
              else
              {
                // This is not the sort column so include no image html
                colImage = "";
              } // if (col.SortExpression == sortExpression)

              // set the title for the column
              col.HeaderText = columnTitle[index] + colImage;
            } // for index

            // set the source of the data for the datagrid control and bind it
            dgBooks.DataSource = ds;
            dgBooks.DataBind( );
          } // try

          finally
          {
            //clean up
            if (dbConn != null)
            {
              dbConn.Close( );
            }
          } // finally
        } // bindData
      } // CH01DatagridWithSortingAndPagingCS
}
```

1.14   Editing Data Within a DataGrid

Problem

You want to allow the user to edit the data within the table displayed by a DataGrid.

Solution

Add an `EditCommandColumn` column type to the `DataGrid` control's display to enable editing of the data fields of each record. A typical example of normal display mode output is shown in Figure 1-17, and an example of edit mode output is shown in Figure 1-18. Examples 1-39 through 1-41 show the *.aspx* and code-behind files for the application that produces this result.

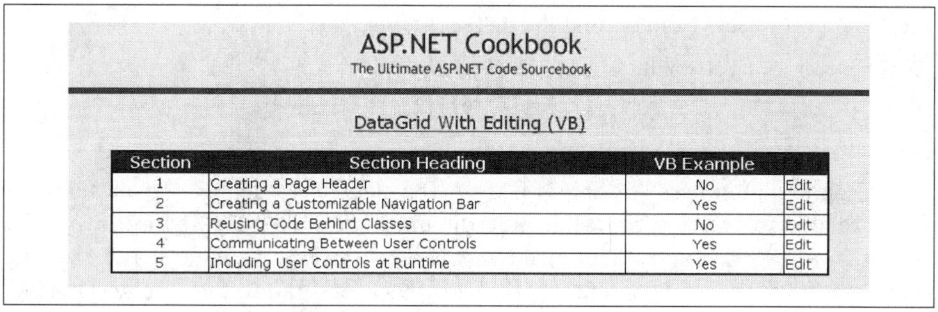

ASP.NET Cookbook
The Ultimate ASP.NET Code Sourcebook

DataGrid With Editing (VB)

Section	Section Heading	VB Example	
1	Creating a Page Header	No	Edit
2	Creating a Customizable Navigation Bar	Yes	Edit
3	Reusing Code Behind Classes	No	Edit
4	Communicating Between User Controls	Yes	Edit
5	Including User Controls at Runtime	Yes	Edit

Figure 1-17. DataGrid with editing—normal mode

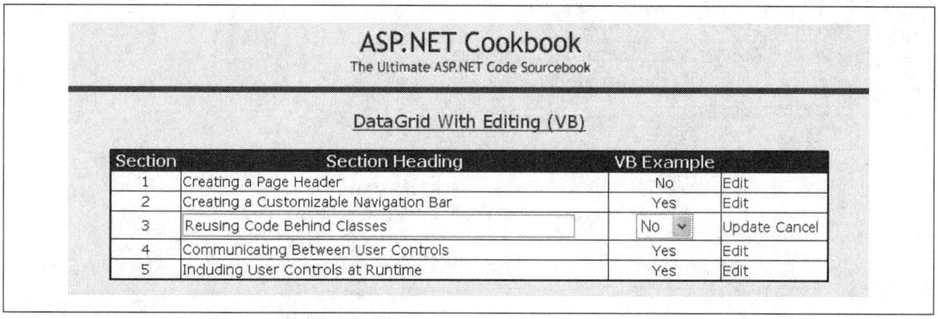

ASP.NET Cookbook
The Ultimate ASP.NET Code Sourcebook

DataGrid With Editing (VB)

Section	Section Heading	VB Example	
1	Creating a Page Header	No	Edit
2	Creating a Customizable Navigation Bar	Yes	Edit
3	Reusing Code Behind Classes	No ⌄	Update Cancel
4	Communicating Between User Controls	Yes	Edit
5	Including User Controls at Runtime	Yes	Edit

Figure 1-18. DataGrid with editing—row edit mode

Discussion

This recipe uses the built-in editing facilities of the `DataGrid` control, in particular the `EditCommandColumn` column type, which provides Edit command buttons for editing data items in each row of a `DataGrid`. The `EditText`, `CancelText`, and `UpdateText` properties define the text to be output for the Edit command button's Edit, Cancel, and Update hyperlinks, respectively.

```
<asp:EditCommandColumn ButtonType="LinkButton"
                       EditText="Edit"
                       CancelText="Cancel"
                       UpdateText="Update" />
```

The `ButtonType` attribute defines the type of button to output. You can specify `LinkButton`, which provides hyperlinked text, or `PushButton`, which outputs an HTML button.

The Edit command button's EditText, CancelText, and UpdateText properties can also be set to HTML. For example, to output an image for the links, you can use <img src="images/buttons/editButton.gif" border="0">.

In our example that implements this solution, three columns are defined for the DataGrid. The first uses an asp:BoundColumn element with the ReadOnly attribute set to True to prevent users from editing the field contents:

```
<asp:BoundColumn DataField="SectionNumber"
               ItemStyle-HorizontalAlign="Center"
               HeaderText="Section"
               ReadOnly="True" />
```

The second column uses an asp:TemplateColumn element to define a layout template for normal display (ItemTemplate) and edit mode display (EditItemTemplate). The EditItemTemplate property defines an asp:TextBox control to control the size and other aspects of the field contents. Both templates are bound to the "SectionHeading" data.

```
<asp:TemplateColumn HeaderText="Section Heading">
    <ItemTemplate>
        <%# DataBinder.Eval(Container.DataItem, _
                        "SectionHeading") %>
    </ItemTemplate>
    <EditItemTemplate>
        <asp:TextBox id="txtSectionHeading" runat="server"
                   size="55" cssClass="TableCellNormal"
                   text='<%# DataBinder.Eval(Container.DataItem, _
                                        "SectionHeading") %>' />
    </EditItemTemplate>
</asp:TemplateColumn>
```

Like the second column, the third column also uses an asp:TemplateColumn tag. In this case, however, the EditItemTemplate property defines an asp:DropDownList control, allowing the user to select only from valid choices for the column. This column is bound to the yesNoSelections ArrayList created in the code-behind. The selection in the drop-down list is initialized to the current value in the database by binding the SelectedIndex to the index of the value in the ArrayList.

```
<asp:TemplateColumn HeaderText="VB Example"
                    ItemStyle-HorizontalAlign="Center">
    <ItemTemplate>
        <%# yesNoSelections.Item(Cint(DataBinder.Eval(Container.DataItem, _
                                    "HasVBExample"))) %>
    </ItemTemplate>
    <EditItemTemplate>
        <asp:DropDownList id="selHasVBSample" runat="server"
          DataSource="<%# yesNoSelections %>"
          DataTextField="Text"
          DataValueField="Value"
```

```
            SelectedIndex='<%# CInt(DataBinder.Eval(Container.DataItem, _
                                    "HasVBExample")) %>' />
          </EditItemTemplate>
        </asp:TemplateColumn>
```

Note that the `Protected yesNoSelections As ArrayList` declaration is added at the class level in the code-behind to provide access to the `ArrayList` from the code in the *.aspx* file.

`Page_Load` just calls `bindData`, as is typical in this chapter's recipes. However, `bindData` is a bit different from the norm in two ways. First, the `ArrayList` is built with the selections that are applicable for the user to select from when changing the value of the "Has VB Example" column. Second, the line `dgProblems.DataKeyField = "EditProblemID"` is added to have the `DataGrid` maintain the primary key value for each row without having to add it to the grid as a column (hidden or visible). This approach stores the primary key value for each row in the view state only so that it can be recovered when needed on the server side. It also has the advantage of hiding the value from prying eyes.

The `dgProblems_EditCommand` method handles the event generated when the user clicks the Edit link within a row. It simply sets the `EditItemIndex` to the selected row, which causes ASP.NET to use the Edit Template when the data for the row is rebound along with the Cancel and Update links in the edit command column.

The `dgProblems_CancelCommand` method handles the event generated when the user clicks the Cancel link in the row being edited. It simply sets the `EditItemIndex` to -1 to display the `DataGrid` in normal mode when the data is rebound.

The `dgProblems_UpdateCommand` method handles the event generated when the user clicks the Update link in the row being edited. It extracts the edited data, updates the data in the database, and resets the `DataGrid` to normal mode when the data is rebound (see comments in the code for more details).

Example 1-39. DataGrid with editing (.aspx)

```
<%@ Page Language="vb" AutoEventWireup="false"
        Codebehind="CH01DataGridWithEditingVB.aspx.vb"
        Inherits="ASPNetCookbook.VBExamples.CH01DataGridWithEditingVB" %>
<!DOCTYPE HTML PUBLIC "-//W3C//DTD HTML 4.0 Transitional//EN">
<html>
  <head>
    <title>DataGrid With Editing</title>
    <link rel="stylesheet" href="css/ASPNetCookbook.css">
  </head>
  <body leftmargin="0" marginheight="0" marginwidth="0" topmargin="0">
    <form id="frmDatagrid" method="post" runat="server">
      <table width="100%" cellpadding="0" cellspacing="0" border="0">
        <tr>
          <td align="center">
            <img src="images/ASPNETCookbookHeading_blue.gif">
          </td>
        </tr>
```

Example 1-39. DataGrid with editing (.aspx) (continued)

```
     <tr>
       <td class="dividerLine">
         <img src="images/spacer.gif" height="6" border="0"></td>
     </tr>
   </table>
   <table width="90%" align="center" border="0">
     <tr>
       <td><img src="images/spacer.gif" height="10" border="0"></td>
     </tr>
     <tr>
       <td align="center" class="PageHeading">
         DataGrid With Editing (VB)
       </td>
     </tr>
     <tr>
       <td><img src="images/spacer.gif" height="10" border="0"></td>
     </tr>
     <tr>
       <td align="center">
         <asp:DataGrid
           id="dgProblems"
           runat="server"
           BorderColor="000080"
           BorderWidth="2px"
           AutoGenerateColumns="False"
           width="100%">

           <HeaderStyle
             HorizontalAlign="Center"
             ForeColor="#FFFFFF"
             BackColor="#000080"
             Font-Bold=true
             CssClass="TableHeader" />

           <ItemStyle
             BackColor="#FFFFE0"
             cssClass="TableCellNormal" />

           <AlternatingItemStyle
             BackColor="#FFFFFF"
             cssClass="TableCellAlternating" />

           <Columns>
             <asp:BoundColumn DataField="SectionNumber"
                         ItemStyle-HorizontalAlign="Center"
                         HeaderText="Section"
                         ReadOnly="True" />

             <asp:TemplateColumn HeaderText="Section Heading">
               <ItemTemplate>
                 <%# DataBinder.Eval(Container.DataItem, _
                             "SectionHeading") %>
```

Example 1-39. DataGrid with editing (.aspx) (continued)

```
          </ItemTemplate>
          <EditItemTemplate>
            <asp:TextBox id="txtSectionHeading" runat="server"
                  size="55" cssClass="TableCellNormal"
                  text='<%# DataBinder.Eval(Container.DataItem, _
                                        "SectionHeading") %>' />
          </EditItemTemplate>
        </asp:TemplateColumn>

        <asp:TemplateColumn HeaderText="VB Example"
                            ItemStyle-HorizontalAlign="Center">
          <ItemTemplate>
      <%# yesNoSelections.Item(Cint(DataBinder.Eval(Container.DataItem, _
                                        "HasVBExample"))) %>
          </ItemTemplate>
          <EditItemTemplate>
            <asp:DropDownList id="selHasVBSample" runat="server"
               DataSource="<%# yesNoSelections %>"
               DataTextField="Text"
               DataValueField="Value"
           SelectedIndex='<%# CInt(DataBinder.Eval(Container.DataItem, _
                                        "HasVBExample")) %>' />
          </EditItemTemplate>
        </asp:TemplateColumn>

        <asp:EditCommandColumn ButtonType="LinkButton"
                            EditText="Edit"
                            CancelText="Cancel"
                            UpdateText="Update" />
        </Columns>
      </asp:DataGrid>
    </td>
   </tr>
  </table>
 </form>
</body>
</html>
```

Example 1-40. DataGrid with editing code-behind (.vb)

```
Option Explicit On
Option Strict On
'---------------------------------------------------------------------------
'
'   Module Name: CH01DataGridWithEditingVB.aspx.vb
'
'   Description: This class provides the code behind for
'                CH01DataGridWithEditingVB
'
'*****************************************************************************
Imports Microsoft.VisualBasic
Imports System
Imports System.Collections
```

Example 1-40. DataGrid with editing code-behind (.vb) (continued)

```vb
Imports System.Configuration
Imports System.Data
Imports System.Data.OleDb
Imports System.Web.UI.WebControls

Namespace ASPNetCookbook.VBExamples
  Public Class CH01DataGridWithEditingVB
    Inherits System.Web.UI.Page

    'controls on form
    Protected WithEvents dgProblems As System.Web.UI.WebControls.DataGrid

    'The following variable contains the list of yes/no selections used in
    'the dropdown lists and is declared protected to provide access to the
    'data from the aspx page
    Protected yesNoSelections As ArrayList

    '***********************************************************************
    '
    '   ROUTINE: Page_Load
    '
    '   DESCRIPTION: This routine provides the event handler for the page load
    '                event.  It is responsible for initializing the controls
    '                on the page.
    '-----------------------------------------------------------------------
    Private Sub Page_Load(ByVal sender As System.Object, _
                    ByVal e As System.EventArgs) _
            Handles MyBase.Load

      If (Not Page.IsPostBack) Then
        bindData()
      End If
    End Sub   'Page_Load

    '***********************************************************************
    '
    '   ROUTINE: dgProblems_EditCommand
    '
    '   DESCRIPTION: This routine provides the event handler for the edit
    '                command click event.  It is responsible for setting the
    '                edit item index to the selected item and rebinding
    '                the data.
    '-----------------------------------------------------------------------
    Private Sub dgProblems_EditCommand(ByVal source As Object, _
              ByVal e As System.Web.UI.WebControls.DataGridCommandEventArgs) _
            Handles dgProblems.EditCommand
      dgProblems.EditItemIndex = e.Item.ItemIndex
      bindData()
    End Sub   'dgProblems_EditCommand

    '***********************************************************************
    '
    '   ROUTINE: dgProblems_CancelCommand
```

Example 1-40. DataGrid with editing code-behind (.vb) (continued)

```vb
'
'    DESCRIPTION: This routine provides the event handler for the cancel
'                 command click event.  It is responsible for resetting the
'                 edit item index to no item and rebinding the data.
'---------------------------------------------------------------------------
Private Sub dgProblems_CancelCommand(ByVal source As Object, _
            ByVal e As System.Web.UI.WebControls.DataGridCommandEventArgs) _
        Handles dgProblems.CancelCommand
  dgProblems.EditItemIndex = -1
  bindData( )
End Sub   'dgProblems_CancelCommand

'***************************************************************************
'
'    ROUTINE: dgProblems_UpdateCommand
'
'    DESCRIPTION: This routine provides the event handler for the update
'                 command click event.  It is responsible for updating
'                 the contents of the database with the date entered for
'                 the item currently being edited.
'---------------------------------------------------------------------------
Private Sub dgProblems_UpdateCommand(ByVal source As Object, _
            ByVal e As System.Web.UI.WebControls.DataGridCommandEventArgs) _
        Handles dgProblems.UpdateCommand

  Dim dbConn As OleDbConnection
  Dim dCmd As OleDbCommand
  Dim sectionHeading As String
  Dim hasVBSample As Integer
  Dim strConnection As String
  Dim strSQL As String
  Dim rowsAffected As Integer

  Try
    'get the edited section heading and "has vb sample" data
    'NOTE: This can be done by using the FindControl method of the edited
    '      item because EditItemTemplates were used and the controls in the
    '      templates were given IDs.  If a standard BoundColumn was used,
    '      the data would have to be acccessed using the cells collection
    '      (e.g. e.Item.Cells(0).Text would access the section number
    '      column in this example.
    sectionHeading = CType(e.Item.FindControl("txtSectionHeading"), _
                          TextBox).Text( )
    hasVBSample = CInt(CType(e.Item.FindControl("selHasVBSample"), _
                          DropDownList).SelectedItem.Value)

    'get the connection string from web.config and open a connection
    'to the database
    strConnection = _
        ConfigurationSettings.AppSettings("dbConnectionString")
    dbConn = New OleDbConnection(strConnection)
    dbConn.Open( )
```

Example 1-40. DataGrid with editing code-behind (.vb) (continued)

```
                'update data in database
                'NOTE: The primary key used to uniquely identify the row being edited
                '      is accessed through the DataKeys collection of the DataGrid.
                strSQL = "UPDATE EditProblem " & _
                        "SET SectionHeading='" & sectionHeading & "'" & _
                        ",HasVBExample=" & hasVBSample & _
                        " WHERE EditProblemID=" & _
                        dgProblems.DataKeys(e.Item.ItemIndex).ToString()
                dCmd = New OleDbCommand(strSQL, dbConn)
                rowsAffected = dCmd.ExecuteNonQuery()
                dbConn.Close()

                'TODO: production code should check the number of rows affected here to
                'make sure it is exactly 1 and output the appropriate success or
                'failure information to the user.

                'reset the edit item and rebind the data
                dgProblems.EditItemIndex = -1
                bindData()

            Finally
                'cleanup
                If (Not IsNothing(dbConn)) Then
                    dbConn.Close()
                End If
            End Try

        End Sub  'dgProblems_UpdateCommand

        '*************************************************************************
        '
        '   ROUTINE: bindData
        '
        '   DESCRIPTION: This routine queries the database for the data to
        '                displayed and binds it to the DataGrid
        '-------------------------------------------------------------------------
        Private Sub bindData()
            Dim dbConn As OleDbConnection
            Dim da As OleDbDataAdapter
            Dim ds As DataSet
            Dim strConnection As String
            Dim strSQL As String

            Try
                'get the connection string from web.config and open a connection
                'to the database
                strConnection = _
                    ConfigurationSettings.AppSettings("dbConnectionString")
                dbConn = New OleDbConnection(strConnection)
                dbConn.Open()

                'build the query string and get the data from the database
```

Example 1-40. DataGrid with editing code-behind (.vb) (continued)

```
        strSQL = "SELECT EditProblemID, SectionNumber" & _
                ", SectionHeading, HasVBExample " & _
                "FROM EditProblem " & _
                "ORDER BY SectionNumber"

        da = New OleDbDataAdapter(strSQL, dbConn)
        ds = New DataSet
        da.Fill(ds)

        'build the arraylist with the acceptable responses to the
        '"Has VB Sample" field
        yesNoSelections = New ArrayList(2)
        yesNoSelections.Add(New ListItem("No", "0"))
        yesNoSelections.Add(New ListItem("Yes", "1"))

        'set the source of the data for the datagrid control and bind it
        dgProblems.DataSource = ds
        dgProblems.DataKeyField = "EditProblemID"
        dgProblems.DataBind( )

    Finally
        'cleanup
        If (Not IsNothing(dbConn)) Then
            dbConn.Close( )
        End If
    End Try
End Sub    'bindData

End Class    'CH01DataGridWithEditingVB
End Namespace
```

Example 1-41. DataGrid with editing code-behind (.cs)

```
//-----------------------------------------------------------------------------
//
//    Module Name: CH01DataGridWithEditingCS.aspx.cs
//
//    Description: This class provides the code behind for
//                 CH01DataGridWithEditingCS.aspx
//
//*****************************************************************************
using System;
using System.Collections;
using System.Configuration;
using System.Data;
using System.Data.OleDb;
using System.Web.UI.WebControls;

namespace ASPNetCookbook.CSExamples
{
    public class CH01DataGridWithEditingCS : System.Web.UI.Page
    {
```

Example 1-41. DataGrid with editing code-behind (.cs) (continued)

```csharp
  // controls on form
  protected System.Web.UI.WebControls.DataGrid dgProblems;

  // The following variable contains the list of yes/no selections used in
  // the dropdown lists and is declared protected to provide access to the
  // data from the aspx page
  protected ArrayList yesNoSelections;

  //***********************************************************************
  //
  //   ROUTINE: Page_Load
  //
  //   DESCRIPTION: This routine provides the event handler for the page
  //                load event.  It is responsible for initializing the
  //                controls on page.
  //-----------------------------------------------------------------------
  private void Page_Load(object sender, System.EventArgs e)
  {
    // wire edit events
    this.dgProblems.CancelCommand +=
      new DataGridCommandEventHandler(this.dgProblems_CancelCommand);
    this.dgProblems.EditCommand +=
      new DataGridCommandEventHandler(this.dgProblems_EditCommand);
    this.dgProblems.UpdateCommand +=
      new DataGridCommandEventHandler(this.dgProblems_UpdateCommand);

    if (!Page.IsPostBack)
    {
      bindData();
    }
  }  // Page_Load

  //***********************************************************************
  //
  //   ROUTINE: dgProblems_EditCommand
  //
  //   DESCRIPTION: This routine provides the event handler for the edit
  //                command click event.  It is responsible for setting the
  //                edit item index to the selected item and rebinding
  //                the data.
  //-----------------------------------------------------------------------
  private void dgProblems_EditCommand(Object source,
                      System.Web.UI.WebControls.DataGridCommandEventArgs e)
  {
    dgProblems.EditItemIndex = e.Item.ItemIndex;
    bindData();
  }  // dgProblems_EditCommand

  //***********************************************************************
  //
  //   ROUTINE: dgProblems_CancelCommand
  //
```

Example 1-41. DataGrid with editing code-behind (.cs) (continued)

```
//    DESCRIPTION: This routine provides the event handler for the cancel
//                 command click event.  It is responsible for resetting the
//                 edit item index to no item and rebinding the data.
//-------------------------------------------------------------------------
private void dgProblems_CancelCommand(Object source,
                   System.Web.UI.WebControls.DataGridCommandEventArgs e)
{
  dgProblems.EditItemIndex = -1;
  bindData( );
}  // dgProblems_CancelCommand

//*************************************************************************
//
//    ROUTINE: dgProblems_UpdateCommand
//
//    DESCRIPTION: This routine provides the event handler for the update
//                 command click event.  It is responsible for updating
//                 the contents of the database with the date entered for
//                 the item currently being edited.
//-------------------------------------------------------------------------
private void dgProblems_UpdateCommand(Object source,
                   System.Web.UI.WebControls.DataGridCommandEventArgs e)
{
  OleDbConnection dbConn = null;
  OleDbCommand dCmd = null;
  String sectionHeading = null;
  int hasCSSample;
  String strConnection = null;
  String strSQL = null;
  int rowsAffected;
  DropDownList ddl = null;

  try
  {
    // get the edited section heading and "has vb sample" data
    // NOTE: This can be done by using the FindControl method of the edited
    //       item because EditItemTemplates were used and the controls in
    //       the templates were given IDs.  If a standard BoundColumn was
    //       used, the data would have to be acccessed using the cells
    //       collection (e.g. e.Item.Cells(0).Text would access the section
    //       number column in this example.
    sectionHeading =
      ((TextBox)(e.Item.FindControl("txtSectionHeading"))).Text;
    ddl =(DropDownList)(e.Item.FindControl("selHasCSSample"));
    hasCSSample = Convert.ToInt32(ddl.SelectedItem.Value);

    // get the connection string from web.config and open a connection
    // to the database
    strConnection =
      ConfigurationSettings.AppSettings["dbConnectionString"];
    dbConn = new OleDbConnection(strConnection);
    dbConn.Open( );
```

Example 1-41. DataGrid with editing code-behind (.cs) (continued)

```
        // update data in database
        // NOTE: The primary key used to uniquely identify the row being edited
        //        is accessed through the DataKeys collection of the DataGrid.
        strSQL = "UPDATE EditProblem " +
                 "SET SectionHeading='" + sectionHeading + "'" +
                 ",HasCSExample=" + hasCSSample +
                 " WHERE EditProblemID=" +
                 dgProblems.DataKeys[e.Item.ItemIndex].ToString();
        dCmd = new OleDbCommand(strSQL, dbConn);
        rowsAffected = dCmd.ExecuteNonQuery();
        dbConn.Close();

        // TODO: production code should check the number of rows affected here to
        // make sure it is exactly 1 and output the appropriate success or
        // failure information to the user.

        // reset the edit item and rebind the data
        dgProblems.EditItemIndex = -1;
        bindData();
      }

      finally
      {
        //cleanup
        if (dbConn != null)
        {
          dbConn.Close();
        }
      }
    }  // dgProblems_UpdateCommand

    //**************************************************************************
    //
    //   ROUTINE: bindData
    //
    //   DESCRIPTION: This routine queries the database for the data to
    //                displayed and binds it to the DataGrid
    //--------------------------------------------------------------------------
    private void bindData()
    {
      OleDbConnection dbConn = null;
      OleDbDataAdapter da = null;
      DataSet ds = null;
      String strConnection = null;
      String strSQL =null;

      try
      {
        // get the connection string from web.config and open a connection
        // to the database
        strConnection =
          ConfigurationSettings.AppSettings["dbConnectionString"];
        dbConn = new OleDbConnection(strConnection);
```

Example 1-41. DataGrid with editing code-behind (.cs) (continued)

```
    dbConn.Open( );

    // build the query string and get the data from the database
    strSQL = "SELECT EditProblemID, SectionNumber" +
            ", SectionHeading, HasCSExample " +
            "FROM EditProblem " +
            "ORDER BY SectionNumber";

    da = new OleDbDataAdapter(strSQL, dbConn);
    ds = new DataSet( );
    da.Fill(ds);

    // build the hashtable with the acceptable responses to the
    // "Has VB Sample" field
    yesNoSelections = new ArrayList(2);
    yesNoSelections.Add(new ListItem("No", "0"));
    yesNoSelections.Add(new ListItem("Yes", "1"));

    // set the source of the data for the datagrid control and bind it
    dgProblems.DataSource = ds;
    dgProblems.DataKeyField = "EditProblemID";
    dgProblems.DataBind( );
  }  // try

  finally
  {
    //clean up
    if (dbConn != null)
    {
      dbConn.Close( );
    }
  }  // finally
}  // bindData
}  // CH01DataGridWithEditingCS
}
```

1.15   Formatting Columnar Data in a DataGrid

Problem

You need to format dates and numbers in your DataGrid controls.

Solution

Use the DataFormatString attribute of the asp:BoundColumn tag.

1. Within the *.aspx* file that contains the DataGrid control, add a BoundColumn tag with the appropriate DataFormatString attribute for each column you want to format.

2. If the DataFormatString does not provide the flexibility you need to format your data, use the ItemDataBound event instead to gain greater flexibility.

Figure 1-19 shows the appearance of an example DataGrid with the Publish Date and List Price columns formatted for dates and currency, respectively. Examples 1-42 through 1-44 show the *.aspx* and code-behind files for an application that produces this result.

ASP.NET Cookbook
The Ultimate ASP.NET Code Sourcebook

DataGrid With Formatted Columns In ASPX (VB)

Title	Publish Date	List Price
.Net Framework Essentials	Feb 01, 2002	$29.95
Access Cookbook	Feb 01, 2002	$49.95
ADO: ActiveX Data Objects	Jun 01, 2001	$44.95
ASP.NET in a Nutshell	May 01, 2002	$34.95
C# Essentials	Jan 01, 2002	$24.95
C# in a Nutshell	Mar 01, 2002	$39.95
COM and .Net Component Services	Sep 01, 2001	$39.95
COM+ Programming with Visual Basic	Jun 01, 2001	$34.95
Developing ASP Components	Mar 01, 2001	$49.95
HTML & XHTML: The Definitive Guide	Aug 01, 2000	$34.95
Java Cookbook	Jan 15, 2001	$44.95
JavaScript Application Cookbook	Oct 01, 1999	$34.95
JavaScript: The Definitive Guide	Dec 15, 2001	$44.95
Perl Cookbook	Aug 01, 1998	$39.95
Programming ASP.NET	Feb 01, 2002	$49.95
Programming C#	Feb 01, 2002	$39.95
Programming Visual Basic .Net	Dec 15, 2001	$39.95
Programming Web Services with SOAP	Dec 15, 2001	$34.95
SQL in a Nutshell	Dec 01, 2000	$29.95
Subclassing & Hooking with Visual Basic	May 15, 2001	$49.95
Transact-SQL Cookbook	Apr 01, 2002	$34.95
Transact-SQL Programming	Apr 01, 1999	$49.95
VB .Net Language in a Nutshell	Oct 15, 2001	$34.95
Web Services Essentials	Feb 01, 2002	$29.95
XML in a Nutshell	Jan 15, 2001	$29.95
XSLT	Aug 15, 2001	$39.95

Figure 1-19. Formatting columnar data in a DataGrid output

Discussion

The formatting of dates and numbers in a DataGrid is performed with the DataFormatString attribute of the asp:BoundColumn element. The general format of the formatting string is {A:B}, where A is the zero-based index number of the property the format applies to (this is generally 0) and B specifies the format.

Numeric formats can be any of the following. Most numeric formats can be followed by an integer defining the number of decimal places displayed.

Format character	Description
C	Displays numeric values in currency format
D	Displays numeric values in decimal format
E	Displays numeric values in scientific (exponential) format
F	Displays numeric values in fixed format

Format character	Description
G	Displays numeric values in general format
N	Displays numeric values in number format
X	Displays numeric values in hexadecimal format

Time/date formats can be any combination of the following:

Format character	Associated property/ description	Example format pattern (en-US)
D	ShortDatePattern	MM/dd/yyyy
D	LongDatePattern	dddd, dd MMMM yyyy
F	Full date and time (long date and short time)	dddd, dd MMMM yyyy HH:mm
F	FullDateTimePattern (long date and long time)	dddd, dd MMMM yyyy HH:mm:ss
G	General (short date and short time)	MM/dd/yyyy HH:mm
G	General (short date and long time)	MM/dd/yyyy HH:mm:ss
m, M	MonthDayPattern	MMMM dd
r, R	RFC1123Pattern	ddd, dd MMM yyyy HH':'mm':'ss 'GMT'
S	SortableDateTimePattern (based on ISO 8601) using local time	yyyy'-'MM'-'dd'T'HH':'mm':'ss
T	ShortTimePattern	HH:mm
T	LongTimePattern	HH:mm:ss
U	UniversalSortableDateTimePattern using universal time	yyyy'-'MM'-'dd HH':'mm':'ss'Z'
U	Full date and time (long date and long time) using universal time	dddd, dd MMMM yyyy HH:mm:ss
y, Y	YearMonthPattern	yyyy MMMM

Formatting can be applied when using data binding to any other control—including text boxes, repeaters, and the like—by passing the same format string described in this recipe as the third parameter of the DataBinder.Eval method. For example:

```
DataBinder.Eval(Container.DataItem,
               " PublishDate ",
               "{0:MMM dd, yyyy}")
DataBinder.Eval(Container.DataItem,
               " ListPrice",
               "{0:C2}")
```

Formatting data in this manner can be costly in terms of performance. A less costly approach is shown next.

If the DataFormatString does not provide the flexibility you need to format your data, the ItemDataBound event can be used to provide total flexibility in the data presented. As with most events in ASP.NET, the ItemDataBound event is passed two parameters.

The first argument is the sender of the event. In this case it will simply be the DataGrid. The second argument is the event arguments. This parameter (by default named e) provides a reference to the item that has just been data bound. By using this argument, each column in the row that has just been data bound can be accessed and the data formatted as required. There are virtually no limits to the reformatting that can be done using the ItemDataBound event. The following code provides an example of using the ItemDataBound event to format the Publish Date and List Price columns in our example.

 Be sure to remove any DataFormatString properties from the BoundColumn elements when using this method of formatting. The additional data conversions and formatting will result in a performance hit as well as potential confusion if the formatting is coded differently.

VB

```
Private Sub dgBooks_ItemDataBound(ByVal sender As Object, _
            ByVal e As System.Web.UI.WebControls.DataGridItemEventArgs) _
        Handles dgBooks.ItemDataBound

    Const DATE_PUBLISHED_COL As Integer = 1
    Const LIST_PRICE_COL As Integer = 2

    Dim cell As TableCell
    Dim datePublished As Date
    Dim listPrice As Single

    'make sure the item data bound is an item or alternating item since
    'this event is also called for the header, footer, pager, etc. and
    'no formatting is required for these items
    If ((e.Item.ItemType = ListItemType.Item) Or _
        (e.Item.ItemType = ListItemType.AlternatingItem)) Then
        'get the date published that was placed in the datagrid during data
        'binding and reformat it as required
        cell = CType(e.Item.Controls(DATE_PUBLISHED_COL), TableCell)
        datePublished = CType(cell.Text, Date)
        cell.Text = datePublished.ToString("MMM dd, yyyy")

        'get the list price that was placed in the datagrid during data
        'binding and reformat it as required
        cell = CType(e.Item.Controls(LIST_PRICE_COL), TableCell)
        listPrice = CType(cell.Text, Single)
        cell.Text = listPrice.ToString("C2")
    End If
End Sub 'dgBooks_ItemDataBound
```

C#

```
private void dgBooks_ItemDataBound(Object sender,
            System.Web.UI.WebControls.DataGridItemEventArgs e)
{
    const int DATE_PUBLISHED_COL = 1;
    const int LIST_PRICE_COL = 2;
```

```csharp
      TableCell cell = null;
      DateTime datePublished;
      Single listPrice;

      // make sure the item data bound is an item or alternating item since
      // this event is also called for the header, footer, pager, etc. and
      // no formatting is required for these items
      if ((e.Item.ItemType == ListItemType.Item) ||
        (e.Item.ItemType == ListItemType.AlternatingItem))
      { // get the date published that was placed in the datagrid during data
        // binding and reformat it as required
        cell = (TableCell)(e.Item.Controls[DATE_PUBLISHED_COL]);
        datePublished = Convert.ToDateTime(cell.Text);
        cell.Text = datePublished.ToString("MMM dd, yyyy");

        // get the list price that was placed in the datagrid during data
        // binding and reformat it as required
        cell = (TableCell)(e.Item.Controls[LIST_PRICE_COL]);
        listPrice = Convert.ToSingle(cell.Text);
        cell.Text = listPrice.ToString("C2");
      }
    } // dgBooks_ItemDataBound
```

Example 1-42. Formatting columnar data in a DataGrid (.aspx)

```
<%@ Page Language="vb" AutoEventWireup="false"
    Codebehind="CH01DatagridWithFormattedColumnsVB1.aspx.vb"
    Inherits="ASPNetCookbook.VBExamples.CH01DatagridWithFormattedColumnsVB1" %>
<!DOCTYPE HTML PUBLIC "-//W3C//DTD HTML 4.0 Transitional//EN">
<html>
  <head>
    <title>DataGrid With Formatted Columns - ASPX</title>
    <link rel="stylesheet" href="css/ASPNetCookbook.css">
  </head>
  <body leftmargin="0" marginheight="0" marginwidth="0" topmargin="0">
    <form id="frmDatagrid" method="post" runat="server">
      <table width="100%" cellpadding="0" cellspacing="0" border="0">
        <tr>
          <td align="center">
            <img src="images/ASPNETCookbookHeading_blue.gif">
          </td>
        </tr>
        <tr>
          <td class="dividerLine">
            <img src="images/spacer.gif" height="6" border="0"></td>
        </tr>
      </table>
      <table width="90%" align="center" border="0">
        <tr>
          <td><img src="images/spacer.gif" height="10" border="0"></td>
        </tr>
        <tr>
          <td align="center" class="PageHeading">
            DataGrid With Formatted Columns In ASPX (VB)
          </td>
```

Example 1-42. Formatting columnar data in a DataGrid (.aspx) (continued)

```
      </tr>
      <tr>
        <td><img src="images/spacer.gif" height="10" border="0"></td>
      </tr>
      <tr>
        <td align="center">
          <asp:DataGrid
            id="dgBooks"
            runat="server"
            BorderColor="000080"
            BorderWidth="2px"
            AutoGenerateColumns="False"
            width="100%">

            <HeaderStyle
              HorizontalAlign="Center"
              ForeColor="#FFFFFF"
              BackColor="#000080"
              Font-Bold=true
              CssClass="TableHeader" />

            <ItemStyle
              BackColor="#FFFFE0"
              cssClass="TableCellNormal" />

            <AlternatingItemStyle
              BackColor="#FFFFFF"
              cssClass="TableCellAlternating" />

            <Columns>
              <asp:BoundColumn HeaderText="Title" DataField="Title" />
              <asp:BoundColumn HeaderText="Publish Date"
                               DataField="PublishDate"
                               ItemStyle-HorizontalAlign="Center"
                               DataFormatString="{0:MMM dd, yyyy}" />
              <asp:BoundColumn HeaderText="List Price"
                               DataField="ListPrice"
                               ItemStyle-HorizontalAlign="Center"
                               DataFormatString="{0:C2}" />
            </Columns>
          </asp:DataGrid>
        </td>
      </tr>
    </table>
  </form>
</body>
</html>
```

Example 1-43. Formatting columnar data in a DataGrid code-behind (.vb)

```
Option Explicit On
Option Strict On
'---------------------------------------------------------------------------
'
```

Example 1-43. Formatting columnar data in a DataGrid code-behind (.vb) (continued)

```vb
'   Module Name: CH01DatagridWithFormattedColumnsVB1.aspx.vb
'
'   Description: This class provides the code behind for
'                CH01DatagridWithFormattedColumnsVB1.aspx
'
'****************************************************************************
Imports Microsoft.VisualBasic
Imports System.Configuration
Imports System.Data
Imports System.Data.OleDb

Namespace ASPNetCookbook.VBExamples
  Public Class CH01DatagridWithFormattedColumnsVB1
    Inherits System.Web.UI.Page

    'controls on form
    Protected dgBooks As System.Web.UI.WebControls.DataGrid

    '****************************************************************************
    '
    '   ROUTINE: Page_Load
    '
    '   DESCRIPTION: This routine provides the event handler for the page load
    '                event.  It is responsible for initializing the controls
    '                on the page.
    '----------------------------------------------------------------------
    Private Sub Page_Load(ByVal sender As System.Object, _
                      ByVal e As System.EventArgs) _
            Handles MyBase.Load
      Dim dbConn As OleDbConnection
      Dim da As OleDbDataAdapter
      Dim ds As DataSet
      Dim strConnection As String
      Dim strSQL As String

      If (Not Page.IsPostBack) Then
        Try
          'get the connection string from web.config and open a connection
          'to the database
          strConnection = _
              ConfigurationSettings.AppSettings("dbConnectionString")
          dbConn = New OleDb.OleDbConnection(strConnection)
          dbConn.Open( )

          'build the query string and get the data from the database
          strSQL = "SELECT Title, PublishDate, ListPrice " & _
                  "FROM Book " & _
                  "ORDER BY Title"

          da = New OleDbDataAdapter(strSQL, dbConn)
          ds = New DataSet
          da.Fill(ds)
```

Example 1-43. Formatting columnar data in a DataGrid code-behind (.vb) (continued)

```
        'set the source of the data for the datagrid control and bind it
        dgBooks.DataSource = ds
        dgBooks.DataBind( )

      Finally
        If (Not IsNothing(dbConn)) Then
          dbConn.Close( )
        End If
      End Try
    End If
  End Sub  'Page_Load
  End Class  'CH01DatagridWithFormattedColumnsVB1
End Namespace
```

Example 1-44. Formatting columnar data in a DataGrid code-behind (.cs)

```
//------------------------------------------------------------------------------
//
//    Module Name: CH01DatagridWithFormattedColumnsCS1.aspx.cs
//
//    Description: This class provides the code behind for
//                 CH01DatagridWithFormattedColumnsCS1.aspx
//
//******************************************************************************
using System;
using System.Configuration;
using System.Data;
using System.Data.OleDb;

namespace ASPNetCookbook.CSExamples
{
  public class CH01DatagridWithFormattedColumnsCS1 : System.Web.UI.Page
  {

    // controls on form
    protected System.Web.UI.WebControls.DataGrid dgBooks;

    //******************************************************************************
    //
    //    ROUTINE: Page_Load
    //
    //    DESCRIPTION: This routine provides the event handler for the page
    //                 load event.  It is responsible for initializing the
    //                 controls on the page.
    //------------------------------------------------------------------------------
    private void Page_Load(object sender, System.EventArgs e)
    {
      OleDbConnection dbConn = null;
      OleDbDataAdapter da = null;
      DataSet ds = null;
      String strConnection = null;
```

Example 1-44. Formatting columnar data in a DataGrid code-behind (.cs) (continued)

```csharp
String strSQL = null;

if (!Page.IsPostBack)
{
  try
  {
    // get the connection string from web.config and open a connection
    // to the database
    strConnection =
      ConfigurationSettings.AppSettings["dbConnectionString"];
    dbConn = new OleDbConnection(strConnection);
    dbConn.Open();

    // build the query string and get the data from the database
    strSQL = "SELECT Title, PublishDate, ListPrice " +
             "FROM Book " +
             "ORDER BY Title";

    da = new OleDbDataAdapter(strSQL, dbConn);
    ds = new DataSet();
    da.Fill(ds);

    // set the source of the data for the datagrid control and bind it
    dgBooks.DataSource = ds;
    dgBooks.DataBind();
  } // try

  finally
  {
    //clean up
    if (dbConn != null)
    {
      dbConn.Close();
    }
  } // finally
}
} // Page_Load
} // CH01DatagridWithFormattedColumnsCS1
}
```

1.16   Allowing Selection Anywhere Within a DataGrid Row

Problem

You are implementing a DataGrid that requires selection of a row, but you do not want to have a Select button in every row of your DataGrid. What you really want is to allow the user to click anywhere within a row, like in a classic Windows application.

Solution

To every row in the DataGrid add a hidden Select button along with an onclick event that performs the same action as if the hidden Select button were clicked.

1. Add a hidden ButtonColumn to the DataGrid.

2. Set the ButtonType attribute to "LinkButton" so that a hidden hyperlinked Select button is rendered in every row.

3. In the ItemDataBound event, add an onclick event to the DataGrid row that performs the same action as clicking the hidden Select button.

The approach produces output like that shown in Figure 1-20. Examples 1-45 through 1-47 show the *.aspx* and code-behind files for the application that produces this result.

ASP.NET Cookbook
The Ultimate ASP.NET Code Sourcebook

DataGrid With Selection Anywhere (VB)

Title	Publish Date	List Price
.Net Framework Essentials	Feb 01, 2002	$29.95
Access Cookbook	Feb 01, 2002	$49.95
ADO: ActiveX Data Objects	Jun 01, 2001	$44.95
ASP.NET in a Nutshell	May 01, 2002	$34.95
C# Essentials	Jan 01, 2002	$24.95
C# in a Nutshell	Mar 01, 2002	$39.95
COM and .Net Component Services	Sep 01, 2001	$39.95
COM+ Programming with Visual Basic	Jun 01, 2001	$34.95
Developing ASP Components	Mar 01, 2001	$49.95
HTML & XHTML: The Definitive Guide	Aug 01, 2000	$34.95
Java Cookbook	Jan 15, 2001	$44.95
JavaScript Application Cookbook	Oct 01, 1999	$34.95
JavaScript: The Definitive Guide	Dec 15, 2001	$44.95
Perl Cookbook	Aug 01, 1998	$39.95
Programming ASP.NET	Feb 01, 2002	$49.95
Programming C#	Feb 01, 2002	$39.95
Programming Visual Basic .Net	Dec 15, 2001	$39.95
Programming Web Services with SOAP	Dec 15, 2001	$34.95
SQL in a Nutshell	Dec 01, 2000	$29.95
Subclassing & Hooking with Visual Basic	May 15, 2001	$49.95
Transact-SQL Cookbook	Apr 01, 2002	$34.95
Transact-SQL Programming	Apr 01, 1999	$49.95
VB .Net Language in a Nutshell	Oct 15, 2001	$34.95
Web Services Essentials	Feb 01, 2002	$29.95
XML in a Nutshell	Jan 15, 2001	$29.95
XSLT	Aug 15, 2001	$39.95

Add   Edit   Delete

Figure 1-20. Output of DataGrid allowing selection anywhere

Discussion

To allow selection of a row of data simply by clicking on it, you create a DataGrid in the usual fashion but add a hidden ButtonColumn. The ButtonType attribute is set to "LinkButton", and the CommandName attribute is set to "Select". This causes the DataGrid to be rendered with a hidden hyperlinked Select button in every row.

```
<Columns>
  <asp:ButtonColumn ButtonType="LinkButton"
                    Visible="False"
                    CommandName="Select" />
  ...
</Columns>
```

In the code-behind, the DataGrid control's ItemDataBound event handler (dgProblems_
ItemDataBound) is used to expand the functionality of the hidden Select button to
encompass the entire row. This method is called for every row of the DataGrid,
including the header and footer, so the item type must be checked to see if this event
applies to a given data row.

When the event applies to a data row, the first thing you must do is get a reference
to the hidden Select button in the row. The LINK_BUTTON_COLUMN and LINK_BUTTON_
CONTROL constants are used to avoid so-called "magic numbers" (hardcoded numbers that seem to appear out of nowhere in the code) and to make the code more
maintainable.

Next, some client-side JavaScript is added to a row's hidden hyperlinked Select button. Its sole purpose is to handle the onclick event for the row in the DataGrid that
has just been data bound and to perform a call to __doPostBack. The JavaScript is
added to the DataGrid row's Attributes collection using the Add method, whose
parameters are the name of the event we want to add to the control and the name of
the function (along with its parameters) that is to be executed when the event occurs.

The Page's GetPostBackClientHyperlink method is used to get the name of the client-
side function created for the hidden Select button in the row being processed. It
returns the name of the event method along with the required parameters. For the
first row in our DataGrid, for example, the GetPostBackClientHyperlink method
returns javascript:__doPostBack('dgProblems:_ctl2:_ctl0','').

Effectively, this adds an onclick event to all the table rows, which causes the method
__doPostBack to be called anytime the user clicks on a data row in the grid. Because
this onclick event is identical to the event created for the hidden Select button in the
row, the postback is processed as a select event, thereby setting the SelectedIndex of
the DataGrid to the clicked row.

Be aware that the selection of a row using this method requires a
round trip to the server to perform the selection.

This example shows the use of Add, Edit, and Delete buttons below the DataGrid,
which is typical of a scenario where a row is selected and then a desired action is performed on it. The methods for the Add, Edit, and Delete events were included in this
recipe but were left empty to keep the code down to a reasonable size.

Example 1-45. DataGrid allowing selection anywhere (.aspx)

```
<%@ Page Language="vb" AutoEventWireup="false"
    Codebehind="CH01DatagridWithSelectionAnywhereVB.aspx.vb"
    Inherits="ASPNetCookbook.VBExamples.CH01DatagridWithSelectionAnywhereVB" %>
<!DOCTYPE HTML PUBLIC "-//W3C//DTD HTML 4.0 Transitional//EN">
<html>
  <head>
    <title>DataGrid With Selection Anywhere</title>
    <link rel="stylesheet" href="css/ASPNetCookbook.css">
  </head>
  <body leftmargin="0" marginheight="0" marginwidth="0" topmargin="0">
    <form id="frmDatagrid" method="post" runat="server">
      <table width="100%" cellpadding="0" cellspacing="0" border="0">
        <tr>
          <td align="center">
            <img src="images/ASPNETCookbookHeading_blue.gif">
          </td>
        </tr>
        <tr>
          <td class="dividerLine">
            <img src="images/spacer.gif" height="6" border="0"></td>
        </tr>
      </table>
      <table width="90%" align="center" border="0">
        <tr>
          <td><img src="images/spacer.gif" height="10" border="0"></td>
        </tr>
        <tr>
          <td align="center" class="PageHeading">
            DataGrid With Selection Anywhere (VB)
          </td>
        </tr>
        <tr>
          <td><img src="images/spacer.gif" height="10" border="0"></td>
        </tr>
        <tr>
          <td align="center">
              <!-- The first column defined in the Columns element is a
                   hidden link button to provide the ability to make
                   clicking anywhere in the row the same as clicking
                   the link button.  See the dgProblems_ItemDataBound
                   method in the code behind page -->
          <asp:DataGrid
            id="dgProblems"
            runat="server"
            BorderColor="000080"
            BorderWidth="2px"
            AutoGenerateColumns="False"
            width="100%">

            <HeaderStyle
              HorizontalAlign="Center"
              ForeColor="#FFFFFF"
```

Example 1-45. DataGrid allowing selection anywhere (.aspx) (continued)

```
              BackColor="#000080"
              Font-Bold=true
              CssClass="TableHeader" />

          <ItemStyle
            BackColor="#FFFFE0"
            cssClass="TableCellNormal" />

          <AlternatingItemStyle
            BackColor="#FFFFFF"
            cssClass="TableCellAlternating" />

          <SelectedItemStyle
            BackColor="#cccccc"
            cssClass="TableCellAlternating" />

          <Columns>
            <asp:ButtonColumn ButtonType="LinkButton"
                              Visible="False"
                              CommandName="Select" />
            <asp:BoundColumn HeaderText="Title"
                             DataField="Title"
                             ItemStyle-HorizontalAlign="Left" />
            <asp:BoundColumn HeaderText="Publish Date"
                             DataField="PublishDate"
                             ItemStyle-HorizontalAlign="Center"
                             DataFormatString="{0:MMM dd, yyyy}"/>
            <asp:BoundColumn HeaderText="List Price"
                             DataField="ListPrice"
                             ItemStyle-HorizontalAlign="Center"
                             DataFormatString="{0:C2}"/>
          </Columns>

      </asp:DataGrid>
    </td>
  </tr>
  <tr>
    <td><img src="images/spacer.gif" height="10" border="0"></td>
  </tr>
  <tr>
    <td align="center">
      <table width="100%">
        <tr>
          <td width="18%"> </td>
          <td width="15%" align="center">
            <asp:ImageButton id="btnAdd" runat="server"
                 ImageUrl="images/buttons/button_add.gif" /></td>
          <td width="10%"> </td>
          <td width="15%" align="center">
            <asp:ImageButton id="btnEdit" runat="server"
                 ImageUrl="images/buttons/button_edit.gif" /></td>
          <td width="10%"> </td>
```

Example 1-45. DataGrid allowing selection anywhere (.aspx) (continued)

```
                <td width="15%" align="center">
                  <asp:ImageButton id="btnDelete" runat="server"
                      ImageUrl="images/buttons/button_delete.gif" /></td>
                <td width="17%"> </td>
              </tr>
            </table>
          </td>
        </tr>
      </table>
    </form>
  </body>
</html>
```

Example 1-46. DataGrid allowing selection anywhere code-behind (.vb)

```
Option Explicit On
Option Strict On
'----------------------------------------------------------------------------
'
'   Module Name: CH01DatagridWithSelectionAnywhereVB.aspx.vb
'
'   Description: This class provides the code behind for
'                CH01DatagridWithSelectionAnywhereVB
'
'****************************************************************************
Imports Microsoft.VisualBasic
Imports System.Configuration
Imports System.Data
Imports System.Data.OleDb
Imports System.Web.UI.WebControls

Namespace ASPNetCookbook.VBExamples
  Public Class CH01DatagridWithSelectionAnywhereVB
    Inherits System.Web.UI.Page

    'controls on form
    Protected WithEvents btnAdd As System.Web.UI.WebControls.ImageButton
    Protected WithEvents btnEdit As System.Web.UI.WebControls.ImageButton
    Protected WithEvents btnDelete As System.Web.UI.WebControls.ImageButton
    Protected WithEvents dgProblems As System.Web.UI.WebControls.DataGrid

    '****************************************************************************
    '
    '   ROUTINE: Page_Load
    '
    '   DESCRIPTION: This routine provides the event handler for the page load
    '                event.  It is responsible for initializing the controls
    '                on the page.
    '----------------------------------------------------------------------------
    Private Sub Page_Load(ByVal sender As System.Object, _
                      ByVal e As System.EventArgs) _
          Handles MyBase.Load
```

Example 1-46. DataGrid allowing selection anywhere code-behind (.vb) (continued)

```vb
    If (Not Page.IsPostBack) Then
      bindData( )
    End If
End Sub  'Page_Load

'*************************************************************************
'
'   ROUTINE: dgProblems_ItemDataBound
'
'   DESCRIPTION: This routine is the event handler that is called for
'                each item in the datagrid after a data bind occurs.  It
'                is responsible for making each row a link button to
'                allow clicking anywhere to select a row.
'------------------------------------------------------------------------
Private Sub dgProblems_ItemDataBound(ByVal sender As Object, _
         ByVal e As System.Web.UI.WebControls.DataGridItemEventArgs) _
      Handles dgProblems.ItemDataBound

  'datagrid column containing link button defined on ASPX page
  Const LINK_BUTTON_COLUMN As Integer = 0
  'index of link button control in the link button column
  Const LINK_BUTTON_CONTROL As Integer = 0

  Dim button As LinkButton

  'check the type of item that was databound and only take action if it
  'was a row in the datagrid
  If ((e.Item.ItemType = ListItemType.Pager) Or _
     (e.Item.ItemType = ListItemType.Header) Or _
     (e.Item.ItemType = ListItemType.Footer)) Then
    'do nothing
  Else
    'the item that was bound is an "Item", "AlternatingItem", "EditItem",
    '"SelectedItem" or "Separator" (in other words a row) so get a
    'reference to the link button column defined in the Columns property
    'of the datagrid (in the aspx page) and add an event handler for the
    'the onclick event for this entire row.  This will make clicking
    'anywhere in the row select the row.
    'NOTE: This is tightly coupled to the definition of the bound columns
    '      in the aspx page.
    button = _
      CType(e.Item.Cells(LINK_BUTTON_COLUMN).Controls(LINK_BUTTON_CONTROL), _
         LinkButton)
    e.Item.Attributes.Add("onclick", _
                     Page.GetPostBackClientHyperlink(button, ""))
  End If
End Sub  'dgProblems_ItemDataBound

'*************************************************************************
'
'   ROUTINE: btnAdd_Click
'
```

Example 1-46. DataGrid allowing selection anywhere code-behind (.vb) (continued)

```vb
'    DESCRIPTION: This routine is the event handler that is called when
'                 the Add button is clicked.
'-------------------------------------------------------------------------
Private Sub btnAdd_Click(ByVal sender As Object, _
                         ByVal e As System.Web.UI.ImageClickEventArgs) _
           Handles btnAdd.Click

  'place code here to perform Add operations
End Sub   'btnAdd_Click


'*************************************************************************
'
'    ROUTINE: btnEdit_Click
'
'    DESCRIPTION: This routine is the event handler that is called when
'                 the Edit button is clicked.
'-------------------------------------------------------------------------
Private Sub btnEdit_Click(ByVal sender As Object, _
                          ByVal e As System.Web.UI.ImageClickEventArgs) _
           Handles btnEdit.Click

  'place code here to perform Edit operations
End Sub   'btnEdit_Click


'*************************************************************************
'
'    ROUTINE: btnDelete_Click
'
'    DESCRIPTION: This routine is the event handler that is called when
'                 the Delete button is clicked.
'-------------------------------------------------------------------------
Private Sub btnDelete_Click(ByVal sender As Object, _
                            ByVal e As System.Web.UI.ImageClickEventArgs) _
           Handles btnDelete.Click

  'place code here to perform Delete operations
End Sub   'btnDelete_Click


'*************************************************************************
'
'    ROUTINE: bindData
'
'    DESCRIPTION: This routine queries the database for the data to
'                 displayed and binds it to the datagrid
'
'-------------------------------------------------------------------------
Private Sub bindData()
  Dim dbConn As OleDbConnection
  Dim dCmd As OleDbCommand
  Dim dReader As OleDbDataReader
  Dim strConnection As String
  Dim strSQL As String
```

Example 1-46. DataGrid allowing selection anywhere code-behind (.vb) (continued)

```
    Try
      'get the connection string from web.config and open a connection
      'to the database
      strConnection = _
          ConfigurationSettings.AppSettings("dbConnectionString")
      dbConn = New OleDb.OleDbConnection(strConnection)
      dbConn.Open( )

      'build the query string and get the data from the database
      strSQL = "SELECT Title, PublishDate, ListPrice " & _
               "FROM Book " & _
               "ORDER BY Title"

      dCmd = New OleDbCommand(strSQL, dbConn)
      dReader = dCmd.ExecuteReader(CommandBehavior.Default)

      'set the source of the data for the datagrid control and bind it
      dgProblems.DataSource = dReader
      dgProblems.DataBind( )

      'select first item in the datagrid
      dgProblems.SelectedIndex = 0

    Finally
      'cleanup
      If (Not IsNothing(dReader)) Then
        dReader.Close( )
      End If

      If (Not IsNothing(dbConn)) Then
        dbConn.Close( )
      End If
    End Try
  End Sub        'bindData
  End Class  'CH01DatagridWithSelectionAnywhereVB
End Namespace
```

Example 1-47. DataGrid allowing selection anywhere code-behind (.cs)

```
//-----------------------------------------------------------------------------
//
//    Module Name: CH01DatagridWithSelectionAnywhereCS.aspx.cs
//
//    Description: This class provides the code behind for
//                 CH01DatagridWithSelectionAnywhereCS.aspx
//
//*****************************************************************************
using System;
using System.Configuration;
using System.Data;
using System.Data.OleDb;
using System.Web.UI;
using System.Web.UI.WebControls;
```

Example 1-47. DataGrid allowing selection anywhere code-behind (.cs) (continued)

```
namespace ASPNetCookbook.CSExamples
{
  public class CH01DatagridWithSelectionAnywhereCS : System.Web.UI.Page
  {
    // controls on form
    protected System.Web.UI.WebControls.ImageButton btnAdd;
    protected System.Web.UI.WebControls.ImageButton btnEdit;
    protected System.Web.UI.WebControls.ImageButton btnDelete;
    protected System.Web.UI.WebControls.DataGrid dgProblems;

    //*********************************************************************
    //
    //   ROUTINE: Page_Load
    //
    //   DESCRIPTION: This routine provides the event handler for the page
    //                load event.  It is responsible for initializing the
    //                controls on the page.
    //---------------------------------------------------------------------
    private void Page_Load(object sender, System.EventArgs e)
    {
      // wire the item data bound and button events
      this.dgProblems.ItemDataBound +=
        new DataGridItemEventHandler(this.dgProblems_ItemDataBound);
      this.btnAdd.Click +=
        new ImageClickEventHandler(this.btnAdd_Click);
      this.btnEdit.Click +=
        new ImageClickEventHandler(this.btnEdit_Click);
      this.btnDelete.Click +=
        new ImageClickEventHandler(this.btnDelete_Click);

      if (!Page.IsPostBack)
      {
        bindData();
      }
    } // Page_Load

    //*********************************************************************
    //
    //   ROUTINE: dgProblems_ItemDataBound
    //
    //   DESCRIPTION: This routine is the event handler that is called for
    //                each item in the datagrid after a data bind occurs.  It
    //                is responsible for making each row a link button to
    //                allow clicking anywhere to select a row.
    //---------------------------------------------------------------------
    private void dgProblems_ItemDataBound(Object sender,
      System.Web.UI.WebControls.DataGridItemEventArgs e)
    {
      // datagrid column containing link button defined on ASPX page
      const int LINK_BUTTON_COLUMN = 0;
      // index of link button control in the link button column
      const int LINK_BUTTON_CONTROL = 0;
```

```csharp
    LinkButton button = null;

    // check the type of item that was databound and only take action if it
    // was a row in the datagrid
    if ((e.Item.ItemType == ListItemType.Pager) ||
        (e.Item.ItemType == ListItemType.Header) ||
        (e.Item.ItemType == ListItemType.Footer))
    {
      // do nothing
    }
    else
    {
      // the item that was bound is an "Item", "AlternatingItem",
      // "EditItem", "SelectedItem" or "Separator" (in other words a row)
      // so get a reference to the link button column defined in the
      // Columns property of the datagrid (in the aspx page) and add an
      // event handler for the the onclick event for this entire row.  This
      // will make clicking anywhere in the row select the row.
      // NOTE: This is tightly coupled to the definition of the bound
      //       columns in the aspx page.
      button =
(LinkButton)(e.Item.Cells[LINK_BUTTON_COLUMN].Controls[LINK_BUTTON_CONTROL]);
      e.Item.Attributes.Add("onclick",
        Page.GetPostBackClientHyperlink(button, ""));
    }
  } // dgProblems_ItemDataBound

  //***********************************************************************
  //
  //   ROUTINE: btnAdd_Click
  //
  //   DESCRIPTION: This routine is the event handler that is called when
  //                the Add button is clicked.
  //-----------------------------------------------------------------------
  private void btnAdd_Click(Object sender,
    System.Web.UI.ImageClickEventArgs e)
  {
    // place code here to perform Add operations
  } // btnAdd_Click

  //***********************************************************************
  //
  //   ROUTINE: btnEdit_Click
  //
  //   DESCRIPTION: This routine is the event handler that is called when
  //                the Edit button is clicked.
  //-----------------------------------------------------------------------
  private void btnEdit_Click(Object sender,
    System.Web.UI.ImageClickEventArgs e)
  {
    // place code here to perform Edit operations
  } // btnEdit_Click
```

```csharp
//***********************************************************************
//
//   ROUTINE: btnDelete_Click
//
//   DESCRIPTION: This routine is the event handler that is called when
//                the Delete button is clicked.
//-----------------------------------------------------------------------
private void btnDelete_Click(Object sender,
  System.Web.UI.ImageClickEventArgs e)
{
  // place code here to perform Delete operations
} // btnDelete_Click


//***********************************************************************
//
//   ROUTINE: bindData
//
//   DESCRIPTION: This routine queries the database for the data to
//                displayed and binds it to the repeater
//-----------------------------------------------------------------------
private void bindData()
{
  OleDbConnection dbConn = null;
  OleDbCommand dCmd = null;
  OleDbDataReader dReader = null;
  String strConnection = null;
  String strSQL =null;

  try
  {
    // get the connection string from web.config and open a connection
    // to the database
    strConnection =
      ConfigurationSettings.AppSettings["dbConnectionString"];
    dbConn = new OleDbConnection(strConnection);
    dbConn.Open();

    // build the query string and get the data from the database
    strSQL = "SELECT Title, PublishDate, ListPrice " +
            "FROM Book " +
            "ORDER BY Title";

    dCmd = new OleDbCommand(strSQL, dbConn);
    dReader = dCmd.ExecuteReader(CommandBehavior.Default);

    // set the source of the data for the datagrid control and bind it
    dgProblems.DataSource = dReader;
    dgProblems.DataBind();

    // select first item in the datagrid
    dgProblems.SelectedIndex = 0;
```

Example 1-47. DataGrid allowing selection anywhere code-behind (.cs) (continued)

```
      }  // try

      finally
      {
        // clean up
        if (dReader != null)
        {
          dReader.Close( );
        }

        if (dbConn != null)
        {
          dbConn.Close( );
        }
      }  // finally
    }  // bindData
  }  // CH01DatagridWithSelectionAnywhereCS
}
```

1.17   Adding a Delete Confirmation Pop Up

Problem

You want to add to a DataGrid row a confirmation pop up that appears whenever a user tries to delete a row in the DataGrid.

Solution

Add a Select button to each row of the DataGrid and a Delete button below the DataGrid. Whenever the Delete button is clicked, execute some client-side script that displays the confirmation pop up, followed by some server-side code that performs the actual deletion.

In the *.aspx* file:

1. Create an extra button column in the DataGrid to display a Select button.
2. Add a Delete button below the DataGrid.

In the code-behind class for the page, use the .NET language of your choice to:

1. Register the client-side script to be executed when the Delete button is clicked.
2. Add an attribute to the Delete button that calls the delete script when the Delete button is clicked.

Figure 1-21 shows a DataGrid with this solution implemented. Examples 1-48 through 1-50 show the *.aspx* and code-behind files for the application that produces this result.

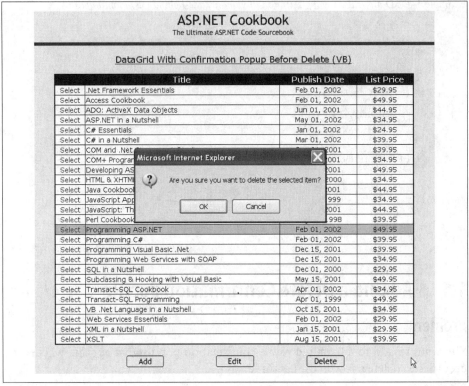

Figure 1-21. Confirmation pop up before deletion in a DataGrid output

Discussion

To display a confirmation pop up when a user attempts to delete a row in a data table, create a DataGrid in the same way you have done so throughout this chapter, except that you add a button column to allow for row selection. Setting the ButtonType to "LinkButton" outputs a hyperlink for selecting the row. (The ButtonType can instead be set to "PushButton" to output an HTML button.) The CommandName defines the action to be taken when the button is clicked, and the Text attribute defines the text that will be output for the button. (Note that the "select anywhere approach" described in Recipe 1.16 can been used here instead.)

```
<Columns>
    <asp:ButtonColumn ButtonType="LinkButton"
                      CommandName="Select"
                      Text="Select"
                      ItemStyle-HorizontalAlign="Center" />
    ...
</Columns>
```

From here on, it's easiest to explain the remaining steps of this recipe in the context of our actual example application. In the Page_Load method of the code-behind, the client-side script block that is to be executed when the Delete button is clicked is created and registered with the page. The `IsClientScriptBlockRegistered` method is used to ensure that the script block is not registered more than once on the page. The `RegisterClientScriptBlock` method is used to output the script block in the page when the page is rendered. This method causes the script to output immediately after the opening `Form` tag. If you prefer the script to be output immediately *before* the `Form` *end* tag, the `RegisterStartupScript` method can be used instead. The client-side script that is output to the browser is shown here:

```
<script language='javascript'>
<!--
function beforeDelete( )
{return(confirm('Are you sure you want to delete the selected item?'));}
//-->
</script>
```

The code that outputs the client-side script block must be executed every time the page is rendered, including postbacks, because the registered script blocks are not persisted in the Page object.

After creating and registering the client script block, an attribute is added to the Delete button control to cause the client script block to be executed when the button is clicked. The resulting HTML for the delete button is shown here:

```
<input type="image" name="btnDelete" id="btnDelete"
    OnClick="return(beforeDelete( ))"
    src="/ASPNetBook/VBExamples/images/buttons/button_delete.gif"
    border="0" />
```

When the user clicks the Delete button, the `beforeDelete` function is called in the client-side code. The `beforeDelete` function outputs a standard HTML confirmation dialog box with the message, "Are you sure you want to delete the selected item?" If the user clicks the Cancel button, the function returns `False`, effectively canceling the postback of the page. If the user clicks the OK button, the function returns `True`, allowing the page to be posted back to the server.

A server-side event handler (`btnDelete_Click`) is added to the code-behind to handle the Delete button's server-side click event. In this method, a check is performed to ensure a row is selected, and then the required deletion code for your application is processed.

The JavaScript registered in the code-behind and the attribute added to the Delete button can also be placed directly in the *.aspx* file. This was not done in this example, though, in the spirit of keeping all code in the code-behind and all presentation aspects in the *.aspx* file, a highly recommended practice. In addition, a library of client-side scripts can be created once and used many times throughout your applications.

Using a radio button for row selection instead of a Select button would be preferable, but a bug in release 1.0 and 1.1 of ASP.NET makes it very difficult. The problem is caused by a unique name and group name being generated for every control in the grid, thus placing the radio buttons on each row in a different group. This has the unfortunate consequence of being able to select multiple radio buttons at the same time. For details of the bug, see Knowledge Base article Q316495 on Microsoft's MSDN web site (*http://msdn.microsoft.com*).

See Also

Recipe 1.16

Example 1-48. Confirmation pop up before deletion in a DataGrid (.aspx)

```
<%@ Page Language="vb" AutoEventWireup="false"
  Codebehind="CH01DatagridWithConfirmBeforeDeleteVB.aspx.vb"
  Inherits="ASPNetCookbook.VBExamples.CH01DatagridWithConfirmBeforeDeleteVB" %>
<!DOCTYPE HTML PUBLIC "-//W3C//DTD HTML 4.0 Transitional//EN">
<html>
  <head>
    <title>DataGrid With Confirmation Popup Before Delete</title>
    <link rel="stylesheet" href="css/ASPNetCookbook.css">
  </head>
  <body leftmargin="0" marginheight="0" marginwidth="0" topmargin="0">
    <form id="frmDatagrid" method="post" runat="server">
      <table width="100%" cellpadding="0" cellspacing="0" border="0">
        <tr>
          <td align="center">
            <img src="images/ASPNETCookbookHeading_blue.gif">
          </td>
        </tr>
        <tr>
          <td class="dividerLine">
            <img src="images/spacer.gif" height="6" border="0"></td>
        </tr>
      </table>
      <table width="90%" align="center" border="0">
        <tr>
          <td><img src="images/spacer.gif" height="10" border="0"></td>
        </tr>
        <tr>
          <td align="center" class="PageHeading">
            DataGrid With Confirmation Popup Before Delete (VB)
          </td>
        </tr>
        <tr>
          <td><img src="images/spacer.gif" height="10" border="0"></td>
        </tr>
        <tr>
          <td align="center">
            <asp:DataGrid
              id="dgBooks"
```

Example 1-48. Confirmation pop up before deletion in a DataGrid (.aspx) (continued)

```
          runat="server"
          BorderColor="000080"
          BorderWidth="2px"
          AutoGenerateColumns="False"
          width="100%">

          <HeaderStyle
            HorizontalAlign="Center"
            ForeColor="#FFFFFF"
            BackColor="#000080"
            Font-Bold=true
            CssClass="TableHeader" />

          <ItemStyle
            BackColor="#FFFFE0"
            cssClass="TableCellNormal" />

          <AlternatingItemStyle
            BackColor="#FFFFFF"
            cssClass="TableCellAlternating" />

          <SelectedItemStyle
            BackColor="#cccccc"
            cssClass="TableCellAlternating" />

          <Columns>
            <asp:ButtonColumn ButtonType="LinkButton"
                              CommandName="Select"
                              Text="Select"
                              ItemStyle-HorizontalAlign="Center" />
            <asp:BoundColumn HeaderText="Title" DataField="Title" />
            <asp:BoundColumn HeaderText="Publish Date"
                             DataField="PublishDate"
                             ItemStyle-HorizontalAlign="Center"
                             DataFormatString="{0:MMM dd, yyyy}" />
            <asp:BoundColumn HeaderText="List Price"
                             DataField="ListPrice"
                             ItemStyle-HorizontalAlign="Center"
                             DataFormatString="{0:C2}" />
          </Columns>
        </asp:DataGrid>
      </td>
    </tr>
    <tr>
      <td><img src="images/spacer.gif" height="10" border="0"></td>
    </tr>
    <tr>
      <td align="center">
        <table width="100%">
          <tr>
            <td width="18%"> </td>
            <td width="15%" align="center">
```

Example 1-48. Confirmation pop up before deletion in a DataGrid (.aspx) (continued)

```
                    <asp:ImageButton id="btnAdd" runat="server"
                            ImageUrl="images/buttons/button_add.gif" /></td>
                    <td width="10%"> </td>
                    <td width="15%" align="center">
                      <asp:ImageButton id="btnEdit" runat="server"
                            ImageUrl="images/buttons/button_edit.gif" /></td>
                    <td width="10%"> </td>
                    <td width="15%" align="center">
                      <asp:ImageButton id="btnDelete" runat="server"
                            ImageUrl="images/buttons/button_delete.gif" /></td>
                    <td width="17%"> </td>
                </tr>
              </table>
            </td>
          </tr>
        </table>
      </form>
    </body>
</html>
```

Example 1-49. Confirmation pop up before deletion in a DataGrid code-behind (.vb)

```
Option Explicit On
Option Strict On
'----------------------------------------------------------------------------
'
'    Module Name: CH01DatagridWithConfirmBeforeDeleteVB.aspx.vb
'
'    Description: This class provides the code behind for
'                 CH01DatagridWithConfirmBeforeDeleteVB
'
'****************************************************************************
Imports Microsoft.VisualBasic
Imports System
Imports System.Configuration
Imports System.Data
Imports System.Data.OleDb

Namespace ASPNetCookbook.VBExamples
  Public Class CH01DatagridWithConfirmBeforeDeleteVB
    Inherits System.Web.UI.Page

    'controls on form
    Protected WithEvents btnAdd As System.Web.UI.WebControls.ImageButton
    Protected WithEvents btnEdit As System.Web.UI.WebControls.ImageButton
    Protected WithEvents btnDelete As System.Web.UI.WebControls.ImageButton
    Protected WithEvents dgBooks As System.Web.UI.WebControls.DataGrid

    '****************************************************************************
    '
    '    ROUTINE: Page_Load
    '
    '    DESCRIPTION: This routine provides the event handler for the page load
```

Example 1-49. Confirmation pop up before deletion in a DataGrid code-behind (.vb) (continued)

```vb
'                event.  It is responsible for initializing the controls
'                on the page.
'-------------------------------------------------------------------------
Private Sub Page_Load(ByVal sender As System.Object, _
                      ByVal e As System.EventArgs) _
         Handles MyBase.Load

  Dim scriptBlock As String

  If (Not Page.IsPostBack) Then
    bindData( )
  End If

  'NOTE: The following code must be processed for every rendering of the
  '      page or the client script will not be output when server click
  '      events are processed.

  'create the script block that will execute when the delete
  'button is clicked and register it
  scriptBlock = "<script language='javascript'>" & vbCrLf & _
               "<!--" & vbCrLf & _
               "function beforeDelete( )" & vbCrLf & _
               "{return(confirm('Are you sure you want to delete " & _
               "the selected item?'));}" & vbCrLf & _
               "//-->" & vbCrLf & _
               "</script>" & vbCrLf
  If (Not IsClientScriptBlockRegistered("deletePromptScript")) Then
    RegisterClientScriptBlock("deletePromptScript", _
                              scriptBlock)
  End If

  'add an attribute to the delete button that will cause the
  'script above to be executed when the button is clicked
  btnDelete.Attributes.Add("OnClick", _
                           "return(beforeDelete( ))")

End Sub    'Page_Load

'************************************************************************
'
'   ROUTINE: btnAdd_Click
'
'   DESCRIPTION: This routine is the event handler that is called when
'                the Add button is clicked.
'-------------------------------------------------------------------------
Private Sub btnAdd_Click(ByVal sender As Object, _
                         ByVal e As System.Web.UI.ImageClickEventArgs) _
           Handles btnAdd.Click

  'place code here to perform Add operations
End Sub    'btnAdd_Click
```

Example 1-49. Confirmation pop up before deletion in a DataGrid code-behind (.vb) (continued)

```
'*************************************************************************
'
'    ROUTINE: btnEdit_Click
'
'    DESCRIPTION: This routine is the event handler that is called when
'                 the Edit button is clicked.
'-------------------------------------------------------------------------
Private Sub btnEdit_Click(ByVal sender As Object, _
                          ByVal e As System.Web.UI.ImageClickEventArgs) _
          Handles btnEdit.Click

   'place code here to perform Edit operations
End Sub  'btnEdit_Click

'*************************************************************************
'
'    ROUTINE: btnDelete_Click
'
'    DESCRIPTION: This routine is the event handler that is called when
'                 the Delete button is clicked.
'-------------------------------------------------------------------------
Private Sub btnDelete_Click(ByVal sender As Object, _
                            ByVal e As System.Web.UI.ImageClickEventArgs) _
          Handles btnDelete.Click

   'make sure an item is selected
   If (dgBooks.SelectedIndex >= 0) Then
     'place code here to perform Delete operations
   End If
End Sub  'btnDelete_Click

'*************************************************************************
'
'    ROUTINE: bindData
'
'    DESCRIPTION: This routine queries the database for the data to
'                 displayed and binds it to the datagrid
'-------------------------------------------------------------------------
Private Sub bindData()
  Dim dbConn As OleDbConnection
  Dim da As OleDbDataAdapter
  Dim ds As DataSet
  Dim strConnection As String
  Dim strSQL As String

  Try
    'get the connection string from web.config and open a connection
    'to the database
    strConnection = _
        ConfigurationSettings.AppSettings("dbConnectionString")
    dbConn = New OleDb.OleDbConnection(strConnection)
    dbConn.Open()
```

Example 1-49. Confirmation pop up before deletion in a DataGrid code-behind (.vb) (continued)

```vb
        'build the query string and get the data from the database
        strSQL = "SELECT Title, PublishDate, ListPrice " & _
                 "FROM Book " & _
                 "ORDER BY Title"

        da = New OleDbDataAdapter(strSQL, dbConn)
        ds = New DataSet
        da.Fill(ds)

        'preselect the first item in the datagrid
        dgBooks.SelectedIndex = 0

        'set the source of the data for the datagrid control and bind it
        dgBooks.DataSource = ds
        dgBooks.DataBind( )

      Finally
        'cleanup
        If (Not IsNothing(dbConn)) Then
          dbConn.Close( )
        End If
      End Try
    End Sub   'bindData

  End Class  'CH01DatagridWithConfirmBeforeDeleteVB
End Namespace
```

Example 1-50. Confirmation pop up before deletion in a DataGrid code-behind (.cs)

```csharp
//----------------------------------------------------------------------------
//
//   Module Name: CH01DatagridWithConfirmBeforeDeleteCS.aspx.cs
//
//   Description: This class provides the code behind for
//                CH01DatagridWithConfirmBeforeDeleteCS.aspx
//
//****************************************************************************
using System;
using System.Configuration;
using System.Data;
using System.Data.OleDb;
using System.Web.UI;
using System.Web.UI.WebControls;

namespace ASPNetCookbook.CSExamples
{
  public class CH01DatagridWithConfirmBeforeDeleteCS : System.Web.UI.Page
  {
    // controls on form
    protected System.Web.UI.WebControls.ImageButton btnAdd;
    protected System.Web.UI.WebControls.ImageButton btnEdit;
    protected System.Web.UI.WebControls.ImageButton btnDelete;
    protected System.Web.UI.WebControls.DataGrid dgBooks;
```

Example 1-50. Confirmation pop up before deletion in a DataGrid code-behind (.cs) (continued)

```csharp
//**********************************************************************
//
//    ROUTINE: Page_Load
//
//    DESCRIPTION: This routine provides the event handler for the page
//                 load event.  It is responsible for initializing the
//                 controls on the page.
//----------------------------------------------------------------------
private void Page_Load(object sender, System.EventArgs e)
{
  String scriptBlock;

  // wire the item data bound and button events
  this.btnAdd.Click +=
    new ImageClickEventHandler(this.btnAdd_Click);
  this.btnEdit.Click +=
    new ImageClickEventHandler(this.btnEdit_Click);
  this.btnDelete.Click +=
    new ImageClickEventHandler(this.btnDelete_Click);

  if (!Page.IsPostBack)
  {
    bindData();
  }

  // NOTE: The following code must be processed for every rendering of the
  //       page or the client script will not be output when server click
  //       events are processed.

  // create the script block that will execute when the delete
  // button is clicked and register it
  scriptBlock = "<script language='javascript'>\n" +
                "<!--\n" +
                "function beforeDelete()\n" +
                "{return(confirm('Are you sure you want to delete " +
                "the selected item?'));}\n" +
                "//-->\n" +
                "</script>\n";
  if (!IsClientScriptBlockRegistered("deletePromptScript"))
  {
    RegisterClientScriptBlock("deletePromptScript",
                              scriptBlock);
  }

  // add an attribute to the delete button that will cause the
  // script above to be executed when the button is clicked
  btnDelete.Attributes.Add("OnClick",
                           "return(beforeDelete())");
}  // Page_Load

//**********************************************************************
//
//    ROUTINE: btnAdd_Click
```

Example 1-50. Confirmation pop up before deletion in a DataGrid code-behind (.cs) (continued)

```
//
//   DESCRIPTION: This routine is the event handler that is called when
//                the Add button is clicked.
//-------------------------------------------------------------------------
private void btnAdd_Click(Object sender,
  System.Web.UI.ImageClickEventArgs e)
{
  // place code here to perform Add operations
} // btnAdd_Click


//*************************************************************************
//
//   ROUTINE: btnEdit_Click
//
//   DESCRIPTION: This routine is the event handler that is called when
//                the Edit button is clicked.
//-------------------------------------------------------------------------
private void btnEdit_Click(Object sender,
  System.Web.UI.ImageClickEventArgs e)
{
  // place code here to perform Edit operations
} // btnEdit_Click


//*************************************************************************
//
//   ROUTINE: btnDelete_Click
//
//   DESCRIPTION: This routine is the event handler that is called when
//                the Delete button is clicked.
//-------------------------------------------------------------------------
private void btnDelete_Click(Object sender,
  System.Web.UI.ImageClickEventArgs e)
{
  // place code here to perform Delete operations
} // btnDelete_Click


//*************************************************************************
//
//   ROUTINE: bindData
//
//   DESCRIPTION: This routine queries the database for the data to
//                displayed and binds it to the repeater
//-------------------------------------------------------------------------
private void bindData( )
{
  OleDbConnection dbConn = null;
  OleDbDataAdapter da = null;
  DataSet ds = null;
  String strConnection = null;
  String strSQL =null;

  try
  {
```

```
      // get the connection string from web.config and open a connection
      // to the database
      strConnection =
        ConfigurationSettings.AppSettings["dbConnectionString"];
      dbConn = new OleDbConnection(strConnection);
      dbConn.Open( );

      // build the query string and get the data from the database
      strSQL = "SELECT Title, PublishDate, ListPrice " +
               "FROM Book " +
               "ORDER BY Title";

      da = new OleDbDataAdapter(strSQL, dbConn);
      ds = new DataSet( );
      da.Fill(ds);

      // preselect the first item in the datagrid
      dgBooks.SelectedIndex = 0;

      // set the source of the data for the datagrid control and bind it
      dgBooks.DataSource = ds;
      dgBooks.DataBind( );
    }  // try

    finally
    {
      // clean up
      if (dbConn != null)
      {
        dbConn.Close( );
      }
    }  // finally
  }  // bindData
}  // CH01DatagridWithConfirmBeforeDeleteCS
}
```

1.18   Displaying a Pop-Up Details Window

Problem

You want to provide additional details for each row in a DataGrid using a pop-up
window.

Solution

Add a Details button to each row in the Datagrid. When the user clicks the button,
open a new browser window, obtain the information from the server, and then display the detailed information in a pop-up window. An example of the output that is

possible with this approach is shown in Figure 1-22 (sample `DataGrid`) and Figure 1-23 (sample pop-up window output). As with the other recipes in this book, we've implemented a complete application that illustrates this approach. The form and code-behind for the page containing the sample `DataGrid` is shown in Examples 1-51 through 1-53, and the form and code-behind for the sample pop-up window is shown in Examples 1-54 through 1-56.

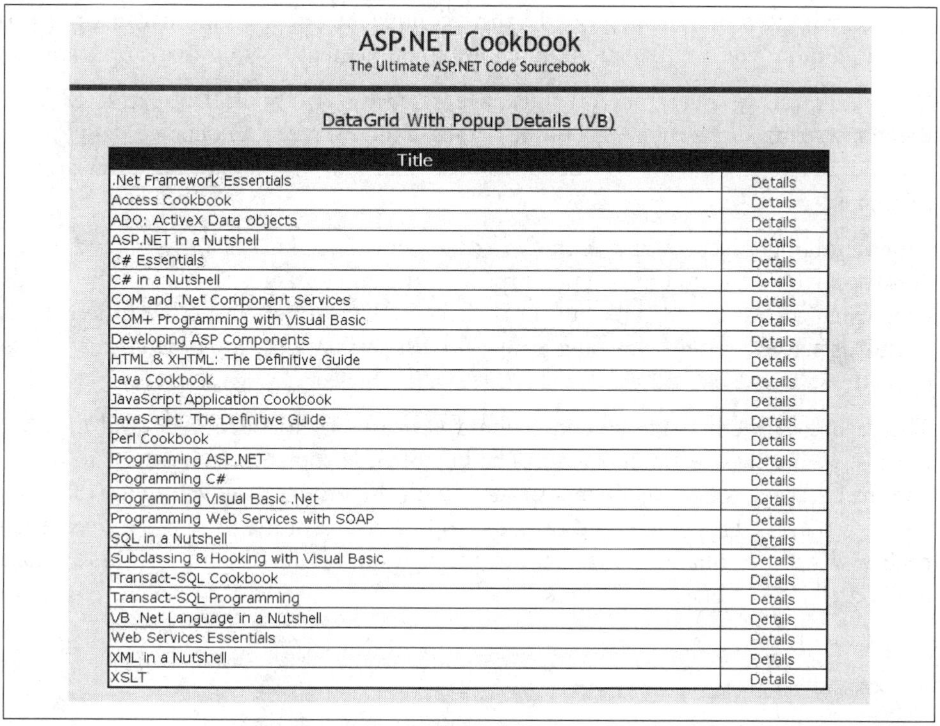

Figure 1-22. DataGrid with pop-up details window output

Figure 1-23. Pop-up details window output

Discussion

To implement this solution, create a DataGrid in the normal fashion, but add a link button column to display a Details link. The idea is that when the user clicks the Details link within a row of the DataGrid, the browser opens a new window and requests the appropriate page from the server. In the context of our example that implements this solution, a book details page is requested. From here on, the recipe's remaining steps are described in the context of our example because we use techniques that you are likely to find helpful in implementing your own application.

In our example, when the book details page is processed, a book ID is extracted from the query string and is then used in the database query to get the detailed data for the specific book, as shown in the setupForm method of Example 1-55 (VB) and Example 1-56 (C#).

When building a Details link in the *.aspx* file, an HTML anchor tag is placed in the ItemTemplate for the column. (The purpose of the anchor tag is to request the details page when the associated link button is clicked.) The target property of the HTML anchor is set to "_blank", causing a new browser window to open when the link is clicked.

The Page_Load method in the code-behind is nearly identical to that used in other recipes, with only one small change. The line of code shown next is added to populate the DataKeys collection of the DataGrid with the primary key values for the rows being displayed. This causes the DataGrid to keep track of the primary key value for each row without our having to output the data in a hidden column. These values are needed later to display the book details.

VB|
```
dgBooks.DataKeyField = "BookID"
```

C#|
```
dgBooks.DataKeyField = "BookID";
```

The DataGrid control's ItemDataBound event is used to set the href value for the "details" HTML anchors added to the DataGrid. Because this event is called independently for every row in the DataGrid, the item type must be checked to see if this event applies for a given data row.

When the event does apply to a data row, the first thing we must do is get the ID of the book being displayed in the row, as shown here:

VB|
```
bookID = CInt(dgBooks.DataKeys(e.Item.ItemIndex))
```

C#|
```
bookID = (int)(dgBooks.DataKeys[e.Item.ItemIndex]);
```

Next, we need to get a reference to the "details" HTML anchor in the row. Because ItemTemplates were used and the anchor controls in the templates were given IDs, we can accomplish this by using the FindControl method of the passed item. If a standard BoundColumn were used instead, the data would have to be accessed using the cells collection (e.g., e.Item.Cells(1).controls(1) would access the anchor control in this example). Providing an ID and using FindControl eliminates the potential for broken code if the columns are later reordered. Note that the control must be cast to an HTMLAnchor because the controls collection is a collection of objects.

After obtaining a reference to the HTML anchor tag, we need to set the href property of the anchor to the name of the details page. In addition, the URL needs to include "BookID = *n*" where *n* is the ID of the book displayed in the row. The resulting anchor tag in the DataGrid for BookID = 1 is shown here:

```
<a href="/ASPNetCookbook/VBExamples/BookDetails.aspx?BookID=1"
   id="dgBooks__ctl3_lnkDetails" target="_blank">
```

 The ID is altered by ASP.NET to ensure all server controls have unique IDs. ASP.NET maintains both the original ID and the unique ID, so the original ID we provided with the FindControl method is handled correctly, sparing us from having to figure out the unique ID or dealing with indexing into items and cells.

Example 1-51. DataGrid with pop-up details window (.aspx)

```
<%@ Page Language="vb" AutoEventWireup="false"
         Codebehind="CH01DatagridWithPopupDetailsVB.aspx.vb"
         Inherits="ASPNetCookbook.VBExamples.CH01DatagridWithPopupDetailsVB" %>
<!DOCTYPE HTML PUBLIC "-//W3C//DTD HTML 4.0 Transitional//EN">
<html>
  <head>
    <title>DataGrid With Popup Details</title>
    <link rel="stylesheet" href="css/ASPNetCookbook.css">
  </head>
  <body leftmargin="0" marginheight="0" marginwidth="0" topmargin="0">
    <form id="frmDatagrid" method="post" runat="server">
      <table width="100%" cellpadding="0" cellspacing="0" border="0">
        <tr>
          <td align="center">
            <img src="images/ASPNETCookbookHeading_blue.gif">
          </td>
        </tr>
        <tr>
          <td class="dividerLine">
            <img src="images/spacer.gif" height="6" border="0"></td>
        </tr>
      </table>
      <table width="90%" align="center" border="0">
        <tr>
          <td><img src="images/spacer.gif" height="10" border="0"></td>
        </tr>
        <tr>
          <td align="center" class="PageHeading">
            DataGrid With Popup Details (VB)
          </td>
        </tr>
        <tr>
```

Example 1-51. DataGrid with pop-up details window (.aspx) (continued)

```
          <td><img src="images/spacer.gif" height="10" border="0"></td>
      </tr>
      <tr>
        <td align="center">
          <asp:DataGrid
            id="dgBooks"
            runat="server"
            BorderColor="000080"
            BorderWidth="2px"
            AutoGenerateColumns="False"
            width="100%">

            <HeaderStyle
              HorizontalAlign="Center"
              ForeColor="#FFFFFF"
              BackColor="#000080"
              Font-Bold=true
              CssClass="TableHeader" />

            <ItemStyle
              BackColor="#FFFFE0"
              cssClass="TableCellNormal" />

            <AlternatingItemStyle
              BackColor="#FFFFFF"
              cssClass="TableCellAlternating" />

            <Columns>
              <asp:BoundColumn HeaderText="Title" DataField="Title" />
              <asp:TemplateColumn ItemStyle-HorizontalAlign="Center">
                <ItemTemplate>
                  <a id="lnkDetails" runat="server"
                      target="_blank">Details</a>
                </ItemTemplate>
              </asp:TemplateColumn>
            </Columns>
          </asp:DataGrid>
        </td>
      </tr>
    </table>
  </form>
  </body>
</html>
```

Example 1-52. DataGrid with pop-up details window code-behind (.vb)

```
Option Explicit On
Option Strict On
'------------------------------------------------------------------------
'
'   Module Name: CH01DatagridWithPopupDetailsVB.aspx.vb
'
```

Example 1-52. DataGrid with pop-up details window code-behind (.vb) (continued)

```vb
'   Description: This class provides the code behind for
'                   CH01DatagridWithPopupDetailsVB
'
'**************************************************************************
Imports Microsoft.VisualBasic
Imports System
Imports System.Configuration
Imports System.Data
Imports System.Data.OleDb
Imports System.Web.UI.HtmlControls
Imports System.Web.UI.WebControls

Namespace ASPNetCookbook.VBExamples
  Public Class CH01DatagridWithPopupDetailsVB
    Inherits System.Web.UI.Page

    'controls on form
    Protected WithEvents dgBooks As System.Web.UI.WebControls.DataGrid

    '**************************************************************************
    '
    '   ROUTINE: Page_Load
    '
    '   DESCRIPTION: This routine provides the event handler for the page load
    '                event.  It is responsible for initializing the controls
    '                on the page.
    '-------------------------------------------------------------------------
    Private Sub Page_Load(ByVal sender As System.Object, _
                          ByVal e As System.EventArgs) _
            Handles MyBase.Load
      Dim dbConn As OleDbConnection
      Dim da As OleDbDataAdapter
      Dim ds As DataSet
      Dim strConnection As String
      Dim strSQL As String

      If (Not Page.IsPostBack) Then
        Try
          'get the connection string from web.config and open a connection
          'to the database
          strConnection = _
              ConfigurationSettings.AppSettings("dbConnectionString")
          dbConn = New OleDb.OleDbConnection(strConnection)
          dbConn.Open()

          'build the query string and get the data from the database
          strSQL = "SELECT BookID, Title " & _
                   "FROM Book " & _
                   "ORDER BY Title"

          da = New OleDbDataAdapter(strSQL, dbConn)
          ds = New DataSet
          da.Fill(ds)
```

Example 1-52. DataGrid with pop-up details window code-behind (.vb) (continued)

```
        'set the source of the data for the datagrid control and bind it
        dgBooks.DataKeyField = "BookID"
        dgBooks.DataSource = ds
        dgBooks.DataBind()

      Finally
        'cleanup
        If (Not IsNothing(dbConn)) Then
          dbConn.Close()
        End If
      End Try
    End If
End Sub  'Page_Load


'***********************************************************************
'
'   ROUTINE: dgBooks_ItemDataBound
'
'   DESCRIPTION: This routine is the event handler that is called for each
'                item in the datagrid after a data bind occurs.  It is
'                responsible for setting the URL of the anchor tags to the
'                page used to display the details for a book
'-----------------------------------------------------------------------
Private Sub dgBooks_ItemDataBound(ByVal sender As Object, _
        ByVal e As System.Web.UI.WebControls.DataGridItemEventArgs) _
      Handles dgBooks.ItemDataBound

  Const DETAIL_PAGE As String = "CH01BookDetailsVB.aspx"

  Dim bookID As Integer
  Dim anchor As HtmlAnchor

  'check the type of item that was databound and only take action if it
  'was a row in the datagrid
  If ((e.Item.ItemType = ListItemType.Pager) Or _
      (e.Item.ItemType = ListItemType.Header) Or _
      (e.Item.ItemType = ListItemType.Footer)) Then
    'do nothing
  Else
    'the item that was bound is an "Item", "AlternatingItem", "EditItem",
    '"SelectedItem" or "Separator" (in other words a row)
    bookID = CInt(dgBooks.DataKeys(e.Item.ItemIndex))

    'get the anchor tag in the row
    'NOTE: This can be done by using the FindControl method of the passed
    '      item because ItemTemplates were used and the anchor controls in
    '      the templates where given IDs.  If a standard BoundColumn was
    '      used, the data would have to be accessed using the cells
    '      collection (e.g. e.Item.Cells(1).controls(1) would access the
    '      anchor control in this example.
    anchor = CType(e.Item.FindControl("lnkDetails"), _
                HtmlAnchor)
```

Example 1-52. DataGrid with pop-up details window code-behind (.vb) (continued)

```
        'set the URL of the anchor tag to the page used to display the book
        'details passing the ID of the book in the querystring
        anchor.HRef = DETAIL_PAGE & "?BookID=" & bookID.ToString( )
      End If

    End Sub   'dgBooks_ItemDataBound
  End Class   'CH01DatagridWithPopupDetailsVB
End Namespace
```

Example 1-53. DataGrid with pop-up details window code-behind (.cs)

```
//---------------------------------------------------------------------------
//
//   Module Name: CH01DatagridWithPopupDetailsCS.aspx.cs
//
//   Description: This class provides the code behind for
//                CH01DatagridWithPopupDetailsCS.aspx
//
//***************************************************************************
using System;
using System.Configuration;
using System.Data;
using System.Data.OleDb;
using System.Web.UI;
using System.Web.UI.WebControls;
using System.Web.UI.HtmlControls;

namespace ASPNetCookbook.CSExamples
{
  public class CH01DatagridWithPopupDetailsCS : System.Web.UI.Page
  {
    // controls on form
    protected System.Web.UI.WebControls.DataGrid dgBooks;

    //***********************************************************************
    //
    //   ROUTINE: Page_Load
    //
    //   DESCRIPTION: This routine provides the event handler for the page
    //                load event.  It is responsible for initializing the
    //                controls on the page.
    //
    //-----------------------------------------------------------------------
    private void Page_Load(object sender, System.EventArgs e)
    {
      OleDbConnection dbConn = null;
      OleDbDataAdapter da = null;
      DataSet ds = null;
      String strConnection = null;
      String strSQL =null;

      // wire the item data bound event
      this.dgBooks.ItemDataBound +=
```

Example 1-53. DataGrid with pop-up details window code-behind (.cs) (continued)

```csharp
      new DataGridItemEventHandler(this.dgBooks_ItemDataBound);

  if (!Page.IsPostBack)
  {
    try
    {
      // get the connection string from web.config and open a connection
      // to the database
      strConnection =
        ConfigurationSettings.AppSettings["dbConnectionString"];
      dbConn = new OleDbConnection(strConnection);
      dbConn.Open( );

      // build the query string and get the data from the database
      strSQL = "SELECT BookID, Title " +
               "FROM Book " +
               "ORDER BY Title";
      da = new OleDbDataAdapter(strSQL, dbConn);
      ds = new DataSet( );
      da.Fill(ds);

      // set the source of the data for the datagrid control and bind it
      dgBooks.DataKeyField = "BookID";
      dgBooks.DataSource = ds;
      dgBooks.DataBind( );
    }  // try

    finally
    {
      // clean up
      if (dbConn != null)
      {
        dbConn.Close( );
      }
    }  // finally
  }
}  // Page_Load

//**************************************************************************
//
//    ROUTINE: dgBooks_ItemDataBound
//
//    DESCRIPTION: This routine is the event handler that is called for each
//                 item in the datagrid after a data bind occurs.  It is
//                 responsible for setting the URL of the anchor tags to the
//                 page used to display the details for a book
//
//--------------------------------------------------------------------------
private void dgBooks_ItemDataBound(Object sender,
  System.Web.UI.WebControls.DataGridItemEventArgs e)
{
  const String DETAIL_PAGE = "CH01BookDetailsCS.aspx";
```

Example 1-53. DataGrid with pop-up details window code-behind (.cs) (continued)

```
        int bookID;
        HtmlAnchor anchor = null;

        // check the type of item that was databound and only take action if it
        // was a row in the datagrid
        if ((e.Item.ItemType == ListItemType.Pager) ||
            (e.Item.ItemType == ListItemType.Header) ||
            (e.Item.ItemType == ListItemType.Footer))
        {
          // do nothing
        }
        else
        {
          // the item that was bound is an "Item", "AlternatingItem",
          // "EditItem", "SelectedItem" or "Separator" (in other words a row)
          bookID = (int)(dgBooks.DataKeys[e.Item.ItemIndex]);

          // get the anchor tag in the row
          // NOTE: This can be done by using the FindControl method of the
          //       passeditem because ItemTemplates were used and the anchor
          //       controls in the templates where given IDs.  If a standard
          //       BoundColumn was used, the data would have to be accessed
          //       using the cells collection (e.g. e.Item.Cells(1).controls(1)
          //       would access the anchor control in this example.
          anchor = (HtmlAnchor)(e.Item.FindControl("lnkDetails"));

          // set the URL of the anchor tag to the page used to display the book
          // details passing the ID of the book in the querystring
          anchor.HRef = DETAIL_PAGE + "?BookID=" + bookID.ToString( );
        }
      } // dgBooks_ItemDataBound
   } // CH01DatagridWithPopupDetailsCS
}
```

Example 1-54. Pop-up detail page (.aspx)

```
<%@ Page Language="vb" AutoEventWireup="false"
        Codebehind="CH01BookDetailsVB.aspx.vb"
        Inherits="ASPNetCookbook.VBExamples.CH01BookDetailsVB" %>
<!DOCTYPE HTML PUBLIC "-//W3C//DTD HTML 4.0 Transitional//EN">
<html>
  <head>
    <title>Book Details</title>
    <meta name="GENERATOR" content="Microsoft Visual Studio.NET 7.0">
    <meta name="CODE_LANGUAGE" content="Visual Basic 7.0">
    <meta name=vs_defaultClientScript content="JavaScript">
    <meta name=vs_targetSchema content="http://schemas.microsoft.com/intellisense/ie5">
    <link rel="stylesheet" href="css/ASPNetCookbook.css">
  </head>
  <body leftmargin="0" marginheight="0" marginwidth="0" topmargin="0">
    <form id="frmDatagrid" method="post" runat="server">
      <table width="100%" cellpadding="0" cellspacing="0" border="0">
        <tr>
```

Example 1-54. Pop-up detail page (.aspx) (continued)

```
      <td align="center">
        <img src="images/ASPNETCookbookHeading_blue.gif">
      </td>
    </tr>
    <tr>
      <td class="dividerLine">
        <img src="images/spacer.gif" height="6" border="0"></td>
    </tr>
  </table>
  <table width="90%" align="center" border="0">
    <tr>
      <td><img src="images/spacer.gif" height="10" border="0"></td>
    </tr>
    <tr>
      <td align="center" class="PageHeading">
        Book Details (VB)
      </td>
    </tr>
    <tr>
      <td><img src="images/spacer.gif" height="10" border="0"></td>
    </tr>
    <tr>
      <td align="center">
        <!-- Put book details here -->
        <table width="600" border="0">
          <tr>
            <td rowspan="6" align="center" width="250">
              <img id="imgBook" runat="server"></td>
            <td class="TableCellNormal" width="150">Title: </td>
            <td id="bookTitle" runat="server"
                class="TableCellNormal" width="325"></td>
          </tr>
          <tr>
            <td class="TableCellNormal">ISBN: </td>
            <td id="isbn" runat="server"
                class="TableCellNormal"></td>
          </tr>
          <tr>
            <td class="TableCellNormal">Publisher: </td>
            <td id="publisher" runat="server"
                class="TableCellNormal"></td>
          </tr>
          <tr>
            <td class="TableCellNormal">Publish Date: </td>
            <td id="publishDate" runat="server"
                class="TableCellNormal"></td>
          </tr>
          <tr>
            <td class="TableCellNormal">List Price: </td>
            <td id="listPrice" runat="server"
                class="TableCellNormal"></td>
```

Example 1-54. Pop-up detail page (.aspx) (continued)

```
            </tr>
            <tr>
              <td class="TableCellNormal">Discounted Price: </td>
              <td id="discountedPrice" runat="server"
                  class="TableCellNormal"></td>
            </tr>
          </table>
        </td>
      </tr>
    </table>
  </form>
 </body>
</html>
```

Example 1-55. Pop-up detail page code-behind (.vb)

```
Option Explicit On
Option Strict On
'-----------------------------------------------------------------------------
'
'   Module Name: CH01BookDetailsVB.aspx.vb
'
'   Description: This class provides the code behind for
'                CH01BookDetailsVB.aspx
'
'*****************************************************************************
Imports Microsoft.VisualBasic
Imports System
Imports System.Configuration
Imports System.Data
Imports System.Data.OleDb

Namespace ASPNetCookbook.VBExamples
  Public Class CH01BookDetailsVB
    Inherits System.Web.UI.Page

    'controls on form
    Protected imgBook As System.Web.UI.HtmlControls.HtmlImage
    Protected bookTitle As System.Web.UI.HtmlControls.HtmlTableCell
    Protected isbn As System.Web.UI.HtmlControls.HtmlTableCell
    Protected publisher As System.Web.UI.HtmlControls.HtmlTableCell
    Protected publishDate As System.Web.UI.HtmlControls.HtmlTableCell
    Protected listPrice As System.Web.UI.HtmlControls.HtmlTableCell
    Protected discountedPrice As System.Web.UI.HtmlControls.HtmlTableCell

    '*************************************************************************
    '
    '   ROUTINE: Page_Load
    '
    '   DESCRIPTION: This routine provides the event handler for the page load
    '                event.  It is responsible for initializing the controls
    '                on the page.
    '-------------------------------------------------------------------------
```

Example 1-55. Pop-up detail page code-behind (.vb) (continued)

```
Private Sub Page_Load(ByVal sender As System.Object, _
                      ByVal e As System.EventArgs) _
      Handles MyBase.Load
  Dim dbConn As OleDbConnection
  Dim dCmd As OleDbCommand
  Dim dReader As OleDbDataReader
  Dim strConnection As String
  Dim strSQL As String
  Dim bookID As String

  If (Not Page.IsPostBack) Then
    Try
      'get the book ID from the querystring in the URL
      If (IsNothing(Request.QueryString.Item("BookID"))) Then
        'production code needs to handle the page request without the needed
        'information in the querystring here
      Else
        bookID = Request.QueryString.Item("BookID").ToString()

        'get the connection string from web.config and open a connection
        'to the database
        strConnection = _
            ConfigurationSettings.AppSettings("dbConnectionString")
        dbConn = New OleDbConnection(strConnection)
        dbConn.Open()

        'build the query string and get the data from the database
        strSQL = "SELECT Title, ISBN, Publisher, PublishDate, " & _
                 "ListPrice, DiscountedPrice, ImageFilename " & _
                 "FROM Book " & _
                 "WHERE BookID=?"

        dCmd = New OleDbCommand(strSQL, dbConn)
        dCmd.Parameters.Add(New OleDbParameter("BookID", bookID))
        dReader = dCmd.ExecuteReader()

        If (dReader.Read) Then
          'set the data in the individual controls on the page
          imgBook.Src = "images/books/" & _
                        dReader.Item("ImageFilename").ToString()
          bookTitle.InnerText = dReader.Item("Title").ToString()
          isbn.InnerText = dReader.Item("ISBN").ToString()
          publisher.InnerText = dReader.Item("Publisher").ToString()
          publishDate.InnerText = Format(dReader.Item("PublishDate"), _
                                  "MMM dd, yyyy")
          listPrice.InnerText = Format(dReader.Item("ListPrice"), _
                                "C2")
      discountedPrice.InnerText = Format(dReader.Item("DiscountedPrice"), _
                                "C2")

        End If
    End If
```

hind (.vb) (continued)

Then

hen

hind (.cs)

----

px.cs

the code behind for
.px

:***************************************

```csharp
public class CH01BookDetailsCS : System.Web.UI.Page
{
  // controls on form
  protected System.Web.UI.HtmlControls.HtmlImage imgBook;
  protected System.Web.UI.HtmlControls.HtmlTableCell bookTitle ;
  protected System.Web.UI.HtmlControls.HtmlTableCell isbn;
  protected System.Web.UI.HtmlControls.HtmlTableCell publisher;
  protected System.Web.UI.HtmlControls.HtmlTableCell publishDate;
  protected System.Web.UI.HtmlControls.HtmlTableCell listPrice;
  protected System.Web.UI.HtmlControls.HtmlTableCell discountedPrice;

  //*************************************************************************
  //
  //   ROUTINE: Page_Load
  //
  //   DESCRIPTION: This routine provides the event handler for the page
  //                load event.  It is responsible for initializing the
  //                controls on the page.
  //
  //-------------------------------------------------------------------------
```

Example 1-56. Pop-up detail page code-behind (.cs) (continued)

```
private void Page_Load(object sender, System.EventArgs e)
{
  OleDbConnection dbConn = null;
  OleDbCommand dCmd = null;
  OleDbDataReader dReader = null;
  String strConnection = null;
  String strSQL = null;
  String bookID = null;
  DateTime pubDate;
  Decimal price;

  if (!Page.IsPostBack)
  {
    try
    {
      // get the book ID from the querystring in the URL
      if (Request.QueryString["BookID"] == null)
      {
        // production code needs to handle the page request without the
        // needed information in the querystring here
      }
      else
      {
        bookID = Request.QueryString["BookID"].ToString();

        // get the connection string from web.config and open a connection
        // to the database
        strConnection =
          ConfigurationSettings.AppSettings["dbConnectionString"];
        dbConn = new OleDbConnection(strConnection);
        dbConn.Open();

        // build the query string and get the data from the database
        strSQL = "SELECT Title, ISBN, Publisher, PublishDate, " +
                 "ListPrice, DiscountedPrice, ImageFilename " +
                 "FROM Book " +
                 "WHERE BookID=?";

        dCmd = new OleDbCommand(strSQL, dbConn);
        dCmd.Parameters.Add(new OleDbParameter("BookID", bookID));
        dReader = dCmd.ExecuteReader();

        if (dReader.Read())
        {
          // set the data in the individual controls on the page
          imgBook.Src = "images/books/" +
                        dReader["ImageFilename"].ToString();
          bookTitle.InnerText = dReader["Title"].ToString();
          isbn.InnerText = dReader["ISBN"].ToString();
          publisher.InnerText = dReader["Publisher"].ToString();

          pubDate = (DateTime)dReader["PublishDate"];
          publishDate.InnerText = pubDate.ToString("MMM dd, yyyy");
```

Example 1-56. Pop-up detail page code-behind (.cs) (continued)

```
               price = (Decimal)dReader["ListPrice"];
               listPrice.InnerText = price.ToString("C2");

               price = (Decimal)dReader["DiscountedPrice"];
               discountedPrice.InnerText = price.ToString("C2");
             }
           }
         } // try

         finally
         {
           // clean up
           if (dReader != null)
           {
             dReader.Close();
           }

           if (dbConn != null)
           {
             dbConn.Close();
           }
         } // finally
       }
     } // Page_Load
   } // CH01BookDetailsCS
}
```

1.19 Adding a Totals Row to a DataGrid

Problem

You have a DataGrid containing numeric information and you need to display a total of the data in the last row of the grid.

Solution

Enable the output of the footer in the DataGrid, accumulate the total for the data in the ItemDataBound event handler, and then output the total in the DataGrid footer.

In the *.aspx* file, set the ShowFooter attribute of the asp:DataGrid element to True.

In the code-behind class for the page, use the .NET language of your choice to:

1. Initialize the totals to 0, and then bind the data to the DataGrid in the normal fashion.

2. In the ItemDataBound event handler, add the values for each data row to the accumulated totals.

3. In the ItemDataBound event handler, set the total values in the footer when the footer is data bound.

Figure 1-24 shows some typical output. Examples 1-57 through 1-59 show the *.aspx* file and code-behind files for an application that produces this output.

ASP.NET Cookbook
The Ultimate ASP.NET Code Sourcebook

DataGrid With Totals Row (VB)

Title	List Price	Discounted Price
.Net Framework Essentials	$29.95	$20.97
Access Cookbook	$49.95	$34.97
ADO: ActiveX Data Objects	$44.95	$31.47
ASP.NET in a Nutshell	$34.95	$24.47
C# Essentials	$24.95	$17.47
C# in a Nutshell	$39.95	$27.97
COM and .Net Component Services	$39.95	$27.97
COM+ Programming with Visual Basic	$34.95	$24.47
Developing ASP Components	$49.95	$34.97
HTML & XHTML: The Definitive Guide	$34.95	$24.47
Java Cookbook	$44.95	$31.47
JavaScript Application Cookbook	$34.95	$24.47
JavaScript: The Definitive Guide	$44.95	$31.47
Perl Cookbook	$39.95	$27.97
Programming ASP.NET	$49.95	$34.97
Programming C#	$39.95	$27.97
Programming Visual Basic .Net	$39.95	$27.97
Programming Web Services with SOAP	$34.95	$24.47
SQL in a Nutshell	$29.95	$20.97
Subclassing & Hooking with Visual Basic	$49.95	$34.97
Transact-SQL Cookbook	$34.95	$24.47
Transact-SQL Programming	$49.95	$34.97
VB .Net Language in a Nutshell	$34.95	$24.47
Web Services Essentials	$29.95	$20.97
XML in a Nutshell	$29.95	$20.97
XSLT	$39.95	$27.97
Total:	$1,013.70	$709.72

Figure 1-24. DataGrid with totals row output

Discussion

The best way to describe the addition of a totals row to a DataGrid is by example. In this recipe, you'll want to create the DataGrid a little differently than normal. In the asp:DataGrid element, set the ShowFooter attribute to True to cause a footer to be output when the control is rendered. You then place the totals data in the footer.

```
<asp:DataGrid
  id="dgBooks"
  runat="server"
  BorderColor="000080"
  BorderWidth="2px"
  AutoGenerateColumns="False"
  width="100%"
  ShowFooter="True">
```

Next, add a FooterStyle element to format all of the columns in the footer with a stylesheet class, background color, and horizontal alignment:

```
<FooterStyle cssClass="TableCellNormal" HorizontalAlign="Right"
        BackColor="#C0C0C0" />
```

All columns are defined in the Columns element as asp:TemplateColumn columns. This provides a lot of flexibility in the display of the columns. The first column contains only an ItemTemplate that is bound to the Title field in the DataSet. The FooterText property of this column is set to "Total:" to simply display the label for the other values in the footer.

```
<asp:TemplateColumn HeaderText="Title" FooterText="Total:">
  <ItemTemplate>
    <%# DataBinder.Eval(Container.DataItem, _
                        "Title") %>
  </ItemTemplate>
</asp:TemplateColumn>
```

The second and third columns contain an ItemTemplate element to define the format of the data placed in the rows of the grid and a FooterTemplate element to define the format of the data placed in the footer of the respective columns:

```
<asp:TemplateColumn HeaderText="List Price"
                    ItemStyle-HorizontalAlign="Right">
  <ItemTemplate>
    <asp:Literal id="lblListPrice" runat="server"
                 text='<%# DataBinder.Eval(Container.DataItem, _
                                           "ListPrice") %>' />
  </ItemTemplate>
  <FooterTemplate>
    <asp:Literal id="lblListPriceTotal" runat="server" />
  </FooterTemplate>
</asp:TemplateColumn>
```

In the code-behind, two private variables (mListPriceTotal and mDiscountedPriceTotal) are declared at the class level to store the accumulated sum for each of the price columns. The bindData method is identical to previous recipes, except for the addition of the code to set mListPriceTotal and mDiscountedPriceTotal to zero before the data binding is performed.

The ItemDataBound event is used to accumulate the sum of the prices as the rows in the DataGrid are bound. You can do this because the data binding always starts at the top of the grid and ends at the bottom. Because the ItemDataBound event method is called for every row in the grid, you must first determine what row this event applies to by checking the ItemType of the passed event arguments. Several groups of item types are needed here, so a Select Case statement (switch in C#) is used.

When the item type is a data row, you need to get the values in the list price and discounted price columns, and then add them to the appropriate total variables. Getting the price values requires getting the price values from the data passed to the method (e.Item.ItemData), adding the price data to the totals, getting a reference to the controls used to display the data, and then setting the price value in the controls for the row. Getting a reference to the control is the trickiest part. The easiest and most flexible approach is to use Literal controls in the ItemTemplates of the DataGrid defined in the *.aspx* file. By setting the IDs of the literal controls, the FindControl method of the row being data bound can be used to get a reference to the desired control.

If the IDs of the controls in the `ItemTemplates` are not defined, the only way to get a reference to a control is to index into the cells and controls collections of the row. In this example, the list price control is in the second column of the grid. Cells in a `DataGrid` are created with a literal control before and after the controls you define in a column; therefore, the list price control is the second control in the controls collection of the cell. Getting a reference to the list price control using this method would be done with `listPriceControl = e.Item.Cells(1).controls(1)`. This approach is very dependent on column layout—rearranging columns would break code that uses this approach. The `FindControl` method is much easier to maintain and less likely to be broken by changing the user interface.

Literal controls are used in this example because they are rendered without the addition of other controls and because accessing the price value is as simple as getting the value of the text property of the control. An `asp:Label` control would seem like a good option here; however, it is created as three literal controls in the `DataGrid`, making it necessary to index into the controls collection of the control returned by the `FindControl` method to get the needed price value.

When the item is the footer, all data rows have been processed and you have the totals for the price columns in the `mListPriceTotal` and `mDiscountedPriceTotal` variables. Now you need to output these totals in the controls placed in the footer. This is done by again using the `FindControl` method of the passed item to get a reference to the controls in the footer. After a reference to the control is obtained, the text property is set to the total for the column. In our example, the totals are also being formatted to be displayed in currency format with two decimal places.

Example 1-57. DataGrid with totals row (.aspx)

```
<%@ Page Language="vb" AutoEventWireup="false"
        Codebehind="CH01DataGridWithTotalsRowVB.aspx.vb"
        Inherits="ASPNetCookbook.VBExamples.CH01DataGridWithTotalsRowVB" %>
<!DOCTYPE HTML PUBLIC "-//W3C//DTD HTML 4.0 Transitional//EN">
<html>
  <head>
    <title>DataGrid With Totals Row</title>
    <link rel="stylesheet" href="css/ASPNetCookbook.css">
  </head>
  <body leftmargin="0" marginheight="0" marginwidth="0" topmargin="0">
    <form id="frmDatagrid" method="post" runat="server">
      <table width="100%" cellpadding="0" cellspacing="0" border="0">
        <tr>
          <td align="center">
            <img src="images/ASPNETCookbookHeading_blue.gif">
          </td>
        </tr>
        <tr>
```

Example 1-57. DataGrid with totals row (.aspx) (continued)

```
      <td class="dividerLine">
        <img src="images/spacer.gif" height="6" border="0"></td>
    </tr>
  </table>
  <table width="90%" align="center" border="0">
    <tr>
      <td><img src="images/spacer.gif" height="10" border="0"></td>
    </tr>
    <tr>
      <td align="center" class="PageHeading">
        DataGrid With Totals Row (VB)
      </td>
    </tr>
    <tr>
      <td><img src="images/spacer.gif" height="10" border="0"></td>
    </tr>
    <tr>
      <td align="center">
        <asp:DataGrid
          id="dgBooks"
          runat="server"
          BorderColor="000080"
          BorderWidth="2px"
          AutoGenerateColumns="False"
          width="100%"
          ShowFooter="True">

          <HeaderStyle
            HorizontalAlign="Center"
            ForeColor="#FFFFFF"
            BackColor="#000080"
            Font-Bold=true
            CssClass="TableHeader" />

          <ItemStyle
            BackColor="#FFFFE0"
            cssClass="TableCellNormal" />

          <AlternatingItemStyle
            BackColor="#FFFFFF"
            cssClass="TableCellAlternating" />

          <FooterStyle cssClass="TableCellNormal" HorizontalAlign="Right"
                       BackColor="#C0C0C0" />

          <Columns>
            <asp:TemplateColumn HeaderText="Title" FooterText="Total:">
              <ItemTemplate>
                <%# DataBinder.Eval(Container.DataItem, "Title") %>
              </ItemTemplate>
            </asp:TemplateColumn>
```

Example 1-57. DataGrid with totals row (.aspx) (continued)

```
                <asp:TemplateColumn HeaderText="List Price"
                                    ItemStyle-HorizontalAlign="Right">
                  <ItemTemplate>
                    <asp:Literal id="lblListPrice" runat="server"
                        text='<%# DataBinder.Eval(Container.DataItem, _
                                            "ListPrice") %>' />
                  </ItemTemplate>
                  <FooterTemplate>
                    <asp:Literal id="lblListPriceTotal" runat="server" />
                  </FooterTemplate>
                </asp:TemplateColumn>

                <asp:TemplateColumn HeaderText="Discounted Price"
                                    ItemStyle-HorizontalAlign="Right">
                  <ItemTemplate>
                    <asp:Literal id="lblDiscountedPrice" runat="server"
                        text='<%# DataBinder.Eval(Container.DataItem, _
                                            "DiscountedPrice") %>' />
                  </asp:Label>
                  </ItemTemplate>
                  <FooterTemplate>
                    <asp:Literal id="lblTotalDiscountedPrice"
                                 runat="server" />
                  </FooterTemplate>
                </asp:TemplateColumn>
              </Columns>

          </asp:DataGrid>
        </td>
      </tr>
    </table>
  </form>
  </body>
</html>
```

Example 1-58. DataGrid with totals row code-behind (.vb)

```
Option Explicit On
Option Strict On
'-----------------------------------------------------------------------------
'
'   Module Name: CH01DataGridWithTotalsRowVB.aspx.vb
'
'   Description: This class provides the code behind for
'               CH01DataGridWithTotalsRowVB
'
'*****************************************************************************
Imports Microsoft.VisualBasic
Imports System.Configuration
Imports System.Data
Imports System.Data.OleDb
Imports System.Web.UI.WebControls
```

Example 1-58. DataGrid with totals row code-behind (.vb) (continued)

```vb
Namespace ASPNetCookbook.VBExamples
  Public Class CH01DataGridWithTotalsRowVB
    Inherits System.Web.UI.Page

    'controls on form
    Protected WithEvents dgBooks As System.Web.UI.WebControls.DataGrid

    'variables used to accumulate the sum of the prices
    Private mListPriceTotal As Decimal
    Private mDiscountedPriceTotal As Decimal

    '*************************************************************************
    '
    '   ROUTINE: Page_Load
    '
    '   DESCRIPTION: This routine provides the event handler for the page load
    '                event.  It is responsible for initializing the controls
    '                on the page.
    '-------------------------------------------------------------------------
    Private Sub Page_Load(ByVal sender As System.Object, _
                          ByVal e As System.EventArgs) _
            Handles MyBase.Load
      Dim dbConn As OleDbConnection
      Dim da As OleDbDataAdapter
      Dim ds As DataSet
      Dim strConnection As String
      Dim strSQL As String

      If (Not Page.IsPostBack) Then
        Try
          'get the connection string from web.config and open a connection
          'to the database
          strConnection = _
              ConfigurationSettings.AppSettings("dbConnectionString")
          dbConn = New OleDb.OleDbConnection(strConnection)
          dbConn.Open()

          'build the query string and get the data from the database
          strSQL = "SELECT Title, ListPrice, DiscountedPrice " & _
                   "FROM Book " & _
                   "ORDER BY Title"
          da = New OleDbDataAdapter(strSQL, dbConn)
          ds = New DataSet
          da.Fill(ds)

          'set total values to 0 before data binding
          mListPriceTotal = 0
          mDiscountedPriceTotal = 0

          'set the source of the data for the datagrid control and bind it
          dgBooks.DataSource = ds
          dgBooks.DataBind()
```

Example 1-58. DataGrid with totals row code-behind (.vb) (continued)

```
      Finally
        'cleanup
        If (Not IsNothing(dbConn)) Then
          dbConn.Close()
        End If
      End Try
    End If
  End Sub  'Page_Load


'**************************************************************************
  '
  '   ROUTINE: dgBooks_ItemDataBound
  '
  '   DESCRIPTION: This routine is the event handler that is called for each
  '               item in the datagrid after a data bind occurs.  It is
  '               responsible for accumlating the total prices and setting
  '               the values in the footer when all rows have been data
  '               bound.
  '--------------------------------------------------------------------------
  Private Sub dgBooks_ItemDataBound(ByVal sender As Object, _
            ByVal e As System.Web.UI.WebControls.DataGridItemEventArgs) _
          Handles dgBooks.ItemDataBound

    Dim rowData As DataRowView
    Dim price As Decimal
    Dim listPriceLabel As System.Web.UI.WebControls.Literal
    Dim discountedPriceLabel As System.Web.UI.WebControls.Literal
    Dim totalLabel As System.Web.UI.WebControls.Literal

    'check the type of item that was databound and only take action if it
    'was a row in the datagrid
    Select Case (e.Item.ItemType)
      Case ListItemType.AlternatingItem, ListItemType.EditItem, _
          ListItemType.Item, ListItemType.SelectedItem
        'get the data for the item being bound
        rowData = CType(e.Item.DataItem, _
                    DataRowView)

        'get the value for the list price and add it to the sum
        price = CDec(rowData.Item("ListPrice"))
        mListPriceTotal += price

        'get the control used to display the list price
        'NOTE: This can be done by using the FindControl method of the
        '       passed item because ItemTemplates were used and the anchor
        '       controls in the templates where given IDs.  If a standard
        '       BoundColumn was used, the data would have to be accessed
        '       using the cellscollection (e.g. e.Item.Cells(1).controls(1)
        '       would access the label control in this example.
        listPriceLabel = CType(e.Item.FindControl("lblListPrice"), _
                          System.Web.UI.WebControls.Literal)
```

Example 1-58. DataGrid with totals row code-behind (.vb) (continued)

```vb
            'now format the list price in currency format
            listPriceLabel.Text = price.ToString("C2")

            'get the value for the discounted price and add it to the sum
            price = CDec(rowData.Item("DiscountedPrice"))
            mDiscountedPriceTotal += price

            'get the control used to display the discounted price
        discountedPriceLabel = CType(e.Item.FindControl("lblDiscountedPrice"), _
                                System.Web.UI.WebControls.Literal)

            'now format the discounted price in currency format
            discountedPriceLabel.Text = price.ToString("C2")

        Case ListItemType.Footer
            'get the control used to display the total of the list prices
            'and set its value to the total of the list prices
            totalLabel = CType(e.Item.FindControl("lblListPriceTotal"), _
                            System.Web.UI.WebControls.Literal)
            totalLabel.Text = mListPriceTotal.ToString("C2")

            'get the control used to display the total of the discounted prices
            'and set its value to the total of the discounted prices
            totalLabel = CType(e.Item.FindControl("lblTotalDiscountedPrice"), _
                            System.Web.UI.WebControls.Literal)
            totalLabel.Text = mDiscountedPriceTotal.ToString("C2")


        Case Else
            'ListItemType.Header, ListItemType.Pager, or ListItemType.Separator
            'no action required
        End Select
    End Sub  'dgBooks_ItemDataBound
  End Class  'CH01DataGridWithTotalsRowVB
End Namespace
```

Example 1-59. DataGrid with totals row code-behind (.cs)

```csharp
//----------------------------------------------------------------------------
//
//   Module Name: CH01DataGridWithTotalsRowCS.aspx.cs
//
//   Description: This class provides the code behind for
//                CH01DataGridWithTotalsRowCS.aspx
//
//****************************************************************************
using System;
using System.Configuration;
using System.Data;
using System.Data.OleDb;
using System.Web.UI.WebControls;

namespace ASPNetCookbook.CSExamples
{
```

Example 1-59. DataGrid with totals row code-behind (.cs) (continued)

```
public class CH01DataGridWithTotalsRowCS : System.Web.UI.Page
{
  // control on form
  protected System.Web.UI.WebControls.DataGrid dgBooks;

  // variables used to accumulate the sum of the prices
  private Decimal mListPriceTotal;
  private Decimal mDiscountedPriceTotal;

  //***********************************************************************
  //
  //   ROUTINE: Page_Load
  //
  //   DESCRIPTION: This routine provides the event handler for the page
  //                load event.  It is responsible for initializing the
  //                controls on the page.
  //-----------------------------------------------------------------------
  private void Page_Load(object sender, System.EventArgs e)
  {
    OleDbConnection dbConn = null;
    OleDbDataAdapter da = null;
    DataSet ds = null;
    String strConnection = null;
    String strSQL =null;

    // wire the item data bound event
    this.dgBooks.ItemDataBound +=
      new DataGridItemEventHandler(this.dgBooks_ItemDataBound);

    if (!Page.IsPostBack)
    {
      try
      {
        // get the connection string from web.config and open a connection
        // to the database
        strConnection =
          ConfigurationSettings.AppSettings["dbConnectionString"];
        dbConn = new OleDbConnection(strConnection);
        dbConn.Open();

        // build the query string and get the data from the database
        strSQL = "SELECT Title, ListPrice, DiscountedPrice " +
                 "FROM Book " +
                 "ORDER BY Title";
        da = new OleDbDataAdapter(strSQL, dbConn);
        ds = new DataSet();
        da.Fill(ds);

        // set total values to 0 before data binding
        mListPriceTotal = 0;
        mDiscountedPriceTotal = 0;
```

Example 1-59. DataGrid with totals row code-behind (.cs) (continued)

```
          // set the source of the data for the datagrid control and bind it
          dgBooks.DataSource = ds;
          dgBooks.DataBind( );
        }  // try

        finally
        {
          //clean up
          if (dbConn != null)
          {
            dbConn.Close( );
          }
        }  // finally
      }
    }  // Page
```

****

```
                                nt handler that is called for each
                                ter a data bind occurs.  It is
                                ing the total prices and setting
                                when all rows have been data

                              ----------------------------
                              nder,
                              s.DataGridItemEventArgs e)

                              abel = null;
                              .PriceLabel = null;
                    ....eral totalLabel = null;

    // check the type of item that was databound and only take action if it
    // was a row in the datagrid
    switch (e.Item.ItemType)
    {
      case ListItemType.AlternatingItem:
      case ListItemType.EditItem:
      case ListItemType.Item:
      case ListItemType.SelectedItem:
        // get the data for the item being bound
        rowData = (DataRowView)(e.Item.DataItem);

        // get the value for the list price and add it to the sum
        price = (Decimal)(rowData["ListPrice"]);
        mListPriceTotal += price;
```

Example 1-59. DataGrid with totals row code-behind (.cs) (continued)

```
                // get the control used to display the list price
                // NOTE: This can be done by using the FindControl method of the
                //       passed item because ItemTemplates were used and the anchor
                //       controls in the templates where given IDs.  If a standard
                //       BoundColumn was used, the data would have to be accessed
                //       using the cellscollection (e.g. e.Item.Cells(1).controls(1)
                //       would access the label control in this example.
                listPriceLabel = (System.Web.UI.WebControls.Literal)
                                (e.Item.FindControl("lblListPrice"));

                // now format the list price in currency format
                listPriceLabel.Text = price.ToString("C2");

                // get the value for the discounted price and add it to the sum
                price = (Decimal)(rowData["DiscountedPrice"]);
                mDiscountedPriceTotal += price;

                // get the control used to display the discounted price
                discountedPriceLabel = (System.Web.UI.WebControls.Literal)
                                      (e.Item.FindControl("lblDiscountedPrice"));

                // now format the discounted price in currency format
                discountedPriceLabel.Text = price.ToString("C2");
                break;

            case ListItemType.Footer:
                // get the control used to display the total of the list prices
                // and set its value to the total of the list prices
                totalLabel = (System.Web.UI.WebControls.Literal)
                            (e.Item.FindControl("lblListPriceTotal"));
                totalLabel.Text = mListPriceTotal.ToString("C2");

                // get the control used to display the total of the discounted
                // prices and set its value to the total of the discounted prices
                totalLabel = (System.Web.UI.WebControls.Literal)
                            (e.Item.FindControl("lblTotalDiscountedPrice"));
                totalLabel.Text = mDiscountedPriceTotal.ToString("C2");
                break;

            default:
                // ListItemType.Header, ListItemType.Pager, or ListItemType.Separator
                // no action required
                break;
        }
    } // dgBooks_ItemDataBound
  } // CH01DataGridWithTotalsRowCS
}
```

CHAPTER 2

Validation

2.0 Introduction

ASP.NET validation controls (also known as *validators*) greatly simplify the task of ensuring that data is entered correctly on forms. For most validations, no code is required in either the *.aspx* file or the code-behind class. You simply add a validator to the *.aspx* file, have it reference an input control (a server control) elsewhere on the page, and set one or more of its validation attributes (such as `MinimumValue` or `MaximumValue`, which specify the minimum and maximum values of a validation range). ASP.NET does all the rest. You can also combine validators to provide multiple validations on a single input, such as a `RequiredFieldValidator` and a `RangeValidator`, which perform as their names imply.

Validation can be performed on the client and the server. By default, validators perform their validation automatically on `postback` in server code. However, if the user has a browser that supports DHTML and client-side validation is enabled, validators can also perform their validation using client script. Client-side validation is handy whenever you want to avoid a round trip to the server for server-side validation, such as when you want to make sure an entry is provided in a text box. Regardless of whether client-side validation is performed, server-side validation is always a good idea, if only to ensure that validation always takes place, even when the user's browser doesn't support DHTML.

This chapter includes a useful collection of recipes for validating data, starting with automatic, attribute-oriented validation and ending with custom validation. When you perform custom validation, you actually intercept an input control's validation call and provide your own validation logic (by adding your own custom JavaScript and server-side code). Custom validation is the focus of the final two recipes of the chapter, which show you how to require a user to make a selection from a drop-down list and how to require valid user input data, such as a password that matches an entry in a database.

All validators, except the `RequiredFieldValidator`, allow the control being validated to be left blank. This is a subtle point but one worth noting, as you may need to account for this behavior in your code when using ASP.NET's automatic validation.

2.1 Requiring that Data be Entered in a Field

Problem

You need to ensure that a user has entered data in a text box, such as a first or last name on a registration form.

Solution

Add a `RequiredFieldValidator` control to the *.aspx* file, and use the event handler of the control that completes the user's entry for the page to verify that validation was successful.

In the *.aspx* file:

1. Add a `RequiredFieldValidator` control for each text box in which data must be entered.

2. Add Save and Cancel (or equivalently named) buttons.

3. Set the Save button's `CausesValidation` attribute to `True` to have validation performed when the button is clicked (set it to `False` for the Cancel button).

In the code-behind class, use the .NET language of your choice to add code to the event handler for the Save button's click event that checks the `Page.IsValid` property and verifies that all validation was successful.

Figure 2-1 shows a typical user input form with fields for First Name and Last Name and several other types of information. Figure 2-2 shows the same form with validation error messages that appear when the user fails to complete the First Name and Last Name fields. Example 2-1 shows the *.aspx* file that implements the form, and Examples 2-2 and 2-3 show the VB and C# code-behind files needed to complete the application.

Discussion

When you need to insist that a user enter data into a text box, a common requirement for forms used to register new users for a site or service, the `RequiredFieldValidator` control provides a straightforward way to enforce the rule. We've used the control to require completion of the First Name and Last Name text boxes of a simple registration form (see Figures 2-1 and 2-2). You need to assign a `RequiredFieldValidator` control to each text box you wish to check. Each validator

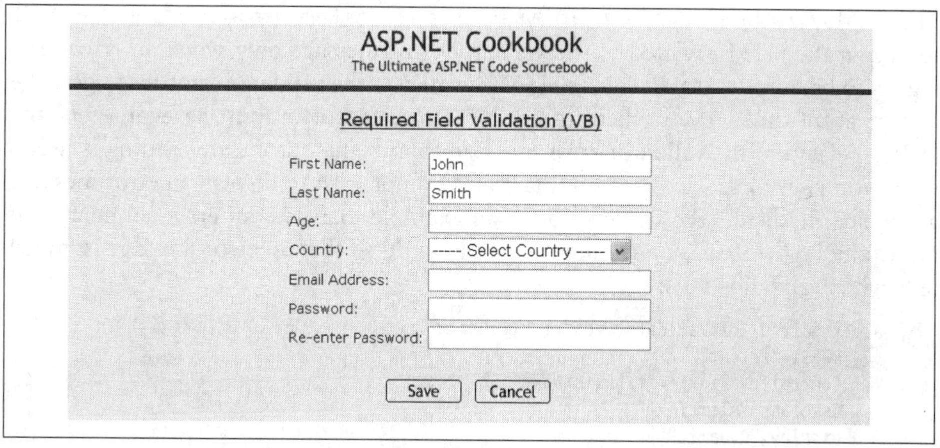

Figure 2-1. Form with required field validation output—normal

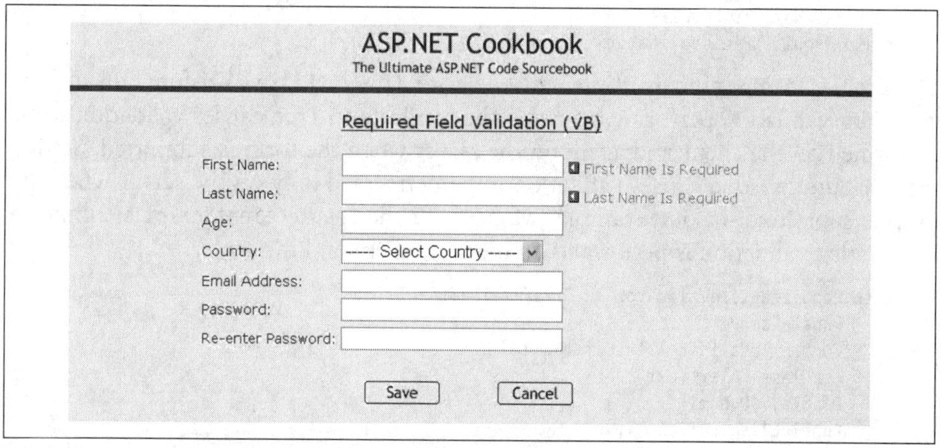

Figure 2-2. Form with required field validation output—with error messages

control must be placed on the form at the exact spot where you want its error message to be displayed (typically just after the text box it validates), and the ControlToValidate attribute of the validator must be set to the ID of the text box, as shown in the following code snippet. In our example, the names of the First Name and Last Name text boxes are txtFirstName and txtLastName, respectively.

```
<asp:RequiredFieldValidator id="rfvFirstName"
    Runat="server"
    ControlToValidate="txtFirstName"
    CssClass="AlertText"
    Display="Dynamic"
    EnableClientScript="True">
  <img src="images/arrow_alert.gif">
  First Name Is Required
</asp:RequiredFieldValidator>
```

The Display attribute must be set to Dynamic, Static, or None. Dynamic causes ASP.NET to output the HTML related to the validator error message only when an error message is to be output. Static causes HTML related to the validator error message to be output at all times, even when an error message is not output. None prevents any HTML related to the validator error message from being output; this setting is useful when you plan to use an error summary and do not wish to display an error message at the specific field. (See Recipe 2.5 for an example that uses an error summary.) In our example, the Display attribute is set to Dynamic so that an error message is issued only when validation fails:

```
<asp:RequiredFieldValidator id="rfvFirstName"
    Runat="server"
    ControlToValidate="txtFirstName"
    CssClass="AlertText"
    Display="Dynamic"
    EnableClientScript="True">
  <img src="images/arrow_alert.gif">
  First Name Is Required
</asp:RequiredFieldValidator>
```

The EnableClientScript attribute can be set to True or False as a function of how you want validation performed. Setting the attribute to True causes validation to be performed on the client and again on the server when the form is submitted. Setting the attribute to False causes validation to be performed only on the server when the form is submitted. In our example, we have set the EnableClientScript attribute to True so that validation is performed on both the client and the server:

```
<asp:RequiredFieldValidator id="rfvFirstName"
    Runat="server"
    ControlToValidate="txtFirstName"
    CssClass="AlertText"
    Display="Dynamic"
    EnableClientScript="True">
  <img src="images/arrow_alert.gif">
  First Name Is Required
</asp:RequiredFieldValidator>
```

The error message that is to be output when validation fails is placed between the open and close tags of the control. The message can include HTML, as shown here, where an HTML image tag comes first, followed by text:

```
<asp:RequiredFieldValidator id="rfvFirstName"
    Runat="server"
    ControlToValidate="txtFirstName"
    CssClass="AlertText"
    Display="Dynamic"
    EnableClientScript="True">
  <img src="images/arrow_alert.gif">
  First Name Is Required
</asp:RequiredFieldValidator>
```

In our application, two buttons are provided on the form to allow the user to submit or cancel the page. The Save button causes the form to be submitted and the data the user has entered to be validated, while the Cancel causes validation to be bypassed. Validation is requested by setting the CausesValidation attribute to True for the Save button and False for the Cancel button:

```
<asp:ImageButton id="btnSave" Runat="server"
    CausesValidation="True"
    ImageUrl="images/buttons/button_save.gif" />

<asp:ImageButton id="btnCancel" Runat="server"
    CausesValidation="False"
    ImageUrl="images/buttons/button_cancel.gif" />
```

With all the setup done in the *.aspx* file, the code-behind requires only a simple check of the Page.IsValid property in the event handler for the Save button's click event. This is done to ensure all client- and server-side validation was successful before processing the form data.

See Also

Recipe 2.5

Example 2-1. Form with required field validation (.aspx)

```
<%@ Page Language="vb" AutoEventWireup="false"
        Codebehind="CH02RequiredFieldValidationVB.aspx.vb"
        Inherits="ASPNetCookbook.VBExamples.CH02RequiredFieldValidationVB" %>
<!DOCTYPE HTML PUBLIC "-//W3C//DTD HTML 4.0 Transitional//EN">
<html>
  <head>
    <title>Validator - Required Field</title>
    <link rel="stylesheet" href="css/ASPNetCookbook.css">
  </head>
  <body leftmargin="0" marginheight="0" marginwidth="0" topmargin="0">
    <form id="frmValidation" method="post" runat="server">
      <table width="100%" cellpadding="0" cellspacing="0" border="0">
        <tr>
          <td align="center">
            <img src="images/ASPNETCookbookHeading_blue.gif">
          </td>
        </tr>
        <tr>
          <td class="dividerLine">
            <img src="images/spacer.gif" height="6" border="0"></td>
        </tr>
      </table>
      <table width="90%" align="center" border="0">
        <tr>
          <td><img src="images/spacer.gif" height="10" border="0"></td>
        </tr>
        <tr>
```

Example 2-1. Form with required field validation (.aspx) (continued)

```
        <td align="center" class="PageHeading">
         Required Field Validation (VB)
        </td>
       </tr>
       <tr>
        <td><img src="images/spacer.gif" height="10" border="0"></td>
       </tr>
       <tr>
        <td align="center">
         <table border="0">
          <tr>
           <td class="LabelText">First Name: </td>
           <td>
            <asp:TextBox id="txtFirstName" Runat="server"
                        Columns="30" CssClass="LabelText" />
            <asp:RequiredFieldValidator id="rfvFirstName"
                Runat="server"
                ControlToValidate="txtFirstName"
                CssClass="AlertText"
                Display="Dynamic"
                EnableClientScript="True">
              <img src="images/arrow_alert.gif">
              First Name Is Required
            </asp:RequiredFieldValidator>
           </td>
          </tr>
          <tr>
           <td class="LabelText">Last Name: </td>
           <td>
            <asp:TextBox id="txtLastName" Runat="server"
                        Columns="30" CssClass="LabelText" />
            <asp:RequiredFieldValidator id="rfvLastName"
                Runat="server"
                ControlToValidate="txtLastName"
                CssClass="AlertText"
                Display="Dynamic"
                EnableClientScript="True">
              <img src="images/arrow_alert.gif">
              Last Name Is Required
            </asp:RequiredFieldValidator>
           </td>
          </tr>
          <tr>
           <td class="LabelText">Age: </td>
           <td>
            <asp:TextBox id="txtAge" Runat="server"
                        Columns="30" CssClass="LabelText" />
           </td>
          </tr>
          <tr>
           <td class="LabelText">Country: </td>
           <td>
```

Example 2-1. Form with required field validation (.aspx) (continued)

```
                <asp:DropDownList id="ddCountry" Runat="server" >
                  <asp:ListItem Selected="True"
                        Value="0">----- Select Country -----</asp:ListItem>
                  <asp:ListItem Value="1">Canada</asp:ListItem>
                  <asp:ListItem Value="2">United States</asp:ListItem>
                </asp:DropDownList>
              </td>
            </tr>
            <tr>
              <td class="LabelText">Email Address: </td>
              <td>
                <asp:TextBox id="txtEmailAddress" Runat="server"
                        Columns="30" CssClass="LabelText" />
              </td>
            </tr>
            <tr>
              <td class="LabelText">Password: </td>
              <td>
                <asp:TextBox id="txtPassword1" Runat="server"
                        TextMode="Password"
                        Columns="30" CssClass="LabelText" />
              </td>
            </tr>
            <tr>
              <td class="LabelText">Re-enter Password: </td>
              <td>
                <asp:TextBox id="txtPassword2" Runat="server"
                        TextMode="Password"
                        Columns="30" CssClass="LabelText" />
              </td>
            </tr>
            <tr>
              <td colspan="2">
                <br>
                <table align="center" width="50%">
                  <tr>
                    <td align="center">
                      <asp:ImageButton id="btnSave" Runat="server"
                          CausesValidation="True"
                          ImageUrl="images/buttons/button_save.gif" />
                    </td>
                    <td align="center">
                      <asp:ImageButton id="btnCancel" Runat="server"
                          CausesValidation="False"
                          ImageUrl="images/buttons/button_cancel.gif" />
                    </td>
                  </tr>
                </table>
              </td>
            </tr>
          </table>
        </td>
```

Example 2-1. Form with required field validation (.aspx) (continued)

```
        </tr>
      </table>
    </form>
  </body>
</html>
```

Example 2-2. Form with required field validation code-behind (.vb)

```vb
Option Explicit On
Option Strict On
'-----------------------------------------------------------------------------
'
'   Module Name: CH02RequiredFieldValidationVB.aspx.vb
'
'   Description: This module provides the code behind for
'                CH02RequiredFieldValidationVB.aspx
'
'*****************************************************************************
Imports System.Web.UI.WebControls

Namespace ASPNetCookbook.VBExamples
  Public Class CH02RequiredFieldValidationVB
    Inherits System.Web.UI.Page

    'controls on form
    Protected WithEvents btnSave As ImageButton

    '*************************************************************************
    '
    '   ROUTINE: Page_Load
    '
    '   DESCRIPTION: This routine provides the event handler for the page load
    '                event.  It is responsible for initializing the controls
    '                on the page.
    '-------------------------------------------------------------------------
    Private Sub Page_Load(ByVal sender As System.Object, _
                      ByVal e As System.EventArgs) _
            Handles MyBase.Load

      If (Not Page.IsPostBack) Then
        'Put user code to initialize the page here
      End If
    End Sub 'Page_Load

    '*************************************************************************
    '
    '   ROUTINE: btnSave_Click
    '
    '   DESCRIPTION: This routine provides the event handler for the save
    '                button click event.  It is responsible for processing the
    '                form data.
    '-------------------------------------------------------------------------
```

Example 2-2. Form with required field validation code-behind (.vb) (continued)

```vb
    Private Sub btnSave_Click(ByVal sender As Object, _
                          ByVal e As System.Web.UI.ImageClickEventArgs) _
            Handles btnSave.Click

      If (Page.IsValid) Then
        'process form data and save as required for application
      End If
    End Sub 'btnSave_Click
  End Class 'CH02RequiredFieldValidationVB
End Namespace
```

Example 2-3. Form with required field validation code-behind (.cs)

```csharp
//-----------------------------------------------------------------------------
//
//    Module Name: CH02RequiredFieldValidationCS.aspx.cs
//
//    Description: This module provides the code behind for
//                 CH02RequiredFieldValidationCS.aspx
//
//****************************************************************************
using System;
using System.Web.UI;
using System.Web.UI.WebControls;

namespace ASPNetCookbook.CSExamples
{
  public class CH02RequiredFieldValidationCS : System.Web.UI.Page
  {
    // controls on form
    protected ImageButton btnSave;

    //****************************************************************************
    //
    //    ROUTINE: Page_Load
    //
    //    DESCRIPTION: This routine provides the event handler for the page
    //                 load event.  It is responsible for initializing the
    //                 controls on the page.
    //-----------------------------------------------------------------------------
    private void Page_Load(object sender, System.EventArgs e)
    {
      // wire the save button click event
      this.btnSave.Click += new ImageClickEventHandler(this.btnSave_Click);

      if (!Page.IsPostBack)
      {
        //Put user code to initialize the page here
      }
    } // Page_Load
```

Example 2-3. Form with required field validation code-behind (.cs) (continued)

```
//**************************************************************************
//
//   ROUTINE: btnSave_Click
//
//   DESCRIPTION: This routine provides the event handler for the save
//                button click event.  It is responsible for processing
//                the form data.
//--------------------------------------------------------------------------
private void btnSave_Click(Object sender,
                           System.Web.UI.ImageClickEventArgs e)

{
    if (Page.IsValid)
    {
        // process form data and save as required for application
    }
}  // btnSave_Click
}  // CH02RequiredFieldValidationCS
}
```

2.2   Requiring Data to Be In a Range

Problem

You need to ensure data entered by a user is within a defined range—for example, between two numbers, currency values, dates, or alphabetic characters.

Solution

Add a RangeValidator control to the *.aspx* file for each TextBox control to be checked, set the minimum and maximum acceptable values for the range, and verify that validation was successful from within the event handler of the control that completes the user's entry for the page.

In the *.aspx* file:

1. Add a RangeValidator control for each text box in which the user must enter data within a specified range.

2. Set the control's MinimumValue and MaximumValue attributes to the minimum and maximum values for the valid range.

3. Add Save and Cancel (or equivalently named) buttons.

4. Set the Save button's CausesValidation attribute to True to have validation performed when the button is clicked (set it to False for the Cancel button).

In the code-behind class for the page, use the .NET language of your choice to add code to the event handler for the Save button's click event to check the Page.IsValid property and verify that all validation was successful. (See Recipe 2.1 for details.)

Figure 2-3 shows the user input form introduced in Recipe 2.1 with normal, error-free output. Figure 2-4 shows the same form with the error message that appears on the form when the data entered into the Age field falls outside a predetermined range. Example 2-4 shows the *.aspx* file that implements the form, and Examples 2-2 and 2-3 (see Recipe 2.1) show the companion code-behind files.

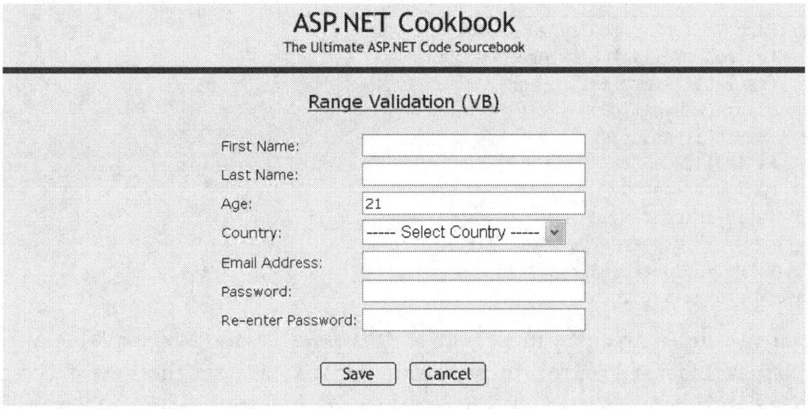

Figure 2-3. Form with range validation output—normal

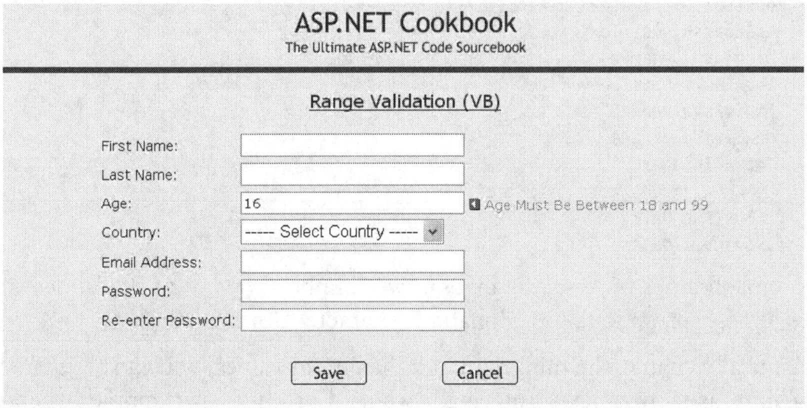

Figure 2-4. Form with range validation output—with error message

Discussion

To make sure a user enters data in a text box within a defined range, place a RangeValidator control on the form and assign it the text box to be validated. To create the form shown in Figures 2-3 and 2-4, for example, we added an asp: RangeValidator control to the *.aspx* file that implements the form, and assigned it to the Age text box to ensure the data entered is within the range 18 to 99. You must place the validator on the form at the exact location where you want the control's error message to be displayed, which in our case is just to the right of the Age text box.

To assign a `RangeValidator` control to a text box or other control type, you must set its `ControlToValidate` attribute to the ID of the control you wish to validate. In our example, the ID of the Age text box is txtAge:

```
<asp:RangeValidator id="rvAge" Runat="server"
    ControlToValidate="txtAge"
    CssClass="AlertText"
    Display="Dynamic"
    EnableClientScript="True"
    MinimumValue="18"
    MaximumValue="99"
    Type="Integer">
  <img src="images/arrow_alert.gif">
  Age Must Be Between 18 and 99
</asp:RangeValidator>
```

To specify a valid range, you must set the `MinimumValue` and `MaximumValue` attributes of the `RangeValidator` control. In our example, we have set the lowest acceptable value to 18 and the highest to 99. These values are inclusive, which means that ages 18 and 99 are both acceptable.

```
<asp:RangeValidator id="rvAge" Runat="server"
    ControlToValidate="txtAge"
    CssClass="AlertText"
    Display="Dynamic"
    EnableClientScript="True"
    MinimumValue="18"
    MaximumValue="99"
    Type="Integer">
  <img src="images/arrow_alert.gif">
  Age Must Be Between 18 and 99
</asp:RangeValidator>
```

Our example focuses on using a range of two numbers, but you can also use a range of dates, times, currency values, alphabetic characters, or the like.

To dynamically change the minimum and maximum values, you can set them in the code-behind, as shown next. You might want to do this, for example, when determining the range on the fly.

VB

```
Dim minAge As Integer
Dim maxAge As Integer


    ..


minAge = 18
maxAge = 99
rvAge.MinimumValue = minAge.ToString()
rvAge.MaximumValue = maxage.ToString()
```

```csharp
int minAge;
int maxAge;

      ..

minAge = 18;
maxAge = 99;
rvAge.MinimumValue = minAge.ToString();
rvAge.MaximumValue = maxAge.ToString();
```

The error message that is to be output when validation fails is placed between the open and close tags:

```
<asp:RangeValidator id="rvAge" Runat="server"
    ControlToValidate="txtAge"
    CssClass="AlertText"
    Display="Dynamic"
    EnableClientScript="True"
    MinimumValue="18"
    MaximumValue="99"
    Type="Integer">
  <img src="images/arrow_alert.gif">
  Age Must Be Between 18 and 99
</asp:RangeValidator>
```

The error message that will be output when a validation error occurs can also be set dynamically in the code-behind, which is something you might find useful when you have also set the maximum and minimum range values on the fly:

```vb
rvAge.Text = "<img src='images/arrow_alert.gif'> " & _
             "Age Must Be Between " & minAge.ToString() & _
             " and " & maxage.ToString()
```

```csharp
rvAge.Text = "<img src='images/arrow_alert.gif'> " +
             "Age Must Be Between " + minAge.ToString() +
             " and " + maxAge.ToString();
```

If you want a text box to be a required field, add a `RequiredFieldValidator` control to the form as well, which is what we have done in our example with the Age text box:

```
<asp:TextBox id="txtAge" Runat="server"
            Columns="30" CssClass="LabelText" />
<asp:RequiredFieldValidator id="rfvAge
    Runat="server"
    ControlToValidate="txtAge"
    CssClass="AlertText"
    Display="Dynamic"
    EnableClientScript="True">
  <img src="images/arrow_alert.gif">
  Age Is Required
</asp:RequiredFieldValidator>
<asp:RangeValidator id="rvAge" Runat="server"
    ControlToValidate="txtAge"
    CssClass="AlertText"
    Display="Dynamic"
```

```
          EnableClientScript="True"
          MinimumValue="18"
          MaximumValue="99"
          Type="Integer">
        <img src="images/arrow_alert.gif">
        Age Must Be Between 18 and 99
    </asp:RangeValidator>
```

All other aspects of the *.aspx* and code-behind are the same as for Recipe 2.1. See that recipe's discussion for comments about the Display, EnableClientScript, and CausesValidation attributes in particular. You'll also find explanations of the Save and Cancel buttons and various other aspects of the code.

See Also

Recipe 2.1

Example 2-4. Form with range validation (.aspx)

```
<%@ Page Language="vb" AutoEventWireup="false"
        Codebehind="CHO2RangeValidationVB.aspx.vb"
        Inherits="ASPNetCookbook.VBExamples.CHO2RangeValidationVB" %>
<!DOCTYPE HTML PUBLIC "-//W3C//DTD HTML 4.0 Transitional//EN">
<html>
  <head>
    <title>Range Validation</title>
    <link rel="stylesheet" href="css/ASPNetCookbook.css">
  </head>
  <body leftmargin="0" marginheight="0" marginwidth="0" topmargin="0">
    <form id="frmValidation" method="post" runat="server">
      <table width="100%" cellpadding="0" cellspacing="0" border="0">
        <tr>
          <td align="center">
            <img src="images/ASPNETCookbookHeading_blue.gif">
          </td>
        </tr>
        <tr>
          <td class="dividerLine">
            <img src="images/spacer.gif" height="6" border="0"></td>
        </tr>
      </table>
      <table width="90%" align="center" border="0">
        <tr>
          <td><img src="images/spacer.gif" height="10" border="0"></td>
        </tr>
        <tr>
          <td align="center" class="PageHeading">
            Range Validation (VB)
          </td>
        </tr>
        <tr>
          <td><img src="images/spacer.gif" height="10" border="0"></td>
        </tr>
```

Example 2-4. Form with range validation (.aspx) (continued)

```
<tr>
  <td align="center">
    <table border="0">
      <tr>
        <td class="LabelText">First Name: </td>
        <td>
          <asp:TextBox id="txtFirstName" Runat="server"
                       Columns="30" CssClass="LabelText" />
        </td>
      </tr>
      <tr>
        <td class="LabelText">Last Name: </td>
        <td>
          <asp:TextBox id="txtLastName" Runat="server"
                       Columns="30" CssClass="LabelText" />
        </td>
      </tr>
      <tr>
        <td class="LabelText">Age: </td>
        <td>
          <asp:TextBox id="txtAge" Runat="server"
                       Columns="30" CssClass="LabelText" />
          <asp:RequiredFieldValidator id="rfvAge"
               Runat="server"
               ControlToValidate="txtAge"
               CssClass="AlertText"
               Display="Dynamic"
               EnableClientScript="True">
            <img src="images/arrow_alert.gif">
            Age Is Required
          </asp:RequiredFieldValidator>
          <asp:RangeValidator id="rvAge" Runat="server"
               ControlToValidate="txtAge"
               CssClass="AlertText"
               Display="Dynamic"
               EnableClientScript="True"
               MinimumValue="18"
               MaximumValue="99"
               Type="Integer">
            <img src="images/arrow_alert.gif">
            Age Must Be Between 18 and 99
          </asp:RangeValidator>
        </td>
      </tr>
      <tr>
        <td class="LabelText">Country: </td>
        <td>
          <asp:DropDownList id="ddCountry" Runat="server" >
            <asp:ListItem Selected="True"
                 Value="0">----- Select Country -----</asp:ListItem>
            <asp:ListItem Value="1">Canada</asp:ListItem>
            <asp:ListItem Value="2">United States</asp:ListItem>
```

Example 2-4. Form with range validation (.aspx) (continued)

```
                    </asp:DropDownList>
                  </td>
              </tr>
              <tr>
                  <td class="LabelText">Email Address: </td>
                  <td>
                    <asp:TextBox id="txtEmailAddress" Runat="server"
                                Columns="30" CssClass="LabelText" />
                  </td>
              </tr>
              <tr>
                  <td class="LabelText">Password: </td>
                  <td>
                    <asp:TextBox id="txtPassword1" Runat="server"
                                TextMode="Password"
                                Columns="30" CssClass="LabelText" />
                  </td>
              </tr>
              <tr>
                  <td class="LabelText">Re-enter Password: </td>
                  <td>
                    <asp:TextBox id="txtPassword2" Runat="server"
                                TextMode="Password"
                                Columns="30" CssClass="LabelText" />
                  </td>
              </tr>
              <tr>
                  <td colspan="2">
                    <br>
                    <table align="center" width="50%">
                      <tr>
                        <td align="center">
                          <asp:ImageButton id="btnSave" Runat="server"
                                CausesValidation="True"
                                ImageUrl="images/buttons/button_save.gif" />
                        </td>
                        <td align="center">
                          <asp:ImageButton id="btnCancel" Runat="server"
                                CausesValidation="False"
                                ImageUrl="images/buttons/button_cancel.gif" />
                        </td>
                      </tr>
                    </table>
                  </td>
              </tr>
          </table>
      </td>
  </tr>
  </table>
  </form>
  </body>
</html>
```

2.3 Requiring that Two Data Input Fields Match

Problem

You need to make sure the data a user enters in two fields on an input form is the same, such as when performing password or email verification.

Solution

Add RequiredFieldValidator controls to the *.aspx* file for both TextBox controls, to prevent a user from skipping one of the fields. Next, add a CompareValidator control to one of the TextBox controls. Finally, verify that validation was successful from within the event handler of the control that completes the user's entry for the page.

In the *.aspx* file:

1. Add a RequiredFieldValidator control for each of the two text boxes in which the user must enter matching data.

2. Add a CompareValidator control to the control that must have its input match the other control.

3. Add Save and Cancel (or equivalently named) buttons.

4. Set the Save button's CausesValidation attribute to True to have validation performed when the button is clicked (set it to False for the Cancel button).

In the code-behind class for the page, use the .NET language of your choice to add code to the event handler for the Save button's click event to check the Page.IsValid property and verify that all validation was successful. (See Recipe 2.1 for details.)

Figure 2-5 shows a typical form with normal output prior to data entry. Figure 2-6 shows the error message that appears on the form when the user enters passwords that do not match. Example 2-5 shows the *.aspx* file for the solution we have implemented to illustrate this recipe. See Examples 2-2 and 2-3 (Recipe 2.1) for the companion code-behind files.

Discussion

The first step in making sure the data a user enters in two fields is the same is to place RequiredFieldValidator controls in the form for the two fields. In our application, for example, RequiredFieldValidator controls are added for the Password and Re-enter Password text boxes.

Next, a CompareValidator control must be added for the second field whose input must match the first field's input. In our example application, a CompareValidator is added for the Re-enter Password, because its input must match the Password's input. The validators are placed to the right of the text boxes, to cause the error messages to be displayed beside the text boxes.

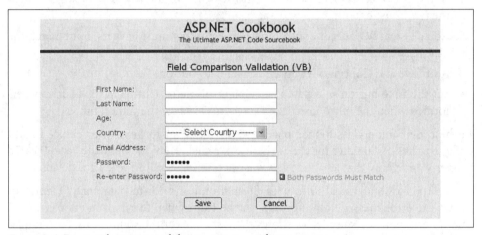

Figure 2-5. Form with compare validation output—normal

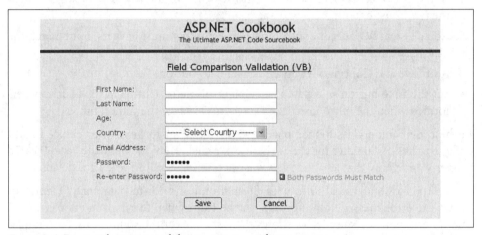

Figure 2-6. Form with compare validation output—with error message

 Because the `CompareValidator` allows empty input, a `RequiredFieldValidator` must be used with each of the controls involved in the comparison. Attempting to use a `CompareValidator` without a `RequiredFieldValidator` will result in odd and undesirable behavior.

In our application, for example, if the `RequiredFieldValidator` were omitted for the Re-enter Password text box, the comparison validation would be performed only if data were entered in the Re-enter Password text box. The end result would be failing to flag a validation error when the user enters data in the Password text box but leaves the Re-enter Password text box empty.

See Recipe 2.1 for more information about how to set up the required field validators.

The `ControlToValidate` attribute of the `CompareValidator` control is set to the ID of the control to validate. On our form, the control to validate is `txtPassword2`, the TextBox in which the user re-enters his password:

```
<asp:CompareValidator ID="cvPassword2" runat="server"
    ControlToValidate="txtPassword2"
    ControlToCompare="txtPassword1"
    CssClass="AlertText"
    Display="Dynamic"
    EnableClientScript="True">
  <img src="images/arrow_alert.gif">
  Both Passwords Must Match
</asp:CompareValidator>
```

The `ControlToCompare` attribute is set to the ID of the control that is used as the reference, in our case `txtPassword1`:

```
<asp:CompareValidator ID="cvPassword2" runat="server"
    ControlToValidate="txtPassword2"
    ControlToCompare="txtPassword1"
    CssClass="AlertText"
    Display="Dynamic"
    EnableClientScript="True">
  <img src="images/arrow_alert.gif">
  Both Passwords Must Match
</asp:CompareValidator>
```

In all other respects, the *.aspx* and code-behind files are the same as those in Recipe 2.1. See that recipe's discussion for comments about the `Display`, `EnableClientScript`, and `CausesValidation` attributes in particular. You'll also find explanations of the Save and Cancel buttons and various other aspects of the code.

See Also

Recipe 2.1

Example 2-5. Form with compare validation (.aspx)

```
<%@ Page Language="vb" AutoEventWireup="false"
        Codebehind="CH02CompareValidationVB.aspx.vb"
        Inherits="ASPNetCookbook.VBExamples.CH02CompareValidationVB" %>
<!DOCTYPE HTML PUBLIC "-//W3C//DTD HTML 4.0 Transitional//EN">
<html>
  <head>
    <title>Compare Validator</title>
    <link rel="stylesheet" href="css/ASPNetCookbook.css">
  </head>
  <body leftmargin="0" marginheight="0" marginwidth="0" topmargin="0">
    <form id="frmValidation" method="post" runat="server">
      <table width="100%" cellpadding="0" cellspacing="0" border="0">
        <tr>
          <td align="center">
            <img src="images/ASPNETCookbookHeading_blue.gif">
          </td>
```

Example 2-5. Form with compare validation (.aspx) (continued)

```
      </tr>
      <tr>
        <td class="dividerLine">
          <img src="images/spacer.gif" height="6" border="0"></td>
      </tr>
    </table>
    <table width="90%" align="center" border="0">
      <tr>
        <td><img src="images/spacer.gif" height="10" border="0"></td>
      </tr>
      <tr>
        <td align="center" class="PageHeading">
          Field Comparison Validation (VB)
        </td>
      </tr>
      <tr>
        <td><img src="images/spacer.gif" height="10" border="0"></td>
      </tr>
      <tr>
        <td align="center">
          <table border="0">
            <tr>
              <td class="LabelText">First Name: </td>
              <td>
                <asp:TextBox id="txtFirstName" Runat="server"
                          Columns="30" CssClass="LabelText" />
              </td>
            </tr>
            <tr>
              <td class="LabelText">Last Name: </td>
              <td>
                <asp:TextBox id="txtLastName" Runat="server"
                          Columns="30" CssClass="LabelText" />
              </td>
            </tr>
            <tr>
              <td class="LabelText">Age: </td>
              <td>
                <asp:TextBox id="txtAge" Runat="server"
                          Columns="30" CssClass="LabelText" />
              </td>
            </tr>
            <tr>
              <td class="LabelText">Country: </td>
              <td>
                <asp:DropDownList id="ddCountry" Runat="server" >
                  <asp:ListItem Selected="True"
                        Value="0">----- Select Country -----</asp:ListItem>
                  <asp:ListItem Value="1">Canada</asp:ListItem>
                  <asp:ListItem Value="2">United States</asp:ListItem>
                </asp:DropDownList>
              </td>
```

Example 2-5. Form with compare validation (.aspx) (continued)

```
      </tr>
      <tr>
        <td class="LabelText">Email Address: </td>
        <td>
          <asp:TextBox id="txtEmailAddress" Runat="server"
                      Columns="30" CssClass="LabelText" />
        </td>
      </tr>
      <tr>
        <td class="LabelText">Password: </td>
        <td>
          <asp:TextBox id="txtPassword1" Runat="server"
                      TextMode="Password"
                      Columns="30" CssClass="LabelText" />
          <asp:RequiredFieldValidator id="rfvPassword1"
              Runat="server"
              ControlToValidate="txtPassword1"
              CssClass="AlertText"
              Display="Dynamic"
              EnableClientScript="True">
            <img src="images/arrow_alert.gif">
            Password Is Required
          </asp:RequiredFieldValidator>
        </td>
      </tr>
      <tr>
        <td class="LabelText">Re-enter Password: </td>
        <td>
          <asp:TextBox id="txtPassword2" Runat="server"
                      TextMode="Password"
                      Columns="30" CssClass="LabelText" />
          <asp:RequiredFieldValidator id="rvPassword2"
              Runat="server"
              ControlToValidate="txtPassword2"
              CssClass="AlertText"
              Display="Dynamic"
              EnableClientScript="True">
            <img src="images/arrow_alert.gif">
            Re-Entered Password Is Required
          </asp:RequiredFieldValidator>
          <asp:CompareValidator ID="cvPassword2" runat="server"
              ControlToValidate="txtPassword2"
              ControlToCompare="txtPassword1"
              CssClass="AlertText"
              Display="Dynamic"
              EnableClientScript="True">
            <img src="images/arrow_alert.gif">
            Both Passwords Must Match
          </asp:CompareValidator>
        </td>
      </tr>
```

Example 2-5. Form with compare validation (.aspx) (continued)

```
      <tr>
        <td colspan="2">
          <br>
          <table align="center" width="50%">
            <tr>
              <td align="center">
                <asp:ImageButton id="btnSave" Runat="server"
                    CausesValidation="True"
                    ImageUrl="images/buttons/button_save.gif" />
              </td>
              <td align="center">
                <asp:ImageButton id="btnCancel" Runat="server"
                    CausesValidation="False"
                    ImageUrl="images/buttons/button_cancel.gif" />
              </td>
            </tr>
          </table>
        </td>
      </tr>
    </table>
  </td>
  </tr>
  </table>
  </form>
  </body>
</html>
```

2.4   Requiring that Data Matches a Predefined Pattern

Problem

You need to make sure the data a user enters matches a specific pattern, such as an email address.

Solution

Add a RegularExpressionValidator control to the *.aspx* file, set the regular expression to perform the pattern matching, and verify that validation was successful from within the event handler of the control that completes the user's entry for the page.

In the *.aspx* file:

1. Add a RegularExpressionValidator control for each text box that must have data matching a specific pattern.

2. Set the ValidationExpression attribute of the RegularExpressionValidator to the regular expression needed to match the required pattern.

3. Add Save and Cancel (or equivalently named) buttons.

4. Set the Save button's CausesValidation attribute to True to have validation performed when the button is clicked (set it to False for the Cancel button).

In the code-behind class for the page, use the .NET language of your choice to add code to the event handler for the Save button's click event to check the Page.IsValid property and verify that all validation was successful. (See Recipe 2.1 for details.)

Figure 2-7 shows a typical form with normal, error-free output. Figure 2-8 shows the error message that appears on the form when an invalid email address is entered. Example 2-6 shows the *.aspx* file for our application that implements the recipe. See Examples 2-2 and 2-3 (Recipe 2.1) for the companion code-behind files.

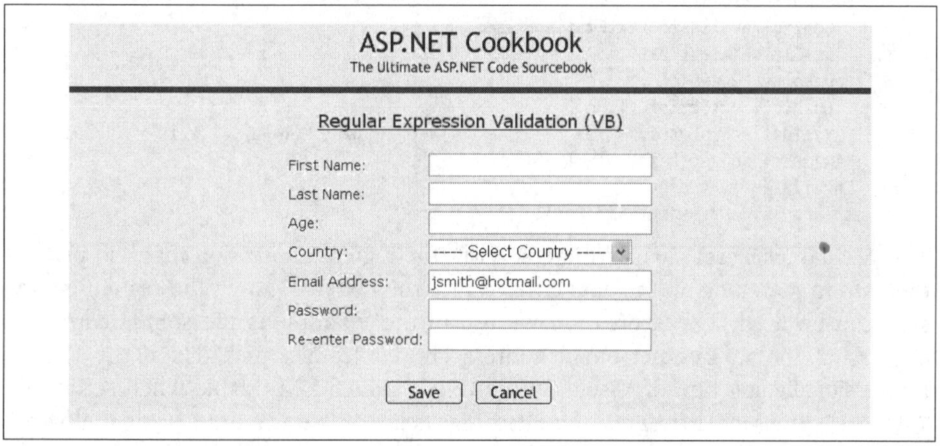

Figure 2-7. Form with pattern validation output—normal

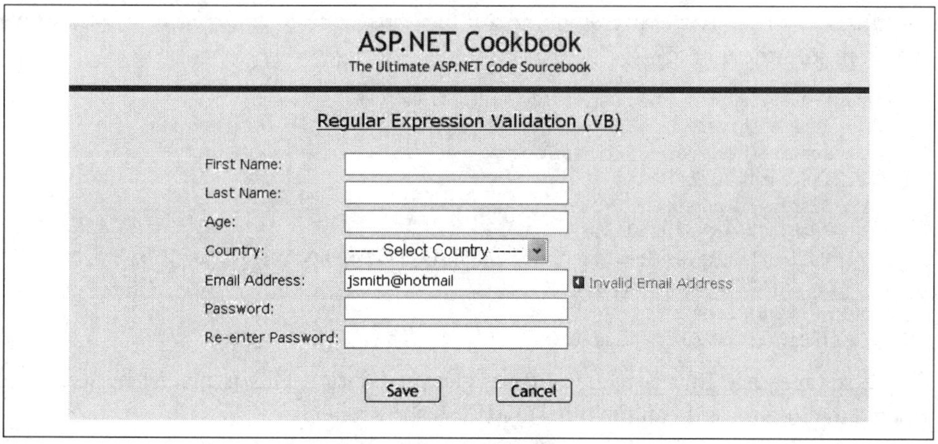

Figure 2-8. Form with pattern validation—with error message

Discussion

One of the more common uses of pattern validation is for checking the form of an email address that has been entered to make sure that it matches the *user@domain* pattern. A RegularExpressionValidator control is added for the Email Address text box in the example. The control is placed to the right of the Email Address text box, to cause the error message to be displayed beside the text box when an invalid email address is entered.

The ControlToValidate attribute of the validation control must be set to the ID of the control to validate, in our case txtEmailAddress:

```
<asp:RegularExpressionValidator id="revEmailAddress"
    Runat="server"
    ControlToValidate="txtEmailAddress"
    CssClass="AlertText"
    Display="Dynamic"
    EnableClientScript="True"
    ValidationExpression="\w+([-+.]\w+)*@\w+([-.]\w+)*\.\w+([-.]\w+)*">
    img src="images/arrow_alert.gif">
  Invalid Email Address
</asp:RegularExpressionValidator>
```

The ValidationExpression attribute is set to the regular expression that will perform the pattern matching on the data entered into the text box. Any valid regular expression can be used. The expression we use in our example is the standard prebuilt expression for an Internet email address chosen from a pick list in the Regular Expression Dialog box of Visual Studio .NET, which is available when setting the ValidateExpression attribute. The Help that is accessible from this same dialog box provides a complete explanation of the syntax and can also be used when writing your own custom regular expressions. Many books are also available that describe all the nuances of regular expressions, including *Mastering Regular Expressions*, so we won't go into them here.

```
<asp:RegularExpressionValidator id="revEmailAddress"
    Runat="server"
    ControlToValidate="txtEmailAddress"
    CssClass="AlertText"
    Display="Dynamic"
    EnableClientScript="True"
    ValidationExpression="\w+([-+.]\w+)*@\w+([-.]\w+)*\.\w+([-.]\w+)*">
    <img src="images/arrow_alert.gif">
  Invalid Email Address
</asp:RegularExpressionValidator>
```

The error message that is to be output when validation fails is placed between the open and close tags. It can include HTML, as shown here:

```
<asp:RegularExpressionValidator id="revEmailAddress"
    Runat="server"
    ControlToValidate="txtEmailAddress"
    CssClass="AlertText"
```

```
         Display="Dynamic"
         EnableClientScript="True"
         ValidationExpression="\w+([-+.]\w+)*@\w+([-.]\w+)*\.\w+([-.]\w+)*">
    <img src="images/arrow_alert.gif">
    Invalid Email Address
</asp:RegularExpressionValidator>
```

 If the email address in this example were required to process the form, a RequiredFieldValidator would need to be added along with the RegularExpressionValidator.

In all other respects, the *.aspx* and code-behind files are identical to Recipe 2.1. See that recipe's discussion for comments about the Display, EnableClientScript, and CausesValidation attributes in particular. You'll also find explanations of the Save and Cancel buttons and various other aspects of the code.

See Also

Recipe 2.1; *Mastering Regular Expressions*, by Jeffrey E. F. Friedl (O'Reilly); the Help that's available from the Regular Expression Dialog box when setting the ValidateExpression attribute in Visual Studio .NET

Example 2-6. Form with pattern validation (.aspx)

```
<%@ Page Language="vb" AutoEventWireup="false"
    Codebehind="CH02RegularExpressionValidationVB.aspx.vb"
    Inherits="ASPNetCookbook.VBExamples.CH02RegularExpressionValidationVB" %>
<!DOCTYPE HTML PUBLIC "-//W3C//DTD HTML 4.0 Transitional//EN">
<html>
  <head>
    <title>Regular Expression Validator</title>
    <link rel="stylesheet" href="css/ASPNetCookbook.css">
  </head>
  <body leftmargin="0" marginheight="0" marginwidth="0" topmargin="0">
    <form id="frmValidation" method="post" runat="server">
      <table width="100%" cellpadding="0" cellspacing="0" border="0">
        <tr>
          <td align="center">
            <img src="images/ASPNETCookbookHeading_blue.gif">
          </td>
        </tr>
        <tr>
          <td class="dividerLine">
            <img src="images/spacer.gif" height="6" border="0"></td>
        </tr>
      </table>
      <table width="90%" align="center" border="0">
        <tr>
          <td><img src="images/spacer.gif" height="10" border="0"></td>
        </tr>
        <tr>
```

Example 2-6. Form with pattern validation (.aspx) (continued)

```
        <td align="center" class="PageHeading">
        Regular Expression Validation (VB)
      </td>
    </tr>
    <tr>
      <td><img src="images/spacer.gif" height="10" border="0"></td>
    </tr>
    <tr>
      <td align="center">
        <table border="0">
          <tr>
            <td class="LabelText">First Name: </td>
            <td>
              <asp:TextBox id="txtFirstName" Runat="server"
                        Columns="30" CssClass="LabelText" />
            </td>
          </tr>
          <tr>
            <td class="LabelText">Last Name: </td>
            <td>
              <asp:TextBox id="txtLastName" Runat="server"
                        Columns="30" CssClass="LabelText" />
            </td>
          </tr>
          <tr>
            <td class="LabelText">Age: </td>
            <td>
              <asp:TextBox id="txtAge" Runat="server"
                        Columns="30" CssClass="LabelText" />
            </td>
          </tr>
          <tr>
            <td class="LabelText">Country: </td>
            <td>
              <asp:DropDownList id="ddCountry" Runat="server" >
                <asp:ListItem Selected="True"
                      Value="0">----- Select Country -----</asp:ListItem>
                <asp:ListItem Value="1">Canada</asp:ListItem>
                <asp:ListItem Value="2">United States</asp:ListItem>
              </asp:DropDownList>
            </td>
          </tr>
          <tr>
            <td class="LabelText">Email Address: </td>
            <td>
              <asp:TextBox id="txtEmailAddress" Runat="server"
                        Columns="30" CssClass="LabelText" />
              <asp:requiredfieldvalidator id="rfvEmailAddress"
                    runat="server"
                    controltovalidate="txtEmailAddress"
                    cssclass="AlertText"
                    display="Dynamic"
```

Example 2-6. Form with pattern validation (.aspx) (continued)

```
                    enableclientscript="True">
                <img src="images/arrow_alert.gif">
                Email Address Is Required
            </asp:requiredfieldvalidator>
            <asp:RegularExpressionValidator id="revEmailAddress"
                Runat="server"
                ControlToValidate="txtEmailAddress"
                CssClass="AlertText"
                Display="Dynamic"
                EnableClientScript="True"
     ValidationExpression="\w+([-+.]\w+)*@\w+([-.]\w+)*\.\w+([-.]\w+)*">
                <img src="images/arrow_alert.gif">
                Invalid Email Address
            </asp:RegularExpressionValidator>
          </td>
        </tr>
        <tr>
          <td class="LabelText">Password: </td>
          <td>
            <asp:TextBox id="txtPassword1" Runat="server"
                        TextMode="Password"
                        Columns="30" CssClass="LabelText" />
          </td>
        </tr>
        <tr>
          <td class="LabelText">Re-enter Password: </td>
          <td>
            <asp:TextBox id="txtPassword2" Runat="server"
                        TextMode="Password"
                        Columns="30" CssClass="LabelText" />
          </td>
        </tr>
        <tr>
          <td colspan="2">
            <br>
            <table align="center" width="50%">
              <tr>
                <td align="center">
                  <asp:ImageButton id="btnSave" Runat="server"
                        CausesValidation="True"
                        ImageUrl="images/buttons/button_save.gif" />
                </td>
                <td align="center">
                  <asp:ImageButton id="btnCancel" Runat="server"
                        CausesValidation="False"
                        ImageUrl="images/buttons/button_cancel.gif" />
                </td>
              </tr>
            </table>
          </td>
        </tr>
      </table>
```

Example 2-6. Form with pattern validation (.aspx) (continued)

```
            </td>
        </tr>
    </table>
  </form>
  </body>
</html>
```

2.5   Requiring that a Drop-Down List Selection Be Made

Problem

You need to make sure a user selects an entry in a drop-down list.

Solution

Add a CustomValidator control to the drop-down list, along with some client-side JavaScript to validate the selection. Next, implement an event handler for the CustomValidator control's ServerValidate event. Finally, check the Page.IsValid property in the event handler for the control that completes the user's entry for the page.

In the *.aspx* file:

1. Add a CustomValidator control for each drop-down list where you must verify that an item has been selected.

2. Add JavaScript to validate the selection on the client side.

3. Add Save and Cancel (or equivalently named) buttons.

4. Set the Save button's CausesValidation attribute to True to have validation performed when the button is clicked (set it to False for the Cancel button).

In the code-behind class for the page, use the .NET language of your choice to:

1. Add an event handler for the CustomValidator control's ServerValidate event whose purpose is to provide the server-side validation to ensure an item has been selected.

2. Add code to the event handler for the Save button's click event to check the Page.IsValid property and verify that all validation was successful (see Recipe 2.1 for details).

Figure 2-9 shows a typical form with normal output prior to data entry. Figure 2-10 shows the form with validation errors. Examples 2-7 through 2-9 show the *.aspx* and code-behind files for our application that implements the solution.

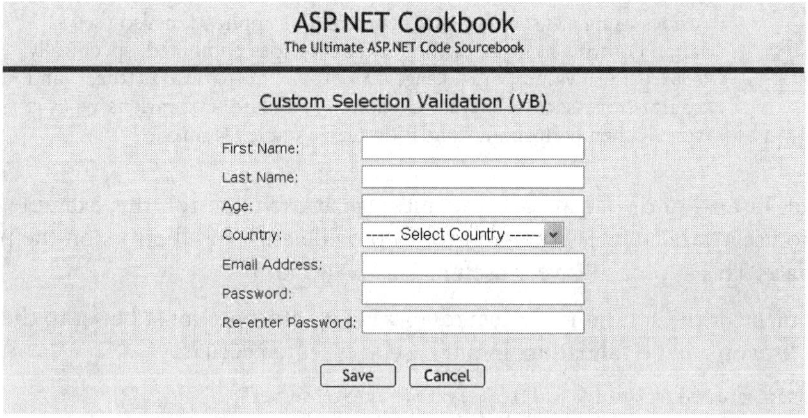

Figure 2-9. Form with selection validation output—normal

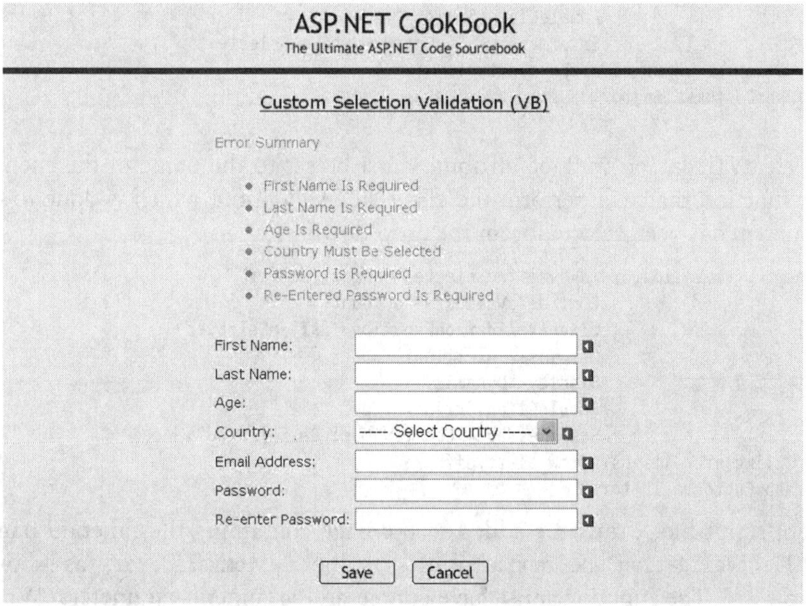

Figure 2-10. Form with selection validation output—with error summary

Discussion

This recipe involves using a CustomValidator control to verify that an item has been selected in a drop-down list. But the approach we advocate is a bit out of the ordinary for a couple of reasons. First, by implementing validation via client-side Java-Script, it allows errors to be detected on the client, thus avoiding unnecessary round trips to the server for server-side validation.

Besides using a CustomValidator control, this application also uses validation controls from all of the previous recipes combined, specifically RequiredFieldValidator, RangeValidator, CompareValidator, and RegularExpressionValidator. Combining validators of various types is typical when performing validation on a complex form.

Second, instead of displaying an error message at each control, this example shows how to use a ValidationSummary control to provide a list of all errors on the page in one place. This approach is very useful for a "busy" form.

To implement the solution, the ControlToValidate attribute must be set to the drop-down list you will be validating. In our case, it is set to ddCountry:

```
<asp:CustomValidator id="valItemSelected" runat="server"
                ControlToValidate="ddCountry"
                ClientValidationFunction="isItemSelected"
                CssClass="AlertText"
                Display="Dynamic"
                EnableClientScript="True"
                ErrorMessage="Country Must Be Selected">
    <img src="images/arrow_alert.gif" />
</asp:CustomValidator>
```

The ClientValidationFunction attribute must be set to the name of the client Java-Script function that will perform the client-side validation, which is done to ensure that an item has been selected from the drop-down:

```
<asp:CustomValidator id="valItemSelected" runat="server"
                ControlToValidate="ddCountry"
                ClientValidationFunction="isItemSelected"
                CssClass="AlertText"
                Display="Dynamic"
                EnableClientScript="True"
                ErrorMessage="Country Must Be Selected">
    <img src="images/arrow_alert.gif" />
</asp:CustomValidator>
```

A client script block must be added to the page containing the function named in the ClientValidationFunction attribute of the CustomValidator, as shown in Example 2-7. The function must have source and argument parameters. When the function is called, the source will be set to a reference to the validator that called the function. In this case, it is the "valItemSelected" validator.

The arguments parameter is a structure containing two elements: Value and IsValid. Value contains the current value of the control that is being validated. In this case, it is the value of the selected item in the drop-down list. In our example, three entries are added to the drop-down list, with the first entry being the "Select Country" instruction with a value of 0. All legitimate selections from the drop-down contain values greater than 0; therefore, if the value of arguments.Value is less than 1, no

selection has been made, and the value of arguments.IsValid is set to False to indicate a validation failure. If arguments.Value is greater than 0, then a selection has
been made, and arguments.IsValid is set to True to indicate the validation passed.

The EnableClientScript attribute is set to True or False according to how you want
validation to be performed. Setting the attribute to True causes validation to be performed on the client and again on the server when the page is submitted. Setting the
attribute to False causes validation to be performed only on the server when the
form is submitted. In our example we are providing client-side JavaScript, so it must
be set to True:

```
<asp:CustomValidator id="valItemSelected" runat="server"
                     ControlToValidate="ddCountry"
                     ClientValidationFunction="isItemSelected"
                     CssClass="AlertText"
                     Display="Dynamic"
                     EnableClientScript="True"
                     ErrorMessage="Country Must Be Selected">
    <img src="images/arrow_alert.gif" />
</asp:CustomValidator>
```

Rather than outputting an error message at each control, as was done in all the previous examples in this chapter, we've added a ValidationSummary control to the form in
this example to provide in one place a summary of all the errors on the form. When a
validation summary is being used, an error message is no longer required between
the start and end tags of the validator element. Instead, the ErrorMessage attribute of
the validator is set to the error message to display. To provide visual feedback of
which control has an error, an arrow image is inserted between the start and end tags
of the validator element in our example:

```
<asp:CustomValidator id="valItemSelected" runat="server"
                     ControlToValidate="ddCountry"
                     ClientValidationFunction="isItemSelected"
                     CssClass="AlertText"
                     Display="Dynamic"
                     EnableClientScript="True"
                     ErrorMessage="Country Must Be Selected">
    <img src="images/arrow_alert.gif" />
</asp:CustomValidator>
```

The DisplayMode attribute of the asp:ValidationSummary control defines how the
summary is displayed. Valid values are BulletList, List, and SingleParagraph.
BulletList will generate a bulleted list of the errors, which is what we've chosen for
our example. List will generate the same list as the BulletList setting but without
the bullets. SingleParagraph generates a single HTML paragraph containing all of the
error information. The HeaderText attribute is set to the title placed at the top of the
list of errors.

```
<asp:ValidationSummary id="vsErrors" Runat="server"
                       CssClass="AlertText"
                       DisplayMode="BulletList"
```

```
                EnableClientScript="True"
                HeaderText="Error Summary" />
```

The sample application's code-behind includes an event handler for the CustomValidator control's ServerValidate event, as shown in Example 2-8 (VB) and Example 2-9 (C#). This event handler provides the server-side validation to ensure a country has been selected using the same technique implemented in the client script.

The code-behind also includes an event handler for the Save button's click event. This event handler checks to make sure the page is valid (all validation passed) and then performs the processing of the form data.

See Also

Recipe 2.1; Recipe 2.2; Recipe 2.3; Recipe 2.4

Example 2-7. Form with selection validation (.aspx)

```
<%@ Page Language="vb" AutoEventWireup="false"
        Codebehind="CH02CustomSelectionValidationVB.aspx.vb"
        Inherits="ASPNetCookbook.VBExamples.CH02CustomSelectionValidationVB" %>
<!DOCTYPE HTML PUBLIC "-//W3C//DTD HTML 4.0 Transitional//EN">
<html>
  <head>
    <title>Custom Selection Validator</title>
    <link rel="stylesheet" href="css/ASPNetCookbook.css">
    <script language="javascript">
    <!--
      function isItemSelected(source, arguments)
      {
        if (arguments.Value < 1)
        {
          arguments.IsValid = false;
        }
        else
        {
          arguments.IsValid = true;
        }
      }
    //-->
    </script>
  </head>
  <body leftmargin="0" marginheight="0" marginwidth="0" topmargin="0">
    <form id="frmValidation" method="post" runat="server">
      <table width="100%" cellpadding="0" cellspacing="0" border="0">
        <tr>
          <td align="center">
            <img src="images/ASPNETCookbookHeading_blue.gif">
          </td>
        </tr>
        <tr>
          <td class="dividerLine">
            <img src="images/spacer.gif" height="6" border="0"></td>
        </tr>
```

Example 2-7. Form with selection validation (.aspx) (continued)

```
    </table>
    <table width="90%" align="center" border="0">
      <tr>
        <td><img src="images/spacer.gif" height="10" border="0"></td>
      </tr>
      <tr>
        <td align="center" class="PageHeading">
          Custom Validation (VB)
        </td>
      </tr>
      <tr>
        <td><img src="images/spacer.gif" height="10" border="0"></td>
      </tr>
      <tr>
        <td align="center">
          <table border="0">
            <tr>
              <td colspan="2" align="left">
                <asp:ValidationSummary id="vsErrors" Runat="server"
                                CssClass="AlertText"
                                DisplayMode="BulletList"
                                EnableClientScript="True"
                                HeaderText="Error Summary" />
              </td>
            </tr>
            <tr>
              <td class="LabelText">First Name: </td>
              <td>
                <asp:TextBox id="txtFirstName" Runat="server"
                          Columns="30" CssClass="LabelText" />
                <asp:RequiredFieldValidator id="rfvFirstName"
                      Runat="server"
                      ControlToValidate="txtFirstName"
                      CssClass="AlertText"
                      Display="Dynamic"
                      EnableClientScript="True"
                      ErrorMessage="First Name Is Required">
                   <img src="images/arrow_alert.gif">
                </asp:RequiredFieldValidator>
              </td>
            </tr>
            <tr>
              <td class="LabelText">Last Name: </td>
              <td>
                <asp:TextBox id="txtLastName" Runat="server"
                          Columns="30" CssClass="LabelText" />
                <asp:RequiredFieldValidator id="rfvLastName"
                      Runat="server"
                      ControlToValidate="txtLastName"
                      CssClass="AlertText"
                      Display="Dynamic"
                      EnableClientScript="True"
                      ErrorMessage="Last Name Is Required">
```

Example 2-7. Form with selection validation (.aspx) (continued)

```
                    <img src="images/arrow_alert.gif">
                </asp:RequiredFieldValidator>
            </td>
        </tr>
        <tr>
            <td class="LabelText">Age: </td>
            <td>
                <asp:TextBox id="txtAge" Runat="server"
                            Columns="30" CssClass="LabelText" />
                <asp:RequiredFieldValidator id="Requiredfieldvalidator1"
                        Runat="server"
                        ControlToValidate="txtAge"
                        CssClass="AlertText"
                        Display="Dynamic"
                        EnableClientScript="True"
                        ErrorMessage="Age Is Required">
                    <img src="images/arrow_alert.gif">
                </asp:RequiredFieldValidator>
                <asp:RangeValidator id="rvAge" Runat="server"
                        ControlToValidate="txtAge"
                        CssClass="AlertText"
                        Display="Dynamic"
                        EnableClientScript="True"
                        MinimumValue="18"
                        MaximumValue="99"
                        Type="Integer"
                        ErrorMessage="Age Must Be Between 18 and 99">
                    <img src="images/arrow_alert.gif">
                </asp:RangeValidator>
            </td>
        </tr>
        <tr>
            <td class="LabelText">Country: </td>
            <td>
                <asp:DropDownList id="ddCountry" Runat="server" >
                    <asp:ListItem Selected="True"
                        Value="0">----- Select Country -----</asp:ListItem>
                    <asp:ListItem Value="1">Canada</asp:ListItem>
                    <asp:ListItem Value="2">United States</asp:ListItem>
                </asp:DropDownList>
                <asp:CustomValidator id="valItemSelected" runat="server"
                            ControlToValidate="ddCountry"
                            ClientValidationFunction="isItemSelected"
                            CssClass="AlertText"
                            Display="Dynamic"
                            EnableClientScript="True"
                            ErrorMessage="Country Must Be Selected">
                    <img src="images/arrow_alert.gif" />
                </asp:CustomValidator>
            </td>
        </tr>
```

Example 2-7. Form with selection validation (.aspx) (continued)

```
<tr>
  <td class="LabelText">Email Address: </td>
  <td>
    <asp:TextBox id="txtEmailAddress" Runat="server"
              Columns="30" CssClass="LabelText" />
    <asp:requiredfieldvalidator id="rfvEmailAddress"
        runat="server"
        controltovalidate="txtEmailAddress"
        cssclass="AlertText"
        display="Dynamic"
        enableclientscript="True">
      <img src="images/arrow_alert.gif">
    </asp:requiredfieldvalidator>
    <asp:RegularExpressionValidator id="revEmailAddress"
        Runat="server"
        ControlToValidate="txtEmailAddress"
        CssClass="AlertText"
        Display="Dynamic"
        EnableClientScript="True"
ValidationExpression="\w+([-+.]\w+)*@\w+([-.]\w+)*\.\w+([-.]\w+)*"
        ErrorMessage="Invalid Email Address">
      <img src="images/arrow_alert.gif">
    </asp:RegularExpressionValidator>
  </td>
</tr>
<tr>
  <td class="LabelText">Password: </td>
  <td>
    <asp:TextBox id="txtPassword1" Runat="server"
              TextMode="Password"
              Columns="30" CssClass="LabelText" />
    <asp:RequiredFieldValidator id="rfvPassword1"
        Runat="server"
        ControlToValidate="txtPassword1"
        CssClass="AlertText"
        Display="Dynamic"
        EnableClientScript="True"
        ErrorMessage="Password Is Required">
      <img src="images/arrow_alert.gif">
    </asp:RequiredFieldValidator>
  </td>
</tr>
<tr>
  <td class="LabelText">Re-enter Password: </td>
  <td>
    <asp:TextBox id="txtPassword2" Runat="server"
              TextMode="Password"
              Columns="30" CssClass="LabelText" />
    <asp:RequiredFieldValidator id="rvPassword2"
        Runat="server"
        ControlToValidate="txtPassword2"
```

Example 2-7. Form with selection validation (.aspx) (continued)

```
                    CssClass="AlertText"
                    Display="Dynamic"
                    EnableClientScript="True"
                    ErrorMessage="Re-Entered Password Is Required">
                <img src="images/arrow_alert.gif">
              </asp:RequiredFieldValidator>
              <asp:CompareValidator ID="cvPassword2" runat="server"
                    ControlToValidate="txtPassword2"
                    ControlToCompare="txtPassword1"
                    CssClass="AlertText"
                    Display="Dynamic"
                    EnableClientScript="True"
                    ErrorMessage="Both Passwords Must Match">
                <img src="images/arrow_alert.gif">
              </asp:CompareValidator>
            </td>
          </tr>
          <tr>
            <td colspan="2">
              <br>
              <table align="center" width="50%">
                <tr>
                  <td align="center">
                    <asp:ImageButton id="btnSave" Runat="server"
                          CausesValidation="True"
                          ImageUrl="images/buttons/button_save.gif" />
                  </td>
                  <td align="center">
                    <asp:ImageButton id="btnCancel" Runat="server"
                          CausesValidation="False"
                          ImageUrl="images/buttons/button_cancel.gif" />
                  </td>
                </tr>
              </table>
            </td>
          </tr>
        </table>
      </td>
    </tr>
  </table>
</form>
</body>
</html>
```

Example 2-8. Form with selection validation code-behind (.vb)

```
Option Explicit On
Option Strict On
'-------------------------------------------------------------------------
'
'   Module Name: CH02CustomSelectionValidationVB.aspx.vb
'
```

Example 2-8. Form with selection validation code-behind (.vb) (continued)

```vb
'    Description: This module provides the code behind for
'                 CH02CustomSelectionValidationVB.aspx
'
'*****************************************************************************
Imports System.Web.UI.WebControls

Namespace ASPNetCookbook.VBExamples
  Public Class CH02CustomSelectionValidationVB
    Inherits System.Web.UI.Page

    'controls on form
    Protected ddCountry As DropDownList
    Protected WithEvents valItemSelected As CustomValidator
    Protected WithEvents btnSave As ImageButton


    '*****************************************************************************
    '
    '    ROUTINE: Page_Load
    '
    '    DESCRIPTION: This routine provides the event handler for the page load
    '                 event.  It is responsible for initializing the controls
    '                 on the page.
    '----------------------------------------------------------------------------
    Private Sub Page_Load(ByVal sender As System.Object, _
                      ByVal e As System.EventArgs) _
          Handles MyBase.Load

      If (Not Page.IsPostBack) Then
        'Put user code to initialize the page here
      End If
    End Sub  'Page_Load


    '*****************************************************************************
    '
    '    ROUTINE: valItemSelected_ServerValidate
    '
    '    DESCRIPTION: This routine provides the event handler for the
    '                 valItemSelected server validate event.  It is responsible
    '                 for validating that a country has been selected
    '----------------------------------------------------------------------------
    Private Sub valItemSelected_ServerValidate(ByVal source As Object, _
          ByVal args As System.Web.UI.WebControls.ServerValidateEventArgs) _
          Handles valItemSelected.ServerValidate

      If (ddCountry.SelectedIndex < 1) Then
        args.IsValid = False
      Else
        args.IsValid = True
      End If
    End Sub  'valItemSelected_ServerValidate
```

Example 2-8. Form with selection validation code-behind (.vb) (continued)

```
'**************************************************************************
'
'     ROUTINE: btnSave_Click
'
'     DESCRIPTION: This routine provides the event handler for the save
'                  button click event.  It is responsible for processing the
'                  form data.
'-----------------------------------------------------------------------
    Private Sub btnSave_Click(ByVal sender As Object, _
                              ByVal e As System.Web.UI.ImageClickEventArgs) _
            Handles btnSave.Click

      If (Page.IsValid) Then
        'process form data and save as required for application
      End If
    End Sub   'btnSave_Click
  End Class   'CHO2CustomSelectionValidationVB
End Namespace
```

Example 2-9. Form with selection validation code-behind (.cs)

```
//--------------------------------------------------------------------------
//
//    Module Name: CHO2CustomSelectionValidationCS.aspx.cs
//
//    Description: This module provides the code behind for
//                 CHO2CustomSelectionValidationCS.aspx
//
//**************************************************************************
using System;
using System.Web.UI;
using System.Web.UI.WebControls;

namespace ASPNetCookbook.CSExamples
{
  public class CHO2CustomSelectionValidationCS : System.Web.UI.Page
  {
    // controls on form
    protected DropDownList ddCountry;
    protected CustomValidator valItemSelected;
    protected ImageButton btnSave;

    //**********************************************************************
    //
    //    ROUTINE: Page_Load
    //
    //    DESCRIPTION: This routine provides the event handler for the page
    //                 load event.  It is responsible for initializing the
    //                 controls on the page.
    //---------------------------------------------------------------------
    private void Page_Load(object sender, System.EventArgs e)
    {
```

Example 2-9. Form with selection validation code-behind (.cs) (continued)

```
      // wire the save button click and the item selected validation events
      this.btnSave.Click += new ImageClickEventHandler(this.btnSave_Click);
      this.valItemSelected.ServerValidate +=
        new ServerValidateEventHandler(this.valItemSelected_ServerValidate);

      if (!Page.IsPostBack)
      {
        //Put user code to initialize the page here
      }
    } // Page_Load

    //*************************************************************************
    //
    //    ROUTINE: valItemSelected_ServerValidate
    //
    //    DESCRIPTION: This routine provides the event handler for the
    //                 valItemSelected server validate event.  It is
    //                 responsible for validating that a country has been
    //                 selected
    //-------------------------------------------------------------------------
    private void valItemSelected_ServerValidate(Object source,
                  System.Web.UI.WebControls.ServerValidateEventArgs args)
    {
      if (ddCountry.SelectedIndex < 1)
      {
        args.IsValid = false;
      }
      else
      {
        args.IsValid = true;
      }
    } // valItemSelected_ServerValidate

    //*************************************************************************
    //
    //    ROUTINE: btnSave_Click
    //
    //    DESCRIPTION: This routine provides the event handler for the save
    //                 button click event.  It is responsible for processing
    //                 the form data.
    //-------------------------------------------------------------------------
    private void btnSave_Click(Object sender,
                          System.Web.UI.ImageClickEventArgs e)
    {
      if (Page.IsValid)
      {
        // process form data and save as required for application
      }
    } // btnSave_Click

  } // CH02CustomSelectionValidationCS
}
```

2.6   Requiring Data to Match a Database Entry

Problem

You need to make sure the data a user enters matches an entry in a database.

Solution

Add a CustomValidator to the *.aspx* file. Then add an event handler to the code-behind for the CustomValidator control's ServerValidate event, whose purpose is to validate the user entries against the database.

In the *.aspx* file:

1. Add a CustomValidator control that validates the entries against the database during server-side validation.

2. Add a Login (or equivalently named) button.

In the code-behind class for the page, use the .NET language of your choice to:

1. Add an event handler for the CustomValidator control's ServerValidate event whose purpose is to provide the server-side validation of the user's entries against the database.

2. Add code to the event handler for the Login button's click event to check the Page.IsValid property and verify that all validation was successful (see Recipe 2. 1 for details).

Figure 2-11 shows a typical form with normal output prior to data entry. Figure 2-12 shows the form with a validation error message. Examples 2-10 through 2-12 show the *.aspx* and code-behind files for our application that implements the solution.

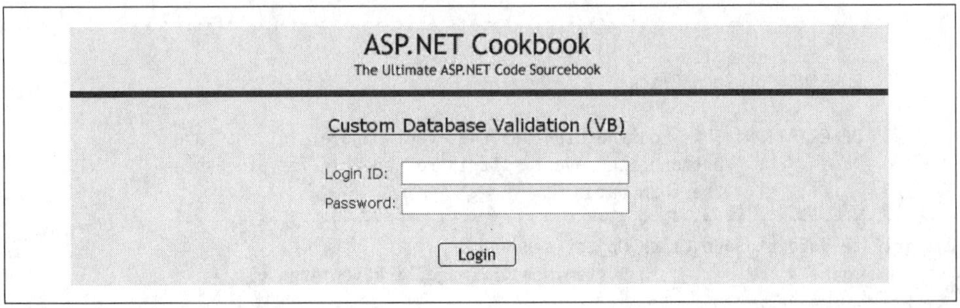

Figure 2-11. Form with database validation output—normal

Discussion

One of the most common examples of when this recipe comes in handy is when implementing a classic login page. The approach we favor in this scenario uses a

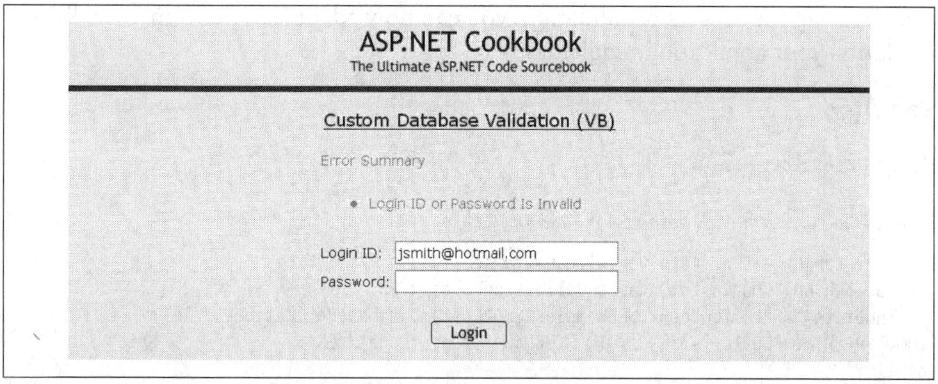

Figure 2-12. Form with database validation output—with error message

`CustomValidator` to perform the user authentication and a `ValidationSummary` to display error information.

In our example, `RequiredFieldValidator` controls are used for the login ID and password fields. (`RequiredFieldValidator` controls are described in Recipe 2.1.) The user must supply both to gain access to her account.

Unlike the other recipes in this chapter, our approach for this recipe has the `CustomValidator` control's `EnableClientScript` attribute set to `False` to disable client-side validation because the database validation can be done only on the server side:

```
<asp:CustomValidator id="cvAuthentication" Runat="server"
            Display="None"
            EnableClientScript="False"
            ErrorMessage="Login ID or Password Is Invalid" />
```

The `ValidationSummary` is set up to display all validation errors. This includes errors from the `RequiredFieldValidator` controls and the `CustomValidator` used for user authentication.

The `ServerValidate` event for the `CustomValidator` (`cvAuthentication_ServerValidate`) is used to perform the user authentication by checking to see if a user exists in the database with the entered login ID and password, as shown in Example 2-11 (VB) and Example 2-12 (C#).

If the user is found in the database, the `args.IsValid` property is set `True` to indicate the validation was successful. Otherwise, it is set `False` to indicate the validation failed.

The event handler for the Login button's click event (`btnLogin_Click`) then checks to see if the page is valid before proceeding with actions required to log the user into the system.

As you may have noticed, the approach used in this recipe is an amalgam of all the approaches used in the chapter's other recipes. Having used this approach to control essentially all the aspects of validation, you can now adapt it to perform virtually any validation your application requires.

See Also

Recipe 2.1; Recipe 2.5

Example 2-10. Form with database validation (.aspx)

```
<%@ Page Language="vb" AutoEventWireup="false"
    Codebehind="CHO2CustomDatabaseValidationVB.aspx.vb"
    Inherits="ASPNetCookbook.VBExamples.CHO2CustomDatabaseValidationVB" %>
<!DOCTYPE HTML PUBLIC "-//W3C//DTD HTML 4.0 Transitional//EN">
<html>
  <head>
    <title>Custom Database Validation</title>
    <link rel="stylesheet" href="css/ASPNetCookbook.css">
  </head>
  <body leftmargin="0" marginheight="0" marginwidth="0" topmargin="0">
    <form id="frmValidation" method="post" runat="server">
      <table width="100%" cellpadding="0" cellspacing="0" border="0">
        <tr>
          <td align="center">
            <img src="images/ASPNETCookbookHeading_blue.gif">
          </td>
        </tr>
        <tr>
          <td class="dividerLine">
            <img src="images/spacer.gif" height="6" border="0"></td>
        </tr>
      </table>
      <table width="90%" align="center" border="0">
        <tr>
          <td><img src="images/spacer.gif" height="10" border="0"></td>
        </tr>
        <tr>
          <td align="center" class="PageHeading">
          Custom Database Validation (VB)
          </td>
        </tr>
        <tr>
          <td><img src="images/spacer.gif" height="10" border="0"></td>
        </tr>
        <tr>
          <td align="center">
            <table border="0">
              <tr>
                <td colspan="2" align="left">
                  <asp:ValidationSummary id="vsErrors" Runat="server"
                                CssClass="AlertText"
                                DisplayMode="BulletList"
                                EnableClientScript="True"
                                HeaderText="Error Summary" />
                  <asp:CustomValidator id="cvAuthentication" Runat="server"
```

Example 2-10. Form with database validation (.aspx) (continued)

```
                        Display="None"
                        EnableClientScript="False"
                        ErrorMessage="Login ID or Password Is Invalid" />
            </td>
        </tr>
        <tr>
          <td class="LabelText">Login ID: </td>
          <td>
            <asp:TextBox id="txtLoginID" Runat="server"
                        Columns="30" CssClass="LabelText" />
            <asp:RequiredFieldValidator id="rfvLoginID"
                    Runat="server"
                    ControlToValidate="txtLoginID"
                    CssClass="AlertText"
                    Display="Dynamic"
                    EnableClientScript="True"
                    ErrorMessage="Login ID Is Required">
                <img src="images/arrow_alert.gif">
            </asp:RequiredFieldValidator>
          </td>
        </tr>
        <tr>
          <td class="LabelText">Password: </td>
          <td>
            <asp:TextBox id="txtPassword" Runat="server"
                        TextMode="Password"
                        Columns="30" CssClass="LabelText" />
            <asp:RequiredFieldValidator id="rfvPassword"
                    Runat="server"
                    ControlToValidate="txtPassword"
                    CssClass="AlertText"
                    Display="Dynamic"
                    EnableClientScript="True"
                    ErrorMessage="Password Is Required">
                <img src="images/arrow_alert.gif">
            </asp:RequiredFieldValidator>
          </td>
        </tr>
        <tr>
          <td colspan="2" align="center">
            <br>
            <asp:ImageButton id="btnLogin" Runat="server"
                    CausesValidation="True"
                    ImageUrl="images/buttons/button_login.gif" />
          </td>
        </tr>
      </table>
    </td>
   </tr>
  </table>
 </form>
 </body>
</html>
```

Example 2-11. Form with database validation code behind (.vb)

```vb
Option Explicit On
Option Strict On
'---------------------------------------------------------------------------
'
'   Module Name: CH02CustomDatabaseValidationVB.aspx.vb
'
'   Description: This module provides the code behind for
'                CH02CustomDatabaseValidationVB.aspx
'
'****************************************************************************
Imports Microsoft.VisualBasic
Imports System.Configuration
Imports System.Data
Imports System.Data.OleDb
Imports System.Web.UI.WebControls

Namespace ASPNetCookbook.VBExamples
  Public Class CH02CustomDatabaseValidationVB
    Inherits System.Web.UI.Page

    'controls on form
    Protected WithEvents cvAuthentication As CustomValidator
    Protected txtLoginID As TextBox
    Protected txtPassword As TextBox
    Protected WithEvents btnLogin As ImageButton

    '****************************************************************************
    '
    '   ROUTINE: Page_Load
    '
    '   DESCRIPTION: This routine provides the event handler for the page load
    '                event.  It is responsible for initializing the controls
    '                on the page.
    '---------------------------------------------------------------------------
    Private Sub Page_Load(ByVal sender As System.Object, _
                          ByVal e As System.EventArgs) _
            Handles MyBase.Load

      If (Not Page.IsPostBack) Then
        'Put user code to initialize the page here
      End If
    End Sub 'Page_Load

    '****************************************************************************
    '
    '   ROUTINE: cvAuthentication_ServerValidate
    '
    '   DESCRIPTION: This routine provides the event handler for the
    '                authentication server validate event.  It is responsible
    '                for checking the login ID and password in the database to
    '                authenticate the user.
    '---------------------------------------------------------------------------
```

Example 2-11. Form with database validation code behind (.vb) (continued)

```vb
Private Sub cvAuthentication_ServerValidate(ByVal source As Object, _
                              ByVal args As ServerValidateEventArgs) _
        Handles cvAuthentication.ServerValidate
  Dim dbConn As OleDbConnection
  Dim dCmd As OleDbCommand
  Dim strConnection As String
  Dim strSQL As String

  Try
    'initially assume credentials are invalid
    args.IsValid = False

    'get the connection string from web.config and open a connection
    'to the database
    strConnection = _
        ConfigurationSettings.AppSettings("dbConnectionString")
    dbConn = New OleDb.OleDbConnection(strConnection)
    dbConn.Open()

    'build the query string and check to see if a user with the entered
    'credentials exists in the database
    strSQL = "SELECT AppUserID FROM AppUser " & _
             "WHERE LoginID=? AND " & _
             "Password=?"
    dCmd = New OleDbCommand(strSQL, dbConn)
    dCmd.Parameters.Add(New OleDbParameter("LoginID", _
                                      txtLoginID.Text))
    dCmd.Parameters.Add(New OleDbParameter("Password", _
                                      txtPassword.Text))

    'check to see if the user was found
    If (Not IsNothing(dCmd.ExecuteScalar())) Then
      args.IsValid = True
    End If

  Finally
    'cleanup
    If (Not IsNothing(dbConn)) Then
      dbConn.Close()
    End If
  End Try
End Sub   'cvAuthentication_ServerValidate

'************************************************************************
'
'   ROUTINE: btnLogin_Click
'
'   DESCRIPTION: This routine provides the event handler for the login
'                button click event.  It is responsible for processing
'                the form data.
'-----------------------------------------------------------------------
Private Sub btnLogin_Click(ByVal sender As Object, _
                      ByVal e As System.Web.UI.ImageClickEventArgs) _
```

Example 2-11. Form with database validation code behind (.vb) (continued)

```vb
        Handles btnLogin.Click

      If (Page.IsValid) Then
        'user has been authenticated so proceed with allowing access
        'to the site
      End If
    End Sub  'btnLogin_Click
  End Class  'CH02CustomDatabaseValidationVB
End Namespace
```

Example 2-12. Form with database validation code behind (.cs)

```cs
//----------------------------------------------------------------------------
//
//   Module Name: CH02CustomDatabaseValidationCS.aspx.cs
//
//   Description: This module provides the code behind for
//                CH02CustomDatabaseValidationCS.aspx
//
//****************************************************************************
using System;
using System.Configuration;
using System.Data;
using System.Data.OleDb;
using System.Web.UI;
using System.Web.UI.WebControls;

namespace ASPNetCookbook.CSExamples
{
  public class CH02CustomDatabaseValidationCS : System.Web.UI.Page
  {
    // controls on form
    protected CustomValidator cvAuthentication;
    protected TextBox txtLoginID;
    protected TextBox txtPassword;
    protected ImageButton btnLogin;

    //****************************************************************************
    //
    //   ROUTINE: Page_Load
    //
    //   DESCRIPTION: This routine provides the event handler for the page
    //                load event.  It is responsible for initializing the
    //                controls on the page.
    //----------------------------------------------------------------------------
    private void Page_Load(object sender, System.EventArgs e)
    {
      // wire the login button click and the authentication validation events
      this.btnLogin.Click += new ImageClickEventHandler(this.btnLogin_Click);
      this.cvAuthentication.ServerValidate +=
        new ServerValidateEventHandler(this.cvAuthentication_ServerValidate);
```

Example 2-12. Form with database validation code behind (.cs) (continued)

```
    if (!Page.IsPostBack)
    {
      //Put user code to initialize the page here
    }
  } // Page_Load

  //*************************************************************************
  //
  //    ROUTINE: cvAuthentication_ServerValidate
  //
  //    DESCRIPTION: This routine provides the event handler for the
  //                 authentication server validate event.  It is
  //                 responsible checking the login ID and password in the
  //                 database to authenticate the user.
  //-------------------------------------------------------------------------
  private void cvAuthentication_ServerValidate(Object source,
                 System.Web.UI.WebControls.ServerValidateEventArgs args)
  {
    OleDbConnection dbConn = null;
    OleDbCommand dCmd = null;
    String strConnection = null;
    String strSQL = null;

    try
    {
      // initially assume credentials are invalid
      args.IsValid = false;

      // get the connection string from web.config and open a connection
      // to the database
      strConnection =
        ConfigurationSettings.AppSettings["dbConnectionString"];
      dbConn = new OleDbConnection(strConnection);
      dbConn.Open( );


      // build the query string and check to see if a user with the
      // entered credentials exists in the database
      strSQL = "SELECT AppUserID FROM AppUser " +
               "WHERE LoginID=? AND " +
               "Password=?";
      dCmd = new OleDbCommand(strSQL, dbConn);
      dCmd.Parameters.Add(new OleDbParameter("LoginID",
                                             txtLoginID.Text));
      dCmd.Parameters.Add(new OleDbParameter("Password",
                                             txtPassword.Text));

      // check to see if the user was found
      if (dCmd.ExecuteScalar( ) != null)
      {
        args.IsValid = true;
      }
```

Example 2-12. Form with database validation code behind (.cs) (continued)

```
    } // try

    finally
    {
      // cleanup
      if (dbConn != null)
      {
        dbConn.Close();
      }
    } // finally
  } // cvAuthentication_ServerValidate


  //**************************************************************************
  //
  //   ROUTINE: btnLogin_Click
  //
  //   DESCRIPTION: This routine provides the event handler for the save
  //                button click event.  It is responsible for processing
  //                the form data.
  //--------------------------------------------------------------------------
  private void btnLogin_Click(Object sender,
                              System.Web.UI.ImageClickEventArgs e)
  {
    if (Page.IsValid)
    {
      // user has been authenticated so proceed with allowing access
      // to the site
    }
  } // btnLogin_Click
} // CH02CustomDatabaseValidationCS
}
```

CHAPTER 3

Forms

3.0 Introduction

Classic ASP developers have become accustomed to certain approaches to performing tasks with forms. The ASP.NET model requires a few changes to these approaches, to say the least.

In particular, one of the toughest things to grow accustomed to is the concept of programming both the server and client sides of an application. Forms are inherently client-side, because that's where they execute and much of their behavior must be handled in the client browser. Sounds simple enough, but getting forms to do your bidding actually requires you to write server-side code that writes the client-side code to be executed when the page is loaded in the browser. And if that weren't enough, consider that the client-side code often needs to be written in JavaScript. Add to that the task of managing the nuances of another scripting language, and you begin to feel as though you're playing 3-D chess.

This chapter provides solutions to many form-related problems that you are likely to encounter in using ASP.NET. By the time you've waded through a recipe or two, the client- and server-side maneuvers required ought to begin to seem fairly manageable.

3.1 Using the Enter Key to Submit a Form

Problem

Ordinarily, a user must click on the Submit button of a form in order to send information entered by a user to a server. You want to use the Enter key for this purpose as well.

Solution

Write some code that generates a client script that captures the keypress event of the browser document object and then checks each keystroke for the Enter key.

In the *.aspx* file, add id and runat attributes to the body element so that the tag's contents can be accessed (and modified) in the code-behind:

```
<body id="pageBody" runat="server"
      leftmargin="0" marginheight="0" marginwidth="0" topmargin="0">
```

In the code-behind class for the page, use the .NET language of your choice to:

1. Call the Add method of the pageBody object's Attributes collection to add the onload attribute to the pageBody control, which causes the captureKeyPress (or equivalently named) client-side script function to be called when the page is first loaded. Your goal is to have HTML like this sent to the browser:

```
<body id="pageBody" leftmargin="0" marginheight="0" marginwidth="0"
      topmargin="0" onload="captureKeyPress();">
```

2. Build a string containing the client-side JavaScript that is to be executed when the page is loaded and that causes it to be output as part of the rendered page. The client-side script must capture the keypress event in the browser, check to see if the key pressed is the Enter key, and perform the form submittal, as the following JavaScript does:

```
<script language='javascript'>
<!--
  function captureKeyPress()
  {
    document.onkeypress = checkForReturn;
  }

  function checkForReturn()
  {
    if (window.event.keyCode==13)
    {
      if (window.event.srcElement.id != 'btnCancel')
      {
        window.event.keyCode=0;
        __doPostBack('btnSave','');
      }
    }
  }
//-->
</script>
```

3. Use the RegisterClientScriptBlock method of the Page object to register the script block so that it is output when the page is rendered.

Examples 3-1 through 3-3 show the *.aspx* and code-behind files for an application that makes use of this solution.

 This code will work only with Internet Explorer. In Netscape, the client script required to capture the keypress event and process the key presses is quite different and beyond the scope of this book; however, the "See Also" section of this recipe references a JavaScript book that can help you through the browser-specific aspects of JavaScript.

Discussion

The idea behind our solution is to use client script to capture the keypress event of the browser document object so you can check each keystroke for the Enter key. After the Enter key is detected, the client script calls the client-side method provided by ASP.NET to perform a postback of the form to the server.

In terms of the client script, the solution we advocate involves starting with some skeleton JavaScript and then generating the rest on the fly. The best way to describe how this is done is by turning to our example.

Before we delve into the example, though, you might be wondering why our solution doesn't place all of the JavaScript code directly in the *.aspx* file from the start instead of generating it on the fly. The reason is that such an approach requires you to hardcode the IDs of the buttons and the name of the ASP.NET-generated postback function in the client script. Our approach has the distinct advantage that it will not break if the IDs of the buttons are changed or if the name of the postback function is changed in a later release of ASP.NET.

Our explanation of the example begins with the client-side JavaScript that we cause to be generated in the code-behind. We then delve into the code in the code-behind that generates it.

The client-side JavaScript that is to be generated by the code-behind is shown next. It consists of two functions: captureKeyPress and checkForReturn.

```
<script language='javascript'>
<!--
  function captureKeyPress()
  {
    document.onkeypress = checkForReturn;
  }

  function checkForReturn()
  {
    if (window.event.keyCode==13)
    {
      if (window.event.srcElement.id != 'btnCancel')
      {
        window.event.keyCode=0;
        __doPostBack('btnSave','');
      }
    }
  }
//-->
</script>
```

The captureKeyPress function sets the checkForReturn function to be executed anytime a key is pressed in the browser.

The checkForReturn function first checks to see if the key pressed is the Enter key (keycode 13). If so, it then checks the source of the event. The Enter key should cause a form postback, with the source of the postback set to the Save button in all cases, except when the Cancel button is the source. This check is important because without it, hitting the Enter key when the Cancel button is the selected control results in a postback with both the Save and Cancel button click events raised.

If the key pressed is the Enter key and the source of the keypress event is not the Cancel button, the event keycode is set to 0 to stop further processing of the keypress event. Then the ASP.NET postback function is called, passing the Save button as the source of the postback (first parameter) and no arguments for the postback event (second parameter).

In this example, the body element is modified in the code-behind. To provide access to the body element in the code-behind, the id and runat attributes are added:

```
<body id="pageBody" runat="server"
      leftmargin="0" marginheight="0" marginwidth="0" topmargin="0">
```

All work in the code-behind is done in the Page_Load method. The first operation performed is to call the Add method of the pageBody object's Attributes collection to add the onload attribute to the pageBody control, which causes the captureKeyPress client-side script function to be called when the page is first loaded.

This results in the following HTML being sent to the browser:

```
<body id="pageBody" leftmargin="0" marginheight="0" marginwidth="0"
      topmargin="0" onload="captureKeyPress();">
```

The remainder of the Page_Load method builds a string containing the client-side JavaScript and causes it to be output as part of the rendered page. This code begins by creating a new StringBuilder object named clientScript and adds the opening script block code to it. It then adds the code to define the captureKeyPress function to the clientScript StringBuilder.

Using the StringBuilder class makes a lot of sense here because of all the appending that is being done to the clientScript string. If the String class had been used instead, ASP.NET would have returned a new String every time a modification was made to clientScript, slowing down execution. This is a good example of where using the StringBuilder class can really improve performance. Refer to Recipe 16.2 for additional information on String performance.

Next, the code adds the checkForReturn function to the clientScript StringBuilder. The following highlighted code sections provide the ASCII value of the Enter keycode, the name of the Cancel button, and the name of the method created by ASP.NET to process the page postback (__doPostBack). Using this approach improves the maintainability of your code by allowing you to change the ID of the Cancel button or the name of the postback function without requiring you to modify this code.

The GetPostBackClientEvent is passed two parameters, as highlighted in the following code. The first is a reference to the control that caused the postback. Setting this to the Save button will cause the Save button's click event to be raised when the page is posted back. The second parameter contains the arguments that are passed to the Save button click event; no arguments are actually required here.

```vb
functionScript = "if (window.event.keyCode==" & Asc(NewLine) & ") " & _
        "{" & NewLine & _
        "if (window.event.srcElement.id!='" & btnCancel.ID & "') " & _
        "{" & NewLine & _
        "window.event.keyCode=0;" & NewLine & _
        GetPostBackClientEvent(btnSave, "") & ";" & NewLine & _
        "}" & NewLine & _
        "}" & NewLine
clientScript.Append("function checkForReturn()" & NewLine)
clientScript.Append("{" & NewLine)
clientScript.Append(functionScript)
clientScript.Append("}" & NewLine)
```

```csharp
functionScript = "if (window.event.keyCode==" +
    System.Convert.ToByte(NEW_LINE).ToString() + ") " +
    "{" + NEW_LINE +
    "if (window.event.srcElement.id!='" + btnCancel.ID + "') " +
    "{" + NEW_LINE +
    "window.event.keyCode=0;" + NEW_LINE +
    GetPostBackClientEvent(btnSave, "") + ";" + NEW_LINE +
    "}" + NEW_LINE +
    "}" + NEW_LINE;
clientScript.Append("function checkForReturn()" + NEW_LINE);
clientScript.Append("{" + NEW_LINE);
clientScript.Append(functionScript);
clientScript.Append("}" + NEW_LINE);
```

Finally, the closing </script> tag is added to the clientScript StringBuilder.

The code shown here registers the script block to be output when the page is rendered:

```vb
Page.RegisterClientScriptBlock("ScriptBlock", _
                            clientScript.ToString())
```

```csharp
Page.RegisterClientScriptBlock("ScriptBlock",
                            clientScript.ToString());
```

 The code shown in the Page_Load method must be executed anytime the page is displayed. In this example, this is accomplished by generating the client script in the Page_Load method without checking to see if the page is initially being displayed or if a postback is being performed. Although this approach works, it can result in generating the client script even when the page is not going to be displayed, such as when a postback results in displaying a different page. Refer to Recipe 3.2 for a more efficient example of generating the client script.

See Also

The sidebar "Building a JavaScript Library" in Recipe 3.5 for information on creating a reusable library of JavaScript functions; Recipe 16.2 for improving String operation performance; *JavaScript: The Definitive Guide*, by David Flanagan (O'Reilly), for more information on browser-specific JavaScript

Example 3-1. Using the Enter key to submit a form (.aspx)

```
<%@ Page Language="vb" AutoEventWireup="false"
        Codebehind="CHO3EnterSubmitVB.aspx.vb"
        Inherits="ASPNetCookbook.VBExamples.CHO3EnterSubmitVB" %>
<!DOCTYPE HTML PUBLIC "-//W3C//DTD HTML 4.0 Transitional//EN">
<html>
  <head>
    <title>Using Enter To Submit Form</title>
    <link rel="stylesheet" href="css/ASPNetCookbook.css">
  </head>
  <body id="pageBody" runat="server"
        leftmargin="0" marginheight="0" marginwidth="0" topmargin="0">
    <form id="frmEnterCapture" method="post" runat="server">
      <table width="100%" cellpadding="0" cellspacing="0" border="0">
        <tr>
          <td align="center">
            <img src="images/ASPNETCookbookHeading_blue.gif">
          </td>
        </tr>
        <tr>
          <td class="dividerLine">
            <img src="images/spacer.gif" height="6" border="0"></td>
        </tr>
      </table>
      <table width="90%" align="center" border="0">
        <tr>
          <td><img src="images/spacer.gif" height="10" border="0"></td>
        </tr>
        <tr>
          <td align="center" class="PageHeading">
            Using Enter To Submit Form (VB)
          </td>
        </tr>
        <tr>
          <td><img src="images/spacer.gif" height="10" border="0"></td>
        </tr>
        <tr>
          <td align="center">
            <table border="0">
              <tr>
                <td class="LabelText">Email Address: </td>
                <td>
                  <asp:TextBox ID="txtEmailAddress" Runat="server"
                               Columns="30" CssClass="LabelText" />
                </td>
              </tr>
```

Example 3-1. Using the Enter key to submit a form (.aspx) (continued)

```
        <tr>
          <td class="LabelText">Password: </td>
          <td>
            <asp:TextBox ID="txtPassword" Runat="server"
                        textmode="Password"
                        Columns="30" CssClass="LabelText" />
          </td>
        </tr>
        <tr>
          <td colspan="2">
            <br>
            <table align="center" width="50%">
              <tr>
                <td align="center">
                  <asp:ImageButton ID="btnLogin" Runat="server"
                        ImageUrl="images/buttons/button_login.gif" />
                </td>
                <td align="center">
                  <asp:ImageButton ID="btnCancel" Runat="server"
                        ImageUrl="images/buttons/button_cancel.gif" />
                </td>
              </tr>
            </table>
          </td>
        </tr>
      </table>
    </td>
  </tr>
    </table>
  </form>
 </body>
</html>
```

Example 3-2. Using the Enter key to submit a form code-behind (.vb)

```
Option Explicit On
Option Strict On
'-----------------------------------------------------------------------------
'
'   Module Name: CH03EnterSubmitVB.aspx.vb
'
'   Description: This module provides the code behind for
'                CH03EnterSubmitVB.aspx
'
'*****************************************************************************
Imports Microsoft.VisualBasic
Imports System.Environment
Imports System.Text

Namespace ASPNetCookbook.VBExamples
  Public Class CH03EnterSubmitVB
    Inherits System.Web.UI.Page
```

```vb
'controls on form
Protected pageBody As System.Web.UI.HtmlControls.HtmlGenericControl
Protected WithEvents btnLogin As System.Web.UI.WebControls.ImageButton
Protected WithEvents btnCancel As System.Web.UI.WebControls.ImageButton

'**************************************************************************
'
'   ROUTINE: Page_Load
'
'   DESCRIPTION: This routine provides the event handler for the page load
'                event.  It is responsible for initializing the controls
'                on the page.
'-------------------------------------------------------------------------
Private Sub Page_Load(ByVal sender As System.Object, _
                     ByVal e As System.EventArgs) Handles MyBase.Load

    Dim clientScript As StringBuilder
    Dim functionScript As String

    'add onload attribute to the page body to add a handler to the
    'keypress event for the page
    pageBody.Attributes.Add("onload", _
                           "captureKeyPress();")

    'generate the opening script tag
    clientScript = New StringBuilder
    clientScript.Append("<script language='javascript'>" & NewLine)
    clientScript.Append("<!--" & NewLine)

    'add the client script used to capture the keypress event
    functionScript = "document.onkeypress = checkForReturn;" & NewLine
    clientScript.Append("function captureKeyPress()" & NewLine)
    clientScript.Append("{" & NewLine)
    clientScript.Append(functionScript)
    clientScript.Append("}" & NewLine)

    'add the client script to check the keypress event
    functionScript = "if (window.event.keyCode==" & Asc(NewLine) & ") " & _
            "{" & NewLine & _
            "if (window.event.srcElement.id!='" & btnCancel.ID & "') " & _
            "{" & NewLine & _
            "window.event.keyCode=0;" & NewLine & _
            GetPostBackClientEvent(btnLogin, "") & ";" & NewLine & _
            "}" & NewLine & _
            "}" & NewLine
    clientScript.Append("function checkForReturn()" & NewLine)
    clientScript.Append("{" & NewLine)
    clientScript.Append(functionScript)
    clientScript.Append("}" & NewLine)

    'generate the closing script tag
    clientScript.Append("//-->" & NewLine)
```

Example 3-2. Using the Enter key to submit a form code-behind (.vb) (continued)

```vb
        clientScript.Append("</script>" & NewLine)

        'register the client script to be output when the page is rendered
        Page.RegisterClientScriptBlock("ScriptBlock", _
                                        clientScript.ToString())
    End Sub 'Page_Load

    '*************************************************************************
    '
    '    ROUTINE: btnLogin_Click
    '
    '    DESCRIPTION: This routine provides the event handler for the login
    '                 button click event.  It is responsible for processing
    '                 the form data.
    '-------------------------------------------------------------------------
    Private Sub btnLogin_Click(ByVal sender As Object, _
                               ByVal e As System.Web.UI.ImageClickEventArgs) _
        Handles btnLogin.Click

        'perform login operations here
    End Sub 'btnLogin_Click

    '*************************************************************************
    '
    '    ROUTINE: btnCancel_Click
    '
    '    DESCRIPTION: This routine provides the event handler for the cancel
    '                 button click event.
    '-------------------------------------------------------------------------
    Private Sub btnCancel_Click(ByVal sender As Object, _
                                ByVal e As System.Web.UI.ImageClickEventArgs) _
        Handles btnCancel.Click

        'perform cancel operations here
    End Sub 'btnCancel_Click
  End Class 'CH03EnterSubmitVB
End Namespace
```

Example 3-3. Using the Enter key to submit a form code-behind (.cs)

```cs
//-----------------------------------------------------------------------------
//
//    Module Name: CH03EnterSubmitCS.aspx.cs
//
//    Description: This module provides the code behind for
//                 CH03EnterSubmitCS.aspx
//
//*************************************************************************
using System;
using System.Text;
using System.Web.UI;
using System.Web.UI.HtmlControls;
using System.Web.UI.WebControls;
```

Example 3-3. Using the Enter key to submit a form code-behind (.cs) (continued)

```
namespace ASPNetCookbook.CSExamples
{
  public class CH03EnterSubmitCS : System.Web.UI.Page
  {
    // controls on form
    protected System.Web.UI.HtmlControls.HtmlGenericControl pageBody;
    protected System.Web.UI.WebControls.ImageButton btnLogin;
    protected System.Web.UI.WebControls.ImageButton btnCancel;

    //*************************************************************************
    //
    //   ROUTINE: Page_Load
    //
    //   DESCRIPTION: This routine provides the event handler for the page
    //                load event.  It is responsible for initializing the
    //                controls on the page.
    //-------------------------------------------------------------------------
    private void Page_Load(object sender, System.EventArgs e)
    {
      const char NEW_LINE = '\r';

      StringBuilder clientScript = null;
      String functionScript = null;

      // wire the login and cancel button click events
      this.btnLogin.Click += new ImageClickEventHandler(this.btnLogin_Click);
      this.btnCancel.Click +=
        new ImageClickEventHandler(this.btnCancel_Click);

      // add onload attribute to the page body to add a handler to the
      // keypress event for the page
      pageBody.Attributes.Add("onload",
                              "captureKeyPress();");

      // generate the opening script tag
      clientScript = new StringBuilder();
      clientScript.Append("<script language='javascript'>" + NEW_LINE);
      clientScript.Append("<!--" + NEW_LINE);

      // add the client script used to capture the keypress event
      functionScript = "document.onkeypress = checkForReturn;" + NEW_LINE;
      clientScript.Append("function captureKeyPress()" + NEW_LINE);
      clientScript.Append("{" + NEW_LINE);
      clientScript.Append(functionScript);
      clientScript.Append("}" + NEW_LINE);

      // add the client script to check the keypress event
      functionScript = "if (window.event.keyCode==" +
                  System.Convert.ToByte(NEW_LINE).ToString() + ") " +
                  "{" + NEW_LINE +
```

```
                    "if (window.event.srcElement.id!='" + btnCancel.ID + "') " +
                    "{" + NEW_LINE +
                    "window.event.keyCode=0;" + NEW_LINE +
                    GetPostBackClientEvent(btnLogin, "") + ";" + NEW_LINE +
                    "}" + NEW_LINE +
                    "}" + NEW_LINE;
        clientScript.Append("function checkForReturn()" + NEW_LINE);
        clientScript.Append("{" + NEW_LINE);
        clientScript.Append(functionScript);
        clientScript.Append("}" + NEW_LINE);

        // generate the closing script tag
        clientScript.Append("//-->" + NEW_LINE);
        clientScript.Append("</script>" + NEW_LINE);

        // register the client script to be output when the page is rendered
        Page.RegisterClientScriptBlock("ScriptBlock",
                                    clientScript.ToString());
    }  // Page_Load

    //*************************************************************************
    //
    //    ROUTINE: btnLogin_Click
    //
    //    DESCRIPTION: This routine provides the event handler for the login
    //                 button click event.  It is responsible for processing
    //                 the form data.
    //
    //-------------------------------------------------------------------------
    private void btnLogin_Click(Object sender,
                                System.Web.UI.ImageClickEventArgs e)
    {
      // perform login operations here
    }  // btnLogin_Click

    //*************************************************************************
    //
    //    ROUTINE: btnCancel_Click
    //
    //    DESCRIPTION: This routine provides the event handler for the cancel
    //                 button click event.
    //
    //-------------------------------------------------------------------------
    private void btnCancel_Click(Object sender,
                                System.Web.UI.ImageClickEventArgs e)
    {
      // perform cancel operations here
    }  // btnCancel_Click
  }  // CHO3EnterSubmitCS
}
```

3.2 Using the Enter Key to Submit a Form After Validation

Problem

You want to use the Enter key to submit the information entered by a user to the server, but your form uses client-side validation that must be performed before the form is submitted.

Solution

Write code that generates some JavaScript that captures the keypress event in the browser, checks to see if the key pressed is the Enter key, performs the client-side validation, and then submits the form.

In the *.aspx* file, add id and runat attributes to the body element so that all the tag's contents can be accessed (and modified) in the code-behind:

```
<body id="pageBody" runat="server"
      leftmargin="0" marginheight="0" marginwidth="0" topmargin="0">
```

In the code-behind class for the page, use the .NET language of your choice to:

1. Call the Add method of the pageBody object's Attributes collection to add the onload attribute to the pageBody control, which causes the captureKeyPress (or equivalently named) client-side script function to be called when the page is first loaded. Your goal is to have HTML like this sent to the browser:

   ```
   <body id="pageBody" leftmargin="0" marginheight="0" marginwidth="0"
         topmargin="0" onload="captureKeyPress();">
   ```

2. Build a string containing the client-side JavaScript that is to be executed when the page is loaded and causes it to be output as part of the rendered page; the client-side script must capture the keypress event in the browser, check to see if the key pressed is the Enter key, perform the client-side validation, and perform the form submittal:

   ```
   <script language='javascript'>
   <!--
     function captureKeyPress()
     {
       document.onkeypress = checkForReturn;
     }

     function checkForReturn()
     {
       if (window.event.keyCode==13)
       {
         if (window.event.srcElement.id!='btnCancel')
         {
   ```

```
              if (typeof(Page_ValidationActive) != 'undefined')
              {
                if (Page_ValidationActive)
                {
                  if (Page_ClientValidate())
                  {
                    window.event.keyCode=0;
                    __doPostBack('btnSave','');
                  }
                }
              }
            }
          }
        }
      }
    }
//-->
</script>
```

3. Use the `RegisterClientScriptBlock` method of the `Page` object to register the script block so that it is output when the page is rendered.

Examples 3-4 through 3-6 show the *.aspx* and code-behind files for an application that implements this solution.

Discussion

In its use of client script to capture the keypress event of the browser document object and watch for use of the Enter key, this solution is like the one we present in Recipe 3.1. What is unique is the way this solution leverages the JavaScript functions provided in the ASP.NET *WebUIValidation.js*. ASP.NET automatically includes this file in rendered pages that use client-side validation. As its name implies, *WebUIValidation.js* is a script library that contains functions housing all of the logic that ASP.NET uses for client-side validation. Indeed, every validation control emits a standard block of client script into the page, whose function is to call relevant code in *WebUIValidation.js*. The validation script library is referenced with the following code, which ASP.NET generates automatically and which you can see when you view the source of a rendered page:

```
<script language="javascript"
  src="/aspnet_client/system_web/1_1_4322/WebUIValidation.js">
</script>
```

 The value for the `src` attribute will vary depending on the version of ASP.NET installed on the web server. However, because this value is automatically generated by ASP.NET when the page is rendered, you can ignore it.

From here on, we concentrate on the validation code used in our example, because that is what is unique about this recipe. See Recipe 3.1 for an explanation of the base code that the two examples share.

In this example, we have added RequiredFieldValidator controls, which perform as their name implies and are highlighted in the code listing shown in Example 3-4. Validators are described in Chapter 2.

The client-side JavaScript generated by this example is shown next. The generated code is similar to the JavaScript in Recipe 3.1, but includes additional code to be processed after the key is identified as the Enter key, provided the Cancel button does not have the focus when Enter is pressed.

```
<script language='javascript'>
<!--
  function captureKeyPress()
  {
    document.onkeypress = checkForReturn;
  }

  function checkForReturn()
  {
    if (window.event.keyCode==13)
    {
      if (window.event.srcElement.id!='btnCancel')
      {
        if (typeof(Page_ValidationActive) != 'undefined')
        {
          if (Page_ValidationActive)
          {
            if (Page_ClientValidate())
            {
              window.event.keyCode=0;
              __doPostBack('btnSave','');
            }
          }
        }
      }
    }
  }
//-->
</script>
```

In the preceding code, a check is made to ensure the validation functions are included in the rendered page. Next, a check is made to ensure validation is active.

If the validation functions are included in the rendered page and validation is active, the client-side validation is performed.

If the client validation passes the tests defined by the validators on the page, the event keycode is set to 0 to stop further processing of the keypress event, and the page is posted back.

The code-behind in Examples 3.2 and 3.3 has been altered to build the client script in a separate routine, generateClientScript, so it can be called by more than one method. The only change to the code used to generate the client-side JavaScript in those examples is in the code that generates the checkForReturn function—it now includes the extra checks mentioned earlier and performs validation.

 The example code shown in this recipe provides a more efficient approach to generating the client script than that in Examples 3-2 and 3-3. In the Page_Load method, a check is made to see if the form is being posted back to the server. If it is, the client script is not generated in the Page_Load method, providing the ability to decide if the page will be redisplayed and thus requiring the client script to be generated in the Save and Cancel button click events. If another page is to be displayed after processing the Save or Cancel click events, the call to generate the client script should not be made, saving unnecessary work.

See Also

Recipe 3.1; Chapter 2 for form validation examples

Example 3-4. Using the Enter key to submit a form after validation (.aspx)

```
<%@ Page Language="vb" AutoEventWireup="false"
         Codebehind="CH03EnterSubmitWithValidationVB.aspx.vb"
         Inherits="ASPNetCookbook.VBExamples.CH03EnterSubmitWithValidationVB" %>
<!DOCTYPE HTML PUBLIC "-//W3C//DTD HTML 4.0 Transitional//EN">
<html>
  <head>
    <title>Using Enter To Submit Form With Validation</title>
    <link rel="stylesheet" href="css/ASPNetCookbook.css">
  </head>
  <body id="pageBody" runat="server"
        leftmargin="0" marginheight="0" marginwidth="0" topmargin="0">
    <form id="frmEnterCapture" method="post" runat="server">
      <table width="100%" cellpadding="0" cellspacing="0" border="0">
        <tr>
          <td align="center">
            <img src="images/ASPNETCookbookHeading_blue.gif">
          </td>
        </tr>
        <tr>
          <td class="dividerLine">
            <img src="images/spacer.gif" height="6" border="0"></td>
        </tr>
      </table>
      <table width="90%" align="center" border="0">
        <tr>
          <td><img src="images/spacer.gif" height="10" border="0"></td>
        </tr>
        <tr>
          <td align="center" class="PageHeading">
            Using Enter To Submit Form With Validation (VB)
          </td>
```

```
      </tr>
      <tr>
        <td><img src="images/spacer.gif" height="10" border="0"></td>
      </tr>
      <tr>
        <td align="center">
          <table border="0">
            <tr>
              <td class="LabelText">Email Address: </td>
              <td>
                <asp:TextBox ID="txtEmailAddress" Runat="server"
                            Columns="30" CssClass="LabelText" />
                <asp:requiredfieldvalidator id="rfvLoginID"
                    runat="server"
                    controltovalidate="txtEmailAddress"
                    cssclass="AlertText"
                    display="Dynamic"
                    enableclientscript="True">
                  <img src="images/arrow_alert.gif"> Email Address Is Required
                </asp:requiredfieldvalidator>
              </td>
            </tr>
            <tr>
              <td class="LabelText">Password: </td>
              <td>
                <asp:TextBox ID="txtPassword" Runat="server"
                            textmode="Password"
                            Columns="30" CssClass="LabelText" />
                <asp:requiredfieldvalidator id="rfvPassword"
                    runat="server"
                    controltovalidate="txtPassword"
                    cssclass="AlertText"
                    display="Dynamic"
                    enableclientscript="True">
                  <img src="images/arrow_alert.gif"> Password Is Required
                </asp:requiredfieldvalidator>
              </td>
            </tr>
            <tr>
              <td colspan="2">
                <br>
                <table align="center" width="50%">
                  <tr>
                    <td align="center">
                      <asp:ImageButton ID="btnLogin" Runat="server"
                          CausesValidation="True"
                          ImageUrl="images/buttons/button_login.gif" />
                    </td>
                    <td align="center">
                      <asp:ImageButton ID="btnCancel" Runat="server"
                          CausesValidation="False"
```

Example 3-4. Using the Enter key to submit a form after validation (.aspx) (continued)

```
                              ImageUrl="images/buttons/button_cancel.gif" />
                      </td>
                    </tr>
                  </table>
                </td>
              </tr>
            </table>
          </td>
        </tr>
      </table>
    </form>
  </body>
</html>
```

Example 3-5. Using the Enter key to submit a form after validation code-behind (.vb)

```vb
Option Explicit On
Option Strict On
'-----------------------------------------------------------------------------
'
'   Module Name: CH03EnterSubmitWithValidationVB.aspx.vb
'
'   Description: This module provides the code behind for
'                CH03EnterSubmitWithValidationVB.aspx
'
'*****************************************************************************
Imports Microsoft.VisualBasic
Imports System.Environment
Imports System.Text

Namespace ASPNetCookbook.VBExamples
  Public Class CH03EnterSubmitWithValidationVB
    Inherits System.Web.UI.Page

    'controls on form
    Protected pageBody As System.Web.UI.HtmlControls.HtmlGenericControl
    Protected WithEvents btnLogin As System.Web.UI.WebControls.ImageButton
    Protected WithEvents btnCancel As System.Web.UI.WebControls.ImageButton

    '*****************************************************************************
    '
    '   ROUTINE: Page_Load
    '
    '   DESCRIPTION: This routine provides the event handler for the page load
    '                event.  It is responsible for initializing the controls
    '                on the page.
    '-----------------------------------------------------------------------------
    Private Sub Page_Load(ByVal sender As System.Object, _
                        ByVal e As System.EventArgs) Handles MyBase.Load
      If (Not Page.IsPostBack) Then
        generateClientScript()
      End If
```

```vb
End Sub   'Page_Load

'************************************************************************
'
'    ROUTINE: btnLogin_Click
'
'    DESCRIPTION: This routine provides the event handler for the login
'                 button click event.  It is responsible processing the
'                 form data.
'-----------------------------------------------------------------------
Private Sub btnLogin_Click(ByVal sender As Object, _
                         ByVal e As System.Web.UI.ImageClickEventArgs) _
        Handles btnLogin.Click

   If (Page.IsValid) Then
     'perform login operations here and redirect to the next page
   Else
     'generate the client JavaScript since the page was not valid and
     'must be redisplayed
     generateClientScript( )
   End If
End Sub   'btnLogin_Click

'************************************************************************
'
'    ROUTINE: btnCancel_Click
'
'    DESCRIPTION: This routine provides the event handler for the cancel
'                 button click event.
'-----------------------------------------------------------------------
Private Sub btnCancel_Click(ByVal sender As Object, _
                         ByVal e As System.Web.UI.ImageClickEventArgs) _
        Handles btnCancel.Click

   'perform cancel operations here
End Sub   'btnCancel_Click

'************************************************************************
'
'    ROUTINE: generateClientScript
'
'    DESCRIPTION: This routine generates the client-side JavaScript used
'                 to capture the Enter key and process it as a form
'                 submittal
'-----------------------------------------------------------------------
Private Sub generateClientScript( )

   Dim clientScript As StringBuilder
   Dim functionScript As String
```

```vb
        'add onload attribute to the page body to add a handler to the
        'keypress event for the page
        pageBody.Attributes.Add("onload", _
                                "captureKeyPress();")

        'generate the opening script tag
        clientScript = New StringBuilder
        clientScript.Append("<script language='javascript'>" & NewLine)
        clientScript.Append("<!--" & NewLine)

        'add the client script used to capture the keypress event
        functionScript = "document.onkeypress = checkForReturn;" & NewLine
        clientScript.Append("function captureKeyPress()" & NewLine)
        clientScript.Append("{" & NewLine)
        clientScript.Append(functionScript)
        clientScript.Append("}" & NewLine)

        'add the client script to check the keypress event
        functionScript = "if (window.event.keyCode==" & Asc(NewLine) & ") " & _
            "{" & NewLine & _
            "if (window.event.srcElement.id!='" & btnCancel.ID & "') " & _
            "{" & NewLine & _
            "if (typeof(Page_ValidationActive) != 'undefined')" & NewLine & _
            "{" & NewLine & _
            "if (Page_ValidationActive)" & NewLine & _
            "{" & NewLine & _
            "if (Page_ClientValidate())" & NewLine & _
            "{" & NewLine & _
            "window.event.keyCode=0;" & NewLine & _
            GetPostBackClientEvent(btnLogin, "") & ";" & NewLine & _
            "}" & NewLine & _
            "}" & NewLine & _
            "}" & NewLine & _
            "}" & NewLine & _
            "}" & NewLine
        clientScript.Append("function checkForReturn()" & NewLine)
        clientScript.Append("{" & NewLine)
        clientScript.Append(functionScript)
        clientScript.Append("}" & NewLine)

        'generate the closing script tag
        clientScript.Append("//-->" & NewLine)
        clientScript.Append("</script>" & NewLine)

        'register the client script to be output when the page is rendered
        Page.RegisterClientScriptBlock("ScriptBlock", _
                                clientScript.ToString())
    End Sub 'generateClientScript
  End Class 'CH03EnterSubmitWithValidationVB
End Namespace
```

Example 3-6. Using the Enter key to submit a form after validation code-behind (.cs)

```
//--------------------------------------------------------------------------
//
//    Module Name: CH03EnterSubmitWithValidationCS.aspx.cs
//
//    Description: This module provides the code behind for
//                 CH03EnterSubmitWithValidationCS.aspx
//
//**************************************************************************
using System;
using System.Text;
using System.Web.UI;
using System.Web.UI.HtmlControls;
using System.Web.UI.WebControls;

namespace ASPNetCookbook.CSExamples
{
  public class CH03EnterSubmitWithValidationCS : System.Web.UI.Page
  {
    // controls on form
    protected System.Web.UI.HtmlControls.HtmlGenericControl pageBody;
    protected System.Web.UI.WebControls.ImageButton btnLogin;
    protected System.Web.UI.WebControls.ImageButton btnCancel;

    //**********************************************************************
    //
    //    ROUTINE: Page_Load
    //
    //    DESCRIPTION: This routine provides the event handler for the page
    //                 load event.  It is responsible for initializing the
    //                 controls on the page.
    //----------------------------------------------------------------------
    private void Page_Load(object sender, System.EventArgs e)
    {
      // wire the login and cancel button click events
      this.btnLogin.Click += new ImageClickEventHandler(this.btnLogin_Click);
      this.btnCancel.Click +=
        new ImageClickEventHandler(this.btnCancel_Click);

      if (!Page.IsPostBack)
      {
        generateClientScript();
      }
    } // Page_Load

    //**********************************************************************
    //
    //    ROUTINE: btnLogin_Click
    //
    //    DESCRIPTION: This routine provides the event handler for the login
    //                 button click event.  It is responsible processing the
    //                 form data.
    //----------------------------------------------------------------------
```

```
private void btnLogin_Click(Object sender,
                            System.Web.UI.ImageClickEventArgs e)
{
  if (Page.IsValid)
  {
    // perform login operations here and redirect to the next page
  }
  else
  {
    // generate the client JavaScript since the page was not valid and
    // 'must be redisplayed
    generateClientScript();
  }
} // btnLogin_Click

//*************************************************************************
//
//    ROUTINE: btnCancel_Click
//
//    DESCRIPTION: This routine provides the event handler for the cancel
//                 button click event.
//-------------------------------------------------------------------------
private void btnCancel_Click(Object sender,
  System.Web.UI.ImageClickEventArgs e)
{
  // perform cancel operations here
} // btnCancel_Click

//*************************************************************************
//
//    ROUTINE: generateClientScript
//
//    DESCRIPTION: This routine generates the client-side JavaScript used
//                 to capture the Enter key and process it as a form
//                 submittal
//-------------------------------------------------------------------------
private void generateClientScript()
{
  const char NEW_LINE = '\r';

  StringBuilder clientScript = null;
  String functionScript = null;

  // add onload attribute to the page body to add a handler to the
  // keypress event for the page
  pageBody.Attributes.Add("onload",
                          "captureKeyPress();");

  // generate the opening script tag
  clientScript = new StringBuilder();
  clientScript.Append("<script language='javascript'>" + NEW_LINE);
  clientScript.Append("<!--" + NEW_LINE);
```

```
        // add the client script used to capture the keypress event
        functionScript = "document.onkeypress = checkForReturn;" + NEW_LINE;
        clientScript.Append("function captureKeyPress()" + NEW_LINE);
        clientScript.Append("{" + NEW_LINE);
        clientScript.Append(functionScript);
        clientScript.Append("}" + NEW_LINE);

        // add the client script to check the keypress event
        functionScript = "if (window.event.keyCode==" +
                System.Convert.ToByte(NEW_LINE).ToString() + ") " +
                "{" + NEW_LINE +
                "if (window.event.srcElement.id!='" + btnCancel.ID + "') " +
                "{" + NEW_LINE +
                "if (typeof(Page_ValidationActive) != 'undefined')" + NEW_LINE +
                "{" + NEW_LINE +
                "if (Page_ValidationActive)" + NEW_LINE +
                "{" + NEW_LINE +
                "if (Page_ClientValidate())" + NEW_LINE +
                "{" + NEW_LINE +
                "window.event.keyCode=0;" + NEW_LINE +
                GetPostBackClientEvent(btnLogin, "") + ";" + NEW_LINE +
                "}" + NEW_LINE +
                "}" + NEW_LINE +
                "}" + NEW_LINE +
                "}" + NEW_LINE +
                "}" + NEW_LINE;
        clientScript.Append("function checkForReturn()" + NEW_LINE);
        clientScript.Append("{" + NEW_LINE);
        clientScript.Append(functionScript);
        clientScript.Append("}" + NEW_LINE);

        // generate the closing script tag
        clientScript.Append("//-->" + NEW_LINE);
        clientScript.Append("</script>" + NEW_LINE);

        // register the client script to be output when the page is rendered
        Page.RegisterClientScriptBlock("ScriptBlock",
                                    clientScript.ToString());
    } // generateClientScript
} // CH03EnterSubmitWithValidationCS
}
```

3.3   Submitting a Form to a Different Page

Problem

You need to submit the information on one page—a form, for example—to another.
You might want to do this in order to use one page to collect form data and a second page to process it.

The ASP.NET model does not "normally" support submitting a form to any page other than itself. If you are willing to revert to the classic ASP model by removing the runat="server" attribute from the form element, the page can be submitted to any other page in the same manner, as was done in ASP pages. We don't recommend this approach, however, because it does not take advantage of the built-in functionality provided by the server controls to automatically recreate the controls and populate them with the data submitted with the form, making your coding tasks much harder.

Solution

There are two ways to solve this problem:

- Use the Server.Transfer method in a button click event handler in the code-behind of the first page to transfer control to a second page, after saving the contents of the first in session scope. Examples 3-7 through 3-12 show the *.aspx* and code-behind files for the application that implements this solution.

- Use the Server.Transfer method in a button click event handler in the code-behind of the first page to transfer control, along with the form contents in the viewstate, to the second page. This approach is described at the end of the "Discussion" section and includes some give-and-take about why one approach might be favored over the other, since neither is entirely perfect.

Discussion

The first solution uses the Server.Transfer method to transfer control to a second page when a button click event handler executes in the code-behind of the first page. As with all the recipes in this chapter, this solution is most easily explained in the context of an example. Before we delve into the example, though, it's useful to relate what happens in ASP.NET when a form is submitted to itself and how the results of that submittal can be used to solve the problem at hand.

The code-behind class for an ASP.NET page is a class that derives from System.Web. UI.Page. This class encapsulates all data and server-side functionality for the page. When a form is submitted to itself, ASP.NET instantiates the page class with the data the user has submitted—that is, ASP.NET uses the data from the form submittal to repopulate the controls to their former state. This object can then be passed to any page, object, or method that has a need for the data.

In order to store the Page class instance representing the first page to session state and retrieve it in the second page, nothing special needs to be done to the *.aspx* file that collects the form data. In the following example, the form is a simple one that contains three text fields to capture the user's first name, last name, and age, and a button to submit the data to the server.

In the code-behind of the page that collects the form data, the data members that are to be accessible to the processing page must have their accessibility set to public. Normally, the accessibility would be set to protected; however, protected members are accessible only by the object itself and other objects that derive from the parent class. In this solution, the second page instantiates a class of type CH03SubmitToAnother_FirstPageVB1 (the class of the first page) rather than deriving from it.

A publicly accessible constant, SES_SUBMITTED_DATA, is provided to name the variable stored in session scope to avoid the problem with "magic values" and improve the maintainability of the code. *Magic values* are literals that have special significance in a system. As a general rule, you should replace magic values with named constants in order to prevent inadvertently varying them somewhere in your code. And when the same magic values appear in many different classes, they should be treated as global constants in your application rather than declaring them repeatedly in each class.

In the click event handler you write for the Submit button, the page object is placed in session scope to provide access to the data by the page that will process the data. This is done by calling the Add method of the Session object and passing it the name of the session-scoped variable (which is defined by the constant SES_SUBMITTED_DATA) and a reference to the current page (represented by the Me keyword in VB.NET and this in C#).

Control is then transferred to the page that will process the form data by calling the Transfer method of the Server class and providing it the URL of the page to which control is to be transferred.

 The second parameter for the Server.Transfer method must be set to False in this example to avoid sending the form data in the viewstate to the processing page. See the alternate example for an approach to using the viewstate to pass the information to the processing form.

The *.aspx* file for the page that processes the form data is nothing special. In this example, it simply has three labels used to display the data from the submitted form. We use Label controls in our example to demonstrate that the two pages can be quite different.

The code-behind for the form data processing page is also quite simple. First, the page object previously stored in session scope is recovered. The session variable is then destroyed to recover the system resources used to store the data by setting it equal to Nothing (in VB) or null (in C#).

The text for the labels on the form processing the data is then set to the values from the previous page. Our example simply displays the values. A real-world example might store the data in a database and would require additional code to handle the data access.

A drawback to the technique of placing the page object in session scope is that it can consume a significant amount of server resources if there are a large number of users on the system and/or the page object is large.

A second approach to submitting a form to another page for processing is to pass the information in the forms collection from the page where the data is entered to the processing page. The forms collection contains all of the data entered on the first page along with any hidden fields, including the viewstate, of the first page. This approach is similar to the classic ASP approach of posting to another page and may be desirable if the project requirements dictate that session scope will not be used for any data storage.

The *.aspx* file for the sending and receiving forms must be modified to disable the "machine authentication check" that is normally performed on the viewstate. By default, ASP.NET adds an encrypted value to the viewstate that is unique to the machine serving the page and the page itself. This allows ASP.NET to verify that the viewstate has not been tampered with by the client. The "machine authentication check" is disabled by setting the EnableViewStateMac attribute in the Page directive to false, as shown here:

```
<%@ Page language="c#" AutoEventWireup="false"
        Codebehind="FormSubmitToAnother_FirstPageCS2.aspx.cs"
        Inherits="ASPNetCookbook.CSExamples.FormSubmitToAnother_FirstPageCS2"
        EnableViewStateMac="False" %>
```

There is a significant drawback to using this approach. By disabling the "machine authentication check," the page submitted back to the server can be altered by the client, resulting in page errors or access to data the client is not authorized to view. You'll have to gauge whether this drawback outweighs the drawback of the previous technique—neither approach is perfect.

In the code-behind for the page that collects the data, the code in the click event for the button is changed to simply transfer control to the processing page with the second parameter of the Server.Transfer method set to True. This preserves the form data from the first page and passes it to the second page for processing.

VB
```
Private Sub btnSubmit_Click(ByVal sender As Object, _
                            ByVal e As System.Web.UI.ImageClickEventArgs) _
            Handles btnSubmit.Click
    Server.Transfer("CH03SubmitToAnother_SecondPageVB2.aspx", True)
End Sub 'btnSubmit_Click
```

C#
```
private void btnSubmit_Click(Object sender,
                            System.Web.UI.ImageClickEventArgs e)
{
    Server.Transfer("CH03SubmitToAnother_SecondPageCS2.aspx", true);
} // btnSubmit_Click
```

The code-behind for the page that processes the form data needs no code for this example. The reason is that, in this example, we are just displaying the data on the page. In a real-world example, the values of the form fields can be accessed just as they would if the form were submitted to itself.

ASP.NET will populate the controls on the second page with the data from the forms collection of the first page. Controls that match by name and datatype will be populated with data from the first form. If the controls on the second form have different names or datatypes, they are not populated. This requires very tight linkage between the pages and can be a significant maintenance issue.

The alternate approach described here may not work correctly in Version 1.1 of the .NET Framework due to a bug in the implementation. The bug is described in Microsoft Knowledge Base article 821758 (*http://support.microsoft.com/default.aspx?kbid=821758*). To work correctly, the hotfix described in article 821156 (*http://support.microsoft.com/default.aspx?kbid=821156*) must be applied.

Example 3-7. Submitting a form to another page—first page (.aspx)

```
<%@ Page Language="vb" AutoEventWireup="false"
        Codebehind="CH03SubmitToAnother_FirstPageVB1.aspx.vb"
        Inherits="ASPNetCookbook.VBExamples.CH03SubmitToAnother_FirstPageVB1" %>
<!DOCTYPE HTML PUBLIC "-//W3C//DTD HTML 4.0 Transitional//EN">
<html>
  <head>
    <title>Form Submission To Another Page</title>
    <link rel="stylesheet" href="css/ASPNetCookbook.css">
  </head>
  <body leftmargin="0" marginheight="0" marginwidth="0" topmargin="0">
    <form id="frmSubmitToAnother" method="post" runat="server">
      <table width="100%" cellpadding="0" cellspacing="0" border="0">
        <tr>
          <td align="center">
            <img src="images/ASPNETCookbookHeading_blue.gif">
          </td>
        </tr>
        <tr>
          <td class="dividerLine">
            <img src="images/spacer.gif" height="6" border="0"></td>
        </tr>
      </table>
      <table width="90%" align="center" border="0">
        <tr>
          <td><img src="images/spacer.gif" height="10" border="0"></td>
        </tr>
        <tr>
          <td align="center" class="PageHeading">
            Form Submission To Another Page - Approach 1 (VB)
          </td>
```

Example 3-7. Submitting a form to another page—first page (.aspx) (continued)

```
          </tr>
          <tr>
            <td><img src="images/spacer.gif" height="10" border="0"></td>
          </tr>
          <tr>
            <td align="center">
              <table border="0">
                <tr>
                  <td class="LabelText">First Name: </td>
                  <td>
                    <asp:TextBox ID="txtFirstName" Runat="server"
                                 Columns="30" CssClass="LabelText" />
                  </td>
                </tr>
                <tr>
                  <td class="LabelText">Last Name: </td>
                  <td>
                    <asp:TextBox ID="txtLastName" Runat="server"
                                 Columns="30" CssClass="LabelText" />
                  </td>
                </tr>
                <tr>
                  <td class="LabelText">Age: </td>
                  <td>
                    <asp:TextBox ID="txtAge" Runat="server"
                                 Columns="30" CssClass="LabelText" />
                  </td>
                </tr>
                <tr>
                  <td align="center" colspan="2">
                    <br>
                    <asp:ImageButton ID="btnSubmit" Runat="server"
                         ImageUrl="images/buttons/button_submit.gif" />
                  </td>
                </tr>
              </table>
            </td>
          </tr>
        </table>
      </form>
    </body>
</html>
```

Example 3-8. Submitting form to another page code-behind—first page (.vb)

```
Option Explicit On
Option Strict On
'---------------------------------------------------------------------------
'
'   Module Name: CH03SubmitToAnother_FirstPageVB1.aspx.vb
'
'   Description: This module provides the code behind for
'                CH03SubmitToAnother_FirstPageVB1.aspx
'
```

Example 3-8. Submitting form to another page code-behind—first page (.vb) (continued)

```
'****************************************************************************

Namespace ASPNetCookbook.VBExamples
  Public Class CH03SubmitToAnother_FirstPageVB1
    Inherits System.Web.UI.Page

    'controls on form
    Public txtFirstName As System.Web.UI.WebControls.TextBox
    Public txtLastName As System.Web.UI.WebControls.TextBox
    Public txtAge As System.Web.UI.WebControls.TextBox
    Protected WithEvents btnSubmit As System.Web.UI.WebControls.ImageButton

    'the following constant is used to define the variable in session scope
    'used to pass the form data
    Public Const SES_SUBMITTED_DATA As String = "SubmittedData"

    '****************************************************************************
    '
    '    ROUTINE: Page_Load
    '
    '    DESCRIPTION: This routine provides the event handler for the page load
    '                 event.  It is responsible for initializing the controls
    '                 on the page.
    '----------------------------------------------------------------------------
    Private Sub Page_Load(ByVal sender As System.Object, _
                          ByVal e As System.EventArgs) Handles MyBase.Load
      If (Not Page.IsPostBack) Then
        'Put user code to initialize the page here
      End If
    End Sub  'Page_Load

    '****************************************************************************
    '
    '    ROUTINE: btnSubmit_Click
    '
    '    DESCRIPTION: This routine provides the event handler for the submit
    '                 button click event.  It is responsible passing the form
    '                 data to another form for processing.
    '----------------------------------------------------------------------------
    Private Sub btnSubmit_Click(ByVal sender As Object, _
                                ByVal e As System.Web.UI.ImageClickEventArgs) _
                Handles btnSubmit.Click

      'add this object to session scope
      Session.Add(SES_SUBMITTED_DATA, Me)

      'transfer control to the page that will process the form data
      'NOTE: Second parameter for the transfer method must be set false to
      '      avoid transferring the viewstate to the next form.  If the
      '      viewstate is transferred without disabling the machine
      '      authentication check, an exception will be thrown due to a
```

```
        '       corrupted viewstate (would fail MAC check)
        Server.Transfer("CH03SubmitToAnother_SecondPageVB1.aspx", False)
    End Sub  'btnSubmit_Click
  End Class  'CH03SubmitToAnother_FirstPageVB1
End Namespace
```

Example 3-9. Submitting a form to another page code-behind—first page (.cs)

```csharp
//--------------------------------------------------------------------------
//
//    Module Name: CH03SubmitToAnother_FirstPageCS1.aspx.cs
//
//    Description: This module provides the code behind for
//                 CH03SubmitToAnother_FirstPageCS1.aspx
//
//**************************************************************************
using System;
using System.Web.UI;

namespace ASPNetCookbook.CSExamples
{
  public class CH03SubmitToAnother_FirstPageCS1 : System.Web.UI.Page
  {
    // controls on form
    public System.Web.UI.WebControls.TextBox txtFirstName;
    public System.Web.UI.WebControls.TextBox txtLastName;
    public System.Web.UI.WebControls.TextBox txtAge;
    protected System.Web.UI.WebControls.ImageButton btnSubmit;

    // the following constant is used to define the variable in session scope
    // used to pass the form data
    public const String SES_SUBMITTED_DATA = "SubmittedData";

    //**************************************************************************
    //
    //    ROUTINE: Page_Load
    //
    //    DESCRIPTION: This routine provides the event handler for the page
    //                 load event.  It is responsible for initializing the
    //                 controls on the page.
    //--------------------------------------------------------------------------
    private void Page_Load(object sender, System.EventArgs e)
    {
      // wire the submit button click event
      this.btnSubmit.Click +=
        new ImageClickEventHandler(this.btnSubmit_Click);

      if (!Page.IsPostBack)
      {
        // Put user code to initialize the page here
      }
    }  // Page_Load
```

Example 3-9. Submitting a form to another page code-behind—first page (.cs) (continued)

```
//*************************************************************************
//
//    ROUTINE: btnSubmit_Click
//
//    DESCRIPTION: This routine provides the event handler for the submit
//                 button click event.  It is responsible processing the
//                 form data.
//
//-------------------------------------------------------------------------
private void btnSubmit_Click(Object sender,
                             System.Web.UI.ImageClickEventArgs e)
{
  // 'add this object to session scope
  Session.Add(SES_SUBMITTED_DATA, this);

  // transfer control to the page that will process the form data
  // NOTE: Second parameter for the transfer method must be set false to
  //       avoid transferring the viewstate to the next form.  If the
  //       viewstate is transferred without disabling the machine
  //       authentication check, an exception will be thrown due to a
  //       corrupted viewstate (would fail MAC check)
  Server.Transfer("CH03SubmitToAnother_SecondPageCS1.aspx", false);
}  // btnSubmit_Click
}  // CH03SubmitToAnother_FirstPageCS1
}
```

Example 3-10. Submitting form to another page—second page (.aspx)

```
<%@ Page Language="vb" AutoEventWireup="false"
    Codebehind="CH03SubmitToAnother_SecondPageVB1.aspx.vb"
    Inherits="ASPNetCookbook.VBExamples.CH03SubmitToAnother_SecondPageVB1" %>
<!DOCTYPE HTML PUBLIC "-//W3C//DTD HTML 4.0 Transitional//EN">
<html>
  <head>
    <title>Form Submission To Another Page - Second Page</title>
    <link rel="stylesheet" href="css/ASPNetCookbook.css">
  </head>
  <body leftmargin="0" marginheight="0" marginwidth="0" topmargin="0">
    <form id="frmSubmitToAnother" method="post" runat="server">
      <table width="100%" cellpadding="0" cellspacing="0" border="0">
        <tr>
          <td align="center">
            <img src="images/ASPNETCookbookHeading_blue.gif">
          </td>
        </tr>
        <tr>
          <td class="dividerLine">
            <img src="images/spacer.gif" height="6" border="0"></td>
        </tr>
      </table>
      <table width="90%" align="center" border="0">
        <tr>
          <td><img src="images/spacer.gif" height="10" border="0"></td>
```

Example 3-10. Submitting form to another page—second page (.aspx) (continued)

```
      </tr>
      <tr>
        <td align="center" class="PageHeading">
          Form Submission To Another Page - Approach 1 (VB)
        </td>
      </tr>
      <tr>
        <td><img src="images/spacer.gif" height="10" border="0"></td>
      </tr>
      <tr>
        <td align="center">
          <table border="0">
            <tr>
              <td colspan="2" align="center" class="PageHeading">
                Data Submitted From Previous Form
              </td>
            </tr>
            <tr>
              <td class="LabelText">First Name: </td>
              <td class="LabelText">
                <asp:Label ID="lblFirstName" Runat="server" />
              </td>
            </tr>
            <tr>
              <td class="LabelText">Last Name: </td>
              <td class="LabelText">
                <asp:Label id="lblLastName" Runat="server" />
              </td>
            </tr>
            <tr>
              <td class="LabelText">Age: </td>
              <td class="LabelText">
                <asp:Label ID="lblAge" Runat="server" />
              </td>
            </tr>
          </table>
        </td>
      </tr>
    </table>
  </form>
  </body>
</html>
```

Example 3-11. Submitting a form to another page code-behind—second page (.vb)

```
Option Explicit On
Option Strict On
'-----------------------------------------------------------------------------
'
'   Module Name: CH03SubmitToAnother_SecondPageVB1.aspx.vb
'
'   Description: This module provides the code behind for
'                CH03SubmitToAnother_SecondPageVB1.aspx
'
```

Example 3-11. Submitting a form to another page code-behind—second page (.vb) (continued)

```vb
'*****************************************************************************

Namespace ASPNetCookbook.VBExamples
  Public Class CH03SubmitToAnother_SecondPageVB1
    Inherits System.Web.UI.Page

    'controls on form
    Protected lblFirstName As System.Web.UI.WebControls.Label
    Protected lblLastName As System.Web.UI.WebControls.Label
    Protected lblAge As System.Web.UI.WebControls.Label

    '*************************************************************************
    '
    '   ROUTINE: Page_Load
    '
    '   DESCRIPTION: This routine provides the event handler for the page load
    '                event.  It is responsible for initializing the controls
    '                on the page.
    '-------------------------------------------------------------------------
    Private Sub Page_Load(ByVal sender As System.Object, _
                          ByVal e As System.EventArgs) Handles MyBase.Load
      Dim submittedPage As CH03SubmitToAnother_FirstPageVB1

      'get the form data from session scope then remove the session variable
      'to conserve resources
      submittedPage = _
        CType(Session.Item(CH03SubmitToAnother_FirstPageVB1.SES_SUBMITTED_DATA), _
            CH03SubmitToAnother_FirstPageVB1)
      Session.Item(CH03SubmitToAnother_FirstPageVB1.SES_SUBMITTED_DATA) = Nothing

      'set the values on this form with the data from the submitted form
      lblFirstName.Text = submittedPage.txtFirstName.Text
      lblLastName.Text = submittedPage.txtLastName.Text
      lblAge.Text = submittedPage.txtAge.Text
    End Sub 'Page_Load
  End Class 'CH03SubmitToAnother_SecondPageVB1
End Namespace
```

Example 3-12. Submitting a form to another page code-behind—second page (.cs)

```csharp
//-----------------------------------------------------------------------------
//
//   Module Name: CH03SubmitToAnother_SecondPageCS1.aspx.cs
//
//   Description: This module provides the code behind for
//                CH03SubmitToAnother_SecondPageCS1.aspx
//
//*****************************************************************************
using System;

namespace ASPNetCookbook.CSExamples
{
```

```
public class CH03SubmitToAnother_SecondPageCS1 : System.Web.UI.Page
{
  // controls on form
  protected System.Web.UI.WebControls.Label lblFirstName;
  protected System.Web.UI.WebControls.Label lblLastName;
  protected System.Web.UI.WebControls.Label lblAge;

  //***********************************************************************
  //
  //    ROUTINE: Page_Load
  //
  //    DESCRIPTION: This routine provides the event handler for the page
  //                 load event.  It is responsible for initializing the
  //                 controls on the page.
  //
  //-----------------------------------------------------------------------
  private void Page_Load(object sender, System.EventArgs e)
  {
    CH03SubmitToAnother_FirstPageCS1 submittedPage;

    // get the form data from session scope then remove the session
    // variable to conserve resources
    submittedPage =
      (CH03SubmitToAnother_FirstPageCS1)
      (Session[CH03SubmitToAnother_FirstPageCS1.SES_SUBMITTED_DATA]);
    Session[CH03SubmitToAnother_FirstPageCS1.SES_SUBMITTED_DATA] = null;

    // set the values on this form with the data from the submitted form
    lblFirstName.Text = submittedPage.txtFirstName.Text;
    lblLastName.Text = submittedPage.txtLastName.Text;
    lblAge.Text = submittedPage.txtAge.Text;
  } // Page_Load
}  // CH03SubmitToAnother_SecondPageCS1
}
```

3.4 Simulating Multipage Forms

Problem

You want to create a form that appears, from the user's prospective, to consist of multiple pages, while keeping all of your code in one *.aspx* file and the code-behind that accompanies it.

Solution

Create one ASP.NET page. Use panels to separate the HTML for each of the "virtual" pages you wish to display, and simulate a multipage form by enabling one panel at a time. The output of a typical three-page form is shown in Figures 3-1 through 3-3. Examples 3-13 through 3-15 show the *.aspx* and code-behind files for an application that implements this solution.

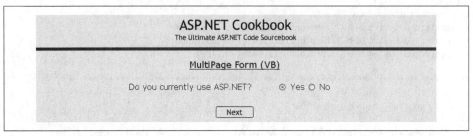

Figure 3-1. Multipage form output (page 1)

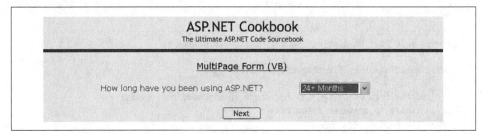

Figure 3-2. Multipage form output (page 2)

Figure 3-3. Multipage form output (page 3)

Discussion

In classic ASP, a series of questions or prompts, such as those on a survey or wizard, are typically implemented using multiple ASP pages with each submitting to the next in turn. ASP.NET allows you to submit a form to itself, which means that you have to rethink how to implement a survey, wizard, or traditionally multipart form. The solution we advocate involves defining multiple panels on a single form with the ASP: Panel control, and showing or hiding the panels as required. For example, the application we've written uses this technique to display a series of questions in a short survey.

 Refer to Recipe 3.3 if you are determined to stick to the multiple form approach.

In our example, the *.aspx* file contains three panels and a Next button. The first panel contains the first question ("Do you currently use ASP.NET?") with two radio buttons for the response. The second panel contains the second question ("How long have you been using ASP.NET?") with a drop-down list for the response. The third panel contains a message thanking the user for taking the survey. A Next button is used to move from one panel to the next.

The code-behind contains a reference to each of the panels to provide you with the ability to show and then hide any particular panel as the survey progresses. For this example, an object, Survey, is used to save the current question number and the response to each question asked. The Survey object is marked as Serializable to allow the objects of this type to be stored in the viewstate. The class is defined as follows:

```vb
<System.Serializable()> Private Class Survey
    Public currentQuestion As Integer
    Public response1 As Boolean
    Public response2 As Integer
End Class
```

```csharp
[System.Serializable()]
private class Survey
{
    public int currentQuestion;
    public Boolean response1;
    public int response2;
}
```

A constant, VS_SURVEY_DATA, is used to define the name of the variable placed in the viewstate. This improves maintainability of the code, because the variable in the viewstate is accessed from several locations in the code.

In the Page_Load method, the Survey object is initialized and stored in the viewstate. The form is then set up to initially display the first question in the series.

When the Next button is clicked, the form is posted back to itself and the btnNext_Click method is executed. The first action performed is to *rehydrate* the Survey object from the viewstate. Next, the current question is checked to see what response should be stored and which panel should next be made visible:

- If the first question was just answered, its response is stored in the Survey object, the question number is incremented, the Survey object is again stored in the viewstate, and the second question is made visible.

- If the second question was just answered, its response is stored in the Survey object (more permanent storage would be used instead if this were a real application), and the thank-you panel is made visible.

This example could be extended in many ways. One enhancement would be to create a totally data-driven survey form. In the *.aspx* file, a panel would be needed for each type of response (free-form, yes/no, selection, etc.). In the code-behind, an

XML document, database, or some other data store could be used and a collection of data defined that contains the questions, type of response, etc. Based on this data, the appropriate panel would be displayed for each question.

Another possible enhancement is that instead of collecting all of the responses and storing them in the viewstate until the survey is completed, the responses could be stored in a database or other data store as the survey proceeds. This would be a better approach if the survey is long or storing partial data is desirable.

See also

Recipe 3.3 for a multiple form approach

Example 3-13. Simulating a multipage form (.aspx)

```
<%@ Page Language="vb" AutoEventWireup="false"
        Codebehind="Ch03MultiPageVB.aspx.vb"
        Inherits="ASPNetCookbook.VBExamples.CH03MultiPageVB" %>
<!DOCTYPE HTML PUBLIC "-//W3C//DTD HTML 4.0 Transitional//EN">
<html>
  <head>
    <title>FormMultiPageVB</title>
    <link rel="stylesheet" href="css/ASPNetCookbook.css">
  </head>
  <body leftmargin="0" marginheight="0" marginwidth="0" topmargin="0">
    <form id="frmMultiPage" method="post" runat="server">
      <table width="100%" cellpadding="0" cellspacing="0" border="0">
        <tr>
          <td align="center">
            <img src="images/ASPNETCookbookHeading_blue.gif">
          </td>
        </tr>
        <tr>
          <td class="dividerLine">
            <img src="images/spacer.gif" height="6" border="0"></td>
        </tr>
      </table>
      <table width="90%" align="center" border="0">
        <tr>
          <td><img src="images/spacer.gif" height="10" border="0"></td>
        </tr>
        <tr>
          <td align="center" class="PageHeading">
            MultiPage Form (VB)
          </td>
        </tr>
        <tr>
          <td><img src="images/spacer.gif" height="10" border="0"></td>
        </tr>
        <tr>
          <td align="center">
            <asp:Panel ID="pnlQuestion1" Runat="server">
              <table width="60%" border="0">
                <tr>
```

Example 3-13. Simulating a multipage form (.aspx) (continued)

```
            <td class="MenuItem">Do you currently use ASP.NET?</td>
            <td>
              <asp:RadioButtonList ID="radQuestion1" Runat="server"
                                   RepeatDirection="Horizontal"
                                   CssClass="MenuItem" >
                <asp:ListItem Value="1">
                  Yes
                </asp:ListItem>
                <asp:ListItem Value="0" Selected="True">
                  No
                </asp:ListItem>
              </asp:RadioButtonList>
            </td>
          </tr>
        </table>
      </asp:Panel>

      <asp:Panel ID="pnlQuestion2" Runat="server">
        <table width="80%" border="0">
          <tr>
            <td class="MenuItem">How long have you been using ASP.NET?</td>
            <td class="MenuItem">
              <select id="selQuestion2" runat="server">
                <option value="0">-- Select One --</option>
                <option value="1">0-6 Months</option>
                <option value="2">7-12 Months</option>
                <option value="3">13-24 Months</option>
                <option value="4">24+ Months</option>
              </select>
            </td>
          </tr>
        </table>
      </asp:Panel>

      <asp:Panel ID="pnlThankyou" Runat="server">
        <table width="60%" border="0">
          <tr>
            <td class="MenuItem" align="center">
              Thank you for taking our survey
            </td>
          </tr>
        </table>
      </asp:Panel>

      <br />
      <asp:ImageButton ID="btnNext" Runat="server"
          ImageUrl="images/buttons/button_nextQuestion.gif" />
    </td>
  </tr>
  </table>
  </form>
  </body>
</html>
```

Example 3-14. Simulating a multipage form code-behind (.vb)

```vb
Option Explicit On
Option Strict On
'-----------------------------------------------------------------------------
'
'   Module Name: CH03MultiPageVB.aspx.vb
'
'   Description: This module provides the code behind for
'                CH03MultiPageVB.aspx
'
'*****************************************************************************

Namespace ASPNetCookbook.VBExamples
  Public Class CH03MultiPageVB
    Inherits System.Web.UI.Page

    'panels on the form
    Protected pnlQuestion1 As System.Web.UI.WebControls.Panel
    Protected pnlQuestion2 As System.Web.UI.WebControls.Panel
    Protected pnlThankyou As System.Web.UI.WebControls.Panel

    'control for response to question 1
    Protected radQuestion1 As System.Web.UI.WebControls.RadioButtonList

    'control for response to question 2
    Protected selQuestion2 As System.Web.UI.HtmlControls.HtmlSelect

    'buttons to navigate through survey
    Protected WithEvents btnNext As System.Web.UI.WebControls.ImageButton

    'the following class defines the container to store the survey data
    <System.Serializable()> Private Class Survey
      Public currentQuestion As Integer
      Public response1 As Boolean
      Public response2 As Integer
    End Class

    'the following constant defines the variable used to store the survey
    'data in the viewstate
    Private VS_SURVEY_DATA As String = "SurveyData"

    '*****************************************************************************
    '
    '   ROUTINE: Page_Load
    '
    '   DESCRIPTION: This routine provides the event handler for the page load
    '                event.  It is responsible for initializing the controls
    '                on the page.
    '-----------------------------------------------------------------------------
    Private Sub Page_Load(ByVal sender As System.Object, _
                          ByVal e As System.EventArgs) Handles MyBase.Load
      Dim surveyData As Survey
```

Example 3-14. Simulating a multipage form code-behind (.vb) (continued)

```vb
    If (Not Page.IsPostBack) Then
      'initialize survey data
      surveyData = New Survey
      surveyData.currentQuestion = 1
      surveyData.response1 = False
      surveyData.response2 = -1

      'store the survey in the viewstate to use on the
      'next submittal
      viewstate.Add(VS_SURVEY_DATA, surveyData)

      'make the first question visible
      pnlQuestion1.Visible = True
      pnlQuestion2.Visible = False
      pnlThankyou.Visible = False
    End If
End Sub   'Page_Load

'*************************************************************************
'
'   ROUTINE: btnNext_Click
'
'   DESCRIPTION: This routine provides the event handler for the next
'                button click event.
'-------------------------------------------------------------------------
Private Sub btnNext_Click(ByVal sender As Object, _
                          ByVal e As System.Web.UI.ImageClickEventArgs) _
           Handles btnNext.Click
   Dim surveyData As Survey

   'get the object from the viewstate with the survey data
   surveyData = CType(viewstate.Item(VS_SURVEY_DATA), Survey)

   Select Case surveyData.currentQuestion
     Case 1
       'store answer to first question
       If (radQuestion1.SelectedItem.Value = "0") Then
         surveyData.response1 = False
       Else
         surveyData.response1 = True
       End If

       'increment the question number
       surveyData.currentQuestion += 1

       'store the survey in the viewstate to use on the
       'next submittal
       viewstate.Add(VS_SURVEY_DATA, surveyData)

       'make 2nd question visible
       pnlQuestion1.Visible = False
       pnlQuestion2.Visible = True
```

Example 3-14. Simulating a multipage form code-behind (.vb) (continued)

```
        Case 2
          'store answer to second question
          surveyData.response2 = CInt(selQuestion2.Value)

          'the survey is complete so store the answers per your
          'applications required (database, etc.)


          'make thank you panel visible
          pnlQuestion2.Visible = False
          pnlThankyou.Visible = True
          btnNext.Visible = False

        Case Else
          'error case
      End Select

    End Sub  'btnNext_Click
  End Class  'CH03MultiPageVB
End Namespace
```

Example 3-15. Simulating a multipage form code-behind (.cs)

```
//----------------------------------------------------------------------------
//
//    Module Name: CH03MultiPageCS.aspx.cs
//
//    Description: This module provides the code behind for
//                 CH03MultiPageCS.aspx
//
//****************************************************************************
using System;
using System.Web.UI;

namespace ASPNetCookbook.CSExamples
{
  public class CH03MultiPageCS : System.Web.UI.Page
  {
    // panels on the form
    protected System.Web.UI.WebControls.Panel pnlQuestion1;
    protected System.Web.UI.WebControls.Panel pnlQuestion2;
    protected System.Web.UI.WebControls.Panel pnlThankyou;

    // control for response to question 1
    protected System.Web.UI.WebControls.RadioButtonList radQuestion1;

    // control for response to question 2
    protected System.Web.UI.HtmlControls.HtmlSelect selQuestion2;

    // buttons to navigate through survey
    protected System.Web.UI.WebControls.ImageButton btnNext;

    // the following class defines the container to store the survey data
```

Example 3-15. Simulating a multipage form code-behind (.cs) (continued)

```csharp
[System.Serializable()]
  private class Survey
{
  public int currentQuestion;
  public Boolean response1;
  public int response2;
}

// the following constant defines the variable used to store the survey
// data in the viewstate
private const String VS_SURVEY_DATA = "SurveyData";

//***********************************************************************
//
//    ROUTINE: Page_Load
//
//    DESCRIPTION: This routine provides the event handler for the page
//                 load event.  It is responsible for initializing the
//                 controls on the page.
//-----------------------------------------------------------------------
private void Page_Load(object sender, System.EventArgs e)
{
  Survey surveyData = null;

  // wire the next button click event
  this.btnNext.Click += new ImageClickEventHandler(this.btnNext_Click);

  if (!Page.IsPostBack)
  {
    // initialize survey data
    surveyData = new Survey();
    surveyData.currentQuestion = 1;
    surveyData.response1 = false;
    surveyData.response2 = -1;

    // store the survey in the viewstate to use on the
    // next submittal
    ViewState.Add(VS_SURVEY_DATA, surveyData);

    /// make the first question visible
    pnlQuestion1.Visible = true;
    pnlQuestion2.Visible = false;
    pnlThankyou.Visible = false;
  }
} // Page_Load

//***********************************************************************
//
//    ROUTINE: btnNext_Click
//
//    DESCRIPTION: This routine provides the event handler for the next
//                 button click event.
//-----------------------------------------------------------------------
```

Example 3-15. Simulating a multipage form code-behind (.cs) (continued)

```csharp
    private void btnNext_Click(Object sender,
                              System.Web.UI.ImageClickEventArgs e)
    {
      Survey surveyData = null;

      // get the object from the viewstate with the survey data
      surveyData = (Survey)(ViewState[VS_SURVEY_DATA]);

      switch (surveyData.currentQuestion)
      {
        case 1:
          // store answer to first question
          if (radQuestion1.SelectedItem.Value == "0")
          {
            surveyData.response1 = false;
          }
          else
          {
            surveyData.response1 = true;
          }

          // increment the question number
          surveyData.currentQuestion ++;

          // store the survey in the viewstate to use on the
          // next submittal
          ViewState.Add(VS_SURVEY_DATA, surveyData);

          // make 2nd question visible
          pnlQuestion1.Visible = false;
          pnlQuestion2.Visible = true;
          break;

        case 2:
          // store answer to second question
          surveyData.response2 = System.Convert.ToInt32(selQuestion2.Value);

          // the survey is complete so store the answers per your
          // applications required (database, etc.)

          // make thank you panel visible
          pnlQuestion2.Visible = false;
          pnlThankyou.Visible = true;
          btnNext.Visible = false;
          break;

        default:
          // error case
          break;
      } // switch (surveyData.currentQuestion)
    } // btnNext_Click
  } // CH03MultiPageCS
}
```

3.5 Setting the Initial Focus to a Specific Control

Problem

You need to set the focus of a page to a specific control when the page is first loaded.

Solution

Create a client-side JavaScript block in the code-behind that sets the focus to the desired control and then writes the block to the rendered page so that it is executed when the page is loaded.

In the code-behind class for the page, use the .NET language of your choice to:

1. Write some code that is called from the Page_Load method and generates a client-side JavaScript block that calls the focus method of the desired control and sets the control's initial focus to itself.

2. Use the RegisterClientScriptBlock method of the Page object to register the script block so that it is output when the page is rendered.

Examples 3-16 through 3-18 show the *.aspx* and code-behind files for the application that implements this solution. (See the sidebar, "Building a JavaScript Library," for the rationale behind our approach.)

Discussion

To implement this solution, nothing special is required in the *.aspx* file. But the code-behind page is another matter. There you need to generate a client-side JavaScript block that calls the focus method of the desired control and sets the control's initial focus to itself.

The application that we've written to implement the solution uses a simple form with only three text boxes to capture the user's first name, last name, and age. The application's code-behind assembles a client-side JavaScript block that calls the set focus method of the first text box control, and then writes the script block to the rendered page. Here is the code that sets the focus of the first text box on the form, txtFirstName:

```
<script language='javascript'>
<!--
  document.frmSetFocus.txtFirstName.focus();
//-->
</script>
```

The client-side JavaScript block is generated by the setFocus method of the code-behind. You pass to setFocus the reference to the control that you want to have the focus when the page is initially displayed in the browser, which is done via controlToFocus.ClientID in our example. The bulk of the method code generates the opening and closing tags of the script block. The line that actually sets the focus to the desired control is built by concatenating the IDs of the form and the desired control:

```
clientScript.Append("document." & frmSetFocus.ID & "." & _
                     controlToFocus.ClientID & ".focus();" & _
                     NewLine)
```

```
clientScript.Append("document." + frmSetFocus.ID + "." +
                     controlToFocus.ClientID + ".focus();\n");
```

The RegisterStartupScript method of the Page object is used to register the client-side script block to be output when the page is displayed in the browser. This method outputs the script block at the bottom of the form. This is important because the script block created in the setFocus method is executed when the browser parses the page, and for it to work correctly, the controls on the form have to have been previously created. If this block were output at the top of the page or at the beginning of the form, a JavaScript error would occur because the control to set the focus to would not yet exist.

To set the initial focus, the Page_Load method calls the setFocus method when the page is initially loaded, passing it a reference to the control that is to have initial focus.

With the basic functionality in place to programmatically set the focus to a control, many options are available. Refer to Recipe 3.6 for an example that uses the same functionality to set the focus to a control that has a validation error.

See Also

Recipe 3.6

Building a JavaScript Library

Client-side JavaScript is frequently required in web pages, and it is not uncommon to want to reuse the same JavaScript block. In classic ASP, reuse is achieved by using include files or by linking to specific JavaScript files. A big drawback to either of these techniques is that when the files are used as libraries, as is commonly done, they typically contain many more functions than are needed by any given pages. This results in slower performance because the excess code has to be downloaded to the browser along with the required code. Other options include using many files, each containing fewer methods, or putting the functionality required for a specific page directly in that page. Both result in duplication of JavaScript in many places and is a maintenance headache when changes are required.

—continued—

—continued—

With ASP.NET, you can generate the JavaScript you need by writing specialized methods that you encapsulate in a custom helper class. You call only the methods required to create the JavaScript you need for a specific page. This approach lets you reuse debugged JavaScript for all of your applications, and it improves performance because only the needed functions are rendered in the HTML page. An example of a client script library class that contains the setFocus method used in this recipe is shown here. To make the method even more useful, we have modified the code to allow you to pass at runtime the identity of the control to receive focus. In addition, the method has the Shared attribute to allow calling the method without instantiating the class.

```vb
Namespace DDIG.Script
  Public Class ClientScripts
    Public Shared Sub setFocus( _
       ByVal pageControl As System.Web.UI.Page, _
       ByVal pageForm As HtmlForm, _
       ByVal controlToFocus As System.Web.UI.Control)

       Dim clientScript As StringBuilder

       'generate the opening script tag
       clientScript = New StringBuilder()
       clientScript.Append("<script & _
                  language='javascript'>" & vbCrLf)
       clientScript.Append("<!--" & vbCrLf)

       'add the client script to set the control focus
       clientScript.Append("document." & _
                  pageForm.ID & "." & _
                  controlToFocus.ClientID & _
                  ".focus();" & _
                  vbCrLf)

       'generate the closing script tag
       clientScript.Append("//-->" & vbCrLf)
       clientScript.Append("</script>" & vbCrLf)

    'register the client script to be output when
       'the page is rendered
       pageControl.RegisterStartupScript( _
                  "setInitialFocus", _
                  clientScript.ToString())
    End Sub  'setFocus
  End Class
End Namespace
```

Example 3-16. Setting focus initially (.aspx)

```
<%@ Page Language="vb" AutoEventWireup="false"
        Codebehind="CH03SetFocusVB.aspx.vb"
        Inherits="ASPNetCookbook.VBExamples.CH03SetFocusVB" %>
<!DOCTYPE HTML PUBLIC "-//W3C//DTD HTML 4.0 Transitional//EN">
<html>
  <head>
    <title>Set Control Focus</title>
    <link rel="stylesheet" href="css/ASPNetCookbook.css">
  </head>
  <body leftmargin="0" marginheight="0" marginwidth="0" topmargin="0">
    <form id="frmSetFocus" method="post" runat="server">
      <table width="100%" cellpadding="0" cellspacing="0" border="0">
        <tr>
          <td align="center">
            <img src="images/ASPNETCookbookHeading_blue.gif">
          </td>
        </tr>
        <tr>
          <td class="dividerLine">
            <img src="images/spacer.gif" height="6" border="0"></td>
        </tr>
      </table>
      <table width="90%" align="center" border="0">
        <tr>
          <td><img src="images/spacer.gif" height="10" border="0"></td>
        </tr>
        <tr>
          <td align="center" class="PageHeading">
            Set Control Focus (VB)
          </td>
        </tr>
        <tr>
          <td><img src="images/spacer.gif" height="10" border="0"></td>
        </tr>
        <tr>
          <td align="center">
            <table border="0">
              <tr>
                <td class="LabelText">First Name: </td>
                <td>
                  <asp:TextBox id="txtFirstName" Runat="server"
                              Columns="30" CssClass="LabelText" />
                  <asp:RequiredFieldValidator id="rfvFirstName"
                        Runat="server"
                        ControlToValidate="txtFirstName"
                        CssClass="AlertText"
                        Display="Dynamic"
                        EnableClientScript="True">
                    <img src="images/arrow_alert.gif"> First Name Is Required
                  </asp:RequiredFieldValidator>
                </td>
              </tr>
```

Example 3-16. Setting focus initially (.aspx) (continued)

```
<tr>
  <td class="LabelText">Last Name: </td>
  <td>
    <asp:TextBox id="txtLastName" Runat="server"
                Columns="30" CssClass="LabelText" />
    <asp:RequiredFieldValidator id="rfvLastName"
        Runat="server"
        ControlToValidate="txtLastName"
        CssClass="AlertText"
        Display="Dynamic"
        EnableClientScript="True">
      <img src="images/arrow_alert.gif"> Last Name Is Required
    </asp:RequiredFieldValidator>
  </td>
</tr>
<tr>
  <td class="LabelText">Age: </td>
  <td>
    <asp:TextBox id="txtAge" Runat="server"
                Columns="30" CssClass="LabelText" />
    <asp:RequiredFieldValidator id="rfvAge"
        Runat="server"
        ControlToValidate="txtAge"
        CssClass="AlertText"
        Display="Dynamic"
        EnableClientScript="True">
      <img src="images/arrow_alert.gif"> Age Is Required
    </asp:RequiredFieldValidator>
    <asp:RangeValidator id="rvAge" Runat="server"
        ControlToValidate="txtAge"
        CssClass="AlertText"
        Display="Dynamic"
        EnableClientScript="True"
        MinimumValue="18"
        MaximumValue="99"
        Type="Integer">
<img src="images/arrow_alert.gif"> Age Must Be Between 18 and 99
    </asp:RangeValidator>
  </td>
</tr>
<tr>
  <td colspan="2">
    <br>
    <table align="center" width="50%">
      <tr>
        <td align="center">
          <asp:ImageButton id="btnSave" Runat="server"
              CausesValidation="True"
              ImageUrl="images/buttons/button_save.gif" />
        </td>
        <td align="center">
```

Example 3-16. Setting focus initially (.aspx) (continued)

```
                        <asp:ImageButton id="btnCancel" Runat="server"
                            CausesValidation="False"
                            ImageUrl="images/buttons/button_cancel.gif" />
                      </td>
                    </tr>
                  </table>
                </td>
              </tr>
            </table>
          </td>
        </tr>
      </table>
    </form>
  </body>
</html>
```

Example 3-17. Setting focus initially code-behind (.vb)

```
Option Explicit On
Option Strict On
'-----------------------------------------------------------------------------
'
'   Module Name: CH03SetFocusVB.aspx.vb
'
'   Description: This module provides the code behind for
'               CH03SetFocusVB.aspx
'
'*****************************************************************************

Imports System.Environment
Imports System.Text

Namespace ASPNetCookbook.VBExamples
  Public Class CH03SetFocusVB
    Inherits System.Web.UI.Page

    'controls on form
    Protected frmSetFocus As System.Web.UI.HtmlControls.HtmlForm
    Protected txtFirstName As System.Web.UI.WebControls.TextBox
    Protected txtLastName As System.Web.UI.WebControls.TextBox
    Protected txtAge As System.Web.UI.WebControls.TextBox
    Protected WithEvents btnSave As System.Web.UI.WebControls.ImageButton
    Protected WithEvents btnCancel As System.Web.UI.WebControls.ImageButton

    '*****************************************************************************
    '
    '   ROUTINE: Page_Load
    '
    '   DESCRIPTION: This routine provides the event handler for the page load
    '               event.  It is responsible for initializing the controls
    '               on the page.
    '-----------------------------------------------------------------------------
```

Example 3-17. Setting focus initially code-behind (.vb) (continued)

```vb
Private Sub Page_Load(ByVal sender As System.Object, _
                      ByVal e As System.EventArgs) _
        Handles MyBase.Load

  If (Not Page.IsPostBack) Then
    setFocus(txtFirstName)
  End If
End Sub 'Page_Load

'*************************************************************************
'
'    ROUTINE: setFocus
'
'    DESCRIPTION: This routine generates the client script to set the focus
'                 to the passed control
'-------------------------------------------------------------------------
Private Sub setFocus(ByVal controlToFocus As System.Web.UI.Control)
  Dim clientScript As StringBuilder

  'generate the opening script tag
  clientScript = New StringBuilder
  clientScript.Append("<script language='javascript'>" & NewLine)
  clientScript.Append("<!--" & NewLine)

  'add the client script to set the control focus
  clientScript.Append("document." & frmSetFocus.ID & "." & _
                      controlToFocus.ClientID & ".focus();" & _
                      NewLine)

  'generate the closing script tag
  clientScript.Append("//-->" & NewLine)
  clientScript.Append("</script>" & NewLine)

  'register the client script to be output when the page is rendered
  Page.RegisterStartupScript("ScriptBlock", _
                             clientScript.ToString())
End Sub   'setFocus

'*************************************************************************
'
'    ROUTINE: btnSave_Click
'
'    DESCRIPTION: This routine provides the event handler for the save
'                 button click event.  It is responsible processing the
'                 form data.
'-------------------------------------------------------------------------
Private Sub btnSave_Click(ByVal sender As Object, _
                          ByVal e As System.Web.UI.ImageClickEventArgs) _
        Handles btnSave.Click

  If (Page.IsValid) Then
    'process form data and save as required for application
```

Example 3-17. Setting focus initially code-behind (.vb) (continued)

```
      End If
    End Sub  'btnSave_Click
  End Class  'CH03SetFocusVB
End Namespace
```

Example 3-18. Setting focus initially code-behind (.cs)

```
//-----------------------------------------------------------------------------
//
//    Module Name: CH03SetFocusCS.aspx.cs
//
//    Description: This module provides the code behind for
//                 CH03SetFocusCS.aspx
//
//*****************************************************************************
using System;
using System.Text;
using System.Web.UI;

namespace ASPNetCookbook.CSExamples
{
  public class CH03SetFocusCS : System.Web.UI.Page
  {
    // controls on form
    protected System.Web.UI.HtmlControls.HtmlForm frmSetFocus;
    protected System.Web.UI.WebControls.TextBox txtFirstName;
    protected System.Web.UI.WebControls.TextBox txtLastName;
    protected System.Web.UI.WebControls.TextBox txtAge;
    protected System.Web.UI.WebControls.ImageButton btnSave;
    protected System.Web.UI.WebControls.ImageButton btnCancel;

    //*****************************************************************************
    //
    //    ROUTINE: Page_Load
    //
    //    DESCRIPTION: This routine provides the event handler for the page
    //                 load event.  It is responsible for initializing the
    //                 controls on the page.
    //-------------------------------------------------------------------------
    private void Page_Load(object sender, System.EventArgs e)
    {
      // wire the save button click event
      this.btnSave.Click += new ImageClickEventHandler(this.btnSave_Click);

      if (!Page.IsPostBack)
      {
        setFocus(txtFirstName);
      }
    }  // Page_Load
```

Example 3-18. Setting focus initially code-behind (.cs) (continued)

```csharp
//**************************************************************************
//
//    ROUTINE: setFocus
//
//    DESCRIPTION: This routine generates the client script to set the
//                 focus to the passed control
//--------------------------------------------------------------------------
private void setFocus(System.Web.UI.Control controlToFocus)
{
   StringBuilder clientScript;

   // generate the opening script tag
   clientScript = new StringBuilder( );
   clientScript.Append("<script language='javascript'>\n");
   clientScript.Append("<!--\n");


   // add the client script to set the control focus
   clientScript.Append("document." + frmSetFocus.ID + "." +
                       controlToFocus.ClientID + ".focus( );\n");

   // generate the closing script tag
   clientScript.Append("//-->\n");
   clientScript.Append("</script>\n");

   // register the client script to be output when the page is rendered
   Page.RegisterStartupScript("ScriptBlock",
                              clientScript.ToString( ));
} // setFocus


//**************************************************************************
//
//    ROUTINE: btnSave_Click
//
//    DESCRIPTION: This routine provides the event handler for the save
//                 button click event.  It is responsible for processing
//                 the form data.
//--------------------------------------------------------------------------
private void btnSave_Click(Object sender,
   System.Web.UI.ImageClickEventArgs e)
{
   if (!Page.IsValid)
   {
     // process form data and save as required for application
   }
} // btnSave_Click
} // CH03SetFocusCS
}
```

3.6   Setting the Focus to a Control with a Validation Error

Problem

You want to set the focus to the first control on your form that has a validation error.

Solution

The solution to this recipe is an extension of the one introduced in Recipe 3.5, where we recommend writing code that generates some client-side JavaScript that calls the focus method of the desired control. For this recipe, we recommend adding some additional JavaScript-generating code that is tied to the Save button's click event handler and that, when executed, searches for a control with a validation error and sets the focus to that control.

In the code-behind class for the page, use the .NET language of your choice to:

1. Write some code that is called from the Page_Load method and generates a client-side JavaScript block that calls the focus method of the desired control and sets the control's initial focus to itself (see Recipe 3.5 for details).

2. Add additional code to the Save (or equivalently named) button's click event handler that searches for a control with a validation error and sets the focus to that control.

3. Use the RegisterClientScriptBlock method of the Page object to register the script block so that it is output when the page is rendered.

Examples 3-19 and 3-20 show routines that are required to implement the last two steps of this solution.

Discussion

As described in Recipe 3.5, you start implementing this solution by creating a client-side JavaScript block in the code-behind that sets the focus to a desired control and then outputs the block to the rendered page so that it is executed when the page is loaded. With this code in place, you can then add some additional code to the Save (or equivalently named) button's click event that determines the first control with a validation error and sets the focus to it via the previously loaded JavaScript code.

This solution relies on the fact that the page object contains a collection of the validation controls on the form. The order of the validators in the collection is the same as the order in which they appear in the .aspx file. (The validators should be placed with the controls they validate for this solution to work correctly.)

To get a feel for how to implement this solution, first take a look at the sample application we created for Recipe 3.5 (Examples 3-16 through 3-18). Next, consider the code in Examples 3-19 and 3-20, which is added to that application to implement this recipe's solution.

The way the additional code works is that when the server-side button's click event is executed, a check is first made to see whether the page is valid. If it is, a save operation is performed. If the page is not valid, the validators are iterated through until the first invalid one is found. This is determined by examining the IsValid property of each validator control; its value is false if the control associated with the validator has failed to pass validation.

When an invalid validator is found, the control it is associated with is identified by calling the FindControl method of the Page object. The control is then passed to the setFocus method. Only one control can have the focus, so after an invalid control is found, the for loop is exited.

> The client-side validation is disabled in this example to simplify the explanation of how to determine which control has a validation error and how to then set the focus to it. If we had kept client-side validation enabled, we would have also had to implement the same approach using client-side JavaScript. Although the latter may ultimately prove to be the most useful for you, we have avoided it here to keep this recipe relatively lean and to the point.

Example 3-19. Set focus to control with validation error (.vb)

```vb
Private Sub btnSave_Click(ByVal sender As Object, _
                    ByVal e As System.Web.UI.ImageClickEventArgs) _
     Handles btnSave.Click

  Dim validator As System.Web.UI.WebControls.BaseValidator

  If (Page.IsValid) Then
    'process form data and save as required for application

  Else
    'page is invalid so iterate through validators to find the first one
    'with an error
    For Each validator In Page.Validators
      If (Not validator.IsValid) Then
        'validator that failed found so set the focus to the control
        'it validates and exit the loop
        setFocus(Page.FindControl(validator.ControlToValidate))
        Exit For
      End If
    Next validator
  End If
End Sub 'btnSave_Click
```

Example 3-20. Set focus to control with validation error (.cs)

```
private void btnSave_Click(Object sender,
                           System.Web.UI.ImageClickEventArgs e)
{
  if (Page.IsValid)
  {
    // process form data and save as required for application
  }
  else
  {
    // page is invalid so iterate through validators to find the first
    // one with an error
    foreach(BaseValidator validator in Page.Validators)
    {
      if (!validator.IsValid)
      {
        // validator that failed found so set the focus to the control
        // it validates and exit the loop
        setFocus(Page.FindControl(validator.ControlToValidate));
        break;
      }
    }
  }
} // btnSave_Click
```

CHAPTER 4

User Controls

4.0 Introduction

User controls provide an excellent mechanism for code reuse in ASP.NET. Indeed, the reuse mechanism is significantly better than the server-side include file method used in classic ASP. For one thing, user controls are compiled and can be cached separately from the page in which they are used, providing a significant increase in performance. (See Chapter 13.) For another, user controls leverage the object model support provided by ASP.NET, which means that you can program against any properties you declare for the control, just like other ASP.NET server controls.

This brings us to another point: user controls exist only on the server. When rendered and sent to the client, they are just part of the flat HTML for a page. Because they exist only on the server, browser compatibility is not an issue. Nor is it necessary to download a control from the server to the client and, in the process, risk that a user might refuse to download a control needed to properly render your web page.

4.1 Sharing a Page Header on Multiple Pages

Problem

You have a header that is common to all pages in a site and do not want to repeat the code on every page.

Solution

Create a user control containing the header code and then add the control to each page.

To create the user control:

1. Create a file with a *.ascx* extension.
2. Place the @ Control directive at the top of the file.

3. Add the HTML you wish to reuse for the header, making sure to avoid using any `<html>`, `<head>`, `<body>`, or `<form>` elements.

In the code-behind class for the control, use the .NET language of your choice to:

1. Create a user control code-behind class that inherits from the `UserControl` class.

2. (Optional) Establish properties for the control that will provide the ability to programmatically control the basic look of the header.

To use the user control in an ASP.NET page:

1. Register the control by using the `@ Register` directive at the top of the page.

2. Place the tag for the user control where you want the control to be rendered.

To demonstrate this solution, we've created a user control that houses some typical header HTML, including `<img>` tags for a header image and a divider image. We then show how to use the user control in three different ways: with default parameters, with parameters set in the *.aspx* file, and with parameters set in the code-behind.

The output of a test page that uses the user control is shown in Figure 4-1. (The second divider line appears in green and the third divider line appears in blue when rendered on the screen.) Example 4-1 shows the *.ascx* file for the user control. Examples 4-2 and 4-3 show the VB and C# code-behind files for the user control. Example 4-4 shows the *.aspx* file that uses the user control in the three different ways previously mentioned. Examples 4-5 and 4-6 show the VB and C# code-behind files for the test page that uses the user control.

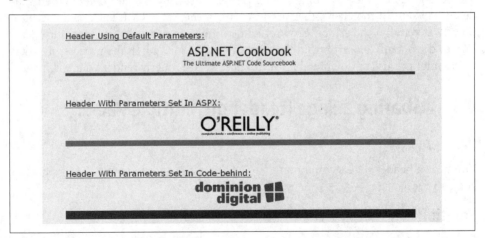

Figure 4-1. Page header user control output

Discussion

User controls provide an easy way to partition pages and reuse the page sections throughout your application. They are very similar to web forms in that they consist of two files: a *.ascx* file (the user interface) and a code-behind file (*.vb* or *.cs*).

Since they constitute page sections, the user interface elements they contain generally do not include <html>, <head>, <body>, or <form> elements. Further, you must place the @ Control directive at the top of the .ascx file instead of the @ Page directive used for web forms. The code-behind class for a user control is very similar to the code-behind class for a web form, with the most noticeable difference being that the user control code-behind class inherits from the UserControl class instead of the Page class.

The example we've provided to demonstrate this solution shows you how to create a user control to be used as a page header. The user control has three custom properties that provide the ability to programmatically control the basic look of the header.

The HTML for the user control (see Example 4-1) contains a table with two rows and a single column. The first row of the table contains a "logo" style image. The src attribute of the image tag is set to the name of the image that will be used for the default image.

The cell in the second row of the table contains a single-pixel transparent image. This is a classic HTML trick to allow manipulation of a table cell to provide dividers with alterable colors and heights as well as to stretch to the size of the cell. The bgcolor and height attributes of the cell are set to the values that will be the defaults for the color and height of the divider line.

The code-behind contains three properties:

headerImage
> Provides the ability to set/get the image that will be displayed in the header

dividerColor
> Provides the ability to set/get the divider color

dividerHeight
> Provides the ability to set/get the divider height

To use a user control in an ASP.NET page, the control must be registered using the @ Register directive at the top of the page. The TagPrefix and TagName attributes are used to uniquely define the "custom tag" on the ASP.NET page. The TagPrefix is typically set to the namespace of the project. The TagName should be set to a value that describes what the control is used for. The Src attribute is set to the name of the .ascx file of the user control. Here is how we set these attributes in our example:

```
<%@ Register TagPrefix="ASPCookbook" TagName="PageHeader"
             Src="CH04UserControlHeaderVB.ascx" %>
```

Additionally, a tag is placed in the HTML where you want the user control rendered. The tag must be given an id and the runat attribute must be set to "server" or else the user control will not be rendered. Here is the syntax we've used for inserting our example user control using the default values:

```
<ASPCookbook:PageHeader id="pageHeader1" runat="server" />
```

If you want to change the properties for a user control, you can set them as attributes in the tag. For instance, here is how we set the header image, the divider color, and the divider height in our example:

```
<ASPCookbook:PageHeader id="pageHeader2" runat="server"
            headerImage="images/oreilly_header.gif"
            dividerColor="#008000"
            dividerHeight=12 />
```

The properties for a user control included in an ASP.NET page can be set in the code-behind in the same manner as setting the attributes for any other HTML or ASP server control. You must declare the control in the class, and then you can set the appropriate values in Page_Load or another method. Here's how we do it in our example:

```
Protected pageHeader3 As ASPNetCookbook.VBExamples.UserControlHeaderVB


    ...


pageHeader3.headerImage = "images/ddig_logo.gif"
pageHeader3.dividerHeight = "18"
pageHeader3.dividerColor = ColorTranslator.ToHtml(Color.DarkBlue)
```

Example 4-1. Page header user control (.ascx)

```
<%@ Control Language="vb" AutoEventWireup="false"
        Codebehind="CH04UserControlHeaderVB.ascx.vb"
        Inherits="ASPNetCookbook.VBExamples.CH04UserControlHeaderVB" %>
<table width="100%" cellpadding="0" cellspacing="0" border="0">
  <tr>
    <td align="center">
      <img id="imgHeader" runat="server"
          src="images/ASPNetCookbookHeading_blue.gif">
    </td>
  </tr>
  <tr>
    <td id="tdDivider" runat="server" bgcolor="#6B0808" height="6">
      <img src="images/spacer.gif"></td>
  </tr>
</table>
```

Example 4-2. Page header user control code-behind (.vb)

```
Option Explicit On
Option Strict On
'-------------------------------------------------------------------------
'
'   Module Name: CH04UserControlHeaderVB.ascx.vb
'
'   Description: This module provides the code behind for
'               CH04UserControlHeaderVB.ascx
'
'*************************************************************************
```

Example 4-2. Page header user control code-behind (.vb) (continued)

```vb
Namespace ASPNetCookbook.VBExamples
  Public MustInherit Class CH04UserControlHeaderVB
    Inherits System.Web.UI.UserControl

    'controls on user control
    Protected imgHeader As System.Web.UI.HtmlControls.HtmlImage
    Protected tdDivider As System.Web.UI.HtmlControls.HtmlTableCell

    '*************************************************************************
    '
    '    ROUTINE: headerImage
    '
    '    DESCRIPTION: This property provides the ability get/set the image
    '                 used in the header user control
    '-------------------------------------------------------------------------
    Public Property headerImage() As String
      Get
        Return (imgHeader.Src)
      End Get

      Set(ByVal Value As String)
        imgHeader.Src = Value
      End Set
    End Property  'headerImage

    '*************************************************************************
    '
    '    ROUTINE: dividerColor
    '
    '    DESCRIPTION: This property provides the ability get/set the divider
    '                 color used at the bottom of the user control
    '-------------------------------------------------------------------------
    Public Property dividerColor() As String
      Get
        Return (tdDivider.BgColor)
      End Get

      Set(ByVal Value As String)
        tdDivider.BgColor = Value
      End Set
    End Property  'dividerColor

    '*************************************************************************
    '
    '    ROUTINE: dividerHeight
    '
    '    DESCRIPTION: This property provides the ability get/set the divider
    '                 height used at the bottom of the user control
    '-------------------------------------------------------------------------
    Public Property dividerHeight() As String
      Get
        Return (tdDivider.Height)
      End Get
```

Example 4-2. Page header user control code-behind (.vb) (continued)

```
      Set(ByVal Value As String)
        tdDivider.Height = Value
      End Set
    End Property    'dividerHeight


    '*************************************************************************
    '
    '    ROUTINE: Page_Load
    '
    '    DESCRIPTION: This routine provides the event handler for the page load
    '                 event.  It is responsible for initializing the controls
    '                 on the user control.
    '-------------------------------------------------------------------------
    Private Sub Page_Load(ByVal sender As System.Object, _
                          ByVal e As System.EventArgs) _
          Handles MyBase.Load
      'place user code here
    End Sub   'Page_Load
  End Class   'CH04UserControlHeaderVB
End Namespace
```

Example 4-3. Page header user control code-behind (.cs)

```
//---------------------------------------------------------------------------
//
//    Module Name: CH04UserControlHeaderCS.ascx.cs
//
//    Description: This module provides the code behind for
//                 CH04UserControlHeaderCS.ascx
//
//***************************************************************************
using System;
using System.Web.UI.HtmlControls;

namespace ASPNetCookbook.CSExamples
{
  public class CH04UserControlHeaderCS : System.Web.UI.UserControl
  {
    // controls on the user control
    protected System.Web.UI.HtmlControls.HtmlImage imgHeader;
    protected System.Web.UI.HtmlControls.HtmlTableCell tdDivider;

    //*********************************************************************
    //
    //    ROUTINE: headerImage
    //
    //    DESCRIPTION: This property provides the ability get/set the image
    //                 used in the header user control
    //-------------------------------------------------------------------
    public String headerImage
    {
      get
      {
        return(imgHeader.Src);
```

Example 4-3. Page header user control code-behind (.cs) (continued)

```
      }
      set
      {
        imgHeader.Src = value;
      }
    }  // headerImage

    //********************************************************************
    //
    //    ROUTINE: dividerColor
    //
    //    DESCRIPTION: This property provides the ability get/set the divider
    //                 color used at the bottom of the user control
    //-------------------------------------------------------------------------
    public String dividerColor
    {
      get
      {
        return(tdDivider.BgColor);
      }
      set
      {
        tdDivider.BgColor = value;
      }
    }  // dividerColor

    //********************************************************************
    //
    //    ROUTINE: dividerHeight
    //
    //    DESCRIPTION: This property provides the ability get/set the divider
    //                 height used at the bottom of the user control
    //-------------------------------------------------------------------------
    public String dividerHeight
    {
      get
      {
        return(tdDivider.Height);
      }
      set
      {
        tdDivider.Height = value;
      }
    }  // dividerHeight

    //********************************************************************
    //
    //    ROUTINE: Page_Load
    //
    //    DESCRIPTION: This routine provides the event handler for the page
    //                 load event.  It is responsible for initializing the
    //                 controls on the user control.
    //-------------------------------------------------------------------------
```

Example 4-3. Page header user control code-behind (.cs) (continued)

```
    private void Page_Load(object sender, System.EventArgs e)
    {
      // Put user code to initialize the page here
    }  // Page_Load
  }  // CH04UserControlHeaderCS
}
```

Example 4-4. Using the page header user control (.aspx)

```
<%@ Page Language="vb" AutoEventWireup="false"
        Codebehind="CH04DisplayHeaderVB.aspx.vb"
        Inherits="ASPNetCookbook.VBExamples.CH04DisplayHeaderVB" %>
<%@ Register TagPrefix="ASPCookbook" TagName="PageHeader"
            Src="CH04UserControlHeaderVB.ascx" %>
<!DOCTYPE HTML PUBLIC "-//W3C//DTD HTML 4.0 Transitional//EN">
<html>
  <head>
    <title>User Control Display Header</title>
    <link rel="stylesheet" href="css/ASPNetCookbook.css">
  </head>
  <body>
    <form id="frmHeaderTest" method="post" runat="server">
      <table width="90%" align="center" border="0">
        <tr>
          <td class="PageHeading">Header Using Default Parameters:</td>
        </tr>
        <tr>
          <td><ASPCookbook:PageHeader id="pageHeader1" runat="server" />
          </td>
        </tr>
        <tr>
          <td class="PageHeading"><br /><br />
              Header With Parameters Set In ASPX:</td>
        </tr>
        <tr>
          <td><ASPCookbook:PageHeader id="pageHeader2" runat="server"
              headerImage="images/oreilly_header.gif"
              dividerColor="#008000"
              dividerHeight="12" />
          </td>
        </tr>
        <tr>
          <td class="PageHeading"><br /><br />
              Header With Parameters Set In Code-behind:</td>
        </tr>
        <tr>
          <td><ASPCookbook:PageHeader id="pageHeader3" runat="server" />
          </td>
        </tr>
      </table>
    </form>
  </body>
</html>
```

Example 4-5. Using the page header user control (.vb)

```vb
Option Explicit On
Option Strict On
'-----------------------------------------------------------------------------
'
'   Module Name: CH04DisplayHeaderVB.aspx.vb
'
'   Description: This module provides the code behind for
'                CH04DisplayHeaderVB.aspx
'
'*****************************************************************************
Imports System.Drawing

Namespace ASPNetCookbook.VBExamples
  Public Class CH04DisplayHeaderVB
    Inherits System.Web.UI.Page

    Protected pageHeader3 As ASPNetCookbook.VBExamples.CH04UserControlHeaderVB

    '*************************************************************************
    '
    '   ROUTINE: Page_Load
    '
    '   DESCRIPTION: This routine provides the event handler for the page load
    '                event.  It is responsible for initializing the controls
    '                on the page.
    '-------------------------------------------------------------------------
    Private Sub Page_Load(ByVal sender As System.Object, _
                          ByVal e As System.EventArgs) Handles MyBase.Load
      'initialize the 3rd page header user control
      pageHeader3.headerImage = "images/ddig_logo.gif"
      pageHeader3.dividerHeight = "18"
      pageHeader3.dividerColor = ColorTranslator.ToHtml(Color.DarkBlue)
    End Sub  'Page_Load
  End Class  'CH04DisplayHeaderVB
End Namespace
```

Example 4-6. Using the page header user control (.cs)

```csharp
//-----------------------------------------------------------------------------
//
//   Module Name: CH04DisplayHeaderCS.ascx.cs
//
//   Description: This module provides the code behind for
//                CH04DisplayHeaderCS.ascx
//
//*****************************************************************************
using System;
using System.Drawing;

namespace ASPNetCookbook.CSExamples
{
  public class CH04DisplayHeaderCS : System.Web.UI.Page
  {
```

Example 4-6. Using the page header user control (.cs) (continued)

```
  // controls on form
  protected ASPNetCookbook.CSExamples.CH04UserControlHeaderCS pageHeader3;

  //**********************************************************************
  //
  //   ROUTINE: Page_Load
  //
  //   DESCRIPTION: This routine provides the event handler for the page
  //                load event.  It is responsible for initializing the
  //                controls on the page.
  //----------------------------------------------------------------------
  private void Page_Load(object sender, System.EventArgs e)
  {
    // initialize the 3rd page header user control
    pageHeader3.headerImage = "images/ddig_logo.gif";
    pageHeader3.dividerHeight = "18";
    pageHeader3.dividerColor = ColorTranslator.ToHtml(Color.DarkBlue);
  }  // Page_Load
}  // CH04DisplayHeaderCS
}
```

4.2   Creating a Customizable Navigation Bar

Problem

You want to create a navigation bar that lets you add or remove items without
changing code so that you can reuse the navigation bar in multiple applications.

Solution

Create an XML document containing the items that will be displayed in the navigation bar, and then create a user control that uses the contents of the XML document
to provide the required customization.

To create the user control:

1. Create a file with a *.ascx* extension.
2. Place the @ Control directive at the top of the file.
3. Add a DataList control configured to render a table with an ItemTemplate defining the cells in the table.

In the code-behind class for the control, use the .NET language of your choice to:

1. Create a user control code-behind class that inherits from the UserControl class.
2. (Optional) Establish properties for the control that will provide the ability to
   programmatically control the basic look of the navigation bar, such as its background color.

To use the user control in an ASP.NET page:

1. Register the control by using the @ Register directive at the top of the page.
2. Place the tag for the user control in the HTML where you want the control rendered.

The output of a test page demonstrating a typical navigation bar user control is shown in Figure 4-2. Example 4-7 shows the XML document we created to define the contents of the navigation bar. Example 4-8 shows the *.ascx* file for the user control. Examples 4-9 and 4-10 show the VB and C# code-behind files for the user control. Example 4-11 shows the *.aspx* file for the test page that uses the user control. Examples 4-12 and 4-13 show the VB and C# code-behind files for the test page.

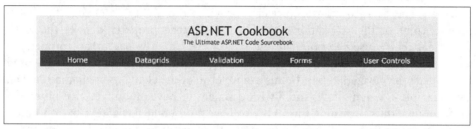

Figure 4-2. Customizable navigation bar output

Discussion

The general strategy for this solution is to create an XML document that defines the contents of the navigation bar user control. You then use the Page_Load method of the user control's code-behind to read into a DataSet the XML document containing the navigation bar data and then bind the dataset to a DataList control. The use of a DataSet and DataList control may sound a little unconventional in this application, but it has these distinct advantages:

- You are not limited to the number of items in the navigation bar.
- Loading the XML document used to define the navigation bar items into a DataSet makes for easy traversal of those items.
- A DataList control configured to render a table with an ItemTemplate provides the flexibility in the display of the columns that is needed for customizing a navigation bar.

The example we have written to implement this solution creates a navigation bar user control whose contents are defined by an XML document. But the example goes a bit further in that it provides the ability to define what buttons appear in the navigation bar as well as the ability to customize the color of the bar, change the name of the XML file used to define the bar, and set other properties.

The XML document that defines our navigation bar consists of a series of elements named Public, as shown in Example 4-7. This is actually the name of the navigation bar (explained later). Each of the Public elements contains three elements: the ButtonLink element defines the URL for the navigation bar button, the ImageSrc element defines the image used for the button, and the AltText element sets the text alternative for the image (i.e., the value of the Alt attribute of the IMG tag used for the button).

The *.ascx* file for our example user control, which is shown in Example 4-8, simply contains a DataList control configured to render a table with an ItemTemplate to define the cells in the table. The ItemTemplate contains an anchor tag used for the navigation and an image tag to display the graphic button.

The code-behind for our example user control, shown in Example 4-9 (VB) and Example 4-10 (C#), contains three properties to enable customization of the navigation bar. The backgroundColor property provides the ability to change the background color of the navigation bar. The xmlFilename property defines the XML document that is used to populate the navigation bar. The navBarName property is used to define the name of the group of elements in the XML document that are used to populate the navigation bar. In this example, all of the elements are named Public. The example's design allows the XML document to have any number of other element groups, thus providing the ability to have a different navigation bar on different pages depending on the page type, user role, context, or the like. If you wanted a different navigation bar for the private pages in the site, for example, you would add a group of Private elements with the information needed to define the private navigation bar. How to select one is described later.

Our approach advocates leveraging a DataList tabular control for the workings of the navigation bar. Here's how we populate the DataList:

1. In the Page_Load method of the code-behind, the XML document containing the navigation bar data is read into a DataSet and then bound to the DataList.

2. The dlNavBar_ItemDataBound method is then called by ASP.NET for each of the items defined in the XML document (rows in the DataSet). Its job is to set the HRef of the anchor tag and then set the image source and alt text for the image tag.

To use the navigation bar user control in an *.aspx* page, the control must be registered with the @ Register directive at the top of the page and then the navigation bar control can be inserted into your page. Example 4-11 shows how this is done in our application, including the use of TagPrefix, TagName, and Src attributes that are set to the namespace of the project, the name of the control, and the name (and virtual path) of the *.ascx* file of the user control, respectively (see Recipe 4.1 for more details on these attributes).

In our example, the three properties of the navigation bar control must also be set. It is possible to set these in the *.aspx* file; however, because the xmlFilename property must be set to a fully qualified XML filename, this is better done in the code-behind, as shown in Example 4-12 (VB) and Example 4-13 (C#).

The navigation bar user control presented here is somewhat bland compared to most others. For instance, many navigation bars we have implemented support a changing image to indicate the active location in the site, complete with mouse-overs for each new image. When implementing this capability yourself, consider adding additional image information in the XML document to support the "on," "off," and "over" images. The typical mouse-over code will need to be added to the *.ascx* file, and the code-behind will need a currentPage property to provide the ability for it to change the images displayed as a function of the currently displayed page.

 The performance of the navigation control shown in this recipe can be significantly improved by caching the control, as described in Recipe 13.5.

See Also

Recipe 13.5 for caching user controls

Example 4-7. XML used for customizable navigation bar

```xml
<?xml version="1.0" encoding="utf-8"?>
<NavBar>
  <Public>
    <ButtonLink>../ChapterMenu.aspx</ButtonLink>
    <ImageSrc>images/nav/button_nav_home_off.gif</ImageSrc>
    <AltText>Home</AltText>
  </Public>
  <Public>
    <ButtonLink>../ProblemMenu.aspx?Chapter=1</ButtonLink>
    <ImageSrc>images/nav/button_nav_datagrids_off.gif</ImageSrc>
    <AltText>Datagrids</AltText>
  </Public>
  <Public>
    <ButtonLink>../ProblemMenu.aspx?Chapter=2</ButtonLink>
    <ImageSrc>images/nav/button_nav_validation_off.gif</ImageSrc>
    <AltText>Validation</AltText>
  </Public>
  <Public>
    <ButtonLink>../ProblemMenu.aspx?Chapter=3</ButtonLink>
    <ImageSrc>images/nav/button_nav_forms_off.gif</ImageSrc>
    <AltText>Forms</AltText>
  </Public>
  <Public>
    <ButtonLink>../ProblemMenu.aspx?Chapter=4</ButtonLink>
    <ImageSrc>images/nav/button_nav_user_controls_off.gif</ImageSrc>
    <AltText>User Controls</AltText>
  </Public>
</NavBar>
```

Example 4-8. Customizable navigation bar (.ascx)

```
<%@ Control Language="vb" AutoEventWireup="false"
            Codebehind="CH04UserControlNavBarVB1.ascx.vb"
            Inherits="ASPNetCookbook.VBExamples.CH04UserControlNavBarVB1" %>
<asp:datalist id="dlNavBar" runat="server"
              borderwidth="0" cellpadding="0" cellspacing="0" height="29"
              repeatdirection="Horizontal" repeatlayout="Table"
              width="100%">
  <itemtemplate>
    <td height="25" align="center">
      <a id="anNavBarLink" runat="server" >
      <img id="imgNavBarImage" runat="server" border="0"/></a></td>
  </itemtemplate>
</asp:datalist>
```

Example 4-9. Customizable navigation bar code-behind (.vb)

```
Option Explicit On
Option Strict On
'-----------------------------------------------------------------------------
'
'   Module Name: CH04UserControlNavBarVB1.ascx.vb
'
'   Description: This module provides the code behind for
'                CH04UserControlNavBarVB1.ascx
'
'*****************************************************************************
Imports System
Imports System.Data
Imports System.Web.UI.HtmlControls
Imports System.Web.UI.WebControls

Namespace ASPNetCookbook.VBExamples
  Public MustInherit Class CH04UserControlNavBarVB1
    Inherits System.Web.UI.UserControl

    'controls on the user control
    Protected WithEvents dlNavBar As System.Web.UI.WebControls.DataList

    'private attributes
    Private mXMLFilename As String
    Private mNavBarName As String

    'The following constants define the elements available
    'in the navigation bar XML document
    Private Const MENU_ITEM_BUTTON_LINK As String = "ButtonLink"
    Private Const MENU_ITEM_IMAGE_SRC As String = "ImageSrc"
    Private Const MENU_ITEM_ALT_TEXT As String = "AltText"

    '*****************************************************************************
    '
    '   ROUTINE: backgroundColor
    '
    '   DESCRIPTION: This property provides the ability get/set the
```

Example 4-9. Customizable navigation bar code-behind (.vb) (continued)

```vb
'                   background color used for the navigation bar
'----------------------------------------------------------------------
Public Property backgroundColor() As System.Drawing.Color
  Get
    Return (dlNavBar.BackColor)
  End Get

  Set(ByVal Value As System.Drawing.Color)
    dlNavBar.BackColor = Value
  End Set
End Property  'backgroundColor

'**********************************************************************
'
'    ROUTINE: xmlFilename
'
'    DESCRIPTION: This property provides the ability get/set the
'                 name of the xml file used to define the navigation bar
'----------------------------------------------------------------------
Public Property xmlFilename() As String
  Get
    Return (mXMLFilename)
  End Get

  Set(ByVal Value As String)
    mXMLFilename = Value
  End Set
End Property  'xmlFilename

'**********************************************************************
'
'    ROUTINE: navBarName
'
'    DESCRIPTION: This property provides the ability get/set the
'                 name of the navigation bar definition in the xml file
'----------------------------------------------------------------------
Public Property navBarName() As String
  Get
    Return (mNavBarName)
  End Get
  Set(ByVal Value As String)
    mNavBarName = Value
  End Set
End Property  'navBarName

'**********************************************************************
'
'    ROUTINE: Page_Load
'
'    DESCRIPTION: This routine provides the event handler for the page load
'                 event.  It is responsible for initializing the controls
'                 on the page.
'----------------------------------------------------------------------
```

Example 4-9. Customizable navigation bar code-behind (.vb) (continued)

```vb
Private Sub Page_Load(ByVal sender As System.Object, _
                        ByVal e As System.EventArgs) _
        Handles MyBase.Load
    Dim dsNavBarData As DataSet

    'load the XML document used to define the navigation bar items
    'into a dataset to provide easy traversal
    dsNavBarData = New DataSet
    dsNavBarData.ReadXml(xmlFilename)

    'bind the nav bar data to the repeater on the control
    dlNavBar.DataSource = dsNavBarData.Tables(navBarName)
    dlNavBar.DataBind()
End Sub 'Page_Load

'**************************************************************************
'
'    ROUTINE: dlNavBar_ItemDataBound
'
'    DESCRIPTION: This routine provides the event handler for the item
'                 data bound event of the datalist control in the nav bar.
'                 It is responsible for setting the anchor and image
'                 attributes for the item being bound.
'-------------------------------------------------------------------------
Private Sub dlNavBar_ItemDataBound(ByVal sender As Object, _
        ByVal e As System.Web.UI.WebControls.DataListItemEventArgs) _
        Handles dlNavBar.ItemDataBound
    'the following constants define the names of the controls in the datalist
    Const ANCHOR_CONTROL As String = "anNavBarLink"
    Const IMAGE_CONTROL As String = "imgNavBarImage"

    Dim anchorControl As HtmlAnchor
    Dim imageControl As HtmlImage
    Dim dRow As DataRowView

    'make sure this is an item or alternating item in the repeater
    If ((e.Item.ItemType = ListItemType.Item) Or _
        (e.Item.ItemType = ListItemType.AlternatingItem)) Then
        'get the data being bound
        dRow = CType(e.Item.DataItem, _
                    DataRowView)

        'find the link control then set it to the url
        anchorControl = CType(e.Item.FindControl(ANCHOR_CONTROL), _
                            HtmlAnchor)
        anchorControl.HRef = CStr(dRow.Item(MENU_ITEM_BUTTON_LINK))

        'find the image control then set the image source and alt text
        imageControl = CType(e.Item.FindControl(IMAGE_CONTROL), _
                            HtmlImage)
        imageControl.Src = CStr(dRow.Item(MENU_ITEM_IMAGE_SRC))
        imageControl.Alt = CStr(dRow.Item(MENU_ITEM_ALT_TEXT))
```

Example 4-9. Customizable navigation bar code-behind (.vb) (continued)

```
      End If
    End Sub    'repNavBarCell_ItemDataBound
  End Class    'CH04UserControlNavBarVB1
End Namespace
```

Example 4-10. Customizable navigation bar code-behind (.cs)

```
//-----------------------------------------------------------------------
//
//    Module Name: CH04UserControlNavBarCS1.ascx.cs
//
//    Description: This module provides the code behind for
//                 CH04UserControlNavBarCS1.ascx
//
//**********************************************************************
namespace ASPNetCookbook.CSExamples
{
  using System;
  using System.Data;
  using System.Drawing;
  using System.Web;
  using System.Web.UI.WebControls;
  using System.Web.UI.HtmlControls;

  public class CH04UserControlNavBarCS1 : System.Web.UI.UserControl
  {
    // controls on the user control
    protected System.Web.UI.WebControls.DataList dlNavBar;

    // private attributes
    private String mXMLFilename;
    private String mNavBarName;

    // The following constants define the elements available
    // in the navigation bar XML document
    private const String MENU_ITEM_BUTTON_LINK  = "ButtonLink";
    private const String MENU_ITEM_IMAGE_SRC  = "ImageSrc";
    private const String MENU_ITEM_ALT_TEXT = "AltText";

    //**********************************************************************
    //
    //    ROUTINE: backgroundColor
    //
    //    DESCRIPTION: This property provides the ability get/set the
    //                 background color used for the navigation bar
    //-----------------------------------------------------------------------
    public System.Drawing.Color backgroundColor
    {
      get
      {
        return(dlNavBar.BackColor);
      }
```

Example 4-10. Customizable navigation bar code-behind (.cs) (continued)

```
    set
    {
      dlNavBar.BackColor = value;
    }
} // backgroundColor

//*************************************************************************
//
//    ROUTINE: xmlFilename
//
//    DESCRIPTION: This property provides the ability get/set the
//                 name of the xml file used to define the navigation bar
//-------------------------------------------------------------------------
public String xmlFilename
{
  get
  {
    return(mXMLFilename);
  }
  set
  {
    mXMLFilename = value;
  }
} // xmlFilename

//*************************************************************************
//
//    ROUTINE: navBarName
//
//    DESCRIPTION: This property provides the ability get/set the
//                 name of the navigation bar defintion in the xml file
//-------------------------------------------------------------------------
public String navBarName
{
  get
  {
    return(mNavBarName);
  }
  set
  {
    mNavBarName = value;
  }
} // navBarName

//*************************************************************************
//
//    ROUTINE: Page_Load
//
//    DESCRIPTION: This routine provides the event handler for the page
//                 load event.  It is responsible for initializing the
//                 controls on the user control.
//-------------------------------------------------------------------------
```

Example 4-10. Customizable navigation bar code-behind (.cs) (continued)

```csharp
private void Page_Load(object sender, System.EventArgs e)
{
  // wire the item data bound event
  this.dlNavBar.ItemDataBound +=
    new DataListItemEventHandler(this.dlNavBar_ItemDataBound);

  // load the XML document used to define the navigation bar items
  // into a dataset to provide easy traversal
  DataSet dsNavBarData = new DataSet( );
  dsNavBarData.ReadXml(xmlFilename);

  // bind the nav bar data to the repeater on the control
  dlNavBar.DataSource = dsNavBarData.Tables[navBarName];
  dlNavBar.DataBind( );
} // Page_Load

//*************************************************************************
//
//   ROUTINE: dlNavBar_ItemDataBound
//
//   DESCRIPTION: This routine provides the event handler for the item
//                data bound event of the datalist control in the nav bar.
//                It is responsible for setting the anchor and image
//                attributes for the item being bound.
//-------------------------------------------------------------------------
private void dlNavBar_ItemDataBound(Object sender,
                      System.Web.UI.WebControls.DataListItemEventArgs e)
{
  // the following constants define the names of the controls in
  // the datalist
  const String ANCHOR_CONTROL = "anNavBarLink";
  const String IMAGE_CONTROL = "imgNavBarImage";

  HtmlAnchor anchorControl = null;
  HtmlImage imageControl = null;
  DataRowView dRow = null;

  // make sure this is an item or alternating item in the repeater
  if ((e.Item.ItemType == ListItemType.Item) ||
      (e.Item.ItemType == ListItemType.AlternatingItem))
  {
    // get the data being bound
    dRow = (DataRowView)(e.Item.DataItem);

    // find the link control then set it to the url
    anchorControl = (HtmlAnchor)(e.Item.FindControl(ANCHOR_CONTROL));
    anchorControl.HRef = (String)(dRow[MENU_ITEM_BUTTON_LINK]);

    // find the image control then set the image source and alt text
    imageControl = (HtmlImage)(e.Item.FindControl(IMAGE_CONTROL));
    imageControl.Src = (String)(dRow[MENU_ITEM_IMAGE_SRC]);
    imageControl.Alt = (String)(dRow[MENU_ITEM_ALT_TEXT]);
  }
```

Example 4-10. Customizable navigation bar code-behind (.cs) (continued)

```
    } // repNavBarCell_ItemDataBound
  } // CH04UserControlNavBarCS1
}
```

Example 4-11. Using the navigation bar (.aspx)

```
<%@ Page Language="vb" AutoEventWireup="false"
        Codebehind="CH04DisplayNavBarVB1.aspx.vb"
        Inherits="ASPNetCookbook.VBExamples.CH04DisplayNavBarVB1" %>
<%@ Register TagPrefix="ASPCookbook" TagName="NavBar"
             Src="CH04UserControlNavBarVB1.ascx" %>
<!DOCTYPE HTML PUBLIC "-//W3C//DTD HTML 4.0 Transitional//EN">
<html>
  <head>
    <title>User Control Display Navigation Bar</title>
    <link rel="stylesheet" href="css/ASPNetCookbook.css">
  </head>
  <body>
    <form id="frmNavBarTest" method="post" runat="server">
      <table width="100%" cellpadding="0" cellspacing="0" border="0">
        <tr>
          <td align="center">
            <img src="images/ASPNETCookbookHeading_blue.gif">
          </td>
        </tr>
        <tr>
          <td class="dividerLine">
            <img src="images/spacer.gif" height="6" border="0"></td>
        </tr>
      </table>
      <table width="100%" align="center" border="0"
             cellpadding="0" cellspacing="0" >
        <tr>
          <td><ASPCookbook:NavBar id="navBar" runat="server" />
          </td>
        </tr>
      </table>
    </form>
  </body>
</html>
```

Example 4-12. Using the navigation bar code-behind (.vb)

```
Option Explicit On
Option Strict On
'-----------------------------------------------------------------------------
'
'   Module Name: CH04DisplayNavBarVB1.aspx.vb
'
'   Description: This module provides the code behind for
'               CH04DisplayNavBarVB1.aspx
'
'*****************************************************************************
```

Example 4-12. Using the navigation bar code-behind (.vb) (continued)

```vb
Imports System.Drawing

Namespace ASPNetCookbook.VBExamples
  Public Class CH04DisplayNavBarVB1
    Inherits System.Web.UI.Page

    'controls on page
    Protected navBar As ASPNetCookbook.VBExamples.CH04UserControlNavBarVB1

    '*************************************************************************
    '
    '    ROUTINE: Page_Load
    '
    '    DESCRIPTION: This routine provides the event handler for the page load
    '                 event.  It is responsible for initializing the controls
    '                 on the page.
    '-------------------------------------------------------------------------
    Private Sub Page_Load(ByVal sender As System.Object, _
                          ByVal e As System.EventArgs) Handles MyBase.Load
      navBar.xmlFilename = Server.MapPath("xml") & "\NavigationBar.xml"
      navBar.navBarName = "Public"
      navBar.backgroundColor = ColorTranslator.FromHtml("#6B0808")
    End Sub  'Page_Load
  End Class  'CH04DisplayNavBarVB1
End Namespace
```

Example 4-13. Using the navigation bar code-behind (.cs)

```csharp
//----------------------------------------------------------------------------
//
//    Module Name: CH04DisplayNavBarCS1.ascx.cs
//
//    Description: This module provides the code behind for
//                 CH04DisplayNavBarCS1.ascx
//
//****************************************************************************
using System;
using System.Drawing;

namespace ASPNetCookbook.CSExamples
{
  public class CH04DisplayNavBarCS1 : System.Web.UI.Page
  {
    // controls on form
    protected ASPNetCookbook.CSExamples.CH04UserControlNavBarCS1 navBar;

    //**************************************************************************
    //
    //    ROUTINE: Page_Load
    //
    //    DESCRIPTION: This routine provides the event handler for the page
    //                 load event.  It is responsible for initializing the
    //                 controls on the page.
```

Example 4-13. Using the navigation bar code-behind (.cs) (continued)

```
  //
  //--------------------------------------------------------------------------
  private void Page_Load(object sender, System.EventArgs e)
  {
    navBar.xmlFilename = Server.MapPath("xml") + "\\NavigationBar.xml";
    navBar.navBarName = "Public";
    navBar.backgroundColor = ColorTranslator.FromHtml("#6B0808");
  }  // Page_Load
  }  // CH04DisplayNavBarCS1
}
```

4.3   Reusing Code-Behind Classes

Problem

You have several page sections that require identical code-behind but the user presentation must be different for each.

Solution

Create a user control for the first page section. For the other page sections, create only the *.ascx* file and link it to the code-behind class for the first page section. For example, to produce the vertically oriented navigation shown in Figure 4-3, create the navigation bar user control described in Recipe 4.2, then create the *.ascx* file shown in Example 4-14, all without writing any VB or C# code.

Figure 4-3. Reuse of code-behind class output

Discussion

The @ Control directive at the top of the *.ascx* page defines the code-behind that will be used with the *.ascx* file. The Codebehind attribute defines the name of the file containing the code-behind code. The Inherits attribute defines the class in the code-behind file that inherits from System.Web.UI.UserControl and provides the actual code-behind code.

By changing the Codebehind and Inherits attributes of the *.ascx* file, you can reuse code. In our example, the attributes are set as shown here to reuse the code-behind from Recipe 4.2:

```
<%@ Control Language="vb" AutoEventWireup="false"
        Codebehind="UserControlNavBarVB1.ascx.vb"
        Inherits="ASPNetCookbook.VBExamples.UserControlNavBarVB1" %>
```

A significant aspect of this approach is that the user control can provide any desired user interface without changing any of the code-behind. The only requirement is that the server controls referenced in the code-behind class must be present in the *.ascx*, and they must be of the same type. Leaving a server control out of the *.ascx* or changing its type will result in an exception being thrown.

See Also

Recipe 4.2

Example 4-14. Reuse of code-behind class (.ascx)

```
<%@ Control Language="vb" AutoEventWireup="false"
        Codebehind="CH04UserControlNavBarVB1.ascx.vb"
        Inherits="ASPNetCookbook.VBExamples.CH04UserControlNavBarVB1" %>
<asp:datalist id="dlNavBar" runat="server"
                borderwidth="0" cellpadding="0" cellspacing="0" height="29"
                repeatdirection="vertical" repeatcolumns="1"
                repeatlayout="Table" width="150" horizontalalign="Left"
                itemstyle-horizontalalign="Center">
  <itemtemplate>
    <a id="anNavBarLink" runat="server" >
    <img id="imgNavBarImage" runat="server" border="0"/></a>
  </itemtemplate>
</asp:datalist>
```

4.4   Communicating Between User Controls

Problem

You have multiple user controls on a page, and one of the user controls needs to send data to another as, for example, when one control takes its form or content from the user's action on another.

Solution

Create a source user control, a destination user control, and a web form that contains both user controls. (See Recipes 4.1 and 4.2 for detailed steps.) In the source user control, create a custom event and raise the event when the required action is performed, such as when a user completes her entry for a form. In the destination user control, create an event handler to receive the event from the source user control. Finally, "wire" the event raised in the source user control to the event handler in the destination user control in the Page_Load event of the web form. The output of a test page showing one user control communicating with another appears in Figure 4-4. The code for our example application that implements the solution is shown in Examples 4-15 through 4-23. Example 4-15 shows the *.ascx* file for the source user control. Examples 4-16 and 4-17 show the VB and C# code-behind for the source user control. Example 4-18 shows the *.ascx* file for the destination user control. Examples 4-19 and 4-20 show the VB and C# code-behind for the destination user control. Example 4-21 shows the *.aspx* file for the web form used to demonstrate the user controls and their interconnection. Examples 4-22 and 4-23 show the VB and C# code-behind for the demonstration web form.

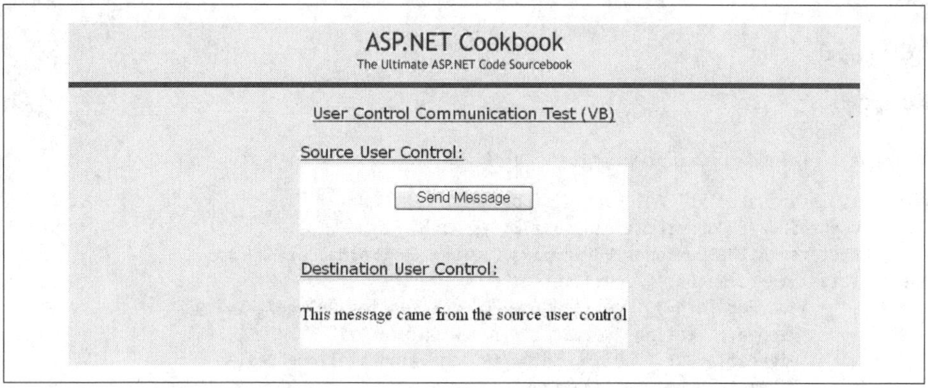

ASP.NET Cookbook
The Ultimate ASP.NET Code Sourcebook

User Control Communication Test (VB)

Source User Control:

Send Message

Destination User Control:

This message came from the source user control

Figure 4-4. Communicating between controls output

Discussion

Rather than focus on the basic content and creation of user controls, which is the focus of the previous recipes in the chapter, this recipe instead focuses on the interaction between user controls. The approach we advocate for handling this interaction involves creating a custom event for the source user control and raising the event when the communication is to be initiated, such as when the user clicks a button to complete his entry for the form. In order to receive the event from the source user control, the destination user control must have an event handler tailored for that purpose.

In our approach, creating the custom event for the source user control involves creating a custom event argument class, which provides the ability to add a message to the event arguments. It also involves using a delegate, which is a convenient way to pass to the destination user control a reference to an event handler for the OnSend event raised by the source user control.

We've created an application to illustrate our approach. Because of the unusually high number of interrelated files, this example may appear a bit overwhelming at first, but it is actually pretty straightforward. Keep in mind that there are three basic pieces:

- A user control that sends a message (the source)
- A user control that receives the message (the destination)
- A web form that contains the two user controls and wires them together

The source user control contains only a button that is used to initiate sending a message.

The source user control code-behind contains the bulk of the code. First, we create a custom event argument class to provide the ability to add the message to the event arguments. This class inherits from System.EventArgs and adds a message property, as shown in Example 4-16 (VB) and Example 4-17 (C#).

Next, we define a new delegate signature, customMessageHandler, to allow the MessageEventArgs object to be passed as the event arguments. Without this delegate, you would have to use the EventArgs object, which does not provide the ability to pass custom information. An event is then defined with this type of delegate.

A *delegate* is a class that can hold a reference to a method. A delegate class has a signature, and it can only hold references to methods that match its signature. The delegate object is passed to code that calls the referenced method, without having to know at compile time which method will actually be invoked. The most common example is building a generic sort routine, one that allows you to sort any type of data, where you pass to it not only the data to be sorted but also a reference to the comparison routine needed to compare the particular data. The situation here is somewhat similar. In this case, we are passing a message to the destination user control (contained within an instance of MessageEventArgs) as well as a reference to an event handler for the OnSend event raised by the source user control. A delegate provides the best, most convenient way to accomplish this.

Our remaining task in the source user control code-behind is to provide a standard event handler for the send message button click event. In this handler, an instance of MessageEventArgs is created and populated with the message being sent. The OnSend event is then raised, passing a reference to the source user control as the event source and a reference to the messageArgs object containing the message being sent. In our example, this is a simple hardwired message, but it demonstrates the basic principal.

In C#, the OnSend event must be checked to make sure it is not null before raising the event. Failure to do so will result in an exception being thrown if no handler is wired to the event. This is not required for VB.

Our example's destination user control, which is shown in Example 4-18, contains only a label used to display the message sent from the source user control.

The destination user control code-behind, which is shown in VB in Example 4-19 and in C# in Example 4-20, contains a single method to handle the event raised from the source user control. The signature of the method must match the customMessageHandler delegate defined in the source user control. The only operation performed is to update the label in the user control with the message passed in the event arguments.

In our example, the *.aspx* file for the web form used to demonstrate the user controls, which appears in Example 4-21, registers the two user controls and instantiates each of the controls.

The code-behind for the demonstration web form, which is shown in VB in Example 4-22 and in C# in Example 4-23, provides the glue for tying the event from the source user control to the destination user control. This is done by adding the updateLabel of the destination user control as an event handler for the OnSend event raised by the source user control. What we're actually doing here is adding a delegate to the source user control's OnSend event's event handler list; that list now consists of just one event handler, but can include more.

Event delegates in .NET are multicast, which allows them to hold references to more than one event handler. This provides the ability for one event to be processed by multiple event handlers. You can try it yourself by adding a label to the demonstration web form, adding a new event handler in the web form, and then adding your new event handler to the OnSend event's event handler list. This will cause the label on the destination user control and the web form to be updated with the message from the source user control. An example that does this with multiple user controls is shown in Recipe 4.5.

In VB, when using the event/delegate model, the keyword WithEvents is not used. (Recall that the WithEvents keyword indicates that a declared object variable refers to a class instance that can raise events.) WithEvents and the event/delegate model can be intermixed, but they should not be used for the same event.

See Also

Programming C# or *Programming Visual Basic .NET*, both by Jesse Liberty (O'Reilly), for more about delegates

Example 4-15. Communicating between controls—source user control (.ascx)

```
<%@ Control Language="vb" AutoEventWireup="false"
    Codebehind="CH04UserControlCommSourceVB.ascx.vb"
    Inherits="ASPNetCookbook.VBExamples.CH04UserControlCommSourceVB" %>
<asp:Button ID="btnSendMessage" runat="server" Text="Send Message" />
```

Example 4-16. Communicating between controls—source user control code-behind (.vb)

```
Option Explicit On
Option Strict On
'-------------------------------------------------------------------------
'
'   Module Name: CH04UserControlCommSourceVB.ascx.vb
'
'   Description: This module provides the code behind for
```

Example 4-16. Communicating between controls—source user control code-behind (.vb) (continued)

```vb
'                    CH04UserControlCommSourceVB.ascx
'
'*****************************************************************************
Imports System

Namespace ASPNetCookbook.VBExamples
  Public MustInherit Class CH04UserControlCommSourceVB
    Inherits System.Web.UI.UserControl

    'controls on the user control
    Protected WithEvents btnSendMessage As System.Web.UI.WebControls.Button

    'define the delegate handler signature and the event that will be raised
    'to send the message
    Public Delegate Sub customMessageHandler(ByVal sender As System.Object, _
                                             ByVal e As MessageEventArgs)
    Public Event OnSend As customMessageHandler

    '*****************************************************************************
    '
    '   ROUTINE: btnSendMessage_Click
    '
    '   DESCRIPTION: This routine provides the event handler for the send
    '                message button click event.  It creates a new
    '                MessageEventArgs object then raises an OnSend event
    '---------------------------------------------------------------------------
    Private Sub btnSendMessage_Click(ByVal sender As Object, _
                                     ByVal e As System.EventArgs) _
              Handles btnSendMessage.Click

      Dim messageArgs As New MessageEventArgs

      messageArgs.message = "This message came from the source user control"
      RaiseEvent OnSend(Me, messageArgs)
    End Sub   'btnSendMessage_Click
End Class   'CH04UserControlCommSourceVB

'The following class provides the definition of the custom event arguments
'used as the event arguments for the message sent from this control
'This class simply inherits from System.EventArgs and adds a message property
Public Class MessageEventArgs
  Inherits EventArgs

  Private mMessage As String
  Public Property message() As String
    Get
      Return (mMessage)
    End Get
    Set(ByVal Value As String)
      mMessage = Value
    End Set
  End Property
```

Example 4-16. Communicating between controls—source user control code-behind (.vb) (continued)

```
  End Class  'MessageEventArgs
End Namespace
```

Example 4-17. Communicating between controls—source user control code-behind (.cs)

```
//-----------------------------------------------------------------------------
//
//    Module Name: CH04UserControlCommSourceCS.ascx.cs
//
//    Description: This module provides the code behind for
//                 CH04UserControlCommSourceCS.ascx
//
//*****************************************************************************
using System;

namespace ASPNetCookbook.CSExamples
{
  public abstract class CH04UserControlCommSourceCS : System.Web.UI.UserControl
  {
    // controls on the user control
    protected System.Web.UI.WebControls.Button btnSendMessage;

    // define the delegate handler signature and the event that will be raised
    // to send the message
    public delegate void customMessageHandler(System.Object sender,
                                              MessageEventArgs e);
    public event customMessageHandler OnSend;

    //*************************************************************************
    //
    //    ROUTINE: Page_Load
    //
    //    DESCRIPTION: This routine provides the event handler for the page
    //                 load event.  It is responsible for initializing the
    //                 controls on the user control.
    //-------------------------------------------------------------------------
    private void Page_Load(object sender, System.EventArgs e)
    {
      // wire the click event for the send button
      this.btnSendMessage.Click +=
        new System.EventHandler(this.btnSendMessage_Click);
    }  // Page_Load

    //*************************************************************************
    //
    //    ROUTINE: btnSendMessage_Click
    //
    //    DESCRIPTION: This routine provides the event handler for the send
    //                 message button click event.  It creates a new
    //                 MessageEventArgs object then raises an OnSend event
    //-------------------------------------------------------------------------
    private void btnSendMessage_Click(Object sender,
                                      System.EventArgs e)
```

```cs
      {
        MessageEventArgs messageArgs = new MessageEventArgs( );
        messageArgs.message = "This message came from the source user control";

        if (OnSend != null)
        {
          OnSend(this, messageArgs);
        }
      }  // btnSendMessage_Click
    }  // CH04UserControlCommSourceCS

    // The following class provides the definition of the custom event
    // arguments used as the event arguments for the message sent from this
    // control.  This class simply inherits from System.EventArgs and adds
    // a message property.
    public class MessageEventArgs : System.EventArgs
    {
      private String mMessage;
      public String message
      {
        get
        {
          return(mMessage);
        }
        set
        {
          mMessage = value;
        }
      }  // message
    }  // MessageEventArgs
}
```

Example 4-18. Communicating between controls—destination user control (.ascx)

```
<%@ Control Language="vb" AutoEventWireup="false"
      Codebehind="CH04UserControlCommDestinationVB.ascx.vb"
      Inherits="ASPNetCookbook.VBExamples.CH04UserControlCommDestinationVB" %>
<asp:Label ID="labMessage" Runat="server">No Message Yet</asp:Label>
```

Example 4-19. Destination user control code-behind (.vb)

```vb
Option Explicit On
Option Strict On
'-----------------------------------------------------------------------------
'
'   Module Name: CH04UserControlCommDestinationVB.ascx.vb
'
'   Description: This module provides the code behind for
'               CH04UserControlCommDestinationVB.ascx
'
'*****************************************************************************
Imports System
```

Example 4-19. Destination user control code-behind (.vb) (continued)

```vb
Namespace ASPNetCookbook.VBExamples
  Public MustInherit Class CH04UserControlCommDestinationVB
    Inherits System.Web.UI.UserControl

    'controls on the user control
    Protected labMessage As System.Web.UI.WebControls.Label

    '*************************************************************************
    '
    '   ROUTINE: updateLabel
    '
    '   DESCRIPTION: This routine provides the event handler that is the
    '                recipient of the event raised by the source user control.
    '-------------------------------------------------------------------------
    Public Sub updateLabel(ByVal sender As System.Object, _
                           ByVal e As MessageEventArgs)
      'update the label with the message in the event arguments
      labMessage.Text = e.message
    End Sub  'updateLabel
  End Class  'CH04UserControlCommDestinationVB
End Namespace
```

Example 4-20. Destination user control code-behind (.cs)

```cs
//-------------------------------------------------------------------------
//
//    Module Name:  CH04UserControlCommDestinationCS.ascx.cs
//
//    Description: This module provides the code behind for
//                 CH04UserControlCommDestinationCS.ascx
//
//*************************************************************************
using System;

namespace ASPNetCookbook.CSExamples
{
  public abstract class CH04UserControlCommDestinationCS :
                        System.Web.UI.UserControl
  {
    // controls on the user control
    protected System.Web.UI.WebControls.Label labMessage;

    //*************************************************************************
    //
    //    ROUTINE: updateLabel
    //
    //    DESCRIPTION: This routine provides the event handler that is the
    //                 recipient of the event raised by the source user
    //                 control.
    //-------------------------------------------------------------------------
    public void updateLabel(System.Object sender,
                            MessageEventArgs e)
    {
```

Example 4-20. Destination user control code-behind (.cs) (continued)

```
        // update the label with the message in the event arguments
        labMessage.Text = e.message;
    } // updateLabel
  } // CH04UserControlCommDestinationCS
}
```

Example 4-21. Communicating between controls—main form (.aspx)

```
<%@ Page Language="vb" AutoEventWireup="false"
        Codebehind="CH04UserControlCommTestVB.aspx.vb"
        Inherits="ASPNetCookbook.VBExamples.CH04UserControlCommTestVB" %>
<%@ Register TagPrefix="ASPCookbook" TagName="SourceControl"
            Src="CH04UserControlCommSourceVB.ascx" %>
<%@ Register TagPrefix="ASPCookbook" TagName="DestinationControl"
            Src="CH04UserControlCommDestinationVB.ascx" %>
<!DOCTYPE HTML PUBLIC "-//W3C//DTD HTML 4.0 Transitional//EN">
<html>
  <head>
    <title>User Control Communication Test</title>
    <link rel="stylesheet" href="css/ASPNetCookbook.css">
  </head>
  <body leftmargin="0" marginheight="0" marginwidth="0" topmargin="0">
    <form id="frmUCCommTest" method="post" runat="server">
      <table width="100%" cellpadding="0" cellspacing="0" border="0">
        <tr>
          <td align="center">
            <img src="images/ASPNETCookbookHeading_blue.gif">
          </td>
        </tr>
        <tr>
          <td class="dividerLine">
            <img src="images/spacer.gif" height="6" border="0"></td>
        </tr>
      </table>
      <table width="90%" align="center" border="0">
        <tr>
          <td><img src="images/spacer.gif" height="10" border="0"></td>
        </tr>
        <tr>
          <td align="center" class="PageHeading">
            User Control Communication Test (VB)
          </td>
        </tr>
        <tr>
          <td><img src="images/spacer.gif" height="10" border="0"></td>
        </tr>
        <tr>
          <td align="center">
            <table border="0">
              <tr>
                <td class="PageHeading">
                  Source User Control:
                </td>
```

Example 4-21. Communicating between controls—main form (.aspx) (continued)

```
            </tr>
            <tr>
              <td bgcolor="#ffffcc" align="center" height="75">
                <ASPCookbook:SourceControl id="ucSource" runat="server" />
              </td>
            </tr>
            <tr>
              <td> </td>
            </tr>
            <tr>
              <td class="PageHeading">
                Destination User Control:
              </td>
            </tr>
            <tr>
              <td bgcolor="#ffffcc" align="center" height="75">
                <ASPCookbook:DestinationControl id="ucDestination"
                                                 runat="server" />
              </td>
            </tr>
          </table>
        </td>
      </tr>
    </table>
  </form>
 </body>
</html>
```

Example 4-22. Communicating between controls—main form code-behind (.vb)

```
Option Explicit On
Option Strict On
'-----------------------------------------------------------------------------
'
'   Module Name: CH04UserControlCommTestVB.aspx.vb
'
'   Description: This module provides the code behind for
'                CH04UserControlCommTestVB.aspx
'
'*****************************************************************************
Namespace ASPNetCookbook.VBExamples
  Public Class CH04UserControlCommTestVB
    Inherits System.Web.UI.Page

    'controls on the form
    Protected ucSource As CH04UserControlCommSourceVB
    Protected ucDestination As CH04UserControlCommDestinationVB

    '*************************************************************************
    '
    '   ROUTINE: Page_Load
    '
```

Example 4-22. Communicating between controls—main form code-behind (.vb) (continued)

```
    '    DESCRIPTION: This routine provides the event handler for the page load
    '                 event.  It is responsible for wiring the source user
    '                 control to the destination user control.
    '------------------------------------------------------------------------
    Private Sub Page_Load(ByVal sender As System.Object, _
                          ByVal e As System.EventArgs) _
            Handles MyBase.Load
      'wire the event to the destination user control handler
      AddHandler ucSource.OnSend, AddressOf ucDestination.updateLabel

    End Sub   'Page_Load
  End Class   'CH04UserControlCommTestVB
End Namespace
```

Example 4-23. Communicating between controls—main form code-behind (.cs)

```
//----------------------------------------------------------------------------
//
//    Module Name: CH04UserControlCommTestCS.aspx.cs
//
//    Description: This module provides the code behind for
//                 CH04UserControlCommTestCS.aspx
//
//****************************************************************************
using ASPNetCookbook.CSExamples;
using System;

namespace ASPNetCookbook.CSExamples
{
  public class CH04UserControlCommTestCS : System.Web.UI.Page
  {
    // controls on the form
    protected CH04UserControlCommSourceCS ucSource;
    protected CH04UserControlCommDestinationCS ucDestination;

    //****************************************************************************
    //
    //    ROUTINE: Page_Load
    //
    //    DESCRIPTION: This routine provides the event handler for the page
    //                 load event.  It is responsible for initializing the
    //                 controls on the page.
    //------------------------------------------------------------------------
    private void Page_Load(object sender, System.EventArgs e)
    {
      // wire the event to the destination user control handler
ucSource.OnSend +=
  new
  CH04UserControlCommSourceCS.customMessageHandler(ucDestination.updateLabel);
    } // Page_Load
  } // CH04UserControlCommTestCS
}
```

4.5   Adding User Controls Dynamically

Problem

You need to programmatically load a group of user controls at runtime because the number of controls required is not known at design time.

Solution

Bind your data to a Repeater control in the normal fashion and then, as data is bound to each row of the Repeater, use the event to dynamically load a user control and place it in a table cell of the Repeater control's ItemTemplate.

Add a Repeater control to the *.aspx* file with a table cell in the ItemTemplate where the user control is to be placed.

In the code-behind class, use the .NET language of your choice to:

1. Bind the data to the Repeater control.

2. Create an event handler method for the ItemDataBound event of the Repeater control.

3. In the method that handles the ItemDataBound event, use the LoadControl method to create an instance of the user control, and then add the loaded control to the controls collection of the table cell in the ItemTemplate.

Figure 4-5 shows a simple form where we start with the user controls created in Recipe 4.4 and dynamically load three user controls at runtime. Example 4-24 shows the *.aspx* file that implements this solution, while Examples 4-25 and 4-26 show the companion VB and C# code-behind files.

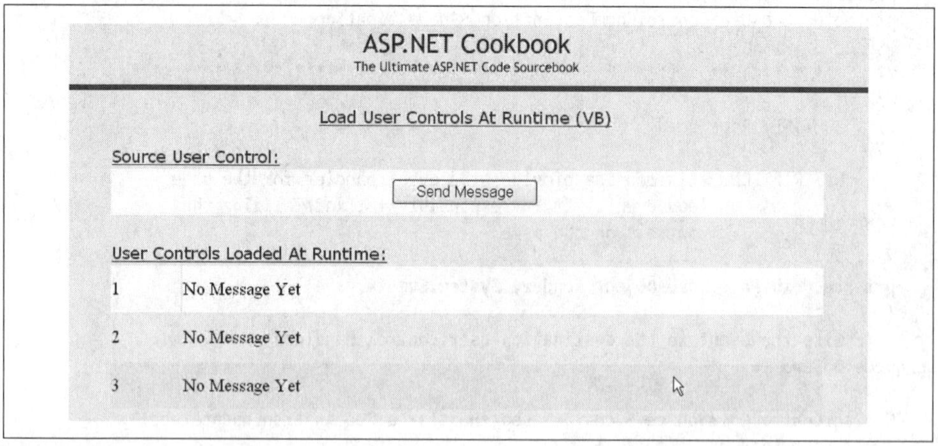

Figure 4-5. User controls loaded at runtime output

Discussion

This recipe demonstrates how to dynamically load a group of user controls into a form, the count for which can be determined only at runtime. A Repeater control is used because it generates a lightweight read-only tabular display and is template-driven. The Repeater control's ItemTemplate element formats the rows of data. The user control dynamically loaded at runtime is strategically placed in a table cell in the ItemTemplate. This loading takes place in the method that handles the ItemDataBound event for each row of the Repeater. More specifically, the LoadControl method is used to create an instance of the user control, and then the loaded control is added to the controls collection of the table cell.

The example we have written to demonstrate the solution starts with the user controls created in Recipe 4.4 and loads the destination user controls at runtime. In addition, it wires them to the source user control to demonstrate the multicast event mechanism in .NET.

An ASP:Repeater control is placed in the *.aspx* file with an ItemTemplate containing two table cells. The first cell is used to hold the dynamically loaded user control's number, and the second cell is used to hold the user control itself. Example 4-24 shows how we've implemented this in our example.

 The dynamically loaded user controls can be added to the Page control collection; however, this will place them at the bottom of the page and they will be rendered outside of the form. Dynamically loaded user controls should be added to the controls collection of some control contained within the form.

In the repUserControls_ItemDataBound method of the code-behind, the user control for the row being bound is loaded at runtime from the *.ascx* file using the LoadControl method. It is then added to the controls collection of the second table cell in the Repeater.

Just to demonstrate the multicast event mechanism in .NET that we mentioned in Recipe 4.4, each of the dynamically loaded user controls is wired to the source user control in the *.aspx* file. This results in each of the dynamically loaded user controls receiving the message event from the source user control.

VB
```
AddHandler ucSource.OnSend, AddressOf ucDest.updateLabel
```

C#
```
ucSource.OnSend +=
    new CH04UserControlCommSourceCS.customMessageHandler(ucDest.updateLabel);
```

The result in this case is that each destination user control is updated with the same text from the source user control—not very exciting. But it is not hard to imagine a more interesting scenario where one destination user control has a text label updated, the second a database, and the third an XML web service, or the like, with all of these updates the result of methods having been registered with the source control's OnSend event's event handler list.

Example 4-24. User controls loaded at runtime (.aspx)

```
<%@ Page Language="vb" AutoEventWireup="false"
        Codebehind="CH04UserControlRuntimeVB.aspx.vb"
        Inherits="ASPNetCookbook.VBExamples.CH04UserControlRuntimeVB" %>
<%@ Register TagPrefix="ASPCookbook" TagName="SourceControl"
            Src="CH04UserControlCommSourceVB.ascx" %>
<!DOCTYPE HTML PUBLIC "-//W3C//DTD HTML 4.0 Transitional//EN">
<html>
  <head>
    <title>Load User Controls At Runtime</title>
    <link rel="stylesheet" href="css/ASPNetCookbook.css">
  </head>
  <body leftmargin="0" marginheight="0" marginwidth="0" topmargin="0">
    <form id="frmUCRuntime" method="post" runat="server">
      <table width="100%" cellpadding="0" cellspacing="0" border="0">
        <tr>
          <td align="center">
            <img src="images/ASPNETCookbookHeading_blue.gif">
          </td>
        </tr>
        <tr>
          <td class="dividerLine">
            <img src="images/spacer.gif" height="6" border="0"></td>
        </tr>
      </table>
      <table width="90%" align="center" border="0">
        <tr>
          <td><img src="images/spacer.gif" height="10" border="0"></td>
        </tr>
        <tr>
          <td align="center" class="PageHeading">
            Load User Controls At Runtime (VB)
          </td>
        </tr>
        <tr>
          <td><img src="images/spacer.gif" height="10" border="0"></td>
        </tr>
        <tr>
          <td align="center">
            <table border="0" width="100%">
              <tr>
                <td class="PageHeading" colspan="2">
                  Source User Control:</td>
              </tr>
              <tr>
                <td bgcolor="#ffffcc" align="center" height="50" colspan="2">
                  <ASPCookbook:SourceControl id="ucSource" runat="server" />
                </td>
              </tr>
```

Example 4-24. User controls loaded at runtime (.aspx) (continued)

```
            <tr>
              <td colspan="2"> </td>
            </tr>
            <tr>
              <td class="PageHeading" colspan="2">
                 User Controls Loaded At Runtime:</td>
            </tr>
            <asp:repeater id="repUserControls" runat="server">
              <itemtemplate>
                <tr id="trControl" runat="server" height="50">
                  <td id="tdCount" runat="server" width="10%"></td>
                  <td id="tdUserControl" runat="server"></td>
                </tr>
              </itemtemplate>
            </asp:repeater>
          </table>
        </td>
      </tr>
    </table>
  </form>
  </body>
</html>
```

Example 4-25. User controls loaded at runtime code-behind (.vb)

```
Option Explicit On
Option Strict On
'----------------------------------------------------------------------------
'
'    Module Name: CH04UserControlRuntimeVB.aspx.vb
'
'    Description: This module provides the code behind for
'                 CH04UserControlRuntimeVB.aspx
'
'****************************************************************************
Imports System.Collections
Imports System.Drawing
Imports System.Web.UI.HtmlControls
Imports System.Web.UI.WebControls

Namespace ASPNetCookbook.VBExamples
  Public Class CH04UserControlRuntimeVB
    Inherits System.Web.UI.Page

    'controls on the form
    Protected ucSource As CH04UserControlCommSourceVB
    Protected WithEvents repUserControls As System.Web.UI.WebControls.Repeater

    'the following variable is used to keep count of the number of controls
    Private controlCount As Integer
```

Example 4-25. User controls loaded at runtime code-behind (.vb) (continued)

```
'***************************************************************************
'
'    ROUTINE: Page_Load
'
'    DESCRIPTION: This routine provides the event handler for the page load
'                 event.  It is responsible for initializing the
'                 controls on the page.
'---------------------------------------------------------------------------
Private Sub Page_Load(ByVal sender As System.Object, _
                      ByVal e As System.EventArgs) _
        Handles MyBase.Load
  Dim values As ArrayList = New ArrayList

  'build array of data to bind to repeater
  'for this example it is just the color of the entry but for a real
  'application the data would normally be from a database, etc.
  values.Add("#ffffcc")
  values.Add("#ccffff")
  values.Add("#ccff99")

  'bind the data to the repeater
  controlCount = 0
  repUserControls.DataSource = values
  repUserControls.DataBind( )
End Sub  'Page_Load


'***************************************************************************
'
'    ROUTINE: repUserControls_ItemDataBound
'
'    DESCRIPTION: This routine provides the event handler for the item
'                 data bound event of the repeater control on the form.
'                 It is responsible for loading the user control and
'                 placing it in the repeater for the item being bound.
'---------------------------------------------------------------------------
Private Sub repUserControls_ItemDataBound(ByVal sender As Object, _
        ByVal e As System.Web.UI.WebControls.RepeaterItemEventArgs) _
        Handles repUserControls.ItemDataBound
  'the following constants are the names of the controls in the repeater
  Const TABLE_ROW As String = "trControl"
  Const COUNT_CELL As String = "tdCount"
  Const USER_CONTROL_CELL As String = "tdUserControl"

  Dim row As HtmlTableRow
  Dim cell As HtmlTableCell
  Dim ucDest As CH04UserControlCommDestinationVB

  'make sure this is an item or alternating item in the repeater
  If ((e.Item.ItemType = ListItemType.Item) Or _
      (e.Item.ItemType = ListItemType.AlternatingItem)) Then
```

Example 4-25. User controls loaded at runtime code-behind (.vb) (continued)

```
        'find the table row and set the background color
        row = CType(e.Item.FindControl(TABLE_ROW), _
                HtmlTableRow)
        row.BgColor = CStr(e.Item.DataItem)

        'find the cell for the control count and set the count
        cell = CType(e.Item.FindControl(COUNT_CELL), _
                HtmlTableCell)
        controlCount += 1
        cell.InnerText = controlCount.ToString()

        'find the cell for the control and load a user control
        cell = CType(e.Item.FindControl(USER_CONTROL_CELL), _
                HtmlTableCell)
        ucDest = CType(LoadControl("CH04UserControlCommDestinationVB.ascx"), _
                CH04UserControlCommDestinationVB)
        cell.Controls.Add(ucDest)
        AddHandler ucSource.OnSend, AddressOf ucDest.updateLabel
      End If
    End Sub  'repUserControls_ItemDataBound
  End Class  'CH04UserControlRuntimeVB
End Namespace
```

Example 4-26. User controls loaded at runtime code-behind (.cs)

```
//----------------------------------------------------------------------------
//
//    Module Name: CH04UserControlRuntimeCS.ascx.cs
//
//    Description: This module provides the code behind for
//                 CH04UserControlRuntimeCS.ascx
//
//****************************************************************************
using ASPNetCookbook.CSExamples;
using System;
using System.Collections;
using System.Drawing;
using System.Web.UI.HtmlControls;
using System.Web.UI.WebControls;

namespace ASPNetCookbook.CSExamples
{
  public class CH04UserControlRuntimeCS : System.Web.UI.Page
  {
    // controls on the form
    protected CH04UserControlCommSourceCS ucSource;
    protected System.Web.UI.WebControls.Repeater repUserControls;

    // the following variable is used to keep count of the number of controls
    private int controlCount;
```

Example 4-26. User controls loaded at runtime code-behind (.cs) (continued)

```
//*************************************************************************
//
//    ROUTINE: Page_Load
//
//    DESCRIPTION: This routine provides the event handler for the page
//                 load event.  It is responsible for initializing the
//                 controls on the page.
//-------------------------------------------------------------------------
private void Page_Load(object sender, System.EventArgs e)
{
  ArrayList values = new ArrayList( );

  // wire the item data bound event
  this.repUserControls.ItemDataBound +=
    new RepeaterItemEventHandler(this.repUserControls_ItemDataBound);

  // build array of data to bind to repeater
  // for this example it is just the color of the entry but for a real
  // application the data would normally be from a database, etc.
  values.Add("#ffffcc");
  values.Add("#ccffff");
  values.Add("#ccff99");

  // bind the data to the repeater
  controlCount = 0;
  repUserControls.DataSource = values;
  repUserControls.DataBind( );
}  // Page_Load

//*************************************************************************
//
//    ROUTINE: repUserControls_ItemDataBound
//
//    DESCRIPTION: This routine provides the event handler for the item
//                 data bound event of the datalist control in the nav bar.
//                 It is responsible for setting the anchor and image
//                 attributes for the item being bound.
//-------------------------------------------------------------------------
private void repUserControls_ItemDataBound(Object sender,
                 System.Web.UI.WebControls.RepeaterItemEventArgs e)
{
  // the following constants are the names of the controls in the repeater
  const String TABLE_ROW = "trControl";
  const String COUNT_CELL = "tdCount";
  const String USER_CONTROL_CELL = "tdUserControl";

  HtmlTableRow row = null;
  HtmlTableCell cell = null;
  CH04UserControlCommDestinationCS ucDest = null;
```

```
      // make sure this is an item or alternating item in the repeater
      if ((e.Item.ItemType == ListItemType.Item) ||
        (e.Item.ItemType == ListItemType.AlternatingItem))
      {
        // find the table row and set the background color
        row = (HtmlTableRow)(e.Item.FindControl(TABLE_ROW));
        row.BgColor = (String)(e.Item.DataItem);

        // find the cell for the control count and set the count
        cell = (HtmlTableCell)(e.Item.FindControl(COUNT_CELL));
        controlCount += 1;
        cell.InnerText = controlCount.ToString( );

        // find the cell for the control and load a user control
        cell = (HtmlTableCell)(e.Item.FindControl(USER_CONTROL_CELL));
        ucDest = (CH04UserControlCommDestinationCS)
                (LoadControl("CH04UserControlCommDestinationCS.ascx"));
        cell.Controls.Add(ucDest);
      ucSource.OnSend +=
        new
          CH04UserControlCommSourceCS.customMessageHandler(ucDest.updateLabel);
      }
    } // repNavBarCell_ItemDataBound
  } // CH04UserControlRuntimeCS
}
```

CHAPTER 5

Custom Controls

5.0   Introduction

Custom controls are compiled controls that function a lot like ASP controls. Like user controls, custom controls can significantly enhance the reusability of code that is repeated many times within a project or over multiple projects. There are important differences, however. In general, user controls are like "mini" web pages in that they contain part of an ASP.NET page. Additionally, they are compiled when first requested, but their user interface can easily be changed as required. With custom controls, on the other hand, the user interface is generated by the code and therefore cannot easily be changed, except through properties and methods that you implement, about which we'll speak more in a minute.

In a broader sense, a custom control is really any control that you create with these common themes: it is typically derived from the `Control` (or `WebControl`) class in the `System.Web.UI` namespace or an existing ASP.NET server control; it generally provides its own user interface; and it may provide its own backend functionality through the methods, properties, and events that you implement for it.

Custom controls range from the simple to the complex. A simple custom control might, for example, write some HTML, perhaps even modifying its HTML-style attributes as it does so. A more complex custom control would offer HTML-style attributes of its own through properties you implement. A custom text box control could, for example, offer one attribute for controlling the color of its label and another to control the width of the control itself. To make it more complex, and ultimately more useful, the control would have to handle `postback` events like the server controls provided with ASP.NET. More complex still would be a custom control that, like the `DataGrid` control, included templates and supported data binding. Because custom controls can be created from scratch or inherited from existing controls, the possibilities are endless.

All of the hypothetical custom controls we've just described are, with the exception of the `templated` control, illustrated in this chapter's recipes. (If you're interested in learning more about `templated` controls, see the example in the *ASP.NET QuickStart*

Tutorials that are part of the *.NET Framework QuickStarts* that ship with Visual Studio .NET or are available via *http://www.gotdotnet.net*.)

This chapter introduces you to some, but not all, of the techniques used to build custom controls. In sticking to the basics, we are implicitly recognizing that custom controls are, after all, "custom" and therefore highly individual. But these basics ought to take you a long way in crafting your own custom controls.

Which Is Better: WebControl or Control?

On the subject of creating custom controls, some books, including several from O'Reilly, recommend inheriting from the WebControl class as opposed to the Control class of System.Web.UI, which we have used for the majority of recipes in this chapter. Using WebControl is certainly a good option, because it serves as the base class that defines the methods, properties, and events common to all web server controls in the System.Web.UI.WebControls namespace. Using this approach, you can control the appearance and behavior of a web server control by setting properties defined in this class—for example, the background color and font color of a control or the border width, color, and style of a control. But to really "get under the hood" in creating a custom control's UI, the class to inherit from is Control, because it makes available the largest number of options. The cost of this increased flexibility is that it requires a bit more planning and execution. The reason is that Control does not have any user interface–specific features. If you are authoring a control that does not have a UI, or combines other controls that render their own UI, derive from Control. Otherwise, if you are authoring a control that can make use of the properties and methods provided by WebControl, derive from WebControl.

5.1   Combining HTML Controls in a Single Custom Control

Problem

You want to create a custom control that combines two or more HTML controls.

Solution

Use the .NET language of your choice to:

1. Create a class that inherits from the Control class in the System.Web.UI namespace.

2. Override the Render method to have it output the HTML controls you wish to include.

3. (Optional) Use the `HtmlTextWriter` class to enhance your chances of writing well-formed HTML.

To use the custom control in an ASP.NET page:

1. Register the assembly containing the control.
2. Insert the tag for the custom control anywhere in the page.

Figure 5-1 shows the output of a custom control that combines a label and text box. Examples 5-1 and 5-2 show the VB and C# class files for the custom control. Example 5-3 shows how to use the custom control in an ASP.NET page.

ASP.NET Cookbook
The Ultimate ASP.NET Code Sourcebook

Quick & Dirty Custom Control - Raw HTML Output (VB)

Enter Age: [   ]

[Submit]

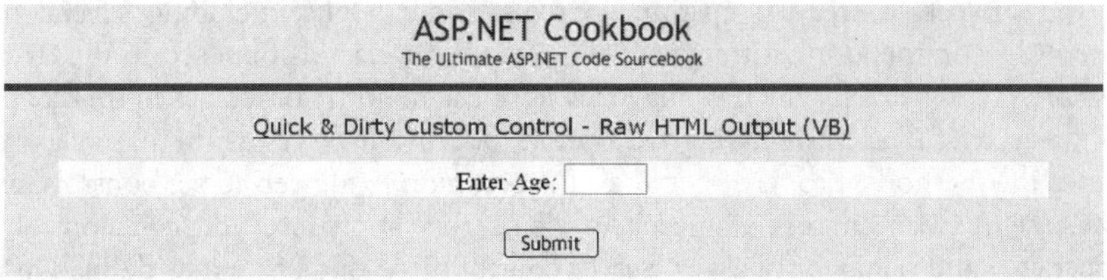

Figure 5-1. Basic custom control output

Discussion

To create a custom control that combines the functionality of two or more HTML controls, you first create a class that inherits from the `Control` class in `System.Web.UI`. The `Control` class is the base class that all ASP.NET server controls inherit from. It provides all of the basic properties, methods, and events necessary to build custom controls.

The only method of `Control` that is required to output HTML is the `Render` method. `Render` is responsible for writing the HTML that will be rendered by the browser. To enhance your ability to write well-formed HTML, you can use other methods of the `HtmlTextWriter` class along with the `HtmlTextWriterAttribute` and `HtmlTextWriterTag` enumerations. We'll talk more about this in a minute, but for now we'll stick with writing our own unvarnished HTML.

The custom control we have implemented in our example contains a label and an input control. The label and input control are output in the `Render` method with the following code:

VB
```
writer.Write("Enter Age: ")
writer.Write("<input type='text' size='3' />")
```

C#
```
writer.Write("Enter Age: ");
writer.Write("<input type='text' size='3' />");
```

To use the custom control, the assembly containing the control must be registered in the target *.aspx* file. The `TagPrefix` attribute defines an alias to use for the namespace in the page. The Namespace attribute must be set to the fully qualified namespace of the control, and the Assembly attribute must be set to the name of the assembly containing the custom control. Here is how you register the assembly in our example:

```
<%@ Register TagPrefix="ASPCookbook" Namespace="ASPNetCookbook.VBExamples"
             Assembly="ASPNetCookbookVB" %>
```

The custom control can be placed anywhere on the page by inserting a tag. The control to insert is identified by naming the tag with the TagPrefix followed by the class name. The tag must include the id and runat="server" attributes for the control to be rendered on the page. This is the tag used in our example:

```
<ASPCookbook:CH05QuickAndDirtyCustomControlVB1
             id="ccQuickAndDirty" runat="server" />
```

In our example, raw HTML is written to the web page using the Render method. For simple HTML, this works well. As the complexity of the HTML you write increases, however, the likelihood that you'll introduce errors increases significantly. Fortunately, HtmlTextWriter includes a variety of methods that simplify the generation of complex HTML. These methods can help you with the nuances of adding HTML attributes (and values) to an HTMLTextWriter output stream, writing beginning and ending tags, flushing buffers so that all buffered data is written to the text stream, and the like. To create the input box in our example, you could use the HtmlTextWriter like this:

```
Protected Overrides Sub Render(ByVal writer As HtmlTextWriter)
  'output label
  writer.Write("Enter Age: ")

  'output input control
  writer.AddAttribute(HtmlTextWriterAttribute.Type, _
                      "text")
  writer.AddAttribute(HtmlTextWriterAttribute.Size, _
                      "3")
  writer.RenderBeginTag(HtmlTextWriterTag.Input)
  writer.RenderEndTag()
End Sub  'Render
```

```
protected override void Render(HtmlTextWriter writer)
{
  //output label
  writer.Write("Enter Age: ");

  //output input control
  writer.AddAttribute(HtmlTextWriterAttribute.Type,
                      "text");
  writer.AddAttribute(HtmlTextWriterAttribute.Size,
                      "3");
  writer.RenderBeginTag(HtmlTextWriterTag.Input);
  writer.RenderEndTag();
}  // Render
```

One advantage of implementing the Render method in this way is that you can use the RenderBeginTag and RenderEndTag methods to output HTML and sidestep having to insert the <, /, and > characters yourself. In addition, using the HtmlTextWriterTag and HtmlTextWriterAttribute enumerations ensures all tags and attributes are correctly spelled.

Another advantage is that you can avoid the hassle of making sure the single and double quotes are handled correctly. Notice in the first example that the values for the attributes of the input tag were output with single quotes, since double quotes mark the beginning and end of strings. Outputting double quotes around the values would have required more complex code with string concatenations. Using the AddAttribute method avoids this problem completely.

 You must call the AddAttribute method immediately before you call the RenderBeginTag method, which writes the opening tag of the associated HTML element. This is required because the HtmlTextWriter builds a collection of attributes to output in the opening tag of the HTML element. When the RenderBeginTag method is called, the attributes are output in the opening tag and then the collection is cleared.

A useful enhancement to this approach would be to add HTML-style attributes to the control to make the control more adaptable and reusable throughout your applications. See Recipe 5.2 for how to do this.

See Also

Recipe 5.2; for additional details on Control, Render, HtmlTextWriterTag, HtmlTextWriterAttribute, and especially HtmlTextWriter, search the MSDN Library

Example 5-1. Quick-and-dirty custom control (.vb)

```
Option Explicit On
Option Strict On
'---------------------------------------------------------------------------
'
'    Module Name: CH05QuickAndDirtyCustomControlVB1.vb
'
'    Description: This class provides the quick and dirty custom control
'                 example which includes a label and a textbox.  The Control
'                 is rendered by writing raw HTML to the output stream.
'
'***************************************************************************
Imports System
Imports System.Web
Imports System.Web.UI

Namespace ASPNetCookbook.VBExamples
    Public Class CH05QuickAndDirtyCustomControlVB1
        Inherits Control
```

Example 5-1. Quick-and-dirty custom control (.vb) (continued)

```
'**********************************************************************
'
'   ROUTINE: Render
'
'   DESCRIPTION: This routine renders the HTML output of the control
'----------------------------------------------------------------------
Protected Overrides Sub Render(ByVal writer As HtmlTextWriter)
  'output label
  writer.Write("Enter Age: ")

  'output input control
  writer.Write("<input type='text' size='3' />")
End Sub  'Render
End Class  'CH05QuickAndDirtyCustomControlVB1
End Namespace
```

Example 5-2. Quick-and-dirty custom control (.cs)

```
//----------------------------------------------------------------------
//
//   Module Name: CustomControlQuickAndDirtyCS1
//
//   Description: This class provides the quick and dirty custom control
//                example which includes a label and a textbox.  The Control
//                is rendered by writing raw HTML to the output stream.
//
//**********************************************************************
using System;
using System.Web;
using System.Web.UI;

namespace ASPNetCookbook.CSExamples
{
  public class CH05QuickAndDirtyCustomControlCS1 : Control
  {
    //**********************************************************************
    //
    //   ROUTINE: Render
    //
    //   DESCRIPTION: This routine renders the HTML output of the control
    //----------------------------------------------------------------------
    protected override void Render(HtmlTextWriter writer)
    {
      //output label
      writer.Write("Enter Age: ");

      //output input control
      writer.Write("<input type='text' size='3' />");
    }  // Render
  }  // CH05QuickAndDirtyCustomControlCS1
}
```

Example 5-3. Using the quick-and-dirty custom control (.aspx)

```
<%@ Page Language="vb" AutoEventWireup="false"
    Codebehind="CH05DisplayQuickAndDirtyControlVB1.aspx.vb"
    Inherits="ASPNetCookbook.VBExamples.CH05DisplayQuickAndDirtyControlVB1" %>
<%@ Register TagPrefix="ASPCookbook" Namespace="ASPNetCookbook.VBExamples"
            Assembly="ASPNetCookbookVB" %>
<!DOCTYPE HTML PUBLIC "-//W3C//DTD HTML 4.0 Transitional//EN">
<html>
  <head>
    <title>Quick And Dirty Custom Control</title>
    <link rel="stylesheet" href="css/ASPNetCookbook.css">
  </head>
  <body leftmargin="0" marginheight="0" marginwidth="0" topmargin="0">
    <form id="frmCustomControl" method="post" runat="server">
      <table width="100%" cellpadding="0" cellspacing="0" border="0">
        <tr>
          <td align="center">
            <img src="images/ASPNETCookbookHeading_blue.gif">
          </td>
        </tr>
        <tr>
          <td class="dividerLine">
            <img src="images/spacer.gif" height="6" border="0"></td>
        </tr>
      </table>
      <table width="90%" align="center" border="0">
        <tr>
          <td><img src="images/spacer.gif" height="10" border="0"></td>
        </tr>
        <tr>
          <td align="center" class="PageHeading">
            Quick & Dirty Custom Control - Raw HTML Output (VB)
          </td>
        </tr>
        <tr>
          <td><img src="images/spacer.gif" height="10" border="0"></td>
        </tr>
        <tr bgcolor="#ffffcc">
          <td align="center">
            <ASPCookbook:CH05QuickAndDirtyCustomControlVB1
                        id="ccQuickAndDirty" runat="server" />
          </td>
        </tr>
        <tr>
          <td align="center">
            <br>
            <asp:ImageButton ID="btnSubmit" Runat="server"
                 ImageUrl="images/buttons/button_submit.gif" />
          </td>
        </tr>
      </table>
    </form>
  </body>
</html>
```

5.2 Creating a Custom Control with Attributes

Problem

You want to create a custom control with HTML-style attributes that can be used to customize the appearance of the control in the *.aspx* file.

Solution

Create the basic custom control (as described in Recipe 5.1), add properties to the class, and then use the values of the properties when rendering the control's HTML output.

Use the .NET language of your choice to:

1. Create a class that inherits from the Control class in the System.Web.UI namespace.
2. Implement support for the HTML-style attributes by adding properties to the class.
3. Override the Render method to have it render the HTML output of the control using the values of the properties.

To use the custom control in an ASP.NET page:

1. Register the assembly containing the control.
2. Insert the tag for the custom control anywhere in the page and set the attributes appropriately.

To illustrate this solution, we started with the sample custom control we built for Recipe 5.1 and then added support for HTML-style attributes, such as an attribute that defines the color used to display label text. Figure 5-2 shows some output using default and modified attributes for the control; in the case of the latter, the Enter Age: label text actually appears in red when rendered on the screen. Examples 5-4 and 5-5 show the VB and C# class files for our custom control. Example 5-6 shows how to use the custom control in an ASP.NET page to produce these results.

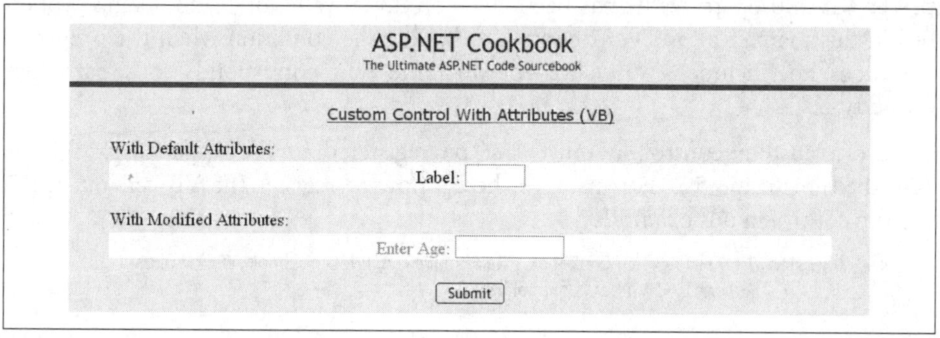

Figure 5-2. Custom control with attributes output

Discussion

Recipe 5.1 describes how to create a basic custom control, so we'll skip that discussion here. Instead we'll focus on implementing HTML-style attributes for a custom control.

Custom control properties provide the ability to programmatically change aspects of the control using HTML-style attributes, which can be set in the *.aspx* file or code-behind. Attributes are a common feature of ASP.NET server controls. For example, the image button control provides an ImageURL attribute that you can set to define the image that is to be displayed when the control is rendered:

```
<asp:ImageButton ID="btnSubmit" Runat="server"
                 ImageUrl="button_submit.gif" />
```

Attributes are implemented in a custom control by adding properties to the class. The properties are no different than properties in a class implemented as a business or data service. The names of the properties define the names of the attributes that can be used with the custom control.

To illustrate this approach, we've provided the code in Example 5-4 (VB) and Example 5-5 (C#) that defines a custom control named CustomControlAttributesVB or CustomControlAttributesCS with the properties shown in Table 5-1.

Table 5-1. Custom control properties

Property	Data type	Description
labelText	String	Defines the text for the label
textColor	Color	Defines the color used to display the label text
textboxWidth	Int or Integer	Defines the width of the text box

When you define custom control properties, you should always initialize each property by assigning it a default value. For example, in Examples 5-4 and 5-5, we've assigned the private variable used to store the labelText property an initial value of "Label: ", the private variable used to store the textColor property value has been given an initial value of Color.Black, and the private variable used to store the textboxWidth property value has been given an initial value of 3. Initializing properties in this manner allows your control to handle the condition when the programmer does not include a value for the attribute that corresponds to a particular property.

To use a custom control, it must first be registered in the target *.aspx* file, as described in Recipe 5.1. For instance, here's how to register the VB version of the custom control in our example:

```
<%@ Register TagPrefix="ASPCookbook" Namespace="ASPNetCookbook.VBExamples"
             Assembly="ASPNetCookbookVB" %>
```

You can use the control as is if the default label text, text color, and text box width are acceptable.

```
<ASPCookbook:CH05CustomControlAttributesVB
              id="ccAttributes1" runat="server" />
```

Or, you can set the attributes to customize the look of the control for a particular page.

```
<ASPCookbook:CH05CustomControlAttributesVB
              id="ccAttributes2" runat="server"
              labelText = "Enter Age: "
              textColor="#FF0000"
              textboxWidth="10" />
```

Before a custom control's attributes can be set in the code-behind, the control must first be declared, just like any other server control. For example, here's how you declare the custom control in the code-behind of our sample application and then set the control's textColor attribute to green:

VB

```
Protected ccAttributes1 As CustomControlAttributesVB

    ..

    ccAttributes1.textColor = Color.Green
```

C#

```
protected CustomControlAttributesCS ccAttributes1;

    ..

    ccAttributes1.textColor = Color.Green;
```

One thing to consider when implementing the properties of a custom control is that ASP.NET will match the names of the attributes in the custom control tag (.*aspx* file) with the names of the properties in the class that implements the custom control. What's more, because all attribute values in the .*aspx* file are effectively strings, ASP.NET provides the type conversion necessary to match the type required for the property.

 If ASP.NET cannot convert the attribute value to the type required for the property, a parse exception will be thrown when the page is displayed. For example, if a property is an integer type and the value "abc" is set as the attribute value, a parse exception will be thrown. If you set the attributes in the .*aspx* file, there really is no way to prevent this other than to make sure you test the code thoroughly. Alternately, you can set the values in the code-behind, which will generally catch errors of this type during compilation instead of at runtime.

See Also

Recipe 5.1

Example 5-4. Custom control with attributes (.vb)

```vb
Option Explicit On
Option Strict On
'-----------------------------------------------------------------------------
'
'    Module Name: CH05CustomControlAttributesVB.vb
'
'    Description: This class provides a custom control with attributes to
'                 provide the ability to alter the control programmically.
'
'*****************************************************************************
Imports System
Imports System.drawing
Imports System.Web
Imports System.Web.UI

Namespace ASPNetCookbook.VBExamples
  Public Class CH05CustomControlAttributesVB
    Inherits Control

    'private copies of attribute data
    Private mLabelText As String = "Label: "
    Private mTextColor As Color = Color.Black
    Private mTextboxWidth As Integer = 3

    '*****************************************************************************
    '
    '    ROUTINE: labelText
    '
    '    DESCRIPTION: This property provides the ability to set the text of
    '                 of the label in the control
    '-----------------------------------------------------------------------------
    Public Property labelText() As String
      Get
        Return (mLabelText)
      End Get
      Set(ByVal Value As String)
        mLabelText = Value
      End Set
    End Property  'labelText

    '*****************************************************************************
    '
    '    ROUTINE: textColor
    '
    '    DESCRIPTION: This property provides the ability to set the color
    '                 of the text in the control
    '-----------------------------------------------------------------------------
    Public Property textColor() As Color
      Get
        Return (mTextColor)
      End Get
      Set(ByVal Value As Color)
        mTextColor = Value
```

Example 5-4. Custom control with attributes (.vb) (continued)

```vb
      End Set
    End Property  'textColor

    '*************************************************************************
    '
    '    ROUTINE: textboxWidth
    '
    '    DESCRIPTION: This property provides the ability to set the width
    '                 of the textbox in the control
    '-------------------------------------------------------------------------
    Public Property textboxWidth( ) As Integer
      Get
        Return (mTextboxWidth)
      End Get
      Set(ByVal Value As Integer)
        mTextboxWidth = Value
      End Set
    End Property  'textboxWidth

    '*************************************************************************
    '
    '    ROUTINE: Render
    '
    '    DESCRIPTION: This routine renders the HTML output of the control
    '-------------------------------------------------------------------------
    Protected Overrides Sub Render(ByVal writer As HtmlTextWriter)
      'output label within a font tag
      writer.AddAttribute("color", _
                          ColorTranslator.ToHtml(textColor))
      writer.RenderBeginTag(HtmlTextWriterTag.Font)
      writer.Write(labelText)
      writer.RenderEndTag( )

      'output input control
      writer.AddAttribute(HtmlTextWriterAttribute.Type, _
                          "text")
      writer.AddAttribute(HtmlTextWriterAttribute.Size, _
                          textboxWidth.ToString( ))
      writer.RenderBeginTag(HtmlTextWriterTag.Input)
      writer.RenderEndTag( )
    End Sub  'Render
  End Class  'CH05CustomControlAttributesVB
End Namespace
```

Example 5-5. Custom control with attributes (.cs)

```cs
//-----------------------------------------------------------------------------
//
//   Module Name: CH05CustomControlAttributesCS
//
//   Description: This class provides a custom control with attributes to
//                provide the ability to alter the control programmatically.
//
//*****************************************************************************
```

Example 5-5. Custom control with attributes (.cs) (continued)

```csharp
using System;
using System.Drawing;
using System.Web;
using System.Web.UI;

namespace ASPNetCookbook.CSExamples
{
  public class CH05CustomControlAttributesCS : Control
  {
    // private copies of attribute data
    private String mLabelText = "Label: ";
    private Color mTextColor = Color.Black;
    private int mTextboxWidth = 3;

    //*************************************************************************
    //
    //   ROUTINE: labelText
    //
    //   DESCRIPTION: This property provides the ability to set the text
    //                of the label in the control
    //-------------------------------------------------------------------------
    public String labelText
    {
      get
      {
        return(mLabelText);
      }
      set
      {
        mLabelText = value;
      }
    }  // labelText

    //*************************************************************************
    //
    //   ROUTINE: textColor
    //
    //   DESCRIPTION: This property provides the ability to set the color
    //                of the text in the control
    //-------------------------------------------------------------------------
    public Color textColor
    {
      get
      {
        return(mTextColor);
      }
      set
      {
        mTextColor = value;
      }
    }  // textColor
```

Example 5-5. Custom control with attributes (.cs) (continued)

```
//**************************************************************************
//
//    ROUTINE: textboxWidth
//
//    DESCRIPTION: This property provides the ability to set the width
//                    of the textbox in the control
//--------------------------------------------------------------------------
public int textboxWidth
{
  get
  {
    return(mTextboxWidth);
  }
  set
  {
    mTextboxWidth = value;
  }
}  // textboxWidth


//**************************************************************************
//
//    ROUTINE: Render
//
//    DESCRIPTION: This routine renders the HTML output of the control
//--------------------------------------------------------------------------
protected override void Render(HtmlTextWriter writer)
{
  //output label
  writer.AddAttribute("color",
                      ColorTranslator.ToHtml(textColor));
  writer.RenderBeginTag(HtmlTextWriterTag.Font);
  writer.Write(labelText);
  writer.RenderEndTag( );

  //output input control
  writer.AddAttribute(HtmlTextWriterAttribute.Type,
                      "text");
  writer.AddAttribute(HtmlTextWriterAttribute.Size,
                      textboxWidth.ToString( ));
  writer.RenderBeginTag(HtmlTextWriterTag.Input);
  writer.RenderEndTag( );
  }  // Render
  }  // CH05CustomControlAttributesCS
}
```

Example 5-6. Using the custom control with attributes (.aspx)

```
<%@ Page Language="vb" AutoEventWireup="false"
    Codebehind="CH05DisplayControlWithAttributesVB.aspx.vb"
    Inherits="ASPNetCookbook.VBExamples.CH05DisplayControlWithAttributesVB" %>
<%@ Register TagPrefix="ASPCookbook" Namespace="ASPNetCookbook.VBExamples"
            Assembly="ASPNetCookbookVB" %>
<!DOCTYPE HTML PUBLIC "-//W3C//DTD HTML 4.0 Transitional//EN">
```

Example 5-6. Using the custom control with attributes (.aspx) (continued)

```html
<html>
  <head>
    <title>Display Custom Control With Attributes</title>
    <link rel="stylesheet" href="css/ASPNetCookbook.css">
  </head>
  <body leftmargin="0" marginheight="0" marginwidth="0" topmargin="0">
    <form id="frmCustomControl" method="post" runat="server">
      <table width="100%" cellpadding="0" cellspacing="0" border="0">
        <tr>
          <td align="center">
            <img src="images/ASPNETCookbookHeading_blue.gif">
          </td>
        </tr>
        <tr>
          <td class="dividerLine">
            <img src="images/spacer.gif" height="6" border="0"></td>
        </tr>
      </table>
      <table width="90%" align="center" border="0">
        <tr>
          <td><img src="images/spacer.gif" height="10" border="0"></td>
        </tr>
        <tr>
          <td align="center" class="PageHeading">
            Custom Control With Attributes (VB)
          </td>
        </tr>
        <tr>
          <td><img src="images/spacer.gif" height="10" border="0"></td>
        </tr>
        <tr>
          <td>With Default Attributes:</td>
        </tr>
        <tr bgcolor="#ffffcc">
          <td align="center">
            <ASPCookbook:CH05CustomControlAttributesVB
                        id="ccAttributes1" runat="server" />
          </td>
        </tr>
        <tr>
          <td><br />With Modified Attributes:</td>
        </tr>
        <tr bgcolor="#ffffcc">
          <td align="center">
            <ASPCookbook:CH05CustomControlAttributesVB
                        id="ccAttributes2" runat="server"
                labelText = "Enter Age: "
                textColor="#FF0000"
                textboxWidth="10" />
          </td>
        </tr>
        <tr>
          <td align="center">
```

Example 5-6. Using the custom control with attributes (.aspx) (continued)

```
        <br>
        <asp:ImageButton ID="btnSubmit" Runat="server"
             ImageUrl="images/buttons/button_submit.gif" />
      </td>
    </tr>
  </table>
 </form>
 </body>
</html>
```

5.3   Creating a Custom Control with State

Problem

You want to create a custom control that remembers its state between postbacks of a form, like the server controls provided with ASP.NET.

Solution

Create a custom control like the one described in Recipe 5.2, implement the IPostBackDataHandler interface to add the functionality to retrieve the values posted to the server, and then update the values in the custom control from the postback data.

Use the .NET language of your choice to:

1. Create a class that inherits from the Control class in the System.Web.UI namespace.

2. Implement support for HTML-style attributes by adding properties to the class.

3. Implement an IPostBackDataHandler as necessary to update the state of the control with the posted data.

4. Override the Render method to have it render the HTML output of the control using the values of the properties.

To use the custom control in an ASP.NET page:

1. Register the assembly containing the control.

2. Insert the tag for the custom control anywhere in the page and set the attributes appropriately.

Examples 5-7 and 5-8 show the VB and C# class files for a custom control that maintains state. Example 5-9 shows how we use the custom control in an ASP.NET page.

A version of the custom control that maintains state and provides the added ability to raise an event when the control data has changed is shown in Example 5-10 (VB) and Example 5-11 (C#). Examples 5-12 through 5-14 show the *.aspx* and code-behind files of an application that uses the custom control with state and provides an event handler for the data-changed event.

Discussion

When implementing a custom control, you will want to make sure that it maintains its state between postbacks to the server. Otherwise, it will lose its values and the user will have to reset them each time. To see what we mean by this, consider the custom controls discussed in Recipes 5.1 and 5.2; if you implement either of these controls, you will notice that anytime you click the Submit button, the value entered into the text box is lost when the page is redisplayed. This is caused by the control's not processing the form data posted back to the server.

To maintain the values in a custom control, it must, like all the controls provided with ASP.NET, implement the `IPostBackDataHandler` interface. The `IPostBackDataHandler` interface requires the implementation of two methods: `LoadPostData` and `RaisePostDataChangedEvent`. The `LoadPostData` method supplies the data posted to the server, which provides the ability to update the state of the control with the posted data. The `RaisePostDataChangedEvent` method provides the ability to raise events if data for the control changes; this method is used to good effect in the second of the two approaches we advocate for this recipe and is discussed at the end of this section. The `LoadPostData` and `RaisePostDataChangedEvent` methods are automatically called by ASP.NET when the form is posted back to the server.

The `LoadPostData` method has the following syntax:

VB
```
LoadPostData(postDataKey As String,
            postCollection As NameValueCollection)
```

C#
```
bool LoadPostData(string postDataKey,
            NameValueCollection postCollection);
```

The `postCollection` argument contains the collection of name/value pairs posted to the server. The `postDataKey` parameter provides the "name" of the key value for this control that is used to access the control's postback value.

 The `postDataKey` parameter will be set to the unique ID value for the custom control. If the custom control contains only one control that posts a value back to the server and its ID was used as the value of the "name" attribute when the control was rendered, the value of the `postDataKey` parameter can be used to obtain the posted value. If the custom control is instead a composite control that contains more than one control with postback data or if the custom control's ID was not used for the control within the custom control, you, as the programmer, will need to provide a unique ID value for each control in the custom control, extract the values individually within the `LoadPostData` method, and then set the appropriate property.

The return value for the `LoadPostData` method should always be set to `False` if the data has not changed or no check is performed to see if the data changed. Setting the return to `False` prevents the `RaisePostDataChangedEvent` method from being called. See the discussion at the end of this section regarding raising events on data changes.

To give you a better feel for how to implement this solution, we now turn to a variation of the custom control we've been working with throughout the chapter, which contains a label and text box. In our first example, the control needs to simply remember the state of the text in the text box of the input HTML control, and so we have added a text property to provide the ability to get/set the text value. Similar properties are also provided for the label text, text color, and text box width. No surprise here.

As you look over the code, you'll notice that, with the exception of the text property, all the properties in this custom control use private variables to store their values. These values are lost when the form is rendered and sent to the browser. Because these values are not changed by the user in the browser, there is no need to remember their previous values. The text property is another matter. To provide the ability to remember its previous value, we use the ViewState to persist the value instead of a private variable. We have implemented the LoadPostData method to process the data posted back from the client and set the text property from the postback data.

Notice that we have also implemented the RaisePostDataChangedEvent method. In this first example, the method is empty and not used but is required as part of the IPostBackDataHandler interface. In the recipe's second example, it is used to raise an event when data for the text control changes (more about this later).

A couple of changes from Recipe 5.2's implementation are also required in the Render event. You must set the name and value attributes of the HTML input control. Set the name attribute to a unique identifier so you'll have the ability to obtain the value posted back to the server. If the control does not have a name attribute, the browser will not include its data in the postback data. Set the value attribute to the current text value for the control.

 If the text value does not exist, the value attribute should not be output. Absent this check, the value attribute will be output without a value, which is not well-formed HTML and is not handled well by some browsers.

In our second example, we build on the basic structure of the first solely to raise an event if the text in the text box changes and to notify the user with a change in the label text. Because the value that was output when the page was rendered is stored in the ViewState, we can compare it to the new value posted back to the server. As shown in Example 5-10 (VB) and Example 5-11 (C#), if the value changes, the LoadPostData method returns True. Otherwise, it returns False.

When the LoadPostData method returns True, ASP.NET will call the RaisePostDataChangedEvent method after all of the controls have had the opportunity to process their postback data. In this method, we simply raise the OnTextChanged event, passing a reference to the custom control and any event arguments that are applicable, as shown in Example 5-10 (VB) and Example 5-11 (C#). In this example, no arguments are required, so `EventArgs.Empty` is used for the event arguments parameter.

The event raised in the `RaisePostDataChangedEvent` must be defined in the custom control class. Further, an event handler in the code-behind of the ASP.NET page hosting the custom control must be "wired" to the event raised by the custom control, as shown here in abridged form (see Examples 5-13 and 5-14 for the complete listing):

VB
```
Protected WithEvents ccAttributes As CustomControlStateVB2

  ..

Private Sub ccAttributes_OnTextChanged(ByVal sender As Object, _
                                    ByVal e As System.EventArgs) _
      Handles ccAttributes.OnTextChanged
  labMessage.Text = "Data Changed"
End Sub  'ccAttributes_OnTextChanged
```

C#
```
protected CustomControlStateCS2 ccAttributes;

  ..

private void Page_Load(object sender, System.EventArgs e)
{

    // wire the event to the text changed event of the custom control
    ccAttributes.OnTextChanged +=
      new EventHandler(this.ccAttributes_OnTextChanged);
}  // Page_Load

  ..

public void ccAttributes_OnTextChanged(System.Object sender,
                                  EventArgs e)
  {
  // update the label with the message in the event arguments
  labMessage.Text = "Data Changed";
}  // ccAttributes_OnTextChanged
```

See Also

Recipe 5.2

Example 5-7. Custom control with state (.vb)

```
Option Explicit On
Option Strict On
'--------------------------------------------------------------------------
'
'  Module Name: CH05CustomControlWithStateVB1.vb
'
```

Example 5-7. Custom control with state (.vb) (continued)

```vb
'   Description: This class provides a custom control that maintains state
'               through postbacks to the server.
'
'***************************************************************************
Imports Microsoft.VisualBasic
Imports System
Imports System.Collections.Specialized
Imports System.Drawing
Imports System.Web
Imports System.Web.UI

Namespace ASPNetCookbook.VBExamples
  Public Class CH05CustomControlWithStateVB1
    Inherits Control
    Implements IPostBackDataHandler

    'private copies of attribute data
    Private mLabelText As String = "Label: "
    Private mTextColor As Color = Color.Black
    Private mTextboxWidth As Integer = 3

    '***************************************************************************
    '
    '   ROUTINE: labelText
    '
    '   DESCRIPTION: This property provides the ability to set the text of
    '               of the label in the control.
    '-------------------------------------------------------------------------
    Public Property labelText() As String
      Get
        Return (mLabelText)
      End Get
      Set(ByVal Value As String)
        mLabelText = Value
      End Set
    End Property

    '***************************************************************************
    '
    '   ROUTINE: textColor
    '
    '   DESCRIPTION: This property provides the ability to set the color
    '               of the text in the control.
    '-------------------------------------------------------------------------
    Public Property textColor() As Color
      Get
        Return (mTextColor)
      End Get
      Set(ByVal Value As Color)
        mTextColor = Value
      End Set
    End Property   'textColor
```

Example 5-7. Custom control with state (.vb) (continued)

```vb
'**************************************************************************
'
'   ROUTINE: textboxWidth
'
'   DESCRIPTION: This property provides the ability to set the width
'                of the textbox in the control.
'--------------------------------------------------------------------------
Public Property textboxWidth() As Integer
  Get
    Return (mTextboxWidth)
  End Get
  Set(ByVal Value As Integer)
    mTextboxWidth = Value
  End Set
End Property  'textboxWidth

'**************************************************************************
'
'   ROUTINE: text
'
'   DESCRIPTION: This property provides the ability to set the text
'                in the textbox in the control.  NOTE: The text value
'                is stored in the ViewState instead of a private variable
'                to provide the ability to check the current and previous
'                values to determine if the text has changed.
'--------------------------------------------------------------------------
Const VS_TEXTBOX_VALUE As String = "TextboxValue"

Public Property text() As String
  Get
    Dim value As String = Nothing
    If (Not IsNothing(viewstate(VS_TEXTBOX_VALUE))) Then
      value = CStr(viewstate(VS_TEXTBOX_VALUE))
    End If
    Return (value)
  End Get
  Set(ByVal Value As String)
    viewstate(VS_TEXTBOX_VALUE) = Value
  End Set
End Property  'text

'**************************************************************************
'
'   ROUTINE: Render
'
'   DESCRIPTION: This routine renders the HTML output of the control.
'--------------------------------------------------------------------------
Protected Overrides Sub Render(ByVal writer As HtmlTextWriter)
  'output label within a font tag
  writer.AddAttribute("color", _
                  ColorTranslator.ToHtml(textColor))
```

Example 5-7. Custom control with state (.vb) (continued)

```
        writer.RenderBeginTag(HtmlTextWriterTag.Font)
        writer.Write(labelText)
        writer.RenderEndTag( )

        'output input control
        writer.AddAttribute(HtmlTextWriterAttribute.Type, _
                            "text")
        writer.AddAttribute(HtmlTextWriterAttribute.Size, _
                            textboxWidth.ToString( ))

        'output name attribute to identify data on postback
        writer.AddAttribute(HtmlTextWriterAttribute.Name, _
                            Me.UniqueID)

        'output value attribute only if value exists
        If (Not IsNothing(text)) Then
          writer.AddAttribute(HtmlTextWriterAttribute.Value, _
                              text)
        End If

        writer.RenderBeginTag(HtmlTextWriterTag.Input)
        writer.RenderEndTag( )
    End Sub   'Render

    '*************************************************************************
    '
    '    ROUTINE: LoadPostData
    '
    '    DESCRIPTION: This routine processes data posted back from the client.
    '-------------------------------------------------------------------------
    Public Overridable Function LoadPostData(ByVal postDataKey As String, _
                ByVal postCollection As NameValueCollection) As Boolean _
            Implements IPostBackDataHandler.LoadPostData

        'set the value of the text property from the postback data
        text = postCollection(postDataKey)
        Return (False)
    End Function   'LoadPostData

    '*************************************************************************
    '
    '    ROUTINE: RaisePostDataChangedEvent
    '
    '    DESCRIPTION: This routine processes data changed events as a result
    '                 of the postback.
    '-------------------------------------------------------------------------
    Public Overridable Sub RaisePostDataChangedEvent( ) _
            Implements IPostBackDataHandler.RaisePostDataChangedEvent

    End Sub   'RaisePostDataChangedEvent
  End Class   'CH05CustomControlWithStateVB1
End Namespace
```

Example 5-8. Custom control with state (.cs)

```
//---------------------------------------------------------------------------
//
//    Module Name: CH05CustomControlWithStateCS1
//
//    Description: This class provides a custom control with attributes to
//                 provide the ability to alter the control programmically.
//
//***************************************************************************
using System;
using System.Collections.Specialized;
using System.Drawing;
using System.Web;
using System.Web.UI;

namespace ASPNetCookbook.CSExamples
{
  public class CH05CustomControlWithStateCS1 : Control, IPostBackDataHandler
  {
    // private copies of attribute data
    private String mLabelText = "Label: ";
    private Color mTextColor = Color.Black;
    private int mTextboxWidth = 3;

    //***********************************************************************
    //
    //    ROUTINE: labelText
    //
    //    DESCRIPTION: This property provides the ability to set the text
    //                 of the label in the control.
    //---------------------------------------------------------------------
    public String labelText
    {
      get
      {
        return(mLabelText);
      }
      set
      {
        mLabelText = value;
      }
    }  // labelText

    //***********************************************************************
    //
    //    ROUTINE: textColor
    //
    //    DESCRIPTION: This property provides the ability to get/set the color
    //                 of the text in the control.
    //---------------------------------------------------------------------
    public Color textColor
    {
      get
      {
```

Example 5-8. Custom control with state (.cs) (continued)

```
          return(mTextColor);
      }
      set
      {
        mTextColor = value;
      }
    }  // textColor

    //***********************************************************************
    //
    //    ROUTINE: textboxWidth
    //
    //    DESCRIPTION: This property provides the ability to get/set the width
    //                 of the textbox in the control.
    //-----------------------------------------------------------------------
    public int textboxWidth
    {
      get
      {
        return(mTextboxWidth);
      }
      set
      {
        mTextboxWidth = value;
      }
    }  // textboxWidth

    //***********************************************************************
    //
    //    ROUTINE: text
    //
    //    DESCRIPTION: This property provides the ability to get/set the text
    //                 in the textbox in the control.
    //-----------------------------------------------------------------------
    const String VS_TEXTBOX_VALUE = "TextboxValue";

    public String text
    {
      get
      {
        String value = null;
        if (ViewState[VS_TEXTBOX_VALUE] != null)
        {
          value = (String)(ViewState[VS_TEXTBOX_VALUE]);
        }
        return (value);
      }
      set
      {
        ViewState[VS_TEXTBOX_VALUE] = value;
      }
    }  // text
```

Example 5-8. Custom control with state (.cs) (continued)

```
//*************************************************************************
//
//    ROUTINE: Render
//
//    DESCRIPTION: This routine renders the HTML output of the control.
//-------------------------------------------------------------------------
protected override void Render(HtmlTextWriter writer)
{
  //output label
  writer.AddAttribute("color",
                      ColorTranslator.ToHtml(textColor));
  writer.RenderBeginTag(HtmlTextWriterTag.Font);
  writer.Write(labelText);
  writer.RenderEndTag();

  //output input control
  writer.AddAttribute(HtmlTextWriterAttribute.Type,
                      "text");
  writer.AddAttribute(HtmlTextWriterAttribute.Size,
                      textboxWidth.ToString());

  // output name attribute to identify data on postback
  writer.AddAttribute(HtmlTextWriterAttribute.Name,
                      this.UniqueID);

  // output value attribute only if value exists
  if (text != null)
  {
    writer.AddAttribute(HtmlTextWriterAttribute.Value,
                        text);
  }

  writer.RenderBeginTag(HtmlTextWriterTag.Input);
  writer.RenderEndTag();
}  // Render

//*************************************************************************
//
//    ROUTINE: LoadPostData
//
//    DESCRIPTION: This routine processes data posted back from the client.
//-------------------------------------------------------------------------
public virtual bool LoadPostData(string postDataKey,
                                 NameValueCollection postCollection)
{
  // set the value of the text property from the postback data
  text = postCollection[postDataKey];
  return (false);
}  // LoadPostData

//*************************************************************************
//
//    ROUTINE: RaisePostDataChangedEvent
```

Example 5-8. Custom control with state (.cs) (continued)

```
    //
    //   DESCRIPTION: This routine processes data changed events as a result
    //               of the postback.
    //-----------------------------------------------------------------------
    public virtual void RaisePostDataChangedEvent( )
    {
    }  // RaisePostDataChangedEvent
  }  // CH05CustomControlWithStateCS1
}
```

Example 5-9. Using the custom control with state (.aspx)

```
<%@ Page Language="vb" AutoEventWireup="false"
    Codebehind="CH05DisplayControlWithStateVB1.aspx.vb"
    Inherits="ASPNetCookbook.VBExamples.CH05DisplayControlWithStateVB1" %>
<%@ Register TagPrefix="ASPCookbook" Namespace="ASPNetCookbook.VBExamples"
         Assembly="ASPNetCookbookVB" %>
<!DOCTYPE HTML PUBLIC "-//W3C//DTD HTML 4.0 Transitional//EN">
<html>
  <head>
    <title>Custom Control With State</title>
    <link rel="stylesheet" href="css/ASPNetCookbook.css">
  </head>
  <body leftmargin="0" marginheight="0" marginwidth="0" topmargin="0">
    <form id="frmCustomControl" method="post" runat="server">
      <table width="100%" cellpadding="0" cellspacing="0" border="0">
        <tr>
          <td align="center">
            <img src="images/ASPNETCookbookHeading_blue.gif">
          </td>
        </tr>
        <tr>
          <td class="dividerLine">
            <img src="images/spacer.gif" height="6" border="0"></td>
        </tr>
      </table>
      <table width="90%" align="center" border="0">
        <tr>
          <td><img src="images/spacer.gif" height="10" border="0"></td>
        </tr>
        <tr>
          <td align="center" class="PageHeading">
            Custom Control With State (VB)
          </td>
        </tr>
        <tr>
          <td><img src="images/spacer.gif" height="10" border="0"></td>
        </tr>
        <tr bgcolor="#ffffcc">
          <td align="center">
            <ASPCookbook:CH05CustomControlWithStateVB1
                id="ccAttributes" runat="server"
                labelText="Enter Age: "
```

Example 5-9. Using the custom control with state (.aspx) (continued)

```
                    textColor="#000080"
                    textboxWidth="5" />
          </td>
        </tr>
        <tr>
          <td align="center">
            <br>
            <asp:ImageButton ID="btnSubmit" Runat="server"
                    ImageUrl="images/buttons/button_submit.gif" />
          </td>
        </tr>
      </table>
    </form>
  </body>
</html>
```

Example 5-10. Custom control with state and changed event (.vb)

```
Option Explicit On
Option Strict On
'----------------------------------------------------------------------------
'
'    Module Name: CH05CustomControlWithStateVB2.vb
'
'    Description: This class provides a custom control that maintains state
'                 through postbacks to the server and raises an event when
'                 the entered data changes.
'
'****************************************************************************
Imports Microsoft.VisualBasic
Imports System
Imports System.Collections.Specialized
Imports System.Drawing
Imports System.Web
Imports System.Web.UI

Namespace ASPNetCookbook.VBExamples
  Public Class CH05CustomControlWithStateVB2
    Inherits Control
    Implements IPostBackDataHandler

    'define an event to be raised if the text changes
    Public Event OnTextChanged As EventHandler

    'private copies of attribute data
    Private mLabelText As String = "Label: "
    Private mTextColor As Color = Color.Black
    Private mTextboxWidth As Integer = 3

    '****************************************************************************
    '
    '    ROUTINE: labelText
    '
```

Example 5-10. Custom control with state and changed event (.vb) (continued)

```vb
'    DESCRIPTION: This property provides the ability to set the text of
'                 of the label in the control.
'-------------------------------------------------------------------------
Public Property labelText() As String
  Get
    Return (mLabelText)
  End Get
  Set(ByVal Value As String)
    mLabelText = Value
  End Set
End Property


'*************************************************************************
'
'    ROUTINE: textColor
'
'    DESCRIPTION: This property provides the ability to set the color
'                 of the text in the control.
'-------------------------------------------------------------------------
Public Property textColor() As Color
  Get
    Return (mTextColor)
  End Get
  Set(ByVal Value As Color)
    mTextColor = Value
  End Set
End Property   'textColor


'*************************************************************************
'
'    ROUTINE: textboxWidth
'
'    DESCRIPTION: This property provides the ability to set the width
'                 of the textbox in the control.
'-------------------------------------------------------------------------
Public Property textboxWidth() As Integer
  Get
    Return (mTextboxWidth)
  End Get
  Set(ByVal Value As Integer)
    mTextboxWidth = Value
  End Set
End Property   'textboxWidth


'*************************************************************************
'
'    ROUTINE: text
'
'    DESCRIPTION: This property provides the ability to set the text
'                 in the textbox in the control.  NOTE: The text value
'                 is stored in the ViewState instead of a private variable
'                 to provide the ability to check the current and previous
```

Example 5-10. Custom control with state and changed event (.vb) (continued)

```
'                   values to determine if the text has changed.
'---------------------------------------------------------------------------
Const VS_TEXTBOX_VALUE As String = "TextboxValue"

Public Property text() As String
  Get
    Dim value As String = Nothing
    If (Not IsNothing(viewstate(VS_TEXTBOX_VALUE))) Then
      value = CStr(viewstate(VS_TEXTBOX_VALUE))
    End If
    Return (value)
  End Get
  Set(ByVal Value As String)
    viewstate(VS_TEXTBOX_VALUE) = Value
  End Set
End Property  'text

'***************************************************************************
'
'    ROUTINE: Render
'
'    DESCRIPTION: This routine renders the HTML output of the control.
'---------------------------------------------------------------------------
Protected Overrides Sub Render(ByVal writer As HtmlTextWriter)
  'output label within a font tag
  writer.AddAttribute("color", _
                      ColorTranslator.ToHtml(textColor))
  writer.RenderBeginTag(HtmlTextWriterTag.Font)
  writer.Write(labelText)
  writer.RenderEndTag()

  'output input control
  writer.AddAttribute(HtmlTextWriterAttribute.Type, _
                      "text")
  writer.AddAttribute(HtmlTextWriterAttribute.Size, _
                      textboxWidth.ToString())

  'output name attribute to identify data on postback
  writer.AddAttribute(HtmlTextWriterAttribute.Name, _
                      Me.UniqueID)

  'output value attribute only if value exists
  If (Not IsNothing(text)) Then
    writer.AddAttribute(HtmlTextWriterAttribute.Value, _
                        text)
  End If

  writer.RenderBeginTag(HtmlTextWriterTag.Input)
  writer.RenderEndTag()
End Sub  'Render
```

Example 5-10. Custom control with state and changed event (.vb) (continued)

```
'*************************************************************************
'
'    ROUTINE: LoadPostData
'
'    DESCRIPTION: This routine processes data posted back from the client.
'-------------------------------------------------------------------------
Public Overridable Function LoadPostData(ByVal postDataKey As String, _
                 ByVal postCollection As NameValueCollection) As Boolean _
        Implements IPostBackDataHandler.LoadPostData

    Dim dataChanged As Boolean = False
    Dim postbackValue As String

    'check to see if the data changed
    postbackValue = postCollection(postDataKey)
    If (Not postbackValue.Equals(text)) Then
        dataChanged = True
    End If

    'set the value of the text property from the postback data
    text = postbackValue

    Return (dataChanged)
End Function   'LoadPostData

'*************************************************************************
'
'    ROUTINE: RaisePostDataChangedEvent
'
'    DESCRIPTION: This routine processes data changed events as a result
'                 of the postback.
'-------------------------------------------------------------------------
Public Overridable Sub RaisePostDataChangedEvent() _
        Implements IPostBackDataHandler.RaisePostDataChangedEvent

    RaiseEvent OnTextChanged(Me, EventArgs.Empty)
End Sub 'RaisePostDataChangedEvent
End Class 'CH05CustomControlWithStateVB2
End Namespace
```

Example 5-11. Custom control with state and changed event (.cs)

```
//-------------------------------------------------------------------------
//
//    Module Name: CH05CustomControlWithStateCS2
//
//    Description: This class provides a custom control that maintains state
//                 through postbacks to the server and raises an event when
//                 the entered data changes.
//
//*************************************************************************
```

```csharp
using System;
using System.Collections.Specialized;
using System.Drawing;
using System.Web;
using System.Web.UI;

namespace ASPNetCookbook.CSExamples
{
  public class CH05CustomControlWithStateCS2 : Control, IPostBackDataHandler
  {
    // define an event to be raised if the text changes
    public event EventHandler OnTextChanged;

    // private copies of attribute data
    private String mLabelText = "Label: ";
    private Color mTextColor = Color.Black;
    private int mTextboxWidth = 3;

    //***********************************************************************
    //
    //    ROUTINE: labelText
    //
    //    DESCRIPTION: This property provides the ability to set the text
    //                 of the label in the control.
    //-----------------------------------------------------------------------
    public String labelText
    {
      get
      {
        return(mLabelText);
      }
      set
      {
        mLabelText = value;
      }
    }  // labelText

    //***********************************************************************
    //
    //    ROUTINE: textColor
    //
    //    DESCRIPTION: This property provides the ability to get/set the color
    //                 of the text in the control.
    //-----------------------------------------------------------------------
    public Color textColor
    {
      get
      {
        return(mTextColor);
      }
      set
      {
```

Example 5-11. Custom control with state and changed event (.cs) (continued)

```
      mTextColor = value;
  }
} // textColor

//**************************************************************************
//
//    ROUTINE: textboxWidth
//
//    DESCRIPTION: This property provides the ability to get/set the width
//                 of the textbox in the control.
//-------------------------------------------------------------------------
public int textboxWidth
{
  get
  {
    return(mTextboxWidth);
  }
  set
  {
    mTextboxWidth = value;
  }
} // textboxWidth

//**************************************************************************
//
//    ROUTINE: text
//
//    DESCRIPTION: This property provides the ability to get/set the text
//                 in the textbox in the control.
//-------------------------------------------------------------------------
const String VS_TEXTBOX_VALUE = "TextboxValue";

public String text
{
  get
  {
    String value = null;
    if (ViewState[VS_TEXTBOX_VALUE] != null)
    {
      value = (String)(ViewState[VS_TEXTBOX_VALUE]);
    }
    return (value);
  }
  set
  {
    ViewState[VS_TEXTBOX_VALUE] = value;
  }
} // text

//**************************************************************************
//
//    ROUTINE: Render
//
```

Example 5-11. Custom control with state and changed event (.cs) (continued)

```csharp
//   DESCRIPTION: This routine renders the HTML output of the control.
//--------------------------------------------------------------------------
protected override void Render(HtmlTextWriter writer)
{
  //output label
  writer.AddAttribute("color",
    ColorTranslator.ToHtml(textColor));
  writer.RenderBeginTag(HtmlTextWriterTag.Font);
  writer.Write(labelText);
  writer.RenderEndTag( );

  //output input control
  writer.AddAttribute(HtmlTextWriterAttribute.Type,
    "text");
  writer.AddAttribute(HtmlTextWriterAttribute.Size,
    textboxWidth.ToString( ));

  // output name attribute to identify data on postback
  writer.AddAttribute(HtmlTextWriterAttribute.Name,
    this.UniqueID);

  // output value attribute only if value exists
  if (text != null)
  {
    writer.AddAttribute(HtmlTextWriterAttribute.Value,
      text);
  }

  writer.RenderBeginTag(HtmlTextWriterTag.Input);
  writer.RenderEndTag( );
} // Render


//**************************************************************************
//
//   ROUTINE: LoadPostData
//
//   DESCRIPTION: This routine processes data posted back from the client.
//--------------------------------------------------------------------------
public virtual bool LoadPostData(string postDataKey,
                                 NameValueCollection postCollection)
{
  bool dataChanged = false;
  String postbackValue;

  // check to see if the data changed
  postbackValue = postCollection[postDataKey];
  if (!postbackValue.Equals(text))
  {
    dataChanged = true;
  }

  // set the value of the text property from the postback data
  text = postbackValue;
```

Example 5-11. Custom control with state and changed event (.cs) (continued)

```
      return (dataChanged);
    }  // LoadPostData

    //**************************************************************************
    //
    //   ROUTINE: RaisePostDataChangedEvent
    //
    //   DESCRIPTION: This routine processes data changed events as a result
    //                of the postback.
    //
    //--------------------------------------------------------------------------
    public virtual void RaisePostDataChangedEvent()
    {
      // raise event if a handler is assigned
      if (OnTextChanged != null)
      {
        OnTextChanged(this, EventArgs.Empty);
      }
    }  // RaisePostDataChangedEvent
  }  // CH05CustomControlWithStateCS2
}
```

Example 5-12. Using the custom control with state and changed event (.aspx)

```
<%@ Page Language="vb" AutoEventWireup="false" Codebehind="CH05DisplayControlWithStateVB2.
aspx.vb" Inherits="ASPNetCookbook.VBExamples.CH05DisplayControlWithStateVB2" %>
<%@ Register TagPrefix="ASPCookbook" Namespace="ASPNetCookbook.VBExamples"
             Assembly="ASPNetCookbookVB" %>
<!DOCTYPE HTML PUBLIC "-//W3C//DTD HTML 4.0 Transitional//EN">
<html>
  <head>
    <title>Custom Control With State</title>
    <link rel="stylesheet" href="css/ASPNetCookbook.css">
  </head>
  <body leftmargin="0" marginheight="0" marginwidth="0" topmargin="0">
    <form id="frmCustomControl" method="post" runat="server">
      <table width="100%" cellpadding="0" cellspacing="0" border="0">
        <tr>
          <td align="center">
            <img src="images/ASPNETCookbookHeading_blue.gif">
          </td>
        </tr>
        <tr>
          <td class="dividerLine">
            <img src="images/spacer.gif" height="6" border="0"></td>
        </tr>
      </table>
      <table width="90%" align="center" border="0">
        <tr>
          <td><img src="images/spacer.gif" height="10" border="0"></td>
        </tr>
        <tr>
          <td align="center" class="PageHeading">
```

Example 5-12. Using the custom control with state and changed event (.aspx) (continued)

```
              Custom Control With State And Events (VB)
          </td>
        </tr>
        <tr>
          <td><img src="images/spacer.gif" height="10" border="0"></td>
        </tr>
        <tr bgcolor="#ffffcc">
          <td align="center">
            <ASPCookbook:CH05CustomControlWithStateVB2
                id="ccAttributes" runat="server"
                labelText="Enter Age: "
                textColor="#000080"
                textboxWidth="5" />
          </td>
        </tr>
        <tr>
          <td align="center">
            <asp:Label ID="labMessage" Runat="server" />
          </td>
        </tr>
        <tr>
          <td align="center">
            <br>
            <asp:ImageButton ID="btnSubmit" Runat="server"
                   ImageUrl="images/buttons/button_submit.gif" />
          </td>
        </tr>
      </table>
    </form>
  </body>
</html>
```

Example 5-13. Using the custom control with state and changed event code-behind (.vb)

```
Option Explicit On
Option Strict On
'----------------------------------------------------------------------------
'
'    Module Name: CH05DisplayControlWithStateVB2.aspx.vb
'
'    Description: This class provides the code behind for
'                 CH05DisplayControlWithStateVB2.aspx
'
'****************************************************************************
Namespace ASPNetCookbook.VBExamples
  Public Class CH05DisplayControlWithStateVB2
    Inherits System.Web.UI.Page

    'controls on the form
    Protected WithEvents ccAttributes As CH05CustomControlWithStateVB2
    Protected labMessage As System.Web.UI.WebControls.Label
```

Example 5-13. Using the custom control with state and changed event code-behind (.vb) (continued)

```vb
'***************************************************************************
'
'    ROUTINE: Page_Load
'
'    DESCRIPTION: This routine provides the event handler for the page load
'                 event.  It is responsible for initializing the controls
'                 on the page.
'---------------------------------------------------------------------------
Private Sub Page_Load(ByVal sender As System.Object, _
                      ByVal e As System.EventArgs) Handles MyBase.Load
   labMessage.Text = ""
End Sub 'Page_Load


'***************************************************************************
'
'    ROUTINE: ccAttributes_OnTextChanged
'
'    DESCRIPTION: This routine provides the event handler for the custom
'                 control text changed event.
'---------------------------------------------------------------------------
Private Sub ccAttributes_OnTextChanged(ByVal sender As Object, _
                                       ByVal e As System.EventArgs) _
        Handles ccAttributes.OnTextChanged
   labMessage.Text = "Data Changed"
End Sub 'ccAttributes_OnTextChanged
End Class 'CH05DisplayControlWithStateVB2
End Namespace
```

Example 5-14. Using the custom control with state and changed event code-behind (.cs)

```csharp
//---------------------------------------------------------------------------
//
//    Module Name: CH05DisplayControlWithStateCS2.ascx.cs
//
//    Description: This module provides the code behind for
//                 CH05DisplayControlWithStateCS2.ascx
//
//***************************************************************************
using System;

namespace ASPNetCookbook.CSExamples
{
  public class CH05DisplayControlWithStateCS2 : System.Web.UI.Page
  {
    // controls on the form
    protected CH05CustomControlWithStateCS2 ccAttributes;
    protected System.Web.UI.WebControls.Label labMessage;

    //***************************************************************************
    //
    //    ROUTINE: Page_Load
    //
```

```
    //   DESCRIPTION: This routine provides the event handler for the page
    //                load event.  It is responsible for initializing the
    //                controls on the page.
    //-------------------------------------------------------------------------
    private void Page_Load(object sender, System.EventArgs e)
    {
      // wire the event to the text changed event of the custom control
      ccAttributes.OnTextChanged +=
        new EventHandler(this.ccAttributes_OnTextChanged);

      labMessage.Text = "";
    }  // Page_Load


    //*************************************************************************
    //
    //   ROUTINE: ccAttributes_OnTextChanged
    //
    //   DESCRIPTION: This routine provides the event handler that is the
    //                recipient of the event raised custom control.
    //-------------------------------------------------------------------------
    public void ccAttributes_OnTextChanged(System.Object sender,
      EventArgs e)
    {
      // update the label with the message in the event arguments
      labMessage.Text = "Data Changed";
    }  // ccAttributes_OnTextChanged
  }  // CH05DisplayControlWithStateCS2
}
```

5.4   Customizing an ASP.NET TextBox Server Control

Problem

You want to customize an ASP.NET TextBox server control to allow only numeric input.

Solution

Create a custom control that inherits from the ASP text box control, and then add code to emit client-side script that limits the input to only numeric values.

Use the .NET language of your choice to:

1. Create a class that inherits from the Control class in the System.Web.UI namespace.

2. Override the OnPreRender method to have it generate the requisite client-side script.

---

3. Override the `AddAttributesToRender` if you need to add an attribute to the rendered control.

To use the custom control in an ASP.NET page:

1. Register the assembly containing the control.
2. Insert the tag for the custom control anywhere in the page.

Examples 5-15 and 5-16 show the VB and C# class files for an example custom control that we have written to illustrate our approach. This custom control emits client-side script that checks key presses and allows only numeric keys to be entered into a text box. Example 5-17 shows how to use the custom control in an ASP.NET page.

Discussion

Extending an existing ASP.NET server control is an easy way to create the functionality you need for an application. By inheriting your custom controls from existing controls, you are left to write only the code you need to add your special functionality.

To illustrate this approach, we've implemented a text box control that allows only numeric input, a common project requirement. Why is it necessary to implement a custom control to accomplish this? First, it turns out that none of the ASP.NET controls provides this functionality. And second, although you can check the data entered in a text box to ensure it is numeric and within a range with a range validator, this does not prevent the user from entering letters into the text box in the first place. Extending the standard text box control by adding client-side script that allows only numeric keys to be processed and their values entered into the text box is a better solution.

The first step in extending the ASP.NET text box control is to create a custom control class that inherits from `System.Web.UI.WebControls.TextBox`.

Next, you must override the `OnPreRender` method to generate the client-side script. (The reason for overriding `OnPreRender` is that you need to get the script onto the page before the control is rendered.) This is done by creating a string containing the script block, and then registering it to be output to the page with the `Page.RegisterClientScriptBlock` method.

The client script must be created and output in an event that occurs before the `Render` event or the script will not be output in the rendered page. This can be done in the `Load` or `PreRender` events.

Be sure to call the base class `OnPreRender` method. Failure to do so can result in lost functionality if the base control performs any operations in the `OnPreRender` method.

It is important to output the client script using the Page. RegisterClientScriptBlock method with the first parameter set to a constant value. This ensures that client script is output to the page only once. If the client script was output directly in the Render event and the page contained multiple instances of the custom control, the client script would be output for each instance of the control.

The client-side script that is output to the page in our example is shown next. It simply checks each key press to see if the keycode is in the 0–9 range and returns true if it is. Otherwise, it returns false.

```
<script language='javascript'>
<!--
  function checkKey( )
  {
    var key = event.keyCode;
    var processKey = false;
    if ((key >= 0x30) && (key <= 0x39))
    {
      processKey = true;
    }
    return(processKey);
  }
//-->
</script>
```

 This script will work only for Internet Explorer. You can use the Page. Request.Browser object in the OnPreRender method to determine the browser type and version so that you can output code specific to the browser requesting the page.

The last step to implement our sample custom control is to add an attribute to the rendered input control to cause the checkKey method to be executed when a key is pressed with the focus set to the input control. This is done by overriding the AddAttributesToRender method and adding the onkeypress attribute.

 If your application has a similar requirement to add an attribute to the rendered input control, be sure to call the base class AddAttributesToRender method. Failure to do so can result in lost functionality if the base control performs any operations in the AddAttributesToRender method.

The rendered HTML input control is shown here:

```
<input name="ccNumericInput" type="text" maxlength="10"
       size="10" id="ccNumericInput" onkeypress="return checkKey( );" />
```

To complete the example, we insert the control into an ASP.NET page by first registering the control (see Example 5-17). We then place the control tag in the page just as if it were a plain-vanilla text box.

One of the great advantages of inheriting from an existing ASP.NET server control is the support for all the control's inherent functionality. In this case, we can set any of the attributes available for the asp:Textbox control, even though we did no coding for those properties in our control.

```
<ASPCookbook:CH05CustomControlNumericInputVB
              id="ccNumericInput" runat="server"
              Columns="10" MaxLength="10" />
```

See Also

JavaScript: The Definitive Guide, by David Flanagan (O'Reilly), for more information on browser-specific JavaScript; *ASP.NET in a Nutshell*, by G. Andrew Duthie and Matthew MacDonald (O'Reilly), and the MSDN Library for more on OnPreRender and AddAttributestoRender

Example 5-15. Numeric input–only text box (.vb)

```
Option Explicit On
Option Strict On
'-----------------------------------------------------------------------------
'
'   Module Name: CH05CustomControlNumericInputVB.vb
'
'   Description: This class provides a custom control that implements an
'                input control that only allows numbers to be input.
'
'*****************************************************************************
Imports System
Imports System.Environment
Imports System.Text
Imports System.Web
Imports System.Web.UI

Namespace ASPNetCookbook.VBExamples
  Public Class CH05CustomControlNumericInputVB
    Inherits System.Web.UI.WebControls.TextBox

    'the following constant defines the name of the name of the client-side
    'JavaScript method used to process keystrokes
    Private Const CHECK_KEY_NAME As String = "checkKey"

    '*****************************************************************************
    '
    '   ROUTINE: OnPreRender
    '
    '   DESCRIPTION: This routine handles the prerender event for the custom
    '                control.  It adds clientside script to process keys
    '                before adding them to the textbox.
    '-----------------------------------------------------------------------------
```

Example 5-15. Numeric input–only text box (.vb) (continued)

```vb
    Protected Overrides Sub OnPreRender(ByVal e As System.EventArgs)
      Dim clientScript As StringBuilder

      MyBase.OnPreRender(e)

      'generate the opening script tag
      clientScript = New StringBuilder
      clientScript.Append("<script language='javascript'>" & NewLine)
      clientScript.Append("<!--" & NewLine)

      'generate code to check the key pressed
      clientScript.Append("function " & CHECK_KEY_NAME & "()" & NewLine)
      clientScript.Append("{" & NewLine)
      clientScript.Append("var key = event.keyCode;" & NewLine)
      clientScript.Append("var processKey = false;" & NewLine)
      clientScript.Append("if ((key >= 0x30) && (key <= 0x39))" & NewLine)
      clientScript.Append("{" & NewLine)
      clientScript.Append("processKey = true;" & NewLine)
      clientScript.Append("}" & NewLine)
      clientScript.Append("return(processKey);" & NewLine)
      clientScript.Append("}" & NewLine)

      'generate the closing script tag
      clientScript.Append("//-->" & NewLine)
      clientScript.Append("</script>" & NewLine)

      'register script to be output when the page is rendered
      Page.RegisterClientScriptBlock(CHECK_KEY_NAME, _
                                     clientScript.ToString())
    End Sub   'OnPreRender

    '***************************************************************************
    '
    '    ROUTINE: AddAttributesToRender
    '
    '    DESCRIPTION: This routine handles the AddAttributeToRender event
    '                 for the custom control.  It adds the onkeypress
    '                 attribute to the textbox to cause processing of all keys
    '                 pressed when the textbox has focus.
    '---------------------------------------------------------------------------
    Protected Overrides Sub AddAttributesToRender( _
                     ByVal writer As System.Web.UI.HtmlTextWriter)
      MyBase.AddAttributesToRender(writer)

      'add an attribute to the textbox to call client script to check
      'keys pressed
      writer.AddAttribute("onkeypress", _
                     "return " & CHECK_KEY_NAME & "();")
    End Sub   'AddAttributesToRender
  End Class   'CH05CustomControlNumericInputVB
End Namespace
```

Example 5-16. Numeric input–only text box (.cs)

```
//---------------------------------------------------------------------------
//
//    Module Name: CH05CustomControlNumericInputCS
//
//    Description: This class provides a custom control that implements an
//                 input control that only allows numbers to be input.
//
//***************************************************************************
using System;
using System.Text;
using System.Web;
using System.Web.UI;

namespace ASPNetCookbook.CSExamples
{
  public class CH05CustomControlNumericInputCS :
              System.Web.UI.WebControls.TextBox
  {
    // the following constant defines the name of the name of the client-side
    // JavaScript method used to process keystrokes
    private const String CHECK_KEY_NAME = "checkKey";

    //***********************************************************************
    //
    //    ROUTINE: OnPreRender
    //
    //    DESCRIPTION: This routine handles the prerender event for the custom
    //                 control.  It adds clientside script to process keys
    //                 before adding them to the textbox.
    //---------------------------------------------------------------------
    protected override void OnPreRender(System.EventArgs e)
    {
      StringBuilder clientScript = null;

      base.OnPreRender(e);

      // generate the opening script tag
      clientScript = new StringBuilder();
      clientScript.Append("<script language='javascript'>\r");
      clientScript.Append("<!--\r");

      // generate code to check the key pressed
      clientScript.Append("function " + CHECK_KEY_NAME + "()\r");
      clientScript.Append("{\r");
      clientScript.Append("var key = event.keyCode;\r");
      clientScript.Append("var processKey = false;\r");
      clientScript.Append("if ((key >= 0x30) && (key <= 0x39))\r");
      clientScript.Append("{\r");
      clientScript.Append("processKey = true;\r");
      clientScript.Append("}\r");
      clientScript.Append("return(processKey);\r");
      clientScript.Append("}\r");
```

Example 5-16. Numeric input–only text box (.cs) (continued)

```csharp
      // generate the closing script tag
      clientScript.Append("//-->\r");
      clientScript.Append("</script>\r");

      // register script to be output when the page is rendered
      Page.RegisterClientScriptBlock(CHECK_KEY_NAME,
                                     clientScript.ToString());
   }  // OnPreRender


   //*************************************************************************
   //
   //   ROUTINE: AddAttributesToRender
   //
   //   DESCRIPTION: This routine handles the AddAttributeToRender event
   //                for the custom control.  It adds the onkeypress
   //                attribute to the textbox to cause processing of all
   //                keys pressed when the textbox has focus.
   //-------------------------------------------------------------------------
   protected override void AddAttributesToRender(
                             System.Web.UI.HtmlTextWriter writer)
   {
      base.AddAttributesToRender(writer);

      // add an attribute to the textbox to call client script to check
      // keys pressed
      writer.AddAttribute("onkeypress", "return " + CHECK_KEY_NAME + "();");
   }  // AddAttributesToRender
}  // CH05CustomControlNumericInputCS
}
```

Example 5-17. Using the numeric input custom control (.aspx)

```aspx
<%@ Page Language="vb" AutoEventWireup="false"
  Codebehind="CH05DisplayControlWIthNumericInputVB.aspx.vb"
  Inherits="ASPNetCookbook.VBExamples.CH05DisplayControlWIthNumericInputVB" %>
<%@ Register TagPrefix="ASPCookbook" Namespace="ASPNetCookbook.VBExamples"
             Assembly="ASPNetCookbookVB" %>
<!DOCTYPE HTML PUBLIC "-//W3C//DTD HTML 4.0 Transitional//EN">
<html>
  <head>
    <title>Custom Control With Numeric Input</title>
    <link rel="stylesheet" href="css/ASPNetCookbook.css">
  </head>
  <body leftmargin="0" marginheight="0" marginwidth="0" topmargin="0">
    <form id="frmCustomControl" method="post" runat="server">
      <table width="100%" cellpadding="0" cellspacing="0" border="0">
        <tr>
          <td align="center">
            <img src="images/ASPNETCookbookHeading_blue.gif">
          </td>
        </tr>
        <tr>
```

Example 5-17. Using the numeric input custom control (.aspx) (continued)

```html
        <td class="dividerLine">
          <img src="images/spacer.gif" height="6" border="0"></td>
      </tr>
    </table>
    <table width="90%" align="center" border="0">
      <tr>
        <td><img src="images/spacer.gif" height="10" border="0"></td>
      </tr>
      <tr>
        <td align="center" class="PageHeading">
          Custom Numeric Input Control (VB)
        </td>
      </tr>
      <tr>
        <td><img src="images/spacer.gif" height="10" border="0"></td>
      </tr>
      <tr bgcolor="#ffffcc">
        <td align="center">
          <ASPCookbook:CH05CustomControlNumericInputVB
              id="ccNumericInput" runat="server"
              Columns="10" MaxLength="10" />
        </td>
      </tr>
      <tr>
        <td align="center">
          <br>
          <asp:ImageButton ID="btnSubmit" Runat="server"
              ImageUrl="images/buttons/button_submit.gif" />
        </td>
      </tr>
    </table>
  </form>
</body>
</html>
```

CHAPTER 6
Maintaining State

6.0 Introduction

Because HTTP is an inherently stateless protocol, you must use special techniques when you want to preserve information about users as they move from one page to the next or when they leave and reenter your application. Saving this information is known as *saving* or *maintaining state*. Why do you need to maintain state in the first place? The reason is that it can improve the user's experience with an ASP.NET application. By maintaining state, you can maintain the continuity between pages and between sessions that users demand of a web-based application, such as keeping track of items in a shopping cart or noting viewing preferences. You can also significantly enhance the performance of heavily used applications by making commonly used data available to any user, without making repeated trips to a database.

You can preserve information at the application, session, and page levels of an ASP.NET application. The recipes in this chapter demonstrate how each is done:

Application state
> By making commonly used data available to all users of an application, you can often improve application performance. Recipe 6.1 shows how to retrieve data from a database and place it in the Application object, thereby making it accessible to all users of an application. This is known as maintaining state at the application level.

Session state
> Experienced web users expect you to remember who they are for the duration of their sessions at your site. Preserving this information, as well as information about their activities, is known as saving *session state*. Recipe 6.2 shows how to use an object to provide a container for some simple personalization data that is used by many pages of an application. The advantage is that you can maintain information for each user without having to access the database each time the data is needed.

Page state

Saving page state involves storing small bits of page information in hidden text fields or in the ViewState. For instance, Recipe 6.3 shows how a page with multiple states can remember the current state value between postbacks. In this instance, information is stored in a hidden field each time a page is submitted to the server so that the state can be restored on return to the client.

In the chapter's last example, page state is used to store a complex object in the ViewState for tracking state information between page submittals. The example also demonstrates how you can emulate two-way data binding, which is available in Windows forms applications but not in ASP.NET applications. With two-way data binding, any changes made to the data in the bound controls are automatically updated in the underlying data container, making updates to the original data source extremely simple. In web forms, because the connection to the underlying data container is broken when the page is rendered, a bit of additional work is required to update the original data source, which the recipe shows you how to do.

Finally, before we move onto the recipes themselves, it is worth mentioning the origin of the application and session states. Classic ASP developers will recognize in their naming the ASP intrinsic objects Application and Session. Indeed, an Application object is used in classic ASP to share information among all users of a given application, while a Session object is maintained for each user that requests a page from an application. Their uses remain essentially unchanged in ASP.NET, although their implementation is considerably more elegant and easier to work with using ASP.NET's classes, properties, and methods, as you will soon see in the recipes that follow.

6.1   Maintaining Information Needed by All Users of an Application

Problem

You want to make certain data available to all users of an application.

Solution

Place the code needed to find and load the data in the Application_Start method of *global.asax* and store it in the Application object.

In the code-behind class for *global.asax*, use the .NET language of your choice to:

1. Create an event handler for the Application_Start event.
2. Load the application data and store it in the Application object.

The code we've written to demonstrate this solution is shown in Examples 6-1 through 6-5. Examples 6-1 and 6-2 show the VB and C# code-behind files for *global.asax*; this code reads data from a database and places it in the Application object. Figure 6-1 shows a simple form that we've created to view the application state data. Example 6-3 shows the *.aspx* file that produces the form. Examples 6-4 and 6-5 show the companion VB and C# code-behind files that demonstrate how to access the application state data.

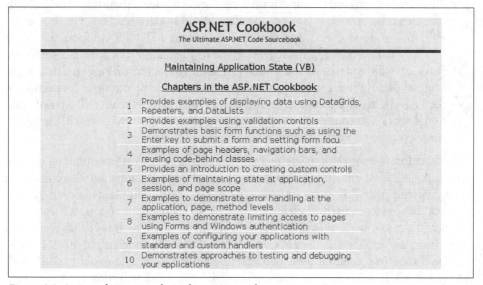

Figure 6-1. A view of some sample application state data

Discussion

The purpose of the Application object is to store information once that can be simultaneously shared with all users of the application without having to access it repeatedly from a database or some other data store. A simple example is when you want to store and then share the number of times an application has been hit by all the users of the application. Another example is when you want to store and then share some common reference information, as illustrated in Figure 6-1. Using the Application object provides the ideal means to accomplish these tasks. The Application object is similar to the Session object (discussed in the next recipe), except that it stores global information as opposed to information about an individual session. The Application object is a property of the Page object that provides the ability to store virtually any data and offer access to it throughout the application by all users. Storing commonly used global data in memory can significantly improve the performance of an application.

The code we've written to illustrate this recipe provides a simple example of loading information from a database and storing it in the Application object so it can be accessed by any user on any page of an application without having to again retrieve the data from the database each time the data is needed.

Data that you want to make available throughout the application should be initialized when the application is started. The Application_Start event handler in the *global.asax.vb* (or *global.asax.cs*) class is the best place to do this, because the Application_Start event is raised the first time the application is accessed.

In our example, the Application_Start event handler reads the titles of the chapters of this book from a database into a DataSet. We then store the table of chapter data as a smaller DataTable object in the Application object.

> Because the chapter data stored in the Application object will be used for read-only data binding, the overhead of a DataSet object is not required. Therefore, a smaller DataTable object, which represents one table in a DataSet, is stored in the Application object instead.

Data stored in the Application object can be accessed from any page of an application. When you access the data, you must cast it to the correct type because all data is stored in the Application object as Objects; without properly casting the data, your code will not compile. Our example retrieves the data and binds it to a Repeater control in the Page_Load method in Examples 6-4 and 6-5. (Data binding is described in Chapter 1.)

> To avoid "hardcoding" names of variables placed in the Application object, we recommend that you instead define public constants in the global class, as shown in Example 6-1 (VB) and Example 6-2 (C#).
>
> Any object placed in the Application object must be free-threaded or else deadlocks, race conditions, and access violations can occur. Any object created from the classes in the Common Language Runtime is free-threaded and can be safely stored in the Application object. VB6 objects are apartment-threaded and should not be placed in the Application object.

You can update data stored in the Application object whenever your application requires it. ASP.NET is multithreaded, so many threads can access the variables within the scope of an application at the same time. Changing the variables' values in an uncontrolled fashion can cause data concurrency issues. To prevent contention between threads, the Application object must be able to block access to itself while changes are made. You can do this by calling the Lock method of the Application object, making your changes, and then calling the UnLock method, as shown here:

VB
```
Application.Lock( )
Application.Add(APP_CHAPTER_DATA, _
            ds.Tables(CHAPTER_TABLE))
Application.UnLock( )
```

```
Application.Lock();
Application.Add(APP_CHAPTER_DATA,
                ds.Tables[CHAPTER_TABLE]);
Application.UnLock();
```

Your application should always minimize the time the `Application` object is locked, because all other threads are held off until the lock is released. To avoid permanent locks, ASP.NET automatically performs the unlock operation when a request is completed, a request times out, or an unhandled exception occurs and causes the request to fail.

Whenever you use the `Application` object in an application, be sure to consider the following points:

- The `Application` object is not shared across servers in a web farm. Each server maintains its own copy of the `Application` object. If the values stored in the application are different on each of the servers in the web farm, your application may operate differently depending on which server was accessed.

- Any data stored in the `Application` object is cleared when the application restarts. If any of that data needs to be persisted, you can place code in the `Application_End` event handler of *global.aspx* to store the data in a database or the like. Be careful in relying on the `Application_End` event handler to persist any important data. It is not called if the application stops abnormally, such as in a power failure or an application crash.

Example 6-1. Maintaining application state (global.asax.vb)

```
Option Explicit On
Option Strict On
'-------------------------------------------------------------------------
'
'   Module Name: Global.asax.vb
'
'   Description: This module provides the code behind for the
'                Global.asax page
'
'*************************************************************************
Imports Microsoft.VisualBasic
Imports System
Imports System.Configuration
Imports System.Data
Imports System.Data.OleDb

Namespace ASPNetCookbook.VBExamples
  Public Class Global
    Inherits System.Web.HttpApplication
```

Example 6-1. Maintaining application state (global.asax.vb) (continued)

```vb
'the following constant used to define the name of the variable used to
'store the chapter data in the application object
Public Const APP_CHAPTER_DATA As String = "ChapterData"

'*************************************************************************
'
'    ROUTINE: Application_Start
'
'    DESCRIPTION: This routine provides the event handler for the
'                 application start event.  It is responsible for
'                 initializing application variables.
'-------------------------------------------------------------------------
Sub Application_Start(ByVal sender As Object, ByVal e As EventArgs)
  Const CHAPTER_TABLE As String = "Chapter"

  Dim dbConn As OleDbConnection
  Dim da As OleDbDataAdapter
  Dim ds As DataSet
  Dim strConnection As String
  Dim strSQL As String

  Try
    'get the connection string from web.config and open a connection
    'to the database
    strConnection = _
        ConfigurationSettings.AppSettings("dbConnectionString")
    dbConn = New OleDbConnection(strConnection)
    dbConn.Open( )

    'build the query string and get the data from the database
    strSQL = "SELECT ChapterNumber, Description " & _
             "FROM Chapter " & _
             "ORDER BY ChapterNumber"

    'fill the dataset with the chapter data
    da = New OleDbDataAdapter(strSQL, dbConn)
    ds = New DataSet
    da.Fill(ds, CHAPTER_TABLE)

    'store the table containing the chapter data in the Application object
    Application.Add(APP_CHAPTER_DATA, _
                    ds.Tables(CHAPTER_TABLE))

  Finally
    If (Not IsNothing(dbConn)) Then
      dbConn.Close( )
    End If
  End Try
End Sub  'Application_Start
End Class  'Global
End Namespace
```

Example 6-2. Maintaining application state (global.asax.cs)

```
//---------------------------------------------------------------------------
//
//    Module Name: Global.asax.cs
//
//    Description: This module provides the code behind for the
//                 Global.asax page
//
//**************************************************************************
using System;
using System.Configuration;
using System.Data;
using System.Data.OleDb;

namespace ASPNetCookbook.CSExamples
{
  public class Global : System.Web.HttpApplication
  {
    // the following constant used to define the name of the variable used to
    // store the chapter data in the application object
    public const String APP_CHAPTER_DATA  = "ChapterData";

    //**********************************************************************
    //
    //    ROUTINE: Application_Start
    //
    //    DESCRIPTION: This routine provides the event handler for the
    //                 application start event.  It is responsible for
    //                 initializing application variables.
    //---------------------------------------------------------------------
    protected void Application_Start(Object sender, EventArgs e)
    {
      const String CHAPTER_TABLE  = "Chapter";

      OleDbConnection dbConn = null;
      OleDbDataAdapter da = null;
      DataSet ds = null;
      String strConnection = null;
      String strSQL = null;

      try
      {
        // get the connection string from web.config and open a connection
        // to the database
        strConnection =
          ConfigurationSettings.AppSettings["dbConnectionString"];
        dbConn = new OleDbConnection(strConnection);
        dbConn.Open();

        // build the query string and get the data from the database
        strSQL = "SELECT ChapterNumber, Description " +
                 "FROM Chapter " +
                 "ORDER BY ChapterNumber";
```

Example 6-2. Maintaining application state (global.asax.cs) (continued)

```
        // fill the dataset with the chapter data
        da = new OleDbDataAdapter(strSQL, dbConn);
        ds = new DataSet( );
        da.Fill(ds, CHAPTER_TABLE);

        // store the table containing the chapter data in the Application object
        Application.Add(APP_CHAPTER_DATA,
                        ds.Tables[CHAPTER_TABLE]);
      }  // try

      finally
      {
        // cleanup
        if (dbConn != null)
        {
          dbConn.Close( );
        }
      } // finally
    } // Application_Start
  }
}
```

Example 6-3. Using application state data (.aspx)

```
<%@ Page Language="vb" AutoEventWireup="false"
        Codebehind="CH06ApplicationStateVB.aspx.vb"
        Inherits="ASPNetCookbook.VBExamples.CH06ApplicationStateVB" %>
<!DOCTYPE HTML PUBLIC "-//W3C//DTD HTML 4.0 Transitional//EN">
<html>
  <head>
    <title>Application State</title>
    <link rel="stylesheet" href="css/ASPNetCookbook.css">
  </head>
  <body leftmargin="0" marginheight="0" marginwidth="0" topmargin="0">
    <form id="frmApplicationState" method="post" runat="server">
      <table width="100%" cellpadding="0" cellspacing="0" border="0">
        <tr>
          <td align="center">
            <img src="images/ASPNETCookbookHeading_blue.gif">
          </td>
        </tr>
        <tr>
          <td class="dividerLine">
            <img src="images/spacer.gif" height="6" border="0"></td>
        </tr>
      </table>
      <table width="90%" align="center" border="0">
        <tr>
          <td><img src="images/spacer.gif" height="10" border="0"></td>
        </tr>
        <tr>
          <td align="center" class="PageHeading">
            Maintaining Application State (VB)
```

Example 6-3. Using application state data (.aspx) (continued)

```
              </td>
          </tr>
          <tr>
            <td><img src="images/spacer.gif" height="10" border="0"></td>
          </tr>
          <tr>
            <td align="center">
              <table width="500" border="0" align="center"
                     cellpadding="0" cellspacing="0">
                <thead>
                  <tr>
                    <th colspan="2"
                        class="PageHeading">Chapters in the ASP.NET Cookbook</th>
                  </tr>
                </thead>
                <tr>
                  <td><img src="images/spacer.gif" height="10" border="0"></td>
                </tr>
                <asp:Repeater id=repMenuItems runat="server">
                  <ItemTemplate>
                    <tr class="MenuItem">
                      <td align="center" width="50">
                        <%# DataBinder.Eval(Container.DataItem, _
                                            "ChapterNumber") %></td>
                      <td width="450">
                        <%# DataBinder.Eval(Container.DataItem, _
                                            "Description") %></td>
                    </tr>
                    <tr height="2">
                      <td bgcolor="#FFFFFF" colspan="2">
                        <img src="images/spacer.gif" border="0"></td>
                    </tr>
                  </ItemTemplate>
                </asp:Repeater>
              </table>
            </td>
          </tr>
        </table>
      </form>
    </body>
</html>
```

Example 6-4. Using application state data code-behind (.vb)

```
Option Explicit On
Option Strict On
'-----------------------------------------------------------------------------
'
'   Module Name: CH06ApplicationStateVB.aspx.vb
'
'   Description: This module provides the code behind for the
'                CH06ApplicationStateVB.aspx page
'
```

Example 6-4. Using application state data code-behind (.vb) (continued)

```vb
'****************************************************************************
Imports Microsoft.VisualBasic
Imports System
Imports System.Data

Namespace ASPNetCookbook.VBExamples
  Public Class CH06ApplicationStateVB
    Inherits System.Web.UI.Page

    'controls on the form
    Protected repMenuItems As System.Web.UI.WebControls.Repeater

    '****************************************************************************
    '
    '    ROUTINE: Page_Load
    '
    '    DESCRIPTION: This routine provides the event handler for the page load
    '                 event.  It is responsible for initializing the controls
    '                 on the page.
    '----------------------------------------------------------------------------
    Private Sub Page_Load(ByVal sender As System.Object, _
                          ByVal e As System.EventArgs) Handles MyBase.Load
      Dim chapterData As DataTable

      If (Not Page.IsPostBack()) Then
        'get the chapter data stored in the application object
        chapterData = CType(Application.Item(Global.APP_CHAPTER_DATA), _
                            DataTable)

        'bind it to the repeater to display the chapter data
        repMenuItems.DataSource = chapterData
        repMenuItems.DataBind()
      End If
    End Sub 'Page_Load
  End Class 'CH06ApplicationStateVB
End Namespace
```

Example 6-5. Using application state data code-behind (.cs)

```csharp
//----------------------------------------------------------------------------
//
//    Module Name: CH06ApplicationStateCS.ascx.cs
//
//    Description: This module provides the code behind for
//                 CH06ApplicationStateCS.ascx
//
//****************************************************************************
using System;
using System.Data;
using System.Web.UI.WebControls;

namespace ASPNetCookbook.CSExamples
{
```

Example 6-5. Using application state data code-behind (.cs) (continued)

```csharp
public class CH06ApplicationStateCS : System.Web.UI.Page
{
  // controls on the form
  protected System.Web.UI.WebControls.Repeater repMenuItems;

  //*************************************************************************
  //
  //   ROUTINE: Page_Load
  //
  //   DESCRIPTION: This routine provides the event handler for the page
  //                load event.  It is responsible for initializing the
  //                controls on the page.
  //-------------------------------------------------------------------------
  private void Page_Load(object sender, System.EventArgs e)
  {
    DataTable chapterData = null;

    if (!Page.IsPostBack)
    {
      // get the chapter data stored in the application object
      chapterData = (DataTable)(Application[Global.APP_CHAPTER_DATA]);

      // bind it to the repeater to display the chapter data
      repMenuItems.DataSource = chapterData;
      repMenuItems.DataBind( );
    }
  } // Page_Load
} // CH06ApplicationStateCS
}
```

6.2   Maintaining Information about a User Throughout a Session

Problem

You want to make personalized information available to the users of your application for as long as each remains active, without having to access a database each time the information is needed and regardless of the number of pages traversed.

Solution

Create a class in which to store the personalized data, instantiate the class and load the data, store the data object in the Session object, and then access the data from the Session object as required.

In the code-behind class for your ASP.NET pages that need access to the data, use the .NET language of your choice to:

1. Check to see if the object used to store the personalized data exists in the Session object.

2. If the object exists, retrieve the object from Session. If the object does not exist, instantiate the class used for the personalized data and store it in the Session object.

3. Use the data as required in your application.

A simple example that illustrates this solution is shown in Examples 6-6 through 6-10. The example uses the class shown in Example 6-6 (CH06PersonalDataVB for VB) and Example 6-7 (CH06PersonalDataCS for C#) to provide a container for some simple personalization data. This class contains properties for each of the data items and a default constructor.

Figure 6-2 shows a simple form that we've created for viewing the current contents of the personalization data stored in the Session object and for entering new session state data values. Example 6-8 shows the .aspx file that produces the form. Examples 6-9 and 6-10 show the companion VB and C# code-behind files.

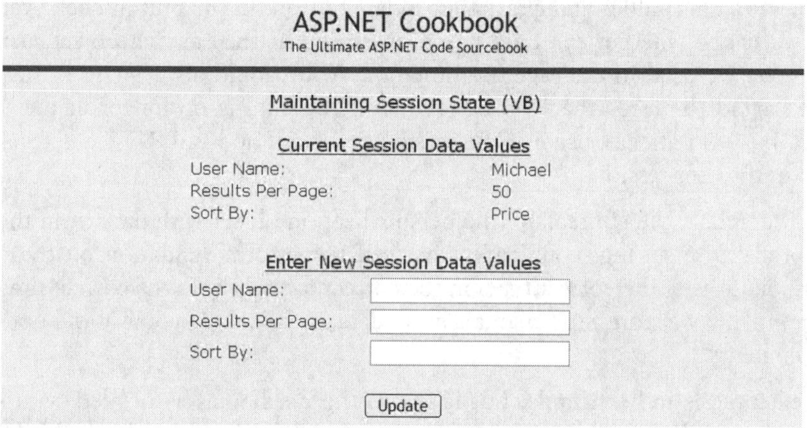

Figure 6-2. Form for viewing and entering session state data values

Discussion

The approach we favor for maintaining personal information about a user for the duration of a session—an approach that is often referred to as *personalization*—is to create a class to hold the data, instantiate and populate the object, store the object in the Session object, and then access the data from the Session object.

As its name implies, you can use the Session object in ASP.NET to store information needed for a particular user session. Variables stored in the Session object are not discarded when the user navigates between the pages of an application. Rather, they are persisted for the entire session.

To illustrate this approach, the code-behind in our example contains the logic needed to access the data in the Session object. We make use of the Page_Load method in Example 6-9 (VB) and Example 6-10 (C#) to first check whether the Session object contains the personalization data. If not, we create a new CH06PersonalDataVB (VB) or CH06PersonalDataCS (C#) object using default values, and store this new data object in the Session object associated with the current session. Otherwise, we retrieve a reference to the object containing the personalized data. Finally, we update the contents of the form by passing the personalization object to a method that uses the data to update the contents of the form.

 In Examples 6-9 and 6-10, a constant, SES_PERSONALIZATION_DATA, is used to define the name of the variable placed in the Session object. This is done to avoid having to hardcode the name of the variable in multiple locations in the code. In an application where the data is accessed in multiple pages, the constant should be stored in *global.asax.vb* (or *global.asax.cs*) or in another class containing global constants.

For this example, the personalization data is updated when the user enters new personalization data values and clicks the Update button. In the button click event handler, we check whether the data has been stored in the Session object, using the same code we used in the Page_Load method. You should always check this condition to avoid the error that will be thrown if the data is no longer in the Session object. Loss of data can occur if the session times out and ASP.NET deletes all variables for the user session.

Next, we update the contents of the personalization object with data from the form. In a production setting, your code will need to perform validation on the data to ensure that it is of the correct type, in the correct form, within the correct range, and so on. Finally, we store the personalization data in the Session object and update the form contents.

This example is rather simple, but it shows the mechanics associated with storing and retrieving data in the Session object. In a full application, the personalization data could be read from a database when the user logs in. If your application uses cookies to identify a user, the Session_Start event handler of *global.asax* provides an ideal place to retrieve the cookie that identifies the user, get the user's personalization data from a database, and then place the data in the Session object.

You can place any object in the Session object, but take care not to overuse the Session object. Large objects can significantly impact the performance of the application by tying up system resources.

To provide the ability to associate session data with a specific user, ASP.NET assigns a session ID to each user session. The session ID is then used by ASP.NET to retrieve the Session object associated with the user requesting a page.

The HTTP protocol is stateless, so some method of associating the incoming requests with a specific user is required. By default, ASP.NET sends a cookie containing the session ID to the client browser as part of its response to the first page request by a user. Subsequent page requests return the cookie data. ASP.NET retrieves the cookie data from the request, extracts the session ID, retrieves the Session object for the specific user, and then processes the requested page.

The cookie sent to the client browser is an in-memory cookie and is not persisted on the client machine. If the user closes the browser, the cookie containing the session ID is destroyed.

To support applications that do not use cookies, ASP.NET provides the ability to automatically modify the URL to contain the session ID (called *URL munging*). This method of tracking the session ID is configured in the *web.config* file and is discussed in Recipe 9.4.

ASP.NET supports three methods of storing the session information. By default, the session data is stored in memory within the ASP.NET process. The session data can also be stored in memory in an out-of-process state server or SQL Server. The storage methods are configured in the *web.config* file and are discussed in Recipe 9.4.

When using the Session object in your application, consider the following points:

- By default, a session times out after 20 minutes of inactivity. When a session times out, the ASP.NET process destroys all session data, and the resources used by the session variables are recovered. The session timeout is configured in the *web.config* file and is discussed in Recipe 9.4.

- If any special operations are required when a user session ends, they can be performed in the Session_End event handler of *global.asax*. This event is raised whenever a session ends, whether it is done programmatically or because the session times out. However, the Session_End event may not be raised if ASP.NET is terminated abruptly.

See Also

Recipe 9.4

Example 6-6. Class used to store data in session object (.vb)

```
Option Explicit On
Option Strict On
'-------------------------------------------------------------------------
'
'   Module Name: CH06PersonalDataVB.vb
'
'   Description: This module provides the container to store personalization
'                data for a user
'
'*************************************************************************
```

Example 6-6. Class used to store data in session object (.vb) (continued)

```
Namespace ASPNetCookbook.VBExamples
  Public Class CH06PersonalDataVB

    'private attributes with default values
    Private mUsername As String = ""
    Private mResultsPerPage As Integer = 25
    Private mSortBy As String = "Title"

    Public Property username( ) As String
      Get
        Return (mUsername)
      End Get
      Set(ByVal Value As String)
        mUsername = Value
      End Set
    End Property   'username

    Public Property resultsPerPage( ) As Integer
      Get
        Return (mResultsPerPage)
      End Get
      Set(ByVal Value As Integer)
        mResultsPerPage = Value
      End Set
    End Property   'resultsPerPage

    Public Property sortBy( ) As String
      Get
        Return (mSortBy)
      End Get
      Set(ByVal Value As String)
        mSortBy = Value
      End Set
    End Property   'sortBy
  End Class   'CH06PersonalDataVB
End Namespace
```

Example 6-7. Class used to store data in session object (.cs)

```
//---------------------------------------------------------------------------
//
//   Module Name: CH06PersonalDataCS
//
//   Description: This module provides the container to store personalization
//                data for a user
//
//***************************************************************************
using System;

namespace ASPNetCookbook.CSExamples
{
  public class CH06PersonalDataCS
  {
```

Example 6-7. Class used to store data in session object (.cs) (continued)

```csharp
   // private attributes with default values
   private String mUsername = "";
   private int mResultsPerPage = 25;
   private String mSortBy = "Title";

   public String username
   {
     get
     {
       return(mUsername);
     }
     set
     {
       mUsername = value;
     }
   }  // username

   public int resultsPerPage
   {
     get
     {
       return(mResultsPerPage);
     }
     set
     {
       mResultsPerPage = value;
     }
   }  // resultsPerPage

   public String sortBy
   {
     get
     {
       return(mSortBy);
     }
     set
     {
       mSortBy = value;
     }
   }  // mSortBy
 }  // CH06PersonalDataCS
}
```

Example 6-8. Maintaining user state (.aspx)

```aspx
<%@ Page Language="vb" AutoEventWireup="false"
        Codebehind="CH06SessionStateVB.aspx.vb"
        Inherits="ASPNetCookbook.VBExamples.CH06SessionStateVB" %>
<!DOCTYPE HTML PUBLIC "-//W3C//DTD HTML 4.0 Transitional//EN">
<html>
  <head>
    <title>State Session</title>
    <link rel="stylesheet" href="css/ASPNetCookbook.css">
```

Example 6-8. Maintaining user state (.aspx) (continued)

```
</head>
<body leftmargin="0" marginheight="0" marginwidth="0" topmargin="0">
  <form id="frmSessionState" method="post" runat="server">
    <table width="100%" cellpadding="0" cellspacing="0" border="0">
      <tr>
        <td align="center">
          <img src="images/ASPNETCookbookHeading_blue.gif">
        </td>
      </tr>
      <tr>
        <td class="dividerLine">
          <img src="images/spacer.gif" height="6" border="0"></td>
      </tr>
    </table>
    <table width="90%" align="center" border="0">
      <tr>
        <td><img src="images/spacer.gif" height="10" border="0"></td>
      </tr>
      <tr>
        <td align="center" class="PageHeading">
          Maintaining Session State (VB)
        </td>
      </tr>
      <tr>
        <td><img src="images/spacer.gif" height="10" border="0"></td>
      </tr>
      <tr>
        <td align="center">
          <table width="60%" align="center">
            <tr>
              <td colspan="2" align="center" class="PageHeading">
                Current Session Data Values</td>
            </tr>
            <tr class="MenuItem">
              <td>User Name: </td>
              <td><asp:Label ID="labUserName" Runat="server" /></td>
            </tr>
            <tr class="MenuItem">
              <td>Results Per Page: </td>
              <td><asp:Label ID="labResultsPerPage" Runat="server" /></td>
            </tr>
            <tr class="MenuItem">
              <td>Sort By: </td>
              <td><asp:Label ID="labSortBy" Runat="server" /></td>
            </tr>
          </table>
          <br />
          <table width="60%" align="center">
            <tr>
              <td colspan="2" align="center" class="PageHeading">
                Enter New Session Data Values</td>
            </tr>
```

Example 6-8. Maintaining user state (.aspx) (continued)

```
            <tr class="MenuItem">
              <td>User Name: </td>
              <td><asp:TextBox ID="txtUserName" Runat="server" /></td>
            </tr>
            <tr class="MenuItem">
              <td>Results Per Page: </td>
              <td><asp:TextBox ID="txtResultsPerPage" Runat="server" /></td>
            </tr>
            <tr class="MenuItem">
              <td>Sort By: </td>
              <td><asp:TextBox ID="txtSortBy" Runat="server" /></td>
            </tr>
            <tr>
              <td colspan="2" align="center">
                <br />
                <asp:ImageButton ID="btnUpdate" Runat="server"
                     ImageUrl="images/buttons/button_update.gif" />
              </td>
            </tr>
          </table>
        </td>
      </tr>
    </table>
  </form>
  </body>
</html>
```

Example 6-9. Maintaining user state (.vb)

```
Option Explicit On
Option Strict On
'-----------------------------------------------------------------------------
'
'   Module Name: CH06SessionStateVB.aspx.vb
'
'   Description: This module provides the code behind for
'                CH06SessionStateVB.aspx
'
'*****************************************************************************
Imports Microsoft.VisualBasic

Namespace ASPNetCookbook.VBExamples
  Public Class CH06SessionStateVB
    Inherits System.Web.UI.Page

    'controls on the form
    Protected labUserName As System.Web.UI.WebControls.Label
    Protected labResultsPerPage As System.Web.UI.WebControls.Label
    Protected labSortBy As System.Web.UI.WebControls.Label

    Protected txtUserName As System.Web.UI.WebControls.TextBox
    Protected txtResultsPerPage As System.Web.UI.WebControls.TextBox
    Protected txtSortBy As System.Web.UI.WebControls.TextBox
```

Example 6-9. Maintaining user state (.vb) (continued)

```
    Protected WithEvents btnUpdate As System.Web.UI.WebControls.ImageButton

    'The following constant defines the name of the session variable used
    'to store the user personalization data
    Public SES_PERSONALIZATION_DATA As String = "PersonalizationData"

    '*************************************************************************
    '
    '   ROUTINE: Page_Load
    '
    '   DESCRIPTION: This routine provides the event handler for the page load
    '                event.  It is responsible for initializing the controls
    '                on the page.
    '-------------------------------------------------------------------------
    Private Sub Page_Load(ByVal sender As System.Object, _
                        ByVal e As System.EventArgs) Handles MyBase.Load

      Dim personalData As CH06PersonalDataVB

      If (Not Page.IsPostBack()) Then
        'check to see if the session data exists
        If (IsNothing(Session(SES_PERSONALIZATION_DATA))) Then
          'data does not exist in session so create a new personalization
          'object and place it in session scope
          personalData = New CH06PersonalDataVB
          Session.Add(SES_PERSONALIZATION_DATA, _
                    personalData)
        Else
          'data exists in session so get a reference to the data
          personalData = CType(Session(SES_PERSONALIZATION_DATA), _
                            CH06PersonalDataVB)
        End If

        'update contents on the form
        updateFormData(personalData)
      End If
    End Sub   'Page_Load

    '*************************************************************************
    '
    '   ROUTINE: btnUpdate_Click
    '
    '   DESCRIPTION: This routine provides the event handler for the update
    '                button click event.  It is responsible for updating the
    '                contents of the session variable used to store the
    '                personalization data and updating the form.
    '-------------------------------------------------------------------------
    Private Sub btnUpdate_Click(ByVal sender As Object, _
                            ByVal e As System.Web.UI.ImageClickEventArgs) _
            Handles btnUpdate.Click

      Dim personalData As CH06PersonalDataVB
```

Example 6-9. Maintaining user state (.vb) (continued)

```vb
      'check to see if the session data exists
      If (IsNothing(Session(SES_PERSONALIZATION_DATA))) Then
        'data does not exist in session so create a new personalization object
        personalData = New CH06PersonalDataVB
      Else
        'data exists in session so get a reference to the data
        personalData = CType(Session(SES_PERSONALIZATION_DATA), _
                              CH06PersonalDataVB)
      End If

      'update contents of session object from form
      personalData.username = txtUserName.Text
      personalData.resultsPerPage = CInt(txtResultsPerPage.Text)
      personalData.sortBy = txtSortBy.Text

      'update contents of session object
      Session(SES_PERSONALIZATION_DATA) = personalData

      'update contents on the form
      updateFormData(personalData)
    End Sub  'btnUpdate_Click

    '*************************************************************************
    '
    '    ROUTINE: updateFormData
    '
    '    DESCRIPTION: This routine updates the contents of the form from the
    '                 passed data.
    '-------------------------------------------------------------------------
    Private Sub updateFormData(ByVal personalData As CH06PersonalDataVB)
      labUserName.Text = personalData.username
      labResultsPerPage.Text = personalData.resultsPerPage.ToString()
      labSortBy.Text = personalData.sortBy
    End Sub  'updateFormData
  End Class  'CH06SessionStateVB
End Namespace
```

Example 6-10. Maintaining user state (.cs)

```csharp
//---------------------------------------------------------------------------
//
//   Module Name: CH06SessionStateCS.ascx.cs
//
//   Description: This module provides the code behind for
//                CH06SessionStateCS.ascx
//
//***************************************************************************
using System;
using System.Web.UI;
using System.Web.UI.WebControls;

namespace ASPNetCookbook.CSExamples
{
```

Example 6-10. Maintaining user state (.cs) (continued)

```csharp
public class CH06SessionStateCS : System.Web.UI.Page
{
  // controls on the form
  protected System.Web.UI.WebControls.Label labUserName;
  protected System.Web.UI.WebControls.Label labResultsPerPage;
  protected System.Web.UI.WebControls.Label labSortBy;

  protected System.Web.UI.WebControls.TextBox txtUserName;
  protected System.Web.UI.WebControls.TextBox txtResultsPerPage;
  protected System.Web.UI.WebControls.TextBox txtSortBy;

  protected System.Web.UI.WebControls.ImageButton btnUpdate;

  // The following constant defines the name of the session variable used
  // to store the user personalization data
  public String SES_PERSONALIZATION_DATA = "PersonalizationData";

  //*************************************************************************
  //
  //    ROUTINE: Page_Load
  //
  //    DESCRIPTION: This routine provides the event handler for the page
  //                 load event.  It is responsible for initializing the
  //                 controls on the page.
  //-------------------------------------------------------------------------
  private void Page_Load(object sender, System.EventArgs e)
  {
    CH06PersonalDataCS personalData = null;

    // wire the update button click event
    this.btnUpdate.Click +=
      new ImageClickEventHandler(this.btnUpdate_Click);

    if (!Page.IsPostBack)
    {
      // check to see if the session data exists
      if (Session[SES_PERSONALIZATION_DATA] == null)
      {
        // data does not exist in session so create a new personalization
        // object and place it in session scope
        personalData = new CH06PersonalDataCS();
        Session.Add(SES_PERSONALIZATION_DATA,
                    personalData);
      }
      else
      {
        // data exists in session so get a reference to the data
        personalData = (CH06PersonalDataCS)
                       (Session[SES_PERSONALIZATION_DATA]);
      }

      // update contents on the form
      updateFormData(personalData);
```

Example 6-10. Maintaining user state (.cs) (continued)

```
  }
} // Page_Load

//************************************************************************
//
//   ROUTINE: btnUpdate_Click
//
//   DESCRIPTION: This routine provides the event handler for the update
//                button click event.  It is responsible for updating the
//                contents of the session variable used to store the
//                personalization data and updating the form.
//------------------------------------------------------------------------
private void btnUpdate_Click(Object sender,
                             System.Web.UI.ImageClickEventArgs e)
{
  CH06PersonalDataCS personalData = null;

  //check to see if the session data exists
  if (Session[SES_PERSONALIZATION_DATA] == null)
  {
    // data does not exist in session so create a new
    // personalization object
    personalData = new CH06PersonalDataCS();
  }
  else
  {
    //data exists in session so get a reference to the data
    personalData = (CH06PersonalDataCS)(Session[SES_PERSONALIZATION_DATA]);
  }

  // update contents of session object from form
  personalData.username = txtUserName.Text;
  personalData.resultsPerPage = Convert.ToInt32(txtResultsPerPage.Text);
  personalData.sortBy = txtSortBy.Text;

  //update contents of session object
  Session[SES_PERSONALIZATION_DATA] = personalData;

  // update contents on the form
  updateFormData(personalData);
} // btnUpdate_Click

//************************************************************************
//
//   ROUTINE: updateFormData
//
//   DESCRIPTION: This routine updates the contents of the form from the
//                passed data.
//------------------------------------------------------------------------
private void updateFormData(CH06PersonalDataCS personalData)
{
  labUserName.Text = personalData.username;
  labResultsPerPage.Text = personalData.resultsPerPage.ToString();
```

Example 6-10. Maintaining user state (.cs) (continued)

```
        labSortBy.Text = personalData.sortBy;
    }  // updateFormData
}  // CH06SessionStateCS
}
```

6.3   Preserving Information Between Postbacks

Problem

You have a page with a state whose value the page needs to remember between postbacks to determine how the page should be displayed.

Solution

Use the `RegisterHiddenField` method of the `Page` object to create a hidden text field in the rendered page.

Nothing special is required in the *.aspx* file. Instead, in the code-behind class for the page, use the .NET language of your choice to:

1. Programmatically insert a hidden text field into the form using the `RegisterHiddenField` method of the `Page` object.

2. Use this field to store the value of the state you wish to preserve between postbacks.

3. Access the hidden text field on subsequent submissions of the page to the server.

Figure 6-3 shows the output of a simple form that preserves the page state using a hidden field. Clicking the Prev/Next buttons decrements/increments the value in the hidden field by one. Example 6-11 shows the *.aspx* file that produces the form. Examples 6-12 and 6-13 show the companion VB and C# code-behind files that demonstrate how to access the application state data.

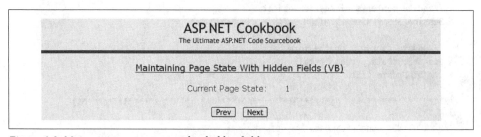

Figure 6-3. Maintaining page state with a hidden field

Discussion

An approach we favor for remembering the current state of a value between postbacks to the server involves programmatically inserting one or more hidden text fields into a form.

A similar technique is commonly used by classic ASP developers, who explicitly place a hidden text field in the form and then set its value in the page code. You can use the same technique in ASP.NET pages. However, ASP.NET, unlike ASP, lets you programmatically insert hidden text fields into a form at runtime. This has two significant advantages. First, all code that you write is kept in the code-behind, allowing the .aspx file to contain only the presentation aspects (hidden fields contain no user interface). Second, the hidden fields are completely decoupled from the .aspx file. Because no hidden fields are explicitly placed in the .aspx file, you do not have the maintenance issues associated with placing the server control in the .aspx file and then declaring it in the code-behind.

One negative aspect of using hidden fields for storing state data is the data is stored in plain text. If you do not want the data to be readily visible in the rendered HTML, you should store the data in the ViewState instead, as described in Recipe 6.4.

As an example of when you might use hidden fields, suppose your application supports complex sorting within a DataGrid, such as a two-way sort that involves both ascending and descending columns and might even be supported by your own sorting expressions. You can use hidden fields to maintain information about how a user has performed a specific sort so that you can preserve the user's sorting order and choice of sorted columns.

Our example that illustrates the solution is kept relatively simple to focus on the concept of storing information in hidden fields each time a page is submitted to the server. The example programmatically inserts a single hidden field into a form and then increments or decrements its value based on the button clicked by the user.

Because the hidden field is accessed from many points in the code-behind, a constant at the class level, PAGE_STATE, defines the name of the hidden field that is programmatically inserted into the rendered page. This avoids hardcoding the hidden field name throughout the code and the associated maintenance issues.

In the Page_Load method, updatePage, which is the method used to update the page based on the page state, is called passing a value of 0 as the initial page state value.

In the updatePage method, a label is updated to indicate the current state value. After updating the page to reflect the current page state, the RegisterHiddenField method of the Page object is used to save the page state value in the rendered page.

The rendered page contains the following hidden form variable that can be retrieved when the page is submitted to the server. The name is set to the value of the PAGE_STATE constant, and the value is set to the current page state:

```
<input type="hidden" name="PageState" value="0" />
```

Hidden fields always store the value as a string. This requires any data saved using the technique to be converted to a string when the RegisterHiddenField method is called.

In this example, two buttons are provided to increment and decrement the page state, respectively. An event handler is added in the code-behind for each of the button click events. The event handler for the increment button is called btnNextState_Click; the event handler for the decrement button is btnPrevState_Click. In the event handlers, the current page state is retrieved from the hidden field, adjusted as required, and then the updatePage method is again called to update the page and save the new page state value in the form when the page is rendered.

Even though the example presented here is simplistic, it nonetheless demonstrates how easy ASP.NET has made it to persist information that is needed for each round trip between the server and the client. For an example of persisting more complex data between page submittals, refer to Recipe 6.4.

See Also

Recipe 6.4

Example 6-11. Maintaining page state with hidden values (.aspx)

```
<%@ Page Language="vb" AutoEventWireup="false"
        Codebehind="CH06HiddenValuesVB.aspx.vb"
        Inherits="ASPNetCookbook.VBExamples.CH06HiddenValuesVB" %>
<!DOCTYPE HTML PUBLIC "-//W3C//DTD HTML 4.0 Transitional//EN">
<html>
  <head>
    <title>Hidden Values</title>
    <link rel="stylesheet" href="css/ASPNetCookbook.css">
  </head>
  <body leftmargin="0" marginheight="0" marginwidth="0" topmargin="0">
    <form id="frmStateHiddenValues" method="post" runat="server">
      <table width="100%" cellpadding="0" cellspacing="0" border="0">
        <tr>
          <td align="center">
            <img src="images/ASPNETCookbookHeading_blue.gif">
          </td>
        </tr>
        <tr>
          <td class="dividerLine">
            <img src="images/spacer.gif" height="6" border="0"></td>
        </tr>
      </table>
      <table width="90%" align="center" border="0">
        <tr>
          <td><img src="images/spacer.gif" height="10" border="0"></td>
        </tr>
        <tr>
          <td align="center" class="PageHeading">
            Maintaining Page State With Hidden Fields (VB)
          </td>
        </tr>
        <tr>
```

```
          <td><img src="images/spacer.gif" height="10" border="0"></td>
        </tr>
        <tr>
          <td align="center">
            <table width="30%" align="center" id="tabState" runat="server">
              <tr class="MenuItem">
                <td>Current Page State: </td>
                <td><asp:Label ID="labPageState" Runat="server" /></td>
              </tr>
              <tr>
                <td colspan="2" align="center">
                  <br />
                  <asp:ImageButton ID="btnPrevState" Runat="server"
                        ImageUrl="images/buttons/button_prev.gif" />
                  <asp:ImageButton ID="btnNextState" Runat="server"
                        ImageUrl="images/buttons/button_next.gif" />
                </td>
              </tr>
            </table>
          </td>
        </tr>
      </table>
    </form>
  </body>
</html>
```

Example 6-12. Maintaining page state with hidden values code-behind (.vb)

```vb
Option Explicit On
Option Strict On
'-----------------------------------------------------------------------------
'
'   Module Name: CH06HiddenValuesVB.aspx.vb
'
'   Description: This module provides the code behind for
'                CH06HiddenValuesVB.aspx
'
'*****************************************************************************

Namespace ASPNetCookbook.VBExamples
  Public Class CH06HiddenValuesVB
    Inherits System.Web.UI.Page

    'controls on the form
    Protected tabState As System.Web.UI.HtmlControls.HtmlTable
    Protected labPageState As System.Web.UI.WebControls.Label
    Protected WithEvents btnPrevState As System.Web.UI.WebControls.ImageButton
    Protected WithEvents btnNextState As System.Web.UI.WebControls.ImageButton

    'The following variable defines the name of the hidden field in the
    'form used to track the page state
    Private PAGE_STATE As String = "PageState"
```

Example 6-12. Maintaining page state with hidden values code-behind (.vb) (continued)

```vb
'************************************************************************
'
'    ROUTINE: Page_Load
'
'    DESCRIPTION: This routine provides the event handler for the page load
'                 event.  It is responsible for initializing the controls
'                 on the page.
'------------------------------------------------------------------------
Private Sub Page_Load(ByVal sender As System.Object, _
                      ByVal e As System.EventArgs) Handles MyBase.Load

  If (Not Page.IsPostBack()) Then
    'not a postback so initialize the page state to 0
    updatePage(0)
  End If
End Sub   'Page_Load


'************************************************************************
'
'    ROUTINE: btnPrevState_Click
'
'    DESCRIPTION: This routine provides the event handler for the previous
'                 state button click event.  It is responsible for setting
'                 the page state back one state.
'------------------------------------------------------------------------
Private Sub btnPrevState_Click(ByVal sender As Object, _
                      ByVal e As System.Web.UI.ImageClickEventArgs) _
           Handles btnPrevState.Click
  Dim pageState As Integer

  pageState = CInt(Request.Form(PAGE_STATE))
  pageState -= 1
  updatePage(pageState)
End Sub   'btnPrevState_Click


'************************************************************************
'
'    ROUTINE: btnNextState_Click
'
'    DESCRIPTION: This routine provides the event handler for the next
'                 state button click event.  It is responsible for setting
'                 the page state ahead one state.
'------------------------------------------------------------------------
Private Sub btnNextState_Click(ByVal sender As Object, _
                      ByVal e As System.Web.UI.ImageClickEventArgs) _
           Handles btnNextState.Click
  Dim pageState As Integer

  pageState = CInt(Request.Form(PAGE_STATE))
  pageState += 1
  updatePage(pageState)
End Sub   'btnNextState_Click
```

Example 6-12. Maintaining page state with hidden values code-behind (.vb) (continued)

```
'***************************************************************************
'
'    ROUTINE: updatePage
'
'    DESCRIPTION: This routine updates the page for the passed page state.
'---------------------------------------------------------------------------
    Private Sub updatePage(ByVal pageState As Integer)

      'update the current page state display
      labPageState.Text = pageState.ToString()

      'register the hidden field used to persist the current page state
      RegisterHiddenField(PAGE_STATE, _
                          pageState.ToString())
    End Sub  'updatePage
  End Class  'CH06HiddenValuesVB
End Namespace
```

Example 6-13. Maintaining page state with hidden values code-behind (.cs)

```
//---------------------------------------------------------------------------
//
//    Module Name: CH06HiddenValuesCS.ascx.cs
//
//    Description: This module provides the code behind for
//                 CH06HiddenValuesCS.ascx
//
//***************************************************************************
using System;
using System.Web.UI;
using System.Web.UI.WebControls;

namespace ASPNetCookbook.CSExamples
{
  public class CH06HiddenValuesCS : System.Web.UI.Page
  {
    // controls on the form
    protected System.Web.UI.HtmlControls.HtmlTable tabState;
    protected System.Web.UI.WebControls.Label labPageState;
    protected System.Web.UI.WebControls.ImageButton btnPrevState;
    protected System.Web.UI.WebControls.ImageButton btnNextState;

    // The following variable defines the name of the hidden field in the
    // form used to track the page state
    private String PAGE_STATE = "PageState";

    //***************************************************************************
    //
    //    ROUTINE: Page_Load
    //
    //    DESCRIPTION: This routine provides the event handler for the page
    //                 load event.  It is responsible for initializing the
    //                 controls on page.
    //---------------------------------------------------------------------------
```

```csharp
private void Page_Load(object sender, System.EventArgs e)
{
  // wire the next and prev button click event handlers
  this.btnPrevState.Click +=
    new ImageClickEventHandler(this.btnPrevState_Click);
  this.btnNextState.Click +=
    new ImageClickEventHandler(this.btnNextState_Click);

  if (!Page.IsPostBack)
  {
    // not a postback so initialize the page state to 0
    updatePage(0);
  }
} // Page_Load

//*************************************************************************
//
//   ROUTINE: btnPrevState_Click
//
//   DESCRIPTION: This routine provides the event handler for the
//                previous state button click event.  It is responsible
//                for setting the page state back one state.
//-------------------------------------------------------------------------
private void btnPrevState_Click(Object sender,
                                System.Web.UI.ImageClickEventArgs e)
{
  int pageState;

  pageState = Convert.ToInt32(Request.Form[PAGE_STATE]);
  pageState -= 1;
  updatePage(pageState);
} // btnPrevState_Click

//*************************************************************************
//
//   ROUTINE: btnNextState_Click
//
//   DESCRIPTION: This routine provides the event handler for the
//                next state button click event.  It is responsible
//                for setting the page state back one state.
//-------------------------------------------------------------------------
private void btnNextState_Click(Object sender,
                                System.Web.UI.ImageClickEventArgs e)
{
  int pageState;

  pageState = Convert.ToInt32(Request.Form[PAGE_STATE]);
  pageState += 1;
  updatePage(pageState);
} // btnNextState_Click
```

```
//**************************************************************************
//
//     ROUTINE: updatePage
//
//     DESCRIPTION: This routine updates the page for the passed page state.
//
//--------------------------------------------------------------------------
private void updatePage(int pageState)
{
    // update the current page state display
    labPageState.Text = pageState.ToString( );

    // register the hidden field used to persist the current page state
    RegisterHiddenField(PAGE_STATE,
                        pageState.ToString( ));
} // updatePage
} // CH06HiddenValuesCS
}
```

6.4   Preserving Information Across Multiple Requests for a Page

Problem

You have a page that contains complex object information you need to preserve between requests for the page. The data contains information you do not want to be readable in the rendered HTML, and you do not want to use a database to preserve the information.

Solution

Use the ViewState property of the Page object to store the data. You can then access the data when the page is submitted back to the server.

In the code-behind class for the page, use the .NET language of your choice to add all the code necessary to handle the storage and recovery of the object data to and from the ViewState.

In a separate class file, use the .NET language of your choice to define the container in which you will store the data in the ViewState.

The application that illustrates this solution is shown in Examples 6-14 through 6-18. Example 6-14 shows the .aspx file. Examples 6-15 and 6-16 show the VB and C# code-behind files. Examples 6-17 and 6-18 show the VB and C# data service class. Figure 6-4 shows the form produced by the application.

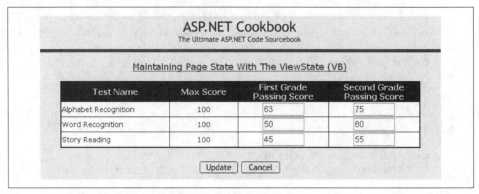

Figure 6-4. Maintaining page state with ViewState

Discussion

The ViewState is an object similar to the Application and Session objects discussed in the previous recipes; however, its method of data storage is quite different. Unlike the Application and Session objects, which are stored in server memory, the ViewState is stored in a hidden form field within the HTML sent to the browser. This property lets you store page state information directly in a page and then retrieve it, without using server resources, when the page is posted back to the server. This technique does result, however, in additional data being transmitted to and from the server.

ASP.NET uses the ViewState to store state information for the server controls on your form so it can rehydrate (or deserialize the data for) the controls upon submittal of the page to the server. You can use the ViewState for storing page state data in your application as well. What we mean by "page state data" in this context is user-specific state values that aren't stored by a control. Values are tracked in ViewState similarly to how they are tracked in Session (described in Recipe 6.2) and Cache (described in Recipe 13.5).

A simple example of when you might want to use ViewState in this way is when you want to display a list of items in a DataGrid, and each user wants to sort the DataGrid's columns differently. In this context, the sort order is a small piece of user-specific page state that you want to maintain when the page is submitted back to the server. ViewState is a fine place to store this type of value, and the Visual Studio .NET help files are replete with examples of this sort.

The example we've written to illustrate this solution is both a bit more ambitious than the aforementioned example and fairly long, but worth the effort. It demonstrates not only the ability to store complex objects in the ViewState for tracking state information between page submittals but also how to emulate the two-way data binding that is available in Windows applications developed with .NET but not available to ASP.NET applications. When used together, these two concepts provide the ability to use many of the features of ASP.NET, which can greatly simplify the code required to develop an application.

The *.aspx* file, shown in Example 6-14, is typical of a page containing a data-bound DataGrid (see Chapter 1). The one difference in this example is the use of constants from the data service class to define the fields bound to the columns in the DataGrid. The constants are described later, during the discussion of the data service class.

> In Example 6-14, the following changes are required to use the *.aspx* file with C#:
>
> - Change the namespace in the imports statement to ASPNetCookbook.CSExamples.
> - In each DataBinder.Eval statement, remove the VB line continuation characters and replace CH06TestDataVB with CH06TestDataCS.

You'll find all code that handles the persistence and recovery of the object data you store in the ViewState in the code-behind, shown in Example 6-15 (VB) and Example 6-16 (C#).

The data service class, shown in Example 6-17 (VB) and Example 6-18 (C#), provides a container for persisting the data in the ViewState. (The data service class is described at the end of this example.)

Because you will want to access the object persisted in the ViewState from multiple places in your code, we've defined a constant in the code-behind, VS_TEST_DATA, to define the name of the variable used to access the object in the ViewState. With this approach, you avoid the problems that arise when you hardcode a variable name throughout your code.

In the Page_Load method of the code-behind, an instance of the data service class is created by calling its constructor. The new object is then passed to the bindData method to bind the data in the object to the DataGrid in the *.aspx* file.

> It is important to create the new object only when the page is originally rendered. Creating it on subsequent postbacks would result in loss of the data entered by the user.

The bindData method performs two operations. First, it binds the data in the passed testData object to the DataGrid. This is done by setting the DataSource to the table in the DataSet of the passed object and calling the BindData method of the DataGrid. In addition, the DataKeyField is set to the field in the table that contains the primary key data. This provides the unique identifier for each row of test data in the rendered DataGrid and is needed to update the data submitted back to the server. The bindData method then persists the passed object to the ViewState. This causes the testData object to be serialized to a string and placed in the ViewState when the page is rendered.

When a page is rendered and sent to the client browser, all objects created in the code-behind are destroyed. This means that the testData object no longer exists after the page is rendered, unless you have persisted it. This is where data binding in web applications differs greatly from data binding in Windows applications. In a Windows application, the underlying DataSet, DataTable, or other data container that is bound to the controls on the Windows form continues to exist and remains connected to the bound controls. Any changes made to the data in the bound controls are updated in the underlying data container, making updates to the original data source extremely simple. In web forms, the connection to the underlying data container is broken when the page is rendered. Emulating the two-way binding and simple data updates available in Windows applications requires a bit of additional work, but it can be well worth the effort.

When the user clicks the Update button, the form is submitted back to the server. ASP.NET takes care of updating the DataGrid server control with the data posted back to the server. However, the underlying data container (the testData object in this example) is not recreated by ASP.NET. Therefore, the testData object is rehydrated from the ViewState in the Update button click event.

After rehydrating the testData object, the contents of the object need to be updated with the current data in the DataGrid. This is done by iterating through the rows in the grid, extracting the individual data values, and then updating the contents of the testData object.

For each row, the primary key value is obtained from the DataKeys collection for the current item. This is possible because the DataKeyField was set to the column containing the primary key when the DataGrid was originally bound.

Next, a reference is obtained to the first grade score text box. This is done by using the FindControl method of the current DataGrid item. This is possible because the text boxes defined in the DataGrid have been assigned IDs that are used here to perform the lookup. After the ID has been retrieved, the first grade score is updated in the testData object with the value in the text box. This process is then repeated for the second grade score text box.

Production code should have validation to ensure only numeric values are entered in the text box. This is best done using validation controls (see Chapter 2) or a custom control that allows only numeric entry as described in Recipe 5.4.

After updating the contents of the object, the update method is called to update the contents of the database with the data in the object, and then the data is again bound to the DataGrid.

The StateTestDataVB class (see Example 6-17 for the VB version and Example 6-18 for the C# version) provides the data services for this example. It encapsulates the data along with the methods for operating on the data. The class is defined with the Serializable attribute to provide the ability to serialize the data in the object created from the class to a string, which can then be stored in the ViewState or another location, such as a database. This string can then be deserialized to rehydrate the original object.

The class is designed to contain a DataSet as the container for the object data. This DataSet also provides the ability to bind a DataGrid or another control directly to the data in the object. To bind to the internal data, two things are required. First, a property (the read-only testData property) must be provided to obtain a reference to the data table that contains the data.

Second, the names of the columns in the data table used for binding must be made available to bind controls to the specific data elements. These are defined as public constants in the class to provide a loose coupling between the code-behind and the data services class. By using the constants, the names of the columns can change without affecting any of the code that uses the StateTestDataVB class.

The constructor for the class queries the database for the test data used in this example and fills the private member mTestData. The only special operation performed is to define the data column that is the primary key for the table in the DataSet. This makes it possible to find a specific row using the primary key value.

 If the primary key is not defined for a table in the DataSet, the code would be required either to filter the data in the table using a DataView or to iterate through all of the rows in the data table to find the row of interest. Both of these approaches can cause a significant performance penalty.

Two properties are defined to set the first and second grade scores. Both of these properties perform the same actions but on different columns in the data table. To set a value, the appropriate row must be located. This is done by using the Find method of the row collection with the testID (primary key) value passed to the property. Note that the find operation will only work if a primary key is defined for the table. After finding the row matching the passed testID, the value is set to the passed score.

When all data has been changed, as required in the object, the Update method is called. This method updates the data from the object to the database. It utilizes the functionality in ADO.NET that will, with just a few lines of code, perform all inserts, updates, and deletes required to match the data in the database with the data in the data table. This basically requires four steps:

1. Open a connection to the database. This is the same process used in the constructor.

2. Create a new data adapter using the same Select statement used to populate the data table originally.

It is important that all of the columns currently contained in the data table be included in the Select statement. For this reason it is good to define the Select statement as a constant or a private member variable to allow the constructor and Update methods to use the same Select statement, as shown in the following code:

VB

```
da = New OleDbDataAdapter(SELECT_STR, dbConn)
```

C#

```
da = new OleDbDataAdapter(SELECT_STR, dbConn);
```

3. Create a new command builder with a reference to the data adapter created in Step 2. The command builder will build the appropriate insert, update, and delete commands from the provided Select command.

4. Call the Update method of the data adapter. This will perform all required inserts, updates, and deletes required to cause the data in the database to match the data in the data table.

The update works because every row in a data table has a status property that indicates if the row in the data table has been modified, added, or deleted. From this status information, the data adapter can determine what actions are required.

This example does not provide the ability to add new tests or delete current tests. You can easily add the functionality to the StateTestDataVB class by adding two methods, addTest and deleteTest. Your addTest method needs to be passed the test name, its maximum score, and the scores for first and second grade. With the passed data, it should add a new row to the data table containing the test data. Likewise, your deleteTest method should delete the required row from the data table using the Delete method of the rows collection. The Delete method does not actually delete the row but marks it for deletion when the update is performed.

Although the technique described in this example is extremely powerful and useful, it should be used carefully. Placing a serialized object in the ViewState can significantly increase the size of the information sent to the client browser, and, because the ViewState information is stored in a hidden form field, it is also sent back to the server when the page is submitted. In most cases, this is not a big issue, because an extra few thousand bytes is not a problem. But if you have a very large object, the overhead could be excessive. One way to use this technique with a large object is to store the object in the Session object instead of the ViewState. The trade-off is the server resources and time required to transmit the data to the Session object. Refer to Recipe 6.2 for information on using the Session object.

See Also

Recipe 5.4; Recipe 6.2; Recipe 13.5

Example 6-14. Maintaining page state using the ViewState (.aspx)

```
<%@ Page Language="vb" AutoEventWireup="false"
        Codebehind="CH06ViewStateVB.aspx.vb"
        Inherits="CH06ViewStateVB" %>
<%@ Import Namespace="ASPNetCookbook.VBExamples" %>
<!DOCTYPE HTML PUBLIC "-//W3C//DTD HTML 4.0 Transitional//EN">
<html>
  <head>
    <title>ViewState Persistence</title>
    <link rel="stylesheet" href="css/ASPNetCookbook.css">
  </head>
  <body leftmargin="0" marginheight="0" marginwidth="0" topmargin="0">
    <form id="frmStateViewState" method="post" runat="server">
      <table width="100%" cellpadding="0" cellspacing="0" border="0">
        <tr>
          <td align="center">
            <img src="images/ASPNETCookbookHeading_blue.gif">
          </td>
        </tr>
        <tr>
          <td class="dividerLine">
            <img src="images/spacer.gif" height="6" border="0"></td>
        </tr>
      </table>
      <table width="90%" align="center" border="0">
        <tr>
          <td><img src="images/spacer.gif" height="10" border="0"></td>
        </tr>
        <tr>
          <td align="center" class="PageHeading">
            Maintaining Page State With The ViewState (VB)
          </td>
        </tr>
        <tr>
          <td><img src="images/spacer.gif" height="10" border="0"></td>
        </tr>
        <tr>
          <td align="center">
            <asp:DataGrid ID="dgScores" Runat="server"
                          Width="100%"
                          AutoGenerateColumns="False"
                          BorderColor="000080"
                          BorderWidth="2px"
                          HeaderStyle-BackColor="#000080"
                          HeaderStyle-CssClass="TableHeader"
                          ItemStyle-CssClass="TableCellNormal"
                          ItemStyle-BackColor="#FFFFFF"  >
              <Columns>
```

```
                <asp:TemplateColumn HeaderStyle-HorizontalAlign="Center"
                                HeaderText="Test Name">
                    <ItemTemplate>
                        <%# DataBinder.Eval(Container.DataItem, _
                                    CH06TestDataVB.TEST_NAME) %>
                    </ItemTemplate>
                </asp:TemplateColumn>
                <asp:TemplateColumn HeaderStyle-HorizontalAlign="Center"
                                ItemStyle-HorizontalAlign="Center"
                                HeaderText="Max Score">
                    <ItemTemplate>
                        <%# DataBinder.Eval(Container.DataItem, _
                                    CH06TestDataVB.MAX_SCORE) %>
                    </ItemTemplate>
                </asp:TemplateColumn>
                <asp:TemplateColumn HeaderStyle-HorizontalAlign="Center"
                                ItemStyle-HorizontalAlign="Center"
                                HeaderText="First Grade<br />Passing Score">
                    <ItemTemplate>
                        <asp:TextBox id="txtFirstGradeScore" runat="server"
                            Columns="5"
                            text='<%# DataBinder.Eval(Container.DataItem, _
                                CH06TestDataVB.FIRST_GRADE_PASSING_SCORE) %>' />
                    </ItemTemplate>
                </asp:TemplateColumn>
                <asp:TemplateColumn HeaderStyle-HorizontalAlign="Center"
                                ItemStyle-HorizontalAlign="Center"
                                HeaderText="Second Grade<br />Passing Score">
                    <ItemTemplate>
                        <asp:TextBox id="txtSecondGradeScore" runat="server"
                            Columns="5"
                            text='<%# DataBinder.Eval(Container.DataItem, _
                                CH06TestDataVB.SECOND_GRADE_PASSING_SCORE) %>' />
                    </ItemTemplate>
                </asp:TemplateColumn>
            </Columns>
          </asp:DataGrid>
        </td>
      </tr>
      <tr>
        <td align="center">
          <br />
          <asp:ImageButton ID="btnUpdate" Runat="server"
                ImageUrl="images/buttons/button_update.gif" />
          <asp:ImageButton ID="btnCancel" Runat="server"
                ImageUrl="images/buttons/button_cancel.gif" />
        </td>
      </tr>
    </table>
  </form>
 </body>
</html>
```

Example 6-15. Maintaining page state using the ViewState (.vb)

```vb
Option Explicit On
Option Strict On
'----------------------------------------------------------------------------
'
'   Module Name: CH06ViewStateVB.aspx.vb
'
'   Description: This module provides the code behind for
'                CH06ViewStateVB.aspx
'
'*****************************************************************************
Imports Microsoft.VisualBasic
Imports System
Imports System.Web.UI.WebControls

Public Class CH06ViewStateVB
  Inherits System.Web.UI.Page

  'controls on the form
  Protected dgScores As System.Web.UI.WebControls.DataGrid
  Protected WithEvents btnUpdate As System.Web.UI.WebControls.ImageButton
  Protected WithEvents btnCancel As System.Web.UI.WebControls.ImageButton

  'the following constant defines the name of the viewstate variable used
  'to store the test data object
  Private Const VS_TEST_DATA As String = "TestData"

  '*****************************************************************************
  '
  '   ROUTINE: Page_Load
  '
  '   DESCRIPTION: This routine provides the event handler for the page load
  '                event.  It is responsible for initializing the controls
  '                on the page.
  '----------------------------------------------------------------------------
  Private Sub Page_Load(ByVal sender As System.Object, _
                        ByVal e As System.EventArgs) Handles MyBase.Load

    Dim testData As CH06TestDataVB

    If (Not Page.IsPostBack()) Then
      'create new test data object and bind to it
      testData = New CH06TestDataVB
      bindData(testData)
    End If
  End Sub  'Page_Load

  '*****************************************************************************
  '
  '   ROUTINE: btnUpdate_Click
  '
  '   DESCRIPTION: This routine provides the event handler for the update
  '                button click event event.  It is responsible for updating
```

Example 6-15. Maintaining page state using the ViewState (.vb) (continued)

```
'                    the contents of the database with the data from the
'                    form.
'-----------------------------------------------------------------------
Private Sub btnUpdate_Click(ByVal sender As Object, _
                            ByVal e As System.Web.UI.ImageClickEventArgs) _
        Handles btnUpdate.Click

  'the following constants define the names of the textboxes in the
  'datagrid rows
  Const FIRST_GRADE_SCORE_TEXTBOX As String = "txtFirstGradeScore"
  Const SECOND_GRADE_SCORE_TEXTBOX As String = "txtSecondGradeScore"

  Dim testData As CH06TestDataVB
  Dim item As System.Web.UI.WebControls.DataGridItem
  Dim txtScore As TextBox
  Dim testID As Integer

  'make sure page contents are valid
  If (Page.IsValid) Then
    'rehydrate the test data object from the viewstate
    testData = CType(viewstate.Item(VS_TEST_DATA), _
                     CH06TestDataVB)

    'copy the contents of the fields in the datagrid to the test data
    'object to emulate the two-way databinding in the Windows world
    For Each item In dgScores.Items
      'get the testID for the test data in the datagrid row
      testID = CInt(dgScores.DataKeys.Item(item.ItemIndex))

      'get a reference to the first grade score textbox in the row
      txtScore = CType(item.FindControl(FIRST_GRADE_SCORE_TEXTBOX), _
                       TextBox)

      'update the first grade score in the test data object
      testData.firstGradeScore(testID) = CInt(txtScore.Text)

      'get a reference to the second grade score textbox in the row
      txtScore = CType(item.FindControl(SECOND_GRADE_SCORE_TEXTBOX), _
                       TextBox)

      'update the first grade score in the test data object
      testData.secondGradeScore(testID) = CInt(txtScore.Text)
    Next item

    'update the test data in the database
    testData.update( )

    'rebind the data to the datagrid
    bindData(testData)
  End If
End Sub  'btnUpdate_Click
```

Example 6-15. Maintaining page state using the ViewState (.vb) (continued)

```vb
'***************************************************************************
'
'   ROUTINE: btnCancel_Click
'
'   DESCRIPTION: This routine provides the event handler for the cancel
'                button click event event.  It is responsible for
'                cancel the current edits.
'---------------------------------------------------------------------------
Private Sub btnCancel_Click(ByVal sender As Object, _
                            ByVal e As System.Web.UI.ImageClickEventArgs) _
        Handles btnCancel.Click

    'perform the actions required to cancel the edits
End Sub   'btnCancel_Click


'***************************************************************************
'
'   ROUTINE: bindData
'
'   DESCRIPTION: This routine binds the data in the passed object to the
'                datagrid then persists the object in the viewstate
'---------------------------------------------------------------------------
Private Sub bindData(ByVal testData As CH06TestDataVB)

    'bind the test data to the datagrid
    dgScores.DataSource = testData.testData()
    dgScores.DataKeyField = testData.TEST_DATA_ID
    dgScores.DataBind()

    'save the test data object in the view state
    viewstate.Add(VS_TEST_DATA, _
                  testData)
    End Sub   'bindData
End Class   'CH06ViewStateVB
```

Example 6-16. Maintaining page state using the ViewState (.cs)

```csharp
//---------------------------------------------------------------------------
//
//   Module Name: CH06ViewStateCS.ascx.cs
//
//   Description: This module provides the code behind for
//                CH06ViewStateCS.ascx
//
//***************************************************************************
using System;
using System.Configuration;
using System.Data;
using System.Web.UI;
using System.Web.UI.WebControls;

namespace ASPNetCookbook.CSExamples
{
```

Example 6-16. Maintaining page state using the ViewState (.cs) (continued)

```csharp
public class CH06ViewStateCS : System.Web.UI.Page
{
  // controls on the form
  protected System.Web.UI.WebControls.DataGrid dgScores;
  protected System.Web.UI.WebControls.ImageButton btnUpdate;
  protected System.Web.UI.WebControls.ImageButton btnCancel;

  // the following constant defines the name of the viewstate variable used
  // to store the test data object
  private const String VS_TEST_DATA = "TestData";

  //*************************************************************************
  //
  //   ROUTINE: Page_Load
  //
  //   DESCRIPTION: This routine provides the event handler for the page
  //                load event.  It is responsible for initializing the
  //                controls on the page.
  //-------------------------------------------------------------------------
  private void Page_Load(object sender, System.EventArgs e)
  {
    CH06TestDataCS testData = null;

    // wire the update and cancel button click events
    this.btnUpdate.Click +=
      new ImageClickEventHandler(this.btnUpdate_Click);
    this.btnCancel.Click +=
      new ImageClickEventHandler(this.btnCancel_Click);

    if (!Page.IsPostBack)
    {
      // create new test data object and bind to it
      testData = new CH06TestDataCS( );
      bindData(testData);
    }
  }  // Page_Load

  //*************************************************************************
  //
  //   ROUTINE: btnUpdate_Click
  //
  //   DESCRIPTION: This routine provides the event handler for the update
  //                button click event event.  It is responsible for
  //                updating the contents of the database with the data
  //                from the form.
  //-------------------------------------------------------------------------
  private void btnUpdate_Click(Object sender,
                               System.Web.UI.ImageClickEventArgs e)
  {
    // the following constants define the names of the textboxes in the
    // datagrid rows
    const String FIRST_GRADE_SCORE_TEXTBOX = "txtFirstGradeScore";
    const string SECOND_GRADE_SCORE_TEXTBOX = "txtSecondGradeScore";
```

Example 6-16. Maintaining page state using the ViewState (.cs) (continued)

```
      CHO6TestDataCS testData = null;
      TextBox txtScore = null;
      int testID;

      // make sure page contents are valid
      if (Page.IsValid)
      {
        // rehydrate the test data object from the viewstate
        testData = (CHO6TestDataCS)(ViewState[VS_TEST_DATA]);

        // copy the contents of the fields in the datagrid to the test data
        // object to emulate the two-way databinding in the Windows world
        foreach (DataGridItem item in dgScores.Items)
        {
          // get the testID for the test data in the datagrid row
          testID = Convert.ToInt32(dgScores.DataKeys[item.ItemIndex]);

          //get a reference to the first grade score textbox in the row
          txtScore = (TextBox)(item.FindControl(FIRST_GRADE_SCORE_TEXTBOX));

          // update the first grade score in the test data object
          testData.set_firstGradeScore(testID,
                                   Convert.ToInt32(txtScore.Text));

          // get a reference to the second grade score textbox in the row
          txtScore = (TextBox)(item.FindControl(SECOND_GRADE_SCORE_TEXTBOX));

          // update the first grade score in the test data object
          testData.set_secondGradeScore(testID,
                                    Convert.ToInt32(txtScore.Text));
        }  // foreach

        // update the test data in the database
        testData.update();

        // rebind the data to the datagrid
        bindData(testData);
      }  // if (Page.IsValid)
    }  // btnUpdate_Click

    //*************************************************************************
    //
    //   ROUTINE: btnCancel_Click
    //
    //   DESCRIPTION: This routine provides the event handler for the cancel
    //                button click event event.  It is responsible for
    //                cancel the current edits.
    //-------------------------------------------------------------------------
    private void btnCancel_Click(Object sender,
                            System.Web.UI.ImageClickEventArgs e)
    {
      // perform the actions required to cancel the edits
    }  // btnCancel_Click
```

Example 6-16. Maintaining page state using the ViewState (.cs) (continued)

```
//*************************************************************************
//
//    ROUTINE: bindData
//
//    DESCRIPTION: This routine binds the data in the passed object to the
//                 datagrid then persists the object in the viewstate
//-------------------------------------------------------------------------
private void bindData(CH06TestDataCS testData)
{
    // bind the test data to the datagrid
    dgScores.DataSource = testData.testData;
    dgScores.DataKeyField = CH06TestDataCS.TEST_DATA_ID;
    dgScores.DataBind( );

    // save the test data object in the view state
    ViewState.Add(VS_TEST_DATA,
                  testData);
    } // bindData
  } // CH06ViewStateCS
}
```

Example 6-17. Data service class for storage in the ViewState (.vb)

```
Option Explicit On
Option Strict On
'-----------------------------------------------------------------------------
'
'    Module Name: CH06TestDataVB.vb
'
'    Description: This class provides an encapsulation of test data and
'                 properties/method to operate on the data.
'
'        NOTE: This class is marked as serializable to provide the ability
'              to serialize the objects created with the class to an
'              XML string.
'
'*************************************************************************
Imports Microsoft.VisualBasic
Imports System
Imports System.Configuration
Imports System.Data
Imports System.Data.OleDb

<Serializable( )> _
Public Class CH06TestDataVB
    'constants used to bind the data in the encapsulated dataset
    Public Const TEST_DATA_ID As String = "TestDataID"
    Public Const TEST_NAME As String = "TestName"
    Public Const FIRST_GRADE_PASSING_SCORE As String = "FirstGradePassingScore"
    Public Const SECOND_GRADE_PASSING_SCORE As String = "SecondGradePassingScore"
    Public Const MAX_SCORE As String = "MaxScore"
```

```vb
'constant to provide the name of the table in the dataset
Private Const TEST_DATA_TABLE As String = "TestData"

'private attributes
Private mTestData As DataSet
Private mConnectionStr As String

'the following constant is used to query the data from the database
Private Const SELECT_STR As String = "SELECT " & TEST_DATA_ID & "," & _
                                     TEST_NAME & "," & _
                                     FIRST_GRADE_PASSING_SCORE & "," & _
                                     SECOND_GRADE_PASSING_SCORE & "," & _
                                     MAX_SCORE & _
                                     " FROM " & TEST_DATA_TABLE


'*************************************************************************
'
'    ROUTINE: testData
'
'    DESCRIPTION: This property provides the ability to get a reference
'                 to the table in the dataset containing the test data.
'-------------------------------------------------------------------------
Public ReadOnly Property testData() As DataTable
  Get
    Return (mTestData.Tables(TEST_DATA_TABLE))
  End Get
End Property   'testData

'*************************************************************************
'
'    ROUTINE: firstGradeScore
'
'    DESCRIPTION: This property provides the ability to get/set the first
'                 grade score for the passed test ID.
'-------------------------------------------------------------------------
Public Property firstGradeScore(ByVal testID As Integer) As Integer
  Get
    Dim dRow As DataRow

    'get row with the passed testID value
    dRow = mTestData.Tables(TEST_DATA_TABLE).Rows.Find(testID)

    'return the first grade passing score
    Return (CInt(dRow.Item(FIRST_GRADE_PASSING_SCORE)))
  End Get

  Set(ByVal Value As Integer)
    Dim dRow As DataRow

    'get row with the passed testID value
    dRow = mTestData.Tables(TEST_DATA_TABLE).Rows.Find(testID)
```

```vb
      'set the first grade passing score
      dRow.Item(FIRST_GRADE_PASSING_SCORE) = Value
   End Set
End Property  'firstGradeScore

'**************************************************************************
'
'   ROUTINE: secondGradeScore
'
'   DESCRIPTION: This property provides the ability to get/set the second
'                grade score for the passed test ID.
'--------------------------------------------------------------------------
Public Property secondGradeScore(ByVal testID As Integer) As Integer
   Get
      Dim dRow As DataRow

      'get row with the passed testID value
      dRow = mTestData.Tables(TEST_DATA_TABLE).Rows.Find(testID)

      'return the first grade passing score
      Return CInt((dRow.Item(SECOND_GRADE_PASSING_SCORE)))

   End Get

   Set(ByVal Value As Integer)
      Dim dRow As DataRow

      'get row with the passed testID value
      dRow = mTestData.Tables(TEST_DATA_TABLE).Rows.Find(testID)

      'set the first grade passing score
      dRow.Item(SECOND_GRADE_PASSING_SCORE) = Value

   End Set
End Property  'secondGradeScore

'**************************************************************************
'
'   ROUTINE: update
'
'   DESCRIPTION: This routine provides the ability to update the test
'                data for this object in the database.
'--------------------------------------------------------------------------
Public Sub update( )
   Dim dbConn As OleDbConnection
   Dim da As OleDbDataAdapter
   Dim cmdBuilder As OleDbCommandBuilder

   Try
      dbConn = New OleDbConnection(mConnectionStr)
      dbConn.Open( )
```

```vb
      da = New OleDbDataAdapter(SELECT_STR, _
                                dbConn)

      'create a command builder which will create the appropriate update,
      'insert, and delete SQL statements
      cmdBuilder = New OleDbCommandBuilder(da)

      'update data in the testdata table
      da.Update(mTestData, _
                TEST_DATA_TABLE)

  Finally
    'cleanup
    If (Not IsNothing(dbConn)) Then
      dbConn.Close()
    End If
  End Try
End Sub  'update

'**************************************************************************
'
'   ROUTINE: New
'
'   DESCRIPTION: This constructor creates the object and populates it
'                with test data from the database
'-------------------------------------------------------------------------
Public Sub New()
  Dim dbConn As OleDbConnection
  Dim da As OleDbDataAdapter
  Dim key(0) As DataColumn

  Try
    'get the connection string from web.config and open a connection
    'to the database
    mConnectionStr = _
        ConfigurationSettings.AppSettings("dbConnectionString")
    dbConn = New OleDbConnection(mConnectionStr)
    dbConn.Open()

    'get the data from the database
    da = New OleDbDataAdapter(SELECT_STR, _
                              dbConn)
    mTestData = New DataSet
    da.Fill(mTestData, _
            TEST_DATA_TABLE)

    'define the testID column in the data table as a primary key column
    'this makes it possible to "lookup" a datarow with the testID value
    'NOTE: The PrimaryKey property expects an array of DataColumn even
    '      when only one column is used as the primary key
    key(0) = mTestData.Tables(TEST_DATA_TABLE).Columns(TEST_DATA_ID)
    mTestData.Tables(TEST_DATA_TABLE).PrimaryKey = key
```

Example 6-17. Data service class for storage in the ViewState (.vb) (continued)

```
      Finally
        'cleanup
        If (Not IsNothing(dbConn)) Then
          dbConn.Close()
        End If
      End Try
    End Sub  'New
End Class  'CH06TestDataVB
```

Example 6-18. Data service class for storage in the ViewState (.cs)

```
//----------------------------------------------------------------------------
//
//    Module Name: CH06TestDataCS
//
//    Description: This class provides an encapsulation of test data and
//                 properties/method to operate on the data.
//
//        NOTE: This class is marked as serializable to provide the ability
//              to serialize the objects created with the class to an
//              XML string.
//
//****************************************************************************
using System;
using System.Configuration;
using System.Data;
using System.Data.OleDb;
using System.Web;

namespace ASPNetCookbook.CSExamples
{
  [Serializable]
  public class CH06TestDataCS
  {
    // constants used to bind the data in the encapsulated dataset
    public const String TEST_DATA_ID = "TestDataID";
    public const String TEST_NAME = "TestName";
    public const String FIRST_GRADE_PASSING_SCORE = "FirstGradePassingScore";
    public const String SECOND_GRADE_PASSING_SCORE= "SecondGradePassingScore";
    public const String MAX_SCORE = "MaxScore";

    // constant to provide the name of the table in the dataset
    private const String TEST_DATA_TABLE = "TestData";

    // private attributes
    private DataSet mTestData = null;
    private String mConnectionStr = null;

    // the following constant is used to query the data from the database
    private const String SELECT_STR = "SELECT " + TEST_DATA_ID + "," +
                                      TEST_NAME + "," +
                                      FIRST_GRADE_PASSING_SCORE + "," +
                                      SECOND_GRADE_PASSING_SCORE + "," +
```

```
                                    MAX_SCORE +
                                    " FROM " + TEST_DATA_TABLE;

//************************************************************************
//
//    ROUTINE: testData
//
//    DESCRIPTION: This property provides the ability to get a reference to
//                 the table in the dataset containing the test data.
//------------------------------------------------------------------------
public DataTable testData
{
  get
  {
    return(mTestData.Tables[TEST_DATA_TABLE]);
  }
} // testData

//************************************************************************
//
//    ROUTINE: set_firstGradeScore
//
//    DESCRIPTION: This routine provides the ability to set the first grade
//                 score for the passed test ID.
//------------------------------------------------------------------------
public void set_firstGradeScore(int testID, int score)
{
  DataRow dRow = null;

  // get row with the passed testID value
  dRow = mTestData.Tables[TEST_DATA_TABLE].Rows.Find(testID);

  // set the first grade passing score
  dRow[FIRST_GRADE_PASSING_SCORE] = score;
} // set_firstGradeScore

//************************************************************************
//
//    ROUTINE: set_secondGradeScore
//
//    DESCRIPTION: This routine provides the ability to set the second
//                 grade score for the passed test ID.
//------------------------------------------------------------------------
public void set_secondGradeScore(int testID, int score)
{
  DataRow dRow = null;

  // get row with the passed testID value
  dRow = mTestData.Tables[TEST_DATA_TABLE].Rows.Find(testID);

  // set the second grade passing score
  dRow[SECOND_GRADE_PASSING_SCORE] = score;
} // set_secondGradeScore
```

Example 6-18. Data service class for storage in the ViewState (.cs) (continued)

```
//***********************************************************************
//
//    ROUTINE: update
//
//    DESCRIPTION: This routine provides the ability to update the test
//                 data for this object in the database.
//-----------------------------------------------------------------------
public void update( )
{
  OleDbConnection dbConn = null;
  OleDbDataAdapter da = null;
  OleDbCommandBuilder cmdBuilder = null;

  try
  {
    dbConn = new OleDbConnection(mConnectionStr);
    dbConn.Open( );

    da = new OleDbDataAdapter(SELECT_STR, dbConn);

    // create a command builder which will create the appropriate update,
    // insert, and delete SQL statements
    cmdBuilder = new OleDbCommandBuilder(da);

    // update data in the testdata table
    da.Update(mTestData,
              TEST_DATA_TABLE);
  }

  finally
  {
    // cleanup
    if (dbConn != null)
    {
      dbConn.Close( );
    }
  }  // finally

}  // update

//***********************************************************************
//
//    ROUTINE: CH06TestDataCS
//
//    DESCRIPTION: This constructor creates the object and populates it
//                 with test data from the database
//-----------------------------------------------------------------------
public CH06TestDataCS( )
{
  OleDbConnection dbConn = null;
  OleDbDataAdapter da = null;
  DataColumn[] key = new DataColumn[1];
```

```
try
{
  // get the connection string from web.config and open a connection
  // to the database
  mConnectionStr =
    ConfigurationSettings.AppSettings["dbConnectionString"];
  dbConn = new OleDbConnection(mConnectionStr);
  dbConn.Open( );

  // get the data from the database
  da = new OleDbDataAdapter(SELECT_STR, dbConn);
  mTestData = new DataSet( );
  da.Fill(mTestData,
          TEST_DATA_TABLE);

  // define the testID column in the data table as a primary key column
  // this makes it possible to "lookup" a datarow with the testID value
  // NOTE: The PrimaryKey property expects an array of DataColumn even
  //       when only one column is used as the primary key
  key[0] = mTestData.Tables[TEST_DATA_TABLE].Columns[TEST_DATA_ID];
  mTestData.Tables[TEST_DATA_TABLE].PrimaryKey = key;
}  // try

finally
{
  // cleanup
  if (dbConn != null)
  {
    dbConn.Close( );
  }
} // finally
}  // CH06TestDataCS
}  // CH06TestDataCS
}
```

CHAPTER 7

Error Handling

7.0   Introduction

Journeyman programmers know that proper error handling is critical to the operation of an application. Without it, your chances of making the application truly fault tolerant are less than remote. Taking the time to plan an error-handling strategy in the early stages of a project can pay off handsomely as the project progresses. Yet, too often error handling is given short shrift, for want of time, interest, awareness, accessibility, or who knows what.

Fortunately, error handling has been greatly improved in ASP.NET, making it much more approachable and much easier to implement than was the case for classic ASP. Taking a page or two from the Java playbook, ASP.NET now provides state of the art handling of errors with exceptions and error-handler events.

The error-handling model in ASP.NET lets you handle errors easily at the method, page, and application levels of your web applications. Most applications will use some combination of these to handle problems when they arise. In this chapter, we have included recipes for handling errors at each level:

Method level

>   When does it make sense to handle errors locally versus letting them propagate up to a higher level? In general, you want to handle recoverable errors in the method where they occur, and let nonrecoverable errors propagate up. Recipe 7.1 delves into this subject in some detail. It also helps you understand all the nuances of the Try...Catch...Finally block, and even includes sets of if...then solution statements and leading questions to help you choose how to properly implement error handling in a routine.

Page level

>   Recipe 7.2 shows you how to trap errors in a page and redirect the user to another page. Why would you want to use this approach? The reason is that it allows you to handle all page-level errors in a uniform way, which can greatly simplify error-handling code and, at the same time, make it much more consistent and robust.

The trick is in keeping all the error-handling code in one place in the original page by leveraging the Page_Error method, as the recipe explains.

Application level

Recipe 7.3 shows you how to handle at the application level the errors that occur on any page of your application. The approach we advocate involves trapping errors that occur and logging them in an event log prior to redirecting the user to another page. By handling all exceptions at the application level, rather than at the method or page level, you can process all errors for the application in a single location. It is our firm belief that doing all error handling in one place in an application is key to writing effective code. It requires understanding what happens to unhandled exceptions at the method, page, and application levels, which this recipe explains.

The final recipe is all about creating user-friendly error messages, which sounds simple enough but actually involves creating a new exception class that inherits from the .NET Framework's base exception classes and adding the functionality your application requires. How to then take advantage of this new class in the Catch block of your code is also explained.

7.1   Handling Errors at the Method Level

Problem

You're uncertain how to best organize your code to handle errors at the method level. In particular, you'd like to take advantage of .NET structured exception handling for dealing with errors, but you're not sure how to best implement it.

Solution

If potential errors are recoverable in the routine
Use a combination of Try...Catch blocks as a retry mechanism for error handling.

If useful information can be added to the exception
Create and throw a new exception with the added information.

If cleanup is required
Perform it in the finally block.

If potential errors are not recoverable in the routine
Recovery should be handled by the calling routine and its error-handling structure.

Discussion

Because .NET structured exception handling is so good, we recommend that you use it, or at least consider using it, with every method that you write. There are a number of ways to implement its functionality.

Basic syntax of Try...Catch...Finally

To begin with, here is the syntax of a .NET Try...Catch...Finally block in VB and C#:

```vb
Private Sub anyRoutine()

    Try
        'Routine code in this block

    Catch err As Exception
        'error handling in this block

    Finally
        'cleanup performed in this block

    End Try
End Sub 'anyRoutine
```

```csharp
private void anyRoutine()
{
    try
    {
        // Routine code in this block
    }

    catch (Exception err)
    {
        // error handling in this block
    }

    finally
    {
        // cleanup performed in this block
    }
} // anyRoutine
```

The try block includes code that implements the method.

The catch block, which is optional, includes code to handle specific errors that you have identified as likely and to recover from them when that is possible.

The finally block code, which is also optional, performs any cleanup required on leaving the method, whether due to an error or not. This typically includes the closing of any open database connections and files, disposing of objects created by the method, and so on. A finally block is guaranteed to be executed, even if an exception is thrown or the code in the routine performs a return.

As noted, the catch and finally blocks are optional. There are times when you'll want to use one or the other, and times when you'll want to use both.

A try block must also contain either a catch or a finally block.

Guidelines for implementing

Developers should make use of .NET exception handling in any method where an error is possible, but the exact technique depends on the circumstances, as summarized in Table 7-1.

Table 7-1. Guidelines for Try...Catch...Finally blocks

Can errors occur?	Recoverable?	Can useful context information be added?	Cleanup required?	Recommended combination of try, catch, and finally
No	N/A	N/A	No	None
No	N/A	N/A	Yes	try and finally only
Yes	No	No	No	None
Yes	No	No	Yes	try and finally only
Yes	No	Yes	No	try and catch only
Yes	No	Yes	Yes	try, catch, and finally
Yes	Yes	N/A	N/A	try and catch only

The .NET Framework does not close database connections, files, and so on when an error occurs. This is your responsibility as a programmer, and you should do it in the finally block. The finally block is the last opportunity to perform any cleanup before the exception-handling infrastructure takes control of the application.

Additional considerations

To help you properly implement error handling in a routine, we've provided the following leading questions. Your answers can help you determine what portions of the Try...Catch...Finally block are needed. Refer to Table 7-1 for how to structure a routine based on your answers.

Can any errors occur in this routine?

    If not, no special error-handling code is required. Do not shortchange the answer to this question, however, because even x = x + 1 can result in an overflow exception.

Are the potential errors recoverable in the routine?

    If an error occurs but nothing useful can be done in the routine, the exception should be allowed to propagate to the calling routine. It serves no useful purpose to catch the exception and simply rethrow it. Bear in mind that this question is different from, "Are the potential errors recoverable at the application level?" For example, if the routine attempts to write a record to a database and finds the record locked, a retry can be attempted in the routine. However, if a value is passed to the routine and the operations on the value result in an overflow or other error, recovery cannot be performed in the routine but should be handled by the calling routine and its error-handling structure.

Can any useful information be added to the exception?

Exceptions that occur in the .NET Framework contain detailed information regarding the actual error. However, the exceptions do not provide any context information about what was being attempted at the application level that may assist in troubleshooting the error or providing more useful information to the user.

A new exception can be created and thrown with the added information. The first parameter for the new exception object should contain the useful context message, while the second parameter should be the original exception. The exception-handling mechanisms in the .NET Framework create a linked list of Exception objects to create a trail from the root of the exception up to the level where the exception is actually handled. By passing the original exception as the second parameter, the linked list from the root exception is maintained. For example:

VB
```
Catch err As Exception
   Throw New Exception("Useful context message", _
                        err)
```

C#
```
catch (Exception err)
{
   throw (new Exception("Useful context message", err));
}
```

Is a combination of Try...Catch *blocks warranted?*

A combination of Try...Catch blocks can be useful for providing a retry mechanism for error handling, as shown in Example 7-1 (VB) and Example 7-2 (C#). These examples show the use of an internal Try...Catch block within a while loop to provide a retry mechanism and an overall Try...Finally block to ensure cleanup is performed.

The catch block should not be used for normal program flow. Normal program flow code should only be placed in the try block, with the abnormal flow being placed in the catch block. Using the catch block in normal program flow will result in significant performance degradation due to the complex operations being performed by the .NET Framework to process exceptions.

The exception-handling mechanisms in the .NET Framework are extremely powerful. Whereas this example just touches on exception handling at the method level, other specific exception types can be caught and processed differently. In addition, you can create new exception classes by inheriting from the base exception classes and adding the functionality required by your applications. An example of this technique is shown in Recipe 7.4.

See Also

Recipe 7.4

Example 7-1. Retrying when an exception occurs (.vb)

```
Private Sub updateData(ByVal problemID As Integer, _
                       ByVal sectionHeading As String)

    Const MAX_RETRIES As Integer = 5

    Dim dbConn As OleDbConnection
    Dim dCmd As OleDbCommand
    Dim strConnection As String
    Dim strSQL As String
    Dim updateOK As Boolean
    Dim retryCount As Integer

    Try
        'get the connection string from web.config and open a connection
        'to the database
        strConnection = _
            ConfigurationSettings.AppSettings("dbConnectionString")
        dbConn = New OleDbConnection(strConnection)
        dbConn.Open( )

        'build the update SQL to update the record in the database
        strSQL = "UPDATE EditProblem " & _
                "SET SectionHeading='" & sectionHeading & "' " & _
                "WHERE EditProblemID=" & problemID.ToString( )
        dCmd = New OleDbCommand(strSQL, _
                                dbConn)

        'provide a loop with a try catch block to facilitate retrying
        'the database update
        updateOK = False
        retryCount = 0
        While ((Not updateOK) And (retryCount < MAX_RETRIES))
            Try
                dCmd.ExecuteNonQuery( )
                updateOK = True

            Catch exc As Exception
                retryCount += 1
                If (retryCount >= MAX_RETRIES) Then
                    'throw a new exception with a context message stating that
                    'the maximum retries was exceeded
                    Throw New Exception("Maximum retries exceeded", _
                                        exc)
```

Example 7-1. Retrying when an exception occurs (.vb) (continued)

```
            End If

        End Try
    End While

  Finally
    'cleanup
    If (Not IsNothing(dbConn)) Then
      dbConn.Close( )
    End If
  End Try
End Sub  'updateData
```

Example 7-2. Retrying when an exception occurs (.cs)

```
private void updateData(int problemID,
                         String sectionHeading)
{
  const int MAX_RETRIES  = 5;

  OleDbConnection dbConn = null;
  OleDbCommand dCmd = null;
  String strConnection = null;
  String strSQL = null;
  bool updateOK;
  int retryCount;

  try
  {
    // get the connection string from web.config and open a connection
    // to the database
    strConnection =
      ConfigurationSettings.AppSettings["dbConnectionString"];
    dbConn = new OleDbConnection(strConnection);
    dbConn.Open( );

    // build the update SQL to update the record in the database
    strSQL = "UPDATE EditProblem " +
            "SET SectionHeading='" + sectionHeading + "' " +
            "WHERE EditProblemID=" + problemID.ToString( );
    dCmd = new OleDbCommand(strSQL, dbConn);

    // provide a loop with a try catch block to facilitate retrying
    // the database update
    updateOK = false;
    retryCount = 0;
    while ((!updateOK) & (retryCount < MAX_RETRIES))
    {
      try
      {
        dCmd.ExecuteNonQuery( );
        updateOK = true;
      } // try
```

Example 7-2. Retrying when an exception occurs (.cs) (continued)

```
        catch (Exception exc)
        {
          retryCount ++;
          if (retryCount >= MAX_RETRIES)
          {
            // throw a new exception with a context message stating that
            // the maximum retries was exceeded
            throw new Exception("Maximum retries exceeded",
                                exc);
          }
        } // catch
      } // While
    } // try

    finally
    {
      // cleanup
      if (dbConn != null)
      {
        dbConn.Close( );
      }
    } // finally
  } // updateData
```

7.2   Handling Errors at the Page Level

Problem

You want to trap any error that occurs on a page and then, using a page-level event handler, redirect the user to another page that displays the information about the problem.

Solution

Add code to the Page_Error event handler of the page to set the ErrorPage property of that page to the URL you want to display to the user when an error occurs.

In the code-behind for the page, use the .NET language of your choice to:

1. Add a Page_Error event handler.

2. In the event handler, get a reference to the last error that occurred using the GetLastError method.

3. Set the ErrorPage property of the Page object to the URL of the page you want displayed after the error, adding querystring parameters to pass error information to the page.

Example 7-3 (VB) and Example 7-4 (C#) show an example that demonstrates this solution. (Because the *.aspx* file for this example contains nothing related to the error handling, it is not included here.)

Discussion

The `Page_Error` event of the ASP.NET `Page` object is raised any time an unhandled error occurs in a page. In C#, be sure to wire the `Page_Error` method to the page error event. This can be done in the `InitializeComponent` method or the `Page_Load` method with the following line of code:

```
this.Error += new System.EventHandler(this.Page_Error);
```

The first action required in the event handler is to get a reference to the last error. After getting the reference, the code should perform the required logging, notifications, and the like. See Recipe 7.3 for an example of writing to the event log.

ASP.NET provides you with the ability to redirect the user to another page when an error occurs. To use this feature, simply set the `ErrorPage` property of the `Page` object to the URL of the page you want the user to see. You can add querystring parameters to the URL to pass specific error messages to the page. For instance, in the code snippets shown next, we've added three querystring parameters to the URL of an error message page: `PageHeader`, `Message1`, and `Message2`. `PageHeader` is simply set to the message "Error Occurred". `Message1` is set to the message in the `lastError` exception. This will be the message from the last exception thrown. `Message2` is a message we've added to say where the error was processed.

VB
```
Page.ErrorPage = "CH07DisplayErrorVB.aspx" & _
                 "?PageHeader=Error Occurred" & _
                 "&Message1=" & lastError.Message & _
                 "&Message2=" & _
                 "This error was processed at the page level"
```

C#
```
Page.ErrorPage = "CH07DisplayErrorCS.aspx" +
                 "?PageHeader=Error Occurred" +
                 "&Message1=" + lastError.Message +
                 "&Message2=" +
                 "This error was processed at the page level";
```

When the `Page_Error` event is completed, ASP.NET will automatically perform a redirect to the URL named in the `ErrorPage` property. You could do this yourself using `Response.Redirect([Page URL])`, but why write a line of code when ASP.NET can do it for you?

 If you do not add any querystring parameters, ASP.NET will append one for you. The name of the parameter will be aspxerrorpath, and the value will be the relative URL to the specified page. In our example, the ASP.NET-added querystring would have been as follows:

```
aspxerrorpath=/aspnetcookbook/VBExamples/
CH07PageLevelErrorHandlingVB.aspx
```

This technique, when coupled with those for handling exceptions at the method level (described in Recipe 7.1) can greatly simplify handling errors in pages. The only place any code is required to gather error information and redirect to another page is in the `Page_Error` event handler. This is a significant improvement over the error-handling code that was required in classic ASP, where exception handling could be done only at the method level.

 By default, ASP.NET displays the full error context in a special ASP.NET page on the local machine. If you access this example from a browser on the web server, the redirection described here will not occur. If you access this example from a different machine, the redirection will be performed. Refer to Chapter 9 for changing the default handling of error messages in *web.config*.

See Also

Recipe 7.1; Recipe 7.3

Example 7-3. Handling errors at the page level (.vb)

```vb
Option Explicit On
Option Strict On
'-------------------------------------------------------------------------
'
'   Module Name: CH07PageLevelErrorHandlingVB.aspx.vb
'
'   Description: This module provides the code behind for
'                CH07PageLevelErrorHandlingVB.aspx
'
'*************************************************************************
Imports System
Imports System.Collections

Namespace ASPNetCookbook.VBExamples
  Public Class CH07PageLevelErrorHandlingVB
    Inherits System.Web.UI.Page

    '*********************************************************************
    '
    '   ROUTINE: Page_Load
    '
    '   DESCRIPTION: This routine provides the event handler for the page load
    '                event.  It is responsible for initializing the controls
    '                on the page.
    '-------------------------------------------------------------------------
    Private Sub Page_Load(ByVal sender As System.Object, _
                          ByVal e As System.EventArgs) Handles MyBase.Load

      Dim values As Hashtable

      'add a key/value pair to the hashtable without first creating
      'the hashtable which will cause a null reference exception error
      values.Add("Key", "Value")
    End Sub  'Page_Load
```

Example 7-3. Handling errors at the page level (.vb) (continued)

```
'************************************************************************
'
'   ROUTINE: Page_Error
'
'   DESCRIPTION: This routine provides the event handler for the page
'                error event.  It builds a URL with the error information
'                then sets the ErrorPage property to the URL.
'------------------------------------------------------------------------
Private Sub Page_Error(ByVal sender As Object, _
                       ByVal e As System.EventArgs) Handles MyBase.Error

  Dim lastError As Exception

  'get the last error that occurred
  lastError = Server.GetLastError()

  'do any logging, notifications, etc. here


  'set the URL of the page that will display the error and
  'include querystring parameters to allow the page to display
  'what happened
  Page.ErrorPage = "CH07DisplayErrorVB.aspx" & _
                   "?PageHeader=Error Occurred" & _
                   "&Message1=" & lastError.Message & _
                   "&Message2=" & _
                   "This error was processed at the page level"
End Sub  'Page_Error
End Class  'CH07PageLevelErrorHandlingVB
End Namespace
```

Example 7-4. Handling errors at the page level (.cs)

```
//-------------------------------------------------------------------------
//
//   Module Name: CH07PageLevelErrorHandlingCS.aspx.cs
//
//   Description: This module provides the code behind for
//                CH07PageLevelErrorHandlingCS.aspx
//
//************************************************************************
using System;
using System.Collections;

namespace ASPNetCookbook.CSExamples
{
  public class CH07PageLevelErrorHandlingCS : System.Web.UI.Page
  {
    //************************************************************************
    //
    //   ROUTINE: Page_Load
    //
    //   DESCRIPTION: This routine provides the event handler for the page
```

Example 7-4. Handling errors at the page level (.cs) (continued)

```csharp
//                   load event.  It is responsible for initializing the
//                   controls on the page.
//-------------------------------------------------------------------------
private void Page_Load(object sender, System.EventArgs e)
{
  Hashtable values = null;

  // wire the page error event
  this.Error += new System.EventHandler(this.Page_Error);

  // add a key/value pair to the hashtable without first creating
  // the hashtable which will cause a null reference exception error
  values.Add("Key", "Value");
} // Page_Load

//*************************************************************************
//
//    ROUTINE: Page_Error
//
//    DESCRIPTION: This routine provides the event handler for the page
//                 error event.  It builds a URL with the error information
//                 then sets the ErrorPage property to the URL.
//-------------------------------------------------------------------------
private void Page_Error(Object sender,
                        System.EventArgs e)
{
  Exception lastError = null;
  // get the last error that occurred
  lastError = Server.GetLastError();

  // do any logging, notifications, etc. here

  // set the URL of the page that will display the error and
  // include querystring parameters to allow the page to display
  // what happened
  Page.ErrorPage = "CH07DisplayErrorCS.aspx" +
                   "?PageHeader=Error Occurred" +
                   "&Message1=" + lastError.Message +
                   "&Message2=" +
                   "This error was processed at the page level";
} // Page_Error
} // CH07PageLevelErrorHandlingCS
}
```

7.3   Handling Errors at the Application Level

Problem

You want to report and log all errors in a common location, regardless of where they arise within the application.

Solution

Incorporate the error handling in methods (described in Recipe 7.1), add code to the `Page_Error` event handler to rethrow the page errors, and add the code to the `Application_Error` event handler to perform the logging and redirection.

In the code-behind class for your ASP.NET pages that need to perform error handling, use the .NET language of your choice to:

1. Create a `Page_Error` event handler.
2. Rethrow the page errors from within the method (this is needed to avoid all errors being wrapped with an `HttpUnhandledException` exception).

In the code-behind for *global.asax*, use the .NET language of your choice to:

1. Create an `Application_Error` event handler.
2. Create a detailed message and write it to the event log.
3. Redirect the user to the error page using `Server.Transfer`.

The code we've written to demonstrate this solution is shown in Examples 7-6 through 7-9. The `Page_Error` code required in all pages is shown in Example 7-6 (VB) and Example 7-7 (C#). The `Application_Error` code required in the *global.asax* code-behind is shown in Example 7-8 (VB) and Example 7-9 (C#). (Because the *.aspx* file for this example contains nothing related to the error handling, it is not included here.)

Discussion

The exception model in ASP.NET provides the ability for exceptions to be handled at any level, from the method level to the application level. An unhandled exception is sequentially rethrown to each method in the call stack. If no methods in the call stack handle the exception, the `Page_Error` event is raised. If the exception is not handled in the `Page_Error` event, the event is rethrown and the `Application_Error` event is raised. The rethrowing of exceptions at the application level allows for processing in a single location for the application.

To process errors at the application level, each page must include the `Page_Error` event handler with a single line of code to rethrow the last exception that occurred, as follows:

```vb
Private Sub Page_Error(ByVal sender As Object, _
                       ByVal e As System.EventArgs) Handles MyBase.Error

    'rethrow the last error that occurred
    Throw Server.GetLastError( )
End Sub 'Page_Error
```

```csharp
private void Page_Error(Object sender,
                        System.EventArgs e)
{
  // rethrow the last error that occurred
  throw Server.GetLastError( );
} // Page_Error
```

Why is this step required? We do this to avoid having the exception information wrapped with an `HttpUnhandledException` exception. It turns out that ASP.NET automatically creates a new `HttpUnhandledException` at the page level unless you simply rethrow the last exception, which from ASP.NET's prospective constitutes handling the exception.

There is a school of thought that says this step isn't necessary and that it's fine to have ASP.NET wrap your exceptions at will; all you have to do is just ignore all the "outer" exceptions and get the first inner exception. We don't subscribe to this view, however, because there are cases, such as page parse errors, that do not get wrapped with the `HttpUnhandledException`. This can make it difficult to extract the "real" exception information when there is no guarantee that the "real" exception information is the first inner exception in the chain of exceptions.

 Visual Studio .NET users can make the insertion of the `Page_Error` code on each page much easier by either using the built-in macro facilities or adding the code block for the `Page_Error` event to the toolbox. Alternately, you can create a base page that contains the `Page_Error` method and have all of your pages inherit from this base page. With this approach you do not have to deal with implementing `Page_Error` in all of your pages.

The error processing for the application is placed in the `Application_Error` event handler (in the *global.asax* code-behind). Much of this code follows a fairly standard pattern, which is illustrated in Example 7-8 (VB) and Example 7-9 (C#). The first step is to get a reference to the last exception that occurred:

[VB]
```
lastException = Server.GetLastError( )
```

[C#]
```
lastException = Server.GetLastError( );
```

The next step is to create a detailed message to insert into the event log. This message should contain the message from the most recent exception and a complete dump of all error information in the link list of exceptions. The complete dump is obtained by calling the `ToString` method of the last exception, as in the following example code:

[VB]
```
message = lastException.Message & _
          vbCrLf & vbCrLf & _
          lastException.ToString( )
```

[C#]
```
message = lastException.Message +
          "\r\r" +
          lastException.ToString( );
```

Next, you can write the message to the event log. As we show in Examples 7-8 and 7-9, this is done by creating a new `EventLog` object, setting the `Source` property to a constant containing the name of the event source to write the information to (the Application log), and then writing the message to the event log. When writing the entry to the event log, the event type can be set to `Error`, `FailureAudit`, `Information`, `SuccessAudit`, and `Warning`, all of which are members of the `EventLogEntryType` enumeration. Here is the code responsible for writing to the event log in our example:

VB
```
Log = New EventLog()
Log.Source = EVENT_LOG_NAME
Log.WriteEntry(message, _
               EventLogEntryType.Error)
```

C#
```
log = new EventLog();
log.Source = EVENT_LOG_NAME;
log.WriteEntry(message,
               EventLogEntryType.Error);
```

The event log entry created by our example is shown in Example 7-5. The entry shows that a `NullReferenceException` occurred at line 64 in the code-behind for the example page. If the exception had been wrapped by throwing new exceptions at each error-handling point in the code, they would all be listed here. This is very useful for troubleshooting runtime errors because the actual source of the error is shown, along with the complete call path to the point the error occurred.

Example 7-5. Event log entry for this example

```
{System.NullReferenceException}
    [System.NullReferenceException]: {System.NullReferenceException}
    HelpLink: Nothing
    InnerException: Nothing
    Message: "Object reference not set to an instance of an object."
    Source: "VBExamples"
    StackTrace: "   at ASPNetCookbook.VBExamples.CH07ApplicationLevelErrorHandlingVB.Page_
Error(Object sender, EventArgs e) in D:\ASPNetBook\Projects\ASPNetCookbookSolution\
UIProjects\VBExamples\CH07ApplicationLevelErrorHandlingVB.aspx.vb:line 64
    at System.Web.UI.TemplateControl.OnError(EventArgs e)
    at System.Web.UI.Page.HandleError(Exception e)
    at System.Web.UI.Page.ProcessRequestMain()
    at System.Web.UI.Page.ProcessRequest()
    at System.Web.UI.Page.ProcessRequest(HttpContext context)
    at System.Web.CallHandlerExecutionStep.System.Web.HttpApplication+IExecutionStep.
Execute()
    at System.Web.HttpApplication.ExecuteStep(IExecutionStep step, Boolean&
completedSynchronously)"
    TargetSite: {System.Reflection.RuntimeMethodInfo}
```

At this point any other notifications, such as sending an email to the system administrator, should be performed. Refer to Recipe 18.7 for information regarding sending emails.

The final step to processing errors at the application level is to clear the error and redirect the user to the page where an error message is displayed:

VB
```
Server.ClearError()
Server.Transfer("CH07DisplayErrorVB.aspx" & _
                "?PageHeader=Error Occurred" & _
```

```
                    "&Message1=" & lastException.Message & _
                     "&Message2=" & _
                    "This error was processed at the application level")
```

```
       Server.ClearError();
       Server.Transfer("CH07DisplayErrorCS.aspx" +
                    "?PageHeader=Error Occurred" +
                    "&Message1=" + lastException.Message +
                    "&Message2=" +
                    "This error was processed at the application level");
```

If you do not clear the error, ASP.NET will assume the error has not been processed and will handle it for you with its infamous "yellow" screen.

You can use either of two methods to redirect the user to the error page. The first method is to call Response.Redirect, which works by returning information to the browser instructing the browser to do a redirect to the page indicated. This results in an additional round trip to the server. As we show in Example 7-8 (VB) and Example 7-9 (C#), the second method is Server.Transfer, which is the method we favor because it transfers the request to the indicated page without the extra browser/server round trip.

By default, Windows 2000 and 2003 Server provides three event sources: Application, Security, and System. Of the three sources, the default ASP.NET user (ASPNET) only has permission to write to the Application log. Attempts to write to the Security or System logs will result in an exception being thrown in the Application_Error event.

You can make the errors for your application easier to find in the event viewer by creating an event source specific to your application. Without escalating the privileges for the ASPNET user to the System level (not a good option), you cannot create a new event source within your ASP.NET application. Two options are available. You can use the registry editor and add a new key to the HKEY_LOCAL_MACHINE\System\CurrentControlSet\Services\EventLog key or create a simple console application to do the work for you. We suggest the console application because it is easy and repeatable.

Create a console application in the usual fashion, add the following code to it, and then run the application while logged in as a user with administrative privileges. This will create an event source specific to your application. The only change that is required to the code described here is to change the EVENT_LOG_NAME constant value to the name of your new event source.

```
       Const EVENT_LOG_NAME As String = "Your Application"

       If (Not EventLog.SourceExists(EVENT_LOG_NAME)) Then
          EventLog.CreateEventSource(EVENT_LOG_NAME, EVENT_LOG_NAME)
       End If
```

```
const String EVENT_LOG_NAME = "Your Application";

if (EventLog.SourceExists(EVENT_LOG_NAME) != null)
{
   EventLog.CreateEventSource(EVENT_LOG_NAME, EVENT_LOG_NAME);
}
```

See Also

Recipe 7.1; Recipe 18.7

Example 7-6. Page_Error code for handling errors at the application level (.vb)

```
'*************************************************************************
'
'   ROUTINE: Page_Error
'
'   DESCRIPTION: This routine handles the error event for the page.  It
'                is used to trap all errors for the page and rethrow the
'                exception.  The rethrow is needed to avoid all errors
'                being wrapped with an "HttpUnhandledException" exception.
'-------------------------------------------------------------------------
Private Sub Page_Error(ByVal sender As Object, _
                    ByVal e As System.EventArgs) Handles MyBase.Error

   'rethrow the last error that occurred
   Throw Server.GetLastError()
End Sub  'Page_Error
```

Example 7-7. Page_Error code for handling errors at the application level (.cs)

```
//*************************************************************************
//
//   ROUTINE: Page_Error
//
//   DESCRIPTION: This routine provides the event handler for the page
//                error event.  It builds a URL with the error information
//                then sets the ErrorPage property to the URL.
//-------------------------------------------------------------------------
private void Page_Error(Object sender,
                    System.EventArgs e)
{
   // rethrow the last error that occurred
   throw Server.GetLastError();
} // Page_Error
```

Example 7-8. Application_Error code for handling errors at the application level (.vb)

```
'*************************************************************************
'
'   ROUTINE: Application_Error
'
'   DESCRIPTION: This routine provides the event handler for the
'                application error event.  It is responsible for
'                processing errors at the application level.
'-------------------------------------------------------------------------
```

```
Sub Application_Error(ByVal sender As Object, ByVal e As EventArgs)
  Const EVENT_LOG_NAME As String = "Application"

  Dim lastException As Exception
  Dim Log As EventLog
  Dim message As String

  'get the last error that occurred
  lastException = Server.GetLastError()

  'create the error message from the message in the last exception along
  'with a complete dump of all of the inner exceptions (all exception
  'data in the linked list of exceptions)
  message = lastException.Message & _
            vbCrLf & vbCrLf & _
            lastException.ToString()

  'Insert error information into the event log
  Log = New EventLog
  Log.Source = EVENT_LOG_NAME
  Log.WriteEntry(message, _
                 EventLogEntryType.Error)

  'perform other notifications, etc. here


  'clear the error and redirect to the page used to display the
  'error information
  Server.ClearError()
  Server.Transfer("CH07DisplayErrorVB.aspx" & _
                  "?PageHeader=Error Occurred" & _
                  "&Message1=" & lastException.Message & _
                  "&Message2=" & _
                  "This error was processed at the application level")
End Sub  'Application_Error
```

Example 7-9. Application_Error code for handling errors at the application level (.cs)

```
//***************************************************************************
//
//   ROUTINE: Application_Error
//
//   DESCRIPTION: This routine provides the event handler for the
//                application error event.  It is responsible for
//                processing errors at the application level.
//---------------------------------------------------------------------------
protected void Application_Error(Object sender, EventArgs e)
{
  const String EVENT_LOG_NAME = "Application";

  Exception lastException = null;
  EventLog log = null;
  String message = null;
```

Example 7-9. Application_Error code for handling errors at the application level (.cs) (continued)

```
        // get the last error that occurred
        lastException = Server.GetLastError();

        // create the error message from the message in the last exception along
        // with a complete dump of all of the inner exceptions (all exception
        // data in the linked list of exceptions)
        message = lastException.Message +
                "\r\r" +
                lastException.ToString();

        // Insert error information into the event log
        log = new EventLog();
        log.Source = EVENT_LOG_NAME;
        log.WriteEntry(message,
                    EventLogEntryType.Error);

        // perform other notifications, etc. here


        // clear the error and redirect to the page used to display the
        // error information
        Server.ClearError();
        Server.Transfer("CH07DisplayErrorCS.aspx" +
                    "?PageHeader=Error Occurred" +
                    "&Message1=" + lastException.Message +
                    "&Message2=" +
                    "This error was processed at the application level");
    }  // Application_Error
```

7.4   Displaying User-Friendly Error Messages

Problem

You want the event-handling methods described in this chapter to write detailed messages to an error log for use in debugging your application, but you want to display friendly, informative messages to the user.

Solution

Create a custom exception class that includes a property to hold the user-friendly message, and then, when an error occurs, instantiate a new exception object of the custom type in the Catch block of your error-handling code, set the property of the exception to the desired message, and then throw the new exception.

Use the .NET language of your choice to create the custom exception class by deriving from System.ApplicationException and adding a property to hold the user-friendly message, giving it a name like userFriendlyMessage.

In the code-behind for the ASP.NET pages of your application that need to perform error handling, use the .NET language of your choice to:

1. In the Catch block of methods where informative messages are useful, instantiate a new exception object of your custom class type, set the userFriendlyMessage property to the desired message, and then throw the new exception.

2. In the Application_Error event handler, write the detailed information provided by the exception object to the event log and then display the message contained in the userFriendlyMessage property of the exception on a common error message page.

The custom exception class we've created to demonstrate this solution is shown in Example 7-10 (VB) and Example 7-11 (C#). The code showing how to create the new exception is shown in Example 7-12 (VB) and Example 7-13 (C#). The code for the Application_Error event handler is shown in Example 7-14 (VB) and Example 7-15 (C#). (Because the *.aspx* file for this example contains nothing related to the error handling, it is not included in this recipe.)

Discussion

The first step to providing user-friendly messages with your exceptions is to create a new class that inherits from System.ApplicationException. (The System.ApplicationException class extends System.Exception but adds no new functionality. It is meant to be used to differentiate between exceptions defined by applications and those defined by the system.) You then need to add a property to the class to support the user-friendly message. The last step in creating the new exception class is to create a constructor that will create the base exception, by calling the base class constructor with the raw message and a reference to the inner exception, and then set the user-friendly message. Example 7-10 (VB) and Example 7-11 (C#) show how we have implemented these steps.

The new exception class is put to use in the Catch block of your code by creating an instance of the new exception class, passing it the original message, a reference to the exception, and the desired user-friendly message. The reference to the original exception is passed to preserve the linked list of exceptions. In this case, your new exception will point to the original exception by using the inner property of the new exception. After the new exception class is created, it is then thrown. Example 7-12 (VB) and Example 7-13 (C#) illustrate a sample Catch block.

As shown in Example 7-14 (VB) and Example 7-15 (C#), our sample Application_Error event handler writes detailed information to the event log and then displays the message contained in the userFriendlyMessage property of the exception. This example event code is actually a variation of the event code described in Recipe 7.3, modified to check whether the exception being processed has a user-friendly message to use instead of the raw exception message.

This recipe's approach can be extended many ways to suite your needs. For example, the custom exception class could contain a "nextPage" property that could be set to pass information on where the user should be taken after reviewing the error message.

See Also

Recipe 7.3

Example 7-10. Custom exception class with user-friendly message property (.vb)

```
Option Explicit On
Option Strict On
'-----------------------------------------------------------------------------
'
'   Module Name: CH07FriendlyExceptionVB.vb
'
'   Description: This class provides an exception class with support for a
'                user friendly message
'
'*****************************************************************************
Imports System

Namespace ASPNetCookbook.VBFriendlyException
  Public Class CH07FriendlyExceptionVB
    Inherits System.ApplicationException

    'private copy of user friendly message
    Private mUserFriendlyMessage As String = ""

    '*****************************************************************************
    '
    '   ROUTINE: Property userFriendlyMessage
    '
    '   DESCRIPTION: Provides access to the message to be displayed to the
    '                user friendly message.
    '-----------------------------------------------------------------------------
    Public Property userFriendlyMessage() As String
      Get
        Return (mUserFriendlyMessage)
      End Get

      Set(ByVal Value As String)
        mUserFriendlyMessage = Value
      End Set
    End Property  'userFriendlyMessage

    '*****************************************************************************
    '
    '   ROUTINE: New
    '
    '   DESCRIPTION: Provides a constructor supporting an error message, a
    '                reference to the exception that threw this exeception,
    '                and a user friendly message for the exception
    '-----------------------------------------------------------------------------
```

Example 7-10. Custom exception class with user-friendly message property (.vb) (continued)

```vb
    Public Sub New(ByVal message As String, _
                   ByVal inner As Exception, _
                   ByVal userFriendlyMessage As String)
      'call base class constructor.  NOTE: This must be the first line in
      'this constructor
      MyBase.New(message, inner)
      mUserFriendlyMessage = userFriendlyMessage
    End Sub  'New
  End Class  'CH07FriendlyExceptionVB
End Namespace
```

Example 7-11. Custom exception class with user-friendly message property (.cs)

```csharp
//----------------------------------------------------------------------------
//
//    Module Name: CH07FriendlyExceptionCS.aspx.cs
//
//    Description: This class provides an exception class with support for a
//                 user friendly message
//
//****************************************************************************
using System;

namespace ASPNetCookbook.CSFriendlyException
{
  public class CH07FriendlyExceptionCS : System.ApplicationException
  {
    // private copy of user friendly message
    private String mUserFriendlyMessage = "";

    //************************************************************************
    //
    //    ROUTINE: userFriendlyMessage
    //
    //    DESCRIPTION: Provides access to the message to be displayed to the
    //                 user friendly message.
    //------------------------------------------------------------------------
    public String userFriendlyMessage
    {
      get
      {
        return(mUserFriendlyMessage);
      }
      set
      {
        mUserFriendlyMessage = value;
      }
    }  // userFriendlyMessage

    //************************************************************************
    //
    //    ROUTINE: CH07FriendlyExceptionCS
    //
```

```
//    DESCRIPTION: Provides a constructor supporting an error message, a
//                 reference to the exception that threw this exeception,
//                 and a user friendly message for the exception.
//------------------------------------------------------------------------
public CH07FriendlyExceptionCS(String message,
                               Exception inner,
                               String userFriendlyMessage) :
        base(message, inner)
{
  mUserFriendlyMessage = userFriendlyMessage;
}
} // CH07FriendlyExceptionCS
}
```

Example 7-12. Creation of new custom exception (.vb)

```
Private Sub Page_Load(ByVal sender As System.Object, _
                      ByVal e As System.EventArgs) Handles MyBase.Load
   Dim values As Hashtable

   Try
      'add a key/value pair to the hashtable without first creating
      'the hashtable which will cause a null exception error
      values.Add("Key", "Value")

   Catch exc As Exception
      Throw New CH07FriendlyExceptionVB(exc.Message, _
                                        exc, _
                                        "The application is currently " & _
                                        "experiencing technical " & _
                                        "difficulties ... " & _
                                        "Please try again later")
   End Try
End Sub  'Page_Load
```

Example 7-13. Creation of new custom exception (.cs)

```
private void Page_Load(object sender,
                       System.EventArgs e)
{
  Hashtable values = null;

  // wire the page error event
  this.Error += new System.EventHandler(this.Page_Error);

  try
  {
    // add a key/value pair to the hashtable without first creating
    // the hashtable which will cause a null exception error
    values.Add("Key", "Value");
  }

  catch (Exception exc)
  {
```

Example 7-13. Creation of new custom exception (.cs) (continued)

```
        throw new CH07FriendlyExceptionCS(exc.Message,
                                          exc,
                                          "The application is currently " +
                                          "experiencing technical " +
                                          "difficulties ... " +
                                          "Please try again later");
    }
} // Page_Load
```

Example 7-14. Application_Error code for displaying a user-friendly message (.vb)

```
'*****************************************************************************
'
'   ROUTINE: Application_Error
'
'   DESCRIPTION: This routine provides the event handler for the
'                application error event.  It is responsible for
'                processing errors at the application level.
'----------------------------------------------------------------------------
Sub Application_Error(ByVal sender As Object, ByVal e As EventArgs)
  Const EVENT_LOG_NAME As String = "Application"

  Dim lastException As Exception
  Dim userFriendlyException As CH07FriendlyExceptionVB
  Dim Log As EventLog
  Dim message As String

  'get the last error that occurred
  lastException = Server.GetLastError()

  'create the error message from the message in the last exception along
  'with a complete dump of all of the inner exceptions (all exception
  'data in the linked list of exceptions)
  message = lastException.Message & _
            vbCrLf & vbCrLf & _
            lastException.ToString()

  'Insert error information into the event log
  Log = New EventLog
  Log.Source = EVENT_LOG_NAME
  Log.WriteEntry(message, _
                 EventLogEntryType.Error)

  'perform other notifications, etc. here

  'check to if the exception has a user friendly message
  If (TypeOf (lastException) Is CH07FriendlyExceptionVB) Then
    'exception has a user friendly message
    userFriendlyException = CType(lastException, _
                                  CH07FriendlyExceptionVB)
    message = userFriendlyException.userFriendlyMessage
  Else
    'exception does not have a user friendly message to just
```

Example 7-14. Application_Error code for displaying a user-friendly message (.vb) (continued)

```vb
        'output the raw message
        message = lastException.Message
    End If

    'clear the error and redirect to the page used to display the
    'error information
    Server.ClearError()
    Server.Transfer("CH07DisplayErrorVB.aspx" & _
                "?PageHeader=Error Occurred" & _
                "&Message1=" & message & _
                "&Message2=" & _
                "This exception used a user friendly mesage")
End Sub  'Application_Error
```

Example 7-15. Application_Error code for displaying a user-friendly message (.cs)

```csharp
//****************************************************************************
//
//   ROUTINE: Application_Error
//
//   DESCRIPTION: This routine provides the event handler for the
//                application error event.  It is responsible for
//                processing errors at the application level.
//----------------------------------------------------------------------------
protected void Application_Error(Object sender, EventArgs e)
{
    const String EVENT_LOG_NAME = "Application";

    Exception lastException = null;
    CH07FriendlyExceptionCS userFriendlyException = null;
    EventLog log = null;
    String message = null;

    // get the last error that occurred
    lastException = Server.GetLastError();

    // create the error message from the message in the last exception along
    // with a complete dump of all of the inner exceptions (all exception
    // data in the linked list of exceptions)
    message = lastException.Message +
            "\r\r" +
            lastException.ToString();

    // Insert error information into the event log
    log = new EventLog();
    log.Source = EVENT_LOG_NAME;
    log.WriteEntry(message,
                EventLogEntryType.Error);

    // perform other notifications, etc. here
```

Example 7-15. Application_Error code for displaying a user-friendly message (.cs) (continued)

```csharp
      // check to if the exception has a user friendly message
      if (lastException.GetType( ) == typeof(CH07FriendlyExceptionCS))
      {
        // exception has a user friendly message
        userFriendlyException = (CH07FriendlyExceptionCS)(lastException);
        message = userFriendlyException.userFriendlyMessage;
      }
      else
      {
        // exception does not have a user friendly message to just
        // output the raw message
        message = lastException.Message;
      }

      // clear the error and redirect to the page used to display the
      // error information
      Server.ClearError( );
      Server.Transfer("CH07DisplayErrorCS.aspx" +
                  "?PageHeader=Error Occurred" +
                  "&Message1=" + message +
                  "&Message2=" +
                  "This exception used a user friendly mesage");
  } // Application_Error
```

CHAPTER 8
Security

8.0   Introduction

ASP.NET provides an infrastructure for authentication and authorization that will meet most of your needs for securing an application. Three authentication schemes are available: Forms, Windows, and Passport.

Forms

> With *Forms authentication* you use a classic custom login page to gather credentials from users and to authenticate the information supplied against a database or other data store of authorized users. You can also leverage the FormsAuthentication APIs built into ASP.NET to issue a cookie back to the client. Recipes in this chapter show you how to use Forms authentication to restrict access to some or all pages of an application. We also show you how to restrict access to pages depending on the role assigned to the user.

Windows

> Implementing *Windows authentication* involves using a standard Windows dialog box to gather user credentials and validating the user against existing Windows accounts. If your application runs on an intranet, you will find that the last recipe in the chapter helps you implement Windows authentication in record time.

Passport

> *Passport authentication* uses Microsoft's Passport service to perform the required authentication. We haven't provided any examples in this chapter, not because Passport authentication is especially difficult but because we doubt many readers are actually implementing it. Irrespective of our personal views, we have yet to see much interest in Passport authentication on a commercial level.

If none of the built-in authentication schemes provided by ASP.NET meets the needs of your application, the .NET Framework provides the ability to create your own authentication scheme. This typically involves writing a custom class that implements the IAuthenticationModule interface and registering it to bypass the built-in .NET authentication. Custom authentication is not covered in this book, because of its individual nature. You can find more details in the MSDN Library by searching for the term "custom authentication".

This chapter provides several recipes for securing your applications using the built-in mechanisms provided by ASP.NET. These are usually adequate to meet the needs of your application.

One of the most important recommendations we can make is that you always have the security features of your application reviewed by key project stakeholders and security specialists. Bringing other perspectives to issues of security is always a good idea, because it is difficult to conceive of all the ways security may be breached in your environment. Having others inspect your plans saves you having to shoulder the entire security burden alone, which is never a wise or comfortable position to be in.

8.1 Restricting Access to All Application Pages

Problem

You want to restrict access to the pages of your application to authorized users only.

Solution

Change the *web.config* settings of your application to specify Forms authentication, and then create an *.aspx* login page to collect user credentials and complete the authentication check.

Modify *web.config* as follows:

1. Set the mode attribute of the <authentication> element to Forms.

2. Add a <forms> child element to the <authentication> element to specify key aspects of the Forms implementation:

```
<authentication mode="Forms">
  <forms name=".ASPNETCookbook"
         loginUrl="Login.aspx"
         protection="All"
         timeout="30"
         path="/">
  </forms>
</authentication>
```

3. Add <deny> and <allow> child elements to the <authorization> element to deny access to anonymous users and allow access to all who have been authenticated:

```
<authorization>
  <deny users="?" /> <!-- Deny anonymous users -->
  <allow users="*" /> <!-- Allow all authenticated users -->
</authorization>
```

In the *.aspx* file for the login page:

1. Add the fields required to collect the data the application needs to authenticate the user. Most applications require, at a minimum, a user login ID and password, but you can specify whatever your application requires.

2. Add a Login button.

3. (Optional) Include a checkbox for users to indicate that they want to be remembered between sessions. (You will need to add some code to the code-behind class to persist the authentication cookie on the client machine.)

In the code-behind class for the login page, use the .NET language of your choice to:

1. Use the Login button click event to verify the user credentials.

2. If the user credentials are valid, create a Forms authentication cookie and add it to the cookie collection returned to the browser by calling the SetAuthCookie method of the FormsAuthentication class.

3. (Optional) Set the Forms authentication cookie to be persisted on the client machine.

4. Redirect the user to the appropriate application start page using Response. Redirect.

The code we've created to illustrate this solution is shown in Examples 8-1 through 8-4. Example 8-1 shows the modifications we make to *web.config* to restrict access to all pages. Example 8-2 shows the *.aspx* file for the login page. Example 8-3 (VB) and Example 8-4 (C#) show the code-behind class for the login page. Figure 8-1 shows the login page produced by the application.

ASP.NET Cookbook
The Ultimate ASP.NET Code Sourcebook

Block Access To All Pages (VB)

Login ID:
Password:
☐ Remember Me

Login

Figure 8-1. Example login page

Discussion

ASP.NET runs within the context of IIS and all requests must first pass through IIS, so setting up the security for an ASP.NET application always starts with setting up security in IIS. For this recipe, we do not want IIS to perform any authentication. Therefore, the web site (or virtual directory) must be set up to allow anonymous access.

(We won't take you through setting up anonymous access in IIS—it is relatively easy to do and is well documented in MSDN. Just search for "IIS authentication".)

The first step to restricting access to all pages of an application is to enable ASP.NET security. This is done by setting the mode attribute of the <authentication> element of the *web.config* file to Forms. (Other options are Windows and Passport.)

The second step is to add a <forms> child element to the <authentication> element in order to specify the details of the Forms implementation. The <forms> element has the following attributes:

name

Defines the name of the HTTP cookie used by ASP.NET to maintain the user authentication information. Care should be taken when naming the cookie. If two applications on the same server use the same cookie name, "cross authentication" could occur.

loginUrl

Defines the page to which ASP.NET will redirect users when they attempt to access pages in your application without being logged in. The login page should provide the fields required to authenticate the user, typically a login ID and password or whatever else your application requires.

protection

Defines the protection method used for the cookie. Possible values are All, None, Encryption, and Validation. Validation specifies that the cookie data will be validated to ensure it was not altered in transit. Encryption specifies that the cookie is encrypted. All specifies that data validation and encryption will be used. None specifies no protection will be provided for the cookie information. The default is All and is highly recommended because it offers the highest level of protection for this authentication cookie.

timeout

Defines the amount of time in minutes before the cookie expires. The value provided here should be at least as long at the timeout for the session. Making the value shorter than the session timeout can result in a user being redirected to the page defined by the loginUrl before the session times out.

path

Defines the path of cookies issued by the application. Be aware that most browsers treat the path as case-sensitive and will not return the cookie for a request that does not match the value provided for the path attribute. The result will be having the users redirected as if they were not logged in. Unless your application requires specifying the path, we recommend that you leave the path as "/".

Here is an example of the <forms> element and its attributes:

```
<authentication mode="Forms">
    <forms name=".ASPNETCookbook"
           loginUrl="Login.aspx"
```

```
        protection="All"
        timeout="30"
        path="/">
    </forms>
</authentication>
```

The next step is to modify *web.config* to deny access to all anonymous users and allow access to all users who have been authenticated. This is done by adding <deny> and <allow> child elements to the <authorization> element:

```
<authorization>
    <deny users="?" /> <!-- Deny anonymous users -->
    <allow users="*" /> <!-- Allow all authenticated users -->
</authorization>
```

Your application login page should provide the fields required to enter the data needed to authenticate the user. This is typically a login ID and password, which you gather via text boxes, but can be whatever your application requires. ASP.NET provides the ability to persist the authentication cookie on the client machine. If your application supports "auto login" from a persistent cookie, you should provide a checkbox for the user to indicate that she wants to be remembered between sessions. In addition, your login page should include a button to initiate the login process after the data has been entered. How we have done this for our application is illustrated in Figure 8-1 and in the *.aspx* file (Example 8-2).

In the code-behind for the login page, use the login button click event to verify the user credentials. In Examples 8-3 and 8-4, for example, the database is queried for a user matching the entered login ID and password using a DataCommand and a DataReader. After the DataReader is created, the record pointer is by default positioned before the first record in the reader. By calling the Read method in the If statement, you can check to see if the user credentials are found and read the user credentials from the database at the same time. If the user credentials are found in the database, the Read method will return True. Otherwise, it will return False.

If the user credentials are valid, the Forms authentication cookie needs to be created and added to the cookie collection returned to the browser. This can be done by calling the SetAuthCookie method of the FormsAuthentication class, passing the user name and a Boolean value indicating whether the value should be persisted on the client machine. To persist the authentication cookie and allow the user to access the application on subsequent sessions without logging in, set the second parameter to True. If the second parameter is set to False, the authentication cookie is stored in memory on the client and is destroyed when the session expires or the user closes the browser.

> Because the SetAuthCookie method is static, it is not necessary to create a FormAuthentication object to use the method. The SetAuthCookie method is the simplest approach to creating and adding the cookie to the cookie collection, but is not very flexible. For an example of a more flexible approach that allows you to store additional data in the authentication cookie, see Recipe 8.3.

After the application has created the authentication cookie, the user should be redirected to the appropriate start page. When ASP.NET redirects the user to the login page defined in your *web.config* file, it automatically appends the name of the originally requested page to the redirected URL, as shown next. You can use this information to redirect users to the originally requested page or simply redirect them to a fixed page, as illustrated in Example 8-3 (VB) and Example 8-4 (C#).

```
http://localhost/ASPNetBook/Login.aspx?ReturnUrl=Home.aspx
```

You must use `Response.Redirect` to redirect the user to the next page. `Response.Redirect` returns information to the browser instructing it to redirect to the indicated page. This round trip to the client browser writes the authentication cookie to the browser so it will be returned to the server on subsequent page requests. This cookie is what ASP.NET uses to determine if the user has been authenticated. Using other mechanisms, such as `Server.Transfer`, will not cause the authentication cookie to be written to the browser, resulting in the user being redirected back to the login page.

 ASP.NET provides in a single method call (the `RedirectFromLoginPage` method of the `FormsAuthentication` class) the ability to create the authentication cookie, add it to the cookie collection, and redirect the user back the original page. This method sounds like it would save a few lines of code; however, if the user was not redirected to the login page (that is, if her original request was the login page), ASP.NET will redirect her to a page named *Default.aspx*. If your application does not use *Default.aspx* as the "home" page, using `RedirectFromLoginPage` creates more problems than it solves.

No other code is required. In other words, by using the simple code just described (without adding code to each page, as is required in classic ASP), access to all of the pages in your application is restricted to logged-in users.

So how does ASP.NET do this so easily? When your application is configured to use Forms authentication, ASP.NET looks for the cookie defined by the name attribute of the <forms> element in *web.config* for every page requested from your application. If the cookie does not exist, ASP.NET assumes the user is not logged in and redirects the user to the page defined by the loginUrl attribute. If the cookie does exist, ASP.NET assumes the user is authenticated and passes the request on to the requesting page. In addition, when the cookie exists, ASP.NET creates a user principal object with the information found in the authentication cookie. The *user principal object* (or *principal object* for short) represents the security context under which code is running. This information is available to your application by accessing the User object in the current context. To get the user name you added to the authentication cookie, use the line of code shown here:

VB
```
userName = Context.User.Identity.Name
```

C#
```
userName = Context.User.Identity.Name;
```

Applications that provide the ability to log in—particularly those that provide the ability to persist the information on the client machine to eliminate the need to log in on subsequent visits—should provide the ability to log out. In this context, logging out simply destroys the authentication cookie on the client machine, which then requires the user to log in again to gain access to your application. This can be accomplished with the line of code shown here:

VB

```
FormsAuthentication.SignOut()
```

C#

```
FormsAuthentication.SignOut();
```

ASP.NET can provide security only for files that are mapped to the ASP.NET ISAPI DLL. By default, these are files with the extensions *.asax*, *.ascx*, *.ashx*, *.asmx*, *.aspx*, *.axd*, *.vsdisco*, *.rem*, *.soap*, *.config*, *.cs*, *.csproj*, *.vb*, *.vbproj*, *.webinfo*, *.licx*, and *.resx* and resources. Any other file types—such as *.gif*, *.jpg*, *.txt*, *.js*, and the like—are not protected by ASP.NET security. If access to these file types must also be restricted, they will have to be added to the list of file types processed by the ASP.NET ISAPI DLL. This can be done in the application configuration section of the IIS properties of your application. Requiring these file types to be processed by ASP.NET will affect performance of your application due to the extra processing required for the images, text files, JavaScript, and the like.

See Also

Recipe 8.3; MSDN documentation for IIS setup (search for "IIS authentication")

Example 8-1. Changes to web.config to restrict access to all pages

```xml
<?xml version="1.0" encoding="utf-8" ?>
<configuration>
  <system.web>

    ..

    <authentication mode="Forms">
      <forms name=".ASPNETCookbookVB"
             loginUrl="Login.aspx"
             protection="All"
             timeout="30"
             path="/">
      </forms>
    </authentication>

    <authorization>
      <deny users="?" /> <!-- Deny anonymous user -->
      <allow users="*" /> <!-- Allow all authenticated users -->
    </authorization>
    ..
```

Example 8-1. Changes to web.config to restrict access to all pages (continued)

```
    </system.web>
</configuration>
```

Example 8-2. Login page (.aspx)

```
<%@ Page Language="vb" AutoEventWireup="false"
        Codebehind="Login.aspx.vb"
        Inherits="ASPNetCookbook.VBSecurity81.Login"%>
<!DOCTYPE HTML PUBLIC "-//W3C//DTD HTML 4.0 Transitional//EN">
<html>
  <head>
    <title>Login</title>
    <link rel="stylesheet" href="css/ASPNetCookbook.css">
  </head>
  <body leftmargin="0" marginheight="0" marginwidth="0" topmargin="0">
    <form id="frmSecurity" method="post" runat="server">
      <table width="100%" cellpadding="0" cellspacing="0" border="0">
        <tr>
          <td align="center">
            <img src="images/ASPNETCookbookHeading_blue.gif">
          </td>
        </tr>
        <tr>
          <td class="dividerLine">
            <img src="images/spacer.gif" height="6" border="0"></td>
        </tr>
      </table>
      <table width="90%" align="center" border="0">
        <tr>
          <td><img src="images/spacer.gif" height="10" border="0"></td>
        </tr>
        <tr>
          <td align="center" class="PageHeading">
            Block Access To All Pages (VB)
          </td>
        </tr>
        <tr>
          <td><img src="images/spacer.gif" height="10" border="0"></td>
        </tr>
        <tr>
          <td align="center">
            <table>
              <tr>
                <td class="LabelText">Login ID: </td>
                <td>
                  <asp:TextBox ID="txtLoginID" Runat="server"
                             CssClass="LabelText" />
                </td>
              </tr>
              <tr>
                <td class="LabelText">Password: </td>
                <td>
```

Example 8-2. Login page (.aspx) (continued)

```
                    <asp:TextBox ID="txtPassword" Runat="server"
                            CssClass="LabelText" TextMode="Password" />
                </td>
            </tr>
            <tr>
                <td colspan="2" align="center">
                    <asp:CheckBox ID="chkRememberMe" Runat="server"
                            CssClass="LabelText" Text="Remember Me" />
                </td>
            </tr>
            <tr>
                <td colspan="2" align="center">
                    <br />
                    <input id="btnLogin" runat="server"
                            type="button" value="Login" />
                </td>
            </tr>
            <tr>
                <td colspan="2" align="center">
                    <br />
                    <input type="button" value="Attempt Access without Login"
                            onclick="document.location='Home.aspx'" />
                </td>
            </tr>
        </table>
      </td>
    </tr>
  </table>
 </form>
 </body>
</html>
```

Example 8-3. Login page code-behind (.vb)

```
Option Explicit On
Option Strict On
'-----------------------------------------------------------------------------
'
'   Module Name: Login.aspx.vb
'
'   Description: This module provides the code behind for the
'               Login.aspx page
'
'*****************************************************************************
Imports Microsoft.VisualBasic
Imports System.Configuration
Imports System.Data
Imports System.Data.OleDb
Imports System.Web.Security
Imports System.Web.UI.HtmlControls
Imports System.Web.UI.WebControls
```

Example 8-3. Login page code-behind (.vb) (continued)

```vb
Namespace ASPNetCookbook.VBSecurity81
  Public Class Login
    Inherits System.Web.UI.Page

    'controls on the form
    Protected txtLoginID As TextBox
    Protected txtPassword As TextBox
    Protected chkRememberMe As CheckBox
    Protected WithEvents btnLogin As HtmlInputButton

    '*************************************************************************
    '
    '   ROUTINE: Page_Load
    '
    '   DESCRIPTION: This routine provides the event handler for the page load
    '                event.  It is responsible for initializing the controls
    '                on the page.
    '-------------------------------------------------------------------------
    Private Sub Page_Load(ByVal sender As System.Object, _
                          ByVal e As System.EventArgs) _
              Handles MyBase.Load
      'Put user code to initialize the page here
    End Sub  'Page_Load

    '*************************************************************************
    '
    '   ROUTINE: btnLogin_ServerClick
    '
    '   DESCRIPTION: This routine provides the event handler for the login
    '                button click event.  It is responsible for authenticating
    '                the user and redirecting to the next page if the user
    '                is authenticated.
    '-------------------------------------------------------------------------
    Private Sub btnLogin_ServerClick(ByVal sender As Object, _
                                     ByVal e As System.EventArgs) _
              Handles btnLogin.ServerClick

      'name of querystring parameter containing return URL
      Const QS_RETURN_URL As String = "ReturnURL"

      Dim dbConn As OleDbConnection
      Dim dCmd As OleDbCommand
      Dim dr As OleDbDataReader
      Dim strConnection As String
      Dim strSQL As String
      Dim nextPage As String

      Try
        'get the connection string from web.config and open a connection
        'to the database
        strConnection = _
            ConfigurationSettings.AppSettings("dbConnectionString")
```

Example 8-3. Login page code-behind (.vb) (continued)

```vb
dbConn = New OleDb.OleDbConnection(strConnection)
dbConn.Open( )

'check to see if the user exists in the database
strSQL = "SELECT (FirstName + ' ' + LastName) AS UserName " & _
        "FROM AppUser " & _
        "WHERE LoginID=? AND " & _
        "Password=?"
dCmd = New OleDbCommand(strSQL, dbConn)
dCmd.Parameters.Add(New OleDbParameter("LoginID", _
                                    txtLoginID.Text))
dCmd.Parameters.Add(New OleDbParameter("Password", _
                                    txtPassword.Text))
dr = dCmd.ExecuteReader( )

If (dr.Read( )) Then
   'user credentials were found in the database so notify the system
   'that the user is authenticated
   FormsAuthentication.SetAuthCookie(CStr(dr.Item("UserName")), _
                                    chkRememberMe.Checked)

   'get the next page for the user
   If (Not IsNothing(Request.QueryString(QS_RETURN_URL))) Then
     'user attempted to access a page without logging in so redirect
     'them to their originally requested page
     nextPage = Request.QueryString(QS_RETURN_URL)
   Else
     'user came straight to the login page so just send them to the
     'home page
     nextPage = "Home.aspx"
   End If

   'Redirect user to the next page
   'NOTE: This must be a Response.Redirect to write the cookie to the
   '      user's browser.  Do NOT change to Server.Transfer which
   '      does not cause around trip to the client browser and thus
   '      will not write the authentication cookie to the client
   '      browser.
   Response.Redirect(nextPage, True)
Else
   'user credentials do not exist in the database - in a production
   'application this should output an error message telling the user
   'that the login ID or password was incorrect
End If

Finally
 'cleanup
 If (Not IsNothing(dr)) Then
   dr.Close( )
 End If

 If (Not IsNothing(dbConn)) Then
```

Example 8-3. Login page code-behind (.vb) (continued)

```vb
            dbConn.Close( )
         End If
      End Try
   End Sub   'btnLogin_ServerClick
 End Class  'Login
End Namespace
```

Example 8-4. Login page code-behind (.cs)

```csharp
//---------------------------------------------------------------------------
//
//   Module Name: Login.aspx.cs
//
//   Description: This module provides the code behind for the
//                Login.aspx page
//
//*************************************************************************
using System;
using System.Configuration;
using System.Data;
using System.Data.OleDb;
using System.Web.Security;
using System.Web.UI.WebControls;
using System.Web.UI.HtmlControls;

namespace ASPNetCookbook.CSSecurity81
{
  public class Login : System.Web.UI.Page
  {
    // controls on the form
    protected System.Web.UI.WebControls.TextBox txtLoginID;
    protected System.Web.UI.WebControls.TextBox txtPassword;
    protected System.Web.UI.WebControls.CheckBox chkRememberMe;
    protected System.Web.UI.HtmlControls.HtmlInputButton btnLogin;

    //*********************************************************************
    //
    //   ROUTINE: Page_Load
    //
    //   DESCRIPTION: This routine provides the event handler for the page
    //                load event.  It is responsible for initializing the
    //                controls on the page.
    //---------------------------------------------------------------------
    private void Page_Load(object sender, System.EventArgs e)
    {
      // wire the login button
      this.btnLogin.ServerClick += new EventHandler(this.btnLogin_ServerClick);
    }  // Page_Load

    //*********************************************************************
    //
    //   ROUTINE: btnLogin_ServerClick
    //
```

Example 8-4. Login page code-behind (.cs) (continued)

```
//    DESCRIPTION: This routine provides the event handler for the login
//                 button click event.  It is responsible for
//                 authenticating the user and redirecting to the next
//                 page if the user is authenticated.
//
//-------------------------------------------------------------------------
private void btnLogin_ServerClick(Object sender,
                                  System.EventArgs e)
{
  // name of querystring parameter containing return URL
  const String QS_RETURN_URL = "ReturnURL";

  OleDbConnection dbConn = null;
  OleDbCommand dCmd = null;
  OleDbDataReader dr = null;
  String strConnection = null;
  String strSQL = null;
  String nextPage = null;

  try
  {
    // get the connection string from web.config and open a connection
    // to the database
    strConnection =
      ConfigurationSettings.AppSettings["dbConnectionString"];
    dbConn = new OleDbConnection(strConnection);
    dbConn.Open();

    // check to see if the user exists in the database
    strSQL = "SELECT (FirstName + ' ' + LastName) AS UserName " +
             "FROM AppUser " +
             "WHERE LoginID=? AND " +
             "Password=?";
    dCmd = new OleDbCommand(strSQL, dbConn);
    dCmd.Parameters.Add(new OleDbParameter("LoginID",
                                           txtLoginID.Text));
    dCmd.Parameters.Add(new OleDbParameter("Password",
                                           txtPassword.Text));
    dr = dCmd.ExecuteReader();

    if (dr.Read())
    {
      // user credentials were found in the database so notify the system
      // that the user is authenticated
      FormsAuthentication.SetAuthCookie((String)(dr["UserName"]),
                                        chkRememberMe.Checked);

      // get the next page for the user
      if (Request.QueryString[QS_RETURN_URL] != null)
      {
        // user attempted to access a page without logging in so redirect
        // them to their originally requested page
```

Example 8-4. Login page code-behind (.cs) (continued)

```csharp
            nextPage = Request.QueryString[QS_RETURN_URL];
        }
        else
        {
            // user came straight to the login page so just send them to the
            // home page
            nextPage = "Home.aspx";
        }

        // Redirect user to the next page
        // NOTE: This must be a Response.Redirect to write the cookie to
        //       the user's browser.  Do NOT change to Server.Transfer
        //       which does not cause around trip to the client browser
        //       and thus will not write the authentication cookie to the
        //       client browser.
        Response.Redirect(nextPage, true);
    }
    else
    {
        // user credentials do not exist in the database - in a production
        //application this should output an error message telling the user
        // that the login ID or password was incorrect.
    }
} // try

finally
{
    // cleanup
    if (dr != null)
    {
        dr.Close();
    }

    if (dbConn != null)
    {
        dbConn.Close();
    }
} // finally
} // btnLogin_ServerClick
} // Login
}
```

8.2   Restricting Access to Selected Application Pages

Problem

You want to restrict access to many, but not all, of the pages in your application (i.e., you want to make some pages accessible to the public).

Solution

Implement the solution described in Recipe 8.1 and then modify the contents of the *web.config* file to list the pages that allow public access and those that require authentication.

Modify *web.config* as follows:

1. Change the `<deny>` child element of the `<authorization>` element to `<deny users="*"/>` and delete the `<allow>` child element to deny access to all users.

2. Add a `<location>` element to the configuration level for each application page to specify whether it is available to the public or only to authenticated users.

Example 8-5 shows how we have implemented this solution with some sample *web.config* entries. We begin by adding settings that deny access to all users. We then add settings that allow public access to *PublicPage.aspx* but restrict access to *Home.aspx* only to authenticated users.

Discussion

The approach we advocate for this recipe is the same as for Recipe 8.1, except for certain aspects of the *web.config* file configuration.

The `<authentication>` element and its `<forms>` child are the same as in Recipe 8.1.

We have modified the `<authorization>` element that we used in Recipe 8.1 to deny access to all users. By denying authorization to all users at the application level, elements can be added to authorize access to particular pages.

Access to the individual pages in the application is controlled by providing a `<location>` element for each page. For pages with public access, the `<location>` element should be set up as follows:

```
<location path="PublicPage.aspx">
  <system.web>
    <authorization>
      <allow users="*"/>
    </authorization>
  </system.web>
</location>
```

The path attribute of the `<location>` element specifies the page that this `<location>` element applies to. The `<authorization>` element defines the access to the page defined in the path attribute. For public access, the `<authorization>` should be set to allow all users (users="*").

To limit access to individual pages, a `<location>` element is provided for each of the restricted pages, as follows:

```
<location path="Home.aspx">
  <system.web>
    <authorization>
```

```
    <deny users="?" />   <!-- Deny anonymous (unauthenticated) users -->
    <allow users="*"/>   <!-- Allow all authenticated users -->
  </authorization>
 </system.web>
</location>
```

The primary difference is the inclusion of two `<authorization>` child elements. The `<deny>` element denies access to anonymous (unauthenticated) users. The `<allow>` element allows access to all authenticated users. Notice that we've used two special identities in the code: ? and *. Here ? refers to the anonymous identity, and * refers to all identities.

At first glance this code sequence would appear to allow access to all users. ASP.NET processes authentication and authorization in a hierarchical fashion, starting at *machine.config*, followed by the *web.config* for the application, and then any *web.config* files located in folders in the path to the requested page. As soon as ASP.NET finds the first access rule that applies to the current user, the rule is applied. The rule evaluation continues, and if any other rules are found that reduce the access, they are applied; otherwise, they are skipped. In this case, the `<deny users="?" />` rule is processed first. The `<allow users="*"/>` rule is processed second, and because it does not reduce the access, it is skipped; therefore, if the user is not authenticated, he is denied access. As you can see by this example, the precise ordering of the `<allow>` and `<deny>` elements is important. They must be in most restrictive order, from top to bottom.

One of the disadvantages of using a `<location>` element for each page you wish to make accessible to authenticated users is the maintenance of all the page names in the `<location>` elements. For an application with 50 pages, it is not a big problem; however, for an application with a large number of pages, it can be a big task. ASP.NET provides another mechanism that is described later to make the process a little easier.

Even though this approach may have some maintenance issues, it does have the advantage of providing more control over the individual pages served by your application. For instance, without modifying the *web.config* file, no one will be able to add a page to your application that will be viewable through the web server. If someone does succeed in adding a page, attempts to access it will result in a redirection to the login page.

If the idea of maintaining a `<location>` element for each page in your application is not appealing, you can structure your application to place public pages and private pages in separate folders, and then provide one `<location>` element for the public folder and a second one for the private pages:

```
<!--
****************************************************************************
    The following location element provides public access to all pages
    in the PublicPages folder.
****************************************************************************
-->
<location path="PublicPages">
  <system.web>
    <authorization>
```

```
        <allow users="*"/>
      </authorization>
    </system.web>
  </location>

  <!--
  *************************************************************************
        The following location element restricts access to all pages
        in the PrivatePages folder.
  *************************************************************************
  -->
  <location path="PrivatePages">
    <system.web>
      <authorization>
        <deny users="?" />  <!-- Deny anonymous (unauthenticated) users -->
        <allow users="*"/>  <!-- Allow all authenticated users -->
      </authorization>
    </system.web>
  </location>
```

Using <location> elements to define separate folders for public and private pages is analogous to their use to set authorization requirements for individual pages, except the path attribute is set to a relative path to an applicable folder rather than to a specific *.aspx* page.

Nothing comes for free. The folder approach to controlling security makes the maintenance of the *web.config* file simpler; however, it has two drawbacks. First, any page that is placed in a designated folder becomes part of your application, whether you want it to or not. Second, sharing images and user controls is much more difficult. This is the result of having to provide a relative path from the requested page to the image or user control. It becomes even more difficult if a user control contains images and is used in the root folder as well as a subfolder.

See Also

Recipe 8.1; MSDN documentation for more information on *web.config* format (search for "Format of ASP.NET Configuration Files")

Example 8-5. web.config entries to restrict access to some pages

```
<?xml version="1.0" encoding="utf-8" ?>
<configuration>
  <system.web>

    ..

    <authentication mode="Forms">
      <forms name=".ASPNETCookbookVB2"
             loginUrl="login.aspx"
             protection="All"
             timeout="30"
```

Example 8-5. web.config entries to restrict access to some pages (continued)

```
            path="/">
        </forms>
    </authentication>

    <authorization>
        <deny users="*" /> <!-- Deny all users -->
    </authorization>

    ..

    <!--
    ****************************************************************************
        The following section provides public access to pages that do not
        require authentication.  An entry must be included for each page
        that does not require authentication.
    ****************************************************************************
    -->
    <location path="PublicPage.aspx">
      <system.web>
        <authorization>
          <allow users="*"/>
        </authorization>
      </system.web>
    </location>

    <!--
    ****************************************************************************
        The following section defines the pages that require authentication
        for access.  An entry must be included for each page that requires
        authentication.
    ****************************************************************************
    -->
    <location path="Home.aspx">
      <system.web>
        <authorization>
          <deny users="?" />  <!-- Deny anonymous (unauthenticated) users -->
          <allow users="*"/>  <!-- Allow all authenticated users -->
        </authorization>
      </system.web>
    </location>
</configuration>
```

8.3   Restricting Access to Application Pages by Role

Problem

You want to assign or make use of predefined roles for the users of your application, and you want to control access to pages as a function of these roles.

Solution

The solution involves the following steps:

1. Implement the solution described in Recipe 8.2, adding to *web.config* the required roles for each of the pages.

2. In the code-behind class for the ASP.NET login page, add the user's role information to the authentication cookie when the user logs in.

3. Add code to the `Application_AuthenticateRequest` method in the *global.asax* code-behind to recover the user role information and build a user principal object.

4. Set the user principal object to the `Context.User` property to provide ASP.NET the data it needs to perform page-by-page authentication.

The code we've written to illustrate this solution appears in Examples 8-6 through 8-10. The `<authentication>` and `<authorization>` elements of *web.config* are shown in Example 8-6. The login page code-behind where the authentication cookie is created is shown in Example 8-7 (VB) and Example 8-8 (C#). (See Recipe 8.1 for the *.aspx* file for a typical login page.) The `Application_AuthenticateRequest` method in the code-behind for *global.asax* is shown in Example 8-9 (VB) and Example 8-10 (C#).

Discussion

The approach we favor for this recipe builds on Recipe 8.2 but quickly takes a tack of its own based on the addition and use of user roles. The `<authentication>` and `<authorization>` elements of the *web.config* file are identical to those used in Recipe 8.2. And like Recipe 8.2, `<location>` elements are used to define the access requirements for each page. The `<location>` elements for the public access pages are also identical.

In this recipe, however, the `<location>` elements for the restricted pages each contains a list of roles required for access to the page it controls. The following code shows an example. For *Home.aspx*, the `User` and `Admin` roles are allowed access. For *AdminPage.aspx*, only the "Admin" role is allowed access:

```
<location path="Home.aspx">
  <system.web>
    <authorization>
      <allow roles="User,
                    Admin"/>
      <deny users="*"/>
    </authorization>
  </system.web>
</location>

<location path="AdminPage.aspx">
  <system.web>
```

```
<authorization>
  <allow roles="Admin"/>
  <deny users="*"/>
</authorization>
  </system.web>
</location>
```

It is important to include the <deny users="*" /> element for all pages
after the list of roles allowed to access the page. This informs ASP.NET
that if the user is not assigned one of the previously listed roles, they
should be denied access to the page.

You might be tempted to use folders to contain pages with similar
access rights, as described in Recipe 8.2. However, this approach is
much more complicated when roles are used, because a user can be
assigned multiple roles and any given page may be accessible by multiple roles. You might be able to initially segment your application to
use the folder approach, but later changes will be very difficult. If you
are using roles to control access to pages in your application, we recommend that you include a <location> element for each page in your
web.config file.

The operations required after the user credentials have been verified are a little different than the previous recipes in this chapter. First, a FormsAuthenticationTicket is
created. This authentication ticket will be used as the authentication cookie. By manually creating the ticket, you can add the user role information to the authentication
cookie.

To manually create the ticket, you must instantiate a System.Web.Security.
FormsAuthenticationTicket object, as shown in a general form here and in a more
application-specific form in Example 8-7 (VB) and Example 8-8 (C#):

```
ticket = New FormsAuthenticationTicket(version, _
                                       name, _
                                       issueDate, _
                                       expiration, _
                                       isPersistent, _
                                       userData)
```

The ticket takes six parameters:

version

> The first parameter is a version number. In our code-behind examples we've
> used the number 1, but you can use any value. In a production application that
> allows persistent cookies to be stored on the client, the version number can be
> used to track and handle changes to the data in the cookie.

name

> The second parameter is the user's name. This can be any string you want to use
> to identify the user.

issueDate

The third parameter is the issue date/time of the authentication ticket. This would normally be set to the current date/time.

expiration

The fourth parameter is the expiration date/time of the authentication ticket. The difference between this value and the issue date/time needs to be greater than or equal to the session timeout value. In Examples 8-7 and 8-8, it is set to 30 minutes in the future.

isPersistent

The fifth parameter is a flag indicating whether the cookie should be persisted on the client (if set to True) or should be memory-based (if set to False).

userData

The sixth parameter can be any string value you want to store with the cookie. It is used in our example to store a comma-delimited list of user roles. This list of roles is used to authorize access to the pages in your application.

> Depending on how the role information is stored for a *user* of your application, you may need to build a comma-delimited string containing the roles and instead use this string as the sixth parameter of the authentication ticket.

After the application creates it, an authentication ticket needs to be converted to an encrypted string. Only strings can be stored in cookies, and encryption prevents the possibility of tampering with the data stored there. To encrypt the string, we call the Encrypt method of the FormsAuthentication class, passing it the ticket that we created. The method returns a string containing the encrypted ticket:

```
encryptedStr = FormsAuthentication.Encrypt(ticket)
```

Now you need to create a cookie from the encrypted string, using the name of the Forms authentication cookie defined in the *web.config* file. Naming the cookie anything else will keep the authentication from working, since ASP.NET will look for the cookie by the name defined in *web.config* and will not find it.

```
cookie = New HttpCookie(FormsAuthentication.FormsCookieName,
                        encryptedStr)
```

Next, you need to set the expiration date and time for the cookie. If the cookie is to be persisted, the expiration should be set significantly in the future. In Examples 8-7 and 8-8, we've set the expiration date 10 years in the future. If the cookie is not to be persisted, the expiration date and time should not be set or the cookie will be made persistent.

The last step before redirecting the user to the appropriate next page (the same as in previous recipes in this chapter) is to add the cookie you created to the cookie collection so it will be sent to the client browser on the redirect. This is done by calling the Add method of the Response object's Cookies collection, and passing it the cookie to be added.

Now that the user is logged in and the role information has been added to the authentication cookie, you need to add the Application_AuthenticateRequest method to the code-behind for *global.asax* (see Examples 8-9 and 8-10). This method is executed for every requested resource that ASP.NET manages and allows the authentication/authorization process to be customized.

In the Application_AuthenticateRequest method, the first thing you need to do is to check to see if the user is currently authenticated by calling the IsAuthenticated method of the Request object. If not, no action needs to be taken.

If the user is authenticated, you need to check to see if the authentication type is set to Forms. If it is not, an exception should be thrown, since there is a significant mismatch between the code and the authentication cookie. This is illustrated by the following code:

VB
```
If (Context.Request.IsAuthenticated) Then
    If (Context.User.Identity.AuthenticationType = "Forms") Then

        ..

    Else
        'application is improperly configured so throw an exception
        Throw New ApplicationException("Application Must Be Configured For Forms
            Authentication")
    End If  'If (Context.User.Identity.AuthenticationType = "Forms")
End If  'If (Context.Request.IsAuthenticated)
```

C#
```
if (Context.Request.IsAuthenticated)
{
    if (Context.User.Identity.AuthenticationType == "Forms")
    {
        ..
    }
    else
    {
        // application is improperly configured so throw an exception
        throw new ApplicationException("Application Must Be Configured For Forms
            Authentication");
    } // if (Context.User.Identity.AuthenticationType = "Forms")
} // if (Context.Request.IsAuthenticated)
```

Next, you need to get the user roles that you added to the Forms authentication cookie. This is done by getting the identity from the Context.User object. You must cast the identity to a FormsIdentity object to get access to the authentication ticket data where the user roles are stored. This casting is the primary reason why the verification was made on the authentication type. If it was not Forms, this casting would throw a generic exception that would be much harder to troubleshoot than an exception that explicitly states what is wrong. The list of roles retrieved from the UserData property of the authentication ticket is the comma-delimited list of the user roles you added to the authentication ticket during login.

VB
```
identity = CType(Context.User.Identity, FormsIdentity)
roles = identity.Ticket.UserData
```

C#
```
identity = (FormsIdentity)(Context.User.Identity);
roles = identity.Ticket.UserData;
```

With the user identity and the roles in hand, you now have the information you need to create a GenericPrincipal object and assign it to the User property of the Context object. This GenericPrincipal object is what ASP.NET uses, along with the information in the *web.config* file, to perform the authorization for the requested page.

The GenericPrincipal constructor requires the user's identity and an array of strings for the roles assigned to the user. The user's identity is the FormsIdentity object you retrieved previously. The comma-delimited list of roles you retrieved previously can easily be converted to an array of strings by using the Split method of the String object, passing a comma as the delimiter used for performing the split. This is illustrated in the following code:

VB
```
Context.User = New GenericPrincipal(identity, _
                               roles.Split(","c))
```

C#
```
Context.User = new GenericPrincipal(identity,
                               roles.Split(','));
```

As with previous recipes in this chapter, you do not need to add any code to the individual pages in your application to handle the authentication and authorization. ASP.NET will now do all of that work for you and let you concentrate on the requirements of the individual pages. If the authorization requirements change for your application and different roles are required to access pages, the only changes required will be to the *web.config* <location> elements.

Even though you do not need to perform any of the authentication and authorization tasks, you may still want access to the information to customize your pages with the user information or to change what is displayed on pages as a function of the user's roles. The username can be obtained as shown here:

VB
```
userName = context.User.Identity.Name
```

C#
```
userName = context.User.Identity.Name;
```

To check the user's role(s), use the following code:

VB
```
If (Context.User.IsInRole("User")) Then

    'perform functions for role

End If
```

```
if (Context.User.IsInRole("User"))
{

    // perform functions for role

}
```

Using the GenericPrincipal object, no mechanism is provided to get the list of roles assigned to the user. You can only check to see if a user can perform a specific role. If your application requires that you have access to the list of roles, you can store the role information in a Session variable, or you can create a custom user principal inheriting from the GenericPrincipal class and adding the functionality needed by your application.

See Also

Recipe 8.1; Recipe 8.2

Example 8-6. web.config for restricting access by user role

```
<?xml version="1.0" encoding="utf-8" ?>
<configuration>

    ..

    <authentication mode="Forms">
      <forms name=".ASPNETCookbookVB3"
             loginUrl="login.aspx"
             protection="All"
             timeout="30"
             path="/">
      </forms>
    </authentication>

    <authorization>
        <deny users="*" /> <!-- Deny all users -->
    </authorization>


    ..

  <!--
  ***********************************************************************
        The following section provides public access to pages that do not
        require authentication.  An entry must be included for each page
        that does not require authentication.
  ***********************************************************************
  -->
  <location path="PublicPage.aspx">
    <system.web>
      <authorization>
        <allow users="*"/>
      </authorization>
```

Example 8-6. web.config for restricting access by user role (continued)

```
    </system.web>
  </location>

  <!--
  ****************************************************************************
      The following section defines the pages that require authentication
      for access.  An entry must be included for each page that requires
      authentication with a list of the roles required for access to
      the page.

      Valid Roles are as follows.
      NOTE: The roles must be entered exactly as listed.

          User
          Admin
  ****************************************************************************
  -->
  <location path="Home.aspx">
    <system.web>
      <authorization>
        <allow roles="User,
                      Admin"/>
        <deny users="*"/>
      </authorization>
    </system.web>
  </location>

  <location path="AdminPage.aspx">
    <system.web>
      <authorization>
        <allow roles="Admin"/>
        <deny users="*"/>
      </authorization>
    </system.web>
  </location>

</configuration>
```

Example 8-7. Login page code-behind (.vb)

```
Option Explicit On
Option Strict On
'----------------------------------------------------------------------------
'
'   Module Name: Login.aspx.vb
'
'   Description: This module provides the code behind for the
'               Login.aspx page
'
'****************************************************************************
Imports Microsoft.VisualBasic
Imports System
```

Example 8-7. Login page code-behind (.vb) (continued)

```vb
Imports System.Configuration
Imports System.Data
Imports System.Data.OleDb
Imports System.Web
Imports System.Web.Security
Imports System.Web.UI.HtmlControls
Imports System.Web.UI.WebControls

Namespace ASPNetCookbook.VBSecurity83
  Public Class Login
    Inherits System.Web.UI.Page

    'controls on the form
    Protected txtLoginID As TextBox
    Protected txtPassword As TextBox
    Protected chkRememberMe As CheckBox
    Protected WithEvents btnLogin As HtmlInputButton

    '*************************************************************************
    '
    '   ROUTINE: Page_Load
    '
    '   DESCRIPTION: This routine provides the event handler for the page load
    '                event.  It is responsible for initializing the controls
    '                on the page.
    '-------------------------------------------------------------------------
    Private Sub Page_Load(ByVal sender As System.Object, _
                    ByVal e As System.EventArgs) _
            Handles MyBase.Load
      'Put user code to initialize the page here
    End Sub 'Page_Load

    '*************************************************************************
    '
    '   ROUTINE: btnLogin_ServerClick
    '
    '   DESCRIPTION: This routine provides the event handler for the login
    '                button click event.  It is responsible for authenticating
    '                the user and redirecting to the next page if the user
    '                is authenticated.
    '-------------------------------------------------------------------------
    Private Sub btnLogin_ServerClick(ByVal sender As Object, _
                                ByVal e As System.EventArgs) _
            Handles btnLogin.ServerClick

      'name of querystring parameter containing return URL
      Const QS_RETURN_URL As String = "ReturnURL"

      Dim dbConn As OleDbConnection
      Dim dCmd As OleDbCommand
      Dim dr As OleDbDataReader
      Dim strConnection As String
```

Example 8-7. Login page code-behind (.vb) (continued)

```vb
Dim strSQL As String
Dim nextPage As String
Dim ticket As FormsAuthenticationTicket
Dim cookie As HttpCookie
Dim encryptedStr As String

Try
    'get the connection string from web.config and open a connection
    'to the database
    strConnection = _
        ConfigurationSettings.AppSettings("dbConnectionString")
    dbConn = New OleDb.OleDbConnection(strConnection)
    dbConn.Open( )

    'check to see if the user exists in the database
    strSQL = "SELECT (FirstName + ' ' + LastName) AS UserName, " & _
            "Role " & _
            "FROM AppUser " & _
            "WHERE LoginID=? AND " & _
            "Password=?"
    dCmd = New OleDbCommand(strSQL, dbConn)
    dCmd.Parameters.Add(New OleDbParameter("LoginID", _
                                            txtLoginID.Text))
    dCmd.Parameters.Add(New OleDbParameter("Password", _
                                            txtPassword.Text))
    dr = dCmd.ExecuteReader( )

    If (dr.Read( )) Then
        'user credentials were found in the database so notify the system
        'that the user is authenticated

        'create an authentication ticket for the user with an expiration
        'time of 30 minutes and placing the user's role in the userData
        'property
        ticket = New FormsAuthenticationTicket(1, _
                                        CStr(dr.Item("UserName")), _
                                        DateTime.Now( ), _
                                        DateTime.Now( ).AddMinutes(30), _
                                        chkRememberMe.Checked, _
                                        CStr(dr.Item("Role")))
        encryptedStr = FormsAuthentication.Encrypt(ticket)

        'add the encrypted authentication ticket in the cookies collection
        'and if the cookie is to be persisted, set the expiration for
        '10 years from now.  Otherwise do not set the expiration or the
        'cookie will be created as a persistent cookie.
        cookie = New HttpCookie(FormsAuthentication.FormsCookieName, _
                            encryptedStr)
        If (chkRememberMe.Checked) Then
            cookie.Expires = ticket.IssueDate.AddYears(10)
        End If

        Response.Cookies.Add(cookie)
```

Example 8-7. Login page code-behind (.vb) (continued)

```vb
                'get the next page for the user
                If (Not IsNothing(Request.QueryString(QS_RETURN_URL))) Then
                    'user attempted to access a page without logging in so redirect
                    'them to their originally requested page
                    nextPage = Request.QueryString(QS_RETURN_URL)
                Else
                    'user came straight to the login page so just send them to the
                    'home page
                    nextPage = "Home.aspx"
                End If

                'Redirect user to the next page
                'NOTE: This must be a Response.Redirect to write the cookie to the
                '      user's browser.  Do NOT change to Server.Transfer which
                '      does not cause around trip to the client browser and thus
                '      will not write the authentication cookie to the client
                '      browser.
                Response.Redirect(nextPage, True)
            Else
                'user credentials do not exist in the database - in a production
                'application this should output an error message telling the user
                'that the login ID or password was incorrect
            End If

        Finally
            'cleanup
            If (Not IsNothing(dr)) Then
                dr.Close()
            End If

            If (Not IsNothing(dbConn)) Then
                dbConn.Close()
            End If
        End Try
    End Sub  'btnLogin_ServerClick
  End Class  'Login
End Namespace
```

Example 8-8. Login page code-behind (.cs)

```csharp
//----------------------------------------------------------------------------
//
//    Module Name: Login.aspx.cs
//
//    Description: This module provides the code behind for the
//                 Login.aspx page
//
//****************************************************************************
using System;
using System.Configuration;
using System.Data;
using System.Data.OleDb;
```

Example 8-8. Login page code-behind (.cs) (continued)

```
using System.Web;
using System.Web.Security;
using System.Web.UI.WebControls;
using System.Web.UI.HtmlControls;

namespace ASPNetCookbook.CSSecurity83
{
  public class Login : System.Web.UI.Page
  {
    // controls on the form
    protected System.Web.UI.WebControls.TextBox txtLoginID;
    protected System.Web.UI.WebControls.TextBox txtPassword;
    protected System.Web.UI.WebControls.CheckBox chkRememberMe;
    protected System.Web.UI.HtmlControls.HtmlInputButton btnLogin;

    //*************************************************************************
    //
    //   ROUTINE: Page_Load
    //
    //   DESCRIPTION: This routine provides the event handler for the page
    //                load event.  It is responsible for initializing the
    //                controls on the page.
    //-------------------------------------------------------------------------
    private void Page_Load(object sender, System.EventArgs e)
    {
      // wire the login button
      this.btnLogin.ServerClick += new EventHandler(this.btnLogin_ServerClick);
    }  // Page_Load

    //*************************************************************************
    //
    //   ROUTINE: btnLogin_ServerClick
    //
    //   DESCRIPTION: This routine provides the event handler for the login
    //                button click event.  It is responsible for
    //                authenticating the user and redirecting to the next
    //                page if the user is authenticated.
    //-------------------------------------------------------------------------
    private void btnLogin_ServerClick(Object sender,
                                      System.EventArgs e)
    {
      // name of querystring parameter containing return URL
      const String QS_RETURN_URL = "ReturnURL";

      OleDbConnection dbConn = null;
      OleDbCommand dCmd = null;
      OleDbDataReader dr = null;
      String strConnection = null;
      String strSQL = null;
      String nextPage = null;
      FormsAuthenticationTicket ticket = null;
      HttpCookie cookie = null;
```

Example 8-8. Login page code-behind (.cs) (continued)

```
String encryptedStr = null;

try
{
  // get the connection string from web.config and open a connection
  // to the database
  strConnection =
    ConfigurationSettings.AppSettings["dbConnectionString"];
  dbConn = new OleDbConnection(strConnection);
  dbConn.Open( );

  // check to see if the user exists in the database
  strSQL = "SELECT (FirstName + ' ' + LastName) AS UserName, " +
           "Role " +
           "FROM AppUser " +
           "WHERE LoginID=? AND " +
           "Password=?";
  dCmd = new OleDbCommand(strSQL, dbConn);
  dCmd.Parameters.Add(new OleDbParameter("LoginID",
                                         txtLoginID.Text));
  dCmd.Parameters.Add(new OleDbParameter("Password",
                                         txtPassword.Text));
  dr = dCmd.ExecuteReader( );

  if (dr.Read( ))
  {
    // user credentials were found in the database so notify the system
    // that the user is authenticated

    // create an authentication ticket for the user with an expiration
    // time of 30 minutes and placing the user's role in the userData
    // property
    ticket = new FormsAuthenticationTicket(1,
                                           (String)(dr["UserName"]),
                                           DateTime.Now,
                                           DateTime.Now.AddMinutes(30),
                                           chkRememberMe.Checked,
                                           (String)(dr["Role"]));
    encryptedStr = FormsAuthentication.Encrypt(ticket);

    // add the encrypted authentication ticket in the cookies collection
    // and if the cookie is to be persisted, set the expiration for
    // 10 years from now.  Otherwise do not set the expiration or the
    // cookie will be created as a persistent cookie.
    cookie = new HttpCookie(FormsAuthentication.FormsCookieName,
                            encryptedStr);
    if (chkRememberMe.Checked)
    {
      cookie.Expires = ticket.IssueDate.AddYears(10);
    }

    Response.Cookies.Add(cookie);
```

Example 8-8. Login page code-behind (.cs) (continued)

```
        // get the next page for the user
        if (Request.QueryString[QS_RETURN_URL] != null)
        {
          // user attempted to access a page without logging in so redirect
          // them to their originally requested page
          nextPage = Request.QueryString[QS_RETURN_URL];
        }
        else
        {
          // user came straight to the login page so just send them to the
          // home page
          nextPage = "Home.aspx";
        }

        // Redirect user to the next page
        // NOTE: This must be a Response.Redirect to write the cookie to
        //       the user's browser.  Do NOT change to Server.Transfer
        //       which does not cause around trip to the client browser
        //       and thus will not write the authentication cookie to the
        //       client browser.
        Response.Redirect(nextPage, true);
      }
      else
      {
        // user credentials do not exist in the database - in a production
        //application this should output an error message telling the user
        // that the login ID or password was incorrect.
      }
    } // try

    finally
    {
      // cleanup
      if (dr != null)
      {
        dr.Close();
      }

      if (dbConn != null)
      {
        dbConn.Close();
      }
    } // finally
  } // btnLogin_ServerClick
} // Login
}
```

Example 8-9. Application_AuthenticateRequest method in global.asax.vb

```
Sub Application_AuthenticateRequest(ByVal sender As Object, _
                                    ByVal e As EventArgs)
  Dim roles As String
  Dim identity As FormsIdentity
```

```vb
    If (Context.Request.IsAuthenticated) Then
      If (Context.User.Identity.AuthenticationType = "Forms") Then
        'get the comma delimited list of roles from the user data
        'in the authentication ticket
        identity = CType(Context.User.Identity, FormsIdentity)
        roles = identity.Ticket.UserData

        'create a new user principal object with the current user identity
        'and the roles assigned to the user
        Context.User = New GenericPrincipal(identity, _
                                            roles.Split(","))
      Else
        'application is improperly configured so throw an exception
        Throw New ApplicationException("Application Must Be Configured For
 Forms Authentication")
      End If  'If (Context.User.Identity.AuthenticationType = "Forms")
    End If  'If (Context.Request.IsAuthenticated)
  End Sub  'Application_AuthenticateRequest
```

Example 8-10. Application_AuthenticateRequest method in global.asax.cs

```csharp
    protected void Application_AuthenticateRequest(Object sender, EventArgs e)
    {
      String roles = null;
      FormsIdentity identity = null;

      if (Context.Request.IsAuthenticated)
      {
        if (Context.User.Identity.AuthenticationType == "Forms")
        {
          // get the comma delimited list of roles from the user data
          // in the authentication ticket
          identity = (FormsIdentity)(Context.User.Identity);
          roles = identity.Ticket.UserData;

          // create a new user principal object with the current user identity
          // and the roles assigned to the user
          Context.User = new GenericPrincipal(identity,
                                              roles.Split(','));
        }
        else
        {
          // application is improperly configured so throw an exception
          throw new ApplicationException("Application Must Be Configured For
 Forms Authentication");
        }  // if (Context.User.Identity.AuthenticationType = "Forms")
      }  // if (Context.Request.IsAuthenticated)
    }  // Application_AuthenticateRequest
```

8.4   Using Windows Authentication

Problem

You want to use existing Windows network accounts for authenticating users of your application.

Solution

Configure IIS to block anonymous access and to require Windows integrated authentication.

Make the following changes to *web.config*:

1. Specify Windows authentication:

    ```
    <authentication mode="Windows" />
    ```

2. Set the `<identity>` element to impersonate:

    ```
    <identity impersonate="true" userName="" password="" />
    ```

3. Configure the `<authorization>` element to deny access to all users:

    ```
    <authorization>
        <deny users="*" /> <!-- Deny all users -->
    </authorization>
    ```

4. Add a `<location>` element for each page to which you want to control access with an `<allow>` child element and attribute (to allow access to the page by certain roles) followed by a `<deny>` child element and attribute (to deny access to all users not listed in the previous roles):

    ```
    <location path="DisplayUserInformation.aspx">
      <system.web>
        <authorization>
          <allow roles="BuiltIn\Users,
                        BuiltIn\Administrators"/>
          <deny users="*"/>
        </authorization>
      </system.web>
    </location>
    ```

In the code-behind class for the ASP.NET page, get the current user's identity and check the user's roles using the `identity` property from the current context:

VB
```
identity = CType(Context.User.Identity, WindowsIdentity)
```

C#
```
identity = (WindowsIdentity)(Context.User.Identity);
```

The code we've implemented to illustrate this solution appears in Examples 8-11 through 8-14. Example 8-11 shows the Windows authentication and role settings in *web.config* for the sample ASP.NET page. Example 8-12 shows the Windows authentication sample *.aspx* file. The code-behind class for the page appears in Example 8-13

(VB) and Example 8-14 (C#). Figure 8-2 shows the Windows authentication dialog box, and Figure 8-3 shows a sample page produced by the application.

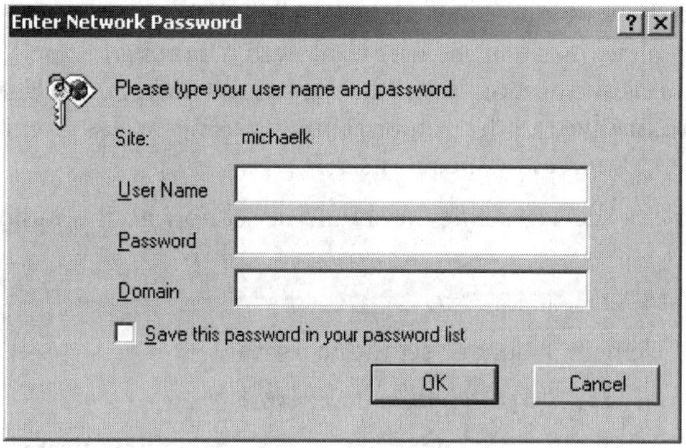

Figure 8-2. Windows authentication dialog box

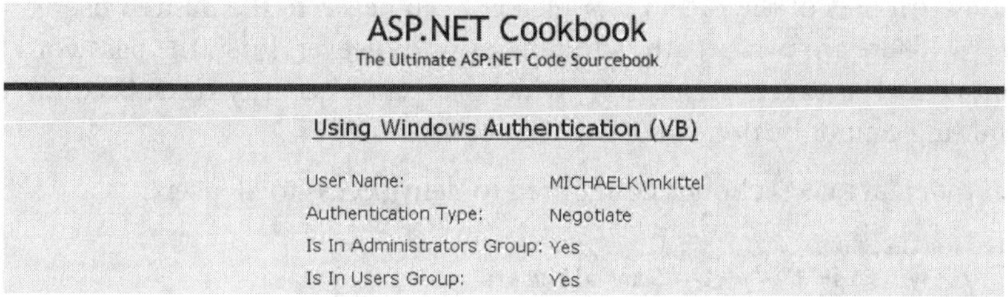

Figure 8-3. Windows authentication sample page

Discussion

Windows authentication is a useful means of authenticating users of web applications that run on an intranet. Windows authentication allows you to assume that each user already has a valid Windows account with appropriate permissions for accessing the network resources. This is an advantage to you as a web application developer because it saves you having to maintain all this information separately in your application.

The setup required for using Windows authentication is very similar to the setup performed for Forms authentication. The big difference is the role IIS plays in the authentication. To support Forms authentication, IIS is configured to allow anonymous access. In other words, IIS does not perform any authentication, leaving the task of authenticating and authorizing users to ASP.NET. (See Recipe 8.1 for more on Forms authentication.)

For Windows authentication, IIS must be configured to block anonymous access and must be configured to use either Windows integrated authentication or basic authentication. We recommend Windows integrated authentication because this method does not send the user password over the network in clear text. With Windows authentication, IIS verifies that the user is allowed to access the application, and then ASP.NET performs the authorization for the requested resource. The operating system can also be involved in the authorization by using Access Control Lists (ACLs) to limit access to resources by specific users.

After setting up IIS, the *web.config* file should be set up with the authentication mode set to Windows:

```
<authentication mode="Windows" />
```

The <identity> element should be set to impersonate:

```
<identity impersonate="true" userName="" password="" />
```

This configures ASP.NET to impersonate the user authenticated by IIS for all resource requests when the userName and password are empty strings. If you want all requests to use a different account than IIS used for authentication, the userName and password attributes of the <identity> element can be set to the desired username and password. There are two negatives to doing this, however. First, the password for the account is in clear text in *web.config*, which can cause security risks. Second, logging and auditing cannot be done on a per-user basis.

The <authorization> section is configured to deny access to all users:

```
<authorization>
    <deny users="*" /> <!-- Deny all users -->
</authorization>
```

This is done because <location> elements will be added to define the authorizations for each page.

To control the access to each page, add a <location> element. This provides the maximum flexibility in controlling access to each page in your application. When using Windows authentication, roles are synonymous with groups. Therefore, the <allow> element should contain the list of groups (roles) allowed to access the given page. The <deny users="*"/> element should always be provided after the <allow> element to deny access to all users not listed in the previous roles. For example:

```
<location path="DisplayUserInformation.aspx">
  <system.web>
    <authorization>
      <allow roles="BuiltIn\Users,
                    BuiltIn\Administrators"/>
      <deny users="*"/>
    </authorization>
  </system.web>
</location>
```

Group (role) names must be fully qualified. When using local "built-in" groups such as Users and Administrators, the fully qualified name is "BuiltIn\Users" and "BuiltIn\Administrators". When using groups you have created, you must include the computer name, such as "<MyComputer>\Testers". When using domain groups, you must include the domain name, such as "<DomainName>\Testers".

As described in Recipe 8.2, you can also place pages with the same access requirements in folders and include a <location> element defining the access to the folders. See Recipes 8.2 and 8.3 for more information on using folders in this way, including a discussion of the pros and cons of various folder-related approaches.

No other code is required in your application to implement Windows authentication.

You can access the user credentials in your application by using the identity property from the current context. Because Windows authentication is being used and more information is available for the user than is available using Forms authentication, the identity property should be cast as a WindowsIdentity type to access these additional properties:

VB
```
identity = CType(Context.User.Identity, WindowsIdentity)
```

C#
```
identity = (WindowsIdentity)(Context.User.Identity);
```

When using Windows authentication, the client browser, IIS, and Windows perform many functions behind the scenes. If you access the application from the same machine or from a machine in the same domain, you may not be prompted to enter your username and password. This is caused by the browser automatically sending your credentials when the challenge is issued by IIS. Whether or not this happens is a function of the requested URL, how IIS is configured, and how your browser is configured. The details of this configuration are beyond the scope of this book. If you're interested in this topic, consult your network administrator; she is likely to know all the fine points.

See Also

Recipe 8.1; Recipe 8.2; Recipe 8.3; MSDN documentation for IIS setup (search for "IIS authentication")

Example 8-11. web.config for Windows authentication

```
<?xml version="1.0" encoding="utf-8" ?>
<configuration>
  <system.web>

    ..
```

Example 8-11. web.config for Windows authentication (continued)

```
<authentication mode="Windows" />
<identity impersonate="true" />
<authorization>
    <deny users="*" /> <!-- Deny all users -->
</authorization>

  ..

<!--
******************************************************************************
      The following section defines the pages in the application and the
      roles (groups) that are allowed to access them.  Any group defined
      in Windows can be used.  NOTE: The groups must be the fully
      qualified names such as BuiltIn\Administrators, etc.
******************************************************************************
-->
<location path="DisplayUserInformation.aspx">
  <system.web>
    <authorization>
      <allow roles="BuiltIn\Users,
                    BuiltIn\Administrators"/>
      <deny users="*"/>
    </authorization>
  </system.web>
</location>

</configuration>
```

Example 8-12. Windows authentication sample page (.aspx)

```
<%@ Page Language="vb" AutoEventWireup="false"
        Codebehind="DisplayUserInformation.aspx.vb"
        Inherits="ASPNetCookbook.VBSecurity84.DisplayUserInformation" %>
<!DOCTYPE HTML PUBLIC "-//W3C//DTD HTML 4.0 Transitional//EN">
<html>
  <head>
    <title>DisplayUserInformation</title>
    <link rel="stylesheet" href="css/ASPNetCookbook.css">
  </head>
  <body leftmargin="0" marginheight="0" marginwidth="0" topmargin="0">
    <form id="frmSecurity" method="post" runat="server">
      <table width="100%" cellpadding="0" cellspacing="0" border="0">
        <tr>
          <td align="center">
            <img src="images/ASPNETCookbookHeading_blue.gif">
          </td>
        </tr>
        <tr>
          <td class="dividerLine">
            <img src="images/spacer.gif" height="6" border="0"></td>
        </tr>
```

Example 8-12. Windows authentication sample page (.aspx) (continued)

```
      </table>
      <table width="90%" align="center" border="0">
        <tr>
          <td><img src="images/spacer.gif" height="10" border="0"></td>
        </tr>
        <tr>
          <td align="center" class="PageHeading">
            Using Windows Authentication (VB)
          </td>
        </tr>
        <tr>
          <td><img src="images/spacer.gif" height="10" border="0"></td>
        </tr>
        <tr>
          <td align="center">
            <table>
              <tr>
                <td class="LabelText">User Name: </td>
                <td>
                  <asp:Label ID="txtUserName" Runat="server"
                              CssClass="LabelText" />
                </td>
              </tr>
              <tr>
                <td class="LabelText">Authentication Type: </td>
                <td>
                  <asp:Label ID="txtAuthenticationType" Runat="server"
                              CssClass="LabelText" />
                </td>
              </tr>
              <tr>
                <td class="LabelText">Is In Administrators Group: </td>
                <td>
                  <asp:Label ID="txtAdminGroup" Runat="server"
                              CssClass="LabelText" />
                </td>
              </tr>
              <tr>
                <td class="LabelText">Is In Users Group: </td>
                <td>
                  <asp:Label ID="txtUsersGroup" Runat="server"
                              CssClass="LabelText" />
                </td>
              </tr>
            </table>
          </td>
        </tr>
      </table>
    </form>
  </body>
</html>
```

Example 8-13. Windows authentication sample page code-behind (.vb)

```vb
Option Explicit On
Option Strict On
'-----------------------------------------------------------------------------
'
'   Module Name: DisplayUserInformation.aspx.vb
'
'   Description: This module provides the code behind for the
'                DisplayUserInformation.aspx page
'
'*****************************************************************************
Imports System.Security.Principal

Namespace ASPNetCookbook.VBSecurity84
  Public Class DisplayUserInformation
    Inherits System.Web.UI.Page

    'controls on the form
    Protected txtUserName As System.Web.UI.WebControls.Label
    Protected txtAuthenticationType As System.Web.UI.WebControls.Label
    Protected txtAdminGroup As System.Web.UI.WebControls.Label
    Protected txtUsersGroup As System.Web.UI.WebControls.Label

    '*****************************************************************************
    '
    '   ROUTINE: Page_Load
    '
    '   DESCRIPTION: This routine provides the event handler for the page load
    '                event.  It is responsible for initializing the controls
    '                on the page.
    '-----------------------------------------------------------------------------
    Private Sub Page_Load(ByVal sender As System.Object, _
                          ByVal e As System.EventArgs) _
              Handles MyBase.Load

        Dim identity As WindowsIdentity

        'get the current user's identity
        identity = CType(Context.User.Identity, WindowsIdentity)

        'output the user's name and authentication type
        txtUserName.Text = identity.Name
        txtAuthenticationType.Text = identity.AuthenticationType

        'check to see if the user is a member of the administators group
        If (Context.User.IsInRole("BuiltIn\Administrators")) Then
          txtAdminGroup.Text = "Yes"
        Else
          txtAdminGroup.Text = "No"
        End If
```

Example 8-13. Windows authentication sample page code-behind (.vb) (continued)

```
      'check to see if the user is a member of the users group
      If (Context.User.IsInRole("BuiltIn\Users")) Then
        txtUsersGroup.Text = "Yes"
      Else
        txtUsersGroup.Text = "No"
      End If
    End Sub    'Page_Load
  End Class    'DisplayUserInformation
End Namespace
```

Example 8-14. Windows authentication sample page code-behind (.cs)

```
//---------------------------------------------------------------------------
//
//    Module Name: DisplayUserInformation.aspx.cs
//
//    Description: This module provides the code behind for the
//                 DisplayUserInformation.aspx page
//
//***************************************************************************
using System;
using System.Security.Principal;

namespace ASPNetCookbook.CSSecurity84
{
  public class DisplayUserInformation : System.Web.UI.Page
  {
    // controls on the form
    protected System.Web.UI.WebControls.Label txtUserName ;
    protected System.Web.UI.WebControls.Label txtAuthenticationType;
    protected System.Web.UI.WebControls.Label txtAdminGroup;
    protected System.Web.UI.WebControls.Label txtUsersGroup ;

    //***********************************************************************
    //
    //    ROUTINE: Page_Load
    //
    //    DESCRIPTION: This routine provides the event handler for the page
    //                 load event.  It is responsible for initializing the
    //                 controls on the page.
    //---------------------------------------------------------------------
    private void Page_Load(object sender, System.EventArgs e)
    {
      WindowsIdentity identity = null;

      // get the current user's identity
      identity = (WindowsIdentity)(Context.User.Identity);

      // output the user's name and authentication type
      txtUserName.Text = identity.Name;
      txtAuthenticationType.Text = identity.AuthenticationType;
```

Example 8-14. Windows authentication sample page code-behind (.cs) (continued)

```csharp
      // check to see if the user is a member of the administators group
      if (Context.User.IsInRole("BuiltIn\\Administrators"))
      {
        txtAdminGroup.Text = "Yes";
      }
      else
      {
        txtAdminGroup.Text = "No";
      }

      // check to see if the user is a member of the users group
      if (Context.User.IsInRole("BuiltIn\\Users"))
      {
        txtUsersGroup.Text = "Yes";
      }
      else
      {
        txtUsersGroup.Text = "No";
      }
    }  // Page_Load
  }  // DisplayUserInformation
}
```

CHAPTER 9

Configuration

9.0 Introduction

ASP.NET provides a convenient, extensible, XML-based mechanism for configuring ASP.NET and applications that run under it. It is a great improvement over the IIS metabase that was awkward to change, required IIS to be restarted, and was not easily replicated on additional servers. By contrast, ASP.NET automatically detects changes to the *web.config* file and transparently restarts the application; there is no need to restart IIS. And replicating an ASP.NET application configuration is as simple as copying the *web.config* file to the new server.

Configuration File Hierarchy

ASP.NET uses a hierarchy of configuration files. The *machine.config* file contains the settings for the server and is located in the *%SystemRoot%\Microsoft.NET\Framework\%VersionNumber%\CONFIG* folder. You can create *web.config* files to configure each of your applications, overriding the settings in *machine.config*. When you create a new ASP.NET web application project, Visual Studio .NET automatically creates a *web.config* file for you in the root directory of the application, which you can modify as required. Folders within the application can also have *web.config* files to customize the configuration of portions of the application.

Structure and Use of web.config

The basic structure of *web.config* has a format similar to *machine.config*. The idea is that you add to *web.config* only those entries for which you want to override settings in *machine.config*. At a minimum, *web.config* must have a <configuration> element and a child element, such as a <system.web> element. The following is a minimal *web.config* file:

```
<?xml version="1.0" encoding="utf-8" ?>
<configuration>
  <system.web>
```

```
      </system.web>
   </configuration>
```

The `<configuration>` and `<system.web>` elements don't do anything special other than to provide the structure for other settings you want to add. By using child elements of these default configuration elements in *web.config*, you can, for example, change the ASP.NET HTTP runtime settings, store key/value pairs in the `<appSettings>` section of *web.config*, and add elements of your own to *web.config*. The recipes in this chapter will show you how to do all these things and more.

Modifying web.config

The *web.config* file is simply an XML file and can be edited with any text editor. As with most XML, the structure of the *web.config* file must conform to a defined schema (in this case, the schema is detailed in the Microsoft documentation). The *web.config* must also be a properly formed XML document. In other words, elements must be placed in the correct sections of the XML document and conform to the case style and exact spelling defined in the schema. If a *web.config* file deviates from the schema in any detail, ASP.NET will throw a parsing error exception.

Dealing with Parse Errors in Debug Mode

Parse errors stemming from the *web.config* file can be confusing when you are running the application in debug mode in Visual Studio. When a parse error occurs, you are typically presented with the message box shown in Figure 9-1, which asks if you want to disable future debugging for this application. You should click No and run the application without debugging, which will tell you exactly what is wrong with *web.config*. If you accidentally click Yes, you will need to re-enable debugging for your application. You can re-enable debugging by doing the following:

1. Select your project in Solution Explorer.
2. Open the property dialog box for the project, either by right-clicking on the project and selecting Properties or by selecting Properties from the project menu.
3. Select "Configuration Properties."
4. Select "Debugging."
5. In the "Debuggers" section, set "Enable ASP.NET Debugging" to True.

This chapter does not attempt to address all of the configuration settings available in *machine.config* and *web.config*. Rather, it provides information on many commonly used features and several that are not well documented. Many other configuration parameters related to security and HTTP handlers are addressed in Chapters 8 and 17, respectively.

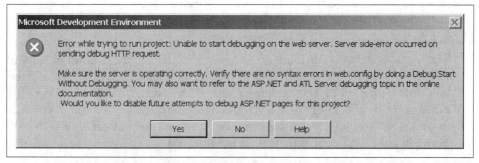

Microsoft Development Environment

Error while trying to run project: Unable to start debugging on the web server. Server side-error occurred on sending debug HTTP request.

Make sure the server is operating correctly. Verify there are no syntax errors in web.config by doing a Debug.Start Without Debugging. You may also want to refer to the ASP.NET and ATL Server debugging topic in the online documentation.
Would you like to disable future attempts to debug ASP.NET pages for this project?

Yes   No   Help

Figure 9-1. Error message displayed with web.config parse errors in debug mode

9.1   Overriding Default HTTP Runtime Parameters in web.config

Problem

You want to change the default HTTP runtime settings for your application, such as the execution timeout setting.

Solution

Modify the *web.config* file by adding ASP.NET HTTP runtime settings to it.

1. Locate the *web.config* file in the root directory of your application (or create one if it does not already exist).

2. Add an `<httpRuntime>` element and set the executionTimeout and other attributes required for your application:

```
<?xml version="1.0" encoding="utf-8" ?>
<configuration>
  <system.web>
    <httpRuntime executionTimeout="90"
                 maxRequestLength="4096"
                 useFullyQualifiedRedirectUrl="false" />
  </system.web>
</configuration>
```

Discussion

It can be useful to modify the default HTTP runtime settings in *web.config* so that users of your application can upload large files, for example. But another, perhaps more important, motivation for this recipe is to demonstrate in a fairly unobtrusive way how you can easily override the predefined settings for your application by adding elements, such as the `<httpRuntime>` element, to the default *web.config* file that Visual Studio .NET creates.

The following is a description of the attributes we've used with the <httpRuntime> element, which are the most commonly used attributes:

executionTimeout

The executionTimeout attribute of <httpRuntime> defines the maximum amount of time in seconds that a request is allowed to run before it is automatically terminated by ASP.NET. The default value is 90 seconds. If your application has requests that take longer, such as a long-running database query, you can increase the value. The value can be any positive integer value (1 to 2,147,483,647), but large numbers are not practical.

maxRequestLength

The maxRequestLength attribute defines the maximum size of a file that can be uploaded by the application. The value is in KB and has a default value of 4096 (4MB). If your application needs to support uploading files larger than 4MB, you can change the value as required. The valid range is 0 to 2,147,483,647.

 Denial-of-service attacks can be launched by initiating the upload of many large files simultaneously. Therefore, the maxRequestLength should be set as small as possible to meet the needs of your application.

useFullyQualifiedRedirectUrl

The useFullyQualifiedRedirectUrl attribute is a flag indicating whether fully qualified URLs should be used when ASP.NET performs a redirection. Setting the value to false (the default) configures ASP.NET to use relative URLs (e.g., */ASPNetCookbook/ProblemMenu.aspx*) for client redirects. Setting the value to true configures ASP.NET to use fully qualified URLs (e.g., *http://localhost/ASPNetCookbook/ProblemMenu.aspx*) for all client redirects. If you are working with mobile applications, be aware that some devices require fully qualified URLs.

The <httpRuntime> element contains other attributes, including those that provide control over threads used by your application and the number of requests that are allowed to be queued before requests are rejected. Consult the Microsoft documentation on the <httpRuntime> element for full details of these attributes.

See Also

MSDN documentation on the httpRuntime element (search for "httpRuntime element")

9.2 Adding Custom Application Settings in web.config

Problem

You have custom configuration information for your application that you would like to store in its *web.config* file.

Solution

Modify the *web.config* file for your application by adding an `<appSettings>` section to contain the custom configuration settings.

1. Locate the *web.config* file in the root directory of your application (or create one if it does not already exist).
2. Add an `<appSettings>` element.
3. Add `<add>` child elements along with key/value pairs to the `<appSettings>` element as required.
4. In the code-behind class for your ASP.NET page, use the .NET language of your choice to access the `<appSettings>` key/value collection through the `ConfigurationSettings` object.

Examples 9-1 through 9-4 show the sample code we've written to implement this solution. Example 9-1 shows our *web.config* file with some key/value pairs. Example 9-2 shows the *.aspx* file for a web form that displays the configuration settings. Example 9-3 (VB) and Example 9-4 (C#) show the code-behind class that accesses the configuration settings using the `ConfigurationSettings` object.

Discussion

ASP.NET lets you add and then access configuration information specific to your application to the *web.config* file by means of a special `<appSettings>` element. You can add application configuration information by adding an `<add>` child element for each parameter, setting the key attribute to the name of the configuration parameter, and then setting the value attribute to the value of the configuration parameter, as shown in Example 9-1.

Notice that the `<appSettings>` element is not a child of `<system.web>`, like some of the other *web.config* elements we discuss in this chapter. Rather, it is a subsection all its own within the `<configuration>` section.

When your application is started, ASP.NET creates a `NameValueCollection` from the key/value pairs in the `<appSettings>` section. You can access this `NameValueCollection` anywhere in your application through the `ConfigurationSettings` object. Any data that can be represented as a string can be stored in the <appSettings> section, but anything other than a string will need to be cast to the appropriate data type for use in your application.

 web.config allows any string for the value of a key/value pair. If the data is actually any nonstring data type, your code needs to include the appropriate exception handling for invalid data in the *web.config* file.

See Also

Recipe 9.6 for how to store an application's configuration information in its own custom section in *web.config*

Example 9-1. Application settings in web.config

```
<?xml version="1.0" encoding="utf-8" ?>
<configuration>

  <appSettings>
    <add key="defaultSortField" value="Title" />
    <add key="defaultSortOrder" value="Ascending" />
    <add key="defaultResultsPerPage" value="25" />
  </appSettings>

</configuration>
```

Example 9-2. Accessing application settings in web.config (.aspx)

```
<%@ Page Language="vb" AutoEventWireup="false"
        Codebehind="CH09GetAppSettingsVB.aspx.vb"
        Inherits="ASPNetCookbook.VBExamples.CH09GetAppSettingsVB"%>
<!DOCTYPE HTML PUBLIC "-//W3C//DTD HTML 4.0 Transitional//EN">
<html>
  <head>
    <title>Get Application Settings</title>
    <link rel="stylesheet" href="css/ASPNetCookbook.css">
  </head>
  <body leftmargin="0" marginheight="0" marginwidth="0" topmargin="0">
    <form id="frmConfiguration" method="post" runat="server">
      <table width="100%" cellpadding="0" cellspacing="0" border="0">
        <tr>
          <td align="center">
            <img src="images/ASPNETCookbookHeading_blue.gif">
          </td>
        </tr>
        <tr>
          <td class="dividerLine">
            <img src="images/spacer.gif" height="6" border="0"></td>
        </tr>
      </table>
```

Example 9-2. Accessing application settings in web.config (.aspx) (continued)

```
      <table width="90%" align="center" border="0">
        <tr>
          <td><img src="images/spacer.gif" height="10" border="0"></td>
        </tr>
        <tr>
          <td align="center" class="PageHeading">
            Application Configuration In web.config (VB)
          </td>
        </tr>
        <tr>
          <td><img src="images/spacer.gif" height="10" border="0"></td>
        </tr>
        <tr>
          <td align="center">
            <table>
              <tr>
                <td class="LabelText">Sort Field: </td>
                <td class="LabelText">
                  <asp:Label ID="labSortField" Runat="server" /></td>
              </tr>
              <tr>
                <td class="LabelText">Sort Order: </td>
                <td class="LabelText">
                  <asp:Label ID="labSortOrder" Runat="server" /></td>
              </tr>
              <tr>
                <td class="LabelText">Number of Pages: </td>
                <td class="LabelText">
                  <asp:Label ID="labNumberOfPages" Runat="server" /></td>
              </tr>
            </table>
          </td>
        </tr>
      </table>
    </form>
  </body>
</html>
```

Example 9-3. Accessing application settings in web.config (.vb)

```
Option Explicit On
Option Strict On
'-----------------------------------------------------------------------------
'
'   Module Name: CH09GetAppSettingsVB.aspx.vb
'
'   Description: This module provides the code behind for the
'                CH09GetAppSettingsVB.aspx page
'
'*****************************************************************************
Imports System
Imports System.Configuration
```

Example 9-3. Accessing application settings in web.config (.vb) (continued)

```vb
Namespace ASPNetCookbook.VBExamples
  Public Class CH09GetAppSettingsVB
    Inherits System.Web.UI.Page

    'controls on the form
    Protected labSortField As System.Web.UI.WebControls.Label
    Protected labSortOrder As System.Web.UI.WebControls.Label
    Protected labNumberOfPages As System.Web.UI.WebControls.Label

    '*************************************************************************
    '
    '   ROUTINE: Page_Load
    '
    '   DESCRIPTION: This routine provides the event handler for the page load
    '               event.  It is responsible for initializing the controls
    '               on the page.
    '-------------------------------------------------------------------------
    Private Sub Page_Load(ByVal sender As System.Object, _
                          ByVal e As System.EventArgs) Handles MyBase.Load

      Dim resultsPerPage As Integer

      'initialize labels on form from values in web.config
      labSortField.Text = ConfigurationSettings.AppSettings("defaultSortField")
      labSortOrder.Text = ConfigurationSettings.AppSettings("defaultSortOrder")

      'get an integer value from web.config and do a little calculating
      resultsPerPage = _
        CInt(ConfigurationSettings.AppSettings("defaultResultsPerPage"))
      labNumberOfPages.Text = Math.Ceiling(1234.0 / resultsPerPage).ToString()
    End Sub  'Page_Load
  End Class  'CH09GetAppSettingsVB
End Namespace
```

Example 9-4. Accessing application settings in web.config (.cs)

```csharp
//---------------------------------------------------------------------------
//
//   Module Name: CH09GetAppSettingsCS.aspx.cs
//
//   Description: This module provides the code behind for the
//               CH09GetAppSettingsCS.aspx page
//
//*************************************************************************
using System;
using System.Configuration;

namespace ASPNetCookbook.CSExamples
{
  public class CH09GetAppSettingsCS : System.Web.UI.Page
  {
    // controls on the form
    protected System.Web.UI.WebControls.Label labSortField;
```

```
    protected System.Web.UI.WebControls.Label labSortOrder;
    protected System.Web.UI.WebControls.Label labNumberOfPages;

    //**********************************************************************
    //
    //   ROUTINE: Page_Load
    //
    //   DESCRIPTION: This routine provides the event handler for the page
    //                load event.  It is responsible for initializing the
    //                controls on the page.
    //----------------------------------------------------------------------
    private void Page_Load(object sender, System.EventArgs e)
    {
      int resultsPerPage;

      // initialize labels on form from values in web.config
      labSortField.Text =
        ConfigurationSettings.AppSettings["defaultSortField"];
      labSortOrder.Text =
        ConfigurationSettings.AppSettings["defaultSortOrder"];

      // get an integer value from web.config and do a little calculating
      resultsPerPage =
  Convert.ToInt32(ConfigurationSettings.AppSettings["defaultResultsPerPage"]);
      labNumberOfPages.Text = Math.Ceiling(1234.0 / resultsPerPage).ToString();
    }  // Page_Load
  }  // CH09GetAppSettingsCS
}
```

9.3   Displaying Custom Error Messages

Problem

You want to replace the generic messages ASP.NET displays whenever an application error occurs with your own custom error messages.

Solution

Create a *web.config* file, add the custom errors element to it, and then create the custom error pages.

1. Locate the *web.config* file in the root directory of your application (or create one if it does not already exist).

2. Add a <customErrors> element to the *web.config* file and add an <error> child element for each custom error page you want to display.

3. Create the custom error pages.

Example 9-5 shows some settings that we've added to a *web.config* file to demonstrate this solution.

Discussion

By default, ASP.NET displays its own error page when any of the standard server errors occurs, such as 401 (access denied), 404 (page not found), or 500 (internal server error). But a default ASP.NET error page will not match the look and feel of your application and may not provide the information you want to convey to your users. ASP.NET provides the ability, via the *web.config* file, to output your own custom error pages. A similar capability is available in IIS, but customizing the *web.config* file is much simpler. Also, because the customization is done in the *web.config* file, moving it to another server is as simple as copying the *web.config* file and the custom error pages to the new location.

First, add a <customErrors> element to your *web.config* file as a child of <system.web>. The mode attribute defines when and where the custom error pages are displayed. Set the mode to RemoteOnly to have the custom error pages displayed only when accessing the application from a remote machine. When set to RemoteOnly, the ASP.NET error pages will not be displayed when accessing the application from the local machine. Set the mode to On to have the custom error messages displayed on local and remote machines. Set the mode to Off to display the ASP.NET error messages on local and remote machines.

Next, add an error element for each server error that you want to redirect to a custom error page. Set the statusCode attribute to the server error code, and set the redirect attribute to the URL of the page to be displayed when the error occurs. You can include parameters in the URL if desired.

When the error is a 404 error (page not found), for example, ASP.NET includes a parameter in the URL to indicate the name of the requested page that was not found. The URL for the redirection of the 404 error just described would be:

```
http://[server]/ASPNetCookbook/PageNotAvailable.aspx?aspxerrorpath=
    /ASPNetCookbook/BadPage.aspx
```

Your application can use the Request.QueryString collection to retrieve the name of the page that was not found and include the information in your custom page:

VB
```
labMessage.Text = Request.QueryString("aspxerrorpath") & _
                  " Is Not Available On This Site"
```

C#
```
labMessage.Text = Request.QueryString["aspxerrorpath"] +
                  " Is Not Available On This Site";
```

Example 9-5. Custom error settings in web.config

```
<?xml version="1.0" encoding="utf-8" ?>
<configuration>
  <system.web>


    ..


    <customErrors mode="RemoteOnly">
```

Example 9-5. Custom error settings in web.config (continued)

```
    <error statusCode="404" redirect="PageNotAvailable.aspx"/>

    ..

  </customErrors>

  ..

  </system.web>

</configuration>
```

9.4   Maintaining Session State Across Multiple Web Servers

Problem

You need to configure your application to maintain session state across multiple web servers.

Solution

When the data stored in session is easy to recreate or is not critical, configure your application to use the ASP.NET State Service using the following steps:

1. Set up a new server with the .NET Framework installed to maintain session state on behalf of your application.

2. Start the ASP.NET State Service on the designated machine.

3. Modify the mode attribute of the <sessionState> element of the application *web.config* file on its current web server to specify the ASP.NET State Service.

4. Copy the contents of the root folder and subfolders of your application on the current web server to the additional web servers.

When it is critical to not lose any session information if server problems arise, use SQL Server to store all session information, as follows:

1. In the instance of SQL Server that you will use for this purpose, install the special tables and stored procedures that ASP.NET requires by running the InstallSqlState.sql script provided with the .NET Framework.

2. Set up a database user with read/write access to the tempDB database.

3. Modify the *web.config* file, as shown next, setting the IP address to the address of your SQL Server machine and replacing *user* and *pwd* with the settings for the database user with read/write access to the tempDB database.

```
    <sessionState
        mode="SQLServer"
```

```
        sqlConnectionString="data source=10.0.1.12;user id=user;password=pwd"
        cookieless="false"
        timeout="20" />
```

Discussion

ASP.NET provides in-process session management much like classic ASP. However, scaling to multiple servers in classic ASP has always been difficult because session information is not shared between ASP servers. There are ways to solve the problem in classic ASP but none is easy and code changes are generally required when you move to a multiple-server configuration.

ASP.NET provides two methods for managing session state when you decide to deploy a web application on multiple servers: the ASP.NET State Service and support for session state storage in SQL Server.

The ASP.NET State Service is an out-of-process, memory-based session management service that is intended to be used when the data stored in session is easy to recreate or is not critical. The SQL Server–based session management uses SQL Server to store all session information and is intended to be used when it is critical to not lose any session information if server problems arise. As you might expect, the performance of SQL Server in maintaining session state management is not as good as that of the ASP.NET State Service, due to the overhead involved in querying and writing session information in a database. The ASP.NET State Service will not have as good a performance as the default in-process storage of an ASP.NET application, due to the out-of-process communications and network hops involved in communicating with other servers across a network.

The out-of-process State Service and SQL Server session management techniques are compatible with each other and require no changes to your code when you move from one technique to another, which you might do, for example, if you are having trouble with losing critical session information.

If you choose to make use of the ASP.NET State Service, it is good practice to install and run it on a server separate from the web servers in the web farm. This allows any one of the web servers to be taken down for maintenance or replacement without interrupting access to your application. If the ASP.NET State Service is running on a server that is also running an instance of the application, when that server requires maintenance, your entire application will be unavailable while the server is down.

You start the ASP.NET State Service the same way you start any other Windows service. Invoke the Services console by clicking on Start → Control Panel and first selecting Administrative Tools, and then Services. In the Services console window, select the ASP.NET State Service, as shown in Figure 9-2.

Right-click the ASP.NET State Service and select Properties to open the ASP.NET State Service Properties dialog box. From the Startup type drop-down menu, select

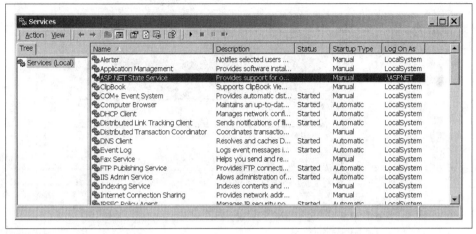

Figure 9-2. Starting the ASP.NET State Service

Automatic to automatically start the service anytime the server is restarted, and then click the Start button to start the service now, as shown in Figure 9-3.

To use the ASP.NET State Service, you must make two changes to the application *web.config* file on its current web server. First, add a <sessionState> element to the *web.config* file in the root directory of your application (unless the element is already present). Next, set (or change) the mode attribute to StateServer and modify the stateConnectionString attribute to include the IP address of the server running the ASP.NET State Service. We'll refer to that machine as the *state server* from here on. Do not change the port number, because this is the port the State Service is listening on. If you must change the port number, you will need to make changes to the registry settings for the State Service, because the port number cannot be changed through the Services console. Here's some sample code that demonstrates the changes we've described:

```
<?xml version="1.0" encoding="utf-8" ?>
<configuration>
  <system.web>

    ..

    <sessionState
          mode="StateServer"
          stateConnectionString="tcpip=10.0.1.11:42424"
          cookieless="false"
          timeout="20" />

    ..

  </system.web>
</configuration>
```

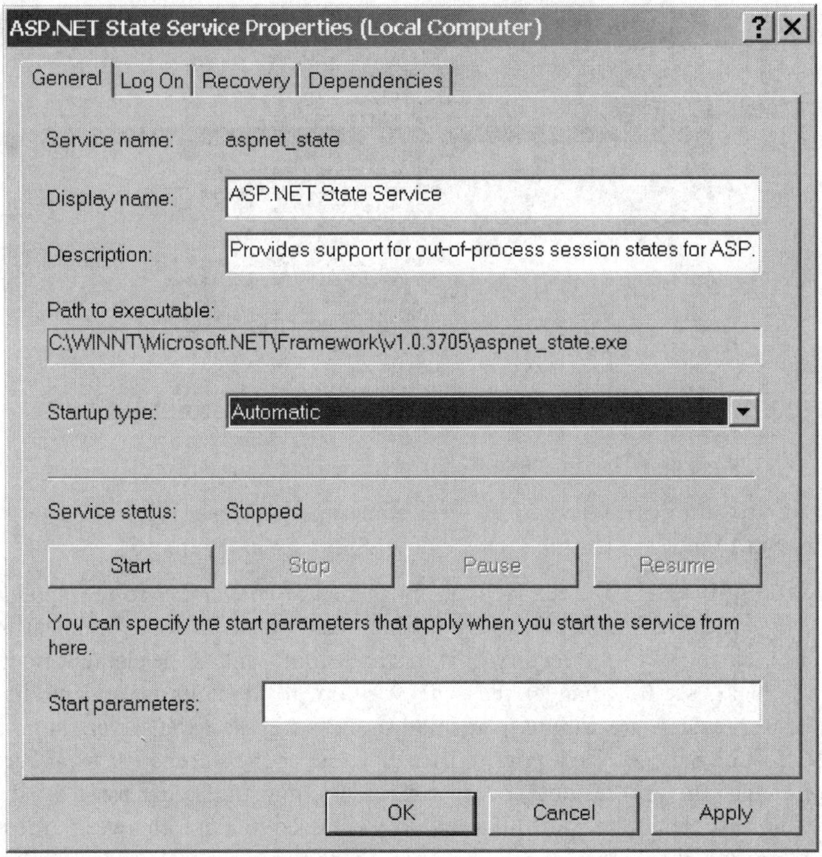

Figure 9-3. Setting the ASP.NET State Service's Startup type property to Automatic

In addition to modifying <sessionState> settings in *web.config*, you also need to alter the keys used for encryption and generation of unique values. Session management uses these keys to generate session IDs and hash values used in the session collection, so all servers must be configured to use the same values. If the values differ from server to server, the session information will not be understood by all of the servers hosting the application. You control encryption through the <machineKey> element, which you will need to add to the *web.config* file. By default, the keys are set to automatically generate values that will result in a different key being used on each server. These values should be set to 40–128 hexadecimal characters as a function of the encryption type and level. Note that *[YourHexValue]* must be replaced with the hexadecimal value you want to use for your application:

```
<?xml version="1.0" encoding="utf-8" ?>
<configuration>
  <system.web>
```

```
<machineKey validationKey="[YourHexValue]"
            decryptionKey="[YourHexValue]"
            validation="SHA1"/>

    ..

    </system.web>
  </configuration>
```

After you've tested your application with the ASP.NET state server enabled, you're
ready to deploy it to the other servers.

> Your system administrator will need to assist in configuring the appro-
> priate network load balancing, failover, etc. These subjects are beyond
> the scope of this book.

An alternate approach to using the ASP.NET state server is to use SQL Server to
store and persist the session information. ASP.NET again makes this a simple configuration change with no code changes required.

The first step to using SQL Server for session management is to install the special
tables and stored procedures that ASP.NET requires in the instance of SQL Server
that you will use for this purpose. You create this support by running the
InstallSqlState.sql script provided with the .NET Framework.

To run the script, open a command prompt and navigate to the folder *\WINNT\
Microsoft.NET\Framework\<version>*, where *<version>* is the version of the .NET
Framework installed on your SQL Server machine. At the command prompt, type
the following, and all of the necessary tables, stored procedures, and the like will be
installed. Note that you will need to substitute for *password* the appropriate password for the sa account.

```
OSQL -S localhost -U sa -P password < InstallSqlState.sql
```

> If you need to uninstall the SQL Server state management objects, use
> the same command line, but substitute UninstallSqlState.sql for
> InstallSqlState.sql.

For a production application, set up a database user with read/write access to the
tempDB database. You will use this database user in the configuration described next.

The only other change required to use SQL Server for state management is to modify
the *web.config* file, as shown here, setting the mode to SQLServer, setting the IP
address to the address of your SQL Server machine, and replacing *user* and *pwd* with
the settings for the database user with read/write access to the tempDB database:

```
<sessionState
    mode="SQLServer"
```

```
sqlConnectionString="data source=10.0.1.12;user id=user;password=pwd"
cookieless="false"
timeout="20" />
```

From now on, when your application runs, it will use SQL Server for storing all of its session information. You can see the results of this by looking at the `ASPStateTempApplications` and `ASPStateTempSessions` tables in the `tempDB` database. You should find entries there for your applications and sessions, respectively. Because the data is stored in binary format, you will not be able to view it.

Two other `sessionState` element attributes are frequently used in conjunction with the other modifications that we've discussed: `cookieless` and `timeout`.

cookieless

> Setting the `cookieless` attribute to `false` (the default) configures ASP.NET's session management to use a non-persistent cookie to remember the session ID between page requests.

> Setting `cookieless` to `true` causes ASP.NET to include the session ID in the URL instead of using a cookie. This is very useful if your application has to be usable by browsers with cookie support disabled. The following URL is an example of how ASP.NET modifies the URL to include the session ID. You might be tempted to quickly shun this approach because your application has some hard-coded links embedded in the pages. Fear not; ASP.NET modifies all URLs in your pages, whether static or dynamically created, to include the session ID, as shown here:

> > *http://localhost/ASPNetCookbook/(3eqccw45tlzqa555hakqrn55)/Chapter-Menu.aspx*

timeout

> The `timeout` attribute is used to define the length of inactivity in a session before the session is terminated. The value is in minutes and is 20 minutes by default.

 You may be aware that you can configure the session timeout in IIS. In an ASP.NET application, however, the session timeout that can be configured in IIS is not used.

9.5 Accessing Other web.config Configuration Elements

Problem

You want to be able to read application information from a *web.config* file that is not available as an `<appSettings>` key/value pair, but present as an attribute or child element of some other element of the file.

Solution

Read the *web.config* file into an XmlDocument object, and access the target element that contains the information you need as you would any other XML document node.

In the code-behind class for your ASP.NET page, use the .NET language of your choice to:

1. Read the *web.config* file into an XmlDocument object.
2. Use the SelectSingleNode method to get a reference to the desired section.
3. Use the attributes collection of the selected node to access the attributes for the section.

Examples 9-6 through 9-8 show an application we've written that implements this solution and retrieves attribute settings from the <trace> element of a *web.config* file. Example 9-6 shows the *.aspx* file that displays the information. Example 9-7 (VB) and Example 9-8 (C#) show the code-behind class for the page that does the work of reading the settings from the <trace> element.

Discussion

Because the *web.config* file is an XML document, you can process it as you would any other XML document and use the XML classes provided in the .NET Framework to access its elements and their children. The first step is to create a new XmlDocument object and load the *web.config* file into it. In our example, we use Server.MapPath to get the fully qualified name for the *web.config* file:

`VB`
```
xmlDoc = New XmlDocument
xmlDoc.Load(Server.MapPath("web.config"))
```

`C#`
```
xmlDoc = new XmlDocument();
xmlDoc.Load(Server.MapPath("web.config"));
```

Next, use the SelectSingleNode method, passing it the fully qualified path from the root of the XML document to the desired section of the *web.config* file. In our application, for example, we want to access the <trace> section:

`VB`
```
xmlNode = xmlDoc.SelectSingleNode("configuration/system.web/trace")
```

`C#`
```
xmlNode = xmlDoc.SelectSingleNode("configuration/system.web/trace");
```

 XML is case-sensitive, and node names are separated by using a forward slash (/).

After getting a reference to the desired section (or *node* in XML terminology), the attributes collection of the node, which contains all of the attribute information for the requested *web.config* section, is available. In our example, we use the GetNamedItem method of the attributes collection to access the specific attributes whose values we want. If you need to display all of the attributes from a section, you can iterate through the attributes collection using the name and value properties of each attribute to read and then output the information.

The approach described in this recipe can provide access to the attributes of any element in the *web.config* file. And, as a bonus, you can use the same method to programmatically change any of those attributes. The following code, for example, changes the value of the enabled attribute of <trace> to true and then saves the *web.config* file with the new value. When the file is saved, ASP.NET, which monitors the *web.config* file for changes, restarts the application.

VB
```
attributes.GetNamedItem("enabled").Value = "true"
xmlDoc.Save(Server.MapPath("web.config"))
```

C#
```
attributes.GetNamedItem("enabled").Value = "true";
xmlDoc.Save(Server.MapPath("web.config"));
```

Example 9-6. Access system configuration information in web.config (.aspx)

```
<%@ Page Language="vb" AutoEventWireup="false"
        Codebehind="CH09AccessSystemConfigVB.aspx.vb"
        Inherits="ASPNetCookbook.VBExamples.CH09AccessSystemConfigVB"%>
<!DOCTYPE HTML PUBLIC "-//W3C//DTD HTML 4.0 Transitional//EN">
<html>
  <head>
    <title>Accessing System Configuration Information</title>
    <link rel="stylesheet" href="css/ASPNetCookbook.css">
  </head>
  <body leftmargin="0" marginheight="0" marginwidth="0" topmargin="0">
    <form id="frmConfiguration" method="post" runat="server">
      <table width="100%" cellpadding="0" cellspacing="0" border="0">
        <tr>
          <td align="center">
            <img src="images/ASPNETCookbookHeading_blue.gif">
          </td>
        </tr>
        <tr>
          <td class="dividerLine">
            <img src="images/spacer.gif" height="6" border="0"></td>
        </tr>
      </table>
      <table width="90%" align="center" border="0">
        <tr>
          <td><img src="images/spacer.gif" height="10" border="0"></td>
        </tr>
        <tr>
          <td align="center" class="PageHeading">
            Accessing System Configuration Information In web.config (VB)
          </td>
        </tr>
```

Example 9-6. Access system configuration information in web.config (.aspx) (continued)

```
    <tr>
      <td><img src="images/spacer.gif" height="10" border="0"></td>
    </tr>
    <tr>
      <td align="center">
        <table width="40%">
          <tr>
            <td align="center" class="SubHeading" colspan="2">
              trace Section Attributes
            </td>
          </tr>
          <tr>
            <td align="right" width="50%" class="LabelText">enabled = </td>
            <td width="50%" class="LabelText">
              <asp:Label ID="labEnabled" runat="server"  />
            </td>
          </tr>
          <tr>
            <td align="right"  class="LabelText">requestLimit = </td>
            <td class="LabelText">
              <asp:Label ID="labRequestLimit" runat="server"  />
            </td>
          </tr>
          <tr>
            <td align="right"  class="LabelText">pageOutput = </td>
            <td class="LabelText">
              <asp:Label ID="labPageOutput" runat="server"  />
            </td>
          </tr>
          <tr>
            <td align="right"  class="LabelText">traceMode = </td>
            <td class="LabelText">
              <asp:Label ID="labTraceMode" runat="server"  />
            </td>
          </tr>
          <tr>
            <td align="right"  class="LabelText">localOnly = </td>
            <td class="LabelText">
              <asp:Label ID="labLocalOnly" runat="server"  />
            </td>
          </tr>
        </table>
      </td>
    </tr>
  </table>
  </form>
  </body>
</html>
```

Example 9-7. Access system configuration information in web.config code-behind (.vb)

```
Option Explicit On
Option Strict On
```

Example 9-7. Access system configuration information in web.config code-behind (.vb) (continued)

```vb
'-----------------------------------------------------------------------
'
'   Module Name: CH09AccessSystemConfigVB.aspx.vb
'
'   Description: This module provides the code behind for the
'                CH09AccessSystemConfigVB.aspx page
'
'***********************************************************************
Imports Microsoft.VisualBasic
Imports System
Imports System.Xml

Namespace ASPNetCookbook.VBExamples
  Public Class CH09AccessSystemConfigVB
    Inherits System.Web.UI.Page

    'controls on the form
    Protected labEnabled As System.Web.UI.WebControls.Label
    Protected labRequestLimit As System.Web.UI.WebControls.Label
    Protected labPageOutput As System.Web.UI.WebControls.Label
    Protected labTraceMode As System.Web.UI.WebControls.Label
    Protected labLocalOnly As System.Web.UI.WebControls.Label

    '***********************************************************************
    '
    '   ROUTINE: Page_Load
    '
    '   DESCRIPTION: This routine provides the event handler for the page load
    '                event.  It is responsible for initializing the controls
    '                on the page.
    '-----------------------------------------------------------------------
    Private Sub Page_Load(ByVal sender As System.Object, _
                          ByVal e As System.EventArgs) Handles MyBase.Load

      Dim xmlDoc As XmlDocument
      Dim xmlNode As XmlNode
      Dim attributes As XmlAttributeCollection

      'load web.config
      xmlDoc = New XmlDocument
      xmlDoc.Load(Server.MapPath("web.config"))

      'get the trace section
      xmlNode = xmlDoc.SelectSingleNode("configuration/system.web/trace")
      If (Not IsNothing(xmlNode)) Then
        'the trace section is a collection or attributes so get the
        'collection then output the individual values
        attributes = xmlNode.Attributes
        labEnabled.Text = attributes.GetNamedItem("enabled").Value
        labRequestLimit.Text = attributes.GetNamedItem("requestLimit").Value
        labPageOutput.Text = attributes.GetNamedItem("pageOutput").Value
        labTraceMode.Text = attributes.GetNamedItem("traceMode").Value
```

```vb
        labLocalOnly.Text = attributes.GetNamedItem("localOnly").Value
      End If
    End Sub  'Page_Load
  End Class  'CH09AccessSystemConfigVB
End Namespace
```

Example 9-8. Access system configuration information in web.config code-behind (.cs)

```csharp
//---------------------------------------------------------------------------
//
//   Module Name: CH09AccessSystemConfigCS.aspx.cs
//
//   Description: This module provides the code behind for the
//                CH09AccessSystemConfigCS.aspx page
//
//***************************************************************************
using System;
using System.Xml;

namespace ASPNetCookbook.CSExamples
{
  public class CH09AccessSystemConfigCS : System.Web.UI.Page
  {
    // controls on the form
    protected System.Web.UI.WebControls.Label labEnabled;
    protected System.Web.UI.WebControls.Label labRequestLimit;
    protected System.Web.UI.WebControls.Label labPageOutput;
    protected System.Web.UI.WebControls.Label labTraceMode;
    protected System.Web.UI.WebControls.Label labLocalOnly;

    //***********************************************************************
    //
    //   ROUTINE: Page_Load
    //
    //   DESCRIPTION: This routine provides the event handler for the page
    //                load event.  It is responsible for initializing the
    //                controls on the page.
    //---------------------------------------------------------------------------
    private void Page_Load(object sender, System.EventArgs e)
    {
      XmlDocument xmlDoc = null;
      XmlNode xmlNode = null;
      XmlAttributeCollection attributes = null;

      // load web.config
      xmlDoc = new XmlDocument();
      xmlDoc.Load(Server.MapPath("web.config"));

      // get the trace section
      xmlNode =
        xmlDoc.SelectSingleNode("configuration/system.web/trace");
      if (xmlNode != null)
      {
```

```
        // the trace section is a collection of attributes so get the
        attributes = xmlNode.Attributes;
        labEnabled.Text = attributes.GetNamedItem("enabled").Value;
        labRequestLimit.Text = attributes.GetNamedItem("requestLimit").Value;
        labPageOutput.Text = attributes.GetNamedItem("pageOutput").Value;
        labTraceMode.Text = attributes.GetNamedItem("traceMode").Value;
        labLocalOnly.Text = attributes.GetNamedItem("localOnly").Value;
      }
    } // Page_Load
  } // CH09AccessSystemConfigCS
}
```

9.6 Adding Your Own Configuration Elements to web.config

Problem

You want to create and add your own configuration elements to *web.config*. No predefined element will do, nor will use of the <appSettings> key/value entries of *web.config*, as described in Recipe 9.2.

Solution

Determine what configuration information you want to store in *web.config*, create your own custom section handler for parsing the element, add the definition of the section handler to *web.config*, add the new configuration element to *web.config*, and then use the configuration information in your application.

1. Determine what configuration information you want to store in *web.config*.

2. Use the .NET language of your choice to create a custom section handler class for parsing your newly defined element.

3. Add the definition of the section handler to the <configSections> section of *web.config*.

4. Add the new configuration element to *web.config* and assign values to its attributes or child elements.

5. In the code-behind class for your ASP.NET page, use the .NET language of your choice to access and put the custom configuration data to work.

The code we've written to illustrate this solution appears in Examples 9-9 through 9-14. Example 9-9 (VB) and Example 9-10 (C#) show the class for a custom section handler. The changes we've made to *web.config* to have it use the custom section handler are shown in Example 9-11. Example 9-12 shows the *.aspx* file for a sample web form that displays some custom configuration settings. Examples 9-13 and 9-14 show the code-behind class that accesses the custom configuration information.

Discussion

Sometimes the predefined configuration elements provided by ASP.NET, including the key/value collection available through the <appSettings> element of *web.config* (described in Recipe 9.2) are not enough. When this is the case, being able to store any configuration information required by your application in its own custom section in *web.config* can be a useful alternative. What's more, having a custom section in *web.config* can be a real boon to program clarity and ease of implementation.

As a prelude to discussing the custom section for *web.config*, it's worthwhile reviewing the basic structure of a *machine.config* file, as shown next, because it is the *machine.config* file whose structure we will mimic. The root node of the XML document is <configuration>. The <configSections> child element is next. It defines the configuration section elements that will follow and the configuration handlers (*classes*) that will handle the configuration information contained in the elements. When <configSections> is present, it must always be the first child element of <configuration>.

```
<?xml version="1.0" encoding="UTF-8"?>
<configuration>

  <configSections>

    ..

  </configSections>


  <!-- sections defined in configSections -->

</configuration>
```

Even if you are used to looking at a *web.config* file, you have probably never seen the <configSections> element. This is because all of the standard configuration handlers are defined in *machine.config*. (Recall that ASP.NET reads the *machine.config* file first and then the *web.config* file(s) for your application. All of the data from the *machine.config* file is used unless a section in *web.config* overrides the equivalent section in *machine.config*.) Because <configSections> is only used to define configuration handlers, it never appears in a *web.config* file, unless your application uses custom configuration handlers like the one described in this example.

In this example, we use a <siteProperties> custom element to hold the information we want to store in *web.config* and that will be used by our custom configuration handler. We have chosen the path of using a custom element (and a custom configuration handler) because of the flexibility it affords us and the clarity with which we can express the information to be stored.

In creating your own custom element, the first thing you need to do is determine the configuration information you want to store in *web.config* and then define the format that you want it stored in. The only limitation is that the data element itself must be a well-formed XML node. You can use attributes, child elements, or any combination of the two to hold your custom configuration information. In our example, we use attributes only. The well-formed XML that defines the section we want to add to our application *web.config* is shown here:

```
<siteProperties applicationName="ASP.NET Cookbook"
                databaseServer="10.0.1.12"
                databaseName="ASPNetCookbook_DB"
                databaseUserName="aspnetcookbook"
                databaseUserPassword="efficient"
                emailServer="mail@mailservices.com" />
```

> The section can be named anything you like as long as it does not conflict with any predefined ASP.NET elements. We recommend that, for consistency, you stick with the mixed-case convention used by ASP.NET. Also, be aware that section names and attributes are case sensitive.

After defining your configuration element and specifying the values of the information it will store, create a custom configuration handler in a separate project. This way the assembly that is created can be reused easily in multiple applications. For our example, the project was named *VBCustomConfigHandlers* (*CSCustomConfigHandlers* for C#), which by default will generate an assembly with the same name.

In your configuration handler project, add a new class named to reflect the configuration element the handler supports. In our example, we've named the class VBSiteConfigHandler (CSSiteConfigHandler for C#), because the section added to *web.config* contains site configuration information.

To act as a custom configuration handler, the class must implement the IConfigurationSectionHandler interface:

VB
```
Namespace VBCustomConfigHandlers

    Public Class VBSiteConfigHandler
      Implements IConfigurationSectionHandler

        ..

    End Class   'VBSiteConfigHandler

End Namespace   'VBCustomConfigHandlers
```

C#
```
namespace CSCustomConfigHandlers
{
    public class CSSiteConfigHandler : IConfigurationSectionHandler
    {
```

```csharp
        ..
      } // CSSiteConfigHandler

    } // CSCustomConfigHandlers
```

The IConfigurationSectionHandler interface requires that you implement a single method, Create, which requires three parameters: parent, configContext, and section. The parent parameter provides a reference to the corresponding parent configuration section, and the configContext parameter provides a reference to the current ASP.NET context. Neither is used in this example. The section parameter provides a reference to the XML node (section) of the *web.config* file that is to be processed. In our example, section will be set to reference the <siteProperties> section added to *web.config*.

```vbnet
Namespace VBCustomConfigHandlers

  Public Class VBSiteConfigHandler
    Implements IConfigurationSectionHandler

    Public Function Create(ByVal parent As Object, _
                           ByVal configContext As Object, _
                           ByVal section As XmlNode) As Object _
        Implements IConfigurationSectionHandler.Create

      ..

    End Function  'Create
  End Class  'VBSiteConfigHandler
End Namespace  'VBCustomConfigHandlers
```

```csharp
namespace CSCustomConfigHandlers
{
  public class CSSiteConfigHandler : IConfigurationSectionHandler
  {
    public Object Create(Object parent,
                         Object configContext,
                         XmlNode section)
    {
      ..

    } // Create
  } // CSSiteConfigHandler
} // CSCustomConfigHandlers
```

The Create method returns an object that contains the configuration information from the passed section. This can be anything you want it to be. The most flexible approach is to define a class that will contain the data and provide easy access by your application. In our example, the class that will be returned is defined in the same file as the VBSiteConfigHandler (CSSiteConfigHandler for C#) class.

```vb
Namespace VBCustomConfigHandlers

    Public Class VBSiteConfigHandler
      Implements IConfigurationSectionHandler

      Public Function Create(ByVal parent As Object, _
                             ByVal configContext As Object, _
                             ByVal section As XmlNode) As Object _
           Implements IConfigurationSectionHandler.Create


        ..

      End Function  'Create

    End Class  'VBSiteConfigHandler

    'The following class provides the container returned by
    'the VBSiteConfigHandler
    Public Class VBSiteConfiguration


        ..

    End Class  'VBSiteConfiguration
End Namespace  'VBCustomConfigHandlers
```

```csharp
namespace CSCustomConfigHandlers
{
    public class CSSiteConfigHandler : IConfigurationSectionHandler
    {
        public Object Create(Object parent,
                             Object configContext,
                             XmlNode section)
        {
            ..

        } // Create
    } // CSSiteConfigHandler

    // The following class provides the container returned by
    // the CSSiteConfigHandler
    public class CSSiteConfiguration
    {
        ..

    } // CSSiteConfiguration
} // CSCustomConfigHandlers
```

The VBSiteConfiguration (CSSiteConfiguration for C#) class needs a constructor that has parameters for each of the configuration items and a read-only property for each of the configuration items. The code for our example is shown in Example 9-9 (VB) and Example 9-10 (C#).

After the class that will be used for the return is defined, the Create method should extract the configuration information from the passed XML section, create a new instance of the VBSiteConfiguration (CSSiteConfiguration for C#) object, and then return a reference to the new instance. For our example, attributes were used for the configuration information in the section. This allows us to get a reference to the attributes collection of the section, and then extract the individual values by using the GetNameItem method of the attributes collection.

```vb
Public Function Create(ByVal parent As Object, _
                       ByVal configContext As Object, _
                       ByVal section As XmlNode) As Object _
       Implements IConfigurationSectionHandler.Create

    Dim siteConfig As VBSiteConfiguration
    Dim attributes As XmlAttributeCollection

    attributes = section.Attributes
    With attributes
      siteConfig = _
        New VBSiteConfiguration(.GetNamedItem("applicationName").Value, _
                                .GetNamedItem("databaseServer").Value, _
                                .GetNamedItem("databaseName").Value, _
                                .GetNamedItem("databaseUserName").Value, _
                                .GetNamedItem("databaseUserPassword").Value, _
                                .GetNamedItem("emailServer").Value)
    End With   'attributes

    Return (siteConfig)
End Function   'Create
```

```csharp
public Object Create(Object parent,
                     Object configContext,
                     XmlNode section)
{
    CSSiteConfiguration siteConfig = null;
    XmlAttributeCollection attributes = null;

    attributes = section.Attributes;
    siteConfig =
      new CSSiteConfiguration(attributes.GetNamedItem("applicationName").Value,
                attributes.GetNamedItem("databaseServer").Value,
                attributes.GetNamedItem("databaseName").Value,
                attributes.GetNamedItem("databaseUserName").Value,
                attributes.GetNamedItem("databaseUserPassword").Value,
                attributes.GetNamedItem("emailServer").Value);

    return (siteConfig);
} // Create
```

With the custom configuration handler in hand, you then need to add the handler information to *web.config* to tell ASP.NET how to handle the <siteProperties> section you've added. Add a <configSections> element at the top of your *web.config* that contains a single section element. The name attribute defines the name of the custom section containing your configuration information. The type attribute defines the class and assembly name in the form type="*class, assembly*" that will process your custom configuration section. The *class* name must be a fully qualified class name. The *assembly* name must be the name of the assembly (dll) created in your configuration handler project, described earlier.

```
<configSections>
  <section name="siteProperties"
    type="VBCustomConfigHandlers.VBSiteConfigHandler, VBCustomConfigHandlers"
  />
</configSections>
```

 When the <configSections> element is present, it must always be the first element in the *web.config* file after the <configuration> element or a parsing exception will be thrown.

The last thing you need to do before you can use the custom configuration in your application is to add a reference to the VBCustomConfigHandlers (CSCustomConfigHandlers for C#) assembly in your application.

Accessing the custom configuration information in your application requires using ConfigurationSettings.GetConfig and passing it the name of your custom section. This method returns an object that must be cast to the object type you returned in your custom configuration handler class. After the reference is obtained, all of the site information is available simply as properties of the object.

VB
```
Dim siteConfig As VBCustomConfigHandlers.VBSiteConfiguration

siteConfig = CType(ConfigurationSettings.GetConfig("siteProperties"), _
                   VBCustomConfigHandlers.VBSiteConfiguration)

labApplicationName.Text = siteConfig.applicationName
labDBServer.Text = siteConfig.databaseServer
labDBName.Text = siteConfig.databaseName
labDBUserName.Text = siteConfig.databaseUserName
labDBUserPassword.Text = siteConfig.databaseUserPassword
labEmailServer.Text = siteConfig.emailServer
```

C#
```
CSCustomConfigHandlers.CSSiteConfiguration siteConfig = null;

siteConfig = (CSCustomConfigHandlers.CSSiteConfiguration)
             (ConfigurationSettings.GetConfig("siteProperties"));

labApplicationName.Text = siteConfig.applicationName;
labDBServer.Text = siteConfig.databaseServer;
labDBName.Text = siteConfig.databaseName;
labDBUserName.Text = siteConfig.databaseUserName;
labDBUserPassword.Text = siteConfig.databaseUserPassword;
labEmailServer.Text = siteConfig.emailServer;
```

Example 9-9. Custom section handler class (.vb)

```
Option Explicit On
Option Strict On
```

Example 9-9. Custom section handler class (.vb) (continued)

```vb
'------------------------------------------------------------------------------
'
'   Module Name: VBSiteConfigHandler.vb
'
'   Description: This class provides a custom site configuration handler.
'
'******************************************************************************
Imports System.Configuration
Imports System.Xml

Namespace VBCustomConfigHandlers
  Public Class VBSiteConfigHandler
    Implements IConfigurationSectionHandler

    '**************************************************************************
    '
    '   ROUTINE: Create
    '
    '   DESCRIPTION: This routine provides the creation of the
    '                VBSiteConfiguration from the passed section of the
    '                web.config file
    '--------------------------------------------------------------------------
    Public Function Create(ByVal parent As Object, _
                           ByVal configContext As Object, _
                           ByVal section As XmlNode) As Object _
          Implements IConfigurationSectionHandler.Create

      Dim siteConfig As VBSiteConfiguration
      Dim attributes As XmlAttributeCollection

      attributes = section.Attributes
      With attributes
        siteConfig = _
        New VBSiteConfiguration(.GetNamedItem("applicationName").Value, _
                                .GetNamedItem("databaseServer").Value, _
                                .GetNamedItem("databaseName").Value, _
                                .GetNamedItem("databaseUserName").Value, _
                                .GetNamedItem("databaseUserPassword").Value, _
                                .GetNamedItem("emailServer").Value)
      End With  'attributes

      Return (siteConfig)
    End Function  'Create
  End Class  'VBSiteConfigHandler

  'The following class provides the container returned by
  'the VBSiteConfigHandler
  Public Class VBSiteConfiguration
    Private mApplicationName As String
    Private mDatabaseServer As String
    Private mDatabaseName As String
    Private mDatabaseUserName As String
```

Example 9-9. Custom section handler class (.vb) (continued)

```vb
   Private mDatabaseUserPassword As String
   Private mEmailServer As String

   Public ReadOnly Property applicationName( ) As String
     Get
       Return (mApplicationName)
     End Get
   End Property   'applicationName

   Public ReadOnly Property databaseServer( ) As String
     Get
       Return (mDatabaseServer)
     End Get
   End Property   'databaseServer

   Public ReadOnly Property databaseName( ) As String
     Get
       Return (mDatabaseName)
     End Get
   End Property   'databaseName

   Public ReadOnly Property databaseUserName( ) As String
     Get
       Return (mDatabaseUserName)
     End Get
   End Property   'databaseUserName

   Public ReadOnly Property databaseUserPassword( ) As String
     Get
       Return (mDatabaseUserPassword)
     End Get
   End Property   'databaseUserPassword

   Public ReadOnly Property emailServer( ) As String
     Get
       Return (mEmailServer)
     End Get
   End Property   'emailServer

   '*************************************************************************
   '
   '   ROUTINE: New
   '
   '   DESCRIPTION: This constructor creates the object and populates the
   '                attributes with the passed values
   '-------------------------------------------------------------------------
   Public Sub New(ByVal applicationName As String, _
                  ByVal databaseServer As String, _
                  ByVal databaseName As String, _
                  ByVal databaseUserName As String, _
                  ByVal databaseUserPassword As String, _
                  ByVal emailServer As String)
```

Example 9-9. Custom section handler class (.vb) (continued)

```
        mApplicationName = applicationName
        mDatabaseServer = databaseServer
        mDatabaseName = databaseName
        mDatabaseUserName = databaseUserName
        mDatabaseUserPassword = databaseUserPassword
        mEmailServer = emailServer
    End Sub   'New
  End Class   'VBSiteConfiguration
End Namespace  'VBCustomConfigHandlers
```

Example 9-10. Custom section handler class (.cs)

```
//---------------------------------------------------------------------------
//
//   Module Name: CSCustomConfigHandlers
//
//   Description: This class provides a custom site configuration handler.
//
//***************************************************************************
using System;
using System.Configuration;
using System.Xml;

namespace CSCustomConfigHandlers
{
  public class CSSiteConfigHandler : IConfigurationSectionHandler
  {
    //***********************************************************************
    //
    //   ROUTINE: Create
    //
    //   DESCRIPTION: This routine provides the creation of the
    //                CSSiteConfiguration from the passed section of the
    //                web.config file
    //-----------------------------------------------------------------------
    public Object Create(Object parent,
                         Object configContext,
                         XmlNode section)
    {
      CSSiteConfiguration siteConfig = null;
      XmlAttributeCollection attributes = null;

      attributes = section.Attributes;
      siteConfig =
        new CSSiteConfiguration(attributes.GetNamedItem("applicationName").Value,
                         attributes.GetNamedItem("databaseServer").Value,
                         attributes.GetNamedItem("databaseName").Value,
                         attributes.GetNamedItem("databaseUserName").Value,
                         attributes.GetNamedItem("databaseUserPassword").Value,
                         attributes.GetNamedItem("emailServer").Value);

      return (siteConfig);
    }  // Create
```

Example 9-10. Custom section handler class (.cs) (continued)

```csharp
}  // CSSiteConfigHandler

// The following class provides the container returned by
// the CSSiteConfigHandler
public class CSSiteConfiguration
{
  private String mApplicationName = null;
  private String mDatabaseServer = null;
  private String mDatabaseName = null;
  private String mDatabaseUserName = null;
  private String mDatabaseUserPassword = null;
  private String mEmailServer = null;

  public String applicationName
  {
    get
    {
      return(mApplicationName);
    }
  }  // applicationName

  public String databaseServer
  {
    get
    {
      return(mDatabaseServer);
    }
  }  // databaseServer

  public String databaseName
  {
    get
    {
      return(mDatabaseName);
    }
  }  // databaseName

  public String databaseUserName
  {
    get
    {
      return(mDatabaseUserName);
    }
  }  // databaseUserName

  public String databaseUserPassword
  {
    get
    {
      return(mDatabaseUserPassword);
    }
  }  // databaseUserPassword
```

Example 9-10. Custom section handler class (.cs) (continued)

```csharp
  public String emailServer
  {
    get
    {
      return(mEmailServer);
    }
  }  // emailServer

//**************************************************************************
//
//    ROUTINE: Constructor
//
//    DESCRIPTION: This constructor creates the object and populates the
//                 attributes with the passed values
//--------------------------------------------------------------------------
  public CSSiteConfiguration(String applicationName,
                             String databaseServer,
                             String databaseName,
                             String databaseUserName,
                             String databaseUserPassword,
                             String emailServer)
  {
    mApplicationName = applicationName;
    mDatabaseServer = databaseServer;
    mDatabaseName = databaseName;
    mDatabaseUserName = databaseUserName;
    mDatabaseUserPassword = databaseUserPassword;
    mEmailServer = emailServer;
  }  // CSSiteConfiguration

  }  // CSSiteConfiguration
}  // CSCustomConfigHandlers
```

Example 9-11. Changes to web.config to use the custom section handler

```xml
<?xml version="1.0" encoding="utf-8"?>
<configuration>

    ..

  <configSections>
    <section name="siteProperties"
      type="VBCustomConfigHandlers.VBSiteConfigHandler, VBCustomConfigHandlers"
/>
  </configSections>

  <system.web>

    ..

  </system.web>

    ..
```

Example 9-11. Changes to web.config to use the custom section handler (continued)

```
<siteProperties applicationName="ASP.NET Cookbook"
                databaseServer="10.0.1.12"
                databaseName="ASPNetCookbook_DB"
                databaseUserName="aspnetcookbook"
                databaseUserPassword="efficient"
                emailServer="mail@mailservices.com" />
</configuration>
```

Example 9-12. Sample web form using custom configuration data (.aspx)

```
<%@ Page Language="vb" AutoEventWireup="false"
        Codebehind="CH09CustomConfigHandlerVB.aspx.vb"
        Inherits="ASPNetCookbook.VBExamples.CH09CustomConfigHandlerVB"%>
<!DOCTYPE HTML PUBLIC "-//W3C//DTD HTML 4.0 Transitional//EN">
<html>
  <head>
    <title>Custom Config Handler</title>
    <link rel="stylesheet" href="css/ASPNetCookbook.css">
  </head>
  <body leftmargin="0" marginheight="0" marginwidth="0" topmargin="0">
    <form id="frmConfiguration" method="post" runat="server">
      <table width="100%" cellpadding="0" cellspacing="0" border="0">
        <tr>
          <td align="center">
            <img src="images/ASPNETCookbookHeading_blue.gif">
          </td>
        </tr>
        <tr>
          <td class="dividerLine">
            <img src="images/spacer.gif" height="6" border="0"></td>
        </tr>
      </table>
      <table width="90%" align="center" border="0">
        <tr>
          <td><img src="images/spacer.gif" height="10" border="0"></td>
        </tr>
        <tr>
          <td align="center" class="PageHeading">
            Writing Custom Configuration Handlers (VB)
          </td>
        </tr>
        <tr>
          <td><img src="images/spacer.gif" height="10" border="0"></td>
        </tr>
        <tr>
          <td align="center">
            <table width="60%">
              <tr>
                <td align="right" width="50%" class="LabelText">
                  applicationName = </td>
                <td width="50%" class="LabelText">
                  <asp:Label ID="labApplicationName" runat="server"  />
                </td>
```

Example 9-12. Sample web form using custom configuration data (.aspx) (continued)

```
                </tr>
                <tr>
                  <td align="right"  class="LabelText">
                    databaseServer = </td>
                  <td class="LabelText">
                    <asp:Label ID="labDBServer" runat="server"  />
                  </td>
                </tr>
                <tr>
                  <td align="right"  class="LabelText">
                    databaseName = </td>
                  <td class="LabelText">
                    <asp:Label ID="labDBName" runat="server"  />
                  </td>
                </tr>
                <tr>
                  <td align="right"  class="LabelText">
                    databaseUserName = </td>
                  <td class="LabelText">
                    <asp:Label ID="labDBUserName" runat="server"  />
                  </td>
                </tr>
                <tr>
                  <td align="right"  class="LabelText">
                    databaseUserPassword = </td>
                  <td class="LabelText">
                    <asp:Label ID="labDBUserPassword" runat="server"  />
                  </td>
                </tr>
                <tr>
                  <td align="right"  class="LabelText">
                    emailServer = </td>
                  <td class="LabelText">
                    <asp:Label ID="labEmailServer" runat="server"  />
                  </td>
                </tr>
              </table>
            </td>
          </tr>
        </table>
      </form>
    </body>
</html>
```

Example 9-13. Sample web form using custom configuration data code-behind (.vb)

```
Option Explicit On
Option Strict On
'---------------------------------------------------------------------------
'
'   Module Name: CH09CustomConfigHandlerVB.aspx.vb
'
'   Description: This module provides the code behind for the
```

Example 9-13. Sample web form using custom configuration data code-behind (.vb) (continued)

```vb
'                    CH09CustomConfigHandlerVB.aspx page
'
'*****************************************************************************
Imports System.Configuration

Namespace ASPNetCookbook.VBExamples
  Public Class CH09CustomConfigHandlerVB
    Inherits System.Web.UI.Page

    'controls on the form
    Protected labApplicationName As System.Web.UI.WebControls.Label
    Protected labDBServer As System.Web.UI.WebControls.Label
    Protected labDBName As System.Web.UI.WebControls.Label
    Protected labDBUserName As System.Web.UI.WebControls.Label
    Protected labDBUserPassword As System.Web.UI.WebControls.Label
    Protected labEmailServer As System.Web.UI.WebControls.Label

    '*****************************************************************************
    '
    '    ROUTINE: Page_Load
    '
    '    DESCRIPTION: This routine provides the event handler for the page load
    '                 event.  It is responsible for initializing the controls
    '                 on the page.
    '-----------------------------------------------------------------------------
    Private Sub Page_Load(ByVal sender As System.Object, _
                    ByVal e As System.EventArgs) Handles MyBase.Load
      Dim siteConfig As VBCustomConfigHandlers.VBSiteConfiguration

      siteConfig = CType(ConfigurationSettings.GetConfig("siteProperties"), _
                    VBCustomConfigHandlers.VBSiteConfiguration)
      labApplicationName.Text = siteConfig.applicationName
      labDBServer.Text = siteConfig.databaseServer
      labDBName.Text = siteConfig.databaseName
      labDBUserName.Text = siteConfig.databaseUserName
      labDBUserPassword.Text = siteConfig.databaseUserPassword
      labEmailServer.Text = siteConfig.emailServer
    End Sub   'Page_Load
  End Class   'CH09CustomConfigHandlerVB
End Namespace
```

Example 9-14. Sample web form using custom configuration data code-behind (.cs)

```csharp
//-----------------------------------------------------------------------------
//
//    Module Name: CH09CustomConfigHandlerCS.aspx.cs
//
//    Description: This module provides the code behind for the
//                 CH09CustomConfigHandlerCS.aspx page
//
//*****************************************************************************
using System;
using System.Configuration;
```

Example 9-14. Sample web form using custom configuration data code-behind (.cs) (continued)

```csharp
namespace ASPNetCookbook.CSExamples
{
  public class CH09CustomConfigHandlerCS : System.Web.UI.Page
  {
    // controls on the form
    protected System.Web.UI.WebControls.Label labApplicationName;
    protected System.Web.UI.WebControls.Label labDBServer;
    protected System.Web.UI.WebControls.Label labDBName;
    protected System.Web.UI.WebControls.Label labDBUserName;
    protected System.Web.UI.WebControls.Label labDBUserPassword;
    protected System.Web.UI.WebControls.Label labEmailServer;

    //*************************************************************************
    //
    //   ROUTINE: Page_Load
    //
    //   DESCRIPTION: This routine provides the event handler for the page
    //                load event.  It is responsible for initializing the
    //                controls on the page.
    //-------------------------------------------------------------------------
    private void Page_Load(object sender, System.EventArgs e)
    {
      CSCustomConfigHandlers.CSSiteConfiguration siteConfig = null;

      siteConfig = (CSCustomConfigHandlers.CSSiteConfiguration)
                  (ConfigurationSettings.GetConfig("siteProperties"));

      labApplicationName.Text = siteConfig.applicationName;
      labDBServer.Text = siteConfig.databaseServer;
      labDBName.Text = siteConfig.databaseName;
      labDBUserName.Text = siteConfig.databaseUserName;
      labDBUserPassword.Text = siteConfig.databaseUserPassword;
      labEmailServer.Text = siteConfig.emailServer;
    } //Page_Load
  } // CH09CustomConfigHandlerCS
}
```

CHAPTER 10

Tracing and Debugging

10.0   Introduction

The recipes in this chapter show you how you can locate problems in your ASP.NET applications by using features that support tracing, debugging, and stress testing.

The first six recipes show you how to use tracing to pinpoint the causes of problems in your code. *Tracing* allows you, through a simple configuration setting or page-level attribute, to have ASP.NET write a whole host of information about the currently executing request to the page or to a trace log. We start by discussing how you initiate page- and application-level tracing. We also show how you can dynamically turn on page-level tracing when an exception occurs. Next, we show you how to make tracing work for components—those that will run on the web, as well as those that will be used elsewhere. The latter technique is important when you don't want your use of tracing-related code to preclude you from using a component outside of ASP.NET. We also show you how to write trace information to a log file from within a component.

Next we discuss *debugging*, specifically how setting conditional breakpoints can be a powerful technique for debugging your ASP.NET applications. Setting conditional breakpoints is especially useful for stopping execution at a specific point in iteration-heavy code, the focus of one of this chapter's recipes.

Finally, we take a look at *stress testing*, using the Application Center Test (ACT) tool, which is available to users of the Enterprise Architect and Enterprise Developer Editions of VS.NET. With ACT, you can fairly easily stress test a web application or service, which is especially useful when scalability is a key goal of your project. The last recipe in the chapter discusses how you might use this tool to analyze the performance of a simple web service.

The recipes in this chapter are intended to help remove some of the mystery of tracing and debugging, and, in the process, help you use these techniques earlier in the development cycle when problems are often less costly to fix.

10.1 Uncovering Page-Level Problems

Problem

You want to find the source of a problem that appears to be associated with a particular page of your application, such as a page that completes its operations more slowly than desired.

Solution

Enable page-level tracing for the page in question by setting the Trace attribute of the @ Page directive in the *.aspx* file to "true" and then using Trace.Write (or Trace.Warn) statements as warranted in your code-behind to write trace information to the trace output.

Examples 10-1 through 10-3 show the code we've written to illustrate this solution. Example 10-1 shows the *.aspx* file for a typical ASP.NET page. The code-behind class for the page appears in Example 10-2 (VB) and Example 10-3 (C#). By running the page and analyzing the trace sequence, you can see how long certain key operations are taking. The output with the trace sequence is shown in Figure 10-1.

ASP.NET Cookbook
The Ultimate ASP.NET Code Sourcebook

Page-Level Tracing (VB)

Request Details

Session Id:	l1xqyy454jbjsnv3nja0e145	Request Type:	GET
Time of Request:	5/17/2003 5:35:38 PM	Status Code:	200
Request Encoding:	Unicode (UTF-8)	Response Encoding:	Unicode (UTF-8)

Trace Information

Category	Message	From First(s)	From Last(s)
aspx.page	Begin Init		
aspx.page	End Init	0.000065	0.000065
Page_Load	Before performing concatenations	0.000109	0.000044
Page_Load	After performing concatenations	12.067026	12.066917
Aver/concat	1.2063	12.067210	0.000185
aspx.page	Begin PreRender	12.067251	0.000041
aspx.page	End PreRender	12.067288	0.000037
aspx.page	Begin SaveViewState	12.067542	0.000255
aspx.page	End SaveViewState	12.068175	0.000633
aspx.page	Begin Render	12.068230	0.000055
aspx.page	End Render	12.069432	0.001202

Figure 10-1. :Sample tracing output

Discussion

Tracing tracks and presents the execution details about an HTTP request. The TraceContext class is actually where ASP.NET stores information about an HTTP request and its trace information. You access the `TraceContext` class through the `Page.Trace` property of an ASP.NET page. To enable tracing for the page, be sure to set the `Trace` attribute of the `@ Page` directive in the *.aspx* file to `"true"`, as shown in Example 10-1.

The `TraceContext` class has two methods for writing statements into the trace log: `Write` and `Warn`. The only difference is that `Warn` outputs statements in red so that they are easier to spot in the trace log. Both methods are overloaded and have three versions. If you pass a single string argument, ASP.NET writes it to the Message column of the trace log, as shown in Figure 10-1. If you use two string arguments, the first string appears in the Category column and the second in the Message column. If you use a third argument, it must be of type Exception and contain information about an error, which ASP.NET then writes to the trace log.

If you've placed `Trace.Write` or `Trace.Warn` statements in your code, you don't have to worry about removing them later. The common language runtime (CLR) will ignore them when tracing is disabled. Just be sure to disable page-level tracing before deploying your application to a production environment.

In our example, `Trace.Write` is used three times to put custom messages into the trace sequence: the first time to mark the start of the concatenations and the second to mark the end of the concatenations. The third message outputs the average time for a string concatenation. The latter shows how inefficient it is to use a classic concatenation operator (& or +) in ASP.NET string operations. (See Recipe 16.2 for more discussion of this code as well as the advantages of using the `StringBuilder` object to build strings over the classic concatenation operators.)

Notice in Figure 10-1 that the trace log (beginning with "Request Details") appears below the standard output for the ASP.NET page that is enabled for `Trace`. Here's an explanation of the "Trace Information" section contents in the trace log:

Category
A custom trace category that you specified as the first argument in a `Trace.Write` (or `Trace.Warn`) method call.

Message
A custom trace message that you specified as the second argument in a `Trace.Write` (or `Trace.Warn`) method call.

From First (s)
The time, in seconds, since the request processing was started (a running total).

From Last (s)
The time, in seconds, since the last message was displayed. This column is especially helpful for seeing how long individual operations are taking.

See Also

Recipe 16.2

Example 10-1. Page-level tracing (.aspx)

```
<%@ Page Trace="True" Language="vb" AutoEventWireup="false"
        Codebehind="CH10TestPageLevelTracingVB.aspx.vb"
        Inherits="ASPNetCookbook.VBExamples.CH10TestPageLevelTracingVB"%>
<!DOCTYPE HTML PUBLIC "-//W3C//DTD HTML 4.0 Transitional//EN">
<html>
  <head>
    <title>Test Page Level Tracing</title>
    <link rel="stylesheet" href="css/ASPNetCookbook.css">
  </head>
  <body leftmargin="0" marginheight="0" marginwidth="0" topmargin="0">
    <form id="frmTracing" method="post" runat="server">
      <table width="100%" cellpadding="0" cellspacing="0" border="0">
        <tr>
          <td align="center">
            <img src="images/ASPNETCookbookHeading_blue.gif">
          </td>
        </tr>
        <tr>
          <td class="dividerLine">
            <img src="images/spacer.gif" height="6" border="0"></td>
        </tr>
      </table>
      <table width="90%" align="center" border="0">
        <tr>
          <td><img src="images/spacer.gif" height="10" border="0"></td>
        </tr>
        <tr>
          <td align="center" class="PageHeading">
            Page-Level Tracing (VB)
          </td>
        </tr>
      </table>
    </form>
  </body>
</html>
```

Example 10-2. Code-behind for page-level tracing (.vb)

```
Option Explicit On
Option Strict On
'----------------------------------------------------------------------------
'
'   Module Name: CH10TestPageLevelTracingVB.aspx.vb
'
'   Description: This class provides the code behind for
'               CH10TestPageLevelTracingVB
'
'****************************************************************************
Imports System
Imports System.Text

Namespace ASPNetCookbook.VBExamples
```

Example 10-2. Code-behind for page-level tracing (.vb) (continued)

```vb
Public Class CH10TestPageLevelTracingVB
  Inherits System.Web.UI.Page

  '*************************************************************************
  '
  '   ROUTINE: Page_Load
  '
  '   DESCRIPTION: This routine provides the event handler for the page load
  '                event.  It is responsible for initializing the controls
  '                on the page.
  '-------------------------------------------------------------------------
  Private Sub Page_Load(ByVal sender As System.Object, _
                        ByVal e As System.EventArgs) Handles MyBase.Load
    Const STRING_SECTION As String = "1234567890"

    Dim testStr As String
    Dim counter As Integer
    Dim startTime As DateTime
    Dim elapsedTime As TimeSpan
    Dim loops As Integer

    'output trace message indicating the start of the concatenations
    Trace.Write("Page_Load", "Before performing concatenations")

    'Measure the elapsed time for 10,000 classic string concatenations
    loops = 10000
    startTime = DateTime.Now( )
    testStr = ""
    For counter = 1 To loops
      testStr &= STRING_SECTION
    Next

    'output trace message indicating the end of the concatenations
    Trace.Write("Page_Load", "After performing concatenations")

    'calculate the elapsed time for the string concatenations
    elapsedTime = DateTime.Now.Subtract(startTime)

    'Write average time per concatenation in milliseconds to trace sequence
    Trace.Write("Aver/concat", _
                (elapsedTime.TotalMilliseconds / loops).ToString("0.0000"))
  End Sub  'Page_Load
End Class  'CH10TestPageLevelTracingVB
End Namespace
```

Example 10-3. Code-behind for page-level tracing (.cs)

```cs
//-------------------------------------------------------------------------
//
//   Module Name: CH10TestPageLevelTracingCS.aspx.cs
//
//   Description: This class provides the code behind for
```

Example 10-3. Code-behind for page-level tracing (.cs) (continued)

```
//                    CH10TestPageLevelTracingCS
//
//*****************************************************************************
using System;
using System.Text;

namespace ASPNetCookbook.CSExamples
{
  public class CH10TestPageLevelTracingCS : System.Web.UI.Page
  {
    //*************************************************************************
    //
    //   ROUTINE: Page_Load
    //
    //   DESCRIPTION: This routine provides the event handler for the page
    //                load event.  It is responsible for initializing the
    //                controls on the page.
    //-------------------------------------------------------------------------
    private void Page_Load(object sender, System.EventArgs e)
    {
      const string STRING_SECTION = "1234567890";

      string testStr = null;
      DateTime startTime;
      TimeSpan elapsedTime;
      int counter;
      int loops;

      // output trace message indicating the start of the concatenations
      Trace.Write("Page_Load", "Before performing concatenations");

      // measure the elapsed time for 10000 classic string concatenations
      loops = 10000;
      startTime = DateTime.Now;
      testStr = "";
      for (counter = 1; counter <= loops; counter++)
      {
        testStr += STRING_SECTION;
      }

      // output trace message indicating the end of the concatenations
      Trace.Write("Page_Load", "After performing concatenations");

      // calculate the elapsed time for the string concatenations
      elapsedTime = DateTime.Now.Subtract(startTime);

      // Write average time per concatenation in milliseconds to trace sequence
      Trace.Write("Aver/concat",
                  (elapsedTime.TotalMilliseconds / loops).ToString("0.0000"));
    }  // Page_Load
  }  // CH10TestPageLevelTracingCS
}
```

10.2 Uncovering Problems Application Wide

Problem

You want to find the sources of problems at any point in an application, but you don't want to have to change every page to do so, nor do you want to disrupt the output of your application pages.

Solution

Enable application-level tracing in the application *web.config* file and then view the AXD application trace log for your application.

1. Locate the *web.config* file in the root directory of your application (or create one if it does not already exist).

2. Enable application-level tracing by adding a `<trace>` element to the `<system.web>` section of *web.config* and setting its enabled attribute to "true":

```
<configuration>
  <system.web>
    <trace enabled="true" />
  </system.web>
</configuration>
```

3. View the application trace log by browsing to the *trace.axd* page from the application root, like this:

   http://localhost/<your application name>/trace.axd

Figure 10-2 shows some sample trace log output.

Application Trace
ASPNETCookbook
[clear current trace]

Physical Directory: c:\inetpub\wwwroot\ASPNETCookbook\

Requests to this Application — Remaining: 0

No.	Time of Request	File	Status Code	Verb	
1	5/17/2003 3:55:58 PM	/PageLevelTracing_VB.aspx	200	GET	View Details
2	5/17/2003 4:18:55 PM	/PageLevelTracing_VB.aspx	200	GET	View Details
3	5/17/2003 4:19:37 PM	/PageLevelTracing_VB.aspx	200	GET	View Details
4	5/17/2003 4:19:44 PM	/PageLevelTracing_VB.aspx	200	GET	View Details
5	5/17/2003 4:19:59 PM	/PageLevelTracing_VB.aspx	200	GET	View Details
6	5/17/2003 4:20:22 PM	/PageLevelTracing_VB.aspx	200	GET	View Details
7	5/17/2003 4:20:43 PM	/PageLevelTracing_VB.aspx	200	GET	View Details
8	5/17/2003 4:20:32 PM	/PageLevelTracing_VB.aspx	200	GET	View Details
9	5/17/2003 4:21:06 PM	/PageLevelTracing_VB.aspx	200	GET	View Details
10	5/17/2003 4:21:06 PM	/PageLevelTracing_VB.aspx	200	GET	View Details

Figure 10-2. Application-level tracing output (trace.axd)

Discussion

By adding a `<trace>` element to *web.config* and setting its enabled attribute to "true", you can activate application-level tracing.

```
<trace enabled="true" />
```

What then happens is that ASP.NET collects trace information for each HTTP request to the application and directs it to the application trace log. You can view the application trace log in the trace viewer. To view the trace viewer, request *trace.axd* from the root of your application directory:

http://localhost/<your application name>/trace.axd

 trace.axd is not an actual page but rather a special URL that is intercepted by ASP.NET. In actuality, *trace.axd* is an HTTP handler, the equivalent of an ISAPI extension. Chapter 17 provides recipes on how to create your own HTTP handlers.

What *trace.axd* actually shows you is a sequential listing of the HTTP requests processed by your application, as shown in Figure 10-2.

Here are some of the more commonly used <trace> element attributes:

requestLimit

The default number of HTTP requests stored in the application trace log is 10. If the limit is reached, ASP.NET automatically disables tracing. You can increase the number of HTTP requests using the requestLimit attribute:

```
<trace enabled="true" requestLimit="40" />
```

Once the limit it reached, no other HTTP requests will be logged until the application is restarted, you hit the "clear current trace" link on the *trace.axd* page (see the upper-right corner of Figure 10-2), or the query string clear=1 is passed to *trace.axd*, like so:

http://localhost/<your application name>/trace.axd?clear=1

pageOutput

If, in addition to viewing the *trace.axd* file, you also want to see trace information displayed at the bottom of the page that it is associated with, add pageOutput="true" to the <trace> element:

```
<trace enabled="true" pageOutput="true" />
```

The trace information you will see is identical to what would appear had you placed Trace="true" in the @ Page directive for the page (see Recipe 10.0 for details).

localOnly

To show trace information to the local user (i.e., the browser making the request is on the machine serving the request) but not to remote users, make sure the <trace> element includes localOnly="true":

```
<trace enabled="true" pageOutput="true" localOnly="true" />
```

If you are viewing the trace log in the trace viewer and you want to see specific information about a request, like the kind you would see in Figure 10-1, click the "View Details" link to the right.

When deploying your application to a production environment, you can explicitly disable *trace.axd* by placing <httpHandler> elements like these in *web.config*:

```
<configuration>
    <system.web>
        <httpHandlers>
            <remove verb="*" path="trace.axd" />
        </httpHandlers>
    </system.web>
</configuration>
```

10.3   Pinpointing the Cause of an Exception

Problem

You want to identify problems only when an exception occurs.

Solution

Dynamically turn on page-level tracing from within the Catch block of your exception handler and write to the trace log.

In the code-behind class for the page, use the .NET language of your choice to:

1. Set Page.Trace.IsEnabled = true in the Catch block of your exception handler.

2. Write to the trace log by using a Trace.Write of the form Trace.Write("Exception", "*Message*", *exc*).

Figure 10-3 shows the appearance of some exception information in the trace sequence. Examples 10-4 through 10-6 show the *.aspx* file and VB and C# code-behind files for the application that produces this result.

Discussion

ASP.NET processes and displays trace statements only when tracing is enabled. However, what if you don't want to see the trace log all the time, but only when an exception occurs? The answer is to turn tracing on dynamically for the page. You can then write the exception information to the trace log and debug the problem from there.

Our example that illustrates this solution is rather primitive, in that it simply forces an exception. While this is not something you would normally do in production code, it does allow us to show the infrastructure needed to control tracing at runtime.

When the exception occurs, the exception handler enables the trace output by setting Trace.IsEnabled to true. In order for the exception information to appear in the trace sequence, you must use a Trace.Write of the form Trace.Write("Exception", "*Message*", *exc*), where *exc* is the Exception object defined in the catch statement.

Additionally, the code limits who sees the trace sequence, something you might want to consider if you are loathe to show tracing information to remote users when an

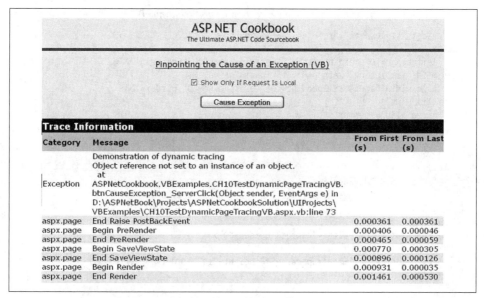

Figure 10-3. Exception information in the trace sequence

exception occurs. Before activating tracing, the program checks to see whether the application is being run from the local machine (i.e., the browser making the request is on the machine serving the request). It does so by using the Request object to get the local IP address from the server variables. It then compares this local address to the *loopback address*, a special IP number (127.0.0.1) that is designated for the software loopback interface of a machine. If it is not equal to the loopback address, a further comparison is then made to see if the local IP address from the server variables is the same as the local IP address that accompanied the request. The results of the comparison are then used to determine whether to enable tracing and display the exception information in the trace sequence.

> The URLs for page requests on the local machine can be in the form *http://localhost/site/page* or *http://[server]/site/page* (where *[server]* is the local server name), so it is necessary to check for the loopback IP address as well as the actual IP address. If the page were requested using the server name in the URL, it would not be detected as a local request if the second check were not performed.

Example 10-4. Pinpointing the cause of an exception (.aspx)

```
<%@ Page Language="vb" AutoEventWireup="false"
        Codebehind="CH10TestDynamicPageTracingVB.aspx.vb"
        Inherits="ASPNetCookbook.VBExamples.CH10TestDynamicPageTracingVB"%>
<!DOCTYPE HTML PUBLIC "-//W3C//DTD HTML 4.0 Transitional//EN">
<html>
  <head>
    <title>Test Dynamic Page Tracing</title>
```

Example 10-4. Pinpointing the cause of an exception (.aspx) (continued)

```
    <link rel="stylesheet" href="css/ASPNetCookbook.css">
  </head>
<body leftmargin="0" marginheight="0" marginwidth="0" topmargin="0">
  <form id="frmTracing" method="post" runat="server">
    <table width="100%" cellpadding="0" cellspacing="0" border="0">
      <tr>
        <td align="center">
          <img src="images/ASPNETCookbookHeading_blue.gif">
        </td>
      </tr>
      <tr>
        <td class="dividerLine">
          <img src="images/spacer.gif" height="6" border="0"></td>
      </tr>
    </table>
    <table width="90%" align="center" border="0">
      <tr>
        <td><img src="images/spacer.gif" height="10" border="0"></td>
      </tr>
      <tr>
        <td align="center" class="PageHeading">
          Pinpointing the Cause of an Exception (VB)
        </td>
      </tr>
      <tr>
        <td><img src="images/spacer.gif" height="10" border="0"></td>
      </tr>
      <tr>
        <td align="center" class="LabelText">
          <input id="chkOnlyLocal" runat="server" type="checkbox">
          Show Only If Request Is Local
        </td>
      </tr>
      <tr>
        <td><img src="images/spacer.gif" height="10" border="0"></td>
      </tr>
      <tr>
        <td align="center">
          <input id="btnCauseException" runat="server" type="button"
                 value="Cause Exception" />
        </td>
      </tr>
    </table>
  </form>
  </body>
</html>
```

Example 10-5. Code-behind for pinpointing the cause of an exception (.vb)

```
Option Explicit On
Option Strict On
'-----------------------------------------------------------------------------
'
```

Example 10-5. Code-behind for pinpointing the cause of an exception (.vb) (continued)

```vb
'   Module Name: CH10TestDynamicPageTracingVB.aspx.vb
'
'   Description: This class provides the code behind for
'                CH10TestDynamicPageTracingVB
'
'*****************************************************************************
Imports System
Imports System.Collections
Imports System.Web
Imports System.Web.UI.HtmlControls
Imports System.Web.UI.WebControls
Imports System.Diagnostics

Namespace ASPNetCookbook.VBExamples
  Public Class CH10TestDynamicPageTracingVB
    Inherits System.Web.UI.Page

    'controls on the form
    Protected chkOnlyLocal As HtmlInputCheckBox
    Protected WithEvents btnCauseException As HtmlInputButton

    '*********************************************************************
    '
    '   ROUTINE: Page_Load
    '
    '   DESCRIPTION: This routine provides the event handler for the page load
    '                event. It is responsible for initializing the controls on
    '                the the page.
    '-------------------------------------------------------------------------
    Private Sub Page_Load(ByVal Sender As Object, _
                          ByVal E As EventArgs) Handles MyBase.Load
      'Put user code to initialize the page here
    End Sub  'Page_Load

    '*********************************************************************
    '
    '   ROUTINE: btnCauseException_ServerClick
    '
    '   DESCRIPTION: This routine provides the event handler for the cause
    '                exception button click event. It is responsible for
    '                causing an exception to demonstrate dynamic tracing
    '-------------------------------------------------------------------------
    Private Sub btnCauseException_ServerClick(ByVal sender As Object, _
                                              ByVal e As System.EventArgs) _
             Handles btnCauseException.ServerClick
      Dim list As ArrayList

      Try
        'force an exception by accessing the list without creating it first
        list.Add(0)

      Catch exc As Exception
```

Example 10-5. Code-behind for pinpointing the cause of an exception (.vb) (continued)

```vb
            'enable tracing and output the exception information
            If ((Not chkOnlyLocal.Checked) OrElse _
                ((chkOnlyLocal.Checked) And (requestIsFromLocalMachine()))) Then
              Trace.IsEnabled = True
              Trace.Write("Exception", _
                          "Demonstration of dynamic tracing", _
                          exc)
            End If
        End Try
    End Sub  'btnCauseException_ServerClick


    '**********************************************************************
    '
    '   ROUTINE: requestIsFromLocalMachine
    '
    '   DESCRIPTION: This routine checks to see if the page request came from
    '                the local machine.
    '
    '   NOTE: Since requests on a local machine can be in the form
    '         http://localhost/site/page or http://server/site/page,
    '         two checks are required.  The first is for the localhost
    '         loopback IP address (127.0.0.1) and the second is for the actual
    '         IP address of the requestor.
    '----------------------------------------------------------------------
    Private Function requestIsFromLocalMachine() As Boolean
      Dim isLocal As Boolean
      Dim localAddress As String

      ' Is browser fielding request from localhost?
      isLocal = Request.UserHostAddress.Equals("127.0.0.1")
      If (Not isLocal) Then
        ' Get local IP address from server variables
        localAddress = Request.ServerVariables.Get("LOCAL_ADDR")

        ' Compare local IP with IP address that accompanied request
        isLocal = Request.UserHostAddress.Equals(localAddress)
      End If

      Return (isLocal)
    End Function  'IsRequestFromLocalMachine
  End Class  'CH10TestDynamicPageTracingVB
End Namespace
```

Example 10-6. Code-behind for pinpointing the cause of an exception (.cs)

```csharp
//------------------------------------------------------------------------
//
//   Module Name: CH10TestDynamicPageTracingCS.aspx.cs
//
//   Description: This class provides the code behind for
//                CH10TestDynamicPageTracingCS
//
//**********************************************************************
```

Example 10-6. Code-behind for pinpointing the cause of an exception (.cs) (continued)

```csharp
using System;
using System.Collections;
using System.Web;
using System.Web.UI.WebControls;
using System.Web.UI.HtmlControls;

namespace ASPNetCookbook.CSExamples
{
  public class CH10TestDynamicPageTracingCS : System.Web.UI.Page
  {
    // controls on form
    protected HtmlInputCheckBox chkOnlyLocal;
    protected HtmlInputButton btnCauseException;

    //*************************************************************************
    //
    //   ROUTINE: Page_Load
    //
    //   DESCRIPTION: This routine provides the event handler for the page
    //                load event.  It is responsible for initializing the
    //                controls on the page.
    //-------------------------------------------------------------------------
    private void Page_Load(object sender, System.EventArgs e)
    {
      // wire the "cause exception" button event handler
      this.btnCauseException.ServerClick +=
        new System.EventHandler(this.btnCauseException_ServerClick);
    }  // Page_Load

    //*************************************************************************
    //
    //   ROUTINE: btnCauseException_ServerClick
    //
    //   DESCRIPTION: This routine provides the event handler for the cause
    //                exception button click event. It is responsible for
    //                causing an exception to demonstrate dynamic tracing
    //-------------------------------------------------------------------------
    private void btnCauseException_ServerClick(object sender,
                                               System.EventArgs e)
    {
      ArrayList list = null;

      try
      {
        // force an exception by accessing the list without creating it first
        list.Add(0);
      }  // try

      catch (Exception exc)
      {
        // enable tracing and output the exception information
        if ((!chkOnlyLocal.Checked) ||
            ((chkOnlyLocal.Checked) && (requestIsFromLocalMachine())))
```

Example 10-6. Code-behind for pinpointing the cause of an exception (.cs) (continued)

```
      {
        Trace.IsEnabled = true;
        Trace.Write("Exception",
                    "Demonstration of dynamic tracing",
                    exc);
      }
    } // catch
  } // btnCauseException_ServerClick


  //**************************************************************************
  //
  //   ROUTINE: requestIsFromLocalMachine
  //
  //   DESCRIPTION: This routine checks to see if the page request came
  //                from the local machine.
  //
  //   NOTE: Since requests on a local machine can be in the form
  //         http://localhost/site/page or http://server/site/page,
  //         two checks are required.  The first is for the localhost
  //         loopback IP address (127.0.0.1) and the second is for the
  //         actual IP address of the requestor.
  //--------------------------------------------------------------------------
  private Boolean requestIsFromLocalMachine( )
  {
    Boolean isLocal;
    string localAddress;

    // Is browser fielding request from localhost?
    isLocal = Request.UserHostAddress.Equals("127.0.0.1");
    if (!isLocal)
    {
      // Get local IP address from server variables
      localAddress = Request.ServerVariables.Get("LOCAL_ADDR");

      // Compare local IP with IP address that accompanied request
      isLocal = Request.UserHostAddress.Equals(localAddress);
    }

    return (isLocal);
  } // IsRequestFromLocalMachine
} // CH10TestDynamicPageTracingCS
}
```

10.4 Uncovering Problems Within Web Application Components

Problem

You want to identify problems within a component of your web application, but your attempts to do so don't seem to work. When you make a call to Trace.Write in the business object, either you get a compilation error or the debugger jumps right over the call and no output ever appears in the trace sequence.

Solution

Import the System.Web namespace and reference the current HTTP context when performing a Trace.Write from within the component.

In the component class, use the .NET language of your choice to:

1. Import the System.Web namespace.

2. Reference the current HTTP context when performing a Trace.Write, as in HTTPContext.Current.Trace.Write.

The sample component we've written to illustrate this solution appears in Example 10-7 (VB) and Example 10-8 (C#). Example 10-9 shows the *.aspx* file used to test the sample component. The code-behind for the test page appears in Example 10-10 (VB) and Example 10-11 (C#). Figure 10-4 shows some sample output, including the resulting trace sequence.

ASP.NET Cookbook
The Ultimate ASP.NET Code Sourcebook

Tracing Within Components (VB)

Request Details

Session Id:	hio1hx550cuiwd45dqc3rc55	Request Type:	GET
Time of Request:	5/18/2003 12:28:38 PM	Status Code:	200
Request Encoding:	Unicode (UTF-8)	Response Encoding:	Unicode (UTF-8)

Trace Information

Category	Message	From First(s)	From Last(s)
aspx.page	Begin Init		
aspx.page	End Init	0.000051	0.000051
In Component	Before performing concatenations	1.336137	1.336086
In Component	After performing concatenations	1.420712	0.084575
In Component	Aver/concat = 0.0781	1.420858	0.000146
aspx.page	Begin PreRender	1.420900	0.000043
aspx.page	End PreRender	1.420939	0.000039
aspx.page	Begin SaveViewState	1.421193	0.000254
aspx.page	End SaveViewState	1.421844	0.000651
aspx.page	Begin Render	1.421899	0.000054
aspx.page	End Render	1.424341	0.002443

Figure 10-4. Trace sequence from testing the component

Discussion

In order for Trace.Write to work from within a component, you must be able to access the context for the current HTTP request. The easiest way to accomplish this is to import the System.Web namespace and access the HTTPContext.Current property from within the component.

If a component is not part of your web application, you will need to add a reference to the System.Web.dll assembly in your project. You do this in Visual Studio .NET by selecting the project containing the component in the Solution Explorer. Right-click, and then select Add Reference. In the .NET tab of the dialog box that is displayed, select System.Web.dll from the list of components, click Select, and finally click OK.

The HTTPContext provides access to the Trace object that allows your application to write trace information, as shown in Example 10-7 (VB) and Example 10-8 (C#).

There is one major caveat to this sample: the disadvantage of referencing the current HTTP context in your component is that it does not allow the component to be used in non-web applications. If you need to share components in web and non-web applications, you may want to consider creating a Listener subclass instead, as described in Recipe 10.5.

See Also

Recipe 10.5

Example 10-7. The business service class (.vb)

```vb
Option Explicit On
Option Strict On
'-----------------------------------------------------------------------------
'
'   Module Name: CH10TestWebComponentVB.vb
'
'   Description: This class provides a "web" component for demonstrating
'                outputting trace information from within a class
'
'*****************************************************************************
Imports System
Imports System.Web

Namespace ASPNetCookbook.VBExamples
  Public Class CH10TestWebComponentVB

    Private mStr As String

    '*****************************************************************************
    '
    '   ROUTINE: theString
    '
    '   DESCRIPTION: This property provides the ability to get/set the
    '                string in the object
    '-----------------------------------------------------------------------------
    Public Property theString() As String
```

Example 10-7. The business service class (.vb) (continued)

```vb
    Get
      Return (mStr)
    End Get
    Set(ByVal Value As String)
      mStr = Value
    End Set
End Property  'theString

'**************************************************************************
'
'    ROUTINE: addToString
'
'    DESCRIPTION: This routine provides the ability to add the passed
'                 string to the private string in this object one or
'                 more times.
'--------------------------------------------------------------------------
Public Sub addToString(ByVal stringToAdd As String, _
                       ByVal numberOfCopies As Integer)
    Dim counter As Integer
    Dim startTime As DateTime
    Dim elapsedTime As TimeSpan
    Dim averageTime As Double

    'output trace message indicating the start of the concatenations
    HttpContext.Current.Trace.Write("In Component", _
                                    "Before performing concatenations")

    'concatenation the passed string as requested
    startTime = DateTime.Now( )
    For counter = 1 To numberOfCopies
      mStr &= stringToAdd
    Next

    'output trace message indicating the end of the concatenations
    HttpContext.Current.Trace.Write("In Component", _
                                    "After performing concatenations")

    'calculate the elapsed time for the string concatenations
    elapsedTime = DateTime.Now.Subtract(startTime)

    'Write average time per concatenation in milliseconds to trace sequence
    averageTime = elapsedTime.TotalMilliseconds / numberOfCopies
    HttpContext.Current.Trace.Write("In Component", _
                       "Aver/concat = " & averageTime.ToString("0.0000"))
End Sub   'addToString

'**************************************************************************
'
'    ROUTINE: New
'
'    DESCRIPTION: This constructor creates the object and initializes the
'                 variables in the object
'--------------------------------------------------------------------------
```

Example 10-7. The business service class (.vb) (continued)

```
    Public Sub New( )
      'initialize string in object
      mStr = ""
    End Sub  'New
  End Class  'CH10TestWebComponentVB
End Namespace
```

Example 10-8. The business service class (.cs)

```
//----------------------------------------------------------------------------
//
//   Module Name: CH10TestWebComponentCS.cs
//
//   Description: This class provides a "web" component for demonstrating
//                outputting trace information from within a class
//
//****************************************************************************
using System;
using System.Web;

namespace ASPNetCookbook.CSExamples
{
  public class CH10TestWebComponentCS
  {
    private String mStr;

    //****************************************************************************
    //
    //   ROUTINE: theString
    //
    //   DESCRIPTION: This property provides the ability to get/set the
    //                string in the object
    //----------------------------------------------------------------------------
    public String theString
    {
      get
      {
        return(mStr);
      }
      set
      {
        mStr = value;
      }
    }  // theString

    //****************************************************************************
    //
    //   ROUTINE: addToString
    //
    //   DESCRIPTION: This routine provides the ability to add the passed
    //                string to the private string in this object one or
    //                more times.
    //----------------------------------------------------------------------------
```

Example 10-8. The business service class (.cs) (continued)

```
  public void addToString(String stringToAdd,
                          int numberOfCopies)
  {
    int counter;
    DateTime startTime;
    TimeSpan elapsedTime;
    Double averageTime;

    // output trace message indicating the start of the concatenations
    HttpContext.Current.Trace.Write("In Component",
                                    "Before performing concatenations");

    // concatenation the passed string as requested
    startTime = DateTime.Now;
    for (counter = 1; counter <numberOfCopies; counter++)
    {
      mStr += stringToAdd;
    }

    // output trace message indicating the end of the concatenations
    HttpContext.Current.Trace.Write("In Component",
                                    "After performing concatenations");

    // calculate the elapsed time for the string concatenations
    elapsedTime = DateTime.Now.Subtract(startTime);

    // Write average time per concatenation in milliseconds to trace sequence
    averageTime = elapsedTime.TotalMilliseconds / numberOfCopies;
    HttpContext.Current.Trace.Write("In Component",
                      "Aver/concat = " + averageTime.ToString("0.0000"));
    } // addToString

  //**********************************************************************
  //
  //    ROUTINE: TestWebComponentCS
  //
  //    DESCRIPTION: This constructor creates the object and initializes the
  //                 variables in the object
  //----------------------------------------------------------------------
  public CH10TestWebComponentCS( )
  {
    // initialize string in object
    mStr = "";
    } // CH10TestWebComponentCS
  } // CH10TestWebComponentCS
}
```

Example 10-9. Code to test tracing in the component (.aspx)

```
<%@ Page Language="vb" AutoEventWireup="false" Trace="True"
    Codebehind="CH10TestTraceWithinWebComponentVB.aspx.vb"
    Inherits="ASPNetCookbook.VBExamples.CH10TestTraceWithinWebComponentVB"%>
```

Example 10-9. Code to test tracing in the component (.aspx) (continued)

```html
<!DOCTYPE HTML PUBLIC "-//W3C//DTD HTML 4.0 Transitional//EN">
<html>
  <head>
    <title>Test Trace Within Web Component</title>
    <link rel="stylesheet" href="css/ASPNetCookbook.css">
  </head>
  <body leftmargin="0" marginheight="0" marginwidth="0" topmargin="0">
    <form id="frmTracing" method="post" runat="server">
      <table width="100%" cellpadding="0" cellspacing="0" border="0">
        <tr>
          <td align="center">
            <img src="images/ASPNETCookbookHeading_blue.gif">
          </td>
        </tr>
        <tr>
          <td class="dividerLine">
            <img src="images/spacer.gif" height="6" border="0"></td>
        </tr>
      </table>
      <table width="90%" align="center" border="0">
        <tr>
          <td><img src="images/spacer.gif" height="10" border="0"></td>
        </tr>
        <tr>
          <td align="center" class="PageHeading">
            Tracing Within Web Components (VB)
          </td>
        </tr>
      </table>
    </form>
  </body>
</html>
```

Example 10-10. Code to test tracing in the component (.vb)

```vb
Option Explicit On
Option Strict On
'----------------------------------------------------------------------------
'
'   Module Name: CH10TestTraceWithinWebComponentVB.aspx.vb
'
'   Description: This class provides the code behind for
'                CH10TestTraceWithinWebComponentVB.aspx
'
'*****************************************************************************

Namespace ASPNetCookbook.VBExamples
  Public Class CH10TestTraceWithinWebComponentVB
    Inherits System.Web.UI.Page

    '*************************************************************************
    '
```

Example 10-10. Code to test tracing in the component (.vb) (continued)

```vb
'    ROUTINE: Page_Load
'
'    DESCRIPTION: This routine provides the event handler for the page load
'                 event.  It is responsible for initializing the controls
'                 on the page.
'
'-----------------------------------------------------------------------
Private Sub Page_Load(ByVal sender As System.Object, _
                      ByVal e As System.EventArgs) Handles MyBase.Load
    Dim webComponent As CH10TestWebComponentVB

    'create the "web aware" component
    webComponent = New CH10TestWebComponentVB

    'add a string to the string in the component 1000 times
    webComponent.addToString("1234567890", _
                             1000)
End Sub   'Page_Load

  End Class  'CH10TestTraceWithinWebComponentVB
End Namespace
```

Example 10-11. Code to test tracing in the component (.cs)

```csharp
//-----------------------------------------------------------------------
//
//    Module Name: CH10TestTraceWithinWebComponentCS.aspx.cs
//
//    Description: This class provides the code behind for
//                 CH10TestTraceWithinWebComponentCS.aspx
//
//***********************************************************************
using System;

namespace ASPNetCookbook.CSExamples
{
  public class CH10TestTraceWithinWebComponentCS : System.Web.UI.Page
  {
    //***********************************************************************
    //
    //    ROUTINE: Page_Load
    //
    //    DESCRIPTION: This routine provides the event handler for the page
    //                 load event.  It is responsible for initializing the
    //                 controls on the page.
    //-----------------------------------------------------------------------
    private void Page_Load(object sender, System.EventArgs e)
    {
      CH10TestWebComponentCS webComponent = null;

      // create the "web aware" component
      webComponent = new CH10TestWebComponentCS();
```

Example 10-11. Code to test tracing in the component (.cs) (continued)

```
    // add a string to the string in the component 1000 times
    webComponent.addToString("1234567890",
                                1000);
  } // Page_Load
 } // CH10TestTraceWithinWebComponentCS
}
```

10.5   Uncovering Problems Within Dual-Use Components

Problem

Because you intend to use a business component in both web and non-web applications, you want to enable tracing within the component without having to reference its current HTTP context.

Solution

Create your own trace listener that inherits from the `TraceListener` class, overrides the `Write` and `WriteLine` methods, and references the current HTTP context to output the message. A sample trace listener we've written to illustrate this solution is shown in Example 10-12 (VB) and Example 10-13 (C#).

Next, modify *web.config*, as shown in Example 10-14, to add the listener to the `Listeners` collection and make it available to your application.

In your non-web-specific components, add plain-vanilla `Trace.Write` statements to output any desired information to the trace log, as shown in our sample component in Example 10-15 (VB) and Example 10-16 (C#).

A web form and the associated VB and C# code-behind we've written to test the tracing in our non-web-specific component are shown in Examples 10-17 through 10-19.

Discussion

The .NET Framework uses the concept of *trace listeners* in its handling of trace messages. By default, the `TraceListeners` collection contains a single listener (`DefaultTraceListener`) when you enable tracing. Additional listeners can be added via the *web.config* file or programmatically. When a `Trace.Write` is executed, all listeners in the `TraceListeners` collection receive and process the message. It is this mechanism that allows you to add trace statements to your components without the need to add a reference to the `System.Web` assembly.

The custom `TraceListener` in our example overrides the `Write` and `WriteLine` methods to write the passed message to the current HTTP context in the same manner we did in Recipe 10.4. The custom `TraceListener` is made available by adding the entry to *web.config* shown in Example 10-14.

 When adding a `TraceListener` to your *web.config* file, it is very important that you specify the type correctly. The type attribute must be specified as shown here.

```
type="namespace, assembly"
```

The namespace must be the fully qualified namespace of the custom `TraceListener`. The assembly must be the name of the assembly into which the custom `TraceListener` is compiled.

Our example business service class is nearly identical to the one we used in Recipe 10.4. Here are the differences:

- The imports (or using) statement at the beginning of the class is changed from `System.Web` to `System.Diagnostics`. (The `System.Diagnostics` namespace provides the abstract base class for the trace listeners.)
- The `HttpContext.Current.Trace.Write` statements are changed to `Trace.Write`.

Our test web form, like our example business service class, is also nearly identical to our test web form used in Recipe 10.4. The only difference is that it uses our example business service class.

There are two advantages to the approach this recipe takes over the previous recipe:

- You can use plain-vanilla `Trace.Writes` in your component; they don't have to reference the current HTTP context, thus maintaining the component's compatibility for non-web uses.
- You can turn tracing on and off via a configuration file.

See Also

Recipe 10.4

Example 10-12. The Listener subclass (.vb)

```vb
Option Explicit On
Option Strict On
'---------------------------------------------------------------------------
'
'   Module Name: CH10WebListenerVB.vb
'
'   Description: This class provides a trace listener that outputs messages
'                that are shown in trace data of an ASPX page.
'
'***************************************************************************
Imports System
Imports System.Diagnostics
Imports System.Web
Imports System.IO
```

Example 10-12. The Listener subclass (.vb) (continued)

```vb
Namespace ASPNetCookbook.VBExamples
  Public Class CH10WebListenerVB
    Inherits TraceListener

    '*************************************************************************
    '
    '   ROUTINE: Write
    '
    '   DESCRIPTION: This routine writes the passed message to the
    '                HttpContext Trace object
    '-------------------------------------------------------------------------
    Public Overloads Overrides Sub Write(ByVal message As String)
      HttpContext.Current.Trace.Write(message)
    End Sub   'Write

    '*************************************************************************
    '
    '   ROUTINE: Write
    '
    '   DESCRIPTION: This routine writes the passed message to the
    '                HttpContext Trace object
    '-------------------------------------------------------------------------
    Public Overloads Overrides Sub Write(ByVal category As String, _
                                         ByVal message As String)
      HttpContext.Current.Trace.Write(category, _
                                      message)
    End Sub   'Write

    '*************************************************************************
    '
    '   ROUTINE: WriteLine
    '
    '   DESCRIPTION: This routine writes the passed message to the
    '                HttpContext Trace object with a CR/LF
    '-------------------------------------------------------------------------
    Public Overloads Overrides Sub WriteLine(ByVal message As String)
      HttpContext.Current.Trace.Write(message)
    End Sub   'WriteLine

    '*************************************************************************
    '
    '   ROUTINE: Write
    '
    '   DESCRIPTION: This routine writes the passed message to the
    '                HttpContext Trace object
    '-------------------------------------------------------------------------
    Public Overloads Overrides Sub WriteLine(ByVal category As String, _
                                             ByVal message As String)
      HttpContext.Current.Trace.Write(category, _
                                      message)
    End Sub   'WriteLine
```

Example 10-12. The Listener subclass (.vb) (continued)

```
  End Class   'CH1OWebListenerVB
End Namespace
```

Example 10-13. The Listener subclass (.cs)

```csharp
//----------------------------------------------------------------------------
//
//   Module Name: CH1OWebListenerCS.cs
//
//   Description: This class provides a trace listener that outputs messages
//                that are shown in trace data of an ASPX page.
//
//****************************************************************************
using System;
using System.Diagnostics;
using System.Web;

namespace ASPNetCookbook.CSExamples
{
  public class CH1OWebListenerCS : TraceListener
  {
    //************************************************************************
    //
    //   ROUTINE: Write
    //
    //   DESCRIPTION: This routine writes the passed message to the
    //                HttpContext Trace object
    //------------------------------------------------------------------------
    public override void Write(String message)
    {
      HttpContext.Current.Trace.Write(message);
    } // Write


    //************************************************************************
    //
    //   ROUTINE: Write
    //
    //   DESCRIPTION: This routine writes the passed message to the
    //                HttpContext Trace object
    //------------------------------------------------------------------------
    public override void Write(String category,
                              String message)
    {
      HttpContext.Current.Trace.Write(category,
                                      message);
    } // Write


    //************************************************************************
    //
    //   ROUTINE: WriteLine
    //
```

Example 10-13. The Listener subclass (.cs) (continued)

```csharp
      //    DESCRIPTION: This routine writes the passed message to the
      //                 HttpContext Trace object
      //-------------------------------------------------------------------------
      public override void WriteLine(String message)
      {
        HttpContext.Current.Trace.Write(message);
      } // WriteLine

      //*********************************************************************
      //
      //    ROUTINE: WriteLine
      //
      //    DESCRIPTION: This routine writes the passed message to the
      //                 HttpContext Trace object
      //-------------------------------------------------------------------------
      public override void WriteLine(String category,
                                     String message)
      {
        HttpContext.Current.Trace.Write(category,
                                        message);
      } // WriteLine
   } // CH10WebListenerCS
}
```

Example 10-14. Web.config settings to add the trace listener

```xml
  <system.diagnostics>
    <trace autoflush="true" indentsize="0">
      <listeners>
        <add name="CookbookWebListener"
            type="ASPNetCookbook.VBExamples.CH10WebListenerVB, VBExamples" />
      </listeners>
    </trace>
  </system.diagnostics>
```

Example 10-15. Business service class with plain-vanilla Trace.Writes (.vb)

```vb
Option Explicit On
Option Strict On
'-----------------------------------------------------------------------------
'
'    Module Name: CH10TestNonWebComponentVB.vb
'
'    Description: This class provides a "non-web" component for demonstrating
'                 outputting trace information from within a class
'
'*****************************************************************************
Imports System
Imports System.Diagnostics

Namespace ASPNetCookbook.VBExamples
  Public Class CH10TestNonWebComponentVB
```

Example 10-15. Business service class with plain-vanilla Trace.Writes (.vb) (continued)

```vb
    Private mStr As String

    '*************************************************************************
    '
    '    ROUTINE: theString
    '
    '    DESCRIPTION: This property provides the ability to get/set the
    '                 string in the object
    '-------------------------------------------------------------------------
    Public Property theString() As String
      Get
        Return (mStr)
      End Get
      Set(ByVal Value As String)
        mStr = Value
      End Set
    End Property   'theString


    '*************************************************************************
    '
    '    ROUTINE: addToString
    '
    '    DESCRIPTION: This routine provides the ability to add the passed
    '                 string to the private string in this object one or
    '                 more times.
    '-------------------------------------------------------------------------
    Public Sub addToString(ByVal stringToAdd As String, _
                           ByVal numberOfCopies As Integer)
      Dim counter As Integer
      Dim startTime As DateTime
      Dim elapsedTime As TimeSpan
      Dim averageTime As Double

      'output trace message indicating the start of the concatenations
      Trace.Write("In Non-web Component", _
                "Before performing concatenations")

      'concatenation the passed string as requested
      startTime = DateTime.Now()
      For counter = 1 To numberOfCopies
        mStr &= stringToAdd
      Next

      'output trace message indicating the end of the concatenations
      Trace.Write("In Non-web Component", _
                "After performing concatenations")

      'calculate the elapsed time for the string concatenations
      elapsedTime = DateTime.Now.Subtract(startTime)

      'Write average time per concatenation in milliseconds to trace sequence
      averageTime = elapsedTime.TotalMilliseconds / numberOfCopies
```

Example 10-15. Business service class with plain-vanilla Trace.Writes (.vb) (continued)

```
    Trace.Write("In Non-web Component", _
                "Aver/concat = " & averageTime.ToString("0.0000"))
    End Sub   'addToString


    '**********************************************************************
    '
    '   ROUTINE: New
    '
    '   DESCRIPTION: This constructor creates the object and initializes the
    '                  variables in the object
    '----------------------------------------------------------------------
    Public Sub New( )
      'initialize string in object
      mStr = ""
    End Sub   'New
  End Class 'CH10TestNonWebComponentVB
End Namespace
```

Example 10-16. Business service class with plain-vanilla Trace.Writes (.cs)

```
//------------------------------------------------------------------------------
//
//    Module Name: CH10TestNonWebComponentCS.cs
//
//    Description: This class provides a "non-web" component for demonstrating
//                 outputting trace information from within a class
//
//******************************************************************************
using System;
using System.Diagnostics;

namespace ASPNetCookbook.CSExamples
{
  public class CH10TestNonWebComponentCS
  {
    private String mStr;

    //**************************************************************************
    //
    //   ROUTINE: theString
    //
    //    DESCRIPTION: This property provides the ability to get/set the
    //                 string in the object
    //--------------------------------------------------------------------------
    public String theString
    {
      get
      {
        return(mStr);
      }
      set
      {
        mStr = value;
```

```
  }
} // theString

//*********************************************************************
//
//   ROUTINE: addToString
//
// DESCRIPTION: This routine provides the ability to add the passed
//              string to the private string in this object one or
//              more times.
//---------------------------------------------------------------------
public void addToString(String stringToAdd,
  int numberOfCopies)
{
  int counter;
  DateTime startTime;
  TimeSpan elapsedTime;
  Double averageTime;

  // output trace message indicating the start of the concatenations
  Trace.Write("In Non-web Component",
              "Before performing concatenations");

  // concatenation the passed string as requested
  startTime = DateTime.Now;
  for (counter = 1; counter <numberOfCopies; counter++)
  {
    mStr += stringToAdd;
  }

  // output trace message indicating the end of the concatenations
  Trace.Write("In Non-web Component",
              "After performing concatenations");

  // calculate the elapsed time for the string concatenations
  elapsedTime = DateTime.Now.Subtract(startTime);

  // Write average time per concatenation in milliseconds to trace sequence
  averageTime = elapsedTime.TotalMilliseconds / numberOfCopies;
  Trace.Write("In Non-web Component",
              "Aver/concat = " + averageTime.ToString("0.0000"));
} // addToString

//*********************************************************************
//
//   ROUTINE: TestNonWebComponentCS
//
// DESCRIPTION: This constructor creates the object and initializes the
//              variables in the object
//---------------------------------------------------------------------
public CH10TestNonWebComponentCS( )
{
```

Example 10-16. Business service class with plain-vanilla Trace.Writes (.cs) (continued)

```
      // initialize string in object
      mStr = "";
    }  // CH10TestNonWebComponentCS
  }  // CH10TestNonWebComponentCS
}
```

Example 10-17. Code to test tracing in the non-web component (.aspx)

```
<%@ Page Language="vb" AutoEventWireup="false" Trace="true"
    Codebehind="CH10TestTraceWithinNonWebComponentVB.aspx.vb"
    Inherits="ASPNetCookbook.VBExamples.CH10TestTraceWithinNonWebComponentVB"%>
<!DOCTYPE HTML PUBLIC "-//W3C//DTD HTML 4.0 Transitional//EN">
<html>
  <head>
    <title>Test Trace Within NonWeb Component</title>
    <link rel="stylesheet" href="css/ASPNetCookbook.css">
  </head>
  <body leftmargin="0" marginheight="0" marginwidth="0" topmargin="0">
    <form id="frmTracing" method="post" runat="server">
      <table width="100%" cellpadding="0" cellspacing="0" border="0">
        <tr>
          <td align="center">
            <img src="images/ASPNETCookbookHeading_blue.gif">
          </td>
        </tr>
        <tr>
          <td class="dividerLine">
            <img src="images/spacer.gif" height="6" border="0"></td>
        </tr>
      </table>
      <table width="90%" align="center" border="0">
        <tr>
          <td><img src="images/spacer.gif" height="10" border="0"></td>
        </tr>
        <tr>
          <td align="center" class="PageHeading">
            Tracing Within Non-Web Components (VB)
          </td>
        </tr>
      </table>
    </form>
  </body>
</html>
```

Example 10-18. Code to test tracing in the non-web component code-behind (.vb)

```
Option Explicit On
Option Strict On
'----------------------------------------------------------------------------
'
'   Module Name: CH10TestTraceWithinNonWebComponentVB.aspx.vb
'
'   Description: This class provides the code behind for
```

Example 10-18. Code to test tracing in the non-web component code-behind (.vb) (continued)

```vb
'                   CH10TestTraceWithinNonWebComponentVB.aspx
'
'**************************************************************************

Namespace ASPNetCookbook.VBExamples
  Public Class CH10TestTraceWithinNonWebComponentVB
    Inherits System.Web.UI.Page

    '**********************************************************************
    '
    '   ROUTINE: Page_Load
    '
    '   DESCRIPTION: This routine provides the event handler for the page load
    '                event.  It is responsible for initializing the controls
    '                on the page.
    '----------------------------------------------------------------------
    Private Sub Page_Load(ByVal sender As System.Object, _
                          ByVal e As System.EventArgs) Handles MyBase.Load
      Dim webComponent As CH10TestNonWebComponentVB

      'create the "web aware" component
      webComponent = New CH10TestNonWebComponentVB

      'add a string to the string in the component 1000 times
      webComponent.addToString("1234567890", _
                               1000)
    End Sub 'Page_Load
  End Class  'CH10TestTraceWithinNonWebComponentVB
End Namespace
```

Example 10-19. Code to test tracing in the non-web component code-behind (.cs)

```csharp
//----------------------------------------------------------------------------
//
//   Module Name: CH10TestTraceWithinNonWebComponentCS.aspx.cs
//
//   Description: This class provides the code behind for
//                CH10TestTraceWithinNonWebComponentCS.aspx
//
//****************************************************************************
using System;

namespace ASPNetCookbook.CSExamples
{
  public class CH10TestTraceWithinNonWebComponentCS : System.Web.UI.Page
  {
    //****************************************************************************
    //
    //   ROUTINE: Page_Load
    //
    //   DESCRIPTION: This routine provides the event handler for the page
    //                load event.  It is responsible for initializing the
    //                controls on the page.
```

Example 10-19. Code to test tracing in the non-web component code-behind (.cs) (continued)

```
//------------------------------------------------------------------------
private void Page_Load(object sender, System.EventArgs e)
{
    CH10TestNonWebComponentCS webComponent = null;

    // create the "web aware" component
    webComponent = new CH10TestNonWebComponentCS();

    // add a string to the string in the component 1000 times
    webComponent.addToString("1234567890",
                             1000);
} // Page_Load
} // CH10TestTraceWithinNonWebComponentCS
}
```

10.6   Writing Trace Data to the Event Log with Controllable Levels

Problem

You want your application to output trace information to the event log and, at the same time, control what level of information is output.

Solution

Create your own trace listener that inherits from the TraceListener class and overrides the Write and WriteLine methods to write their output to the event log. A sample trace listener we've written to demonstrate this solution is shown in Example 10-20 (VB) and Example 10-21 (C#).

Next, modify your *web.config* file to add the custom TraceListener and TraceSwitch, as shown in Example 10-22.

In the classes you want to output trace information, create a TraceSwitch object using the name of the TraceSwitch you added to the *web.config* file, and then use the WriteIf and WriteLineIf methods of the Trace class to output the required messages, as we demonstrate in our class in Example 10-23 (VB) and Example 10-24 (C#).

Discussion

The technique we advocate for writing trace information to the event log involves creating your own custom trace listener that overrides the Write and WriteLine methods and directs their output to the event log. We also find it useful to control the level of messages that are output to the event log, such as outputting only error messages or outputting error and warning messages. Controlling the level of messages that are output involves the use of switches (more about this in a minute).

As discussed in Recipe 10.5, you can add additional listeners to the TraceListeners collection via the *web.config* file. When a Trace.Write or Trace.WriteLine is executed, all listeners in the TraceListeners collection receive and process their output.

The support that the .NET Framework provides for the writing of custom TraceListeners, as shown here and in other recipes in this chapter, is even more powerful when coupled with switches. *Switches* provide the ability to control when trace information is sent to the TraceListeners configured for your application.

Two switch types are provided in the .NET Framework: BooleanSwitch and TraceSwitch. The BooleanSwitch class supports two states (on and off) that literally turn the trace output on and off. The TraceSwitch class supports five levels (off, error, warning, info, and verbose) to provide the ability to output messages only for the configured levels.

In our example, we created a custom TraceListener similar to the one created in Recipe 10.5, except that the messages are written to the event log rather than the current page, as shown in Example 10-20 (VB) and Example 10-21 (C#).

 For additional information on writing to the event log, refer to Recipe 7.3.

You must first add the switch and listener information to your *web.config* file, as shown in Example 10-22. The switch data includes the name of the switch and the value for the switch. The switch name is the name used in your code to access the switch configuration. The value defines the message level to output, as shown in Table 10-1.

Table 10-1. Switch level values

Value	Meaning
0	Output no messages
1	Output only error messages
2	Output error and warning messages
3	Output error, warning, and informational messages
4	Output all messages

To output trace messages that use the switch information, you first need to create a TraceSwitch object passing the name of the switch and a general description of the switch. After creating the TraceSwitch, you use it with the WriteIf and WriteLineIf methods of the Trace class to output your messages. The first parameter of either method defines the level for which the message should be output. In other words, if you only want the message to be output when the switch is configured for "warnings," set the first parameter to the TraceWarning property of the switch you created. The second parameter should be set to the message you want to output.

We are not outputting the trace information to the web form, as we have in other examples in this chapter, so it is not necessary to add the trace="true" statement to the @ Page directive in the *.aspx* page or to turn on application-level tracing in the *web.config* file.

 The name used in the constructor of the TraceSwitch must match the name of the switch in the *web.config* file. Failing to use the exact name defined in the *web.config* file can cause you to spend a significant amount of time trying to determine why your messages are not being output as expected.

 In a web application, referencing the Trace class without further qualifying the namespace will actually reference the System.Web.Trace class, which does not support the WriteIf and WriteLineIf methods. To access the Trace class in the System.Diagnostics namespace that provides the WriteIf and WriteLineIf methods, fully qualify the reference:

```
System.Diagnostics.Trace.WriteIf(level,
                                 Message)
```

See Also

Recipe 7.3; for a discussion of trace listeners, see Recipe 10.5

Example 10-20. Custom TraceListener for writing to the event log (.vb)

```
Option Explicit On
Option Strict On
'----------------------------------------------------------------------------
'
'   Module Name: CH10EventLogListenerVB.vb
'
'   Description: This class provides a trace listener that outputs messages
'                to the application event log.
'
'****************************************************************************
Imports System
Imports System.Diagnostics

Namespace ASPNetCookbook.VBExamples
  Public Class CH10EventLogListenerVB
    Inherits TraceListener

    'the following constant defines the event log to which messages are
    'written
    Const EVENT_LOG_NAME As String = "Application"

    '********************************************************************
    '
    '   ROUTINE: Write
    '
```

```vb
'   DESCRIPTION: This routine writes the passed message to the
'                HttpContext Trace object
'-----------------------------------------------------------------------
Public Overloads Overrides Sub Write(ByVal message As String)
  writeLogEntry(message)
End Sub  'Write

'*************************************************************************
'
'   ROUTINE: Write
'
'   DESCRIPTION: This routine writes the passed message to the
'                HttpContext Trace object
'-----------------------------------------------------------------------
Public Overloads Overrides Sub Write(ByVal category As String, _
                                     ByVal message As String)
  writeLogEntry(category & ": " & message)
End Sub  'Write

'*************************************************************************
'
'   ROUTINE: WriteLine
'
'   DESCRIPTION: This routine writes the passed message to the
'                HttpContext Trace object with a CR/LF
'-----------------------------------------------------------------------
Public Overloads Overrides Sub WriteLine(ByVal message As String)
  writeLogEntry(message)
End Sub  'WriteLine

'*************************************************************************
'
'   ROUTINE: WriteLine
'
'   DESCRIPTION: This routine writes the passed message to the
'                HttpContext Trace object
'-----------------------------------------------------------------------
Public Overloads Overrides Sub WriteLine(ByVal category As String, _
                                         ByVal message As String)
  writeLogEntry(category & ": " & message)
End Sub  'WriteLine

'*************************************************************************
'
'   ROUTINE: writeLogEntry
'
'   DESCRIPTION: This routine writes the passed message to the event log
'-----------------------------------------------------------------------
Private Sub writeLogEntry(ByVal message As String)
  Dim log As EventLog

  'Insert error information into the event log
```

Example 10-20. Custom TraceListener for writing to the event log (.vb) (continued)

```
        log = New EventLog
        log.Source = EVENT_LOG_NAME
        log.WriteEntry(message, _
                       EventLogEntryType.Error)

    End Sub  'writeLogEntry
  End Class  'CH10EventLogListenerVB
End Namespace
```

Example 10-21. Custom TraceListener for writing to the event log (.cs)

```
//---------------------------------------------------------------------------
//
//   Module Name: CH10EventLogListenerCS.cs
//
//   Description: This class provides a trace listener that outputs messages
//                to the application event log.
//
//***************************************************************************
using System;
using System.Diagnostics;

namespace ASPNetCookbook.CSExamples
{
  public class CH10EventLogListenerCS : TraceListener
  {
    // the following constant defines the event log to which messages are
    // written
    const String EVENT_LOG_NAME = "Application";

    //***********************************************************************
    //
    //   ROUTINE: Write
    //
    //   DESCRIPTION: This routine writes the passed message to the
    //                HttpContext Trace object
    //-----------------------------------------------------------------------
    public override void Write(String message)
    {
      writeLogEntry(message);
    } // Write

    //***********************************************************************
    //
    //   ROUTINE: Write
    //
    //   DESCRIPTION: This routine writes the passed message to the
    //                HttpContext Trace object
    //-----------------------------------------------------------------------
    public override void Write(String category,
                              String message)
    {
```

```
      writeLogEntry(category + ": " + message);
    } // Write

    //************************************************************************
    //
    //   ROUTINE: WriteLine
    //
    //   DESCRIPTION: This routine writes the passed message to the
    //                HttpContext Trace object
    //------------------------------------------------------------------------
    public override void WriteLine(String message)
    {
      writeLogEntry(message);
    } // WriteLine

    //************************************************************************
    //
    //   ROUTINE: WriteLine
    //
    //   DESCRIPTION: This routine writes the passed message to the
    //                HttpContext Trace object
    //------------------------------------------------------------------------
    public override void WriteLine(String category,
                                   String message)
    {
      writeLogEntry(category + ": " + message);
    } // WriteLine

    //************************************************************************
    //
    //   ROUTINE: writeLogEntry
    //
    //   DESCRIPTION: This routine writes the passed message to the event log
    //------------------------------------------------------------------------
    private void writeLogEntry(String message)
    {
      EventLog log;

      // Insert error information into the event log
      log = new EventLog( );
      log.Source = EVENT_LOG_NAME;
      log.WriteEntry(message,
                     EventLogEntryType.Error);
    }  // writeLogEntry
  }  // CH10EventLogListenerCS
}
```

Example 10-22. web.config settings for adding the trace listener and trace switch

```
<system.diagnostics>
  <switches>
    <!-- This switch controls messages written to the event log.
         To control the level of message written to the log set
```

Example 10-22. web.config settings for adding the trace listener and trace switch (continued)

```
        the value attribute as follows:
        "0" - output no messages
        "1" - output only error messages
        "2" - output error and warning messages
        "3" - output error, warning, and informational messages
        "4" - output all messages
    -->
    <add name="EventLogSwitch" value="0" />
  </switches>

  <trace autoflush="true" indentsize="0">
    <listeners>
      <add name="CookbookEventLogListener"
       type="ASPNetCookbook.VBExamples.CH10EventLogListenerVB,
           ASPNetCookbookVB" />
    </listeners>
  </trace>
</system.diagnostics>
```

Example 10-23. Writing trace information as a function of trace level (.vb)

```
Dim generalTraceSwitch As TraceSwitch

'create the trace switch
generalTraceSwitch = New TraceSwitch("EventLogSwitch", _
                                    "Used throughout the application")

'write trace data if error level is enabled
System.Diagnostics.Trace.WriteIf(generalTraceSwitch.TraceError, _
                                "This is an error message")

'write trace data if warning level is enabled
System.Diagnostics.Trace.WriteIf(generalTraceSwitch.TraceWarning, _
                                "This is an warning message")

'write trace data if info level is enabled
System.Diagnostics.Trace.WriteIf(generalTraceSwitch.TraceInfo, _
                                "This is an info message")

'write trace data if verbose level is enabled
System.Diagnostics.Trace.WriteIf(generalTraceSwitch.TraceVerbose, _
                                "This is an verbose message")
```

Example 10-24. Writing trace information as a function of trace level (.cs)

```
TraceSwitch generalTraceSwitch = null;

// create the trace switch
generalTraceSwitch = new TraceSwitch("EventLogSwitch",
                                    "Used throughout the application");

// write trace data if error level is enabled
System.Diagnostics.Trace.WriteIf(generalTraceSwitch.TraceError,
```

```
                                "This is an error message");

    // write trace data if warning level is enabled
    System.Diagnostics.Trace.WriteIf(generalTraceSwitch.TraceWarning,
                                "This is an warning message");

    // write trace data if info level is enabled
    System.Diagnostics.Trace.WriteIf(generalTraceSwitch.TraceInfo,
                                "This is an info message");

    // write trace data if verbose level is enabled
    System.Diagnostics.Trace.WriteIf(generalTraceSwitch.TraceVerbose,
                                "This is an verbose message");
```

10.7 Using a Breakpoint to Stop Execution of an Application When a Condition Is Met

Problem

You have some fairly complicated code that is having a problem after many iterations, and you need an easy way to stop execution when the conditions are met.

Solution

Set a conditional breakpoint using an expression in the Visual Studio debugger. The value of the expression will determine whether program execution breaks when the breakpoint is hit.

To set a conditional breakpoint in the Visual Studio debugger:

1. Set a breakpoint in the usual fashion by clicking in the gray border to the left of the line where you want execution to break.

2. Right-click the breakpoint and select the Breakpoint Properties command from the menu.

3. Use the Breakpoint Properties dialog box to set the conditions for the break, as shown in Figure 10-5. Typically, you'll use the Function tab, select the Breakpoints button, and set a conditional expression like any of these:

   VB
   ```
   counter = 5000

   i=100 AND j=150

   message.Length > 0
   ```

   C#
   ```
   counter == 5000

   i==100 && j==150

   message.Length > 0
   ```

When you run the program, execution will break at the location when the expression is true or has changed, depending on the option you've chosen in the dialog box.

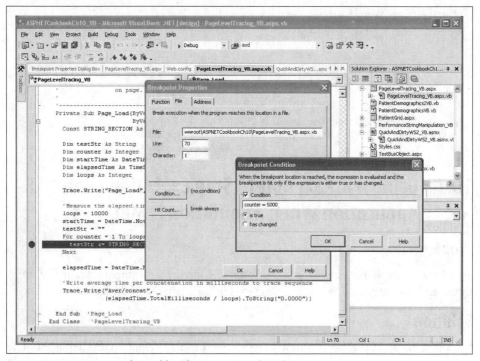

Figure 10-5. Setting a conditional breakpoint in Visual Studio

Discussion

You can view the contents of the Visual Studio Locals window to verify the values of the variables involved in the expression. Access the Locals window by selecting the Debug → Windows → Locals command; the Locals window is accessible only when the VS.NET Debugger is active.

Another approach is to set a hit count within the Function tab. The hit count lets you specify how many times the breakpoint is hit before the debugger enters break mode. For example, you might choose to break when the hit count is equal to 100. The debugger will break only when the hit count reaches the target number.

See Also

All the rules for setting breakpoint expressions are available from Visual Studio Help under the "Expressions in the Debugger" topic, which is accessible from the Breakpoint Properties dialog box (the expression evaluator accepts most expressions written in Visual Basic or C#).

10.8   Stress Testing a Web Application or Service

Problem

You want to stress test your ASP.NET web application or service to analyze its performance and identify any scalability problems.

Solution

Use the Application Center Test (ACT), included in the Enterprise Architect and Enterprise Developer editions of Visual Studio .NET, to simulate a large group of users by opening multiple connections to the server and rapidly sending HTTP requests. The easiest way to accomplish this is to record a test script and then modify the test properties to match the stress test you want to simulate. In the case of a web service, you can record the steps you'd take to manually enter settings into the web service's test page, and then have the ACT tool automatically replay the test script to simulate a large number of users simultaneously accessing the service.

For example, to stress test our sample web service in Recipe 11.1, follow these steps:

1. Add a new Application Center Test project to the Solution Explorer (available under Other Projects in the Project Types list).

2. Click on the new ACT project in Solution Explorer, select File → Add New Item from the menu, and choose "Browser Recorded Test (.vbs)" from the list of templates.

3. Start Browser Record mode and when the browser opens, navigate to the web service's ASMX page, choose a method to stress test, enter the appropriate values (as shown in Figure 10-6), and invoke the method.

4. When you see the XML returned by the web service, click Stop on the recorder dialog box.

You'll then see the contents of the *.vbs* script where you can edit commands as necessary, as shown in Figure 10-7. You can also use the Properties window to modify the number of simultaneous browser connections (also known as the *stress level*), iterations or time in seconds to run the test, test warm-up time, and the like. Start the test by right-clicking the *.vbs* file in Solution Explorer and choosing "Start Test."

Discussion

Stress testing is the process of assessing your web applications or services under load. It allows you to determine how well your applications or services scale under the stress of user demand.

Although you can record and run a stress test within Visual Studio .NET, there are distinct advantages to using ACT's standalone user interface instead. Besides being easier to work with, the standalone UI provides more in-depth reporting information

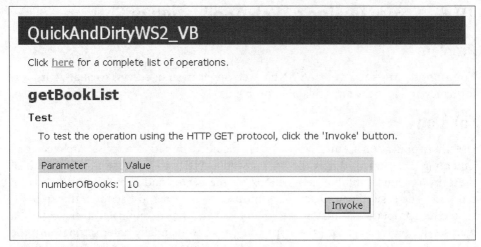

Figure 10-6. Settings for stress testing a sample web service

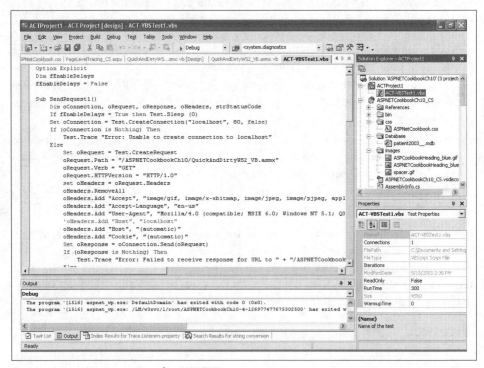

Figure 10-7. ACT test script within VS.NET

and graphs, as shown in Figure 10-8. For example, it provides the only way to add additional performance counters to a report.

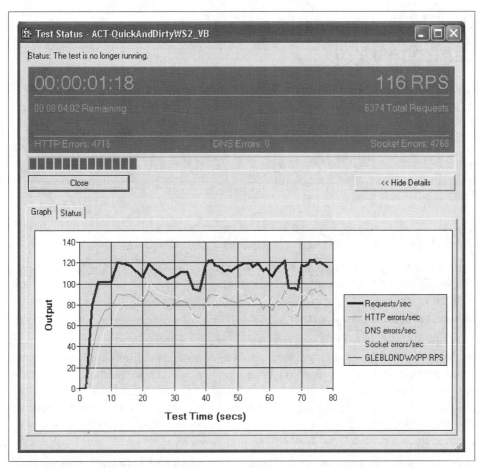

Figure 10-8. Results of a stress test in ACT

ACT tests can run for either a length of time or a number of script iterations. When setting the number of iterations, be aware how it relates to the number of simultaneous browser connections. The number of requests that are issued for the test is the product of the two settings. For example, if you set the number of iterations to 10 and the simultaneous browser connections to 10, the web service will actually receive 100 requests before the test completes.

When stress testing a web service, you can learn a lot by estimating what the expected production load will be and setting the stress level accordingly. Another good approach is to hike the stress level to the point where you start to see significant numbers of HTTP, Socket, and/or DNS errors. You can then iterate on the stress level to find out the web service's maximum capacity. In the process, you wind up better understanding where the bottlenecks exist in your software, hardware, and network capacity.

CHAPTER 11

Web Services

11.0 Introduction

Web services hold the promise of revolutionizing the way that organizations of all kinds share data. They provide a standard, universal means of data exchange that is well within the grasp of the average programmer. And beyond that, they are remarkably easy to get started with.

For those who are new to the subject, web services are modular applications that can be described, published, located, and invoked over standard Internet protocols using standardized XML messaging. Applications use the XML-based SOAP for the exchange of information in a loosely coupled, distributed environment. Applications posted to the Web are described with the Web Services Description Language (WSDL) and registered with a private or public service registry using the UDDI standard, such as *http://uddi.microsoft.com* or *http://uddi.ibm.com*.

This chapter shows you how to deal with a number of common web service scenarios and overcome some of the typical problems you might encounter. Detailed coverage of web services would require an entire book. For a tutorial on web services, we recommend *Programming .NET Web Services*, by Alex Ferrara and Matthew MacDonald (O'Reilly).

11.1 Creating a Web Service

Problem

You want to create a web service.

Solution

Use Visual Studio to create a new web service and then add methods to expose the functionality required for your web service.

To create the new web service:

1. On the Visual Studio .NET File menu, choose New → Project....
2. When the New Project dialog box is displayed, go to the left pane and select either Visual Basic Projects or Visual C# Projects.
3. Go to the right pane and click on the ASP.NET Web Service icon.
4. Enter the name of the web service in the Location text box and click OK.

Visual Studio .NET creates a virtual directory in IIS and a project that contains a *.asmx* file and code-behind files for the web service, like those shown in Examples 11-2 through 11-5. The web service is fully functional at this point but is just a shell with no useful functionality.

You need to add methods to the code-behind to expose the functionality required for your web service. The code-behind shown in Example 11-6 (VB) and Example 11-7 (C#) shows a method we have added to our example web service to return a list of books from a database. The code generated by Visual Studio .NET to support the component designer has been omitted from Examples 11-6 and 11-7 for clarity.

You can add a web service to an existing web application by selecting the project in the Solution Explorer, and then selecting Add New Item from the File menu. When the Add New Item dialog box is displayed, select Web Service, enter the desired name of the web service, and click Open. Any number of web services can be added to a web application.

Discussion

Web services are a useful tool for communicating with remote systems or with systems built with technologies different from those used to build your application.

Visual Studio .NET greatly simplifies the creation of web services. With just a few menu selections, you can quickly build a web service shell that you can use to create the functionality required by your application.

In .NET, a web service consists of an *.asmx* file and a code-behind class that provides the required functionality. The content of an *.asmx* file consists of a single line that contains a WebService directive. The line is just like the @ Page directive used in the *.aspx* file, but with Page replaced by WebService:

```
<%@ WebService Language="vb" Codebehind="CH11QuickWebServiceVB1.asmx.vb"
        Class="VBWebServices.CH11QuickWebServiceVB1" %>
```

```
<%@ WebService Language="c#" Codebehind="CH11QuickWebServiceCS1.asmx.cs"
        Class="CSWEbServices.CH11QuickWebServiceCS1" %>
```

The code-behind file for a web service consists of a class that inherits from System.Web.Services.WebService.

```
VB   Public Class CH11QuickWebServiceVB1
        Inherits System.Web.Services.WebService
        ...

     End Class
```

```
C#   public class CH11QuickWebServiceCS1 : System.Web.Services.WebService
     {
        ...
     }
```

In addition, Visual Studio .NET adds a WebService attribute to the class definition. While not explicitly required, the WebService attribute lets you define the namespace for the web service. By default, the namespace is set to *http://tempuri.org/*, but you will typically want to set this to the URI representing your company, such as *http://www.dominiondigital.com/*.

```
VB   <WebService(Namespace:="http://tempuri.org/ ")> _
     Public Class CH11QuickWebServiceVB1
        Inherits System.Web.Services.WebService


        ...

     End Class
```

```
C#   [WebService(Namespace="http://tempuri.org/")]
     public class CH11QuickWebServiceCS1 : System.Web.Services.WebService
     {
        ...
     }
```

Other than the constructor it creates for the class, all of the code added by Visual Studio .NET is necessary to support the Web Services Designer and is not required for the web service itself.

To add useful functionality to the web service, you create methods just as you would for any other class, except that you precede each method definition with a WebMethod attribute. The WebMethod attribute informs Visual Studio that the method is to be exposed as part of the web service.

For instance, the getBookList method shown in our example queries a database for a list of books and returns the list in a DataSet. The number of books retrieved is defined by the numberOfBooks parameter. Nothing special is done in the code to support the web service. Visual Studio .NET and the .NET Framework take care of the creation of the XML and the SOAP wrapper used to transfer the data to the client.

One of the big advantages to creating web services with Visual Studio .NET and ASP.NET is the testing and debugging functionality provided. ASP.NET provides a series of web pages that effectively create a test harness that can be used to test all the exposed methods of the web service. Visual Studio .NET lets you set breakpoints in your web service code so you can step through it to verify its operation.

To test a web service, run your project in Visual Studio .NET in debug mode and access the *.asmx* file for the web service. ASP.NET will display a page listing all of the methods exposed by the web service, as shown in Figure 11-1.

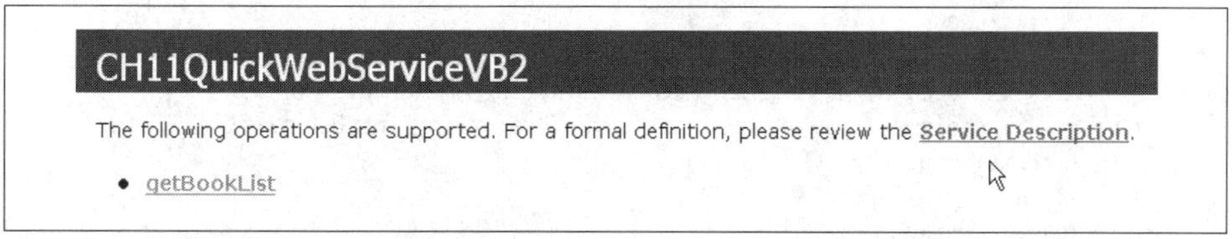

CH11QuickWebServiceVB2

The following operations are supported. For a formal definition, please review the Service Description.

- getBookList

Figure 11-1. Methods exposed by the web service

In this example, clicking on the getBookList method displays another page where you can enter the required numberOfBooks parameter value and invoke (execute) the method. Although not shown in Figure 11-2, this page also displays the content of the XML-encoded request and response messages for the method using SOAP, Http Get, and Http Post. These samples allow you to examine the data that is exchanged when the method is called.

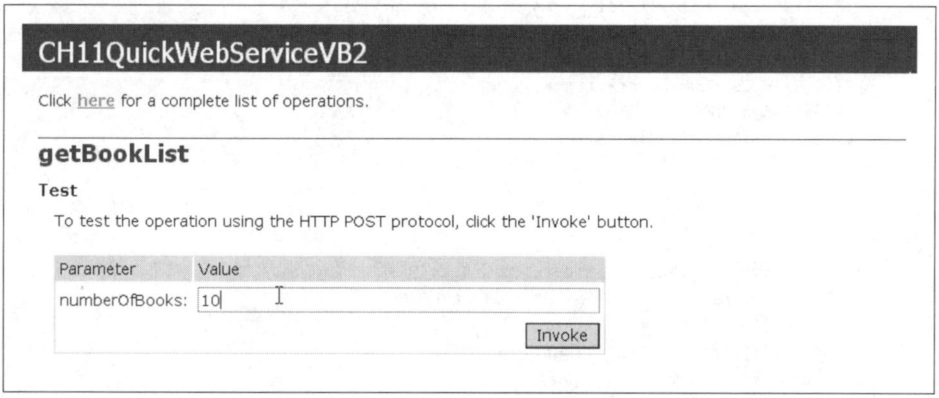

CH11QuickWebServiceVB2

Click here for a complete list of operations.

getBookList

Test

To test the operation using the HTTP POST protocol, click the 'Invoke' button.

Parameter	Value
numberOfBooks:	10
	Invoke

Figure 11-2. Invoking the method

When you click the Invoke button, ASP.NET generates an Http Get request and submits it to the web service. The web service responds with an Http response containing the requested data. In our example, the XML shown in Example 11-1 is returned from the web service when the numberOfBooks parameter is set to 10.

Example 11-1. XML returned with numberOfBooks parameter set to 10

```
<?xml version="1.0" encoding="utf-8"?>
<DataSet xmlns="http://www.dominiondigital.com">
  <xs:schema id="NewDataSet" xmlns=""
      xmlns:xs="http://www.w3.org/2001/XMLSchema"
      xmlns:msdata="urn:schemas-microsoft-com:xml-msdata">
    <xs:element name="NewDataSet" msdata:IsDataSet="true">
      <xs:complexType>
```

Example 11-1. XML returned with numberOfBooks parameter set to 10 (continued)

```xml
        <xs:choice maxOccurs="unbounded">
          <xs:element name="Table">
            <xs:complexType>
              <xs:sequence>
                <xs:element name="Title" type="xs:string" minOccurs="0" />
                <xs:element name="ISBN" type="xs:string" minOccurs="0" />
                <xs:element name="Publisher" type="xs:string" minOccurs="0" />
              </xs:sequence>
            </xs:complexType>
          </xs:element>
        </xs:choice>
      </xs:complexType>
    </xs:element>
  </xs:schema>
  <diffgr:diffgram xmlns:msdata="urn:schemas-microsoft-com:xml-msdata"
    xmlns:diffgr="urn:schemas-microsoft-com:xml-diffgram-v1">
    <NewDataSet xmlns="">
      <Table diffgr:id="Table1" msdata:rowOrder="0">
        <Title>.Net Framework Essentials</Title>
        <ISBN>0-596-00302-1</ISBN>
        <Publisher>O'Reilly</Publisher>
      </Table>
      <Table diffgr:id="Table2" msdata:rowOrder="1">
        <Title>Access Cookbook</Title>
        <ISBN>0-596-00084-7</ISBN>
        <Publisher>O'Reilly</Publisher>
      </Table>

      ...

      <Table diffgr:id="Table10" msdata:rowOrder="9">
        <Title>HTML &amp; XHTML: The Definitive Guide</Title>
        <ISBN>0-596-00026-X</ISBN>
        <Publisher>O'Reilly</Publisher>
      </Table>
    </NewDataSet>
  </diffgr:diffgram>
</DataSet>
```

Example 11-2. Quick web service .asmx file (.vb)

```vb
<%@ WebService Language="vb" Codebehind="CH11QuickWebServiceVB1.asmx.vb"
    Class="VBWebServices.CH11QuickWebServiceVB1" %>
```

Example 11-3. Quick web service code-behind (.vb)

```vb
Imports System.Web.Services

Namespace VBWebServices
  <WebService(Namespace:="http://tempuri.org/ ")> _
  Public Class CH11QuickWebServiceVB1
    Inherits System.Web.Services.WebService
```

Example 11-3. Quick web service code-behind (.vb) (continued)

```
' WEB SERVICE EXAMPLE
' The HelloWorld( ) example service returns the string Hello World.
' To build, uncomment the following lines then save and build the project.
' To test this web service, ensure that the .asmx file is the start page
' and press F5.
'
'<WebMethod( )> _
'Public Function HelloWorld( ) As String
'    Return "Hello World"
'End Function

  End Class
End Namespace
```

Example 11-4. Quick web service .asmx file (.cs)

```
<%@ WebService Language="c#" Codebehind="QuickAndDirtyWS1_CS.asmx.cs"
               Class="CSWebServices.QuickAndDirtyWS1_CS" %>
```

Example 11-5. Quick web service code-behind (.cs)

```
using System;
using System.ComponentModel;
using System.Web.Services;

namespace CSWEbServices
{
  [WebService(Namespace="http://tempuri.org/")]
  public class CH11QuickWebServiceCS1 : System.Web.Services.WebService
  {
    public CH11QuickWebServiceCS1( )
    {
      //CODEGEN: This call is required by the ASP.NET Web Services Designer
      InitializeComponent( );
    }
    // WEB SERVICE EXAMPLE
    // The HelloWorld( ) example service returns the string Hello World
    // To build, uncomment the following lines then save and build the project
    // To test this web service, press F5

//    [WebMethod]
//    public string HelloWorld( )
//    {
//      return "Hello World";
//    }
  }
}
```

Example 11-6. Code-behind with method for obtaining a list of books (.vb)

```
Option Explicit On
Option Strict On
'--------------------------------------------------------------------------
```

Example 11-6. Code-behind with method for obtaining a list of books (.vb) (continued)

```
'
'    Module Name: CH11QuickWebServiceVB2.asmx.vb
'
'    Description: This class provides the code-behind for
'                 CH11QuickWebServiceVB2.asmx
'
'***************************************************************************
Imports Microsoft.VisualBasic
Imports System
Imports System.Configuration
Imports System.Data
Imports System.Data.OleDb
Imports System.Web.Services

Namespace VBWebServices
  <WebService(Namespace:="http://www.dominiondigital.com/")> _
  Public Class CH11QuickWebServiceVB2
    Inherits System.Web.Services.WebService

    '***************************************************************************
    '
    '    ROUTINE: getBooklist
    '
    '    DESCRIPTION: This routine gets the list of books from the database.
    '-------------------------------------------------------------------------
    <WebMethod()> _
    Function getBookList(ByVal numberOfBooks As Integer) As DataSet
      Dim dbConn As OleDbConnection
      Dim da As OleDbDataAdapter
      Dim dSet As DataSet
      Dim strConnection As String
      Dim strSQL As String

      Try
        'get the connection string from web.config and open a connection
        'to the database
        strConnection = _
            ConfigurationSettings.AppSettings("dbConnectionString")
        dbConn = New OleDbConnection(strConnection)
        dbConn.Open()

        'build the query string used to get the data from the database
        strSQL = "SELECT Top " & numberOfBooks.ToString() & " " & _
                "Title, ISBN, Publisher " & _
                "FROM Book " & _
                "ORDER BY Title"

        'create a new dataset and fill it with the book data
        dSet = New DataSet
        da = New OleDbDataAdapter(strSQL, dbConn)
        da.Fill(dSet)
```

Example 11-6. Code-behind with method for obtaining a list of books (.vb) (continued)

```vb
         'return the list of books
         Return (dSet)

      Finally
         'clean up
         If (Not IsNothing(dbConn)) Then
           dbConn.Close()
         End If
      End Try
   End Function  'getBookList
  End Class  'CH11QuickWebServiceVB2
End Namespace
```

Example 11-7. Code-behind with method for obtaining a list of books (.cs)

```csharp
//----------------------------------------------------------------------------
//
//   Module Name: CH11QuickWebServiceCS2.aspx.cs
//
//   Description: This module provides the code behind for the
//                CH11QuickWebServiceCS2.aspx page
//
//****************************************************************************
using System;
using System.ComponentModel;
using System.Configuration;
using System.Data;
using System.Data.OleDb;
using System.Web;
using System.Web.Services;

namespace CSWebServices
{
  [WebService(Namespace="http://www.dominiondigital.com/")]
  public class CH11QuickWebServiceCS2 : System.Web.Services.WebService
  {
    //********************************************************************
    //
    //   ROUTINE: getBookList
    //
    //   DESCRIPTION: This routine gets the list of books from the database.
    //--------------------------------------------------------------------
    [WebMethod] public DataSet getBookList(int numberOfBooks)
    {
      OleDbConnection dbConn = null;
      OleDbDataAdapter da = null;
      DataSet dSet = null;
      String strConnection = null;
      String strSQL = null;

      try
      {
```

Example 11-7. Code-behind with method for obtaining a list of books (.cs) (continued)

```
            // get the connection string from web.config and open a connection
            // to the database
            strConnection =
              ConfigurationSettings.AppSettings["dbConnectionString"];
            dbConn = new OleDbConnection(strConnection);
            dbConn.Open( );

            //build the query string used to get the data from the database
            strSQL = "SELECT Top " + numberOfBooks.ToString( ) + " " +
                    "Title, ISBN, Publisher " +
                    "FROM Book " +
                    "ORDER BY Title";

            // create a new dataset and fill it with the book data
            dSet = new DataSet( );
            da = new OleDbDataAdapter(strSQL, dbConn);
            da.Fill(dSet);

            //return the list of books
            return (dSet);

        }  // try

        finally
        {
          // cleanup
          if (dbConn != null)
          {
            dbConn.Close( );
          }
        }  // finally
      }  // getBookList
  }  // CH11QuickWebServiceCS2
}
```

11.2 Consuming a Web Service

Problem

You need to use a web service created by another group in your company to access data your application requires.

Solution

Add a web reference to an existing ASP.NET project using Visual Studio .NET. Create an instance of the web service class in your application and call its methods.

To add a web reference to an ASP.NET project in Visual Studio .NET:

1. Select the project in the Solution Explorer, and then select Add Web Reference from the Project menu.

2. In the Add Web Reference dialog box, enter the URL of the web service you want to consume, as shown in Figure 11-3, and then click the Add Reference button.

Visual Studio .NET will create all of the files needed to consume the web service.

After adding the web reference, create an instance of the web service class and call its methods in the code-behind class for the page. Examples 11-8 through 11-10 show the .aspx file and VB and C# code-behind files for an example we've written to create an instance of the web service class from Recipe 11.1 and call its methods.

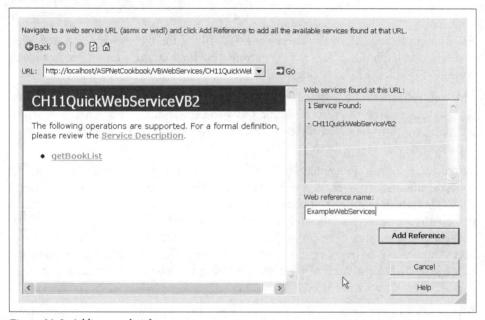

Figure 11-3. Adding a web reference

Discussion

Visual Studio .NET makes consumption of a web service a trivial task by creating all of the plumbing for you. You don't have to worry about creating proxy classes and the SOAP messages; it's all done for you when you add a web reference.

In our example that illustrates the solution, the web service created in Recipe 11.1 is used to obtain a list of books and display the list in a DataGrid. We have accomplished this by writing just a few lines of code.

The first step in consuming a web service is to add a web reference to your project by selecting the project in the Solution Explorer, and then selecting Add Web Reference from the Project menu or by right-clicking the project in the Solution Explorer and selecting Add Web Reference from the context menu. You need to enter the URL of the web service you want to consume. This is normally the full URL of the *.asmx* file or the WSDL file of the web service. But when the web service resides on your own computer, as is the case with our example for this recipe, a URL like the following will do:

http://localhost/ASPNetCookbook/VBWebServices/CH11QuickWebServiceVB2.asmx

 When adding a web reference be sure to select Add Web Reference, *not* Add Reference. Add Reference is used to add a reference to an assembly on the local server. Add Web Reference is used to add a reference to a web service.

After entering the URL of the *.asmx* or WSDL file of the web service, the Add Web Reference dialog box displays the operations provided by the web service in the left pane.

The web reference name should be changed to remove the tight coupling to a specific server, because the server hosting the web service can always change. For our example, we have renamed the web reference to ExampleWebServices, as shown in Figure 11-3.

When you click Add Reference, Visual Studio .NET creates and adds to your project all of the files needed to make a web service available to your application, including a disco file, which helps the application locate the service, and a WSDL file, which defines the services available from the web service. It then creates a proxy class that you use to access the web service. (The *proxy* class interfaces with the web service and provides a local representation of the service.) The web reference is given the name provided in the Add Web Reference dialog box and the proxy class is named Reference, as shown in Figure 11-4.

After you add a web reference to the service you plan to employ, you need to create an instance of the proxy class. For instance, here's how we create an instance of the proxy class for the example web service in Recipe 11.1:

VB
```
bookServices = New ExampleWebServices.CH11QuickWebServiceVB2
```

C#
```
bookServices = new ExampleWebServices.CH11QuickWebServiceCS2( );
```

In our example, the getBookList method of the proxy class is then called to obtain a DataSet containing the book list. Even though this method call looks like a standard method call, the proxy class is actually calling the web service to get the data.

VB
```
books = bookServices.getBookList(NUMBER_OF_BOOKS)
```

C#
```
books = bookServices.getBookList(NUMBER_OF_BOOKS);
```

Figure 11-4. The default web reference in Solution Explorer

For our example, the DataSet returned by the web service is bound to a DataGrid on the form to display the list of books.

VB
```
dgBooks.DataSource = books
dgBooks.DataBind( )
```

C#
```
dgBooks.DataSource = books;
dgBooks.DataBind( );
```

By creating all of the plumbing required to access web services, which would be both tedious to write and error prone if you had to do it yourself, Visual Studio .NET makes using web services in your applications much more practical. This is particularly true if the web service provider and consumer are both .NET implementations, because most of the data types provided by the Common Language Runtime (CLR) can be used in the web service interfaces. (See the ".NET Web Service Idiosyncrasies" sidebar in Recipe 11.3 for more on this topic.)

Web services provided by other technology platforms, such as Java, can be consumed by .NET applications. Java and other platforms do not have a set of rich data types that match the CLR data types, so the interface must be designed using simple data types. The details of consuming a web service from other technologies are beyond the scope of this book.

See Also

If you need to use web services created with Java, see *Java Web Services*, by Dave Chappell and Tyler Jewell (O'Reilly), for information

Example 11-8. Consuming a web service (.aspx)

```
<%@ Page Language="vb" AutoEventWireup="false"
        Codebehind="CH11ConsumingAWebServiceVB.aspx.vb"
        Inherits="ASPNetCookbook.VBExamples.CH11ConsumingAWebServiceVB"%>
<!DOCTYPE HTML PUBLIC "-//W3C//DTD HTML 4.0 Transitional//EN">
<html>
  <head>
    <title>Consuming A WebService</title>
    <link rel="stylesheet" href="css/ASPNetCookbook.css">
  </head>
  <body leftmargin="0" marginheight="0" marginwidth="0" topmargin="0">
    <form id="frmConfiguration" method="post" runat="server">
      <table width="100%" cellpadding="0" cellspacing="0" border="0">
        <tr>
          <td align="center">
            <img src="images/ASPNETCookbookHeading_blue.gif">
          </td>
        </tr>
        <tr>
          <td class="dividerLine">
            <img src="images/spacer.gif" height="6" border="0"></td>
        </tr>
      </table>
      <table width="90%" align="center" border="0">
        <tr>
          <td><img src="images/spacer.gif" height="10" border="0"></td>
        </tr>
        <tr>
          <td align="center" class="PageHeading">
            Consuming a Web Service (VB)
          </td>
        </tr>
        <tr>
          <td><img src="images/spacer.gif" height="10" border="0"></td>
        </tr>
        <tr>
          <td align="center" class="MenuItem">
            <!-- Minimal datagrid -->
            <asp:DataGrid id="dgBooks"
                          runat="server"
                          BorderColor="000080"
                          BorderWidth="2px"
                          AutoGenerateColumns="True"
                          width="100%" />
          </td>
        </tr>
      </table>
    </form>
  </body>
</html>
```

Example 11-9. Consuming a web service code-behind (.vb)

```vb
Option Explicit On
Option Strict On
'----------------------------------------------------------------------------
'
'   Module Name: CH11ConsumingAWebServiceVB.aspx.vb
'
'   Description: This module provides the code behind for the
'                CH11ConsumingAWebServiceVB.aspx page
'
'****************************************************************************
Imports Microsoft.VisualBasic
Imports System
Imports System.Data

Namespace ASPNetCookbook.VBExamples
  Public Class CH11ConsumingAWebServiceVB
    Inherits System.Web.UI.Page

    'controls on the form
    Protected dgBooks As System.Web.UI.WebControls.DataGrid

    '****************************************************************************
    '
    '   ROUTINE: Page_Load
    '
    '   DESCRIPTION: This routine provides the event handler for the page load
    '                event.  It is responsible for initializing the controls
    '                on the page.
    '----------------------------------------------------------------------------
    Private Sub Page_Load(ByVal sender As System.Object, _
                          ByVal e As System.EventArgs) _
             Handles MyBase.Load
      Const NUMBER_OF_BOOKS As Integer = 10

      Dim bookServices As ExampleWebServices.CH11QuickWebServiceVB2
      Dim books As DataSet

      If (Not Page.IsPostBack) Then
        'create an instance of the web service proxy class
        bookServices = New ExampleWebServices.CH11QuickWebServiceVB2

        'get the books from the service
        books = bookServices.getBookList(NUMBER_OF_BOOKS)

        'bind the book list to the datagrind on the form
        dgBooks.DataSource = books
        dgBooks.DataBind()
      End If
    End Sub  'Page_Load
  End Class  'CH11ConsumingAWebServiceVB
End Namespace
```

Example 11-10. Consuming a web service code-behind (.cs)

```
//-------------------------------------------------------------------------
//
//   Module Name: CH11ConsumingAWebServiceCS.aspx.cs
//
//   Description: This module provides the code behind for the
//                CH11ConsumingAWebServiceCS.aspx page
//
//***********************************************************************
using System;
using System.Data;

namespace ASPNetCookbook.CSExamples
{
  public class CH11ConsumingAWebServiceCS : System.Web.UI.Page
  {
    // controls on the form
    protected System.Web.UI.WebControls.DataGrid dgBooks;

    //***********************************************************************
    //
    //   ROUTINE: Page_Load
    //
    //   DESCRIPTION: This routine provides the event handler for the page
    //                load event.  It is responsible for initializing the
    //                controls on the page.
    //-------------------------------------------------------------------------
    private void Page_Load(object sender, System.EventArgs e)
    {
      const int NUMBER_OF_BOOKS = 10;

      ExampleWebServices.CH11QuickWebServiceCS2 bookServices = null;
      DataSet books = null;

      if (!Page.IsPostBack)
      {
        // create an instance of the web service proxy class
        bookServices = new ExampleWebServices.CH11QuickWebServiceCS2();

        // get the books from the service
        books = bookServices.getBookList(NUMBER_OF_BOOKS);

        // bind the book list to the datagrind on the form
        dgBooks.DataSource = books;
        dgBooks.DataBind();
      }
    } // Page_Load
  } // CH11ConsumingAWebServiceCS
}
```

11.3   Creating a Web Service That Returns a Custom Object

Problem

You want to create a web service that returns a custom object, because none of the .NET data types meets your needs.

Solution

Create a class that encapsulates the data you need and use it as the return type of a method of your web service.

To demonstrate this solution, we have created the custom class, BookData, shown in Example 11-11 (VB) and Example 11-12 (C#). The class encapsulates information about books stored in a database. A class that uses a web service that returns book information from a database using the custom class is shown in Example 11-13 (VB) and Example 11-14 (C#). Examples 11-15 through 11-17 show the *.aspx* file and VB and C# code-behind files for our application that demonstrates how we use the web service.

Discussion

Web services use XML to transfer data, and rely on the common language runtime (CLR) to serialize most data types to XML. If you create an object that contains public properties or variables of the types the CLR can serialize, the CLR will serialize the object for you with no additional coding when it is used as the return type of a web service.

A custom object that is to be returned by a web service must meet two requirements. First, the object must contain only data types that can be serialized (they must implement the ISerializable interface). All of the .NET base data types and the majority of its complex data types can be serialized. The notable exceptions are DataTable, DataRow, and DataView.

Second, the class defining the object must include a public default constructor (one with no parameters). The CLR uses this constructor to serialize the object.

Let's take a look at the code we have written to illustrate this solution. To begin with, we have created the class shown in Example 11-11 (VB) and Example 11-12 (C#), which encapsulates the object that a method of the web service will return. The class consists of the four sections shown in Table 11-1.

Table 11-1. Elements of the class returned by the sample web service

Element	Description
Private attributes	Used to store the object data
Public properties	Used to access the object data
First constructor	Used to create the object and populate it with data for a specific book
Second constructor	Provides the default public constructor required for serialization and provides the ability to create an object with all default values

The class shown in Example 11-13 (VB) and Example 11-14 (C#) implements our web service. To make our example more useful, the getBookList method described in Recipe 11.1 is included in this class. For more on the getBookList web service method, refer to Recipe 11.1.

In our example, the getBookData method creates an instance of the BookData class and uses it as the return type for the method. The ID of the required book and the current HttpContext are passed to provide the constructor the information it needs to create the object and populate it with the requested book data.

VB
```
bookInfo = New BookData(bookID, _
                        Context)
Return (bookInfo)
```

C#
```
bookInfo = new BookData(bookID,
                        Context);
return (bookInfo);
```

Our *.aspx* file shown in Example 11-15 uses a ListBox to display a list of available books and a group of Literal controls to display the Title, ISBN, and other details about the book.

The Page_Load method in our example's code-behind, shown in Example 11-16 (VB) and Example 11-17 (C#), is responsible for populating the ListBox with the list of available books. Our first step is to create an instance of the web service proxy class.

 In our example, the web reference was renamed to ExampleBookServices and the class that implements the web service is named CH11BookServicesVB (or CH11BookServicesCS).

VB
```
bookServices = New ExampleBookServices.CH11BookServicesVB
```

C#
```
bookServices = new ExampleBookServices.CH11BookServicesCS( );
```

Our next step is to call the getBookList method of the proxy class to get a list of available books.

VB
```
books = bookServices.getBookList(NUMBER_OF_BOOKS)
```

C#
```
books = bookServices.getBookList(NUMBER_OF_BOOKS);
```

After getting the list, the data is bound to the ListBox by setting the DataSource property to the DataSet containing the list of books. The DataTextField is set to the column in the DataSet containing the title of the book to define what will be displayed in the ListBox. The DataValueField is set to the column in the DataSet containing the BookID to uniquely identify the book when an item is selected. Finally, the DataBind method is called to bind the data in the DataSet to the ListBox.

VB
```
lstBooks.DataSource = books
lstBooks.DataTextField = "Title"
lstBooks.DataValueField = "BookID"
lstBooks.DataBind()
```

C#
```
lstBooks.DataSource = books;
lstBooks.DataTextField = "Title";
lstBooks.DataValueField = "BookID";
lstBooks.DataBind();
```

Rather than attempting to handle the case where the user does not select a book in the ListBox, we have simplified our example by selecting the first book in the list and then calling the getBookDetails method (described next).

VB
```
lstBooks.SelectedIndex = 0
getBookDetails()
```

C#
```
lstBooks.SelectedIndex = 0;
getBookDetails();
```

The getBookDetails method is responsible for calling the web service that retrieves the details of the selected book. The getBookData method that is exposed by the web service is responsible for returning a custom object.

First, the method gets the ID of the selected book from the ListBox.

VB
```
bookID = CInt(lstBooks.SelectedItem.Value)
```

C#
```
bookID = System.Convert.ToInt32(lstBooks.SelectedItem.Value);
```

Next, an instance of the web service proxy class is created and the getBookData method is called to get the details of the book from the web service.

VB
```
bookServices = New ExampleBookServices.CH11BookServicesVB
bookInfo = bookServices.getBookData(bookID)
```

C#
```
bookServices = new ExampleBookServices.CH11BookServicesCS();
bookInfo = bookServices.getBookData(bookID);
```

The controls used to display the book details are then initialized with the data in the BookData object returned from the web service.

VB
```
litTitle.Text = bookInfo.title
litIsbn.Text = bookInfo.Isbn
litDescription.Text = bookInfo.description
litPublisher.Text = bookInfo.publisher
litListPrice.Text = bookInfo.listPrice.ToString("0.00")
litDate.Text = bookInfo.publishDate.ToShortDateString()
```

```csharp
litTitle.Text = bookInfo.title;
litIsbn.Text = bookInfo.Isbn;
litDescription.Text = bookInfo.description;
litPublisher.Text = bookInfo.publisher;
litListPrice.Text = bookInfo.listPrice.ToString("0.00");
litDate.Text = bookInfo.publishDate.ToShortDateString();
```

One of the primary benefits of encapsulating data as we have in this example is the improvement in the performance of the web service. By returning the custom BookData object from our web service, all of the data is retrieved in a single call. If each piece of data for the book is obtained using separate calls, the application's performance will be significantly reduced. When you use a web service to retrieve data, it is usually best to return the largest possible block of data for each call. This reduces the significant overhead of serializing the data to XML and wrapping it with SOAP and HTTP protocol wrappers.

.NET Web Service Idiosyncrasies

Web services that are produced and consumed by .NET applications can use any of the data types of the Common Language Runtime (CLR) that implement the ISerializable interface. If your web services need to be consumed by other technologies, such as Java, it will be necessary to limit the data types to simple types, such as integer, string, etc. In addition, .NET web services use Document Literal encoding by default, while many other technologies use RPC encoding. These factors must be considered when developing web services that are produced and consumed by different technologies.

Web Services Return Data Only

Web services let you pass simple or complex data between applications; however, they cannot pass behavior. If you create a typical class that provides methods to act upon the data in the instantiated object and use it as the return type from a web service method, you will find the methods to act upon the data are not available when the object is returned. While the object created by the web service and the object created by the application consuming the web service have the same name, they are not created from the same class. The BookData proxy class (VB version) created for our example is shown here. You will notice that it does not resemble the BookData class shown in Example 11-11. Essentially, it is just a structure containing the data exposed by the class returned by the web service.

—continued—

—continued—

```
<System.Xml.Serialization.XmlTypeAttribute([Namespace]:="http://
    www.dominiondigital.com")> _
Public Class BookData

    '<remarks/>
    Public title As String

    '<remarks/>
    Public Isbn As String

    '<remarks/>
    Public description As String

    '<remarks/>
    Public publisher As String

    '<remarks/>
    Public listPrice As Single

    '<remarks/>
    Public publishDate As Date

    '<remarks/>
    Public bookID As Integer
End Class
```

See Also

Recipe 11.1

Example 11-11. Custom class (.vb)

```
Option Explicit On
Option Strict On
'-----------------------------------------------------------------------------
'
'   Module Name: BookData.vb
'
'   Description: This class provides the data class used to encapsulate
'                book data returned from a web service
'
'*****************************************************************************
Imports Microsoft.VisualBasic
Imports System
Imports System.Configuration
Imports System.Data
Imports System.Data.OleDb
Imports System.Web
```

Example 11-11. Custom class (.vb) (continued)

```
Namespace VBWebServices
  Public Class BookData
    'private attributes
    Private mBookID As Integer
    Private mTitle As String
    Private mIsbn As String
    Private mDescription As String
    Private mPublisher As String
    Private mListPrice As Single
    Private mPublishDate As DateTime

    '*************************************************************************
    '
    '   ROUTINE: bookID
    '
    '   DESCRIPTION: This property provides the ability to get/set the
    '                book ID
    '-------------------------------------------------------------------------
    Public Property bookID( ) As Integer
      Get
        Return (mBookID)
      End Get
      Set(ByVal Value As Integer)
        mBookID = Value
      End Set
    End Property   'bookID

    '*************************************************************************
    '
    '   ROUTINE: title
    '
    '   DESCRIPTION: This property provides the ability to get/set the
    '                title
    '-------------------------------------------------------------------------
    Public Property title( ) As String
      Get
        Return (mTitle)
      End Get
      Set(ByVal Value As String)
        mTitle = Value
      End Set
    End Property   'title

    '*************************************************************************
    '
    '   ROUTINE: Isbn
    '
    '   DESCRIPTION: This property provides the ability to get/set the
    '                ISBN
    '-------------------------------------------------------------------------
    Public Property Isbn( ) As String
      Get
        Return (mIsbn)
```

Example 11-11. Custom class (.vb) (continued)

```vb
    End Get  '
    Set(ByVal Value As String)
      mIsbn = Value
    End Set
  End Property  'Isbn

  '************************************************************************
  '
  '    ROUTINE: description
  '
  '    DESCRIPTION: This property provides the ability to get/set the
  '                 description
  '------------------------------------------------------------------------
  Public Property description() As String
    Get
      Return (mDescription)
    End Get
    Set(ByVal Value As String)
      mDescription = Value
    End Set
  End Property  'description

  '************************************************************************
  '
  '    ROUTINE: publisher
  '
  '    DESCRIPTION: This property provides the ability to get/set the
  '                 publisher
  '------------------------------------------------------------------------
  Public Property publisher() As String
    Get
      Return (mPublisher)
    End Get
    Set(ByVal Value As String)
      mPublisher = Value
    End Set
  End Property  'publisher

  '************************************************************************
  '
  '    ROUTINE: listPrice
  '
  '    DESCRIPTION: This property provides the ability to get/set the
  '                 listPrice
  '------------------------------------------------------------------------
  Public Property listPrice() As Single
    Get
      Return (mListPrice)
    End Get
    Set(ByVal Value As Single)
      mListPrice = Value
    End Set
  End Property  'listPrice
```

Example 11-11. Custom class (.vb) (continued)

```vb
'**************************************************************************
'
'    ROUTINE: publishDate
'
'    DESCRIPTION: This property provides the ability to get/set the
'                 publishDate
'-------------------------------------------------------------------------
Public Property publishDate( ) As DateTime
  Get
    Return (mPublishDate)
  End Get
  Set(ByVal Value As Date)
    mPublishDate = Value
  End Set
End Property   'publishDate


'**************************************************************************
'
'    ROUTINE: New
'
'    DESCRIPTION: This constructor creates the object and populates it
'                 with data for the passed book ID.
'-------------------------------------------------------------------------
Public Sub New(ByVal ID As Integer, _
               ByVal context As HttpContext)
  Dim dbConn As OleDbConnection
  Dim da As OleDbDataAdapter
  Dim dTable As DataTable
  Dim dRow As DataRow
  Dim strConnection As String
  Dim strSQL As String

  Try
    'get the connection string from web.config and open a connection
    'to the database
    strConnection = _
        ConfigurationSettings.AppSettings("dbConnectionString")
    dbConn = New OleDbConnection(strConnection)
    dbConn.Open( )

    'build the query string used to get the data from the database
    strSQL = "SELECT BookID, Title, ISBN, Description, Publisher, " & _
             "ListPrice, PublishDate " & _
             "FROM Book " & _
             "WHERE BookID=" & ID.ToString( )

    'create a new data table and fill it with the book data
    dTable = New DataTable
    da = New OleDbDataAdapter(strSQL, dbConn)
    da.Fill(dTable)
```

Example 11-11. Custom class (.vb) (continued)

```
        'populate object with the book data read from the database
        dRow = dTable.Rows(0)
        bookID = CInt(dRow.Item("BookID"))
        title = CStr(dRow.Item("Title"))
        Isbn = CStr(dRow.Item("ISBN"))
        description = CStr(dRow.Item("Description"))
        publisher = CStr(dRow.Item("Publisher"))
        listPrice = CSng(dRow.Item("ListPrice"))
        publishDate = CDate(dRow.Item("PublishDate"))

    Finally
      'clean up
      If (Not IsNothing(dbConn)) Then
        dbConn.Close()
      End If
    End Try
  End Sub   'New


  '**************************************************************************
  '
  '    ROUTINE: New
  '
  '    DESCRIPTION: This constructor creates the object will default values
  '--------------------------------------------------------------------------
  Public Sub New()
    bookID = -1
    title = ""
    Isbn = ""
    description = ""
    publisher = ""
    listPrice = 0
    publishDate = DateTime.MinValue
  End Sub   'New
  End Class   'BookData
End Namespace
```

Example 11-12. Custom class (.cs)

```
//--------------------------------------------------------------------------
//
//    Module Name: BookData.cs
//
//    Description: This class provides the data class used to encapsulate
//                 book data returned from a web service
//
//**************************************************************************
using System;
using System.Configuration;
using System.Data;
using System.Data.OleDb;
using System.Web;
```

Example 11-12. Custom class (.cs) (continued)

```csharp
namespace CSWebServices
{
  public class BookData
  {
    // private attributes
    private int mBookID;
    private string mTitle;
    private string mIsbn;
    private string mDescription;
    private string mPublisher;
    private Decimal mListPrice;
    private DateTime mPublishDate;

    //**********************************************************************
    //
    //    ROUTINE: bookID
    //
    //    DESCRIPTION: This property provides the ability to get/set the
    //                 book ID
    //----------------------------------------------------------------------
    public int bookID
    {
      get
      {
        return(mBookID);
      }
      set
      {
        mBookID = value;
      }
    }  // bookID

    //**********************************************************************
    //
    //    ROUTINE: title
    //
    //    DESCRIPTION: This property provides the ability to get/set the
    //                 title
    //----------------------------------------------------------------------
    public string title
    {
      get
      {
        return(mTitle);
      }
      set
      {
        mTitle = value;
      }
    }  // title
```

Example 11-12. Custom class (.cs) (continued)

```
//***********************************************************************
//
//    ROUTINE: Isbn
//
//    DESCRIPTION: This property provides the ability to get/set the
//                 ISBN
//-----------------------------------------------------------------------
public string Isbn
{
  get
  {
    return(mIsbn);
  }
  set
  {
    mIsbn = value;
  }
} // Isbn


//***********************************************************************
//
//    ROUTINE: description
//
//    DESCRIPTION: This property provides the ability to get/set the
//                 description
//-----------------------------------------------------------------------
public string description
{
  get
  {
    return(mDescription);
  }
  set
  {
    mDescription = value;
  }
} // description

//***********************************************************************
//
//    ROUTINE: publisher
//
//    DESCRIPTION: This property provides the ability to get/set the
//                 publisher
//-----------------------------------------------------------------------
public string publisher
{
  get
  {
    return(mPublisher);
  }
  set
  {
```

Example 11-12. Custom class (.cs) (continued)

```
      mPublisher = value;
    }
  }  // publisher

  //**********************************************************************
  //
  //    ROUTINE: listPrice
  //
  //    DESCRIPTION: This property provides the ability to get/set the
  //                 listPrice
  //------------------------------------------------------------------------
  public Decimal listPrice
  {
    get
    {
      return(mListPrice);
    }
    set
    {
      mListPrice = value;
    }
  }  // listPrice

  //**********************************************************************
  //
  //    ROUTINE: publishDate
  //
  //    DESCRIPTION: This property provides the ability to get/set the
  //                 publishDate
  //------------------------------------------------------------------------
  public DateTime publishDate
  {
    get
    {
      return(mPublishDate);
    }
    set
    {
      mPublishDate = value;
    }
  }  // publishDate

  //**********************************************************************
  //
  //    ROUTINE: BookData
  //
  //    DESCRIPTION: This constructor creates the object and populates it
  //                 with data for the passed book ID.
  //------------------------------------------------------------------------
  public BookData(int ID,
                  HttpContext context)
  {
    OleDbConnection dbConn = null;
```

Example 11-12. Custom class (.cs) (continued)

```
    OleDbDataAdapter da = null;
    DataTable dTable = null;
    DataRow dRow = null;
    string strConnection = null;
    string strSQL = null;

    try
    {
      // get the connection string from web.config and open a connection
      // to the database
      strConnection =
        ConfigurationSettings.AppSettings["dbConnectionString"];
      dbConn = new OleDbConnection(strConnection);
      dbConn.Open( );

      //build the query string used to get the data from the database
      strSQL = "SELECT BookID, Title, ISBN, Description, Publisher, " +
               "ListPrice, PublishDate " +
               "FROM Book " +
               "WHERE BookID=" + ID.ToString( );

      // create a new data table and fill it with the book data
      dTable = new DataTable( );
      da = new OleDbDataAdapter(strSQL, dbConn);
      da.Fill(dTable);

      // populate object with the book data read from the database
      dRow = dTable.Rows[0];
      bookID = (int)(dRow["BookID"]);
      title = (string)(dRow["Title"]);
      Isbn = (string)(dRow["ISBN"]);
      description = (string)(dRow["Description"]);
      publisher = (string)(dRow["Publisher"]);
      listPrice = (Decimal)(dRow["ListPrice"]);
      publishDate = (DateTime)(dRow["PublishDate"]);
    }

    finally
    {
      // cleanup
      if (dbConn != null)
      {
        dbConn.Close( );
      }
    }  // finally
  }

  //*************************************************************************
  //
  //   ROUTINE: BookData
  //
  //   DESCRIPTION: This constructor creates the object will default values
  //-------------------------------------------------------------------------
```

Example 11-12. Custom class (.cs) (continued)

```
   public BookData( )
   {
     bookID = -1;
     title = "";
     Isbn = "";
     description = "";
     publisher = "";
     listPrice = 0;
     publishDate = DateTime.MinValue;
   }
 }  // BookData
}  // CSWebServices
```

Example 11-13. Web service returning a custom object (.vb)

```
Option Explicit On
Option Strict On
'-----------------------------------------------------------------------------
'
'   Module Name: CH11BookServicesVB.asmx.vb
'
'   Description: This class provides the code-behind for
'                CH11BookServicesVB.asmx.  It provides several methods for
'                accessing book information.
'
'*****************************************************************************
Imports Microsoft.VisualBasic
Imports System
Imports System.Configuration
Imports System.Data
Imports System.Data.OleDb
Imports System.Web.Services

Namespace VBWebServices
  <WebService(Namespace:="http://www.dominiondigital.com/")> _
  Public Class CH11BookServicesVB
    Inherits System.Web.Services.WebService

    '*************************************************************************
    '
    '   ROUTINE: getBooklist
    '
    '   DESCRIPTION: This routine gets the list of books from the database.
    '-------------------------------------------------------------------------
    <WebMethod( )> _
    Function getBookList(ByVal numberOfBooks As Integer) As DataSet
      Dim dbConn As OleDbConnection
      Dim da As OleDbDataAdapter
      Dim dSet As DataSet
      Dim strConnection As String
```

Example 11-13. Web service returning a custom object (.vb) (continued)

```
      Dim strSQL As String

      Try
        'get the connection string from web.config and open a connection
        'to the database
        strConnection = _
            ConfigurationSettings.AppSettings("dbConnectionString")
        dbConn = New OleDbConnection(strConnection)
        dbConn.Open( )

        'build the query string used to get the data from the database
        strSQL = "SELECT Top " & numberOfBooks.ToString( ) & " " & _
              "BookID, Title, ISBN, Publisher " & _
              "FROM Book " & _
              "ORDER BY Title"

        'create a new dataset and fill it with the book data
        dSet = New DataSet
        da = New OleDbDataAdapter(strSQL, dbConn)
        da.Fill(dSet)

        'return the list of books
        Return (dSet)

      Finally
        'clean up
        If (Not IsNothing(dbConn)) Then
          dbConn.Close( )
        End If
      End Try
    End Function   'getBookList

    '***************************************************************************
    '
    '    ROUTINE: getBookData
    '
    '    DESCRIPTION: This routine gets the data for the passed book
    '---------------------------------------------------------------------------
    <WebMethod( )> _
    Function getBookData(ByVal bookID As Integer) As BookData

      Dim bookInfo As BookData

      'create a new BookData object containing the requested data
      bookInfo = New BookData(bookID, _
                              Context)
      Return (bookInfo)
    End Function   ' getBookData
  End Class   'CH11BookServicesVB
End Namespace
```

Example 11-14. Web service returning a custom object (.cs)

```
//----------------------------------------------------------------------------
//
//    Module Name: CH11BookServicesCS.aspx.cs
//
//    Description: This module provides the code behind for the
//                 CH11BookServicesCS.aspx page
//
//****************************************************************************
using System;
using System.Configuration;
using System.ComponentModel;
using System.Data;
using System.Data.OleDb;
using System.Web.Services;

namespace CSWebServices
{
  [WebService(Namespace="http://www.dominiondigital.com/")]
  public class CH11BookServicesCS : System.Web.Services.WebService
  {
    //****************************************************************************
    //
    //    ROUTINE: getBookList
    //
    //    DESCRIPTION: This routine gets the list of books from the database.
    //----------------------------------------------------------------------------
    [WebMethod] public DataSet getBookList(int numberOfBooks)
    {
      OleDbConnection dbConn = null;
      OleDbDataAdapter da = null;
      DataSet dSet = null;
      String strConnection = null;
      String strSQL = null;

      try
      {
        // get the connection string from web.config and open a connection
        // to the database
        strConnection =
          ConfigurationSettings.AppSettings["dbConnectionString"];
        dbConn = new OleDbConnection(strConnection);
        dbConn.Open();

        //build the query string used to get the data from the database
        strSQL = "SELECT Top " + numberOfBooks.ToString() + " " +
                 "BookID, Title, ISBN, Publisher " +
                 "FROM Book " +
                 "ORDER BY Title";

        // create a new dataset and fill it with the book data
        dSet = new DataSet();
        da = new OleDbDataAdapter(strSQL, dbConn);
```

Example 11-14. Web service returning a custom object (.cs) (continued)

```
      da.Fill(dSet);

      //return the list of books
      return (dSet);
    } // try

    finally
    {
      // cleanup
      if (dbConn != null)
      {
        dbConn.Close( );
      }
    } // finally
  } // getBookList


  //*************************************************************************
  //
  //    ROUTINE: getBookData
  //
  //    DESCRIPTION: This routine gets the data for the passed book
  //-------------------------------------------------------------------------
  [WebMethod] public BookData getBookData(int bookID)
  {
    BookData bookInfo = null;

    // create a new BookData object containing the requested data
    bookInfo = new BookData(bookID,
                            Context);
    return (bookInfo);
  } // getBookData
} // CH11BookServicesCS
}
```

Example 11-15. Using the web service returning a custom object (.aspx)

```
<%@ Page Language="vb" AutoEventWireup="false"
    Codebehind="CH11CustomObjectWithWebServiceVB.aspx.vb"
    Inherits="ASPNetCookbook.VBExamples.CH11CustomObjectWithWebServiceVB"%>
<!DOCTYPE HTML PUBLIC "-//W3C//DTD HTML 4.0 Transitional//EN">
<html>
  <head>
    <title>Web Service Returning A Custom Object</title>
    <link rel="stylesheet" href="css/ASPNetCookbook.css">
  </head>
  <body leftmargin="0" marginheight="0" marginwidth="0" topmargin="0">
    <form id="frmWebService" method="post" runat="server">
      <table width="100%" cellpadding="0" cellspacing="0" border="0">
        <tr>
          <td align="center">
            <img src="images/ASPNETCookbookHeading_blue.gif">
          </td>
        </tr>
```

```
        <tr>
          <td class="dividerLine">
            <img src="images/spacer.gif" height="6" border="0"></td>
        </tr>
      </table>
      <table width="90%" align="center" border="0">
        <tr>
          <td><img src="images/spacer.gif" height="10" border="0"></td>
        </tr>
        <tr>
          <td align="center" class="PageHeading">
            Returning a Custom Object From a Web Service (VB)
          </td>
        </tr>
        <tr>
          <td><img src="images/spacer.gif" height="10" border="0"></td>
        </tr>
        <tr>
          <td align="center" class="MenuItem">
            Available Books<br /><br />
            <asp:ListBox ID="lstBooks" Runat="server" AutoPostBack="True" />
          </td>
        </tr>
        <tr>
          <td>
            <br />
            <table width="60%" align="center"
                   border="1" bordercolor="#000080"
                   cellpadding="5" cellspacing="0" class="MenuItem">
              <tr>
                <td width="25%" align="right">Title: </td>
                <td width="75%">
                  <asp:Literal ID="litTitle" Runat="server" /></td>
              </tr>
              <tr>
                <td width="25%" align="right">ISBN: </td>
                <td width="75%">
                  <asp:Literal ID="litIsbn" Runat="server" /></td>
              </tr>
              <tr>
                <td width="25%" align="right">Description: </td>
                <td width="75%">
                  <asp:Literal ID="litDescription" Runat="server" /></td>
              </tr>
              <tr>
                <td width="25%" align="right">Publisher: </td>
                <td width="75%">
                  <asp:Literal ID="litPublisher" Runat="server" /></td>
              </tr>
              <tr>
                <td width="25%" align="right">List Price: </td>
                <td width="75%">
```

```
                <asp:Literal ID="litListPrice" Runat="server" /></td>
            </tr>
            <tr>
              <td width="25%" align="right">Date: </td>
              <td width="75%">
                <asp:Literal ID="litDate" Runat="server" /></td>
            </tr>
          </table>
        </td>
      </tr>
    </table>
  </form>
  </body>
</html>
```

Example 11-16. Using the web service returning a custom object code-behind (.vb)

```vb
Option Explicit On
Option Strict On
'------------------------------------------------------------------------------
'
'   Module Name: CH11CustomObjectWithWebServiceVB.aspx.vb
'
'   Description: This module provides the code behind for the
'               CH11CustomObjectWithWebServiceVB.aspx page
'
'******************************************************************************
Imports Microsoft.VisualBasic
Imports System
Imports System.Data

Namespace ASPNetCookbook.VBExamples
  Public Class CH11CustomObjectWithWebServiceVB
    Inherits System.Web.UI.Page

    'controls on the form
    Protected WithEvents lstBooks As System.Web.UI.WebControls.ListBox
    Protected btnDetails As System.Web.UI.WebControls.ImageButton
    Protected litTitle As System.Web.UI.WebControls.Literal
    Protected litIsbn As System.Web.UI.WebControls.Literal
    Protected litDescription As System.Web.UI.WebControls.Literal
    Protected litPublisher As System.Web.UI.WebControls.Literal
    Protected litListPrice As System.Web.UI.WebControls.Literal
    Protected litDate As System.Web.UI.WebControls.Literal

    '******************************************************************************
    '
    '   ROUTINE: Page_Load
    '
    '   DESCRIPTION: This routine provides the event handler for the page load
    '               event.  It is responsible for initializing the controls
    '               on the page.
    '------------------------------------------------------------------------------
```

Example 11-16. Using the web service returning a custom object code-behind (.vb) (continued)

```
   Private Sub Page_Load(ByVal sender As System.Object, _
                         ByVal e As System.EventArgs) _
             Handles MyBase.Load
      Const NUMBER_OF_BOOKS As Integer = 20

      Dim bookServices As ExampleBookServices.CH11BookServicesVB
      Dim books As DataSet

      If (Not Page.IsPostBack) Then
        'create an instance of the web service proxy class
        bookServices = New ExampleBookServices.CH11BookServicesVB

        'get the books from the service
        books = bookServices.getBookList(NUMBER_OF_BOOKS)

        'bind the book list to the listbox on the form
        lstBooks.DataSource = books
        lstBooks.DataTextField = "Title"
        lstBooks.DataValueField = "BookID"
        lstBooks.DataBind()

        'select the first item in the list and get the details
        lstBooks.SelectedIndex = 0
        getBookDetails()
      End If
   End Sub   'Page_Load

   '*************************************************************************
   '
   '    ROUTINE: lstBooks_SelectedIndexChanged
   '
   '    DESCRIPTION: This routine provides the event handler for the book
   '                 listbox selected index changed event.  It is responsible
   '                 for getting the book data for the selected book
   '-------------------------------------------------------------------------
   Private Sub lstBooks_SelectedIndexChanged(ByVal sender As Object, _
                                   ByVal e As System.EventArgs) _
             Handles lstBooks.SelectedIndexChanged

      'get the data for the selected book
      getBookDetails()
   End Sub   'lstBooks_SelectedIndexChanged

   '*************************************************************************
   '
   '    ROUTINE: getBookDetails
   '
   '    DESCRIPTION: This routine gets the details for the currently
   '                 selected book and initializes the controls on the
   '                 with the data.
   '-------------------------------------------------------------------------
```

```vb
    Private Sub getBookDetails()
      Dim bookServices As ExampleBookServices.CH11BookServicesVB
      Dim bookInfo As ExampleBookServices.BookData
      Dim bookID As Integer

      'get the currently selected book
      bookID = CInt(lstBooks.SelectedItem.Value)

      'create an instance of the web service proxy class
      'and get the book data
      bookServices = New ExampleBookServices.CH11BookServicesVB
      bookInfo = bookServices.getBookData(bookID)

      'set the controls on the form to display the book data
      litTitle.Text = bookInfo.title
      litIsbn.Text = bookInfo.Isbn
      litDescription.Text = bookInfo.description
      litPublisher.Text = bookInfo.publisher
      litListPrice.Text = bookInfo.listPrice.ToString("0.00")
      litDate.Text = bookInfo.publishDate.ToShortDateString()
    End Sub    'getBookDetails
  End Class    'CH11CustomObjectWithWebServiceVB
End Namespace
```

Example 11-17. Using the web service returning a custom object code-behind (.cs)

```csharp
//-----------------------------------------------------------------------------
//
//    Module Name: CH11CustomObjectWithWebServiceCS.aspx.cs
//
//    Description: This module provides the code behind for the
//                 CH11CustomObjectWithWebServiceCS.aspx page
//
//*****************************************************************************
using System;
using System.Data;

namespace ASPNetCookbook.CSExamples
{
  public class CH11CustomObjectWithWebServiceCS : System.Web.UI.Page
  {
    // controls on the form
    protected System.Web.UI.WebControls.ListBox lstBooks;
    protected System.Web.UI.WebControls.ImageButton btnDetails;
    protected System.Web.UI.WebControls.Literal litTitle;
    protected System.Web.UI.WebControls.Literal litIsbn;
    protected System.Web.UI.WebControls.Literal litDescription;
    protected System.Web.UI.WebControls.Literal litPublisher;
    protected System.Web.UI.WebControls.Literal litListPrice;
    protected System.Web.UI.WebControls.Literal litDate;
```

Example 11-17. Using the web service returning a custom object code-behind (.cs) (continued)

```csharp
//**************************************************************************
//
//    ROUTINE: Page_Load
//
//    DESCRIPTION: This routine provides the event handler for the page
//                 load event.  It is responsible for initializing the
//                 controls on the page.
//--------------------------------------------------------------------------
private void Page_Load(object sender, System.EventArgs e)
{
  const int NUMBER_OF_BOOKS = 20;

  ExampleBookServices.CH11BookServicesCS bookServices = null;
  DataSet books = null;

  // wire the selected index changed event
  this.lstBooks.SelectedIndexChanged +=
    new System.EventHandler(this.lstBooks_SelectedIndexChanged);

  if (!Page.IsPostBack)
  {
    // create an instance of the web service proxy class
    bookServices = new ExampleBookServices.CH11BookServicesCS( );

    // get the books from the service
    books = bookServices.getBookList(NUMBER_OF_BOOKS);

    // bind the book list to the listbox on the form
    lstBooks.DataSource = books;
    lstBooks.DataTextField = "Title";
    lstBooks.DataValueField = "BookID";
    lstBooks.DataBind( );

    // select the first item in the list and get the details
    lstBooks.SelectedIndex = 0;
    getBookDetails( );
  }
} // Page_Load

//**************************************************************************
//
//    ROUTINE: lstBooks_SelectedIndexChanged
//
//    DESCRIPTION: This routine provides the event handler for the book
//                 listbox selected index changed event.  It is
//                 responsible for getting the book data for the
//                 selected book
//--------------------------------------------------------------------------
private void lstBooks_SelectedIndexChanged(Object sender,
                                           System.EventArgs e)
{
  // get the data for the selected book
  getBookDetails( );
```

Example 11-17. Using the web service returning a custom object code-behind (.cs) (continued)

```
    }  // lstBooks_SelectedIndexChanged

    //*************************************************************************
    //
    //   ROUTINE: getBookDetails
    //
    //   DESCRIPTION: This routine gets the details for the currently
    //                selected book and initializes the controls on the
    //                with the data.
    //-------------------------------------------------------------------------
    private void getBookDetails()
    {
      ExampleBookServices.CH11BookServicesCS bookServices = null;
      ExampleBookServices.BookData bookInfo = null;
      int bookID;

      // get the currently selected book
      bookID = System.Convert.ToInt32(lstBooks.SelectedItem.Value);

      // create an instance of the web service proxy class
      // and get the book data
      bookServices = new ExampleBookServices.CH11BookServicesCS();
      bookInfo = bookServices.getBookData(bookID);

      // set the controls on the form to display the book data
      litTitle.Text = bookInfo.title;
      litIsbn.Text = bookInfo.Isbn;
      litDescription.Text = bookInfo.description;
      litPublisher.Text = bookInfo.publisher;
      litListPrice.Text = bookInfo.listPrice.ToString("0.00");
      litDate.Text = bookInfo.publishDate.ToShortDateString();
    }  // getBookDetails
  }  // CH11CustomObjectWithWebServiceCS
}
```

11.4   Setting the URL of a Web Service at Runtime

Problem

You need to set the URL of the web service at runtime.

Solution

In the code-behind class for your page, set the URL property of the proxy class to the required URL after instantiating the proxy object, as shown here:

VB
```
    bookServices = New ExampleBookServices.CH11BookServicesVB()
    bookServices.Url = "http://michaelk/aspnetcookbook/CH11BookServicesVB.asmx"
```

```
bookServices = new ExampleBookServices.CH11BookServicesCS( );
bookServices.Url = "http://michaelk/aspnetcookbook/CH11BookServicesCS.asmx";
```

Better still, by storing the URL in *web.config* and setting the URL property of the proxy class at runtime from the *web.config* setting, you can avoid having to change the code whenever the URL changes.

Discussion

The ability to configure an application without having to recompile its code every time you make a change in the location of its resources can be a real time-saver. Since the URL for a web service can change, it is a good idea to code your application to set the URL at runtime.

Whenever you add a web reference to a project, Visual Studio creates a proxy class for the web service using the URL you enter. For example, the constructor for the class from Recipe 11.3 is shown here with a hardcoded value for the URL that Visual Studio added using the value we entered when adding the web reference:

```
Public Class BookServices_VB
    Inherits System.Web.Services.Protocols.SoapHttpClientProtocol

  Public Sub New( )
    MyBase.New
    Me.Url = _
      "http://localhost/ASPNetCookbook/VBWebServices/CH11BookServicesVB.asmx"
  End Sub

    ...

End Class
```

```
public class BookServices_CS :
    System.Web.Services.Protocols.SoapHttpClientProtocol
{
  public BookServices_CS( )
  {
    this.Url =
      http://localhost/ASPNetCookbook/CSWebServices/CH11BookServicesCS.asmx";
  }
    ...
}
```

If the URL changes and your code does not provide the ability to set the URL at runtime, we would need to delete the current web reference, add a web reference to the new URL, recompile the code, and then deploy the application. This is a lot of work simply to change a URL.

By storing the URL in a configuration file, such as *web.config*, and setting the URL property of the proxy class at runtime, no code changes are required when the URL changes. By selecting the web reference in the Solution Explorer window and then changing the URL Behavior property in the Properties window to Dynamic, as shown in

Figure 11-5, Visual Studio .NET alters the constructor of the proxy class to read the URL from *web.config* and set the URL property if the setting was found in *web.config* or use the hardcoded value if it was not found. The following code snippets show the code Visual Studio .NET creates for the constructor when the URL Behavior property is set to Dynamic.

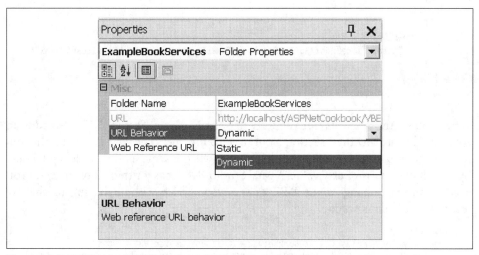

Figure 11-5. Setting the URL Behavior to Dynamic in web.config

VB
```
Public Class CH11BookServicesVB
    Inherits System.Web.Services.Protocols.SoapHttpClientProtocol

  Public Sub New()
    MyBase.New
    Dim urlSetting As String = _
      System.Configuration.ConfigurationSettings.AppSettings( _
      "VBExamples.ExampleBookServices.CH11BookServicesVB")
    If (Not (urlSetting) Is Nothing) Then
      Me.Url = String.Concat(urlSetting, "")
    Else
      Me.Url = _
        "http://michaelk/ASPNetCookbook/VBWebServices/CH11BookServicesVB.asmx"
    End If
  End Sub

    ...

End Class
```

C#
```
public class CH11BookServicesCS:
    System.Web.Services.Protocols.SoapHttpClientProtocol
{
  public BookServices_CS()
  {
    string urlSetting =
```

```
C#           System.Configuration.ConfigurationSettings.
                AppSettings["CSExamples.ExampleBookServices.CH11BookServicesCS"];

        if ((urlSetting != null))
        {
            this.Url = string.Concat(urlSetting, "");
        }
        else
        {
            this.Url =
                "http://localhost/ASPNetCookbook/CSWebServices/CH11BookServicesCS.asmx";
        }
    }
    ...
}
```

When you set the URL Behavior property to Dynamic, Visual Studio .NET also adds an entry in the appSettings section your *web.config* file. The key is set to the full namespace of the proxy class, and the value is set the same as the hardcoded value. By just changing a property value, Visual Studio .NET has written all of the code you need to support changing the URL of the web service without having to change, recompile, and deploy code.

```
<appSettings>
 <add key="VBExamples.ExampleBookServices.CH11BookServicesVB"
   value="http://michaelk/ASPNetCookbook/VBWebServices/CH11BookServicesVB.asmx"/>
 </appSettings>
```

CHAPTER 12

Dynamic Images

12.0 Introduction

The ability to draw or retrieve and display graphic images on your web pages on the fly can add powerful functionality to an application. This is a nearly impossible task in classic ASP, unless you use a third-party component of some kind. By contrast, the drawing library provided in the .NET Framework makes it relatively easy to create your own images when you need them. Indeed, it provides the ability to do almost anything you can imagine in the way of image generation. The examples shown in this chapter show you how to:

- Draw button images on the fly using text generated during the running of your application
- Create bar charts on the fly
- Display images stored in a database
- Display thumbnails from full-sized images stored in a database

These represent just a sampling of what you can do with the .NET drawing libraries and a little bit of custom code.

12.1 Drawing Button Images on the Fly

Problem

You need to create a button image on the fly using text generated during the running of your application.

Solution

Create a web form that is responsible for creating the button image using the System. Drawing classes and then streaming the image to the Response object.

In the *.aspx* file, enter an @ Page directive, but omit any head or body tags. The @ Page directive links the ASP.NET page to the code-behind class that draws the image.

In the code-behind class for the page, use the .NET language of your choice to:

1. Import the System.Drawing and System.Drawing.Imaging namespaces.

2. Create a makeButton (or similarly named) method that creates a bitmap for a button using text generated during the running of the application—for example, text passed in on the URL.

3. Create a MemoryStream object and save the bitmap in JPEG format (or other format) to the memory stream.

4. Write the resulting binary stream to Response object.

Examples 12-1 through 12-3 show the *.aspx* file and VB and C# code-behind files for an application that creates a button image whose label is provided by the application user.

To use a dynamically generated image in your application, you need to set the Src attribute of the image tags for your button bitmaps to the URL of the ASP.NET page that creates the images, passing the image text in the URL.

In the *.aspx* file for the page, add an img tag for displaying the dynamically created image.

In the code-behind class for the page that uses the image, use the .NET language of your choice to set to the Src attribute of the image tag to the URL for the web form that will draw the image, passing the text it needs in the URL.

Examples 12-4 through 12-6 show the *.aspx* file and VB and C# code-behind files for an application that uses the dynamic image generation. Figure 12-1 shows some typical output from the application.

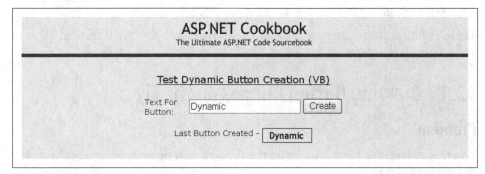

Figure 12-1. Creating a button image on the fly

Discussion

Creating button images on the fly can be handy for a couple of related reasons. First, using button images may help provide the look you want for your application. Second, generating them on the fly can avoid you having to create and save a whole series of button images to the filesystem on the prospect that they may be needed someday. For example, you might want to use images to improve the appearance of reports.

The approach we favor for generating images on the fly involves first drawing them and then streaming the images to the Response object. How does this work? The process begins when the browser first makes a request for a page to display. During the rendering of the page, whenever the browser encounters an image tag, it sends a request for that image to the server. The browser expects the server to stream the requested image back to the browser with the content type set to indicate an image of a certain type is being returned—for example, "image/jpg", indicating an image in JPEG format. Our approach does exactly that, but with a unique twist. Instead of a static image, which is the norm, our approach returns an image that has been created on the fly on the server. The browser neither knows nor cares where the stream is coming from, which is why our approach works just fine.

Two web forms are used in our example that illustrates this solution. The first one renders no HTML but instead processes a user request for a dynamically created button image. A second web form is used to display the requested image.

The *.aspx* file of the first form contains no head or body; it simply contains the @ Page directive to link the code-behind class for the page.

In the Page_Load event of the code-behind of the first page, the text for the image button passed in the URL is retrieved and passed to the makeButton method to create the button image.

The makeButton method first creates the font that will be used to label the button image and then measures the space that will be required to display the text. Because we have no Graphics object in this scenario and a Graphics object cannot be created by itself (it must always be associated with a specific device context), we have to create a Bitmap solely for the purpose of creating the Graphics object. Here a dummy 1-pixel-by-1-pixel bitmap is created:

```
bfont = New Font("Trebuchet MS", 10)
button = New Bitmap(1, 1, PixelFormat.Format32bppRgb)
g = Graphics.FromImage(button)
tSize = g.MeasureString(buttonText, bfont)
```

```
bfont = new Font("Trebuchet MS", 10);
button = new Bitmap(1, 1, PixelFormat.Format32bppRgb);
g = Graphics.FromImage(button);
tSize = g.MeasureString(buttonText, bfont);
```

Next, we need to calculate the size of the image required to contain the text, allowing for some space around the text. The constants HORT_PAD and VERT_PAD are used to define the space at the ends of the text and above/below the text.

```
buttonWidth = CInt(Math.Ceiling(tSize.Width + (HORT_PAD * 2)))
buttonHeight = CInt(Math.Ceiling(tSize.Height + (VERT_PAD * 2)))
```

```
buttonWidth = Convert.ToInt32(Math.Ceiling(tSize.Width +
                         (HORT_PAD * 2)));
buttonHeight = Convert.ToInt32(Math.Ceiling(tSize.Height +
                          (VERT_PAD * 2)));
```

Now that we know how big to create the image, the `Bitmap` that will be used for the button image can be created. The `PixelFormat.Format32bppRgb` defines the `Bitmap` to be 32 bits per pixel, using 8 bits each for the red, green, and blue color components. For the image being created here, the format is not that important. For more graphically appealing images, however, the format plays a significant role.

```
button = New Bitmap(buttonWidth, _
                    buttonHeight, _
                    PixelFormat.Format32bppRgb)
```

```
button = new Bitmap(buttonWidth,
                    buttonHeight,
                    PixelFormat.Format32bppRgb);
```

Next, the entire image is filled with a background color. This requires creating a brush with the desired color and calling the `FillRectangle` method with the full size of the image being created. (Remember, the graphics coordinates always start at 0.) The `FromHtml` method of the `ColorTranslator` class is used to convert the HTML style color designation to the color required for the brush being created.

 When filling an image with a background color, be careful of the color choices you make, since browsers do not consistently display all colors. It is best to stick to the 216 colors of the web-safe palette.

```
g = Graphics.FromImage(button)
g.FillRectangle(New SolidBrush(ColorTranslator.FromHtml("#F0F0F0")), _
                0, _
                0, _
                buttonWidth - 1, _
                buttonHeight - 1)
```

```
g = Graphics.FromImage(button);
g.FillRectangle(new SolidBrush(ColorTranslator.FromHtml("#F0F0F0")),
                0,
                0,
                buttonWidth - 1,
                buttonHeight - 1);
```

After filling the button image background color, a border is drawn around the perimeter of the image. This requires creating a pen with the desired color and width to do the drawing.

```
g.DrawRectangle(New Pen(Color.Navy, 1), _
                0, _
                0, _
                buttonWidth - 1, _
                buttonHeight - 1)
```

```
C#   g.DrawRectangle(new Pen(Color.Navy, 1),
                     0,
                     0,
                     buttonWidth - 1,
                     buttonHeight - 1);
```

Finally, the text is drawn in the center of the image button. The centering is accomplished by offsetting the upper-left corner of the text block by the same amount as the spacing that was allowed around the text.

```
VB   g.DrawString(buttonText, _
                  bfont, _
                  New SolidBrush(Color.Navy), _
                  HORT_PAD, _
                  VERT_PAD)
```

```
C#   g.DrawString(buttonText,
                  bfont,
                  new SolidBrush(Color.Navy),
                  HORT_PAD,
                  VERT_PAD);
```

When the button image bitmap is returned to the Page_Load method, we need to create a MemoryStream object and save the bitmap in JPEG format to the memory stream. (We chose the JPEG format because it happened to work well with the images in this example. Depending on the circumstances, you may need to use another format, such as GIF.)

```
VB   ms = New MemoryStream
     button.Save(ms, ImageFormat.Jpeg)
```

```
C#   ms = new MemoryStream( );
     button.Save(ms, ImageFormat.Jpeg);
```

The final step in generating the button image is to write the binary stream to the Response object. This requires setting the ContentType property to match the format we saved the image to in the memory stream. In this example, the image was saved in JPEG format, so the ContentType must be set to "image/jpg". This informs the browser that the stream being returned is an image of the proper type. We then use the BinaryWrite method to write the image to the Response object.

```
VB   Response.ContentType = "image/jpg"
     Response.BinaryWrite(ms.ToArray( ))
```

```
C#   Response.ContentType = "image/jpg";
     Response.BinaryWrite(ms.ToArray( ));
```

Using our example web form that dynamically creates button images merely requires setting the Src attribute of the image tag to the URL for the web form just described, passing the text for the image in the URL. A sample URL is shown here:

```
src="CH12CreateButtonVB.aspx?ButtonText=Test Button"
```

In our example, the Src attribute of the img tag is set in the create button click event of the test page code-behind. To make things a little easier and avoid hardcoding page names and QueryString information, two constants (PAGE_NAME and QS_BUTTON_TEXT) are defined in the code-behind of the image creation page and are used here in building the URL.

 Dynamically generating images can be resource intensive. To improve the performance of your application, the generated images should be cached. Recipe 13.2 provides an example of how to cache the results as a function of the data passed in the QueryString.

See Also

Recipe 13.2; MSDN Help for more on the .NET drawing libraries

Example 12-1. Create images dynamically (.aspx)

```
<%@ Page Language="vb" AutoEventWireup="false"
        Codebehind="CH12CreateButtonVB.aspx.vb"
        Inherits="ASPNetCookbook.VBExamples.CH12CreateButtonVB" %>
```

Example 12-2. Create images dynamically code-behind (.vb)

```
Option Explicit On
Option Strict On
'----------------------------------------------------------------------------
'
'   Module Name: CH12CreateButtonVB.aspx.vb
'
'   Description: This module provides the code behind for the
'                CH12CreateButtonVB.aspx page.  It streams a dynamically
'                created button image to the browser.
'
'****************************************************************************
Imports System
Imports System.Drawing
Imports System.Drawing.Imaging
Imports System.IO

Namespace ASPNetCookbook.VBExamples
  Public Class CH12CreateButtonVB
    Inherits System.Web.UI.Page

    'constants used to create URLs to this page
    Public Const PAGE_NAME As String = "CH12CreateButtonVB.aspx"
    Public Const QS_BUTTON_TEXT As String = "ButtonText"

    '****************************************************************************
    '
    '   ROUTINE: Page_Load
    '
```

Example 12-2. Create images dynamically code-behind (.vb) (continued)

```
'    DESCRIPTION: This routine provides the event handler for the page load
'                 event.  It is responsible for initializing the controls
'                 on the page.
'----------------------------------------------------------------------------
Private Sub Page_Load(ByVal sender As System.Object, _
                      ByVal e As System.EventArgs) Handles MyBase.Load

   Dim buttonText As String
   Dim button As Bitmap
   Dim ms As MemoryStream

   'get button text from the query string and create the image
   buttonText = Request.QueryString(QS_BUTTON_TEXT)
   button = makeButton(buttonText)

   'write image to response object
   ms = New MemoryStream
   button.Save(ms, ImageFormat.Jpeg)
   Response.ContentType = "image/jpg"
   Response.BinaryWrite(ms.ToArray( ))
End Sub  'Page_Load

'**************************************************************************
'
'    ROUTINE: MakeButton
'
'    DESCRIPTION: This routine creates a button with the passed text.
'----------------------------------------------------------------------------
Private Function makeButton(ByVal buttonText As String) As Bitmap
   'define the space around the text on the button
   Const HORT_PAD As Integer = 10
   Const VERT_PAD As Integer = 2

   Dim button As Bitmap
   Dim g As Graphics
   Dim bfont As Font
   Dim tSize As SizeF
   Dim buttonHeight As Integer
   Dim buttonWidth As Integer

   'create the font that will used then create a dummy button to get
   'a graphics object that provides the ability to measure the height
   'and width required to display the passed string
   bfont = New Font("Trebuchet MS", 10)
   button = New Bitmap(1, 1, PixelFormat.Format32bppRgb)
   g = Graphics.FromImage(button)
   tSize = g.MeasureString(buttonText, bfont)

   'calculate the size of button required to display the text adding
   'some space around the text
   buttonWidth = CInt(Math.Ceiling(tSize.Width + (HORT_PAD * 2)))
   buttonHeight = CInt(Math.Ceiling(tSize.Height + (VERT_PAD * 2)))
```

Example 12-2. Create images dynamically code-behind (.vb) (continued)

```vb
        'create a new button using the calculated size
        button = New Bitmap(buttonWidth, _
                            buttonHeight, _
                            PixelFormat.Format32bppRgb)

        'fill the button area
        g = Graphics.FromImage(button)
        g.FillRectangle(New SolidBrush(ColorTranslator.FromHtml("#F0F0F0")), _
                        0, _
                        0, _
                        buttonWidth - 1, _
                        buttonHeight - 1)

        'draw a rectangle around the button perimeter using a pen width of 1
        g.DrawRectangle(New Pen(Color.Navy, 1), _
                        0, _
                        0, _
                        buttonWidth - 1, _
                        buttonHeight - 1)

        'draw the text on the button (centered)
        g.DrawString(buttonText, _
                     bfont, _
                     New SolidBrush(Color.Navy), _
                     HORT_PAD, _
                     VERT_PAD)
        g.Dispose()
        Return (button)
    End Function  'makeButton
  End Class  'CH12CreateButtonVB
End Namespace
```

Example 12-3. Create images dynamically code-behind (.cs)

```csharp
//------------------------------------------------------------------------------
//
//   Module Name: CH12CreateButtonCS.aspx.cs
//
//   Description: This module provides the code behind for the
//                CH12CreateButtonCS.aspx page
//
//******************************************************************************
using System;
using System.Drawing;
using System.Drawing.Imaging;
using System.IO;

namespace ASPNetCookbook.CSExamples
{
  public class CH12CreateButtonCS : System.Web.UI.Page
  {
```

Example 12-3. Create images dynamically code-behind (.cs) (continued)

```
// constants used to create URLs to this page
public const String PAGE_NAME = "CH12CreateButtonCS.aspx";
public const String QS_BUTTON_TEXT = "ButtonText";

//*********************************************************************
//
//   ROUTINE: Page_Load
//
//   DESCRIPTION: This routine provides the event handler for the page
//                load event.  It is responsible for initializing the
//                controls on the page.
//---------------------------------------------------------------------
private void Page_Load(object sender, System.EventArgs e)
{
  String buttonText = null;
  Bitmap button = null;
  MemoryStream ms = null;

  // get button text from the query string and create image
  buttonText = Request.QueryString[QS_BUTTON_TEXT];
  button = makeButton(buttonText);

  // write image to response object
  ms = new MemoryStream();
  button.Save(ms, ImageFormat.Jpeg);
  Response.ContentType = "image/jpg";
  Response.BinaryWrite(ms.ToArray());
} // Page_Load

//*********************************************************************
//
//   ROUTINE: makeButton
//
//   DESCRIPTION: This routine creates a button with the passed text.
//---------------------------------------------------------------------
private Bitmap makeButton(String buttonText)
{
  // define the space around the text on the button
  const int HORT_PAD = 10;
  const int VERT_PAD = 2;

  Bitmap button = null;
  Graphics g = null;
  Font bfont = null;
  SizeF tSize;
  int buttonHeight;
  int buttonWidth;

  // create the font that will used then create a dummy button to get
  // a graphics object that provides the ability to measure the height
  // and width required to display the passed string
```

Example 12-3. Create images dynamically code-behind (.cs) (continued)

```
        bfont = new Font("Trebuchet MS", 10);
        button = new Bitmap(1, 1, PixelFormat.Format32bppRgb);
        g = Graphics.FromImage(button);
        tSize = g.MeasureString(buttonText, bfont);

        // calculate the size of button required to display the text adding
        // some space around the text
        buttonWidth = Convert.ToInt32(Math.Ceiling(tSize.Width +
                                      (HORT_PAD * 2)));
        buttonHeight = Convert.ToInt32(Math.Ceiling(tSize.Height +
                                       (VERT_PAD * 2)));

        // create a new button using the calculated size
        button = new Bitmap(buttonWidth,
                            buttonHeight,
                            PixelFormat.Format32bppRgb);

        // fill the button area
        g = Graphics.FromImage(button);
        g.FillRectangle(new SolidBrush(ColorTranslator.FromHtml("#F0F0F0")),
                        0,
                        0,
                        buttonWidth - 1,
                        buttonHeight - 1);

        // draw a rectangle around the button perimeter using a pen width of 1
        g.DrawRectangle(new Pen(Color.Navy, 1),
                        0,
                        0,
                        buttonWidth - 1,
                        buttonHeight - 1);

        // draw the text on the button (centered)
        g.DrawString(buttonText,
                     bfont,
                     new SolidBrush(Color.Navy),
                     HORT_PAD,
                     VERT_PAD);
        g.Dispose();
        return (button);
    } // makeButton
  } // CH12CreateButtonCS
}
```

Example 12-4. Using the dynamically created images (.aspx)

```
<%@ Page Language="vb" AutoEventWireup="false"
    Codebehind="CH12TestCreateButtonVB.aspx.vb"
    Inherits="ASPNetCookbook.VBExamples.CH12TestCreateButtonVB" %>
<!DOCTYPE HTML PUBLIC "-//W3C//DTD HTML 4.0 Transitional//EN">
<html>
  <head>
    <title>Test Dynamic Button Creation</title>
```

Example 12-4. Using the dynamically created images (.aspx) (continued)

```html
      <link rel="stylesheet" href="css/ASPNetCookbook.css">
   </head>
<body leftmargin="0" marginheight="0" marginwidth="0" topmargin="0">
   <form id="frmTestCreateButton" method="post" runat="server">
      <table width="100%" cellpadding="0" cellspacing="0" border="0">
         <tr>
            <td align="center">
               <img src="images/ASPNETCookbookHeading_blue.gif">
            </td>
         </tr>
         <tr>
            <td class="dividerLine">
               <img src="images/spacer.gif" height="6" border="0"></td>
         </tr>
      </table>
      <table width="90%" align="center" border="0">
         <tr>
            <td align="center"> </td>
         </tr>
         <tr>
            <td align="center" class="PageHeading">
               Test Dynamic Button Creation (VB)
            </td>
         </tr>
         <tr>
            <td><img src="images/spacer.gif" height="10" border="0"></td>
         </tr>
         <tr>
            <td align="center">
               <table width="50%">
                  <tr>
                     <td class="LabelText">Text For Button: </td>
                     <td>
                        <asp:TextBox ID="txtButtonText" Runat="server" />
                     </td>
                     <td>
                        <input id="btnCreate" runat="server" type="button"
                               value="Create" name="btnCreate">
                     </td>
                  </tr>
                  <tr>
                     <td id="tdCreatedButton" runat="server"
                         colspan="3" align="center" class="LabelText"><br />
                        Last Button Created -
                        <img id="imgButton" runat="server"
                             border="0" align="middle">
                     </td>
                  </tr>
               </table>
            </td>
         </tr>
      </table>
```

Example 12-4. Using the dynamically created images (.aspx) (continued)

```
    </form>
  </body>
</html>
```

Example 12-5. Using the dynamically created images code-behind (.vb)

```vb
Option Explicit On
Option Strict On
'-----------------------------------------------------------------------------
'
'   Module Name: CH12TestCreateButtonVB.aspx.vb
'
'   Description: This module provides the code behind for the
'                CH12TestCreateButtonVB.aspx page.
'
'*****************************************************************************
Namespace ASPNetCookbook.VBExamples
  Public Class CH12TestCreateButtonVB
    Inherits System.Web.UI.Page

    'controls on the form
    Protected txtButtonText As System.Web.UI.WebControls.TextBox
    Protected WithEvents btnCreate As System.Web.UI.HtmlControls.HtmlInputButton
    Protected tdCreatedButton As System.Web.UI.HtmlControls.HtmlTableCell
    Protected imgButton As System.Web.UI.HtmlControls.HtmlImage

    '*************************************************************************
    '
    '   ROUTINE: Page_Load
    '
    '   DESCRIPTION: This routine provides the event handler for the page load
    '                event.  It is responsible for initializing the controls
    '                on the page.
    '-------------------------------------------------------------------------
    Private Sub Page_Load(ByVal sender As System.Object, _
                          ByVal e As System.EventArgs) Handles MyBase.Load

      If (Not Page.IsPostBack) Then
        'make image button table cell invisible initially
        tdCreatedButton.Visible = False
      End If
    End Sub  'Page_Load

    '*************************************************************************
    '
    '   ROUTINE: btnCreate_Click
    '
    '   DESCRIPTION: This routine provides the event handler for the create
    '                button click event.  It is responsible for initializing
    '                the source property of the image button to the URL of
    '                the dynamic button creation page.
    '-------------------------------------------------------------------------
```

Example 12-5. Using the dynamically created images code-behind (.vb) (continued)

```vb
    Private Sub btnCreate_ServerClick(ByVal sender As Object, _
                                    ByVal e As System.EventArgs) _
                Handles btnCreate.ServerClick
      'update the image tag with the URL to the page that will
      'create the button and with the button text in the URL
      imgButton.Src = CH12CreateButtonVB.PAGE_NAME & _
                    "?" & CH12CreateButtonVB.QS_BUTTON_TEXT & _
                    "=" & txtButtonText.Text
      tdCreatedButton.Visible = True
    End Sub  'btnCreate_Click
  End Class  'CH12TestCreateButtonVB
End Namespace
```

Example 12-6. Using the dynamically created images code-behind (.cs)

```csharp
//----------------------------------------------------------------------------
//
//    Module Name: CH12TestCreateButtonCS.aspx.cs
//
//    Description: This module provides the code behind for the
//                 CH12TestCreateButtonCS.aspx page
//
//****************************************************************************
using System;

namespace ASPNetCookbook.CSExamples
{
  public class CH12TestCreateButtonCS : System.Web.UI.Page
  {
    // controls on the form
    protected System.Web.UI.WebControls.TextBox txtButtonText ;
    protected System.Web.UI.HtmlControls.HtmlInputButton btnCreate;
    protected System.Web.UI.HtmlControls.HtmlTableCell tdCreatedButton;
    protected System.Web.UI.HtmlControls.HtmlImage imgButton;


    //****************************************************************************
    //
    //    ROUTINE: Page_Load
    //
    //    DESCRIPTION: This routine provides the event handler for the page
    //                 load event.  It is responsible for initializing the
    //                 controls on the page.
    //----------------------------------------------------------------------------
    private void Page_Load(object sender, System.EventArgs e)
    {
      // wire the create button click event
      this.btnCreate.ServerClick +=
        new EventHandler(this.btnCreate_ServerClick);

      if (!Page.IsPostBack)
      {
        // make image button table cell invisible initially
        tdCreatedButton.Visible = false;
```

```
    }
  }  // Page_Load

  //*************************************************************************
  //
  //    ROUTINE: btnCreate_ServerClick
  //
  //    DESCRIPTION: This routine provides the event handler for the create
  //                 button click event.  It is responsible for initializing
  //                 the source property of the image button to the URL of
  //                 the dynamic button creation page.
  //-------------------------------------------------------------------------
  private void btnCreate_ServerClick(Object sender,
                                     System.EventArgs e)
  {
    // update the image tag with the URL to the aspx page that will
    // create the button and with the button text in the URL
    imgButton.Src = CH12CreateButtonCS.PAGE_NAME +
                    "?" + CH12CreateButtonCS.QS_BUTTON_TEXT +
                    "=" + txtButtonText.Text;
    tdCreatedButton.Visible = true;
  }  // btnCreate_ServerClick
}  // CH12TestCreateButtonCS
}
```

12.2   Creating Bar Charts on the Fly

Problem

You want to create a simple bar chart on the fly without having to resort to a commercial package to do so.

Solution

Use a combination of data binding with a Repeater control and the well-known HTML trick of stretching an image to create the bars.

In the *.aspx* file, add a Repeater control with an ItemTemplate.

In the code-behind class for the page, use the .NET language of your choice to:

1. Assign the data source to the Repeater control and bind it.

2. In the ItemDataBound event handler that is called for each item in the Repeater, set the width of the bar in the passed Repeater row.

Figure 12-2 shows some typical output. Examples 12-7 through 12-9 show the *.aspx* file and VB and C# code-behind files for an application that implements this solution.

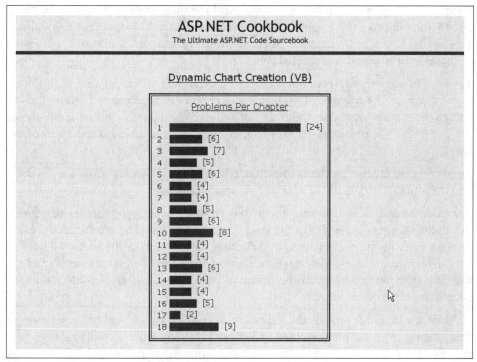

ASP.NET Cookbook
The Ultimate ASP.NET Code Sourcebook

Dynamic Chart Creation (VB)

Problems Per Chapter

Figure 12-2. Create bar chart output dynamically

Discussion

This recipe provides a rather simple approach that combines data binding and HTML tricks to create a bar graph with very little coding, and without the need to purchase any additional components. By using more complex HTML, you can add more labels and other enhancements to this recipe, which may make it more useful for your situation.

The example we use to illustrate this solution generates a bar chart from chapter and problem data in a database. (The source of the data is not that important. Rather, it's the technique for generating the graph on the fly that is the main focus of this recipe.) The bar chart is created from an HTML table, with the top row used to label the chart.

This recipe advocates using a Repeater control to generate the rows in a table that represent the bars on the chart. The rows generated by the Repeater are defined in the ItemTemplate element, which in our example contains two columns. The first column is used to output the chapter number. In our example, the chapter number is obtained by binding the cell text to the Chapter column in the data source.

The second column contains the bar representing the number of problems in the chapter. The bar is created by using an HTML image tag with the source set to a 1-pixel-by-1-pixel image. The height and width attributes of the image "stretch" the image to the size of the bar needed to represent the number of problems in the chapter. In our example, the height is set to a fixed value of 15 pixels, but the width is adjusted to represent the number of problems in the chapter. The width is adjusted in the code-behind and is discussed later.

The second column also contains a label to indicate the actual number of problems in the chapter. The number of problems in a chapter is obtained by binding the cell text to the ProblemCount column in the data source. This label is placed at the end of the bar with a nonbreaking space ( ) to separate the label from the end of the bar.

The Page_Load method in the example code-behind reads the data from the database and then binds the data to the Repeater control on the page.

The code-behind class also implements the ItemDataBound event handler to provide the ability to adjust the width of the image used for the bar. The ItemDataBound event fires once per row in the Repeater as the row is data bound. In this event we need to get a reference to the HTML image in the row using the FindControl method of the row and then set the width of the image to reflect the number of problems in the chapter represented by the row.

If this recipe does not provide the richness you need for your chart, you can create an image using the concepts presented in Recipe 12.1. The System.Drawing classes provide all of the functionality to create very sophisticated charts using the GDI+. They do require considerably more coding, however, as you must build your graphs from the ground up using the basic ingredients of pen, brush, point, rectangle, and the like.

See Also

Recipe 12.1; MSDN Help for more information on the System.Drawing class

Example 12-7. Create bar chart dynamically (.aspx/.vb)

```
<%@ Page Language="vb" AutoEventWireup="false"
        Codebehind="CH12CreateChartVB.aspx.vb"
        Inherits="ASPNetCookbook.VBExamples.CH12CreateChartVB" %>
<!DOCTYPE HTML PUBLIC "-//W3C//DTD HTML 4.0 Transitional//EN">
<html>
  <head>
    <title>Create Chart</title>
    <link rel="stylesheet" href="css/ASPNetCookbook.css">
  </head>
  <body leftmargin="0" marginheight="0" marginwidth="0" topmargin="0">
    <form id="frmTestDynamicChart" method="post" runat="server">
      <table width="100%" cellpadding="0" cellspacing="0" border="0">
        <tr>
          <td align="center">
            <img src="images/ASPNETCookbookHeading_blue.gif">
          </td>
```

Example 12-7. Create bar chart dynamically (.aspx/.vb) (continued)

```
      </tr>
      <tr>
        <td class="dividerLine">
          <img src="images/spacer.gif" height="6" border="0"></td>
      </tr>
    </table>
    <table width="90%" align="center" border="0">
      <tr>
        <td align="center"> </td>
      </tr>
      <tr>
        <td align="center" class="PageHeading">
          Dynamic Chart Creation (VB)
        </td>
      </tr>
      <tr>
        <td><img src="images/spacer.gif" height="10" border="0"></td>
      </tr>
      <tr>
        <td align="center">
          <table border="2" bordercolor="#000080"  cellpadding="10">
            <tr>
              <td>
                <table cellpadding="0" cellspacing="0" border="0">
                  <tr>
                    <td align="center" colspan="2" class="SubHeading">
                      Problems Per Chapter<br /><br /></td>
                  </tr>
<asp:Repeater ID="repChartBar" Runat="server">
  <ItemTemplate>
    <tr>
      <td class="LabelText">
        <%# DataBinder.Eval(Container.DataItem, "Chapter") %> 
      </td>
      <td class="LabelText">
        <img id="imgChartBar" runat="server"
            src="images/blueSpacer.gif" border="0"
            Height="15" align="middle" >
           [<%# DataBinder.Eval(Container.DataItem, "ProblemCount") %>]
      </td>
    </tr>
  </ItemTemplate>
</asp:Repeater>
                </table>
              </td>
            </tr>
          </table>
        </td>
      </tr>
    </table>
  </form>
 </body>
</html>
```

Example 12-8. Create bar chart dynamically code-behind (.vb)

```vb
Option Explicit On
Option Strict On
'----------------------------------------------------------------------------
'
'   Module Name: CH12CreateChartVB.aspx.vb
'
'   Description: This module provides the code behind for the
'                CH12CreateChartVB.aspx page.
'
'****************************************************************************
Imports Microsoft.VisualBasic
Imports System
Imports System.Configuration
Imports System.Data
Imports System.Data.Common
Imports System.Data.OleDb

Namespace ASPNetCookbook.VBExamples
  Public Class CH12CreateChartVB
    Inherits System.Web.UI.Page

    'controls on the form
    Protected WithEvents repChartBar As System.Web.UI.WebControls.Repeater

    '****************************************************************************
    '
    '   ROUTINE: Page_Load
    '
    '   DESCRIPTION: This routine provides the event handler for the page load
    '                event.  It is responsible for initializing the controls
    '                on the page.
    '----------------------------------------------------------------------------
    Private Sub Page_Load(ByVal sender As System.Object, _
                          ByVal e As System.EventArgs) Handles MyBase.Load
      Dim dbConn As OleDbConnection
      Dim dc As OleDbCommand
      Dim dr As OleDbDataReader
      Dim strConnection As String
      Dim strSQL As String

      If (Not Page.IsPostBack) Then
        Try
          'get the connection string from web.config and open a connection
          'to the database
          strConnection = _
              ConfigurationSettings.AppSettings("dbConnectionString")
          dbConn = New OleDb.OleDbConnection(strConnection)
          dbConn.Open()

          'build the query string and get the data from the database
          strSQL = "SELECT DISTINCT ChapterID AS Chapter, " & _
                   "count(*) AS ProblemCount " & _
                   "FROM Problem " & _
```

Example 12-8. Create bar chart dynamically code-behind (.vb) (continued)

```vb
                  "GROUP BY ChapterID"

         dc = New OleDbCommand(strSQL, dbConn)
         dr = dc.ExecuteReader( )

         'set the source of the data for the repeater control and bind it
         repChartBar.DataSource = dr
         repChartBar.DataBind( )

      Finally
        'cleanup
        If (Not IsNothing(dbConn)) Then
          dbConn.Close( )
        End If
      End Try
    End If
  End Sub


  '*************************************************************************
  '
  '    ROUTINE: repChartBar_ItemDataBound
  '
  '    DESCRIPTION: This routine is the event handler that is called for each
  '                 item in the datagrid after a data bind occurs.  It is
  '                 responsible for setting the width of the bar in the
  '                 passed repeater row to reflect the number of problems in
  '                 the chapter the row represents
  '--------------------------------------------------------------------------
  Private Sub repChartBar_ItemDataBound(ByVal sender As Object, _
            ByVal e As System.Web.UI.WebControls.RepeaterItemEventArgs) _
         Handles repChartBar.ItemDataBound
    Dim img As System.Web.UI.HtmlControls.HtmlImage

      'get a reference to the image used for the bar in the row
      img = CType(e.Item.FindControl("imgChartBar"), _
                System.Web.UI.HtmlControls.HtmlImage)

      'set the width to the number of problems in the chapter for this row
      'multiplied by a constant to stretch the bar a bit more
      img.Width = _
        CInt(CType(e.Item.DataItem, DbDataRecord)("ProblemCount")) * 10
    End Sub  'repChartBar_ItemDataBound
  End Class  'CH12CreateChartVB
End Namespace
```

Example 12-9. Create bar chart dynamically code-behind (.cs)

```cs
//------------------------------------------------------------------------
//
//    Module Name: CH12CreateChartCS.aspx.cs
//
//    Description: This module provides the code behind for the
//                 CH12CreateChartCS.aspx page
```

Example 12-9. Create bar chart dynamically code-behind (.cs) (continued)

```csharp
//
//****************************************************************************
using System;
using System.Configuration;
using System.Data;
using System.Data.Common;
using System.Data.OleDb;
using System.Web.UI.WebControls;

namespace ASPNetCookbook.CSExamples
{
  public class CH12CreateChartCS : System.Web.UI.Page
  {
    // controls on the form
    protected System.Web.UI.WebControls.Repeater repChartBar;

    //****************************************************************************
    //
    //   ROUTINE: Page_Load
    //
    //   DESCRIPTION: This routine provides the event handler for the page
    //                load event.  It is responsible for initializing the
    //                controls on the page.
    //----------------------------------------------------------------------
    private void Page_Load(object sender, System.EventArgs e)
    {
      OleDbConnection dbConn = null;
      OleDbCommand dc = null;
      OleDbDataReader dr = null;
      string strConnection = null;
      String strSQL = null;

      // bind the item data bound event
      this.repChartBar.ItemDataBound +=
        new RepeaterItemEventHandler(this.repChartBar_ItemDataBound);

      if (!Page.IsPostBack)
      {
        try
        {
          // get the connection string from web.config and open a connection
          // to the database
          strConnection =
            ConfigurationSettings.AppSettings["dbConnectionString"];
          dbConn = new OleDbConnection(strConnection);
          dbConn.Open();

          // build the query string and get the data from the database
          strSQL = "SELECT DISTINCT ChapterID AS Chapter, " +
                   "count(*) AS ProblemCount " +
                   "FROM Problem " +
                   "GROUP BY ChapterID";
          dc = new OleDbCommand(strSQL, dbConn);
```

Example 12-9. Create bar chart dynamically code-behind (.cs) (continued)

```
        dr = dc.ExecuteReader( );

        // set the source of the data for the repeater control and bind it
        repChartBar.DataSource = dr;
        repChartBar.DataBind( );
    }

    finally
    {
      // clean up
      if (dbConn != null)
      {
        dbConn.Close( );
      }
    }
  }
} // Page_Load

//************************************************************************
//
//    ROUTINE: repChartBar_ItemDataBound
//
//    DESCRIPTION: This routine is the event handler that is called for
//                 each item in the datagrid after a data bind occurs.  It
//                 is responsible for setting the width of the bar in the
//                 passed repeater row to reflect the number of problems
//                 in the chapter the row represents.
//------------------------------------------------------------------------
private void repChartBar_ItemDataBound(Object sender,
          System.Web.UI.WebControls.RepeaterItemEventArgs e)
{
  System.Web.UI.HtmlControls.HtmlImage img = null;

  // get a reference to the image used for the bar in the row
  img = (System.Web.UI.HtmlControls.HtmlImage)
        (e.Item.FindControl("imgChartBar"));

  // set the width to the number of problems in the chapter for this row
  // multiplied by a constant to stretch the bar a bit more
  img.Width =
    (int)(((DbDataRecord)(e.Item.DataItem))["ProblemCount"]) * 10;
  } // repChartBar_ItemDataBound
} // CH12CreateChartCS
}
```

12.3   Displaying Images Stored in a Database

Problem

Your application stores images in a database that you want to display on a web form.

Solution

Create a web form that reads the image data from the database and streams the image to the Response object.

In the *.aspx* file, enter an @ Page directive—omitting any head or body tags to link the *.aspx* page to the code-behind class that retrieves and displays the images.

1. Read the image ID that is generated by the running application—for example, the image ID passed in the URL for accessing the web form.
2. Open a connection to the database that contains the images.
3. Build a query string, and read the byte array of the desired image from the database.
4. Set the content type for the image and write it to the Response object.

Examples 12-10 through 12-12 show the *.aspx* file and VB and C# code-behind files for an application that implements the image-building portion of the solution.

To use this dynamic image generation technique in your application, set the src attribute of the image tags used to display the images to the URL of the ASP.NET page that reads the images from the database, passing the image ID in the URL.

In the *.aspx* file for the page, add an img tag for displaying the image.

In the code-behind class for the page that uses the image, use the .NET language of your choice to set the src attribute of the image tag to the URL for the web form just described, passing the ID of the image in the URL.

Examples 12-13 through 12-15 show the *.aspx* file and VB and C# code-behind files for an application that uses the dynamic image generation. Figure 12-3 shows some typical output from the application.

Discussion

If you have images in a database that you want to display on a web form, chances are you've considered using an image tag to display them. Nevertheless, you may be searching for a practical way to set the image tag's src attribute and move the image data to the browser while maintaining the maximum flexibility in selecting the images you need.

The solution we favor that meets these requirements involves creating a web form that reads an image from a database and streams it to the Response object. A convenient way to specify the image to read from the database is to include an image ID in the URL used to call the web form that retrieves and returns the image to the browser.

Our example that illustrates this solution consists of two web forms. The first web form renders no HTML but instead processes the request for reading an image from the database. The second web form is used to demonstrate displaying an image from the database.

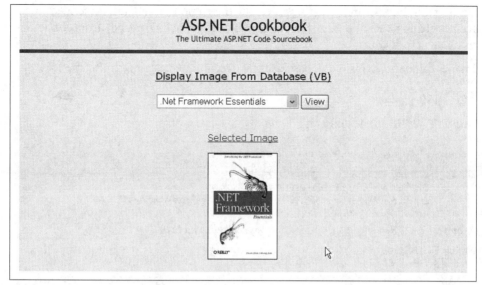

Figure 12-3. Displaying images from a database

The *.aspx* file of the first form contains no head or body; it simply contains the @ Page directive to link the page to its code-behind class.

The Page_Load method of the code-behind performs the following steps to retrieve the requested image from the database and then send it to the browser:

1. Retrieve the ID of the requested image from the URL

2. Read the byte array of the image from the database

3. Set the ContentType of the type of image stored in the database (GIF in this example)

4. Write the byte array of the image to the Response object

To use the ASP.NET page to retrieve images from the database, we need to set the src attribute of an image tag to the name of the page just described, passing the ID of the desired image in the URL. A sample URL is shown here:

```
src="CH12ImageFromDatabaseVB.aspx?ImageID=5"
```

In our example, the src attribute of an img tag is set in the view image button click event of the test page code-behind. To make things a little easier and avoid hardcoding page names and querystring information, two constants (PAGE_NAME and QS_IMAGE_ID) are defined in the code-behind of the page that reads the images from the database and are used here in building the URL.

The performance of this solution can be significantly improved by caching the images retrieved from the database instead of retrieving them for each request. Refer to Recipe 13.2 for an example of how to cache the results as a function of the data passed in the QueryString.

An `HttpHandler` can be used to implement the same functionality described in this recipe. Refer to Recipe 17.1 for an example of retrieving images from a database using an `HttpHandler`.

Images can be stored in a database using the technique described in Recipe 15.4.

See Also

Recipe 13.2; Recipe 15.4; Recipe 17.1

Example 12-10. Reading images from a database (.aspx)

```
<%@ Page Language="vb" AutoEventWireup="false"
        Codebehind="CH12ImageFromDatabaseVB.aspx.vb"
        Inherits="ASPNetCookbook.VBExamples.CH12ImageFromDatabaseVB" %>
```

Example 12-11. Reading images from a database code-behind (.vb)

```
Option Explicit On
Option Strict On
'-------------------------------------------------------------------------------
'
'   Module Name: CH12ImageFromDatabaseVB.aspx.vb
'
'   Description: This module provides the code behind for the
'                CH12ImageFromDatabaseVB.aspx page.
'
'*******************************************************************************
Imports Microsoft.VisualBasic
Imports System
Imports System.Configuration
Imports System.Data
Imports System.Data.OleDb
Imports System.IO

Namespace ASPNetCookbook.VBExamples
  Public Class CH12ImageFromDatabaseVB
    Inherits System.Web.UI.Page

    'constants used to create URLs to this page
    Public Const PAGE_NAME As String = "CH12ImageFromDatabaseVB.aspx"
    Public Const QS_IMAGE_ID As String = "ImageID"

    '*******************************************************************************
    '
    '   ROUTINE: Page_Load
    '
    '   DESCRIPTION: This routine provides the event handler for the page load
    '                event.  It is responsible for initializing the controls
    '                on the page.
    '-------------------------------------------------------------------------------
    Private Sub Page_Load(ByVal sender As System.Object, _
                ByVal e As System.EventArgs) Handles MyBase.Load
```

Example 12-11. Reading images from a database code-behind (.vb) (continued)

```vb
        Dim dbConn As OleDbConnection
        Dim dCmd As OleDbCommand
        Dim imageData( ) As Byte
        Dim strConnection As String
        Dim strSQL As String
        Dim imageID As String

        If (Not Page.IsPostBack) Then
          Try
            'get the ID of the image to retrieve from the database
            imageID = Request.QueryString(QS_IMAGE_ID)

            'get the connection string from web.config and open a connection
            'to the database
            strConnection = _
                ConfigurationSettings.AppSettings("dbConnectionString")
            dbConn = New OleDb.OleDbConnection(strConnection)
            dbConn.Open( )

            'build the query string and get the data from the database
            strSQL = "SELECT ImageData " & _
                     "FROM BookImage " & _
                     "WHERE BookImageID=?"
            dCmd = New OleDbCommand(strSQL, dbConn)
            dCmd.Parameters.Add(New OleDbParameter("BookImageID", imageID))
            imageData = CType(dCmd.ExecuteScalar( ), Byte( ))

            'set the content type for the image and write it to the response
            Response.ContentType = "image/gif"
            Response.BinaryWrite(imageData)


          Finally
            'clean up
            If (Not IsNothing(dbConn)) Then
              dbConn.Close( )
            End If
          End Try
        End If
      End Sub   'Page_Load
    End Class   'CH12ImageFromDatabaseVB
End Namespace
```

Example 12-12. Reading images from a database code-behind (.cs)

```cs
//-----------------------------------------------------------------------------
//
//   Module Name: CH12ImageFromDatabaseCS.aspx.cs
//
//   Description: This module provides the code behind for the
//                CH12ImageFromDatabaseCS.aspx page
//
//*****************************************************************************
```

Example 12-12. Reading images from a database code-behind (.cs) (continued)

```csharp
using System;
using System.Configuration;
using System.Data;
using System.Data.OleDb;

namespace ASPNetCookbook.CSExamples
{
  public class CH12ImageFromDatabaseCS : System.Web.UI.Page
  {
    // constants used to create URLs to this page
    public const String PAGE_NAME = "CH12ImageFromDatabaseCS.aspx";
    public const String QS_IMAGE_ID = "ImageID";

    //*************************************************************************
    //
    //   ROUTINE: Page_Load
    //
    //   DESCRIPTION: This routine provides the event handler for the page
    //                load event.  It is responsible for initializing the
    //                controls on the page.
    //-------------------------------------------------------------------------
    private void Page_Load(object sender, System.EventArgs e)
    {
      OleDbConnection dbConn = null;
      OleDbCommand dCmd = null;
      byte[] imageData = null;
      String strConnection = null;
      String strSQL = null;
      String imageID = null;

      if (!Page.IsPostBack)
      {
        try
        {
          // get the ID of the image to retrieve from the database
          imageID = Request.QueryString[QS_IMAGE_ID];

          // get the connection string from web.config and open a connection
          // to the database
          strConnection =
            ConfigurationSettings.AppSettings["dbConnectionString"];
          dbConn = new OleDbConnection(strConnection);
          dbConn.Open();

          // build the query string and get the data from the database
          strSQL = "SELECT ImageData " +
                   "FROM BookImage " +
                   "WHERE BookImageID=?";
          dCmd = new OleDbCommand(strSQL, dbConn);
          dCmd.Parameters.Add(new OleDbParameter("BookImageID", imageID));
          imageData = (byte[])(dCmd.ExecuteScalar());
```

Example 12-12. Reading images from a database code-behind (.cs) (continued)

```csharp
          // set the content type for the image and write it to the response
          Response.ContentType = "image/gif";
          Response.BinaryWrite(imageData);
        }

        finally
        {
          // clean up
          if (dbConn != null)
          {
            dbConn.Close( );
          }
        }
      }
    }  // Page_Load
  }  // CH12ImageFromDatabaseCS
}
```

Example 12-13. Displaying images from a database (.aspx)

```aspx
<%@ Page Language="vb" AutoEventWireup="false"
        Codebehind="CH12TestImageFromDatabaseVB.aspx.vb"
        Inherits="ASPNetCookbook.VBExamples.CH12TestImageFromDatabaseVB" %>
<!DOCTYPE HTML PUBLIC "-//W3C//DTD HTML 4.0 Transitional//EN">
<html>
  <head>
    <title>Test Image From Database</title>
    <link rel="stylesheet" href="css/ASPNetCookbook.css">
  </head>
  <body leftmargin="0" marginheight="0" marginwidth="0" topmargin="0">
    <form id="frmTestImageDB" method="post" runat="server">
      <table width="100%" cellpadding="0" cellspacing="0" border="0">
        <tr>
          <td align="center">
            <img src="images/ASPNETCookbookHeading_blue.gif">
          </td>
        </tr>
        <tr>
          <td class="dividerLine">
            <img src="images/spacer.gif" height="6" border="0"></td>
        </tr>
      </table>
      <table width="90%" align="center" border="0">
        <tr>
          <td align="center"> </td>
        </tr>
        <tr>
          <td align="center" class="PageHeading">
            Display Image From Database (VB)
          </td>
        </tr>
        <tr>
```

Example 12-13. Displaying images from a database (.aspx) (continued)

```
        <td><img src="images/spacer.gif" height="10" border="0"></td>
      </tr>
      <tr>
        <td align="center">
          <table>
            <tr>
              <td>
                <asp:DropDownList ID="ddImages" Runat="server" />
              </td>
              <td>
                <input id="btnViewImage" runat="server" type="button"
                       value="View">
              </td>
            </tr>
            <tr>
              <td id="tdSelectedImage" runat="server"
                  colspan="2" align="center" class="SubHeading">
                <br /><br />
                Selected Image<br /><br />
                <img id="imgBook" runat="server" border="0">
              </td>
            </tr>
          </table>
        </td>
      </tr>
    </table>
  </form>
</body>
</html>
```

Example 12-14. Displaying images from a database code-behind (.vb)

```
Option Explicit On
Option Strict On
'-----------------------------------------------------------------------------
'
'   Module Name: CH12TestImageFromDatabaseVB.aspx.vb
'
'   Description: This module provides the code behind for the
'                CH12TestImageFromDatabaseVB.aspx page.
'
'*****************************************************************************
Imports Microsoft.VisualBasic
Imports System
Imports System.Configuration
Imports System.Data
Imports System.Data.OleDb

Namespace ASPNetCookbook.VBExamples
  Public Class CH12TestImageFromDatabaseVB
    Inherits System.Web.UI.Page
```

Example 12-14. Displaying images from a database code-behind (.vb) (continued)

```vb
    'controls on the form
Protected ddImages As System.Web.UI.WebControls.DropDownList
Protected WithEvents btnViewImage As System.Web.UI.HtmlControls.HtmlInputButton
Protected imgBook As System.Web.UI.HtmlControls.HtmlImage
Protected tdSelectedImage As System.Web.UI.HtmlControls.HtmlTableCell

    '*************************************************************************
    '
    '    ROUTINE: Page_Load
    '
    '    DESCRIPTION: This routine provides the event handler for the page load
    '                 event.  It is responsible for initializing the controls
    '                 on the page.
    '-------------------------------------------------------------------------
    Private Sub Page_Load(ByVal sender As System.Object, _
                          ByVal e As System.EventArgs) Handles MyBase.Load
      Dim dbConn As OleDbConnection
      Dim dc As OleDbCommand
      Dim dr As OleDbDataReader
      Dim strConnection As String
      Dim strSQL As String

      If (Not Page.IsPostBack) Then
        'initially hide the selected image since one is not selected
        tdSelectedImage.Visible = False

        Try
          'get the connection string from web.config and open a connection
          'to the database
          strConnection = _
              ConfigurationSettings.AppSettings("dbConnectionString")
          dbConn = New OleDb.OleDbConnection(strConnection)
          dbConn.Open()

          'build the query string and get the data from the database
          strSQL = "SELECT BookImageID, Title " & _
                  "FROM BookImage"
          dc = New OleDbCommand(strSQL, dbConn)
          dr = dc.ExecuteReader()

          'set the source of the data for the repeater control and bind it
          ddImages.DataSource = dr
          ddImages.DataTextField = "Title"
          ddImages.DataValueField = "BookImageID"
          ddImages.DataBind()

        Finally
          'clean up
          If (Not IsNothing(dbConn)) Then
            dbConn.Close()
          End If
        End Try
```

Example 12-14. Displaying images from a database code-behind (.vb) (continued)

```
      End If
    End Sub  'Page_Load

    '*************************************************************************
    '
    '    ROUTINE: btnViewImage_ServerClick
    '
    '    DESCRIPTION: This routine provides the event handler for the view
    '                 image click event.  It is responsible for setting the
    '                 src attibute of the imgBook tag to the page that will
    '                 retrieve the image data from the database and stream
    '                 it to the browser.
    '-------------------------------------------------------------------------
    Private Sub btnViewImage_ServerClick(ByVal sender As Object, _
              ByVal e As System.EventArgs) _
              Handles btnViewImage.ServerClick
      'set the source for the selected image tag
      imgBook.Src = CH12ImageFromDatabaseVB.PAGE_NAME & "?" & _
                    CH12ImageFromDatabaseVB.QS_IMAGE_ID & "=" & _
                    ddImages.SelectedItem.Value.ToString( )

      'make the selected image visible
      tdSelectedImage.Visible = True
    End Sub  'btnViewImage_ServerClick
  End Class  'CH12TestImageFromDatabaseVB
End Namespace
```

Example 12-15. Displaying images from a database code-behind (.cs)

```
//-----------------------------------------------------------------------------
//
//   Module Name: CH12TestImageFromDatabaseCS.aspx.cs
//
//   Description: This module provides the code behind for the
//                CH12TestImageFromDatabaseCS.aspx page
//
//*****************************************************************************
using System;
using System.Configuration;
using System.Data;
using System.Data.OleDb;

namespace ASPNetCookbook.CSExamples
{
  public class CH12TestImageFromDatabaseCS : System.Web.UI.Page
  {
    // controls on the form
    protected System.Web.UI.WebControls.DropDownList ddImages;
    protected System.Web.UI.HtmlControls.HtmlInputButton btnViewImage;
    protected System.Web.UI.HtmlControls.HtmlImage imgBook;
    protected System.Web.UI.HtmlControls.HtmlTableCell tdSelectedImage;
```

Example 12-15. Displaying images from a database code-behind (.cs) (continued)

```
//*********************************************************************
//
//   ROUTINE: Page_Load
//
//   DESCRIPTION: This routine provides the event handler for the page
//                load event.  It is responsible for initializing the
//                controls on the page.
//---------------------------------------------------------------------
private void Page_Load(object sender, System.EventArgs e)
{
  OleDbConnection dbConn = null;
  OleDbCommand dc = null;
  OleDbDataReader dr = null;
  String strConnection = null;
  String strSQL = null;

  // wire the view button click event
  this.btnViewImage.ServerClick +=
    new EventHandler(this.btnViewImage_ServerClick);

  if (!Page.IsPostBack)
  {
    // initially hide the selected image since one is not selected
    tdSelectedImage.Visible = false;

    try
    {
      // get the connection string from web.config and open a connection
      // to the database
      strConnection =
        ConfigurationSettings.AppSettings["dbConnectionString"];
      dbConn = new OleDbConnection(strConnection);
      dbConn.Open( );

      // build the query string and get the data from the database
      strSQL = "SELECT BookImageID, Title " +
               "FROM BookImage";
      dc = new OleDbCommand(strSQL, dbConn);
      dr = dc.ExecuteReader( );

      // set the source of the data for the repeater control and bind it
      ddImages.DataSource = dr;
      ddImages.DataTextField = "Title";
      ddImages.DataValueField = "BookImageID";
      ddImages.DataBind( );
    }

    finally
    {
      // clean up
      if (dbConn != null)
      {
```

```
            dbConn.Close( );
        }
    }
  }
} // Page_Load

//**************************************************************************
//
//  ROUTINE: btnViewImage_ServerClick
//
//  DESCRIPTION: This routine provides the event handler for the view
//               image click event.  It is responsible for setting the
//               src attibute of the imgBook tag to the page that will
//               retrieve the image data from the database and stream
//               it to the browser.
//--------------------------------------------------------------------------
private void btnViewImage_ServerClick(Object sender,
                                   System.EventArgs e)
{
  // set the source for the selected image tag
  imgBook.Src = CH12ImageFromDatabaseCS.PAGE_NAME + "?" +
                CH12ImageFromDatabaseCS.QS_IMAGE_ID + "=" +
                ddImages.SelectedItem.Value.ToString( );

  // make the selected image visible
  tdSelectedImage.Visible = true;
} // btnViewImage_ServerClick
} // CH12TestImageFromDatabaseCS
}
```

12.4   Displaying Thumbnail Images

Problem

You want to be able to display a page of images stored in your database in thumbnail format.

Solution

Implement the first of the two ASP.NET pages described in Recipe 12.3, changing the Page_Load method in the code-behind class to scale the full-sized image retrieved from the database to the appropriate size for a thumbnail presentation.

In the Page_Load method of the code-behind class for the page, use the .NET language of your choice to:

1. Create a System.Drawing.Image object from the byte array retrieved from the database.

2. Use a constant to define the height of the thumbnail and then calculate the width to maintain the aspect ratio of the image.

3. Use the `GetThumbnailImage` method of the `Image` object to scale the image to the desired size.

4. Load the thumbnail image into a `MemoryStream` and then write it to the `Response` object.

Examples 12-16 and 12-17 show the VB and C# code-behind class for our example that illustrates this solution. (See the `CH12ImageFromDatabaseVB` .*aspx* file and VB and C# code-behind files in Recipe 12.3 for our starting point.)

To display the thumbnails, create another ASP.NET page, add a `DataList` control with image tags in the `ItemTemplate`, and then use data binding to set the `src` attributes of the image tags.

In the *.aspx* file for the page:

1. Use a `DataList` control to provide the ability to generate a list using data binding.

2. Use a `HeaderTemplate` to label the table of images.

3. Use an `ItemTemplate` to define an image that is displayed in the `DataList`.

In the code-behind class for the page, use the .NET language of your choice to:

1. Open a connection to the database.

2. Build a query string, and read the list of images from the database.

3. Assign the data source to the `DataList` control and bind it.

4. Set the `src` attribute of the image tags used to display the thumbnail images in the `ItemDataBound` event of the `DataList`.

Examples 12-18 through 12-20 show the *.aspx* file and VB and C# code-behind files for the application that uses the dynamically generated images. The output produced by the page is shown in Figure 12-4.

Discussion

The rationale for this recipe is similar to that of Recipe 12.3. That is, you need a convenient way to display images from a database, in this case a page of thumbnail images, and it must efficiently move the image data to the browser while maintaining the maximum flexibility in selecting images from the data store.

This recipe uses the same approach as in Recipe 12.3 where, with one page, an image is retrieved from the database and streamed to the browser, and a second page is used to generate the image requests and display the results, which in this case is a set of thumbnails. Additionally, the image retrieval page must scale the images to thumbnail size.

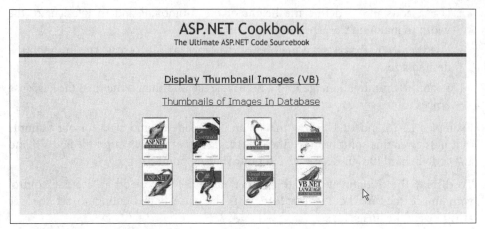

Figure 12-4. Display thumbnails output

In our example that demonstrates the solution, the Page_Load method of the code-behind for the image building page (the CH12ThumbnailFromDatabase page) is modified to scale the full-sized image retrieved from the database to the appropriate size for a thumbnail presentation.

The first step to scale the image is to create a System.Drawing.Image object from the byte array retrieved from the database. This requires loading the byte array into a MemoryStream and then using the FromStream method of the Image class to create the image.

Next, we need to calculate how much to reduce the image. A constant is used to define the height of the thumbnail, and the width is calculated by determining how much the height is being reduced and multiplying the value times the width of the full-size image.

It is important to reduce the height and width by the same scale factor to keep the aspect ratio correct. If the height or width is reduced by a different amount, the image will be distorted.

Handling mixed calculations of integers and doubles can result in unexpected results. Visual Basic is more tolerant and will allow the division of two integers with the quotient set to a variable of type double and result in the correct value. C# will return an integer result from the division of two integers, effectively truncating the result. It is best to cast at least the numerator to the type of the resultant variable.

Now that the width and height of the thumbnail are determined, the GetThumbnailImage method of the full-size image can be used to return a scaled-down image to use as the thumbnail.

Once the thumbnail image is created it can be loaded into a MemoryStream and then written to the Response object in the same manner described in Recipe 12.1.

The web form used to display the thumbnails uses a DataList control to provide the ability to generate the list using data binding. The DataList is configured to display four columns horizontally by setting the RepeatColumns attribute to "4" and the RepeatDirection attribute to "Horizontal". This will start a new row in the table used to display the images after every fourth image.

A HeaderTemplate is used to label the table of images. The template can contain any HTML that can be properly displayed in a table. In this example, the template consists of a single table row containing a single cell with the heading for the table. The colspan attribute is set to "4" to cause the cell to span across all columns in the table, and the align attribute is set to "center" to center the heading.

An ItemTemplate is used to define an item that is displayed in the DataList. In this example, the template consists of an img tag that simply has the ID and Runat attributes set to provide access to the item from the code-behind.

The Page_Load method in the code-behind reads the list of images from the database and binds them to the DataList control. This is accomplished by opening a connection to the database, querying for a list of the image IDs, then setting the DataSource and calling the dataBind method of the DataList. The only data we need from the database is the list of IDs for the images. These will be used to set the image sources, and the actual reading of the image data will be done by the code described earlier.

The src attribute of the image tags used to display the thumbnail images is set in the ItemDataBound event of the DataList. The ItemDataBound event is called for every item in the DataList, including the header. Therefore, it is important to check the item type, since image tags only appear in the data items. Data items can be an Item or an AlternatingItem.

If the item is actually a data item, we need to get a reference to the image control in the item. This is accomplished by using the FindControl method of the item to locate the image control using the ID assigned in the .aspx file. This reference must be cast to an HtmlImage type since the return type of FindControl is an Object.

Once a reference to the image is obtained, the src attribute can be set to the name of the ASP.NET page that is used to generate the thumbnail image passing the ID of the image in the URL. As with Recipe 12.3, constants are used for the name of the page and the name of the item passed in the URL.

The ID of the image is obtained from the DataItem method of the item. This must be cast to a DbDataRecord type to allow "looking up" the ID of the image using the name of the column included in the SQL query used in the bindData method described earlier.

This example presents a useful method of displaying thumbnails of images stored in a database. When used with reasonably small images, the performance is acceptable for most applications. If the images are very large, however, you may want to create the thumbnail images offline and store them in the database to avoid the performance hit for real-time conversion.

See Also

Recipe 12.1; Recipe 12.3

Example 12-16. Page_Load method for generating thumbnail image (.vb)

```vb
Private Sub Page_Load(ByVal sender As System.Object, _
                      ByVal e As System.EventArgs) Handles MyBase.Load
    'height of the thumbnail created from the original image
    Const THUMBNAIL_HEIGHT As Integer = 75

    Dim dbConn As OleDbConnection
    Dim dc As OleDbCommand
    Dim imageData() As Byte
    Dim strConnection As String
    Dim strSQL As String
    Dim ms As MemoryStream
    Dim fullsizeImage As image
    Dim thumbnailImage As image
    Dim thumbnailWidth As Integer
    Dim imageID As String

    If (Not Page.IsPostBack) Then
      Try
        'get the ID of the image to retrieve from the database
        imageID = Request.QueryString(QS_IMAGE_ID)

        'get the connection string from web.config and open a connection
        'to the database
        strConnection = _
            ConfigurationSettings.AppSettings("dbConnectionString")
        dbConn = New OleDb.OleDbConnection(strConnection)
        dbConn.Open()

        'build the query string and get the data from the database
        strSQL = "SELECT ImageData " & _
                 "FROM BookImage " & _
                 "WHERE BookImageID=" & imageID
        dc = New OleDbCommand(strSQL, dbConn)
        imageData = CType(dc.ExecuteScalar(), Byte())

        'create an image from the byte array
        ms = New MemoryStream(imageData)
        fullsizeImage = System.Drawing.Image.FromStream(ms)

        'calculate the amount to shink the height and width
        thumbnailWidth = _
          CInt(Math.Round((CDbl(THUMBNAIL_HEIGHT) / _
                          fullsizeImage.Height) * fullsizeImage.Width))
```

Example 12-16. Page_Load method for generating thumbnail image (.vb) (continued)

```vb
      'create the thumbnail image
      thumbnailImage = fullsizeImage.GetThumbnailImage(thumbnailWidth, _
                                                       THUMBNAIL_HEIGHT, _
                                                       Nothing, _
                                                       IntPtr.Zero)

      'write thumbnail to the response object
      ms = New MemoryStream
      thumbnailImage.Save(ms, ImageFormat.Jpeg)
      Response.ContentType = "image/jpg"
      Response.BinaryWrite(ms.ToArray())

    Finally
      'clean up
      If (Not IsNothing(dbConn)) Then
        dbConn.Close()
      End If
    End Try
  End If
End Sub  'Page_Load
```

Example 12-17. getImage method for generating thumbnail image (.cs)

```csharp
private void Page_Load(object sender, System.EventArgs e)
{
  // height of the thumbnail created from the original image
  const int THUMBNAIL_HEIGHT = 75;

  OleDbConnection dbConn = null;
  OleDbCommand dc = null;
  byte[] imageData = null;
  String strConnection = null;
  String strSQL = null;
  MemoryStream ms = null;
  System.Drawing.Image fullsizeImage  = null;
  System.Drawing.Image thumbnailImage = null;
  int thumbnailWidth;
  String imageID = null;

  if (!Page.IsPostBack)
  {
    try
    {
      // get the ID of the image to retrieve from the database
      imageID = Request.QueryString[QS_IMAGE_ID];

      // get the connection string from web.config and open a connection
      // to the database
      strConnection =
        ConfigurationSettings.AppSettings["dbConnectionString"];
      dbConn = new OleDbConnection(strConnection);
      dbConn.Open();
```

Example 12-17. getImage method for generating thumbnail image (.cs) (continued)

```
            // build the query string and get the data from the database
            strSQL = "SELECT ImageData " +
                     "FROM BookImage " +
                     "WHERE BookImageID=" + imageID;
            dc = new OleDbCommand(strSQL, dbConn);
            imageData = (byte[])(dc.ExecuteScalar());

            // create an image from the byte array
            ms = new MemoryStream(imageData);
            fullsizeImage = System.Drawing.Image.FromStream(ms);

            // calculate the amount to shink the height and width
            thumbnailWidth =
              Convert.ToInt32(Math.Round((Convert.ToDouble(THUMBNAIL_HEIGHT) /
                            fullsizeImage.Height) * fullsizeImage.Width));

            // create the thumbnail image
            thumbnailImage = fullsizeImage.GetThumbnailImage(thumbnailWidth,
                                                   THUMBNAIL_HEIGHT,
                                                   null,
                                                   IntPtr.Zero);

            // write thumbnail to the response object
            ms = new MemoryStream();
            thumbnailImage.Save(ms, ImageFormat.Jpeg);
            Response.ContentType = "image/jpg";
            Response.BinaryWrite(ms.ToArray());
        }

        finally
        {
          if (dbConn != null)
          {
            dbConn.Close();
          }
        }
      }
    }  // Page_Load
```

Example 12-18. Display thumbnail images (.aspx)

```
<%@ Page Language="vb" AutoEventWireup="false"
        Codebehind="CH12TestThumbnailsFromDatabaseVB.aspx.vb"
        Inherits="ASPNetCookbook.VBExamples.CH12TestThumbnailsFromDatabaseVB" %>
<!DOCTYPE HTML PUBLIC "-//W3C//DTD HTML 4.0 Transitional//EN">
<html>
  <head>
    <title>Display Thumbnails</title>
    <link rel="stylesheet" href="css/ASPNetCookbook.css">
  </head>
  <body leftmargin="0" marginheight="0" marginwidth="0" topmargin="0">
    <form id="frmDisplayThumbnails" method="post" runat="server">
      <table width="100%" cellpadding="0" cellspacing="0" border="0">
```

Example 12-18. Display thumbnail images (.aspx) (continued)

```
      <tr>
        <td align="center">
          <img src="images/ASPNETCookbookHeading_blue.gif">
        </td>
      </tr>
      <tr>
        <td class="dividerLine">
          <img src="images/spacer.gif" height="6" border="0"></td>
      </tr>
    </table>
    <table width="90%" align="center" border="0">
      <tr>
        <td align="center"> </td>
      </tr>
      <tr>
        <td align="center" class="PageHeading">
          Display Thumbnail Images (VB)
        </td>
      </tr>
      <tr>
        <td><img src="images/spacer.gif" height="10" border="0"></td>
      </tr>
      <tr>
        <td align="center">
          <asp:DataList ID="dlImages" Runat="server"
                        RepeatColumns="4" RepeatDirection="Horizontal"
                        RepeatLayout="Table" Width="50%">
            <HeaderTemplate>
              <tr>
                <td colspan="4" class="SubHeading" align="center">
                  Thumbnails of Images In Database<br /><br />
                </td>
              </tr>
            </HeaderTemplate>
            <ItemTemplate>
              <img id="imgThumbnail" runat="server" border="0" >
            </ItemTemplate>
          </asp:DataList>
        </td>
      </tr>
    </table>
  </form>
  </body>
</html>
```

Example 12-19. Display thumbnail images code-behind (.vb)

```
Option Explicit On
Option Strict On
'-----------------------------------------------------------------------------
'
'   Module Name: CH12TestThumbnailsFromDatabaseVB.aspx.vb
'
```

Example 12-19. Display thumbnail images code-behind (.vb) (continued)

```
'    Description: This module provides the code behind for the
'                 CH12TestThumbnailsFromDatabaseVB.aspx page.
'
'*****************************************************************************
Imports Microsoft.VisualBasic
Imports System
Imports System.Configuration
Imports System.Data
Imports System.Data.Common
Imports System.Data.OleDb
Imports System.Web.UI.WebControls

Namespace ASPNetCookbook.VBExamples
  Public Class CH12TestThumbnailsFromDatabaseVB
    Inherits System.Web.UI.Page

    'controls on the form
    Protected WithEvents dlImages As System.Web.UI.WebControls.DataList

    '*************************************************************************
    '
    '    ROUTINE: Page_Load
    '
    '    DESCRIPTION: This routine provides the event handler for the page load
    '                 event.  It is responsible for initializing the controls
    '                 on the page.
    '
    '-------------------------------------------------------------------------
    Private Sub Page_Load(ByVal sender As System.Object, _
                          ByVal e As System.EventArgs) Handles MyBase.Load
      Dim dbConn As OleDbConnection
      Dim dc As OleDbCommand
      Dim dr As OleDbDataReader
      Dim strConnection As String
      Dim strSQL As String

      If (Not Page.IsPostBack) Then
        Try
          'get the connection string from web.config and open a connection
          'to the database
          strConnection = _
              ConfigurationSettings.AppSettings("dbConnectionString")
          dbConn = New OleDb.OleDbConnection(strConnection)
          dbConn.Open( )

          'build the query string and get the data from the database
          strSQL = "SELECT BookImageID " & _
                   "FROM BookImage"
          dc = New OleDbCommand(strSQL, dbConn)
          dr = dc.ExecuteReader( )

          'set the source of the data for the repeater control and bind it
          dlImages.DataSource = dr
```

Example 12-19. Display thumbnail images code-behind (.vb) (continued)

```vb
        dlImages.DataBind( )

      Finally
        'clean up
        If (Not IsNothing(dbConn)) Then
          dbConn.Close( )
        End If
      End Try
    End If
  End Sub  'Page_Load

  '**************************************************************************
  '
  '   ROUTINE: dlImages_ItemDataBound
  '
  '   DESCRIPTION: This routine is the event handler that is called for each
  '               item in the datalist after a data bind occurs.  It is
  '               responsible for setting the source of the image tag to
  '               the URL of the page that will generate the thumbnail
  '               images with the ID of the appropriate image for the item.
  '--------------------------------------------------------------------------
  Private Sub dlImages_ItemDataBound(ByVal sender As Object, _
             ByVal e As System.Web.UI.WebControls.DataListItemEventArgs) _
         Handles dlImages.ItemDataBound

    Dim img As System.Web.UI.HtmlControls.HtmlImage

    'make sure this is an item in the data list (not header etc.)
    If ((e.Item.ItemType = ListItemType.Item) Or _
       (e.Item.ItemType = ListItemType.AlternatingItem)) Then
      'get a reference to the image used for the bar in the row
      img = CType(e.Item.FindControl("imgThumbnail"), _
               System.Web.UI.HtmlControls.HtmlImage)

      'set the source to the page that generates the thumbnail image
      img.Src = CH12ThumbnailFromDatabaseVB.PAGE_NAME & "?" & _
               CH12ThumbnailFromDatabaseVB.QS_IMAGE_ID & "=" & _
               CStr(CType(e.Item.DataItem, DbDataRecord)("BookImageID"))
    End If
  End Sub  'dlImages_ItemDataBound
  End Class  'CH12TestThumbnailsFromDatabaseVB
End Namespace
```

Example 12-20. Display thumbnail images code-behind (.cs)

```csharp
//--------------------------------------------------------------------------
//
//   Module Name: CH12TestThumbnailsFromDatabaseCS.aspx.cs
//
//   Description: This module provides the code behind for the
//               CH12TestThumbnailsFromDatabaseCS.aspx page
//
//**************************************************************************
```

Example 12-20. Display thumbnail images code-behind (.cs) (continued)

```csharp
using System;
using System.Configuration;
using System.Data;
using System.Data.Common;
using System.Data.OleDb;
using System.Web.UI.WebControls;

namespace ASPNetCookbook.CSExamples
{
  public class CH12TestThumbnailsFromDatabaseCS : System.Web.UI.Page
  {
    // controls on the form
    protected System.Web.UI.WebControls.DataList dlImages;

    //*************************************************************************
    //
    //   ROUTINE: Page_Load
    //
    //   DESCRIPTION: This routine provides the event handler for the page
    //                load event.  It is responsible for initializing the
    //                controls on the page.
    //-------------------------------------------------------------------------
    private void Page_Load(object sender, System.EventArgs e)
    {
      OleDbConnection dbConn = null;
      OleDbCommand dc = null;
      OleDbDataReader dr = null;
      String strConnection = null;
      String strSQL = null;

      // wire the item data bound event
      this.dlImages.ItemDataBound +=
        new DataListItemEventHandler(this.dlImages_ItemDataBound);

      if (!Page.IsPostBack)
      {
        try
        {
          // get the connection string from web.config and open a connection
          // to the database
          strConnection =
            ConfigurationSettings.AppSettings["dbConnectionString"];
          dbConn = new OleDbConnection(strConnection);
          dbConn.Open();

          // build the query string and get the data from the database
          strSQL = "SELECT BookImageID " +
                   "FROM BookImage";
          dc = new OleDbCommand(strSQL, dbConn);
          dr = dc.ExecuteReader();
```

Example 12-20. Display thumbnail images code-behind (.cs) (continued)

```
        // set the source of the data for the repeater control and bind it
        dlImages.DataSource = dr;
        dlImages.DataBind( );
      }

      finally
      {
        // clean up
        if (dbConn != null)
        {
          dbConn.Close( );
        }
      }
    }
  }  // Page_Load

  //*************************************************************************
  //
  //    ROUTINE: dlImages_ItemDataBound
  //
  //    DESCRIPTION: This routine is the event handler that is called for
  //                 each item in the datalist after a data bind occurs.
  //                 It is responsible for setting the source of the image
  //                 tag to the URL of the page that will generate the
  //                 thumbnail images with the ID of the appropriate image
  //                 for the item.
  //-------------------------------------------------------------------------
  private void dlImages_ItemDataBound(Object sender,
              System.Web.UI.WebControls.DataListItemEventArgs e)
  {
    System.Web.UI.HtmlControls.HtmlImage img = null;

    // make sure this is an item in the data list (not header etc.)
    if ((e.Item.ItemType == ListItemType.Item) ||
        (e.Item.ItemType == ListItemType.AlternatingItem))
    {
      // get a reference to the image used for the bar in the row
      img = (System.Web.UI.HtmlControls.HtmlImage)
            (e.Item.FindControl("imgThumbnail"));

      // set the source to the page that generates the thumbnail image
      img.Src = CH12ThumbnailFromDatabaseCS.PAGE_NAME + "?" +
              CH12ThumbnailFromDatabaseCS.QS_IMAGE_ID + "=" +
              (((DbDataRecord)(e.Item.DataItem))["BookImageID"]).ToString( );
    }
  }  // dlImages_ItemDataBound
}  // CH12TestThumbnailsFromDatabaseCS
}
```

CHAPTER 13

Caching

13.0 Introduction

ASP.NET gives you the ability to cache the output of pages or portions of pages in memory to significantly improve performance. The main reason to cache is to reduce the latency and increase the scalability of an application while reducing the server resources required to deliver its page content. *Latency* is a measure of the time it takes for an application to respond to a user request. *Scalability* is the ability of an application to handle increased numbers of users. If a page is cached on the server, the rendered HTML stored in memory is served instead of a freshly generated page from the server. Because it takes less time for the client to get the page and display it, your web site will seem more responsive.

If pages are completely static, deciding to cache them is a no-brainer. But the decision gets trickier if pages must vary their content in response to one of the following:

- Query string parameters
- Client browser type (e.g., Internet Explorer, Netscape, and so on)
- Custom parameters

Sometimes it makes sense to cache such pages, and sometimes not, as you will soon see.

ASP.NET also provides the ability to cache data items to enhance performance. But what if the data items occasionally change? Does it still make sense to cache them? The answer is a definite "yes," provided you know how to refresh the cache when the data changes.

The nuances of all of these topics are covered in the recipes that follow.

13.1 Caching Pages

Problem

You want to cache the pages in your application.

Solution

Add the @ OutputCache directive to the top of the .*aspx* file of each page you want to cache with the VaryByParam attribute set to "none", as shown here:

```
<%@ Page Language="vb" AutoEventWireup="false"
        Codebehind="CH13CachePageVB.aspx.vb"
        Inherits="ASPNetCookbook.VBExamples.CH13CachePageVB" %>
<%@ OutputCache Duration="5" VaryByParam="none" %>
<!DOCTYPE HTML PUBLIC "-//W3C//DTD HTML 4.0 Transitional//EN">
<html>
  ...
</html>
```

Discussion

This recipe shows the minimum changes required to an .*aspx* file to cache a page of your ASP.NET application. Only one @ OutputCache directive can be included per page, and the Duration and VaryByParam attributes are required.

You specify how long the page is to be retained in the cache by setting the Duration attribute to the desired time in seconds. In our example directive, the page will be rendered on the first request for the page and placed in the cache. For five seconds all subsequent requests for the page will be delivered from the cached copy. After five seconds, the page will again be rendered.

The duration can be set to any positive integer value (1–2,147,483,647), which allows caching a page for approximately 68 years. You may be tempted to use very large numbers; however, every cached page uses server resources and if the page is not needed frequently, you will tie up server resources unnecessarily.

The VaryByParam attribute is used to define parameters that determine which cached copy of a page should be sent to the client. If your page does not vary, simply set the VaryByParam attribute to "none" and a single copy of the page will be saved in the cache. For an example of caching multiple copies of a rendered page as a function of the values in the query string, see Recipe 13.2.

Not all pages should be cached. In fact, caching pages that are used for data input or login functions can result in some very odd behavior. Table 13-1 provides some guidelines for deciding when to cache a page.

Table 13-1. Suggestions for caching pages

Page type	Should it be cached?	Comment
Completely static	Yes	A single copy of the rendered page will be saved in the cache.
Contents change as a function of query string values	Possibly	Multiple copies of the rendered page will need to be saved in the cache (see Recipe 13.2).
Static, but rendered page varies by client browser	Yes	One copy of the rendered page will be saved in the cache for each major version of a browser (see Recipe 13.3).

Table 13-1. Suggestions for caching pages (continued)

Page type	Should it be cached?	Comment
Input form	No	Caching an input form page can result in the data entered by one user being displayed to another.
Dynamically created from database	Possibly	If the contents of the database change at a known interval, as is the case with currency exchange data, the page can be cached without danger of displaying stale data. If the contents of the database change erratically, the page generally should not be cached.

See Also

Recipe 13.2; Recipe 13.3

13.2 Caching Pages Based on Query String Parameter Values

Problem

You want to use page caching to improve the performance of your application, but the contents of your pages vary depending on the values of parameters in the query string.

Solution

Add the @ OutputCache directive to the *.aspx* file of each page you want to cache with the VaryByParam attribute set to the names of the parameters used in the query string, as shown here:

```
<%@ Page Language="vb" AutoEventWireup="false"
        Codebehind="CH13CachePageByQuerystringVB.aspx.vb"
        Inherits="ASPNetCookbook.VBExamples.CH13CachePageByQuerystringVB" %>
<%@ OutputCache Duration="10" VaryByParam="DistrictID;SchoolID" %>
<!DOCTYPE HTML PUBLIC "-//W3C//DTD HTML 4.0 Transitional//EN">
<html>
  ...
</html>
```

Discussion

It is fairly common practice to pass information in the query string that is used to define what is displayed on a page. Because the page content is dependent upon one or more parameters, the basic caching example shown in Recipe 13.1 cannot be used. Fortunately, ASP.NET provides the ability to cache multiple copies of a page by defining the dependent parameters.

You define the parameters ASP.NET will use to cache copies of a page by setting the VaryByParam attribute to a semicolon-separated list of the parameters used in the query string to define the page contents. For each page request, ASP.NET checks the values of the indicated parameters in the query string. If the parameter values match the parameter values of a copy of the page in the cache, the copy from the cache will be sent to the browser. If the parameter values do not match, the page will be rendered by your code, added to the cache, and then sent to the browser.

In our example, the VaryByParam attribute is set to "DistrictID;SchoolID", which causes ASP.NET to check the URL of each page request for the DistrictID and SchoolID parameters in the query string. An example URL is shown here:

```
http://localhost/ASPNetCookbook/CH13CachePageByQuerystringVB.
aspx?DistrictID=1&SchoolID=2
```

When ASP.NET receives the request for this page, it will check to see if a copy of the page exists in the cache for DistrictID=1 and SchoolID=2. If the copy exists in the cache, it will be sent to the browser without rerendering the page, which can significantly improve the responsiveness of your application, especially if database access was required to render the page. If a copy for DistrictID=1 and SchoolID=2 is not in the cache, the page will be rendered by the server.

The VaryByParam attribute can be set to "*" to cause ASP.NET to cache a copy of the rendered page for every variation in parameters. This can result in caching more copies than you anticipate and generally should not be used.

> Care should be taken in defining the duration the page is stored in the cache. If the duration is set to a large value and a large number of unique page requests are received within the duration period, server resources could be depleted.

This recipe deals with how to cache different versions of a rendered page as a function of its query string parameters. This same approach can be used to cache different versions of a page depending on form data when the page is posted back to the server. To cache versions as a function of posted parameters, use the names of the controls on the form (text boxes, checkboxes, and the like) in the VaryByParam attribute.

13.3 Caching Pages Based on Browser Type and Version

Problem

You have a page with static content that you want to cache, but the page is rendered differently for some browsers.

Solution

Add the @ OutputCache directive to the *.aspx* file of each page you want to cache with the VaryByCustom attribute set to "browser", as shown here:

```
<%@ Page Language="vb" AutoEventWireup="false"
        Codebehind="CH13CacheByBrowserVB.aspx.vb"
        Inherits="ASPNetCookbook.VBExamples.CH13CacheByBrowserVB" %>
<%@ OutputCache Duration="30" VaryByParam="none"
               VaryByCustom="browser" %>
<!DOCTYPE HTML PUBLIC "-//W3C//DTD HTML 4.0 Transitional//EN">
<html>
   ...
</html>
```

Discussion

The way in which a page is rendered often depends on the characteristics and version number of the browser making the request. ASP.NET handles most of this variation behind the scenes by sensing the browser type and its version and then rendering the HTML and JavaScript in a suitable format.

The variation in a rendered page from one browser type to another can cause problems if you implement caching as described in Recipe 13.1. For example, if a request is made for a page of this type by Internet Explorer 6.x, the page is rendered and stored in the cache. If a request for the same page is made by a Netscape 4.x browser before the cached copy expires, the Internet Explorer 6.x version will be sent to the browser. This generally results in a poorly displayed or improperly functioning page.

ASP.NET provides the ability to cache browser-specific versions of the rendered page by setting the VaryByCustom attribute of the OutputCache element to "browser". When VaryByCustom is set to "browser", ASP.NET will check the browser name and major version of the browser making the page request (4.x, 5.x, 6.x, and the like) to see if there is a copy of the rendered page stored in the cache that matches them. If so, the cached version is sent as the response. Otherwise, the page will be rendered as usual, stored in the cache, and then delivered to the browser.

The only VaryByCustom attribute value that ASP.NET provides built-in support for is "browser"; however, with additional coding, this attribute can be used to control the caching of a page by any variation you choose. Recipe 13.4 provides an example of using the VaryByCustom attribute to cache a page based on the browser type and full version number.

 The VaryByParam attribute is required even though it is not being used in this example. Setting the value to "none" effectively disables the caching by parameter. Failure to include the VaryByParam attribute will result in a parse error when the page is requested.

See also

Recipe 13.4 for an example of caching based on browser type and full version number

13.4 Caching Pages Based on Developer-Defined Custom Strings

Problem

You have pages in your application that you want to cache but ASP.NET does not provide built-in support for the dependencies you need, such as browser type and full version number.

Solution

Add the @ OutputCache directive at the top of the *.aspx* file of each page you want to cache. Set the VaryByCustom attribute to the name of a custom string, such as "BrowserFullVersion", as shown in the following code snippet:

```
<%@ Page Language="vb" AutoEventWireup="false"
        Codebehind="CH13CacheByCustomStringVB.aspx.vb"
        Inherits="ASPNetCookbook.VBExamples.CH13CacheByCustomStringVB" %>
<%@ OutputCache Duration="10" VaryByParam="none"
                VaryByCustom="BrowserFullVersion" %>
<!DOCTYPE HTML PUBLIC "-//W3C//DTD HTML 4.0 Transitional//EN">
<html>
    ...
</html>
```

Next, override the GetVaryByCustomString method in *Global.aspx.vb* (*Global.aspx.cs* in C#) and write code that builds a unique string for the value you have assigned to the VaryByCustom attribute. Examples 13-1 and 13-2 show VB and C# class files for overriding this method to return a full browser version number.

Discussion

ASP.NET provides the ability to control the caching of pages as a function of custom strings that you provide, which gives you the ability to control the caching by variations not directly supported by ASP.NET. In the example we use to illustrate this solution, we show how to cache pages based on the browser type, its major version number (integer portion of version number), and its minor version number (the decimal portion of the version number).

The first step in this recipe is to add the @ OutputCache directive shown earlier to the *.aspx* file of the page you plan to cache. Set the VaryByCustom attribute to the name of the string that is to be used to determine caching. In our example we have named the string "BrowserFullVersion".

Next, you need to override the GetVaryByCustomString method in *global.asax.vb* (or *global.asax.cs* for C#) to return the full browser version when the passed parameter (arg) is set to "BrowserFullVersion". This provides a unique string for each browser and version to allow ASP.NET to differentiate between the browsers and use the cached version of the page accordingly.

This technique is not limited to caching by browser version. You can use almost any information to uniquely identify pages that should be cached separately. For example, you could use a value stored in a cookie to determine the uniqueness of a page. The cookie collection is accessed through the Request object in the same manner as the Browser data (context.Request.Cookies).

One thing you cannot use is Session information. The reason for this is that at the time GetVaryByCustomString is called, session information has not been retrieved from session storage. The session ID is available but not the session data. If you need to use a value related to a specific session, the data must first be stored in a cookie and used as described earlier.

 Unlike other attributes in the @ OutputCache directive, the VaryByCustom attribute can contain only one value. It cannot be set to a semicolon-delimited string, because the entire unparsed value is passed to the GetVaryByCustomString method. Your code in the GetVaryByCustomString will have to perform the parsing if you want to use multiple values for a single page.

See Also

Recipe 13.3

Example 13-1. GetVaryByCustomString method (.vb)

```
'***********************************************************************
'
'    ROUTINE: GetVaryByCustomString
'
'    DESCRIPTION: This routine provides the ability to set custom string
'                 values to control the page or page fragment caching
'                 based on values assigned to the VaryByCustom attribute
'                 of the OutputCache directive.
'----------------------------------------------------------------------
Public Overrides Function GetVaryByCustomString( _
                       ByVal context As System.Web.HttpContext, _
                       ByVal arg As String) As String
    Dim value As String = Nothing

    'if argument is requesting the full browser version, build a string
    'containing the browser name, major version, and minor version
    If (arg = "BrowserFullVersion") Then
      value = "BrowserFullVersion =" & _
```

Example 13-1. GetVaryByCustomString method (.vb) (continued)

```vb
                context.Request.Browser.Browser & _
                context.Request.Browser.MajorVersion.ToString() & "." & _
                context.Request.Browser.MinorVersion.ToString()
        End If

        Return (value)
    End Function   'GetVaryByCustomString
```

Example 13-2. GetVaryByCustomString method (.cs)

```csharp
//*************************************************************************
//
//    ROUTINE: GetVaryByCustomString
//
//    DESCRIPTION: This routine provides the ability to set custom string
//                 values to control the page or page fragment caching
//                 based on values assigned to the VaryByCustom attribute
//                 of the OutputCache directive.
//-------------------------------------------------------------------------
public override string GetVaryByCustomString(System.Web.HttpContext context,
   string arg)
{
  String value = null;

  // if argument is requesting the full browser version, build a string
  // containing the browser name, major version, and minor version
  if (arg == "BrowserFullVersion")
  {
    value = "BrowserFullVersion =" +
            context.Request.Browser.Browser +
            context.Request.Browser.MajorVersion.ToString() + "." +
            context.Request.Browser.MinorVersion.ToString();
  }

  return(value);
}  // GetVaryByCustomString
```

13.5 Caching User Controls

Problem

You have data-entry pages in your application that cannot be cached, but the pages contain user controls that do not change and you want to cache them.

Solution

Add the @ OutputCache directive at the top of each *.ascx* file of the user controls you want to cache:

```
<%@ OutputCache Duration="5" VaryByParam="None" %>
```

Discussion

This solution is exactly the same as that described in Recipe 13.1, except that it is applied to a user control. In fact, all of the solutions described previously in this chapter can be applied to user controls.

User controls have one caching feature that is not available to pages. A user control can be cached as a function of its properties. This is quite handy because many times a user control, like a header or global navigation bar, varies as a function of its properties, not the parameters passed to the page on which it is used.

To see this in action for yourself, we suggest implementing the user control example described in Recipe 4.1, and then adding the @ OutputCache directive shown here at the top of the *.ascx* file for the header user control:

```
<%@ OutputCache Duration="15"
                VaryByControl="headerImage;dividerColor;dividerHeight" %>
```

A copy of the user control will then be cached for every combination of the headerImage, dividerColor, and dividerHeight property values used in the application.

While this example is not all that useful, since the header on a page is generally consistent within an application, the example demonstrates the ability to cache user controls as a function of the property values. A more practical example (but much longer) would be the implementation of a global navigation bar that incorporates different images as a function of the page currently displayed in the application.

 When caching user controls in pages, it is important to verify that the control is valid before accessing any properties of the control. When the page is first displayed, the user control will be created and will be available to the page. Subsequent page requests, while the user control is in the cache, will not create the control and the variable used to reference the control will be set to "Nothing" (VB) or "null" (C#). Attempts to access the user control without checking its validity will result in a null reference exception being thrown.

See Also

Recipe 4.1

13.6   Caching Application Data

Problem

Your application draws on data that is expensive to create from a performance perspective, so you want to store it in memory, where it can be accessed by users throughout the lifetime of the application. The problem is that the data changes occasionally and you need to refresh the data when it changes.

Solution

Place the data in the Cache object with a dependency set to the source of the data so the data will be reloaded when it changes. Examples 13-3 and 13-4 show the code we've written to demonstrate this solution. In this case, these are VB and C# code-behind files for *Global.asax* that place some sample XML book data in the Cache object. In our example, the book data is automatically removed from the cache anytime the XML file is changed.

Discussion

The Cache object in ASP.NET provides the ability to store application data in a manner similar to the storing of data in the Application object. The Cache object, unlike the Application object, lets you specify that the cached data is to be replaced at a specified time or whenever there is a change to the original source of the data.

In Examples 13-3 and 13-4, two methods have been added to *global.asax.vb* (or *global.asax.cs* for C#). The first method (getBookData) provides access to the data stored in the Cache object with the appropriate checking (to ensure the data is still valid) and reloading as required. The getBookData method performs the following operations:

1. Gets a reference to the book data in the Cache object
2. Checks the reference to ensure the data is still valid and reloads the data using the loadBookDataInCache method if it is not
3. Returns a reference to the book data

The second method (loadBookDataInCache) provides the ability to initially load the book data into the Cache. It performs the following operations:

1. Reads the book data from the XML file into a DataSet
2. Stores the DataTable in the DataSet in the Cache object
3. Returns a reference to the book data

When the DataTable in the DataSet is stored in the Cache object, three parameters are passed to the Insert method of the Cache object. The first parameter is the "key" value used to access the data in the cache. A constant is used here since the key value is needed in several places in the code. The second parameter is the DataTable containing the book data. The third parameter is the dependency on the XML file that was the original source of the data. By adding this dependency, the data is automatically removed from the cache anytime the XML file is changed.

> A DataTable is being stored in the Cache object instead of a DataSet because it uses less system resources and the extra functionality of a DataSet is not needed.

VB
```
context.Cache.Insert(CAC_BOOK_DATA, _
                     ds.Tables(BOOK_TABLE), _
                     New CacheDependency(xmlFilename))
```

C#
```
context.Cache.Insert(CAC_BOOK_DATA,
                     ds.Tables[BOOK_TABLE],
                     new CacheDependency(xmlFilename));
```

The getBookData method is added to *global.asax.vb* (or *global.asax.cs* for C#) to provide access to the data stored in the Cache object with the appropriate checking to ensure the data is still valid and reloading it as required.

The first step to retrieving the cached data is to get a reference to the book data in the Cache object:

VB
```
bookData = CType(context.Cache.Item(CAC_BOOK_DATA), _
                 DataTable)
```

C#
```
bookData = (DataTable)(context.Cache[CAC_BOOK_DATA]);
```

Next, the reference must be checked to ensure the data is still valid and, if it is not, the data must be reloaded using the loadBookDataInCache method:

VB
```
If (IsNothing(bookdata)) Then
   'data is not in the cache so load it
   bookData = loadBookDataInCache(context)
End If
```

C#
```
if (bookData == null)
{
   // data is not in the cache so load it
   bookData = loadBookDataInCache(context);
}
```

Finally, the book data is returned to the caller.

The caching object provides many additional features not described in our example, including the ability to replace the data based on a specified time and the ability to have one object in the cache be dependent on another object in the cache. For more information on these topics, refer to the MSDN documentation on the Cache and CacheDependency objects.

One dependency that is not provided is the ability to replace the data when data in a database changes. A workaround is to write the data to an XML document when the application starts, and then use the approach shown in this example. When an operation changes the data in the database, the XML document can be regenerated, which will cause the data to be removed from the cache and then reloaded when it is needed the next time.

See Also

MSDN documentation on the Cache and CacheDependency objects

Avoiding Race Conditions

The code shown in our example is designed to avoid a race condition that can result in a very difficult-to-find error. The race condition is best described by example. Assume the following code was used (VB code shown):

```
1 If (IsNothing(context.Cache.Item(CAC_BOOK_DATA)) then
2    loadBookDataInCache(context)
3 End If
4 bookData = Ctype(context.Cache.Item(CAC_BOOK_DATA), _
                   DataTable)
```

The code shown on line 1 checks to see if the book data exists in the cache, but it does not retrieve the data. If the data was valid, the next line of code that would execute would be line 4. If the dependency caused the data to be removed from the cache between the execution of lines 1 and 4, a null reference exception would be thrown at line 4. because the data is no longer in the cache.

This example precludes the problem by retrieving the data as the first step then checks to see if the data is valid. Because you already have a copy of the data, you do not care if the data is removed from the cache. Likewise, the loadBookDataInCache method returns the data to avoid the same race condition problem.

Example 13-3. Using application data in cache (.vb)

```vb
Option Explicit On
Option Strict On
'------------------------------------------------------------------------
'
'    Module Name: Global.asax.vb
'
'    Description: This module provides the code behind for the
'                 Global.asax page
'
'****************************************************************************
Imports Microsoft.VisualBasic
Imports System
Imports System.Configuration
Imports System.Data
Imports System.Data.OleDb
Imports System.Diagnostics
Imports System.Web
Imports System.Web.Caching

Namespace ASPNetCookbook.VBExamples
  Public Class Global
    Inherits System.Web.HttpApplication

    'the following constant used to define the name of the variable used to
    'store the book data in the cache object
    Private Const CAC_BOOK_DATA As String = "BookData"
```

Example 13-3. Using application data in cache (.vb) (continued)

```vb
'**************************************************************************
'
'    ROUTINE: loadBookDataInCache
'
'    DESCRIPTION: This routine reads the book data from an XML file and
'                 places it in the cache object.
'--------------------------------------------------------------------------
Private Shared Function loadBookDataInCache(ByVal context As HttpContext) _
            As DataTable
  Const BOOK_TABLE As String = "Book"

  Dim xmlFilename As String
  Dim ds As DataSet

  'read book data from XML file
  xmlFilename = context.Server.MapPath("xml") & "\books.xml"
  ds = New DataSet
  ds.ReadXml(xmlFilename)

  'store datatable with book data in cache scope with a
  'dependency to the original XML file
  context.Cache.Insert(CAC_BOOK_DATA, _
                    ds.Tables(BOOK_TABLE), _
                    New CacheDependency(xmlFilename))

  'return the data added to the cache
  Return (ds.Tables(BOOK_TABLE))
End Function 'loadBookDataInCache


'**************************************************************************
'
'    ROUTINE: loadBookDataInCache
'
'    DESCRIPTION: This routine gets the book data from cache and reloads
'                 the cache if required.
'--------------------------------------------------------------------------
Public Shared Function getBookData(ByVal context As HttpContext) _
        As DataTable
  Dim bookData As DataTable

  'get the book data from the cache
  bookData = CType(context.Cache.Item(CAC_BOOK_DATA), _
                   DataTable)

  'make sure the data is valid
  If (IsNothing(bookData)) Then
    'data is not in the cache so load it
    bookData = loadBookDataInCache(context)
  End If

  Return (bookData)
End Function  'getBookData
```

Example 13-3. Using application data in cache (.vb) (continued)

```
  End Class   'Global
End Namespace
```

Example 13-4. Using application data in cache (.cs)

```csharp
//----------------------------------------------------------------------------
//
//    Module Name: Global.asax.cs
//
//    Description: This module provides the code behind for the
//                 Global.asax page
//
//****************************************************************************
using System;
using System.Configuration;
using System.Data;
using System.Data.OleDb;
using System.Diagnostics;
using System.Web;
using System.Web.Caching;

namespace ASPNetCookbook.CSExamples
{
  public class Global : System.Web.HttpApplication
  {
    // the following constant used to define the name of the variable used to
    // store the book data in the cache object
    private const String CAC_BOOK_DATA = "BookData";

    //****************************************************************************
    //
    //    ROUTINE: loadBookDataInCache
    //
    //    DESCRIPTION: This routine reads the book data from an XML file and
    //                 places it in the cache object.
    //----------------------------------------------------------------------------
    private static DataTable loadBookDataInCache(HttpContext context)
    {
      const String BOOK_TABLE = "Book";

      String xmlFilename = null;
      DataSet ds = null;

      // read book data from XML file
      xmlFilename = context.Server.MapPath("xml") + "\\books.xml";
      ds = new DataSet();
      ds.ReadXml(xmlFilename);

      // store datatable with book data in cache scope with a
      // dependency to the original XML file
      context.Cache.Insert(CAC_BOOK_DATA,
                           ds.Tables[BOOK_TABLE],
                           new CacheDependency(xmlFilename));
```

Example 13-4. Using application data in cache (.cs) (continued)

```
      // return the data added to the cache
      return (ds.Tables[BOOK_TABLE]);
   } // loadBookDataInCache


   //************************************************************************
   //
   //    ROUTINE: getBookData
   //
   //    DESCRIPTION: This routine gets the book data from cache and reloads
   //                 the cache if required.
   //------------------------------------------------------------------------
   public static DataTable getBookData(HttpContext context)
   {
      DataTable bookData = null;

      // get the book data from the cache
      bookData = (DataTable)(context.Cache[CAC_BOOK_DATA]);

      // make sure the data is valid
      if (bookData == null)
      {
         // data is not in the cache so load it
         bookData = loadBookDataInCache(context);
      }
      return (bookData);
   } // getBookData
} // Global
}
```

CHAPTER 14

Internationalization

14.0 Introduction

Internationalizing an application requires explicit planning during the initial design. It generally consists of three steps:

1. Designing for globalization by ensuring the application is culture and language neutral. In other words, any content whose display depends on culture or language cannot be hardcoded in the HTML or program code.

2. Designing for localization by ensuring that no data that is culture or language specific is contained in the code and that the required data is obtained from resource files.

3. Creating specific resource files to support each culture and language.

The full details of internationalizing an application would require a significant portion of this book. Instead, a few samples of internationalization are included. If you need to internationalize an application, you would do well to obtain training or purchase one of the many books dedicated to the subject.

14.1 Localizing Request/Response Encoding

Problem

You are developing an application for a specific region and you want to tell the browser which character set to use in rendering the page.

Solution

Set the `requestEncoding` and `responseEncoding` properties of the `<globalization>` element in *web.config* to the desired character set, as shown here:

```
<system.web>
    <globalization requestEncoding="iso-8859-1" responseEncoding="iso-8859-1" />
</system.web>
```

Discussion

The HTTP header returned to the browser in response to a request contains information that is not displayed but nevertheless controls how the browser displays the content it receives. Included in the header is information that specifies which character set has been used to encode the response data and, by implication, which character set the browser should use to display it.

ASP.NET lets you specify the character set used to encode the response data using the responseEncoding attribute of the <globalization> element in the *web.config* file, as shown earlier. The responseEncoding attribute can be set to any valid character set. Table 14-1 lists some of the more common character sets used for Latin-based languages (English, French, German, and others).

Table 14-1. Common character sets

Character set name	Description
iso-8859-1	Commonly called Latin 1 and covers the Western European languages
iso-8859-2	Commonly called Latin 2 and covers the Central and Eastern European languages
Windows-1252	Windows version of the character set covering the Western European languages
utf-8	Technically not a character set but an encoding scheme to provide the ability to encode Unicode characters as a sequence of bytes

> The character set information provided in the response header is not guaranteed to be honored, because the client machine may not have the suggested character set installed. If Internet Explorer is being used, it will prompt the user to install the required character set. If the character set is not installed, IE will use the character set defined by the computer's region locale setting. Other browsers may respond differently.

The requestEncoding attribute is used to specify the assumed encoding for incoming requests. This includes posted data as well as data passed in the URL. Generally, the requestEncoding attribute is set to the same character set as the responseEncoding attribute.

If your *web.config* file does not contain a <globalization> element with responseEncoding and requestEncoding attributes set to a particular character set, the values defined in the *machine.config* file are used instead. By default requests and responses are encoded in utf-8 format. If your *machine.config* file does not contain a <globalization> element with the responseEncoding and requestEncoding attributes set to the given character set, the encoding defaults to the computer's region locale setting.

The character set can be defined on a page-by-page basis by placing the <meta> tag shown here in the header section of the HTML (or *.aspx*) file:

```
<meta http-equiv="Content-Type" content="text/html;
charset=iso-8859-1">
```

This approach is not recommended for two reasons. First, you need to add a <meta> tag to every page of your application, which implies some associated maintenance should any changes be required. Second, some browsers interpret meta tags only after they have rendered a page, which can cause the page to be rendered twice.

14.2   Providing Multiple Language Support

Problem

You want to support multiple languages in your application without developing multiple versions of each page.

Solution

Use resource files to provide the text for each user interface element in the languages you wish to support, and then set the text to use at runtime based on the language setting in the browser.

You don't need to make any changes to the *.aspx* files of your application for them to output text in multiple languages.

In the code-behind class for each page that needs to support multiple languages, use the .NET language of your choice to:

1. Determine the user's preferred language from the collection of acceptable languages returned with the page request.

2. Create a `CultureInfo` object from the user's language.

3. Set the `CurrentCulture` and the `CurrentUICulture` to the user's culture object (for controlling the formatting of dates and numbers and locating the appropriate resource file for the selected culture, respectively).

4. Create a `ResourceManager` object that will be used to obtain the strings to be displayed in the user's language.

5. Set the text for the individual controls using the `GetString` method of the `ResourceManager`.

6. Set the values of the language, current date, and sample currency.

Examples 14-1 through 14-3 show the *.aspx* file and VB and C# code-behind files for an application we've written to demonstrate this solution. The output is shown in Figure 14-1 (English) and Figure 14-2 (German).

Figure 14-1. Multiple language output—English

Figure 14-2. Multiple language support—German

Discussion

ASP.NET provides extensive support for internationalizing applications. With just a few lines of code and the appropriate resource files, an application can display text in the language set in the browser and can format dates, times, and currency as the user would expect to see them.

In the example we have provided to demonstrate multiple language support, the code determines the user's preferred language when the page is requested. Using the preferred language, a welcome message, the language setting, the current date, and a currency sample are displayed.

The *.aspx* file in our example contains nothing specific to support outputting text in multiple languages. Several ASP literal controls are used to display the information in the user's preferred language.

The Page_Load method in the code-behind provides all of the code required to display the form data in the user's preferred language. Our first step is to get the user's preferred language from the collection of acceptable languages returned with the page request. The language collection can contain zero or more languages, so we must make sure there is at least one language in the collection. Because the language collection usually lists the languages in the order preferred by the user, selecting the first language in the list is generally acceptable.

 In a production application, you may want to verify that your application supports the first language in the collection, and if it does not, continue through the collection looking for a supported language.

Your next step is to create a CultureInfo object whose culture value is set to the user's language. You'll use this information to set the CurrentCulture and CurrentUICulture properties of the CurrentThread. CurrentCulture cannot be set to a neutral culture value (one without the subculture specified), so the CreateSpecificCulture method is used to add the subculture information as required. This is necessary because Internet Explorer and other browsers allow the user to select a language, such as German, without specifying the specific country or locale in which the user resides.

Now we set the CurrentCulture and the CurrentUICulture to the user's culture object. The CurrentCulture is used to format dates and numbers, while the CurrentUICulture is used by the resource manager to locate the appropriate resource file for the selected culture.

Next, you must create a ResourceManager object to gather the strings to be displayed in the user's language. The constructor for the ResourceManager requires you to pass it the root name of the resource files for the application (resource file naming is described later) and a reference to the main assembly for the resources. The root name must be fully qualified with the default namespace name you use for the project. In our example, the default namespace in the project properties has been left blank so only the root name of the resource file "Strings" is used. In this example, the root resource file is compiled into the main assembly, so a reference to the currently executing assembly can be obtained using the GetExecutingAssembly method.

Now that you have set the current culture and UI culture and a ResourceManager is available, you can set the text for the individual controls using the GetString method of the ResourceManager. The values you pass to the GetString method are the keys you use identify the desired text strings in the resource files.

The last thing to do is to set the values of the language, current date, and sample currency. These are done in exactly the same manner as a single-language application.

The ResourceManager handles all of the dirty work of finding the resource file for the user's language, as well as defaulting to the root resource file if a language is requested that is not supported by your application. It is able to find the appropriate resource file because of a very strict naming convention used for the files.

The root resource file can be named most anything, but it is best to keep it simple and avoid using names that include additional periods and dashes. In our example, the root filename is *Strings*.

The names for additional language files must include the root name combined with the culture and subculture information in the format shown next, where *Rootname* is the root filename, *<languagecode>* defines the two-letter language code derived from ISO-639-1, and *<country/regioncode>* defines the two-letter country or region code from ISO-3166. The *languagecode* should be in lowercase and the *country/ regioncode* in uppercase.

> *Rootname.<languagecode>-<country/regioncode>*

For instance, the resource file containing text in German for our example is named *Strings.de-DE*, where *de* indicates the German language and *DE* designates the German localization of the language (as opposed to Austrian, Swiss, and others).

To find the required resource file, the resource manager uses the root name of the resource file then appends the UI Culture name to create the name of the resource file applicable to the user's language. The resource manager then attempts to locate the resource file using a fairly complex set of rules. For our example, let's keep it simple and just say that if the specific resource file is not found on a first attempt, then the root resource file will be used instead. (Refer to "Packaging and Deploying Resources" in the MSDN documentation for the full set of rules defining where the .NET runtime looks for resource files.)

Resource files can be created in many different ways. If you are using Visual Studio .NET, you can simply add a new "Assembly Resource File" to your project. Visual Studio will create an empty XML file (*.resx*) to contain your resources. You can double-click on the file in your project and start typing the names of the keys and the values (text to display). Visual Studio will take care of the creation and placement of the compiled resource files in the *bin* directory. The English (root) resource file for our example is shown here, with the in-line schema deleted for clarity:

```
<?xml version="1.0" encoding="utf-8"?>
<root>

    ...

    <data name="txtWelcome">
        <value>Welcome to Localization</value>
    </data>
    <data name="txtLanguageSetting">
        <value>Language Setting</value>
    </data>
    <data name="txtCurrencySample">
        <value>Currency Sample</value>
    </data>
    <data name="txtDateSample" mimetype=" ">
        <value>Date Sample</value>
    </data>
</root>
```

If you are not using Visual Studio, you can create text files containing the names of the keys and the required values. The root text file and the German text file for our example are shown here:

English (root)

```
txtLanguageSetting=Language Setting
txtWelcome=Welcome to Localization
txtDateSample=Date Sample
txtCurrencySample=Currency Sample
```

German

```
txtLanguageSetting=SprachencEinstellung
txtWelcome=Willkommen zur Lokalisation
txtDate=Datum-Probe
txtCurrencySample=Währung-Probe
```

After creating text resource files, you need to compile them into .NET resource files by entering the following in a command prompt:

English (root)

```
resgen Strings.txt
```

German

```
resgen Strings.de-DE.txt
```

The resulting *Strings.resources* and *Strings.de-DE.resources* files must be copied to the *bin* directory of our application.

Testing your application for the supported languages can be performed by changing the preferred language in Internet Explorer. You can change the language by selecting Tools → Internet Options from the IE menu. Next, click the Languages button and the Language Preference dialog box will be displayed, as shown in Figure 14-3. Add the languages you need to test your application. To test a specific language, move it to the top of the list of languages.

Using resource files in an international application provides a very cost-effective method of implementing the needed support for multiple languages. One thing to keep in mind when designing your application is the performance impact caused by "looking up" every string at runtime. This will result in longer rendering times for the pages. Your international application may require a more powerful web server than you would generally specify for a domestic application.

See Also

"Packaging and Deploying Resources" in the MSDN documentation for the full set of rules defining where the .NET runtime looks for resource files

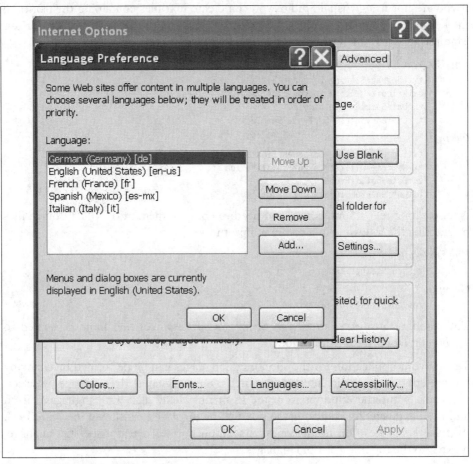

Figure 14-3. Setting language preference in IE

Example 14-1. Multiple language support (.aspx)

```
<%@ Page Language="vb" AutoEventWireup="false"
        Codebehind="CH14InternationalCultureVB.aspx.vb"
        Inherits="ASPNetCookbook.VBExamples.CH14InternationalCultureVB" %>
<!DOCTYPE HTML PUBLIC "-//W3C//DTD HTML 4.0 Transitional//EN">
<html>
  <head>
    <title>Internationalization - Culture and UI Culture</title>
    <link rel="stylesheet" href="css/ASPNetCookbook.css">
  </head>
  <body leftmargin="0" marginheight="0" marginwidth="0" topmargin="0">
    <form id="frmInternationalization" method="post" runat="server">
      <table width="100%" cellpadding="0" cellspacing="0" border="0">
        <tr>
          <td align="center">
            <img src="images/ASPNETCookbookHeading_blue.gif">
```

Example 14-1. Multiple language support (.aspx) (continued)

```
        </td>
      </tr>
      <tr>
        <td class="dividerLine">
          <img src="images/spacer.gif" height="6" border="0"></td>
      </tr>
    </table>
    <table width="90%" align="center" border="0">
      <tr>
        <td align="center"> </td>
      </tr>
      <tr>
        <td align="center" class="PageHeading">
          Internationalization - Culture and UI Culture (VB)
        </td>
      </tr>
      <tr>
        <td><img src="images/spacer.gif" height="10" border="0"></td>
      </tr>
      <tr>
        <td>
          <table width="60%" align="center" border="0">
            <tr>
              <td align="center" colspan="2">
                <asp:Literal id="litWelcome" Runat="server" />
              </td>
            </tr>
            <tr>
              <td align="right" width="50%">
                <asp:Literal id="litLanguageSettingLabel" Runat="server" />
                : 
              </td>
              <td width="50%">
                <asp:Literal id="litLanguageSetting" Runat="server" />
              </td>
            </tr>
            <tr>
              <td align="right" width="50%">
                <asp:Literal id="litDateLabel" Runat="server" />: 
              </td>
              <td width="50%">
                <asp:Literal id="litDate" Runat="server" />
              </td>
            </tr>
            <tr>
              <td align="right" width="50%">
                <asp:Literal id="litCostLabel" Runat="server" />: 
              </td>
              <td width="50%">
                <asp:Literal id="litCost" Runat="server" />
              </td>
```

Example 14-1. Multiple language support (.aspx) (continued)

```
            </tr>
          </table>
        </td>
      </tr>
    </table>
  </form>
  </body>
</html>
```

Example 14-2. Multiple language support code-behind (.vb)

```
Option Explicit On
Option Strict On
'----------------------------------------------------------------------------
'
'   Module Name: CH14InternationalCultureVB.aspx.vb
'
'   Description: This module provides the code behind for the
'                CH14InternationalCultureVB.aspx page
'
'****************************************************************************
Imports System.Resources
Imports System.Globalization
Imports System.Reflection
Imports System.Threading

Namespace ASPNetCookbook.VBExamples
  Public Class CH14InternationalCultureVB
    Inherits System.Web.UI.Page

    'controls on the form
    Protected litWelcome As System.Web.UI.WebControls.Literal
    Protected litLanguageSettingLabel As System.Web.UI.WebControls.Literal
    Protected litLanguageSetting As System.Web.UI.WebControls.Literal
    Protected litCostLabel As System.Web.UI.WebControls.Literal
    Protected litCost As System.Web.UI.WebControls.Literal
    Protected litDateLabel As System.Web.UI.WebControls.Literal
    Protected litDate As System.Web.UI.WebControls.Literal

    '****************************************************************************
    '
    '   ROUTINE: Page_Load
    '
    '   DESCRIPTION: This routine provides the event handler for the page load
    '                event.  It is responsible for initializing the controls
    '                on the page.
    '----------------------------------------------------------------------------
    Private Sub Page_Load(ByVal sender As System.Object, _
                          ByVal e As System.EventArgs) Handles MyBase.Load

      Const sampleValue As Single = 12345.67
```

Example 14-2. Multiple language support code-behind (.vb) (continued)

```
        Dim locRM As ResourceManager
        Dim userLanguage As String
        Dim culture As CultureInfo

        'make sure at least one language is set in the browser
        If (Request.UserLanguages.Length > 0) Then
          'select the first language in browser's accept language list
          userLanguage = Request.UserLanguages(0)

          'create a culture object from the user's language by using the
          'CreateSpecificCulture method to ensure subculture information
          'is included.  Culture cannot be set to a neutral culture.
          culture = CultureInfo.CreateSpecificCulture(userLanguage)

          'set the culture and UICulture
          Thread.CurrentThread.CurrentCulture = culture
          Thread.CurrentThread.CurrentUICulture = culture
        End If

        'create a new resource manager from the currently executing assembly
        locRM = New ResourceManager("Strings", _
                           System.Reflection.Assembly.GetExecutingAssembly())

        'set the labels on the form with the strings obtained through the
        'resource manager from the applicable resource file
        litWelcome.Text = locRM.GetString("txtWelcome")
        litLanguageSettingLabel.Text = locRM.GetString("txtLanguageSetting")
        litDateLabel.Text = locRM.GetString("txtDateSample")
        litCostLabel.Text = locRM.GetString("txtCurrencySample")

        'set the control displaying the browser culture setting
        litLanguageSetting.Text = userLanguage

        'set the sample date to the current date
        litDate.Text = Date.Now.ToShortDateString()

        'set the sample currency value
        litCost.Text = sampleValue.ToString("C")
      End Sub  'Page_Load
    End Class  'CH14InternationalCultureVB
End Namespace
```

Example 14-3. Multiple language support code-behind (.cs)

```
//-----------------------------------------------------------------------------
//
//   Module Name: CH14InternationalCultureCS.aspx.cs
//
//   Description: This module provides the code behind for the
//                CH14InternationalCultureCS.aspx page
//
//*****************************************************************************
```

Example 14-3. Multiple language support code-behind (.cs) (continued)

```csharp
using System;
using System.Resources;
using System.Globalization;
using System.Reflection;
using System.Threading;
using System.Web.UI.WebControls;

namespace ASPNetCookbook.CSExamples
{
  public class CH14InternationalCultureCS : System.Web.UI.Page
  {
    protected System.Web.UI.WebControls.Literal litWelcome;
    protected System.Web.UI.WebControls.Literal litLanguageSettingLabel;
    protected System.Web.UI.WebControls.Literal litLanguageSetting;
    protected System.Web.UI.WebControls.Literal litCostLabel;
    protected System.Web.UI.WebControls.Literal litCost;
    protected System.Web.UI.WebControls.Literal litDateLabel;
    protected System.Web.UI.WebControls.Literal litDate;

    //***************************************************************************
    //
    //   ROUTINE: Page_Load
    //
    //   DESCRIPTION: This routine provides the event handler for the page
    //                load event.  It is responsible for initializing the
    //                controls on the page.
    //---------------------------------------------------------------------------
    private void Page_Load(object sender, System.EventArgs e)
    {
      const double sampleValue = 12345.67;

      ResourceManager locRM =null;
      String userLanguage = null;
      CultureInfo culture = null;

      // make sure at least one language is set in the browser
      if (Request.UserLanguages.Length > 0)
      {
        // select the first language in browser's accept language list
        userLanguage = Request.UserLanguages[0];

        // create a culture object from the user's language by using the
        // CreateSpecificCulture method to ensure subculture information
        // is included.  Culture cannot be set to a neutral culture.
        culture = CultureInfo.CreateSpecificCulture(userLanguage);

        // set the culture and UICulture
        Thread.CurrentThread.CurrentCulture = culture;
        Thread.CurrentThread.CurrentUICulture = culture;
      }  // if (Request.UserLanguages.Length > 0)
```

Example 14-3. Multiple language support code-behind (.cs) (continued)

```
    // create a new resource manager from the currently executing assembly
    locRM = new ResourceManager("Strings",
                         System.Reflection.Assembly.GetExecutingAssembly());

    // set the labels on the form with the strings obtained through the
    // resource manager from the applicable resource file
    litWelcome.Text = locRM.GetString("txtWelcome");
    litLanguageSettingLabel.Text = locRM.GetString("txtLanguageSetting");
    litDateLabel.Text = locRM.GetString("txtDateSample");
    litCostLabel.Text = locRM.GetString("txtCurrencySample");

    // set the control displaying the browser culture setting
    litLanguageSetting.Text = userLanguage;

    // set the sample date to the current date
    litDate.Text = DateTime.Now.ToShortDateString();

    // set the sample currency value
    litCost.Text = sampleValue.ToString("C");
  } // Page_Load
 } // CH14InternationalCultureCS
}
```

14.3   Overriding Currency Formatting

Problem

You have an international application that must always display currency with the U.S. dollar symbol but all other text must follow the language setting in the browser.

Solution

Implement the solution described in Recipe 14.2, and then use a `CultureInfo` object to override the default currency format of the currency value in the code-behind class for the page, as shown here:

VB
```
    litCost.Text = sampleValue.ToString("C", _
                                 New CultureInfo("en-US"))
```

C#
```
    litCost.Text = sampleValue.ToString("C",
                                 new CultureInfo("en-US"));
```

Discussion

It is not uncommon to have an international application that needs to display dates, a currency value, or other data in a format specific to a language or culture that is not the default. For example, you might need to display currency values in U.S. format but all text and dates in the local language of the user.

The simplest solution in such cases is to implement the example described in Recipe 14.2 and then use the ToString method of the number to override its default currency setting. Use the "C" string format code to indicate the number should be formatted as a currency value and a CultureInfo object to require U.S. English with the en-US language code. If you have many places where the alternate currency formatting is required, you should implement a single method to perform it. This will make changes much simpler when they are required.

If your application does not need to display non-currency values such as dates or other numbers in the user's local language format, an even simpler solution is to leave the CurrentCulture property of the current thread unset. This way all formatting of dates and numbers will follow the regional settings of your web server without any additional coding.

CHAPTER 15

File Operations

15.0 Introduction

Downloading a file from a server is a fairly common requirement of web applications, whereas uploading a file is less so. For example, you might want your application to allow users to download PDF, binary, or image files to their browsers. Alternatively, you might have a content management system to which you want to let users upload images or binary files.

ASP.NET provides an easy-to-use and flexible infrastructure you can use to complete either task. You can easily download a file to the browser for display, storage, or printing by streaming it to the Response object, a fairly simple task in ASP.NET.

Uploading a file to the web server for storage is also easy, but you need to know a few tricks about how to set up an Upload button and how to encode the Form element for the page that sends user input to the server.

Sometimes you may want to upload a file to the server for processing only, without storing it there, and at other times you may need to store the contents of an uploaded file to a database. For example, you might want to do the former to avoid having to deal with problems associated with files being uploaded with the same names, inadvertently filling the hard drive, or allowing the ASPNET write privileges on the local filesystem. Storing an uploaded file in a database is useful when you want to keep a complete record of the file set apart from the web server's filesystem. The recipes in this chapter show you how to do all of these things.

15.1 Downloading a File from the Web Server

Problem

You need to provide the ability for a user to download a file from the web server.

Solution

Use the `Directory` and `FileInfo` classes to gather and present the names of the files you want to make available for download to the user. Display their names in a listbox with a button to initiate the download. When the user clicks the button, stream the selected file to the browser.

In the *.aspx* file, add a listbox and a Download (or equivalently named) button.

In the code-behind class for the page, use the .NET language of your choice to:

1. Create a list of available files to download using the `GetFiles` method of the `Directory` class.

2. Populate the `ListBox` with the filenames by binding the list of files to the `ListBox`.

3. Process the Download button click event and stream the selected file to the browser using the `Response` object.

Examples 15-1 through 15-3 show the *.aspx* file and VB and C# code-behind files for an application that illustrates our solution by populating the listbox with a list of files located in the application's images directory. The populated listbox is shown in Figure 15-1, and the prompt that is output when the user selects a file and clicks Download is shown in Figure 15-2.

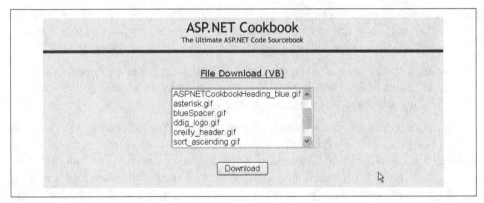

Figure 15-1. Listing files to be downloaded

Discussion

Downloading a file to the browser for display, storage, or printing is a common requirement of a web application. PDF and Word files are perhaps the most ubiquitous download files types, although image, audio, video, and text files are quite common as well.

Downloading a file from a server is a two-step process. The first step is to gather and present to the user a list of the available files that can be downloaded along with a

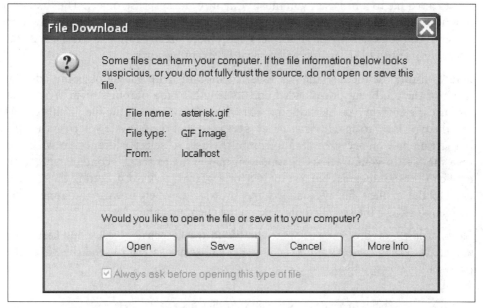

Figure 15-2. File download user prompt

button to initiate the download. The second step is to process the button click event and stream the selected file to the browser.

In our example, we use a listbox to present a list of available files to the user. The list is populated in the Page_Load method of the code-behind with a list of files located in the images directory of the application. (In a production application, you may want to create a download folder instead.)

To populate the listbox, we use the GetFiles method of the Directory class to gather the fully qualified filenames of the files in the specified folder and return them as an array. The GetFiles method returns a fully qualified filename for each file it finds, so our code needs to remove the path information for each file to simplify the list we present to the user.

Next, we bind the files array to the listbox and select the first entry in the list.

 Selecting the first entry in the list simplifies the code because no validation is required if we can always assume an item is selected.

When the user clicks the Download button to initiate the download, the btnDownload_ServerClick method in the code-behind executes. In this routine, we use the MapPath method of the Server class to create a fully qualified filename, which we use to instantiate a FileInfo object to provide easy access to the length of the file that is needed for the download.

To stream a file to a browser, you must write it to the Response object. The first step in writing a file to the Response object is to call its Clear method to remove any data currently in the buffer stream. If the Response object already contains data, when you attempt to write a file to it, you will receive a corrupt file error.

Before writing the file, use the AddHeader method of the Response object to add the name of the file being downloaded and its length to the output stream. You must also use the ContentType method to specify the content type of the file. In this example, the type is set to application/octet-stream so that the browser will treat the output stream as a binary stream and prompt the user to select a location to which to save the file. In your own application you may want to set the content type to an explicit file type, such as application/PDF or application/msword. Setting the content type to the explicit file type allows the browser to open it with the application defined to handle the specified file type on the client machine.

Now, at last, you are ready to write the file to the Response object using Response. WriteFile. When the operation is complete, call Response.End to send the file to the browser.

Things to remember when downloading files:

- Any code that appears after the Response.End statement will not be executed. The Response.End statement sends all buffered data in the Response object to the client, stops the execution of the page, and raises the Application_EndRequest event. For more information on the application behavior when calling Response. End, refer to Knowledge Base article KB312629.

- The only data that can be included in the Response stream is the file to download. If any other data is included, the downloaded file will be corrupted. This may occur if your application uses the Application_EndRequest method to append a footer to all pages.

In our example, a list of files currently residing on the filesystem is presented to the user to select from and download. If your application is going to dynamically create the file, it is not necessary to present a list or to save the file to the filesystem. Instead, remove the listbox and add whatever controls are needed to collect the information you need to dynamically create the file. When the user clicks Download, create your file and generate a byte array containing the file data. Instead of using the WriteFile method of the Response object, use the BinaryWrite method, as shown here:

VB

```
Response.BinaryWrite([your byte array])
```

C#

```
Response.BinaryWrite([your byte array]);
```

For another approach to implementing the solution described in this example using an HTTP handler, refer to Recipe 17.2.

See Also

Recipe 17.2 for implementing file downloads with an HTTP handler; Knowledge Base article KB312629 for more information on the system operation when `Response.End`, `Response.Redirect`, and `Server.Transfer` are called

Example 15-1. Downloading a file (.aspx)

```
<%@ Page Language="vb" AutoEventWireup="false"
        Codebehind="CH15FileDownloadVB.aspx.vb"
        Inherits="ASPNetCookbook.VBExamples.CH15FileDownloadVB" %>
<!DOCTYPE HTML PUBLIC "-//W3C//DTD HTML 4.0 Transitional//EN">
<html>
  <head>
    <title>File Download</title>
    <link rel="stylesheet" href="css/ASPNetCookbook.css">
  </head>
  <body leftmargin="0" marginheight="0" marginwidth="0" topmargin="0">
    <form id="frmDownload" method="post" runat="server">
      <table width="100%" cellpadding="0" cellspacing="0" border="0">
        <tr>
          <td align="center">
            <img src="images/ASPNETCookbookHeading_blue.gif">
          </td>
        </tr>
        <tr>
          <td class="dividerLine">
            <img src="images/spacer.gif" height="6" border="0"></td>
        </tr>
      </table>
      <table width="90%" align="center" border="0">
        <tr>
          <td align="center"> </td>
        </tr>
        <tr>
          <td align="center" class="PageHeading">
            File Download (VB)
          </td>
        </tr>
        <tr>
          <td><img src="images/spacer.gif" height="10" border="0"></td>
        </tr>
        <tr>
          <td align="center">
            <asp:ListBox ID="lstFiles" Runat="server" Rows="6" />
          </td>
        </tr>
        <tr>
          <td align="center">
            <br />
            <input id="btnDownload" runat="server"
                   type="button" value="Download">
          </td>
```

Example 15-1. Downloading a file (.aspx) (continued)

```
        </tr>
      </table>
    </form>
  </body>
</html>
```

Example 15-2. Downloading a file code-behind (.vb)

```vb
Option Explicit On
Option Strict On
'----------------------------------------------------------------------
'
'   Module Name: CH15FileDownloadVB.aspx.vb
'
'   Description: This module provides the code behind for the
'                CH15FileDownloadVB.aspx page
'
'**********************************************************************
Imports System
Imports System.IO
Imports System.Web.UI

Namespace ASPNetCookbook.VBExamples
  Public Class CH15FileDownloadVB
    Inherits System.Web.UI.Page

    'controls on the form
    Protected lstFiles As System.Web.UI.WebControls.ListBox
    Protected WithEvents btnDownload As HtmlControls.HtmlInputButton


    '**********************************************************************
    '
    '   ROUTINE: Page_Load   .
    '
    '   DESCRIPTION: This routine provides the event handler for the page load
    '                event.  It is responsible for initializing the controls
    '                on the page.
    '----------------------------------------------------------------------
    Private Sub Page_Load(ByVal sender As System.Object, _
                          ByVal e As System.EventArgs) Handles MyBase.Load
      Dim files() As String
      Dim index As Integer

      If (Not Page.IsPostBack) Then
        'get list of files in the images directory (just for example here)
        files = Directory.GetFiles(Server.MapPath("images"))

        'for display purposes, remove the path to the file
        For index = 0 To files.Length - 1
          files(index) = New FileInfo(files(index)).Name
        Next index
```

Example 15-2. Downloading a file code-behind (.vb) (continued)

```vb
        'bind the list of files to the listbox on the form
        lstFiles.DataSource = files
        lstFiles.DataBind( )

        'select the first entry in the list
        'NOTE: This is done to simplify the example since preselecting an
        '      item eliminates the need to verify an item was selected
        lstFiles.SelectedIndex = 0
      End If
    End Sub   'Page_Load

    '***************************************************************************
    '
    '    ROUTINE: btnDownload_ServerClick
    '
    '    DESCRIPTION: This routine provides the event handler for the download
    '                 button click event.  It is responsible for reading the
    '                 selected file from the file system and streaming it to
    '                 the browser.
    '---------------------------------------------------------------------------
    Private Sub btnDownload_ServerClick(ByVal sender As Object, _
                                        ByVal e As System.EventArgs) _
              Handles btnDownload.ServerClick
      Dim file As FileInfo
      Dim filename As String

      'get the fully qualified name of the selected file
      filename = Server.MapPath("images") & "\" & _
                 lstFiles.SelectedItem.Text

      'get the file data since the length is required for the download
      file = New FileInfo(filename)

      'write it to the browser
      Response.Clear( )
      Response.AddHeader("Content-Disposition", _
                         "attachment; filename=" & lstFiles.SelectedItem.Text)
      Response.AddHeader("Content-Length", _
                         file.Length.ToString( ))
      Response.ContentType = "application/octet-stream"
      Response.WriteFile(filename)
      Response.End( )
    End Sub   'btnDownload_ServerClick
  End Class   'CH15FileDownloadVB
End Namespace
```

Example 15-3. Downloading a file code-behind (.cs)

```csharp
//---------------------------------------------------------------------------
//
//   Module Name: CH15FileDownloadCS.aspx.cs
//
```

Example 15-3. Downloading a file code-behind (.cs) (continued)

```
//    Description: This module provides the code behind for the
//                 CH15FileDownloadCS.aspx page
//
//****************************************************************************
using System;
using System.IO;

namespace ASPNetCookbook.CSExamples
{
  public class CH15FileDownloadCS : System.Web.UI.Page
  {
    // controls on the form
    protected System.Web.UI.WebControls.ListBox lstFiles;
    protected System.Web.UI.HtmlControls.HtmlInputButton btnDownload;

    //********************************************************************
    //
    //    ROUTINE: Page_Load
    //
    //    DESCRIPTION: This routine provides the event handler for the page
    //                 load event.  It is responsible for initializing the
    //                 controls on the page.
    //--------------------------------------------------------------------
    private void Page_Load(object sender, System.EventArgs e)
    {
      string[] files = null;
      int index;

      // wire the download button event handler
      this.btnDownload.ServerClick +=
        new EventHandler(this.btnDownload_ServerClick);

      if (!Page.IsPostBack)
      {
        // get list of files in the images directory
        files = Directory.GetFiles(Server.MapPath("images"));

        // for display purposes, remove the path to the file
        for (index = 0; index < files.Length; index++)
        {
          files[index] = new FileInfo(files[index]).Name;
        }

        // bind the list of files to the listbox on the form
        lstFiles.DataSource = files;
        lstFiles.DataBind();

        // select the first entry in the list
        // NOTE: This is done to simplify the example since preselecting an
        //       item eliminates the need to verify an item was selected
        lstFiles.SelectedIndex = 0;
      }
```

Example 15-3. Downloading a file code-behind (.cs) (continued)

```
    }  // Page_Load

    //**************************************************************************
    //
    //    ROUTINE: btnDownload_ServerClick
    //
    //    DESCRIPTION: This routine provides the event handler for the download
    //                 button click event.  It is responsible for reading the
    //                 selected file from the file system and streaming it to
    //                 the browser.
    //-------------------------------------------------------------------------
    private void btnDownload_ServerClick(object sender,
                                         System.EventArgs e)
    {
      FileInfo file = null;
      string filename = null;

      // get the fully qualified name of the selected file
      filename = Server.MapPath("images") + "\\" +
                 lstFiles.SelectedItem.Text;

      // get the file data since the length is required for the download
      file = new FileInfo(filename);

      // write it to the browser
      Response.Clear();
      Response.AddHeader("Content-Disposition",
                         "attachment; filename=" + lstFiles.SelectedItem.Text);
      Response.AddHeader("Content-Length",
                         file.Length.ToString());
      Response.ContentType = "application/octet-stream";
      Response.WriteFile(filename);
      Response.End();
    }  // btnDownload_ServerClick
  }  // CH15FileDownloadCS
}
```

15.2   Uploading a File to the Web Server

Problem

You need to provide the ability for a user to upload a file to the filesystem of the web server.

Solution

To enable a page to upload a file to the server, the form encoding type must be set to multipart/form-data and the form must include an input control with the type set to file and a button to initiate the upload process. When the user clicks the button, the code-behind can save the file to the filesystem.

In the *.aspx* file:

1. Set the form encoding type to `multipart/form-data`.

2. Add an HTML `input` control with the type set to `file`.

3. Add an Upload (or equivalently named) button.

In the code-behind class for the page, use the .NET language of your choice to:

1. Verify, in the Upload button click event handler, that the file content has been uploaded by checking the filename length and the content length to make sure they are not 0.

2. Save the file to the local filesystem on the server using the `SaveAs` method of the `PostedFile` object.

Example 15-4 shows the *.aspx* file for an application we've written to demonstrate this solution by allowing you to browse for a file and then uploading the chosen file to your web server's local filesystem when you click the Upload button. The code-behind files for the application are shown in Example 15-5 (VB) and Example 15-6 (C#). The UI for uploading a file is shown in Figure 15-3.

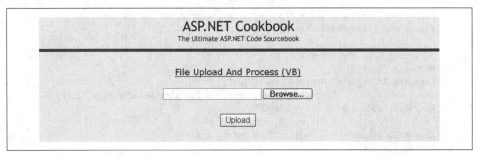

Figure 15-3. UI for uploading a file

Discussion

Uploading files to a web server is not a feature that most applications require. Nevertheless, here are a few examples of applications for which this capability comes in handy:

Departmental content management system
    Uploading images or documents

Technical support site
    Uploading error logs and defective documents or files

Graphics library
    Allowing users to be able to make their own graphics file submissions

When uploading files is needed, the support provided by ASP.NET makes the implementation straightforward.

The application we've written to illustrate the solution allows you to browse for a file and then upload the chosen file to your web server's local filesystem when you click the Upload button. For all that it accomplishes, the application requires a remarkably small amount of code.

To enable an application to submit a form to a server with a file attached, you must set the encoding type of the Form element of the *.aspx* file to multipart/form-data, as shown in our example.

The *.aspx* file must also include an input element with its type set to file. This causes the browser to render the input element with a "Browse…" button to allow the user to browse to the file to upload.

To give your user the ability to initiate the upload, you'll want to add an Upload button to your *.aspx* file. Your *.aspx* file can contain as many controls as you need to allow users to interact with the application, such as other input controls or dropdowns. Their data will be submitted just like any other form for use on the server side.

Place code to save the uploaded file to the server in the Upload button click event handler of the code-behind. Before saving the file, be sure to confirm that the file upload completed successfully. This can be done by checking the length, after trimming, of the filename of the uploaded file to make sure it is not 0 and checking the file's content length to make sure it is not 0. A production application should use validation controls to check these conditions and output an error message to the user. Refer to Chapter 2 for a discussion of validation controls.

After you verify that the file has been uploaded, it can be saved to the filesystem. The SaveAs method of the PostedFile object saves the uploaded file contents to a file on the web server. It requires a fully qualified filename on the web server. Unfortunately, the name of the file in the txtUpload.PostedFile object of our example is a fully qualified filename to the file on the client's machine. As shown in the example, we must extract the name of the file from the txtUpload.PostedFile and then build a fully qualified filename for the storage location and name on the web server.

 By default, the ASPNET account under which ASP.NET runs does not have permission to write files to the filesystem of the server. You will need to modify the security settings on the folder used for uploads to allow the ASPNET user to write to the folder. The steps for doing so vary somewhat for the different flavors of Windows, but the basic steps are these:

1. Using Windows Explorer, browse to the folder where the uploaded files will be saved.

2. Access the security settings by right-clicking on the folder, select Properties, and then select the Security tab.

3. Add the ASPNET user and allow write access.

By default, file uploads are limited to 4M. Any attempt to upload a file larger that 4M will result in an error message. The error message is generated by ASP.NET before any of your code runs; therefore, you have no control over the message being displayed.

You can change the maximum file size that can be uploaded by changing the maxRequestLength attribute of the httpRuntime element in the *web.config* file, as shown here (the value must be set in kilobytes):

```
<httpRuntime executionTimeout="90"
             maxRequestLength="4096"
             useFullyQualifiedRedirectUrl="false"
             minFreeThreads="8"
             minLocalRequestFreeThreads="4"
             appRequestQueueLimit="100"/>
```

See Also

Chapter 2 for validation examples

Example 15-4. File upload (.aspx)

```
<%@ Page Language="vb" AutoEventWireup="false"
        Codebehind="CH15FileUploadVB.aspx.vb"
        Inherits="ASPNetCookbook.VBExamples.CH15FileUploadVB" %>
<!DOCTYPE HTML PUBLIC "-//W3C//DTD HTML 4.0 Transitional//EN">
<html>
  <head>
    <title>File Upload</title>
    <link rel="stylesheet" href="css/ASPNetCookbook.css">
  </head>
  <body leftmargin="0" marginheight="0" marginwidth="0" topmargin="0">
    <form id="frmUpload" method="post" runat="server"
          enctype="multipart/form-data">
      <table width="100%" cellpadding="0" cellspacing="0" border="0">
        <tr>
          <td align="center">
            <img src="images/ASPNETCookbookHeading_blue.gif">
          </td>
        </tr>
        <tr>
          <td class="dividerLine">
            <img src="images/spacer.gif" height="6" border="0"></td>
        </tr>
      </table>
      <table width="90%" align="center" border="0">
        <tr>
          <td align="center"> </td>
        </tr>
        <tr>
          <td align="center" class="PageHeading">
            File Upload (VB)
          </td>
```

Example 15-4. File upload (.aspx) (continued)

```
        </tr>
        <tr>
          <td><img src="images/spacer.gif" height="10" border="0"></td>
        </tr>
        <tr>
          <td align="center">
            <input id="txtUpload" runat="server" type="file" >
          </td>
        </tr>
        <tr>
          <td align="center">
            <br />
            <input id="btnUpload" runat="server"
                   type="button" value="Upload">
          </td>
        </tr>
      </table>
    </form>
  </body>
</html>
```

Example 15-5. File upload code-behind (.vb)

```
Option Explicit On
Option Strict On
'-----------------------------------------------------------------------------
'
'   Module Name: CH15FileUploadVB.aspx.vb
'
'   Description: This module provides the code behind for the
'                CH15FileUploadVB.aspx page
'*****************************************************************************
Imports System
Imports System.IO
Imports System.Web.UI

Namespace ASPNetCookbook.VBExamples
  Public Class CH15FileUploadVB
    Inherits System.Web.UI.Page

    'controls on the form
    Protected txtUpload As System.Web.UI.HtmlControls.HtmlInputFile
    Protected WithEvents btnUpload As HtmlControls.HtmlInputButton

    '*********************************************************************
    '
    '   ROUTINE: Page_Load
    '
    '   DESCRIPTION: This routine provides the event handler for the page load
    '                event.  It is responsible for initializing the controls
    '                on the page.
    '-----------------------------------------------------------------------------
```

Example 15-5. File upload code-behind (.vb) (continued)

```vb
Private Sub Page_Load(ByVal sender As System.Object, _
                      ByVal e As System.EventArgs) Handles MyBase.Load
    'Nothing is required for this example
End Sub  'Page_Load


'*************************************************************************
'
'    ROUTINE: btnUpload_ServerClick
'
'    DESCRIPTION: This routine provides the event handler for the upload
'                 button click event.  It is responsible saving the file
'                 to the local file system.
'------------------------------------------------------------------------
Private Sub btnUpload_ServerClick(ByVal sender As Object, _
                                  ByVal e As System.EventArgs) _
         Handles btnUpload.ServerClick
    Dim filename As String
    Dim file As FileInfo

    'make sure file was specified and was found
    filename = txtUpload.PostedFile.FileName.Trim
    If ((filename.Length > 0) And _
        (txtUpload.PostedFile.ContentLength > 0)) Then
      'get a fileInfo object to simplify extraction of the filename
      'from the fully qualified filename
      file = New FileInfo(filename)

      'save the file to the local file system
      txtUpload.PostedFile.SaveAs(Server.MapPath("uploads") & _
                                  "\" & file.Name)
    End If
  End Sub  'btnUpload_ServerClick
  End Class  'CH15FileUploadVB
End Namespace
```

Example 15-6. File upload code-behind (.cs)

```cs
//------------------------------------------------------------------------
//
//    Module Name: CH15FileUploadCS.aspx.cs
//
//    Description: This module provides the code behind for the
//                 CH15FileUploadCS.aspx page
//
//*************************************************************************
using System;
using System.IO;

namespace ASPNetCookbook.CSExamples
{
```

Example 15-6. File upload code-behind (.cs) (continued)

```csharp
public class CH15FileUploadCS : System.Web.UI.Page
{
  // controls on the form
  protected System.Web.UI.HtmlControls.HtmlInputFile txtUpload;
  protected System.Web.UI.HtmlControls.HtmlInputButton btnUpload;

  //**********************************************************************
  //
  //    ROUTINE: Page_Load
  //
  //    DESCRIPTION: This routine provides the event handler for the page
  //                 load event.  It is responsible for initializing the
  //                 controls on the page.
  //----------------------------------------------------------------------
  private void Page_Load(object sender, System.EventArgs e)
  {
    // wire the upload button event handler
    this.btnUpload.ServerClick +=
      new EventHandler(this.btnUpload_ServerClick);
  } // Page_Load

  //**********************************************************************
  //
  //    ROUTINE: btnUpload_ServerClick
  //
  //    DESCRIPTION: This routine provides the event handler for the upload
  //                 button click event.  It is responsible saving the file
  //                 to the local file system.
  //----------------------------------------------------------------------
  private void btnUpload_ServerClick(object sender, System.EventArgs e)
  {
    string filename = null;
    FileInfo file = null;

    // make sure file was specified and was found
    filename = txtUpload.PostedFile.FileName.Trim( );
    if ((filename.Length > 0) &&
        (txtUpload.PostedFile.ContentLength > 0))
    {
      // get a fileInfo object to simplify extraction of the filename
      // from the fully qualified filename
      file = new FileInfo(filename);

      // save the file to the local file system
      txtUpload.PostedFile.SaveAs(Server.MapPath("uploads") +
                                  "\\" + file.Name);
    }
  } // btnUpload_ServerClick
} // CH15FileUploadCS
}
```

15.3 Processing an Uploaded File Without Storing It on the Filesystem

Problem

You want a user to be able to upload a file to the web server for immediate processing, without having to first store the file.

Solution

Implement the solution described in Recipe 15.2 but instead of writing the file to the filesystem, use the input stream containing the uploaded file to process the data.

For the *.aspx* file, follow the steps for implementing the *.aspx* file in Recipe 15.2 and then, if you like, add a control that will show the results of the processing—for example, a DataGrid control to display the contents of an uploaded XML file.

In the code-behind file for the page, use the .NET language of your choice to:

1. Verify, in the Upload button click event handler, that the file has been uploaded—that is, that the length of the filename and the file contents are both greater than 0—and (if appropriate) that it is a valid XML file.

2. Load the updated data and, if you elected to include a control for showing the contents of the uploaded file, bind the uploaded data to the control—for example, a DataGrid control.

Examples 15-8 through 15-10 show the *.aspx* file and VB and C# code-behind files for an application we've written to illustrate this solution. The initial output is identical to Recipe 15.2's example output and is shown in Figure 15-3.

Discussion

This recipe demonstrates the concept of uploading files and processing them without having to store them to the local filesystem, as you might do with the contents of an XML file for example. This eliminates the problems of files being uploaded with the same names, inadvertently filling the hard drive, and the security aspects of allowing the ASPNET write privileges on the local filesystem.

The example that we've written to illustrate this solution is similar to that described in Recipe 15.2, except that instead of saving the file contents to the filesystem, we process it immediately by loading the uploaded data into a DataSet and then binding the DataSet to a DataGrid. What's more, our example uses the basic *.aspx* file described in Recipe 15.2 with a few changes to support using the page for uploading an XML file and displaying its contents.

In the Page_Load method of the code-behind, the table containing the upload controls is made visible and the DataGrid invisible. (We'll switch the visibility of the two at a later stage to display the contents of the processed file.)

When the user clicks the Upload button, the btnUpload_ServerClick method is executed. The code for making sure a file was uploaded is identical to our example code in Recipe 15.2. An additional check has been added in this example to ensure the uploaded file is an XML file because this example is expecting XML data. Because the same page is used to display the contents of the uploaded file, the table containing the upload controls now needs to be made invisible and the DataGrid used to display the contents of the uploaded file made visible.

Next, we use PostedFile.InputStream to load the data into the DataSet. In our example, the XML file shown in Example 15-7 is being uploaded and because of its formatting can be read directly into the DataSet. With other types of data, you may need to do other processing. In addition, production code should validate the content type of the posted file as well as the contents of the file itself to ensure the uploaded file is valid.

Example 15-7. XML file uploaded

```
<Root>
  <Book>
    <BookID>1</BookID>
    <Title>Access Cookbook</Title>
    <ISBN>0-596-00084-7</ISBN>
    <Publisher>O'Reilly</Publisher>
  </Book>
  <Book>
    <BookID>2</BookID>
    <Title>Perl Cookbook</Title>
    <ISBN>1-565-92243-3</ISBN>
    <Publisher>O'Reilly</Publisher>
  </Book>
  <Book>
    <BookID>3</BookID>
    <Title>Java Cookbook</Title>
    <ISBN>0-596-00170-3</ISBN>
    <Publisher>O'Reilly</Publisher>
  </Book>
  <Book>
    <BookID>4</BookID>
    <Title>JavaScript Application Cookbook</Title>
    <ISBN>1-565-92577-7</ISBN>
    <Publisher>O'Reilly</Publisher>
  </Book>
  <Book>
    <BookID>5</BookID>
    <Title>VB .Net Language in a Nutshell</Title>
    <ISBN>0-596-00092-8</ISBN>
    <Publisher>O'Reilly</Publisher>
  </Book>
  <Book>
    <BookID>6</BookID>
    <Title>Programming Visual Basic .Net</Title>
    <ISBN>0-596-00093-6</ISBN>
```

Example 15-7. XML file uploaded (continued)

```
    <Publisher>O'Reilly</Publisher>
  </Book>
  <Book>
    <BookID>7</BookID>
    <Title>Programming C#</Title>
    <ISBN>0-596-00117-7</ISBN>
    <Publisher>O'Reilly</Publisher>
  </Book>
  <Book>
    <BookID>8</BookID>
    <Title>.Net Framework Essentials</Title>
    <ISBN>0-596-00165-7</ISBN>
    <Publisher>O'Reilly</Publisher>
  </Book>
  <Book>
    <BookID>9</BookID>
    <Title>COM and .Net Component Services</Title>
    <ISBN>0-596-00103-7</ISBN>
    <Publisher>O'Reilly</Publisher>
  </Book>
</Root>
```

The last step in our example is to bind the DataGrid on the form to the DataSet containing the uploaded XML file. Figure 15-4 shows the output for the uploaded and processed file. For more information on data binding, refer to the recipes in Chapter 1.

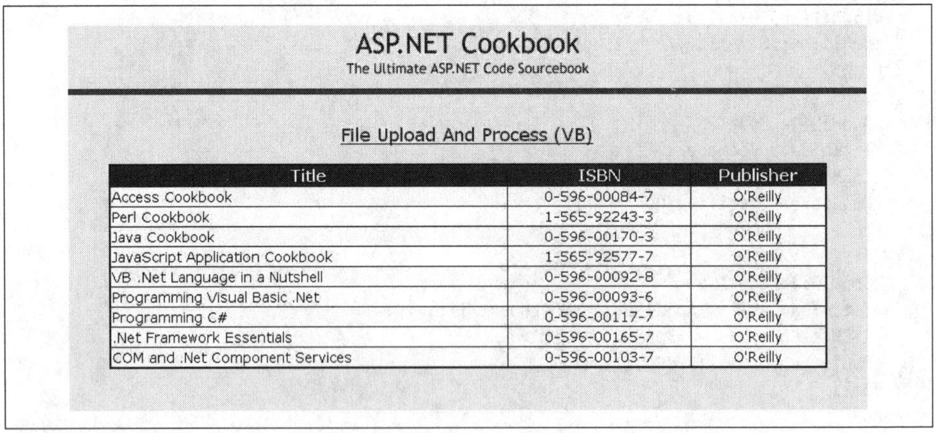

ASP.NET Cookbook
The Ultimate ASP.NET Code Sourcebook

File Upload And Process (VB)

Title	ISBN	Publisher
Access Cookbook	0-596-00084-7	O'Reilly
Perl Cookbook	1-565-92243-3	O'Reilly
Java Cookbook	0-596-00170-3	O'Reilly
JavaScript Application Cookbook	1-565-92577-7	O'Reilly
VB .Net Language in a Nutshell	0-596-00092-8	O'Reilly
Programming Visual Basic .Net	0-596-00093-6	O'Reilly
Programming C#	0-596-00117-7	O'Reilly
.Net Framework Essentials	0-596-00165-7	O'Reilly
COM and .Net Component Services	0-596-00103-7	O'Reilly

Figure 15-4. Uploaded and processed file output

See Also

Chapter 2 for validation controls; HtmlInputFile class documentation in the MSDN library for more information on file uploads

Example 15-8. Upload file and process (.aspx)

```
<%@ Page Language="vb" AutoEventWireup="false"
        Codebehind="CH15FileUploadAndProcessVB.aspx.vb"
        Inherits="ASPNetCookbook.VBExamples.CH15FileUploadAndProcessVB" %>
<!DOCTYPE HTML PUBLIC "-//W3C//DTD HTML 4.0 Transitional//EN">
<html>
  <head>
    <title>File Upload And Process</title>
    <link rel="stylesheet" href="css/ASPNetCookbook.css">
  </head>
  <body leftmargin="0" marginheight="0" marginwidth="0" topmargin="0">
    <form id="frmUpload" method="post" runat="server"
          enctype="multipart/form-data">
      <table width="100%" cellpadding="0" cellspacing="0" border="0">
        <tr>
          <td align="center">
            <img src="images/ASPNETCookbookHeading_blue.gif">
          </td>
        </tr>
        <tr>
          <td class="dividerLine">
            <img src="images/spacer.gif" height="6" border="0"></td>
        </tr>
      </table>
      <table width="90%" align="center" border="0">
        <tr>
          <td align="center"> </td>
        </tr>
        <tr>
          <td align="center" class="PageHeading">
            File Upload And Process (VB)
          </td>
        </tr>
        <tr>
          <td><img src="images/spacer.gif" height="10" border="0"></td>
        </tr>
        <tr>
          <td align="center">
            <!-- The following table is displayed when the user is
                 uploading a file -->
            <table id="tabUpload" runat="server" width="60%" border="0">
              <tr>
                <td align="center">
                  <input id="txtUpload" runat="server" type="file" >
                </td>
              </tr>
              <tr>
                <td align="center">
                  <br />
                  <input id="btnUpload" runat="server"
                         type="button" value="Upload" name="btnUpload">
                </td>
              </tr>
            </table>
```

Example 15-8. Upload file and process (.aspx) (continued)

```
              <!-- The following datagrid is displayed to show the data from
                   the uploaded file -->
              <asp:DataGrid id="dgBooks" runat="server"
                            BorderColor="000080"
                            BorderWidth="2px"
                            AutoGenerateColumns="False"
                            width="100%">

                 <HeaderStyle HorizontalAlign="Center"
                              ForeColor="#FFFFFF"
                              BackColor="#000080"
                              Font-Bold=true
                              CssClass="TableHeader" />

                 <ItemStyle BackColor="#FFFFE0"
                            cssClass="TableCellNormal" />

                 <AlternatingItemStyle BackColor="#FFFFFF"
                                       cssClass="TableCellAlternating" />

                 <Columns>
                   <asp:BoundColumn HeaderText="Title" DataField="Title" />
                   <asp:BoundColumn HeaderText="ISBN" DataField="ISBN"
                                    ItemStyle-HorizontalAlign="Center" />
                   <asp:BoundColumn HeaderText="Publisher" DataField="Publisher"
                                    ItemStyle-HorizontalAlign="Center" />
                 </Columns>
              </asp:DataGrid>
            </td>
          </tr>
        </table>
      </form>
    </body>
</html>
```

Example 15-9. Upload file and process code-behind (.vb)

```
Option Explicit On
Option Strict On
'-------------------------------------------------------------------------
'
'   Module Name: CH15FileUploadAndProcessVB.aspx.vb
'
'   Description: This module provides the code behind for the
'                CH15FileUploadAndProcessVB.aspx page
'
'*************************************************************************
Imports Microsoft.VisualBasic
Imports System
Imports System.Data
Imports System.IO
Imports System.Web.UI
```

Example 15-9. Upload file and process code-behind (.vb) (continued)

```
Namespace ASPNetCookbook.VBExamples
  Public Class CH15FileUploadAndProcessVB
    Inherits System.Web.UI.Page

    'controls on the form
    Protected tabUpload As System.Web.UI.HtmlControls.HtmlTable
    Protected txtUpload As System.Web.UI.HtmlControls.HtmlInputFile
    Protected WithEvents btnUpload As HtmlControls.HtmlInputButton
    Protected dgBooks As System.Web.UI.WebControls.DataGrid

    '*************************************************************************
    '
    '   ROUTINE: Page_Load
    '
    '   DESCRIPTION: This routine provides the event handler for the page load
    '                event.  It is responsible for initializing the controls
    '                on the page.
    '-------------------------------------------------------------------------
    Private Sub Page_Load(ByVal sender As System.Object, _
                          ByVal e As System.EventArgs) Handles MyBase.Load
      If (Not Page.IsPostBack) Then
        'make the table containing the upload controls visible and
        'the datagrid with the uploaded data invisible
        tabUpload.Visible = True
        dgBooks.Visible = False
      End If
    End Sub  'Page_Load

    '*************************************************************************
    '
    '   ROUTINE: btnUpload_ServerClick
    '
    '   DESCRIPTION: This routine provides the event handler for the upload
    '                button click event.  It is responsible processing the
    '                file and displaying the contents.
    '-------------------------------------------------------------------------
    Private Sub btnUpload_ServerClick(ByVal sender As Object, _
                                      ByVal e As System.EventArgs) _
            Handles btnUpload.ServerClick

      Dim ds As DataSet
      Dim filename As String

      'make sure file was specified, was found, and is an xml file
      filename = txtUpload.PostedFile.FileName.Trim
      If ((filename.Length > 0) And _
          (txtUpload.PostedFile.ContentLength > 0) And _
          (txtUpload.PostedFile.ContentType.Equals("text/xml"))) Then
        'make the table containing the upload controls invisible and
        'the datagrid with the uploaded data visible
        tabUpload.Visible = False
        dgBooks.Visible = True
```

Example 15-9. Upload file and process code-behind (.vb) (continued)

```vb
        'load uploaded data into the dataset
        ds = New DataSet
        ds.ReadXml(txtUpload.PostedFile.InputStream)

        'bind the data to the datagrid on the form
        dgBooks.DataSource = ds
        dgBooks.DataBind()
      Else
        'production code should notify user of upload error here
      End If
    End Sub  'btnUpload_ServerClick
  End Class  'CH15FileUploadAndProcessVB
End Namespace
```

Example 15-10. Upload file and process code-behind (.cs)

```csharp
//----------------------------------------------------------------------------
//
//   Module Name: CH15FileUploadAndProcessCS.aspx.cs
//
//   Description: This module provides the code behind for the
//                CH15FileUploadAndProcessCS.aspx page
//
//****************************************************************************
using System;
using System.Data;
using System.IO;

namespace ASPNetCookbook.CSExamples
{
  public class CH15FileUploadAndProcessCS : System.Web.UI.Page
  {
    // controls on the form
    protected System.Web.UI.HtmlControls.HtmlTable tabUpload;
    protected System.Web.UI.HtmlControls.HtmlInputFile txtUpload;
    protected System.Web.UI.HtmlControls.HtmlInputButton btnUpload;
    protected System.Web.UI.WebControls.DataGrid dgBooks;

    //****************************************************************************
    //
    //   ROUTINE: Page_Load
    //
    //   DESCRIPTION: This routine provides the event handler for the page
    //                load event.  It is responsible for initializing the
    //                controls on the page.
    //----------------------------------------------------------------------------
    private void Page_Load(object sender, System.EventArgs e)
    {
      // wire the upload button event handler
      this.btnUpload.ServerClick +=
        new EventHandler(this.btnUpload_ServerClick);
```

Example 15-10. Upload file and process code-behind (.cs) (continued)

```csharp
    if (!Page.IsPostBack)
    {
      // make the table containing the upload controls visible and
      // the datagrid with the uploaded data invisible
      tabUpload.Visible = true;
      dgBooks.Visible = false;
    }
  } // Page_Load

  //***********************************************************************
  //
  //    ROUTINE: btnUpload_ServerClick
  //
  //    DESCRIPTION: This routine provides the event handler for the upload
  //                 button click event.  It is responsible processing the
  //                 file and displaying the contents.
  //-----------------------------------------------------------------------
  private void btnUpload_ServerClick(object sender, System.EventArgs e)
  {
    string filename = null;
    DataSet ds = null;

    // make sure file was specified, was found, and is an xml file
    filename = txtUpload.PostedFile.FileName.Trim();
    if ((filename.Length > 0) &&
        (txtUpload.PostedFile.ContentLength > 0) &&
        (txtUpload.PostedFile.ContentType.Equals("text/xml")))
    {
      // make the table containing the upload controls invisible and
      // the datagrid with the uploaded data visible
      tabUpload.Visible = false;
      dgBooks.Visible = true;

      //load uploaded data into the dataset
      ds = new DataSet();
      ds.ReadXml(txtUpload.PostedFile.InputStream);

      // bind the data to the datagrid on the form
      dgBooks.DataSource = ds;
      dgBooks.DataBind();
    }
    else
    {
      // production code should notify user of upload error here
    }
  } // btnUpload_ServerClick
} // CH15FileUploadAndProcessCS
}
```

15.4   Storing the Contents of an Uploaded File in a Database

Problem

You need to provide the ability for a user to upload a file to the web server that will be processed later, so you want to store the file in the database.

Solution

Implement the solution described in Recipe 15.2, but when the user clicks a button to initiate the upload process, instead of writing the file to the filesystem, use the input stream containing the uploaded file along with ADO.NET to write the file to a database.

For the *.aspx* file, follow the steps for implementing the *.aspx* file in Recipe 15.2.

In the code-behind class for the page, use the .NET language of your choice to:

1. Process the Upload button click event and verify that a file has been uploaded.

2. Open a connection to the database.

3. Build the command used to add the data to the database and insert the file data.

The application we've written to demonstrate this solution uses the same *.aspx* file as Recipe 15.2's example (see Example 15-4). The code-behind for our application is shown in Example 15-11 (VB) and Example 15-12 (C#). The initial output is the same as Recipe 15.2's example output and is shown in Figure 15-3.

Discussion

Storing an uploaded file in a database is useful when a complete, unmodified record of the upload is required to be set apart from the web server's filesystem, when the file contains sensitive information, or when additional metadata needs to be stored with the file. It is also quite common to store the uploaded data in a database and then process the data either immediately or by another program outside of the web application, although we don't go into that here.

The example we've written to demonstrate this solution includes a button to initiate the upload process and uses the input stream containing the uploaded file along with ADO.NET to write the file to a database. The example uses the same code as Recipe 15.2, changing only the actions performed in the btnUpload_ServerClick method of the code-behind. After verifying that a file is actually uploaded, a connection is made to the database.

An OleDbCommand is then created with the CommandText property set to a parameter- ized SQL INSERT statement to store the filename, the file size, and the contents of the file in the database. A parameterized query is used to handle the binary data contained in the file.

The FileData column of our database needs to be able to handle the binary data contained in the file. For SQL Server, the data type should be VarBinary or image. Even if the uploaded files are text files, it is best to use a binary field for storage of the data. Text files can contain Unicode or UTF-8 encoded characters that SQL Server cannot store in text fields, which results in a SQL exception being thrown.

Next, three parameters are added to the parameter collection of the command object and the values are set with the uploaded file information. Because our example uses OleDb, which does not support named parameters like the SQL provider does, the parameters must be added in the same order they appear in the INSERT statement.

The Filename and Filesize parameters each require creating the parameter and setting the value. The Filedata parameter is created in the same manner; however, the value must be set to a byte array. This requires creating a new BinaryReader stream from the posted file input stream and then using the ReadBytes method of the BinaryReader to create the required byte array.

The last step is to set the connection property of the command to the connection opened earlier and executing the command. The ExecuteNonQuery method of the command object is used because no data is being returned by the command.

See Also

Recipe 15.2 for the base code used for this recipe and a discussion of the size limits on uploaded files

Example 15-11. Storing uploaded file to database code-behind (.vb)

```vb
Private Sub btnUpload_ServerClick(ByVal sender As Object, _
                                  ByVal e As System.EventArgs) _
            Handles btnUpload.ServerClick
    Dim dbConn As OleDbConnection
    Dim dcmd As OleDbCommand
    Dim bReader As BinaryReader
    Dim strConnection As String
    Dim filename As String
    Dim filesize As Integer

    Try
        'make sure file was specified and was found
        filename = txtUpload.PostedFile.FileName.Trim
        If ((filename.Length > 0) And _
            (txtUpload.PostedFile.ContentLength > 0)) Then
            'get the connection string from web.config and open a connection
            'to the database
            strConnection = _
                ConfigurationSettings.AppSettings("dbConnectionString")
```

```
        dbConn = New OleDbConnection(strConnection)
        dbConn.Open( )

        'build the command used to add the data to the database
        dcmd = New OleDbCommand
        dcmd.CommandText = "INSERT INTO FileUpload " & _
                    "(Filename,  Filesize, FileData) " & _
                    "VALUES " & _
                    "(?, ?, ?)"

        'create the paramters and set the values for the file data
        dcmd.Parameters.Add(New OleDbParameter("Filename", _
                                        filename))

        filesize = txtUpload.PostedFile.ContentLength
        dcmd.Parameters.Add(New OleDbParameter("Filesize", _
                                        filesize))

        bReader = New BinaryReader(txtUpload.PostedFile.InputStream)
        dcmd.Parameters.Add(New OleDbParameter("FileData", _
                                        bReader.ReadBytes(filesize)))

        'insert the file data
        dcmd.Connection = dbConn
        dcmd.ExecuteNonQuery( )
      End If

    Finally
      If (Not IsNothing(dbConn)) Then
        dbConn.Close( )
      End If

      If (Not IsNothing(bReader)) Then
        bReader.Close( )
      End If
    End Try
  End Sub  'btnUpload_ServerClick
```

Example 15-12. Storing uploaded file to database code-behind (.cs)

```
  private void btnUpload_ServerClick(object sender, System.EventArgs e)
  {
    OleDbConnection dbConn = null;
    OleDbCommand dcmd = null;
    BinaryReader bReader = null;
    string strConnection = null;
    string filename = null;
    int filesize;

    try
    {
```

Example 15-12. Storing uploaded file to database code-behind (.cs) (continued)

```
      // make sure file was specified and was found
      filename = txtUpload.PostedFile.FileName.Trim( );
      if ((filename.Length > 0) &&
          (txtUpload.PostedFile.ContentLength > 0))
      {
        // get the connection string from web.config and open a connection
        // to the database
        strConnection =
          ConfigurationSettings.AppSettings["dbConnectionString"];
        dbConn = new OleDbConnection(strConnection);
        dbConn.Open( );

        // build the command used to add the data to the database
        dcmd = new OleDbCommand( );
        dcmd.CommandText = "INSERT INTO FileUpload " +
                           "(Filename,  Filesize, FileData) " +
                           "VALUES " +
                           "(?, ?, ?)";

        // create the paramters and set the values for the file data
        dcmd.Parameters.Add(new OleDbParameter("Filename",
                                               filename));

        filesize = txtUpload.PostedFile.ContentLength;
        dcmd.Parameters.Add(new OleDbParameter("Filesize",
                                               filesize));

        bReader = new BinaryReader(txtUpload.PostedFile.InputStream);
        dcmd.Parameters.Add(new OleDbParameter("FileData",
                                               bReader.ReadBytes(filesize)));

        // insert the file data
        dcmd.Connection = dbConn;
        dcmd.ExecuteNonQuery( );
      }
    } // try

    finally
    {
      if (dbConn != null)
      {
        dbConn.Close( );
      }

      if (bReader != null)
      {
        bReader.Close( );
      }
    } // finally
  } // btnUpload_ServerClick
```

CHAPTER 16

Performance

16.0 Introduction

Performance has been a concern of ours throughout this book, and we have endeavored to provide you production-ready code that will perform well in any setting. And when a recipe involves trade-offs between performance and ease of implementation, we strive to bring these to your attention. Nevertheless, when an application is not performing as well as you would like, you can often improve matters by altering its handling of the following elements:

ViewState

> You can often improve a page's performance by disabling the ViewState for the page or some of its controls, but you have to be aware of the consequences.

String manipulation

> You've probably heard that it is better to use the StringBuilder object to build strings rather than the classic concatenation operators (& and +). But you may be wondering just how much better and whether it really applies to your situation.

Data access

> With the different options available for data access, it's little wonder that there are ways to improve data access performance, especially when choosing between the two primary methods for reading data from a database—i.e., via a DataReader or a DataAdapter.

SQL Server managed provider

> For the sake of database interoperability, the bulk of the recipes in this book show how to access data using the OleDB managed provider. Yet because of the performance that can be garnered, there is much to be said for using the SQL Server managed provider instead when you know the application will always access SQL Server 7.0 or later.

All of these topics are addressed in the recipes in this chapter.

Like all other programming tools, ASP.NET and the common language runtime (CLR) provide many different ways to accomplish a given task. And because each application is unique and there is no one "right" way to approach it, we believe that every application's performance is worthy of review, mitigated by its frequency of use and its significance. With this in mind, you may want to consider these performance-oriented recipes as much for their approaches to performance tuning as for their line-for-line coding techniques.

As you evaluate the comparisons we've made in this chapter between different data access methods, you should know that the measurements were made on a 1.7 GHz Pentium 4 PC with 1G of memory. Your mileage may vary.

 The side-by-side test results presented in this chapter's examples should be used to compare the relative difference between data access methods. The actual time to retrieve data is a function of the hardware, the database, the fragmentation of the data, and other variables.

16.1 Reducing Page Size by Selectively Disabling the ViewState

Problem

You want to reduce the size of your application pages to improve performance.

Solution

Review each page of your application and each of its controls to determine if the ViewState is required. Disable the ViewState where it is not explicitly needed.

In the code-behind class for the page, use the .NET language of your choice to do either of the following:

- Disable the ViewState for the page by setting Page.EnableViewState to False.
- Disable the ViewState for individual controls by setting the control's EnableViewState property to False.

To illustrate these performance improvements, we took two examples from Chapter 1 and optimized them by disabling the ViewState. In the first example, we took the ASP.NET page created for Recipe 1.19, which displays a grid containing books and price data, and disabled the ViewState at the page level. Table 16-1 shows the page and ViewState size before and after the optimization.

Table 16-1. ViewState performance improvement for Recipe 1.19 example

	Before optimization	After optimization
Page size	18,175 bytes	11,271 bytes
ViewState **size**	6,953 bytes	49 bytes

In the second example, we have used the ASP.NET page created in Recipe 1.12, replaced the table used for the page header with the header user control created in Recipe 4.1, and then disabled the ViewState for the header control as well as the row controls within the DataGrid that appears within the page body. Example 16-1 shows the *.aspx* file for this application. The code-behind class for the application is shown in Example 16-2 (VB) and Example 16-3 (C#). Table 16-2 shows the page and ViewState sizes before and after optimization.

Table 16-2. ViewState performance improvement for Recipe 1.12 example

	Before optimization	After optimization
Page size	14,643 bytes	9,251 bytes
ViewState **size**	6,665 bytes	1,273 bytes

Discussion

The ViewState is used to keep track of the state of each control on a page and to rehydrate the control upon postback to the server. Because of its ability to maintain state when a page is posted back to the server, the use of the ViewState significantly reduces the amount of code you would otherwise have to write. Thanks to the ViewState, you no longer need to extract values from the posted form for processing or reset the control values when you display the page again, as was the case with classic ASP. The controls are simply accessed as they were when the page was initially generated.

While use of the ViewState significantly reduces your coding and maintenance efforts, it comes at a cost. All of the data required to keep track of the control's state is stored in a hidden input control in the HTML page, as shown next. Depending on the number and types of controls you use on your pages, the ViewState can get very large, resulting in a significant decrease in performance. Because the ViewState data is sent to the browser when the page is rendered and returned to the server as part of the postback, a performance hit occurs when the page is first displayed as well as when the page is posted back to the server. Performance is degraded not so much by the generation of the ViewState data itself when the page is first rendered, but rather by the transfer of the extra ViewState data to and from the browser on post-backs, as well as by the processing of the data *by* the browser. Here is a typical ViewState input control:

```
<input type="hidden" name="__VIEWSTATE"
    value="dDwtOTQzNjg3NDE1O3Q802w8aTwxPjs"/>
```

While "byte counters" will be quick to completely disable the ViewState because of its inevitable negative impact on performance, there is a compromise available that provides the best of both worlds: selectively disable ViewState because it is not needed for all pages or controls. By reviewing each of the pages in your application, you can significantly improve the performance of the application without losing the benefits of the ViewState.

The first step when reviewing a page is to determine if the page does a postback to itself. If not, then the ViewState can be disabled for the entire page. This is done by placing this line of code in the Page_Load method:

```
Page.EnableViewState = False
```

```
Page.EnableViewState = False;
```

Even with the ViewState disabled for a page, a few bytes will remain in the value setting of the hidden input control. If you are absolutely determined to remove all traces of the ViewState, you must either remove the form element or remove the runat="server" attribute from the form element. Either action can cause maintenance issues later and the resulting savings of less than 50 bytes in a 20K page has no measurable performance impact, so we do not recommend such an extreme remedy.

If the page does a postback to itself, you will need to review each of the controls on the page. For each control you need to determine whether any state information is required by the control upon postback. If no state information is required, the ViewState for the control can be disabled.

The example page created in Recipe 1.19 displays a grid containing books and price data. The page contains two "action" controls that are anchors used to access other pages; therefore, this page has no mechanism to postback to itself and is a good candidate for disabling the ViewState at the page level, a conclusion borne out by the results shown in Table 16-1. After this optimization, the page size is 62% of the original size and the ViewState represents less than 0.5% of the optimized page.

The example page created in Recipe 1.12 is also a good candidate for performance improvement. As mentioned, we replaced the table used for the page header at the top of the page with the header user control created in Recipe 4.1. This change better illustrates our point and is shown in the .aspx file in Example 16-1. This page is similar to the page created in Recipe 1.19 but has three additional "action" controls used to sort the data in the grid. Clicking on the column headers in the grid causes the page to be posted back to itself with the data sorted by the column clicked; therefore, this page cannot have the ViewState disabled at the page level.

Because the ViewState cannot be disabled at the page level, we need to instead review each control to determine if the ViewState is needed. The page contains two controls, a header control and a DataGrid control. The header control contains no "action" controls and no programmatically set content; therefore, the ViewState for the header control can be disabled using the code shown here:

```
pageHeader.EnableViewState = False
```

```
pageHeader.EnableViewState = false;
```

While you might be tempted to disable the ViewState for the DataGrid, because all of the data is regenerated on each postback, you cannot. ASP.NET needs the ViewState information for the controls within the header of the DataGrid to process its click events and to execute the dgBooks_SortCommand method. If you disable the ViewState for the DataGrid, the postback will occur but none of the event handlers will be called.

A DataGrid is itself a container of controls. At its highest level, a DataGrid consists of a header control and one or more row controls. In this example, only the header contains "action" controls and because the data in each row is regenerated with each postback, the ViewState for the row controls can be disabled using the code shown here:

VB
```vb
For Each item In dgBooks.Items
    item.EnableViewState = False
Next
```

C#
```csharp
foreach (DataGridItem item in dgBooks.Items)
{
    item.EnableViewState = false;
}
```

 When programmatically disabling the ViewState of individual controls, the code that performs the disabling must be executed anytime the page is rendered. In addition, the disabling of controls within a DataGrid must be performed after data binding.

The results in Table 16-2 confirm the advantage of this optimization. By disabling the ViewState for the page header and for each row in the DataGrid, we have significantly reduced the size of the ViewState and the overall page size as well. After optimization, the page size is 63% of the original size and the ViewState represents less than 14% of the optimized page.

See Also

Recipe 1.12; Recipe 1.19; Recipe 4.1

Example 16-1. Modified .aspx file from Recipe 1.12

```
<%@ Page Language="vb" AutoEventWireup="false"
        Codebehind="CH16ViewStatePerformanceVB2.aspx.vb"
        Inherits="ASPNetCookbook.VBExamples.CH16ViewStatePerformanceVB2"%>
<%@ Register TagPrefix="ASPCookbook" TagName="PageHeader"
        Src="CH04UserControlHeaderVB.ascx" %>
<!DOCTYPE HTML PUBLIC "-//W3C//DTD HTML 4.0 Transitional//EN">
<html>
  <head>
    <title>View State Performance</title>
    <link rel="stylesheet" href="css/ASPNetCookbook.css">
  </head>
  <body leftmargin="0" marginheight="0" marginwidth="0" topmargin="0">
    <form id="frmDatagrid" method="post" runat="server">
      <ASPCookbook:PageHeader id="Pageheader" runat="server" />
      <table width="90%" align="center" border="0">
        <tr>
```

Example 16-1. Modified .aspx file from Recipe 1.12 (continued)

```
        <td><img src="images/spacer.gif" height="10" border="0"></td>
      </tr>
      <tr>
        <td align="center" class="PageHeading">
          Improving ViewState Performance of Recipe 1-12 (VB)
        </td>
      </tr>
      <tr>
        <td><img src="images/spacer.gif" height="10" border="0"></td>
      </tr>
      <tr>
        <td align="center">
          <asp:datagrid
            id="dgBooks"
            runat="server"
            bordercolor="000080"
            borderwidth="2px"
            autogeneratecolumns="False"
            width="100%"
            allowsorting="True">

            <headerstyle
              horizontalalign="Center"
              forecolor="#FFFFFF"
              backcolor="#000080"
              font-bold=true
              cssclass="TableHeader" />

            <itemstyle
              backcolor="#FFFFE0"
              cssclass="TableCellNormal" />

            <alternatingitemstyle
              backcolor="#FFFFFF"
              cssclass="TableCellAlternating" />

            <columns>
            <asp:boundcolumn datafield="Title"
                             sortexpression="Title" />
            <asp:boundcolumn datafield="ISBN"
                             itemstyle-horizontalalign="Center"
                             sortexpression="ISBN" />
            <asp:boundcolumn datafield="Publisher"
                             itemstyle-horizontalalign="Center"
                             sortexpression="Publisher" />
            </columns>
          </asp:datagrid>
        </td>
      </tr>
    </table>
  </form>
  </body>
</html>
```

Example 16-2. Optimized code-behind forRecipe 1.12 (.vb)

```vb
Option Explicit On
Option Strict On
'-----------------------------------------------------------------------------
'
'   Module Name: CH16ViewStatePerformanceVB2.aspx.vb
'
'   Description: This module provides the code behind for the
'                CH16ViewStatePerformanceVB2.aspx page
'
'*****************************************************************************
Imports Microsoft.VisualBasic
Imports System.Configuration
Imports System.Data
Imports System.Data.OleDb
Imports System.Web.UI.WebControls

Namespace ASPNetCookbook.VBExamples
  Public Class CH16ViewStatePerformanceVB2
    Inherits System.Web.UI.Page

    'controls on the form
    Protected WithEvents dgBooks As System.Web.UI.WebControls.DataGrid
    Protected pageHeader As ASPNetCookbook.VBExamples.CH04UserControlHeaderVB

    'the following enumeration is used to define the sort orders
    Private Enum enuSortOrder
      soAscending = 0
      soDescending = 1
    End Enum

    'strings to use for the sort expressions and column title
    'separate arrays are used to support the sort expression and titles
    'being different
    Private ReadOnly sortExpression() As String = {"Title", "ISBN", "Publisher"}
    Private ReadOnly columnTitle() As String = {"Title", "ISBN", "Publisher"}

    'the names of the variables placed in the viewstate
    Private Const VS_CURRENT_SORT_EXPRESSION As String = "currentSortExpression"
    Private Const VS_CURRENT_SORT_ORDER As String = "currentSortOrder"

    '*****************************************************************************
    '
    '   ROUTINE: Page_Load
    '
    '   DESCRIPTION: This routine provides the event handler for the page load
    '                event.  It is responsible for initializing the controls
    '                on the page.
    '-----------------------------------------------------------------------------
    Private Sub Page_Load(ByVal sender As System.Object, _
                          ByVal e As System.EventArgs) _
            Handles MyBase.Load
```

Example 16-2. Optimized code-behind forRecipe 1.12 (.vb) (continued)

```
      Dim defaultSortExpression As String
      Dim defaultSortOrder As enuSortOrder

      If (Not Page.IsPostBack) Then
        'sort by title, ascending as the default
        defaultSortExpression = sortExpression(0)
        defaultSortOrder = enuSortOrder.soAscending

        'store current sort expression and order in the viewstate then
        'bind data to the DataGrid
        viewstate(VS_CURRENT_SORT_EXPRESSION) = defaultSortExpression
        viewState(VS_CURRENT_SORT_ORDER) = defaultSortOrder
        bindData(defaultSortExpression, _
                 defaultSortOrder)

       'disable the ViewState for controls that do not need it
        disableViewState( )
      End If
    End Sub   'Page_Load

    '*************************************************************************
    '
    '    ROUTINE: dgBooks_SortCommand
    '
    '    DESCRIPTION: This routine provides the event handler for the datagrid
    '                 sort event.  It is responsible re-binding the data to the
    '                 datagrid by the selected column.
    '-------------------------------------------------------------------------
    Private Sub dgBooks_SortCommand(ByVal source As Object, _
                                    ByVal e As DataGridSortCommandEventArgs) _
            Handles dgBooks.SortCommand

      Dim newSortExpression As String
      Dim currentSortExpression As String
      Dim currentSortOrder As enuSortOrder

      'get the current sort expression and order from the viewstate
      currentSortExpression = CStr(viewstate(VS_CURRENT_SORT_EXPRESSION))
      currentSortOrder = CType(viewstate(VS_CURRENT_SORT_ORDER), enuSortOrder)

      'check to see if this is a new column or the sort order
      'of the current column needs to be changed.
      newSortExpression = e.SortExpression
      If (newSortExpression = currentSortExpression) Then
        'sort column is the same so change the sort order
        If (currentSortOrder = enuSortOrder.soAscending) Then
          currentSortOrder = enuSortOrder.soDescending
        Else
          currentSortOrder = enuSortOrder.soAscending
        End If
      Else
```

Example 16-2. Optimized code-behind forRecipe 1.12 (.vb) (continued)

```
        'sort column is different so set the new column with ascending
        'sort order
        currentSortExpression = newSortExpression
        currentSortOrder = enuSortOrder.soAscending
      End If

      'update the view state with the new sort information
      viewstate(VS_CURRENT_SORT_EXPRESSION) = currentSortExpression
      viewstate(VS_CURRENT_SORT_ORDER) = currentSortOrder

      'rebind the data in the datagrid
      bindData(currentSortExpression, _
               currentSortOrder)

    'disable the ViewState for controls that do not need it
    disableViewState( )
  End Sub    'dgBooks_SortCommand

  '*************************************************************************
  '
  '    ROUTINE: bindData
  '
  '    DESCRIPTION: This routine queries the database for the data to
  '                 displayed and binds it to the datagrid
  '-------------------------------------------------------------------------
  Private Sub bindData(ByVal sortExpression As String, _
                       ByVal sortOrder As enuSortOrder)
    Dim dbConn As OleDbConnection
    Dim da As OleDbDataAdapter
    Dim ds As DataSet
    Dim strConnection As String
    Dim strSQL As String
    Dim index As Integer
    Dim col As DataGridColumn
    Dim colImage As String
    Dim strSortOrder As String

    Try
      'get the connection string from web.config and open a connection
      'to the database
      strConnection = _
         ConfigurationSettings.AppSettings("dbConnectionString")
      dbConn = New OleDbConnection(strConnection)
      dbConn.Open( )

      'build the query string and get the data from the database
      If (sortOrder = enuSortOrder.soAscending) Then
        strSortOrder = " ASC"
      Else
        strSortOrder = " DESC"
      End If
```

Example 16-2. Optimized code-behind forRecipe 1.12 (.vb) (continued)

```vb
        strSQL = "SELECT Title, ISBN, Publisher " & _
                 "FROM Book " & _
                 "ORDER BY " & sortExpression & _
                 strSortOrder

      da = New OleDbDataAdapter(strSQL, dbConn)
      ds = New DataSet
      da.Fill(ds)

      'loop through the columns in the datagrid updating the heading to
      'mark which column is the sort column and the sort order
      For index = 0 To dgBooks.Columns.Count - 1
        col = dgBooks.Columns(index)

        'check to see if this is the sort column
        If (col.SortExpression = sortExpression) Then
          'this is the sort column so determine whether the ascending or
          'descending image needs to be included
          If (sortOrder = enuSortOrder.soAscending) Then
            colImage = " <img src='images/sort_ascending.gif' border='0'>"
          Else
            colImage = " <img src='images/sort_descending.gif' border='0'>"
          End If
        Else
          'This is not the sort column so include no image html
          colImage = ""
        End If  'If (col.SortExpression = sortExpression)

        'set the title for the column
        col.HeaderText = columnTitle(index) & colImage
      Next index

      'set the source of the data for the datagrid control and bind it
      dgBooks.DataSource = ds
      dgBooks.DataBind( )

    Finally
      'cleanup
      If (Not IsNothing(dbConn)) Then
        dbConn.Close( )
      End If
    End Try
  End Sub  'bindData

  '*************************************************************************
  '
  '    ROUTINE: disableViewState
  '
  '    DESCRIPTION: This routine disables the ViewState for all controls
  '                 on the page that do not need to use it.
  '-------------------------------------------------------------------------
```

Example 16-2. Optimized code-behind forRecipe 1.12 (.vb) (continued)

```
    Private Sub disableViewState( )
      Dim item As DataGridItem

      'disable the ViewState for the page header
      pageHeader.EnableViewState = False

      'disable the ViewState for each row in the DataGrid
      For Each item In dgBooks.Items
        item.EnableViewState = False
      Next item
    End Sub  'disableViewState
  End Class  'CH16ViewStatePerformanceVB2
End Namespace
```

Example 16-3. Optimized code-behind for Recipe 1.12 (.cs)

```
//-----------------------------------------------------------------------------
//
//   Module Name: CH16ViewStatePerformanceCS2.aspx.cs
//
//   Description: This class provides the code behind for
//                CH16ViewStatePerformanceCS2.aspx
//
//*****************************************************************************
using System;
using System.Configuration;
using System.Data;
using System.Data.OleDb;
using System.Web.UI.WebControls;

namespace ASPNetCookbook.CSExamples
{
  public class CH16ViewStatePerformanceCS2 : System.Web.UI.Page
  {
    // controls on the form
    protected System.Web.UI.WebControls.DataGrid dgBooks;
    protected ASPNetCookbook.CSExamples.CH04UserControlHeaderCS pageHeader;

    // the following enumeration is used to define the sort orders
    private enum enuSortOrder : int
    {
      soAscending = 0,
      soDescending = 1
    }

    // strings to use for the sort expressions and column title
    // separate arrays are used to support the sort expression and titles
    // being different
    static readonly String [] sortExpression =
                            new String [] {"Title", "ISBN", "Publisher"};
    static readonly String[] columnTitle =
                            new String [] {"Title", "ISBN", "Publisher"};
```

Example 16-3. Optimized code-behind for Recipe 1.12 (.cs) (continued)

```
// the names of the variables placed in the viewstate
static readonly String VS_CURRENT_SORT_EXPRESSION =
                                       "currentSortExpression";
static readonly String VS_CURRENT_SORT_ORDER = "currentSortOrder";

//*************************************************************************
//
//   ROUTINE: Page_Load
//
//   DESCRIPTION: This routine provides the event handler for the page
//                load event.  It is responsible for initializing the
//                controls on the page.
//-------------------------------------------------------------------------
private void Page_Load(object sender, System.EventArgs e)
{
  String defaultSortExpression;
  enuSortOrder defaultSortOrder;

  // wire the event handler for the sort command
  this.dgBooks.SortCommand +=
    new DataGridSortCommandEventHandler(this.dgBooks_SortCommand);

  if (!Page.IsPostBack)
  {
    // sort by title, ascending as the default
    defaultSortExpression = sortExpression[0];
    defaultSortOrder = enuSortOrder.soAscending;

    // bind data to the DataGrid
    this.ViewState.Add(VS_CURRENT_SORT_EXPRESSION, defaultSortExpression);
    this.ViewState.Add(VS_CURRENT_SORT_ORDER, defaultSortOrder);
    bindData(defaultSortExpression,
            defaultSortOrder);

    // disable the ViewState for controls that do not need it
    disableViewState( );
  }
} // Page_Load

//*************************************************************************
//
//   ROUTINE: dgBooks_SortCommand
//
//   DESCRIPTION: This routine provides the event handler for the
//                datagrid sort event.  It is responsible re-binding
//                the data to the datagrid by the selected column.
//-------------------------------------------------------------------------
private void dgBooks_SortCommand(Object source,
  System.Web.UI.WebControls.DataGridSortCommandEventArgs e)
{
  String newSortExpression = null;
  String currentSortExpression = null;
```

Example 16-3. Optimized code-behind for Recipe 1.12 (.cs) (continued)

```
    enuSortOrder currentSortOrder;

    // get the current sort expression and order from the viewstate
    currentSortExpression =
                    (String)(this.ViewState[VS_CURRENT_SORT_EXPRESSION]);
    currentSortOrder =
                    (enuSortOrder)(this.ViewState[VS_CURRENT_SORT_ORDER]);

    // check to see if this is a new column or the sort order
    // of the current column needs to be changed.
    newSortExpression = e.SortExpression;
    if (newSortExpression == currentSortExpression)
    {
      // sort column is the same so change the sort order
      if (currentSortOrder == enuSortOrder.soAscending)
      {
        currentSortOrder = enuSortOrder.soDescending;
      }
      else
      {
        currentSortOrder = enuSortOrder.soAscending;
      }
    }
    else
    {
      // sort column is different so set the new column with ascending
      // sort order
      currentSortExpression = newSortExpression;
      currentSortOrder = enuSortOrder.soAscending;
    }

    // update the view state with the new sort information
    this.ViewState.Add(VS_CURRENT_SORT_EXPRESSION, currentSortExpression);
    this.ViewState.Add(VS_CURRENT_SORT_ORDER, currentSortOrder);

    // rebind the data in the datagrid
    bindData(currentSortExpression,
            currentSortOrder);

    // disable the ViewState for controls that do not need it
    disableViewState( );
} // dgBooks_SortCommand

//***********************************************************************
//
//    ROUTINE: bindData
//
//    DESCRIPTION: This routine queries the database for the data to
//                 displayed and binds it to the repeater
//-----------------------------------------------------------------------
private void bindData(String sortExpression,
    enuSortOrder sortOrder)
```

Example 16-3. Optimized code-behind for Recipe 1.12 (.cs) (continued)

```
{
  OleDbConnection dbConn = null;
  OleDbDataAdapter da = null;
  DataSet ds = null;
  String strConnection = null;
  String strSQL =null;
  int index = 0;
  DataGridColumn col = null;
  String colImage = null;
  String strSortOrder = null;

  try
  {
    // get the connection string from web.config and open a connection
    // to the database
    strConnection =
      ConfigurationSettings.AppSettings["dbConnectionString"];
    dbConn = new OleDbConnection(strConnection);
    dbConn.Open( );

    // build the query string and get the data from the database
    if (sortOrder == enuSortOrder.soAscending)
    {
      strSortOrder = " ASC";
    }
    else
    {
      strSortOrder = " DESC";
    }

    strSQL = "SELECT Title, ISBN, Publisher " +
             "FROM Book " +
             "ORDER BY " + sortExpression +
             strSortOrder;

    da = new OleDbDataAdapter(strSQL, dbConn);
    ds = new DataSet( );
    da.Fill(ds, "Table");

    // loop through the columns in the datagrid updating the heading to
    // mark which column is the sort column and the sort order
    for (index = 0; index < dgBooks.Columns.Count; index++)
    {
      col = dgBooks.Columns[index];
      // check to see if this is the sort column
      if (col.SortExpression == sortExpression)
      {
        // this is the sort column so determine whether the ascending or
        // descending image needs to be included
        if (sortOrder == enuSortOrder.soAscending)
        {
          colImage = " <img src='images/sort_ascending.gif' border='0'>";
```

Example 16-3. Optimized code-behind for Recipe 1.12 (.cs) (continued)

```
            }
            else
            {
               colImage = " <img src='images/sort_descending.gif' border='0'>";
            }
         }
         else
         {
            // This is not the sort column so include no image html
            colImage = "";
         }  // if (col.SortExpression == sortExpression)

         // set the title for the column
         col.HeaderText = columnTitle[index] + colImage;
      }  // for index

      // set the source of the data for the datagrid control and bind it
      dgBooks.DataSource = ds;
      dgBooks.DataBind();
   }  // try

   finally
   {
      //clean up
      if (dbConn != null)
      {
         dbConn.Close();
      }
   }  // finally
}  // bindData


//*************************************************************************
//
//   ROUTINE: disableViewState
//
//   DESCRIPTION: This routine disables the ViewState for all controls
//                on the page that do not need to use it.
//-------------------------------------------------------------------------
private void disableViewState()
{
   // disable the ViewState for the header
   pageHeader.EnableViewState = false;

   // disable the ViewState for each row in the DataGrid
   foreach (DataGridItem item in dgBooks.Items)
   {
      item.EnableViewState = false;
   }
}  // disableViewState
}  // CH16ViewStatePerformanceCS2
}
```

16.2 Speeding up String Concatenation with a StringBuilder

Problem

You want to reduce the time spent concatenating strings in an application that performs this operation repeatedly.

Solution

Concatenate strings with a StringBuilder object instead of the classic & and + concatenation operators.

Examples 16-4 through 16-6 show the .aspx file and the VB and C# code-behind files for our application that demonstrates the performance difference between using the classic string operators and a StringBuilder object to perform concatenation. Our example concatenates two strings repeatedly, and then calculates the average time per concatenation for the two approaches. The output of the application is shown in Figure 16-1.

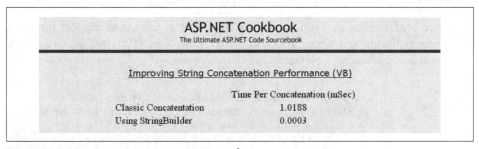

Figure 16-1. Measuring string concatenation performance output

Discussion

In the common language runtime (CLR), strings are immutable, which means that once they have been created they cannot be changed. If you concatenate the two strings, str1 and str2, shown in the following code fragment, the resulting value of str1 is "1234567890".

VB

```
str1 = "12345"
str2 = "67890"
str1 = str1 & str2
```

C#

```
str1 = "12345";
str2 = "67890";
str1 = str1 + str2;
```

The way in which this concatenation is accomplished may come as a bit of a surprise to you. Since str1 cannot be changed (it is immutable), it is actually disposed of and a new string str1 is created that contains the concatenation of str1 and str2. As you might expect, there is a lot of overhead associated with this operation.

The StringBuilder object provides a much faster method of concatenating strings. A StringBuilder object treats strings as an array of characters that can be altered without recreating the object. When a StringBuilder object is created, the CLR allocates a block of memory in which to store the string. As characters are added to a StringBuilder object, they are stored in the already available block of memory. If the additional characters will not fit within the current block, additional memory is allocated to store the new data.

The default capacity of a StringBuilder is 16 characters, but the number can be set to any value up to 2,147,483,647 characters, the maximum size of an integer type. If you know approximately how long the final string will be, you can improve performance further by setting the maximum size when the StringBuilder is created, which reduces the number of additional memory allocations that must be performed.

As Figure 16-1 shows, the performance difference between classic concatenation and concatenation using a StringBuilder object is dramatic. Classic concatenation averaged 1.0188 milliseconds per concatenation, while using a StringBuilder object averaged 0.0003 milliseconds per concatenation, which is nearly 3,000 times faster.

StringBuilder objects are not limited to concatenation: they also support inserting, removing, replacing, and appending formatted strings. The StringBuilder is a significant improvement over the classic manipulation of strings.

 The question always arises as to when classic string manipulation or a StringBuilder should be used. Every application is different. However, if you are performing a simple concatenation of less than 5–10 strings outside of a loop (done only once), you should probably use classic string manipulation due to the overhead of creating a StringBuilder object. Anytime you are performing string manipulations within a loop or are combining many string fragments, a StringBuilder should be used. If you are not sure, set up a test similar to the one we use in our examples for this recipe and measure the two approaches yourself.

See Also

In the MSDN Library, search for "Use StringBuilder for Complex String Manipulation"

Example 16-4. Measuring string concatenation performance (.aspx)

```
<%@ Page Language="vb" AutoEventWireup="false"
    Codebehind="CH16StringManipulationPerformanceVB.aspx.vb"
    Inherits="ASPNetCookbook.VBExamples.CH16StringManipulationPerformanceVB" %>
<!DOCTYPE HTML PUBLIC "-//W3C//DTD HTML 4.0 Transitional//EN">
<html>
  <head>
    <title>String Concatenation Performance</title>
    <link rel="stylesheet" href="css/ASPNetCookbook.css">
```

Example 16-4. Measuring string concatenation performance (.aspx) (continued)

```
  </head>
  <body leftmargin="0" marginheight="0" marginwidth="0" topmargin="0">
    <form id="frmStringPerformance" method="post" runat="server">
      <table width="100%" cellpadding="0" cellspacing="0" border="0">
        <tr>
          <td align="center">
            <img src="images/ASPNETCookbookHeading_blue.gif">
          </td>
        </tr>
        <tr>
          <td class="dividerLine">
            <img src="images/spacer.gif" height="6" border="0"></td>
        </tr>
      </table>
      <table width="90%" align="center" border="0">
        <tr>
          <td align="center"> </td>
        </tr>
        <tr>
          <td align="center" class="PageHeading">
            Improving String Concatenation Performance (VB)
          </td>
        </tr>
        <tr>
          <td><img src="images/spacer.gif" height="10" border="0"></td>
        </tr>
        <tr>
          <td align="center">
            <table width="70%" align="center" border="0">
              <tr>
                <td> </td>
                <td align="center">Time Per Concatenation (mSec)</td>
              </tr>
              <tr>
                <td>Classic Concatentation</td>
                <td id="cellClassic" runat="server" align="center"></td>
              </tr>
              <tr>
                <td>Using StringBuilder</td>
                <td id="cellSB" runat="server" align="center"></td>
              </tr>
            </table>
          </td>
        </tr>
      </table>
    </form>
  </body>
</html>
```

Example 16-5. Measuring string concatenation performance code-behind (.vb)

```
Option Explicit On
Option Strict On
```

```vb
'-----------------------------------------------------------------------------
'
'    Module Name: CH16StringManipulationPerformanceVB.aspx.vb
'
'    Description: This module provides the code behind for the
'                 CH16StringManipulationPerformanceVB.aspx page
'*****************************************************************************
Imports System
Imports System.Text

Namespace ASPNetCookbook.VBExamples
  Public Class CH16StringManipulationPerformanceVB
    Inherits System.Web.UI.Page

    'controls on the form
    Protected cellClassic As System.Web.UI.HtmlControls.HtmlTableCell
    Protected cellSB As System.Web.UI.HtmlControls.HtmlTableCell

    '*****************************************************************************
    '
    '    ROUTINE: Page_Load
    '
    '    DESCRIPTION: This routine provides the event handler for the page load
    '                 event.  It is responsible for initializing the controls
    '                 on the page.
    '-----------------------------------------------------------------------------
    Private Sub Page_Load(ByVal sender As System.Object, _
                          ByVal e As System.EventArgs) Handles MyBase.Load

      Const STRING_SECTION As String = "1234567890"

      Dim testStr As String
      Dim testStrBuilder As StringBuilder
      Dim counter As Integer
      Dim startTime As DateTime
      Dim elapsedTime As TimeSpan
      Dim loops As Integer

      'measure the elapsed time for 10000 classic string concatenation
      loops = 10000
      startTime = DateTime.Now()
      testStr = ""
      For counter = 1 To loops
        testStr &= STRING_SECTION
      Next

      elapsedTime = DateTime.Now.Subtract(startTime)

      'set the table cell value to the average time per concatenation
      'in milliseconds
      cellClassic.InnerText = _
        (elapsedTime.TotalMilliseconds / loops).ToString("0.0000")
```

Example 16-5. Measuring string concatenation performance code-behind (.vb) (continued)

```
      'measure the elapsed time for 1,000,000 classic string concatenation
      'NOTE: Many more loops were used to provide a measureable time period
      loops = 1000000
      startTime = DateTime.Now( )
      testStrBuilder = New StringBuilder
      For counter = 1 To loops
        testStrBuilder.Append(STRING_SECTION)
      Next

      elapsedTime = DateTime.Now.Subtract(startTime)

      'set the table cell value to the average time per concatenation
      'in milliseconds
      cellSB.InnerText = _
        (elapsedTime.TotalMilliseconds / loops).ToString("0.0000")
    End Sub  'Page_Load
  End Class  'CH16StringManipulationPerformanceVB
End Namespace
```

Example 16-6. Measuring string concatenation performance code-behind (.cs)

```
//-----------------------------------------------------------------------------
//
//   Module Name: CH16StringManipulationPerformanceCS.aspx.cs
//
//   Description: This class provides the code behind for
//                CH16StringManipulationPerformanceCS.aspx
//
//*****************************************************************************
using System;
using System.Text;

namespace ASPNetCookbook.CSExamples
{
  public class CH16StringManipulationPerformanceCS : System.Web.UI.Page
  {
    // controls on the form
    protected System.Web.UI.HtmlControls.HtmlTableCell cellClassic;
    protected System.Web.UI.HtmlControls.HtmlTableCell cellSB;

    //*****************************************************************************
    //
    //   ROUTINE: Page_Load
    //
    //   DESCRIPTION: This routine provides the event handler for the page
    //                load event.  It is responsible for initializing the
    //                controls on the page.
    //-----------------------------------------------------------------------------
    private void Page_Load(object sender, System.EventArgs e)
    {
      const string STRING_SECTION = "1234567890";

      string testStr = null;
```

```csharp
    StringBuilder testStrBuilder = null;
    DateTime startTime;
    TimeSpan elapsedTime;
    int counter;
    int loops;

    // measure the elapsed time for 10000 classic string concatenation
    loops = 10000;
    startTime = DateTime.Now;
    testStr = "";
    for (counter = 1; counter <= loops; counter++)
    {
      testStr += STRING_SECTION;
    }

    elapsedTime = DateTime.Now.Subtract(startTime);

    // set the table cell value to the average time per concatenation
    // in milliseconds
    cellClassic.InnerText =
      (elapsedTime.TotalMilliseconds / loops).ToString("0.0000");

    // measure the elapsed time for 1,000,000 classic string concatenation
    // NOTE: Many more loops were used to provide a measureable time period
    loops = 1000000;
    startTime = DateTime.Now;
    testStrBuilder = new StringBuilder();
    for (counter = 1; counter <= loops; counter++)
    {
      testStrBuilder.Append(STRING_SECTION);
    }

    elapsedTime = DateTime.Now.Subtract(startTime);

    // set the table cell value to the average time per concatenation
    // in milliseconds
    cellSB.InnerText =
      (elapsedTime.TotalMilliseconds / loops).ToString("0.0000");
  } // Page_Load
} // CH16StringManipulationPerformanceCS
}
```

16.3   Speeding Up Read-Only Data Access

Problem

You want to speed up read-only data access to a database in your application.

Solution

Use a DataReader instead of a DataAdapter to access the data.

Examples 16-7 through 16-9 show the *.aspx* file and VB and C# code-behind files for our application that demonstrates the performance difference between a DataReader and a DataAdapter using the OleDB managed provider. Figure 16-2 shows the output of the application. Refer to Recipe 16.4 for an equivalent example using the SQL Server managed provider.

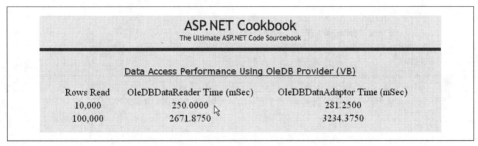

Figure 16-2. Measuring data reader and data adapter performance output

Discussion

The common language runtime (CLR) provides two primary methods for reading data from a database. The first is to use a DataReader, and the second is to use a DataAdapter in conjunction with a DataTable or DataSet.

The DataReader provides forward, read-only access to the data read from the database. It provides no mechanisms for randomly accessing the data.

A DataAdapter, along with a DataTable or DataSet, provides random access to data. In addition, the data can be changed in the DataTable or DataSet and the DataAdapter can be used to update the data in the database.

Of the two access methods, the DataReader is the lightest and fastest and is preferable when you only need to read the data, as reflected in the results we show for our sample application in Figure 16-2. Our example reads 10K and 100K records from a SQL Server database table containing 500K rows. The table contains five columns, of which three are retrieved in the query. The data indicates that using a DataAdapter is anywhere from 12% to 21% slower than using a DataReader.

See Also

Recipe 16.4

Example 16-7. Measuring data reader and data adapter performance (.aspx)

```
<%@ Page Language="vb" AutoEventWireup="false"
        Codebehind="CH16DataAccessPerformanceVB.aspx.vb"
        Inherits="ASPNetCookbook.VBExamples.CH16DataAccessPerformanceVB" %>
<!DOCTYPE HTML PUBLIC "-//W3C//DTD HTML 4.0 Transitional//EN">
<html>
  <head>
    <title>Data Access Performance</title>
```

```
    <link rel="stylesheet" href="css/ASPNetCookbook.css">
  </head>
  <body leftmargin="0" marginheight="0" marginwidth="0" topmargin="0">
    <form id="frmDataAccessPerformance" method="post" runat="server">
      <table width="100%" cellpadding="0" cellspacing="0" border="0">
        <tr>
          <td align="center">
            <img src="images/ASPNETCookbookHeading_blue.gif">
          </td>
        </tr>
        <tr>
          <td class="dividerLine">
            <img src="images/spacer.gif" height="6" border="0"></td>
        </tr>
      </table>
      <table width="90%" align="center" border="0">
        <tr>
          <td align="center"> </td>
        </tr>
        <tr>
          <td align="center" class="PageHeading">
            Data Access Performance Using OleDB Provider (VB)
          </td>
        </tr>
        <tr>
          <td><img src="images/spacer.gif" height="10" border="0"></td>
        </tr>
        <tr>
          <td align="center">
            <table width="100%" align="center" border="0">
              <tr>
                <td align="center">Rows Read</td>
                <td align="center">OleDBDataReader Time (mSec)</td>
                <td align="center">OleDBDataAdaptor Time (mSec)</td>
              </tr>
              <tr>
                <td align="center">10,000</td>
                <td id="cellDR10K" runat="server" align="center"></td>
                <td id="cellDA10K" runat="server" align="center"></td>
              </tr>
              <tr>
                <td align="center">100,000</td>
                <td id="cellDR100K" runat="server" align="center"></td>
                <td id="cellDA100K" runat="server" align="center"></td>
              </tr>
            </table>
          </td>
        </tr>
      </table>
    </form>
  </body>
</html>
```

Example 16-8. Measuring data reader and data adapter performance code-behind (.vb)

```vb
Option Explicit On
Option Strict On
'----------------------------------------------------------------------
'
'   Module Name: CH16DataAccessPerformanceVB.aspx.vb
'
'   Description: This module provides the code behind for the
'                CH16DataAccessPerformanceVB.aspx page
'
'**********************************************************************
Imports Microsoft.VisualBasic
Imports System
Imports System.Configuration
Imports System.Data
Imports System.Data.OleDb

Namespace ASPNetCookbook.VBExamples
  Public Class CH16DataAccessPerformanceVB
    Inherits System.Web.UI.Page

    'controls on the form
    Protected cellDR10K As System.Web.UI.HtmlControls.HtmlTableCell
    Protected cellDR100K As System.Web.UI.HtmlControls.HtmlTableCell
    Protected cellDA10K As System.Web.UI.HtmlControls.HtmlTableCell
    Protected cellDA100K As System.Web.UI.HtmlControls.HtmlTableCell

    '**********************************************************************
    '
    '   ROUTINE: Page_Load
    '
    '   DESCRIPTION: This routine provides the event handler for the page load
    '                event.  It is responsible for initializing the controls
    '                on the page.
    '----------------------------------------------------------------------
    Private Sub Page_Load(ByVal sender As System.Object, _
                          ByVal e As System.EventArgs) Handles MyBase.Load
      Dim strConnection As String
      Dim elapsedTime As TimeSpan

      'get the connection string from web.config
      strConnection = _
        ConfigurationSettings.AppSettings("dbConnectionString")

      'get times for 10,000 records
      elapsedTime = getDataAdapterTime(strConnection, 10000)
      cellDA10K.InnerText = elapsedTime.TotalMilliseconds.ToString("0.0000")

      elapsedTime = getDataReaderTime(strConnection, 10000)
      cellDR10K.InnerText = elapsedTime.TotalMilliseconds.ToString("0.0000")

      'get times for 100,000 records
      elapsedTime = getDataAdapterTime(strConnection, 100000)
      cellDA100K.InnerText = elapsedTime.TotalMilliseconds.ToString("0.0000")
```

Example 16-8. Measuring data reader and data adapter performance code-behind (.vb) (continued)

```vb
      elapsedTime = getDataReaderTime(strConnection, 100000)
      cellDR100K.InnerText = elapsedTime.TotalMilliseconds.ToString("0.0000")
End Sub   'Page_Load

'*************************************************************************
'
'    ROUTINE: getDataReaderTime
'
'    DESCRIPTION: This routine retrieves the passed number of records from
'                 the database using an OleDBDataReader and returns the
'                 elapsed time
'------------------------------------------------------------------------
Private Function getDataReaderTime(ByVal strConnection As String, _
                                   ByVal numberOfRecords As Integer) _
             As TimeSpan

   Dim dbConn As OleDbConnection
   Dim dCmd As OleDbCommand
   Dim dr As OleDbDataReader
   Dim strSQL As String
   Dim startTime As DateTime
   Dim elapsedTime As TimeSpan
   Dim bookTitle As String
   Dim isbn As String
   Dim price As Decimal

   Try
     'open connection to database
     dbConn = New OleDbConnection(strConnection)
     dbConn.Open( )

     startTime = DateTime.Now( )

     'build the query string and get the data from the database
     strSQL = "SELECT Top " & numberOfRecords.ToString( ) & " " & _
              "BookTitle, ISBN, Price " & _
              "FROM PerformanceTesting " & _
              "ORDER BY PerformanceTestingID"

     'read the data from the database
     dCmd = New OleDbCommand(strSQL, dbConn)
     dr = dCmd.ExecuteReader( )
     Do While (dr.Read( ))
       bookTitle = CStr(dr.Item("BookTitle"))
       isbn = CStr(dr.Item("ISBN"))
       price = CDec(dr.Item("Price"))
     Loop

     'return the elapsed time
     elapsedTime = DateTime.Now.Subtract(startTime)
     getDataReaderTime = elapsedTime
```

Example 16-8. Measuring data reader and data adapter performance code-behind (.vb) (continued)

```
    Finally
      'clean up
      If (Not IsNothing(dbConn)) Then
        dbConn.Close( )
      End If
    End Try
  End Function   'getDataReaderTime

  '*************************************************************************
  '
  '   ROUTINE: getDataAdapterTime
  '
  '   DESCRIPTION: This routine retrieves the passed number of records from
  '                the database using an OleDbDataAdapter and returns the
  '                elapsed time
  '-------------------------------------------------------------------------
  Private Function getDataAdapterTime(ByVal strConnection As String, _
                             ByVal numberOfRecords As Integer) _
                As TimeSpan
    Dim dbConn As OleDbConnection
    Dim da As OleDbDataAdapter
    Dim dTable As DataTable
    Dim strSQL As String
    Dim startTime As DateTime
    Dim elapsedTime As TimeSpan

    Try
      'open connection to database
      dbConn = New OleDbConnection(strConnection)
      dbConn.Open( )

      startTime = DateTime.Now( )

      'build the query string and get the data from the database
      strSQL = "SELECT Top " & numberOfRecords.ToString( ) & " " & _
               "BookTitle, ISBN, Price " & _
               "FROM PerformanceTesting " & _
               "ORDER BY PerformanceTestingID"

      'read the data from the database
      da = New OleDbDataAdapter(strSQL, dbConn)
      dTable = New DataTable
      da.Fill(dTable)

      'return the elapsed time
      elapsedTime = DateTime.Now.Subtract(startTime)
      getDataAdapterTime = elapsedTime

    Finally
      'clean up
      If (Not IsNothing(dbConn)) Then
        dbConn.Close( )
```

Example 16-8. Measuring data reader and data adapter performance code-behind (.vb) (continued)

```vb
        End If
      End Try
    End Function  'getDataAdapterTime
  End Class   'CH16DataAccessPerformanceVB
End Namespace
```

Example 16-9. Measuring data reader and data adapter performance code-behind (.cs)

```csharp
//-----------------------------------------------------------------------------
//
//   Module Name: CH16DataAccessPerformanceCS.aspx.cs
//
//   Description: This module provides the code behind for the
//                CH16DataAccessPerformanceCS.aspx page
//
//****************************************************************************
using System;
using System.Configuration;
using System.Data;
using System.Data.OleDb;

namespace ASPNetCookbook.CSExamples
{
  public class CH16DataAccessPerformanceCS : System.Web.UI.Page
  {
    // controls on the form
    protected System.Web.UI.HtmlControls.HtmlTableCell cellDR10K;
    protected System.Web.UI.HtmlControls.HtmlTableCell cellDR100K;
    protected System.Web.UI.HtmlControls.HtmlTableCell cellDA10K;
    protected System.Web.UI.HtmlControls.HtmlTableCell cellDA100K;


    //****************************************************************************
    //
    //   ROUTINE: Page_Load
    //
    //   DESCRIPTION: This routine provides the event handler for the page
    //                load event.  It is responsible for initializing the
    //                controls on the page.
    //-------------------------------------------------------------------------
    private void Page_Load(object sender, System.EventArgs e)
    {
      String strConnection;
      TimeSpan elapsedTime;

      // get the connection string from web.config
      strConnection =
          ConfigurationSettings.AppSettings["dbConnectionString"];

      // get times for 10,000 records
      elapsedTime = getDataAdapterTime(strConnection, 10000);
      cellDA10K.InnerText = elapsedTime.TotalMilliseconds.ToString("0.0000");

      elapsedTime = getDataReaderTime(strConnection, 10000);
```

Example 16-9. Measuring data reader and data adapter performance code-behind (.cs) (continued)

```
      cellDR10K.InnerText = elapsedTime.TotalMilliseconds.ToString("0.0000");

      // get times for 100,000 records
      elapsedTime = getDataAdapterTime(strConnection, 100000);
      cellDA100K.InnerText = elapsedTime.TotalMilliseconds.ToString("0.0000");

      elapsedTime = getDataReaderTime(strConnection, 100000);
      cellDR100K.InnerText = elapsedTime.TotalMilliseconds.ToString("0.0000");
   }  // Page_Load

   //*************************************************************************
   //
   //   ROUTINE: getDataReaderTime
   //
   //   DESCRIPTION: This routine retrieves the passed number of records from
   //                the database using an OleDBDataReader and returns the
   //                elapsed time.
   //-------------------------------------------------------------------------
   private TimeSpan getDataReaderTime(String strConnection,
                                      int numberOfRecords)
   {
      OleDbConnection dbConn = null;
      OleDbCommand dCmd = null;
      OleDbDataReader dr = null;
      string strSQL = null;
      DateTime startTime;
      TimeSpan elapsedTime;
      String bookTitle;
      String isbn;
      Decimal price;

      try
      {
         // open connection to database
         dbConn = new OleDbConnection(strConnection);
         dbConn.Open( );

         startTime = DateTime.Now;

         // build the query string used to get the data from the database
         strSQL = "SELECT Top " + numberOfRecords.ToString( ) + " " +
                  "BookTitle, ISBN, Price " +
                  "FROM PerformanceTesting " +
                  "ORDER BY PerformanceTestingID";

         // read the data from the database
         dCmd = new OleDbCommand(strSQL, dbConn);
         dr = dCmd.ExecuteReader( );
         while (dr.Read( ))
         {
            bookTitle = (String)(dr["BookTitle"]);
            isbn = (String)(dr["ISBN"]);
            price = Convert.ToDecimal(dr["Price"]);
```

```
  }

    //return the elapsed time
    elapsedTime = DateTime.Now.Subtract(startTime);
    return(elapsedTime);
  }

  finally
  {
    // clean up
    if (dbConn != null)
    {
      dbConn.Close();
    }
  }
} // getDataReaderTime

//***********************************************************************
//
//   ROUTINE: getDataAdapterTime
//
//   DESCRIPTION: This routine retrieves the passed number of records from
//                the database using an OleDbDataAdapter and returns the
//                elapsed time.
//-----------------------------------------------------------------------
private TimeSpan getDataAdapterTime(String strConnection,
                                    int numberOfRecords)
{
  OleDbConnection dbConn = null;
  OleDbDataAdapter da = null;
  DataTable dTable = null;
  string strSQL = null;
  DateTime startTime;
  TimeSpan elapsedTime;

  try
  {
    // open connection to database
    dbConn = new OleDbConnection(strConnection);
    dbConn.Open();

    startTime = DateTime.Now;

    // build the query string used to get the data from the database
    strSQL = "SELECT Top " + numberOfRecords.ToString() + " " +
             "BookTitle, ISBN, Price " +
             "FROM PerformanceTesting " +
             "ORDER BY PerformanceTestingID";

    // read the data from the database
    da = new OleDbDataAdapter(strSQL, dbConn);
    dTable = new DataTable();
    da.Fill(dTable);
```

```
        // return the elapsed time
        elapsedTime = DateTime.Now.Subtract(startTime);
        return(elapsedTime);
    }

    finally
    {
        // clean up
        if (dbConn != null)
        {
            dbConn.Close( );
        }
    }
    } // getDataAdapterTime
  } // CH16DataAccessPerformanceCS
}
```

16.4 Speeding Up Data Access to a SQL Server Database Using the SQL Provider

Problem

You want to speed up data access in an application that will always be used with SQL Server.

Solution

Use the SQL Server managed provider instead of the OleDB managed provider for accessing the data in the database.

In the code-behind class for the page, open a connection to a SQL Server database using the SQLConnection class.

To test the SQL provider, we have implemented our example from Recipe 16.3 and replaced the getDataReaderTime and getDataAdapterTime methods in the code-behind with the code shown in Example 16-10 (VB) and Example 16-11 (C#). The output of the test is shown in Figure 16-3.

Rows Read	SqlDataReader Time (mSec)	SqlDataAdaptor Time (mSec)
10,000	125.0000	156.2500
100,000	1406.2500	1921.8750

Figure 16-3. Performance using SQL managed provider output

Discussion

The common language runtime (CLR) provides four managed providers for accessing data in a database: SQL, OleDB, ODBC, and Oracle. The OleDB and ODBC providers can be used to access virtually any database—including SQL Server, Access, Oracle, and many others—using an OleDB (or ODBC) layer. OleDB communicates to a data source through both the OleDB service component, which provides connection pooling and transaction services, and the OleDB provider for the data source. In contrast, the SQL Server provider uses a proprietary protocol to directly access SQL Server, eliminating the additional layer of the OleDB service component and thereby improving performance. It can only be used to access SQL Server 7.0 or later release, however.

Comparing the results in Example 16-10 (VB) and Example 16-11 (C#) with the results shown in Recipe 16.3 indicates that the SQL Server provider is substantially faster than the OleDB provider when accessing SQL Server; access using a DataReader is nearly twice as fast, while access using a DataAdapter is 65–80% faster.

The data also indicates that when using the SQL Server provider, the difference between using the DataReader and the DataAdapter is more significant. The DataAdapter is 25–35% slower than the DataReader with the SQL Server provider.

See Also

Recipe 16.3; search for "The .NET Framework Data Provider for SQL Server" in the MSDN Library

Example 16-10. Methods using SQL provider (.vb)

```
'*****************************************************************************
'
'    ROUTINE: getDataReaderTime
'
'    DESCRIPTION: This routine retrieves the passed number of records from
'                 the database using an SqlDataReader and returns the
'                 elapsed time
'----------------------------------------------------------------------------
Private Function getDataReaderTime(ByVal strConnection As String, _
                           ByVal numberOfRecords As Integer) _
                As TimeSpan

   Dim dbConn As SqlConnection
   Dim dCmd As SqlCommand
   Dim dr As SqlDataReader
   Dim strSQL As String
   Dim startTime As DateTime
   Dim elapsedTime As TimeSpan
   Dim bookTitle As String
   Dim isbn As String
   Dim price As Decimal
```

Example 16-10. Methods using SQL provider (.vb) (continued)

```vb
    Try
      'open connection to database
      dbConn = New SqlConnection(strConnection)
      dbConn.Open( )

      startTime = DateTime.Now( )

      'build the query string and get the data from the database
      strSQL = "SELECT Top " & numberOfRecords.ToString( ) & " " & _
               "BookTitle, ISBN, Price " & _
               "FROM PerformanceTesting " & _
               "ORDER BY PerformanceTestingID"

      'read the data from the database
      dCmd = New SqlCommand(strSQL, dbConn)
      dr = dCmd.ExecuteReader( )
      Do While (dr.Read( ))
        bookTitle = CStr(dr.Item("BookTitle"))
        isbn = CStr(dr.Item("ISBN"))
        price = CDec(dr.Item("Price"))
      Loop

      'return the elapsed time
      elapsedTime = DateTime.Now.Subtract(startTime)
      getDataReaderTime = elapsedTime

    Finally
      'clean up
      If (Not IsNothing(dbConn)) Then
        dbConn.Close( )
      End If
    End Try
  End Function  'getDataReaderTime

  '**************************************************************************
  '
  '    ROUTINE: getDataAdapterTime
  '
  '    DESCRIPTION: This routine retrieves the passed number of records from
  '                 the database using an SqlDataAdapter and returns the
  '                 elapsed time
  '--------------------------------------------------------------------------
  Private Function getDataAdapterTime(ByVal strConnection As String, _
                                      ByVal numberOfRecords As Integer) _
                   As TimeSpan
    Dim dbConn As SqlConnection
    Dim da As SqlDataAdapter
    Dim dTable As DataTable
    Dim strSQL As String
    Dim startTime As DateTime
    Dim elapsedTime As TimeSpan
```

Example 16-10. Methods using SQL provider (.vb) (continued)

```
  Try
    'open connection to database
    dbConn = New SqlConnection(strConnection)
    dbConn.Open( )

    startTime = DateTime.Now( )

    'build the query string and get the data from the database
    strSQL = "SELECT Top " & numberOfRecords.ToString( ) & " " & _
            "BookTitle, ISBN, Price " & _
            "FROM PerformanceTesting " & _
            "ORDER BY PerformanceTestingID"

    'read the data from the database
    da = New SqlDataAdapter(strSQL, dbConn)
    dTable = New DataTable
    da.Fill(dTable)

    'return the elapsed time
    elapsedTime = DateTime.Now.Subtract(startTime)
    getDataAdapterTime = elapsedTime

  Finally
    'clean up
    If (Not IsNothing(dbConn)) Then
      dbConn.Close( )
    End If
  End Try
End Function   'getDataAdapterTime
```

Example 16-11. Methods using SQL provider (.cs)

```
//************************************************************************
//
//   ROUTINE: getDataReaderTime
//
//   DESCRIPTION: This routine retrieves the passed number of records from
//                the database using an SqlDataReader and returns the
//                elapsed time.
//------------------------------------------------------------------------
private TimeSpan getDataReaderTime(String strConnection,
  int numberOfRecords)
{
  SqlConnection dbConn = null;
  SqlCommand dCmd = null;
  SqlDataReader dr = null;
  string strSQL = null;
  DateTime startTime;
  TimeSpan elapsedTime;
  String bookTitle;
  String isbn;
  Decimal price;
```

Example 16-11. Methods using SQL provider (.cs) (continued)

```csharp
    try
    {
      // open connection to database
      dbConn = new SqlConnection(strConnection);
      dbConn.Open( );

      startTime = DateTime.Now;

      // build the query string used to get the data from the database
      strSQL = "SELECT Top " + numberOfRecords.ToString( ) + " " +
               "BookTitle, ISBN, Price " +
               "FROM PerformanceTesting " +
               "ORDER BY PerformanceTestingID";

      // read the data from the database
      dCmd = new SqlCommand(strSQL, dbConn);
      dr = dCmd.ExecuteReader( );
      while (dr.Read( ))
      {
        bookTitle = (String)(dr["BookTitle"]);
        isbn = (String)(dr["ISBN"]);
        price = Convert.ToDecimal(dr["Price"]);
      }

      //return the elapsed time
      elapsedTime = DateTime.Now.Subtract(startTime);
      return(elapsedTime);
    }

    finally
    {
      // clean up
      if (dbConn != null)
      {
        dbConn.Close( );
      }
    }
  } // getDataReaderTime

//************************************************************************
//
//    ROUTINE: getDataAdapterTime
//
//    DESCRIPTION: This routine retrieves the passed number of records from
//                 the database using an SqlDataAdapter and returns the
//                 elapsed time.
//------------------------------------------------------------------------
private TimeSpan getDataAdapterTime(String strConnection,
  int numberOfRecords)
{
  SqlConnection dbConn = null;
  SqlDataAdapter da = null;
```

Example 16-11. Methods using SQL provider (.cs) (continued)

```csharp
    DataTable dTable = null;
    string strSQL = null;
    DateTime startTime;
    TimeSpan elapsedTime;

    try
    {
      // open connection to database
      dbConn = new SqlConnection(strConnection);
      dbConn.Open( );

      startTime = DateTime.Now;

      // build the query string used to get the data from the database
      strSQL = "SELECT Top " + numberOfRecords.ToString( ) + " " +
               "BookTitle, ISBN, Price " +
               "FROM PerformanceTesting " +
               "ORDER BY PerformanceTestingID";

      // read the data from the database
      da = new SqlDataAdapter(strSQL, dbConn);
      dTable = new DataTable( );
      da.Fill(dTable);

      // return the elapsed time
      elapsedTime = DateTime.Now.Subtract(startTime);
      return(elapsedTime);
    }

    finally
    {
      // clean up
      if (dbConn != null)
      {
        dbConn.Close( );
      }
    }
  } // getDataAdapterTime
```

CHAPTER 17

HTTP Handlers

17.0 Introduction

An *HTTP handler* is a class that intercepts and handles requests for a resource of a given type on a web server. HTTP handlers are a key feature of ASP.NET. For instance, when you request an *.aspx* file, a built-in HTTP handler intercepts the request and takes charge of loading and executing the *.aspx* file. ASP.NET also provides built-in HTTP handlers for *.asmx*, *.ascx*, *.cs*, and *.vb* files, as well as other file types. The <httpHandlers> element of the *machine.config* file contains a list of the standard HTTP handlers configured for your web server.

It's possible to extend the built-in handlers provided by ASP.NET or to write your own. A custom HTTP handler is useful when you want to handle requests by your application for a given resource on your own. For example, custom handlers are useful for returning binary data, such as the contents of an image file, or for handling the processing necessary to access a resource stored in a database. HTTP handlers also provide a good mechanism for building reusable assemblies for your web applications, such as a general purpose file download module able to handle requests for virtually any file type. Each of these ideas is illustrated in the recipes in this chapter.

Overriding ASP.NET's Built-in HTTP Handlers

The <httpHandlers> element in *machine.config* defines how ASP.NET handles requests for all of the standard file extensions found in most ASP.NET applications. These include *.aspx*, *.asmx*, *.ascx*, *.cs*, *.vb*, *.vbproj*, *.csproj*, *.soap*, and many others. By placing your own handler settings in *web.config*, you can override those defined in *machine. config*. The override maps incoming requests to the appropriate IHttpHandler class you define (see Recipe 17.1's "Discussion" section for more details). The override can be for a single URL or for all requests with a given extension.

HTTP handlers are similar to the ISAPI extensions used to implement classic ASP for IIS. But, whereas ISAPI extensions are difficult to implement and can only be implemented in C++, HTTP handlers are supported by ASP.NET and can be implemented in any .NET language.

17.1 Creating a Reusable Image Handler

Problem

You want to create a reusable assembly that retrieves image data from a database and processes it before sending it to a browser.

Solution

Create an HTTP handler to read the image data from the database and send it to the browser.

To implement a custom, reusable HTTP handler:

1. Create a separate Class Library project in Visual Studio.
2. Create a class in the project that implements the IHttpHandler interface and place code to handle the request in the ProcessRequest method.
3. Compile the project as an assembly and place the assembly in the *bin* directory of your web project.
4. Add an <httpHandlers> element to the *web.config* file in your web project referencing your custom HTTP handler.
5. Reference the URL of the HTTP handler in your application.

Examples 17-3 and 17-4 show the VB and C# class files we've written to implement an image handler as an HTTP handler. Examples 17-5 through 17-7 show the *.aspx* file and VB and C# code-behind files for our application that demonstrates the use of the HTTP handler.

Discussion

HTTP handlers are simply classes that implement the IHttpHandler interface. Implementing the IHttpHandler interface requires the implementation of two methods: IsReusable and ProcessRequest. IsReusable is a property that explicitly returns a Boolean value that indicates whether the HTTP handler can be reused by other HTTP requests. For synchronous handlers, like our example, the property should always return false so the handler is not pooled (kept in memory). The ProcessRequest method is where the actual work is performed and you should place code that processes the requests here.

To create a *reusable* HTTP handler, you need to eliminate all application-specific code from the class. You must also compile the class as a separate .NET assembly and place the assembly in the *bin* directory of each application that uses it.

To create an assembly that contains only the handler code, you need to create a separate Class Library project in Visual Studio. In our example, we have named the project VBImageHandler (or CSImageHandler for C#) resulting in an assembly that has the same name as the project. We then compile the assembly, place it in the *bin* directory of the web project, and add a reference to the assembly.

When you create a new "Class Library" project for your HTTP handler, you will need to add a reference to the System.Web assembly. This is required because the IHttpHandler interface and HttpContext class used by the HTTP handler are defined in the System.Web assembly.

In our example that demonstrates this solution, we have stored GIF images in a database that can be retrieved and displayed in a browser using our HTTP handler just as if they were standard image files. To demonstrate the HTTP handler, we created an ASP.NET page that contains a DropDownList, a View button, and an HTML img tag. The DropDownList displays the descriptions of the images stored in the database. When you make a selection from the list and click the View button, the src attribute for the img tag is set to the URL of our HTTP handler with the ID of the image in the URL. When the page is then displayed, the browser requests the image from our HTTP handler, which retrieves the ID of the requested image from the URL, reads the data from the database for the image, and then streams the image data to the browser. Figure 17-1 shows the output of the page used to test our HTTP handler.

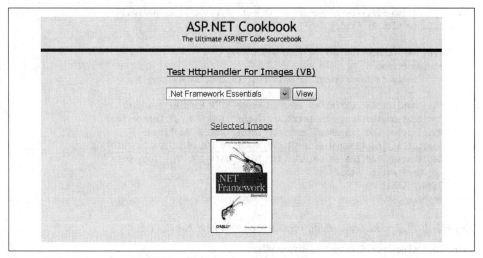

Figure 17-1. Output from HTTPHandler test page

The image handler implemented in our example needs several pieces of data to retrieve an image from the database. These include the following:

- The connection string for the database
- The name of the table containing the image data
- The name of the column that uniquely identifies an image (the primary key)
- The name of the column containing the image data
- A unique identifier (ID) for the image that is to be displayed

To be reusable, none of this data can be coded directly into the handler. To get around this problem in our example, we declare four public constants in the image handler class that we can use to specify the names of the variables in `Application` scope that contain the database information. In addition, the ID of the image that is to be downloaded will be passed in the URL used to access the handler (described later).

The application variables defined by the constants are initialized in the `Application_Start` method of the *global.asax.vb* (VB) or *global.asax.cs* (C#) class, which is executed when an application is first started. If you initialize your application variables in the `Application_Start` method, they will always be available when HTTP requests are processed. The code to implement this approach is in Examples 17-1 and 17-2.

Example 17-1. Application variable initialization for image handler (.vb)

```
Imports ASPNetCookbook.VBExamples.HttpHandlers

Namespace ASPNetCookbook.VBExamples
 Public Class Global
 Inherits System.Web.HttpApplication

 Sub Application_Start(ByVal sender As Object, ByVal e As EventArgs)
 Dim strConnection As String

     'get the connection string from web.config
     strConnection = _
        ConfigurationSettings.AppSettings("dbConnectionString")

     'Set application variables used in image HTTP handler example
     Application.Add(ImageHandlerVB.APP_CONNECTION_STR, strConnection)
     Application.Add(ImageHandlerVB.APP_IMAGE_TABLE, "BookImage")
     Application.Add(ImageHandlerVB.APP_IMAGE_ID_COLUMN, "BookImageID")
     Application.Add(ImageHandlerVB.APP_IMAGE_DATA_COLUMN, "ImageData")
 End Sub 'Application_Start
 End Class 'Global
End Namespace
```

Example 17-2. Application variable initialization for image handler (.cs)

```
using ASPNetCookbook.CSExamples.HttpHandlers;

namespace ASPNetCookbook.CSExamples
{
```

```
public class Global : System.Web.HttpApplication
{
  protected void Application_Start(Object sender, EventArgs e)
  {
    String strConnection = null;

    // get the connection string from web.config
    strConnection =
      ConfigurationSettings.AppSettings["dbConnectionString"];

    // Set application variables used in image HTTP handler example
    Application.Add(ImageHandlerCS.APP_CONNECTION_STR, strConnection);
    Application.Add(ImageHandlerCS.APP_IMAGE_TABLE, "BookImage");
    Application.Add(ImageHandlerCS.APP_IMAGE_ID_COLUMN, "BookImageID");
    Application.Add(ImageHandlerCS.APP_IMAGE_DATA_COLUMN, "ImageData");
  } // Application_Start
} // Global
}
```

To create the image handler, you next need to create a class that implements IHttpHandler and its two methods: IsReusable and ProcessRequest. Add the code to process requests made to the handler to the ProcessRequest method. As mentioned, IsReusable is a property that returns a Boolean value indicating whether the HTTP handler can be reused by other HTTP requests. Because our example is a synchronous handler, the property returns false so the handler is not pooled (kept in memory).

In our example, the first step in processing a request for an image is to get the ID of the requested image from the URL that is being processed by the handler.

Next, a connection to the database needs to be opened. The connection string is obtained from an Application scope variable defined by the APP_CONNECTION_STR constant shown in Example 17-1(VB) and Example 17-2 (C#). The name of the database table along with the columns containing the unique identifier and the image data are also obtained from the Application scope variables described earlier. These are then used to create the SQL statement required to read the image data from the database.

The next step in our example is to read the image data from the database using the ExecuteScalar method of the command object. The ExecuteScalar method returns a generic Object, so the return value must be cast to the type of data stored in the database. In this case it must be cast to a byte array.

The image data stored in the database for our example is in the GIF format, so the content type is set to "image/GIF" to inform the browser of the type of data being sent. After setting the content type, the image data is written to the Response object using the BinaryWrite method.

If your image is of another type, you will need to set the ContentType accordingly. Other choices for images include "image/jpeg", "images/tiff", and "images/png".

In order to use the handler, we next have to add information to the <httpHandlers> element of the *web.config* file of the application to tell ASP.NET which URL requests it should route to our custom image handler. You insert this information using an add element and its attributes. The verb attribute defines the types of requests that are routed to the HTTP handler. The allowable values are *, GET, HEAD, and POST. The value * is a wildcard that specifies that all request types are to be routed to the handler.

The path attribute defines the URL(s) that are to be processed by the HTTP handler. The path can be set to a single URL, or to a less specific value such as "*.images" to have the HTTP handler process all requests for URLs with an images extension. In our example, we are setting the path to a specific URL (*ImageHandlerVB.aspx*).

IIS routes requests with the extensions *.asax, .ascx, .ashx, .asmx, .aspx, .axd, .config, .cs, .csproj, .lic, .rem, .resources, .resx, .soap, .vb, .vbproj, .vsdisco*, and *.webinfo* to ASP.NET for processing.

To use an HTTP handler for requests with other extensions, IIS must be configured to send the requests with the desired extensions to the *aspnet_isapi.dll*.

The type attribute defines the name of the assembly and class within the assembly that will process the request in the format type="*class name, assembly*". The class name must be identified by its full namespace. Here is the code necessary to add a reference to the image handler to an application *web.config* file:

VB
```
<configuration>
  <system.web>
    <httpHandlers>
      <add verb="*" path="ImageHandlerVB.aspx"
          type="ASPNetCookbook.VBExamples.HttpHandlers.ImageHandlerVB,
              VBImageHandler" />
    </httpHandlers>
  </system.web>
</configuration>
```

C#
```
<configuration>
  <system.web>
    <httpHandlers>
      <add verb="*" path="ImageHandlerCS.aspx"
          type="ASPNetCookbook.CSExamples.HttpHandlers.ImageHandlerCS,
              CSImageHandler" />
    </httpHandlers>
  </system.web>
</configuration>
```

To use the HTTP handler to retrieve images from the database, we need to set the src attribute of image tags that will use the HTTP handler to the name of the HTTP handler defined in the path attribute of the entry added to *web.config*, passing the ID of the desired image in the URL. In our example, the src attribute of an img tag is set in the view image button click event of the test page code-behind. A sample URL is shown here:

```
src="ImageHandlerVB.aspx?ImageID=5"
```

 The HTTP handler does not have to be implemented in the same language as the application. The C# image handler can be used in VB projects or vice versa.

Example 17-3. Image HTTP handler (.vb)

```vb
Option Explicit On
Option Strict On
'-----------------------------------------------------------------------------
'
'     Module Name: ImageHandlerVB.vb
'
'     Description: This class provides an image handler as an HTTP handler.
'
'*****************************************************************************
Imports Microsoft.VisualBasic
Imports System.Configuration
Imports System.Data
Imports System.Data.OleDb
Imports System.Web

Namespace ASPNetCookbook.VBExamples.HttpHandlers
   Public Class ImageHandlerVB
      Implements IHttpHandler

      'The following constant is used in the URL used to access this handler to
      'define the image required
      Public Const QS_IMAGE_ID As String = "ImageID"

      'The following constants define the name of the application variables
      'used to define the database connection string and database table
      'information required to retrieve the required image
      Public Const APP_CONNECTION_STR As String = "DBConnectionStr"
      Public Const APP_IMAGE_TABLE As String = "DBImageTable"
      Public Const APP_IMAGE_ID_COLUMN As String = "DBImageIDColumn"
      Public Const APP_IMAGE_DATA_COLUMN As String = "DBImageDataColumn"

      '*****************************************************************************
      '
      '     ROUTINE: IsReusable
      '
      '     DESCRIPTION: This property defines whether another HTTP handler can
      '                  reuse this instance of the handler.
      '
```

Example 17-3. Image HTTP handler (.vb) (continued)

```
'         NOTE: False is always returned since this handler is synchronous
'              and is not pooled.
'-------------------------------------------------------------------------
Public ReadOnly Property IsReusable() As Boolean _
  Implements IHttpHandler.IsReusable
  Get
    Return (False)
  End Get
End Property  'IsReusable


'*************************************************************************
'
'   ROUTINE: ProcessRequest
'
'   DESCRIPTION: This routine provides the processing for the http request.
'                It is responsible for reading image data from the
'                database and writing it to the response object.
'-------------------------------------------------------------------------
Public Sub ProcessRequest(ByVal context As HttpContext) _
  Implements IHttpHandler.ProcessRequest

    Dim dbConn As OleDbConnection
    Dim dCmd As OleDbCommand
    Dim strConnection As String
    Dim imageTable As String
    Dim imageIDColumn As String
    Dim imageDataColumn As String
    Dim strSQL As String
    Dim imageID As String
    Dim imageData() As Byte


    Try
      'get the ID of the required image from the querystring
      imageID = context.Request.QueryString(QS_IMAGE_ID)

      'get the connection string and open a connection to the database
      strConnection = CStr(context.Application(APP_CONNECTION_STR))
      dbConn = New OleDbConnection(strConnection)
      dbConn.Open()

      'get the name of the database table and columns where the image
      'data is stored then create the SQL to read the data from
      'the database
      imageTable = CStr(context.Application(APP_IMAGE_TABLE))
      imageIDColumn = CStr(context.Application(APP_IMAGE_ID_COLUMN))
      imageDataColumn = CStr(context.Application(APP_IMAGE_DATA_COLUMN))

      strSQL = "SELECT " & imageDataColumn & _
               " FROM " & imageTable & _
               " WHERE " & imageIDColumn & "=?"

      dCmd = New OleDbCommand(strSQL, dbConn)
```

Example 17-3. Image HTTP handler (.vb) (continued)

```vb
        dCmd.Parameters.Add(New OleDbParameter("ImageID", _
                                                imageID))

        'get the image data
        imageData = CType(dCmd.ExecuteScalar( ), Byte( ))

        'write the image data to the reponse object
        context.Response.ContentType = "image/gif"
        context.Response.BinaryWrite(imageData)

    Finally
        'clean up
        If (Not IsNothing(dbConn)) Then
          dbConn.Close( )
        End If
    End Try
  End Sub    'ProcessRequest
  End Class    'ImageHandlerVB
End Namespace
```

Example 17-4. Image HTTP handler (.cs)

```cs
//-----------------------------------------------------------------------------
//
//    Module Name: ImageHandlerCS
//
//    Description: This class provides an image handler as an HTTP handler.
//
//*****************************************************************************
using System;
using System.Data;
using System.Data.OleDb;
using System.Web;

namespace ASPNetCookbook.CSExamples.HttpHandlers
{
  public class ImageHandlerCS : IHttpHandler
  {
    // The following constant is used in the URL used to access this handler
    // to define the image required
    public const string QS_IMAGE_ID = "ImageID";

    // The following constants defines the name of the application variables
    // used to define the database connection string and database table
    // information required to retrieve the required image
    public const string APP_CONNECTION_STR = "DBConnectionStr";
    public const string APP_IMAGE_TABLE = "DBImageTable";
    public const string APP_IMAGE_ID_COLUMN = "DBImageIDColumn";
    public const string APP_IMAGE_DATA_COLUMN = "DBImageDataColumn";

    //*****************************************************************************
    //
    //    ROUTINE: IsReusable
    //
```

Example 17-4. Image HTTP handler (.cs) (continued)

```csharp
//     DESCRIPTION: This property defines whether another HTTP handler can
//                  reuse this instance of the handler.
//
//          NOTE: false is always returned since this handler is synchronous
//                and is not pooled.
//----------------------------------------------------------------------------
public bool IsReusable
{
  get
  {
    return(false);
  }
} // IsReusable

//****************************************************************************
//
//     ROUTINE: ProcessRequest
//
//     DESCRIPTION: This routine provides the processing for the http
//                  request. It is responsible for reading image data from
//                  the database and writing it to the response object.
//----------------------------------------------------------------------------
public void ProcessRequest(HttpContext context)
{
  OleDbConnection dbConn = null;
  OleDbCommand dCmd = null;
  String strConnection = null;
  String imageTable = null;
  String imageIDColumn = null;
  String imageDataColumn = null;
  String strSQL = null;
  String imageID = null;
  byte[] imageData = null;

  try
  {
    // get the ID of the required image from the querystring
    imageID = context.Request.QueryString[QS_IMAGE_ID];

    // get connection string from application scope and open connection
    // to the database
    strConnection = (String)(context.Application[APP_CONNECTION_STR]);
    dbConn = new OleDbConnection(strConnection);
    dbConn.Open();

    // get the name of the database table and columns where the image
    // data is stored then create the SQL to read the data from
    // the database
    imageTable = (String)(context.Application[APP_IMAGE_TABLE]);
    imageIDColumn = (String)(context.Application[APP_IMAGE_ID_COLUMN]);
    imageDataColumn = (String)(context.Application[APP_IMAGE_DATA_COLUMN]);
```

Example 17-4. Image HTTP handler (.cs) (continued)

```
      strSQL = "SELECT " + imageDataColumn +
               " FROM " + imageTable +
               " WHERE " + imageIDColumn + "=?";

      dCmd = new OleDbCommand(strSQL, dbConn);
      dCmd.Parameters.Add(new OleDbParameter("ImageID",
                                              imageID));
      imageData = (byte[])(dCmd.ExecuteScalar());

      // write the image data to the reponse object
      context.Response.ContentType = "image/gif";
      context.Response.BinaryWrite(imageData);
    }  // try

    finally
    {
      // clean up
      if (dbConn != null)
      {
        dbConn.Close();
      }
    }  // finally
  }  // ProcessRequest
}  // ImageHandlerCS
}
```

Example 17-5. Using the image HTTP handler (.aspx)

```
<%@ Page Language="vb" AutoEventWireup="false"
        Codebehind="CH17TestHTTPImageHandlerVB.aspx.vb"
        Inherits="ASPNetCookbook.VBExamples.CH17TestHTTPImageHandlerVB" %>
<!DOCTYPE HTML PUBLIC "-//W3C//DTD HTML 4.0 Transitional//EN">
<html>
  <head>
    <title>Test HTTP Image Handler</title>
    <link rel="stylesheet" href="css/ASPNetCookbook.css">
  </head>
  <body leftmargin="0" marginheight="0" marginwidth="0" topmargin="0">
    <form id="frmTestImageHandler" method="post" runat="server">
      <table width="100%" cellpadding="0" cellspacing="0" border="0">
        <tr>
          <td align="center">
            <img src="images/ASPNETCookbookHeading_blue.gif">
          </td>
        </tr>
        <tr>
          <td class="dividerLine">
            <img src="images/spacer.gif" height="6" border="0"></td>
        </tr>
      </table>
      <table width="90%" align="center" border="0">
        <tr>
```

Example 17-5. Using the image HTTP handler (.aspx) (continued)

```
          <td align="center"> </td>
        </tr>
        <tr>
          <td align="center" class="PageHeading">
            Test HttpHandler For Images (VB)
          </td>
        </tr>
        <tr>
          <td><img src="images/spacer.gif" height="10" border="0"></td>
        </tr>
        <tr>
          <td align="center">
            <table>
              <tr>
                <td>
                  <asp:DropDownList ID="ddImages" Runat="server" />
                </td>
                <td>
                  <input id="btnViewImage" runat="server"
                         type="button" value="View">
                </td>
              </tr>
              <tr>
                <td id="tdSelectedImage" runat="server"
                    colspan="2" align="center" class="SubHeading">
                  <br /><br />
                  Selected Image<br /><br />
                  <img id="imgBook" runat="server" border="0">
                </td>
              </tr>
            </table>
          </td>
        </tr>
      </table>
    </form>
  </body>
</html>
```

Example 17-6. Using the image HTTP handler code-behind (.vb)

```
Option Explicit On
Option Strict On
'-----------------------------------------------------------------------------
'
'   Module Name: CH17TestHTTPImageHandlerVB.aspx.vb
'
'   Description: This module provides the code behind for the
'                CH17TestHTTPImageHandlerVB.aspx page.
'
'*****************************************************************************
Imports ASPNetCookbook.VBExamples.HttpHandlers
Imports Microsoft.VisualBasic
Imports System
```

Example 17-6. Using the image HTTP handler code-behind (.vb) (continued)

```vb
Imports System.Configuration
Imports System.Data
Imports System.Data.OleDb

Namespace ASPNetCookbook.VBExamples
  Public Class CH17TestHTTPImageHandlerVB
    Inherits System.Web.UI.Page

    'controls on the form
    Protected ddImages As System.Web.UI.WebControls.DropDownList
    Protected WithEvents btnViewImage As _
      System.Web.UI.HtmlControls.HtmlInputButton
    Protected imgBook As System.Web.UI.HtmlControls.HtmlImage
    Protected tdSelectedImage As System.Web.UI.HtmlControls.HtmlTableCell

    '*****************************************************************************
    '
    '   ROUTINE: Page_Load
    '
    '   DESCRIPTION: This routine provides the event handler for the page load
    '                event.  It is responsible for initializing the controls
    '                on the page.
    '-----------------------------------------------------------------------------
    Private Sub Page_Load(ByVal sender As System.Object, _
                          ByVal e As System.EventArgs) Handles MyBase.Load
      Dim dbConn As OleDbConnection
      Dim dCmd As OleDbCommand
      Dim dr As OleDbDataReader
      Dim strConnection As String
      Dim strSQL As String

      If (Not Page.IsPostBack) Then
        Try
          'initially hide the selected image since one is not selected
          tdSelectedImage.Visible = False

          'get the connection string from web.config and open a connection
          'to the database
          strConnection = _
              ConfigurationSettings.AppSettings("dbConnectionString")
          dbConn = New OleDbConnection(strConnection)
          dbConn.Open()

          'build the query string used to get the data from the database
          strSQL = "SELECT BookImageID, Title " & _
                  "FROM BookImage"

          dCmd = New OleDbCommand(strSQL, dbConn)
          dr = dCmd.ExecuteReader()

          'set the source of the data for the repeater control and bind it
          ddImages.DataSource = dr
          ddImages.DataTextField = "Title"
```

Example 17-6. Using the image HTTP handler code-behind (.vb) (continued)

```vb
          ddImages.DataValueField = "BookImageID"
          ddImages.DataBind()

      Finally
        'clean up
        If (Not IsNothing(dbConn)) Then
          dbConn.Close()
        End If
      End Try
    End If
  End Sub  'Page_Load

  '**************************************************************************
  '
  '    ROUTINE: btnViewImage_ServerClick
  '
  '    DESCRIPTION: This routine provides the event handler for the view
  '                 image click event.  It is responsible for setting the
  '                 src attibute of the imgBook tag to the URL of the
  '                 HTTP handler that will deliver the image content.
  '--------------------------------------------------------------------------
  Private Sub btnViewImage_ServerClick(ByVal sender As Object, _
            ByVal e As System.EventArgs) _
            Handles btnViewImage.ServerClick
    'set the source for the selected image tag
    imgBook.Src = "ImageHandlerVB.aspx?" & _
                ImageHandlerVB.QS_IMAGE_ID & "=" & _
                ddImages.SelectedItem.Value.ToString()

    'make the selected image visible
    tdSelectedImage.Visible = True
  End Sub  'btnViewImage_ServerClick
  End Class  'CH17TestHTTPImageHandlerVB
End Namespace
```

Example 17-7. Using the image HTTP handler code-behind (.cs)

```csharp
//--------------------------------------------------------------------------
//
//   Module Name: CH17TestHTTPImageHandlerCS.aspx.cs
//
//   Description: This module provides the code behind for the
//                CH17TestHTTPImageHandlerCS.aspx page
//
//**************************************************************************
using ASPNetCookbook.CSExamples.HttpHandlers;
using System;
using System.Configuration;
using System.Data;
using System.Data.OleDb;

namespace ASPNetCookbook.CSExamples
{
```

Example 17-7. Using the image HTTP handler code-behind (.cs) (continued)

```csharp
public class CH17TestHTTPImageHandlerCS : System.Web.UI.Page
{
  protected System.Web.UI.WebControls.DropDownList ddImages;
  protected System.Web.UI.HtmlControls.HtmlInputButton btnViewImage;
  protected System.Web.UI.HtmlControls.HtmlImage imgBook;
  protected System.Web.UI.HtmlControls.HtmlTableCell tdSelectedImage;

  //*************************************************************************
  //
  //    ROUTINE: Page_Load
  //
  //    DESCRIPTION: This routine provides the event handler for the page
  //                 load event.  It is responsible for initializing the
  //                 controls on the page.
  //-------------------------------------------------------------------------
  private void Page_Load(object sender, System.EventArgs e)
  {
    OleDbConnection dbConn = null;
    OleDbCommand dc = null;
    OleDbDataReader dr = null;
    String strConnection = null;
    String strSQL = null;

    // wire the view button click event
    this.btnViewImage.ServerClick +=
      new EventHandler(this.btnViewImage_ServerClick);

    if (!Page.IsPostBack)
    {
      try
      {
        // initially hide the selected image since one is not selected
        tdSelectedImage.Visible = false;

        // get the connection string from web.config and open a connection
        // to the database
        strConnection =
          ConfigurationSettings.AppSettings["dbConnectionString"];
        dbConn = new OleDbConnection(strConnection);
        dbConn.Open();

        // build the query string and get the data from the database
        strSQL = "SELECT BookImageID, Title " +
                 "FROM BookImage";
        dc = new OleDbCommand(strSQL, dbConn);
        dr = dc.ExecuteReader();

        // set the source of the data for the repeater control and bind it
        ddImages.DataSource = dr;
        ddImages.DataTextField = "Title";
        ddImages.DataValueField = "BookImageID";
        ddImages.DataBind();
      }
```

Example 17-7. Using the image HTTP handler code-behind (.cs) (continued)

```
      finally
      {
        // clean up
        if (dbConn != null)
        {
          dbConn.Close( );
        }
      }
    }
  } // Page_Load

  //************************************************************************
  //
  //   ROUTINE: btnViewImage_ServerClick
  //
  //   DESCRIPTION: This routine provides the event handler for the view
  //                image click event.  It is responsible for setting the
  //                src attibute of the imgBook tag to the page that will
  //                retrieve the image data from the database and stream
  //                it to the browser.
  //
  //------------------------------------------------------------------------
  private void btnViewImage_ServerClick(Object sender,
                                        System.EventArgs e)
  {
    // set the source for the selected image tag
    imgBook.Src = "ImageHandlerCS.aspx?" +
                  ImageHandlerCS.QS_IMAGE_ID + "=" +
                  ddImages.SelectedItem.Value.ToString( );

    // make the selected image visible
    tdSelectedImage.Visible = true;
  } // btnViewImage_ServerClick
  } // CH17TestHTTPImageHandlerCS
}
```

17.2   Creating a File Download Handler

Problem

You want to create a general purpose file handler to download files of any type.

Solution

Create an HTTP handler to read the required file from the filesystem and send it to the browser. The steps for creating an HTTP handler are defined in Recipe 17.1.

Examples 17-8 and 17-9 show the VB and C# class files we've written to implement a file download HTTP handler. Examples 17-10 through 17-12 show the *.aspx* file

---

and the VB and C# code-behind files for our application that demonstrates the use of the file download HTTP handler.

Discussion

Of the many ways you might implement a reusable file download routine that can handle virtually any file type, creating an HTTP handler makes the most sense. HTTP handlers are designed specifically to process requests for resources, and a file download request is merely a special instance of such a request.

The file download HTTP handler described in our example downloads a file from the local filesystem to the user's system. The name of the file to download is passed in the URL used to access the HTTP handler.

The first step in implementing the file download HTTP handler is to create a class that implements IHttpHandler. The class can be part of your web project, or, if you want it to be reusable across applications, place it in a project by itself so a separate assembly can be created, as described in Recipe 17.1.

As discussed in the previous recipe, implementing the IHttpHandler interface requires the implementation of two methods: IsReusable and ProcessRequest. IsReusable is a property that explicitly returns a Boolean value that indicates whether the HTTP handler can be reused by other HTTP requests. For synchronous handlers like our example, the property should always return false so the handler is not pooled (kept in memory).

The ProcessRequest method provides all of the functionality required to download the file. The first step is to retrieve the name of the file that is to be downloaded from the URL that is being processed by the handler.

In our example, we provide only the filename in the URL that calls the handler, because all files to be downloaded are intended to be located in a single *Downloads* directory associated with the application. However, because a fully qualified filename is required for the download along with the size of the file, a FileInfo object is created passing the fully qualified name of the file to the constructor. The path to the *Downloads* directory is obtained using Server.MapPath, which translates a relative path within the web application to a fully qualified path on the web server's filesystem.

 It is important to carefully review how you've implemented your file download handler to make sure it is not possible for a hacker to download files you do not intend to have downloaded. For example, if you do not restrict downloadable files to a single area, like we have done in our example, a hacker could possibly enter the following to download your *web.config* file:

http://aspnetcookbook/FileDownloadHandlerVB.aspx?filename=web.config

By restricting downloadable files to a single area and providing the path information in your code instead of in the URL, you can block a hacker from accessing restricted folders.

To send a file to the browser, you must write it to the Response object. Passing data in the response object is the only way to return data to the browser. Based on the content type (described later), the browser processes the data returned using the Response object.

The first step in writing the data to the Response object is to clear any data currently in the object, because no other data can be included with the file or a corrupted file error will occur.

The AddHeader method of the Response object is then used to add the name of the file being downloaded and its length.

The content type then needs to be set. In our example it is set to "application/octet-stream" so it will be treated by the browser as a binary stream and prompt the user to select the location to save the file. For your application, you may want to set the content type to the explicit file type, such as "application/PDF" or "application/msword". Setting the content type to the explicit file type allows the browser to open it with the application defined to handle the specified file type on the client machine. For more information on content types, consult *http://www.w3c.org*.

The file is then written to the Response object and the response is ended to send the file to the browser.

The *web.config* file for our application must have an entry in the <httpHandlers> element to tell ASP.NET which URL requests need to routed to the file download HTTP handler. You use the add element and its attributes to specify each custom handler. The verb attribute of the add element defines the types of requests that are routed to the HTTP handler. The allowable values are *, GET, HEAD, and POST. The value * is a wildcard for all request types.

The path attribute defines the URL(s) that are to be processed by the HTTP handler. The path can be a single URL, as shown later, or it can be set to something like "*.download" to have the HTTP handler process all requests for URLs with a download extension. (See the note in Recipe 17.1 regarding request extensions.)

The type attribute defines the name of the assembly and class within the assembly that will process the request in the format type="*class name, assembly*". The class must be identified by its full namespace. The following code shows how to add a reference to the file download handler to the *web.config* file of our sample application:

```
<configuration>
  <system.web>
    <httpHandlers>
      <add verb="*" path="FileDownloadHandlerVB.aspx"
           type="ASPNetCookbook.VBExamples.HttpHandlers.FileDownloadHandlerVB,
                 VBFileDownloadHandler"/>
    </httpHandlers>
  </system.web>
</configuration>
```

```
<configuration>
  <system.web>
    <httpHandlers>
      <add verb="*" path="FileDownloadHandlerCS.aspx"
           type="ASPNetCookbook.CSExamples.HttpHandlers.FileDownloadHandlerCS,
                 CSFileDownloadHandler"/>
    </httpHandlers>
  </system.web>
</configuration>
```

To use the HTTP handler described earlier to download files, we need to set the href attribute of an HTML anchor tag to the name of the file download HTTP handler defined in the path attribute of the entry added to *web.config*, passing the name of the file to download in the URL. In our example, the href attribute of the anchor tag is set in the Page_Load method of the test page. A sample of the URL is shown here:

```
href="FileDownloadHandlerVB.aspx?Filename=SampleDownload.txt"
```

This example demonstrates downloading a file that already exists on the web server. The code can easily be altered to pass additional data in the URL, then programmatically generate the file and send it to the browser without saving it to the filesystem. This could be useful if you are dynamically creating a PDF or a CSV file requested by the user.

See Also

Recipe 17.1 for techniques on how to create a generic, reusable HTTP handler; *http://www.w3c.org* for information on content types

Example 17-8. File download HTTP handler (.vb)

```
Option Explicit On
Option Strict On
'-----------------------------------------------------------------------
'
'   Module Name: FileDownloadHandlerVB.vb
'
'   Description: This class provides a file download handler as an HTTP
'                handler.
'
'*************************************************************************
Imports System.IO
Imports System.Web

Namespace ASPNetCookbook.VBExamples.HttpHandlers
  Public Class FileDownloadHandlerVB
    Implements IHttpHandler

    'The following constant is used in the URL used to access this handler to
    'define the file to download
    Public Const QS_FILENAME As String = "Filename"
```

Example 17-8. File download HTTP handler (.vb) (continued)

```vb
    'the following constant defines the folder containing downloadable files
    Private Const DOWNLOAD_FOLDER As String = "Downloads"

    '*************************************************************************
    '
    '    ROUTINE: IsReusable
    '
    '    DESCRIPTION: This property defines whether another HTTP handler can
    '                 reuse this instance of the handler.
    '
    '       NOTE: False is always returned since this handler is synchronous
    '             and is not pooled.
    '-------------------------------------------------------------------------
    Public ReadOnly Property IsReusable() As Boolean _
      Implements IHttpHandler.IsReusable
      Get
        Return (False)
      End Get
    End Property  'IsReusable

    '*************************************************************************
    '
    '    ROUTINE: ProcessRequest
    '
    '    DESCRIPTION: This routine provides the processing for the http request.
    '                 It is responsible for reading the file from the local
    '                 file system and writing it to the response object.
    '-------------------------------------------------------------------------
    Public Sub ProcessRequest(ByVal context As HttpContext) _
      Implements IHttpHandler.ProcessRequest

      Dim file As FileInfo
      Dim filename As String

      'get the filename from the querystring
      filename = context.Request.QueryString(QS_FILENAME)

      'get the file data since the length is required for the download
      file = New FileInfo(context.Server.MapPath(DOWNLOAD_FOLDER) & "\" & _
                      filename)

      'write it to the browser
      context.Response.Clear()
      context.Response.AddHeader("Content-Disposition", _
                          "attachment; filename=" & filename)
      context.Response.AddHeader("Content-Length", _
                          file.Length.ToString())
      context.Response.ContentType = "application/octet-stream"
      context.Response.WriteFile(file.FullName)
      context.Response.End()
    End Sub  'ProcessRequest
  End Class  'FileDownloadHandlerVB
End Namespace
```

Example 17-9. File download HTTP handler (.cs)

```
//---------------------------------------------------------------------------
//
//    Module Name: FileDownloadHandlerCS
//
//    Description: This class provides a file download handler as an HTTP
//                 handler.
//
//***************************************************************************
using System;
using System.IO;
using System.Web;

namespace ASPNetCookbook.CSExamples.HttpHandlers
{
  public class FileDownloadHandlerCS : IHttpHandler
  {
    // The following constant is used in the URL used to access this handler
    // to define the file to download
    public const string QS_FILENAME = "Filename";


    //the following constant defines the folder containing downloadable files
    private const string DOWNLOAD_FOLDER = "Downloads";

    //***************************************************************************
    //
    //    ROUTINE: IsReusable
    //
    //    DESCRIPTION: This property defines whether another HTTP handler can
    //                 reuse this instance of the handler.
    //
    //        NOTE: false is always returned since this handler is synchronous
    //              and is not pooled.
    //---------------------------------------------------------------------------
    public bool IsReusable
    {
      get
      {
        return(false);
      }
    }  // IsReusable

    //***************************************************************************
    //
    //    ROUTINE: ProcessRequest
    //
    //    DESCRIPTION: This routine provides the processing for the http
    //                 request. It is responsible for reading image data from
    //                 the database and writing it to the response object.
    //---------------------------------------------------------------------------
    public void ProcessRequest(HttpContext context)
    {
      FileInfo file = null;
```

Example 17-9. File download HTTP handler (.cs) (continued)

```
    string filename = null;

    // get the filename from the querystring
    filename = context.Request.QueryString[QS_FILENAME];

    // get the file data since the length is required for the download
    file = new FileInfo(context.Server.MapPath(DOWNLOAD_FOLDER) + "\\" +
                        filename);

    // write it to the browser
    context.Response.Clear( );
    context.Response.AddHeader("Content-Disposition",
                               "attachment; filename=" + filename);
    context.Response.AddHeader("Content-Length",
                               file.Length.ToString( ));
    context.Response.ContentType = "application/octet-stream";
    context.Response.WriteFile(file.FullName);
    context.Response.End( );
  } // ProcessRequest
} // FileDownloadHandlerCS
}
```

Example 17-10. Using the file download HTTP handler (.aspx)

```
<%@ Page Language="vb" AutoEventWireup="false"
    Codebehind="CH17TestHTTPFileDownloadHandlerVB.aspx.vb"
    Inherits="ASPNetCookbook.VBExamples.CH17TestHTTPFileDownloadHandlerVB" %>
<!DOCTYPE HTML PUBLIC "-//W3C//DTD HTML 4.0 Transitional//EN">
<html>
  <head>
    <title>Test HTTP File Download Handler</title>
    <link rel="stylesheet" href="css/ASPNetCookbook.css">
  </head>
  <body leftmargin="0" marginheight="0" marginwidth="0" topmargin="0">
    <form id="frmTestFileDownloadHandler" method="post" runat="server">
      <table width="100%" cellpadding="0" cellspacing="0" border="0">
        <tr>
          <td align="center">
            <img src="images/ASPNETCookbookHeading_blue.gif">
          </td>
        </tr>
        <tr>
          <td class="dividerLine">
            <img src="images/spacer.gif" height="6" border="0"></td>
        </tr>
      </table>
      <table width="90%" align="center" border="0">
        <tr>
          <td align="center"> </td>
        </tr>
        <tr>
          <td align="center" class="PageHeading">
```

Example 17-10. Using the file download HTTP handler (.aspx) (continued)

```
              HTTP Handler For File Downloads (VB)
          </td>
        </tr>
        <tr>
          <td><img src="images/spacer.gif" height="10" border="0"></td>
        </tr>
        <tr>
          <td align="center" class="SubHeading">
            Click the link below to download the sample file using
            an HTTP Handler<br />
            <br />
            <a id="anDownload" runat="server" ></a>
          </td>
        </tr>
      </table>
    </form>
  </body>
</html>
```

Example 17-11. Using the file download HTTP handler code-behind (.vb)

```
Option Explicit On
Option Strict On
'-----------------------------------------------------------------------------
'
'   Module Name: CH17TestHTTPFileDownloadHandlerVB.aspx.vb
'
'   Description: This module CH17TestHTTPFileDownloadHandlerVB the code-behind
'                for the CH17TestHTTPFileDownloadHandlerVB.aspx page.
'
'*****************************************************************************
Imports ASPNetCookbook.VBExamples.HttpHandlers

Namespace ASPNetCookbook.VBExamples
  Public Class CH17TestHTTPFileDownloadHandlerVB
    Inherits System.Web.UI.Page

    'controls on the form
    Protected anDownload As System.Web.UI.HtmlControls.HtmlAnchor

    '*****************************************************************************
    '
    '   ROUTINE: Page_Load
    '
    '   DESCRIPTION: This routine provides the event handler for the page load
    '                event.  It is responsible for initializing the controls
    '                on the page.
    '-----------------------------------------------------------------------------
    Private Sub Page_Load(ByVal sender As System.Object, _
                          ByVal e As System.EventArgs) Handles MyBase.Load

      Const FILE_TO_DOWNLOAD As String = "SampleDownload.txt"
```

Example 17-11. Using the file download HTTP handler code-behind (.vb) (continued)

```
        'set the text and href of the download anchor
        anDownload.InnerText = FILE_TO_DOWNLOAD
        anDownload.HRef = "FileDownloadHandlerVB.aspx?" & _
                          FileDownloadHandlerVB.QS_FILENAME & "=" & _
                          FILE_TO_DOWNLOAD
    End Sub  'Page_Load
  End Class  'HTTPFileDownloadHandlerDemo_VB
End Namespace
```

Example 17-12. Using the file download HTTP handler code-behind (.cs)

```
//-----------------------------------------------------------------------------
//
//   Module Name: CH17TestHTTPFileDownloadHandlerCS.aspx.cs
//
//   Description: This module provides the code behind for the
//                CH17TestHTTPFileDownloadHandlerCS.aspx page
//
//*****************************************************************************
using ASPNetCookbook.CSExamples.HttpHandlers;
using System;

namespace ASPNetCookbook.CSExamples
{
  public class CH17TestHTTPFileDownloadHandlerCS : System.Web.UI.Page
  {
    // controls on the form
    protected System.Web.UI.HtmlControls.HtmlAnchor anDownload;

    //*************************************************************************
    //
    //   ROUTINE: Page_Load
    //
    //   DESCRIPTION: This routine provides the event handler for the page
    //                load event.  It is responsible for initializing the
    //                controls on the page.
    //-------------------------------------------------------------------------
    private void Page_Load(object sender, System.EventArgs e)
    {
      const string FILE_TO_DOWNLOAD = "SampleDownload.txt";

      // set the text and href of the download anchor
      anDownload.InnerText = FILE_TO_DOWNLOAD;
      anDownload.HRef = "FileDownloadHandlerCS.aspx?" +
                        FileDownloadHandlerCS.QS_FILENAME + "=" +
                        FILE_TO_DOWNLOAD;
    } // Page_Load
  } // CH17TestHTTPFileDownloadHandlerCS
}
```

CHAPTER 18

Assorted Tips

18.0 Introduction

This chapter contains an assortment of recipes that don't fit conveniently into the other chapters of the book. If there is a common theme among them, it is that they illustrate that the .NET Framework's class library—specifically the classes that support ASP.NET—is much more expansive than you might expect. Indeed, it is not overstating the case to say that ASP.NET provides the functionality to support most everything an application needs. You just have to be willing to dig deep enough to find it.

18.1 Accessing HTTP-Specific Information from Within a Class

Problem

You want to create a business service class that can be used by any page in your site, and you want it to have access to the HTTP-specific information available in web pages—that is, all the server objects used by the application.

Solution

Add a reference to the System.Web assembly in your business service project and a companion Imports statement (or using statement in C#) to your class, and then use the Current property of the HttpContext object to access the desired server objects.

In the business service class, use the .NET language of your choice to:

1. Add a reference to System.Web.
2. Import the System.Web namespace.
3. Reference the current HTTP context when accessing server objects, as in HTTPContext.Current.Session.

Examples 18-1 and 18-2 show the VB and C# class files for an example business service that implements this solution.

Discussion

By referencing the Current property of the HttpContext object in the business class, your code has full access to all the server objects used in web applications. This includes the ability to access all information about the request being made, the response being returned, session data, and application data. For more information, refer to the HttpContext class in the MSDN documentation.

When you create an ASP.NET application with Visual Studio .NET, all the pages and classes of the web project have access to the HTTP-specific information. This is because Visual Studio automatically adds a reference to System.Web when you create the project. When you create a Class Library project, the technique commonly used to create reusable assemblies, Visual Studio does not automatically add the reference to System.Web. You can easily do so manually, however, by right-clicking the project in the Solution Explorer and then selecting Add Reference from the context menu. When the Add Reference dialog box appears, choose the *System.Web.dll* component from the .NET tab.

If you are not using Visual Studio for your project, you can add the reference as part of the compile command. The following fragments show how we do this for our example:

VB
```
vbc /target:library /reference:System.Web.dll /out:BusinessService.dll
   BusinessService.vb
```

C#
```
csc /target:library /reference:System.Web.dll /out:BusinessService.dll
   BusinessService.cs
```

In the class requiring access to the HTTP-specific information, add an Imports statement (or using statement in C#) for the System.Web assembly. Adding this statement imports the namespace and provides access to the HTTP objects without having to fully qualify each reference to the object, making the code more readable and easier to maintain. The difference in access methods is shown here:

VB
```
'access to the Session object when Imports statement is included
value = CStr(HttpContext.Current.Session("someData"))

'access to the Session object when the Imports statement is NOT included
value = CStr(System.Web.HttpContext.Current.Session("someData"))
```

C#
```
// access to the Session object when Imports statement is included
value = (string)(HttpContext.Current.Session["someData"]);

// access to the Session object when the Imports statement is NOT included
value = (string)(System.Web.HttpContext.Current.Session["someData"]);
```

By adding the reference and Imports (or using) statement to your business service projects, your code now has full access to all the server objects used in web applications.

 Providing access to the server objects in your business classes is useful and necessary for some services, but it should not be universally applied. When your business service requires access to the HTTP-specific information, it can no longer be used in non-web applications, reducing its reusability.

See Also

HttpContext class documentation in the MSDN Library

Example 18-1. Accessing HTTP-specific information (.vb)

```
Imports System.Web

Public Class BusinessService

   Public Sub doSomething()
      Dim value As String

      value = CStr(HttpContext.Current.Session("someData"))

      'use the data from session as required
   End Sub
End Class   'BusinessService
```

Example 18-2. Accessing HTTP-specific information (.cs)

```
using System.Web;

namespace CSMisc
{
   public class BusinessService
   {
      public BusinessService()
      {
         string value;

         value = (string)(HttpContext.Current.Session["someData"]);

         // use the data from session as required
      }
   }
}
```

18.2 Executing External Applications

Problem

You need to run an external application from your web application to perform a required operation.

Solution

Use the System.Diagnostics.Process.Start method to call your external application.

In the code-behind class for the page, use the .NET language of your choice to:

1. Import the System.Diagnostics namespace.
2. Create a ProcessStartInfo object, passing the name of the external application to run along with any required command-line parameters.
3. Set the working directory to the location of the external application.
4. Start the external application process by calling the Start method of the Process class, passing the ProcessStartInfo object.

Examples 18-3 and 18-4 show the relevant portion of the sample VB and C# code-behind files that illustrate this solution.

Discussion

Applications frequently must interface with other applications or systems that use different technologies. At the same time, it is not always practical to migrate these applications to the new platforms or to provide web service wrappers to gain access to the applications. Sometimes, the only practical solution is to execute another program to perform the required operation. For example, you may have an existing application that exports data from your Cobol accounting program to a format usable by other systems. The common language runtime (CLR) provides a set of classes to support running other applications from within the .NET environment. These classes are part of the System.Diagnostics assembly.

The first step to running an external application from within ASP.NET applications is to create a ProcessStartInfo object, and to pass it the name of the application to run along with any command-line parameters it might require. In our example, we use the Java runtime to execute a Java program called AJavaProgram. In our case, the name of the application to run is *java* and the name of the Java program to run, *AJavaProgram*, is the only command-line parameter required.

```
VB
        si = New ProcessStartInfo("java", _
                            "AJavaProgram")
```

```
C#
        si = new ProcessStartInfo("java",
                            "AJavaProgram");
```

Next, the working directory is set to the location of the Java application. For this example, the Java application (`AJavaProgram.class`) is located in the root directory of the ASP.NET application, so `Server.MapPath` is passed "." to get the fully qualified path to the root directory:

VB
```
si.WorkingDirectory = Server.MapPath(".")
```

C#
```
si.WorkingDirectory = Server.MapPath(".");
```

The application is then started by calling the `Start` method of the `Process` class passing the `ProcessStartInfo` object containing the application information. The `Start` method is shared (or static), which does not require instantiating a `Process` object.

VB
```
proc = Process.Start(si)
```

C#
```
proc = Process.Start(si);
```

To wait for the process to complete before continuing execution of the ASP.NET application, the `WaitForExit` method is called, optionally passing a maximum time to wait. Once the `WaitForExit` method is called, page execution is paused until the process completes or the timeout occurs. If you do not need to wait on the process to complete, it is not necessary to call the `WaitForExit` method.

VB
```
proc.WaitForExit( )
```

C#
```
proc.WaitForExit( );
```

> If the process takes longer to complete than the passed timeout value, the process is not terminated; it will continue until completion. If you do not want the process to continue executing, your application can terminate it by calling the `kill` method of the process object.

By default, external applications are run using the ASPNET user account. As a result, you may need to change the permissions for the ASPNET account depending on the operations the external application performs. Take care when giving the ASPNET user additional permissions to avoid creating security problems on your server.

> The user account used by ASP.NET is defined in the `userName` attribute of the `processModel` element in the *machine.config* file. By default, the `userName` attribute is set to "machine", which is a special username indicating the ASPNET user. The `userName` can be set to any local or domain username that you want ASP.NET to run under.

Example 18-3. Running an external application (.vb)

```
Private Sub Page_Load(ByVal sender As System.Object, _
                      ByVal e As System.EventArgs) Handles MyBase.Load
  Dim proc As Process
  Dim si As ProcessStartInfo
```

Example 18-3. Running an external application (.vb) (continued)

```
    'create a new start information object with the program to execute
    'and the command line parameters
    si = New ProcessStartInfo("java", _
                        "AJavaProgram")

    'set the working directory where the legacy program is located
    si.WorkingDirectory = Server.MapPath(".")

    'start a new process using the start information object
    proc = Process.Start(si)

    'wait for process to complete before continuing
    proc.WaitForExit()
End Sub    'Page_Load
```

Example 18-4. Running an external application (.cs)

```
private void Page_Load(object sender, System.EventArgs e)
{
    Process proc = null;
    ProcessStartInfo si = null;

    // create a new start information object with the program to execute
    // and the command line parameters
    si = new ProcessStartInfo("java",
                        "AJavaProgram");

    // set the working directory where the legacy program is located
    si.WorkingDirectory = Server.MapPath(".");

    // start a new process using the start information object
    proc = Process.Start(si);

    // wait for process to complete before continuing
    proc.WaitForExit();
}   // Page_Load
```

18.3   Transforming XML to HTML

Problem

The content for your application is in XML format, and you need to transform it to HTML for display in a browser.

Solution

Use an ASP.NET XML control and set its DocumentSource property to the XML document you need to transform and the TransformSource property to the XSLT document that specifies the transformation to be performed.

In the *.aspx* file, place an asp:Xml control where you want the HTML from the transformation to be placed in the page.

In the code-behind class for the page, use the .NET language of your choice to:

1. Set the DocumentSource property of the XML control to the relative path to the XML document to convert.

2. Set the TransformSource property to the relative path to the XSLT document.

Examples 18-5 through 18-7 show the *.aspx* file and VB and C# code-behind files for an application that demonstrates this solution. The XML used as the source is shown in Example 18-8, and the XSLT used to transform the XML is shown in Example 18-9. The output transformed to HTML is shown in Figure 18-1.

ASP.NET Cookbook
The Ultimate ASP.NET Code Sourcebook

Transform XML To HTML (VB)

Title	ISBN	Publisher
Access Cookbook	0-596-00084-7	O'Reilly
Perl Cookbook	1-565-92243-3	O'Reilly
Java Cookbook	0-596-00170-3	O'Reilly
JavaScript Application Cookbook	1-565-92577-7	O'Reilly
VB .Net Language in a Nutshell	0-596-00092-8	O'Reilly
Programming Visual Basic .Net	0-596-00093-6	O'Reilly
Programming C#	0-596-00117-7	O'Reilly
.Net Framework Essentials	0-596-00165-7	O'Reilly
COM and .Net Component Services	0-596-00103-7	O'Reilly

Figure 18-1. Transforming XML to HTML output

Discussion

XML is quickly becoming the predominant format for storing content. XML provides a platform-independent format that can easily be converted to many other formats, including HTML. By storing the content for your web application in XML, the same content can be transformed to the HTML needed for display in a standard browser or the HTML needed for a PDA.

In our example to illustrate this problem, an XML document containing book information (Example 18-8) is transformed into an HTML table using an XSLT document (Example 18-9). The transformation is performed by an Xml server control.

When you use an Xml control to do the work, you need to set only two of its properties to convert XML to HTML. The DocumentSource property needs to be set to the relative path to the XML document to convert, and the TransformSource property needs to be set to the relative path to the XSLT document, as we have done in our example.

 Most controls that use files require a fully qualified name of the file on the web server. However, the Xml control requires a relative path from the root folder of the web site to the XML and XSLT files. Setting the properties to fully qualified paths will result in an exception being thrown.

VB
```
xmlTransform.DocumentSource = "xml/books.xml"
xmlTransform.TransformSource = "xml/books.xslt"
```

C#
```
xmlTransform.DocumentSource = "xml//books.xml";
xmlTransform.TransformSource = "xml//books.xslt";
```

The majority of the work to perform an XSL transformation is in the creation of the XSLT. An XSLT document is a specially formatted XML document and, as such, requires a declaration defining the version of XML and the encoding of the document. In addition, elements indicating that the document is an XSL stylesheet and defining the output method are required, as shown here:

```
<?xml version="1.0" encoding="UTF-8"?>
<xsl:stylesheet version="1.0" xmlns:xsl="http://www.w3.org/1999/XSL/Transform">
  <xsl:output method="xml" version="1.0" encoding="UTF-8" indent="yes"/>

    ...

</xsl:stylesheet>
```

In XSLT, templates are used to replace specific content in the XML document with the template defined in an xsl:template element. In our example, two templates are used. The first template defines the base structure of the HTML table that will be used to display the XML content when it is converted to HTML, as shown here:

```
<!-- output main table with header row -->
<xsl:template match="Root">
  <table width="80%" border="1" cellspacing="0" cellpadding="4">
    <tr class="TableHeader" bgcolor="#000080">
      <td width="50%" align="center">Title</td>
      <td width="25%" align="center">ISBN</td>
      <td width="25%" align="center">Publisher</td>
    </tr>
    <xsl:apply-templates select="Book"/>
  </table>
</xsl:template>
```

This template also instructs the conversion to apply additional templates using the Book element of the XML document as a source for the data.

```
<xsl:apply-templates select="Book"/>
```

The xsl:apply-templates element is roughly equivalent to a for loop that would iterate through each Book element in the XML document applying our second template, as shown here:

```
<!-- output a row in the table for each Book node in the XML document -->
<xsl:template match="Book">
  <tr class="TableCellNormal" bgcolor="#ffffe0">
    <td width="50%">
      <xsl:value-of select="Title"/>
    </td>
    <td width="25%" align="center">
      <xsl:value-of select="ISBN"/>
    </td>
    <td width="25%" align="center">
      <xsl:value-of select="Publisher"/>
    </td>
  </tr>
</xsl:template>
```

This template generates a row for the base HTML table for each Book element in the XML document. Each cell in the table contains an xsl:value-of element that instructs the transformation to insert the value of the element indicated by the select attribute in the cell.

XSLT is very powerful and can be used to perform very complex transformations, including transformations that dynamically vary according to passed parameters, and is not limited to converting XML to HTML. To learn the techniques of XSLT, these books are highly recommended: *XSLT* and the *XSLT Cookbook*, both from O'Reilly.

See Also

XSLT, by Doug Tidwell (O'Reilly); *XSLT Cookbook*, by Sal Mangano (O'Reilly)

Example 18-5. Transforming XML to HTML (.aspx)

```
<%@ Page Language="vb" AutoEventWireup="false"
        Codebehind="CH18TransformingXMLToHTMLVB.aspx.vb"
        Inherits="ASPNetCookbook.VBExamples.CH18TransformingXMLToHTMLVB" %>
<!DOCTYPE HTML PUBLIC "-//W3C//DTD HTML 4.0 Transitional//EN">
<html>
  <head>
    <title>Transforming XML To HTML</title>
    <link rel="stylesheet" href="css/ASPNetCookbook.css">
  </head>
  <body leftmargin="0" marginheight="0" marginwidth="0" topmargin="0">
    <form id="frmTransformXML" method="post" runat="server" >
      <table width="100%" cellpadding="0" cellspacing="0" border="0">
        <tr>
          <td align="center">
            <img src="images/ASPNETCookbookHeading_blue.gif">
          </td>
        </tr>
```

Example 18-5. Transforming XML to HTML (.aspx) (continued)

```
      <tr>
        <td class="dividerLine">
          <img src="images/spacer.gif" height="6" border="0"></td>
      </tr>
    </table>
    <table width="90%" align="center" border="0">
      <tr>
        <td><img src="images/spacer.gif" height="10" border="0"></td>
      </tr>
      <tr>
        <td align="center" class="PageHeading">
          Transform XML To HTML (VB)
        </td>
      </tr>
      <tr>
        <td><img src="images/spacer.gif" height="10" border="0"></td>
      </tr>
      <tr>
        <td align="center" class="MenuItem">
          <asp:Xml ID="xmlTransform" Runat="server" />
        </td>
      </tr>
    </table>
  </form>
  </body>
</html>
```

Example 18-6. Transforming XML to HTML code-behind (.vb)

```
Option Explicit On
Option Strict On
'----------------------------------------------------------------------------
'
'   Module Name: CH18TransformingXMLToHTMLVB.aspx.vb
'
'   Description: This module provides the code behind for the
'                CH18TransformingXMLToHTMLVB.aspx page
'
'****************************************************************************
Imports System

Namespace ASPNetCookbook.VBExamples
  Public Class CH18TransformingXMLToHTMLVB
    Inherits System.Web.UI.Page

    'controls on the form
    Protected xmlTransform As System.Web.UI.WebControls.Xml

    '****************************************************************************
    '
    '   ROUTINE: Page_Load
    '
```

Example 18-6. Transforming XML to HTML code-behind (.vb) (continued)

```vb
'   DESCRIPTION: This routine provides the event handler for the page load
'               event.  It is responsible for initializing the controls
'               on the page.
'----------------------------------------------------------------------
Private Sub Page_Load(ByVal sender As System.Object, _
                      ByVal e As System.EventArgs) Handles MyBase.Load

    'set the names of the XML and XSLT documents used in the
    'transformation
    xmlTransform.DocumentSource = "xml/books.xml"
    xmlTransform.TransformSource = "xml/books.xslt"
    End Sub 'Page_Load
  End Class 'CH18TransformingXMLToHTMLVB
End Namespace
```

Example 18-7. Transforming XML to HTML code-behind (.cs)

```csharp
//----------------------------------------------------------------------
//
//   Module Name: CH18TransformingXMLToHTMLCS.aspx.cs
//
//   Description: This module provides the code behind for the
//                CH18TransformingXMLToHTMLCS.aspx page
//
//**********************************************************************
using System;

namespace ASPNetCookbook.CSExamples
{
  public class CH18TransformingXMLToHTMLCS : System.Web.UI.Page
  {
    // controls on the page
    protected System.Web.UI.WebControls.Xml xmlTransform;

    //******************************************************************
    //
    //   ROUTINE: Page_Load
    //
    //   DESCRIPTION: This routine provides the event handler for the page
    //                load event.  It is responsible for initializing the
    //                controls on the page.
    //------------------------------------------------------------------
    private void Page_Load(object sender, System.EventArgs e)
    {
      // set the names of the XML and XSLT documents used in the
      // transformation
      xmlTransform.DocumentSource = "xml//books.xml";
      xmlTransform.TransformSource = "xml//books.xslt";
    }  // Page_Load
  }  // CH18TransformingXMLToHTMLCS
}
```

Example 18-8. XML source used for transformation

```
<Root>
  <Book>
    <BookID>1</BookID>
    <Title>Access Cookbook</Title>
    <ISBN>0-596-00084-7</ISBN>
    <Publisher>O'Reilly</Publisher>
  </Book>
  <Book>
    <BookID>2</BookID>
    <Title>Perl Cookbook</Title>
    <ISBN>1-565-92243-3</ISBN>
    <Publisher>O'Reilly</Publisher>
  </Book>
  <Book>
    <BookID>3</BookID>
    <Title>Java Cookbook</Title>
    <ISBN>0-596-00170-3</ISBN>
    <Publisher>O'Reilly</Publisher>
  </Book>
  <Book>
    <BookID>4</BookID>
    <Title>JavaScript Application Cookbook</Title>
    <ISBN>1-565-92577-7</ISBN>
    <Publisher>O'Reilly</Publisher>
  </Book>
  <Book>
    <BookID>5</BookID>
    <Title>VB .Net Language in a Nutshell</Title>
    <ISBN>0-596-00092-8</ISBN>
    <Publisher>O'Reilly</Publisher>
  </Book>
  <Book>
    <BookID>6</BookID>
    <Title>Programming Visual Basic .Net</Title>
    <ISBN>0-596-00093-6</ISBN>
    <Publisher>O'Reilly</Publisher>
  </Book>
  <Book>
    <BookID>7</BookID>
    <Title>Programming C#</Title>
    <ISBN>0-596-00117-7</ISBN>
    <Publisher>O'Reilly</Publisher>
  </Book>
  <Book>
    <BookID>8</BookID>
    <Title>.Net Framework Essentials</Title>
    <ISBN>0-596-00165-7</ISBN>
    <Publisher>O'Reilly</Publisher>
  </Book>
  <Book>
    <BookID>9</BookID>
    <Title>COM and .Net Component Services</Title>
```

Example 18-8. XML source used for transformation (continued)

```
    <ISBN>0-596-00103-7</ISBN>
    <Publisher>O'Reilly</Publisher>
  </Book>
</Root>
```

Example 18-9. XSLT used to transform HTML

```
<?xml version="1.0" encoding="UTF-8"?>
<xsl:stylesheet version="1.0" xmlns:xsl="http://www.w3.org/1999/XSL/Transform">
  <xsl:output method="xml" version="1.0" encoding="UTF-8" indent="yes"/>

  <!-- output main table with header row -->
  <xsl:template match="Root">
    <table width="80%" border="1" cellspacing="0" cellpadding="4" align="center">
      <tr class="TableHeader" bgcolor="#000080">
        <td width="50%" align="center" >Title</td>
        <td width="25%" align="center" >ISBN</td>
        <td width="25%" align="center" >Publisher</td>
      </tr>
      <xsl:apply-templates select="Book" />
    </table>
  </xsl:template>

  <!-- output a row in the table for each Book node in the XML document -->
  <xsl:template match="Book" >
    <tr class="TableCellNormal" bgcolor="#FFFFE0">
    <td width="50%"><xsl:value-of select="Title"/></td>
    <td width="25%" align="center"><xsl:value-of select="ISBN" /></td>
    <td width="25%" align="center"><xsl:value-of select="Publisher" /></td>
    </tr>
  </xsl:template>
</xsl:stylesheet>
```

18.4   Determining the User's Browser Type

Problem

Your application requires the use of a specific browser and you want to determine whether the required browser is being used before allowing a user to access your application.

Solution

Use the properties of the Request.Browser object to determine the browser type and version, and then take the action required by your application.

In the code-behind class for the page, use the .NET language of your choice to:

1. Use the Browser property of the Request.Browser object to return a string representing the full browser type, such as "IE" in the case of Internet Explorer.

2. Use the `Version` property of the `Request.Browser` object to return a string that represents the major and minor version of the browser, such as "6.0" in the case of IE 6.0.

3. Take action accordingly, such as outputting a message indicating whether the user's browser is compatible with the application.

Examples 18-10 through 18-12 show the *.aspx* file and the VB and C# code-behind files for an application that demonstrates the solution. The output of our example program is shown in Figure 18-2.

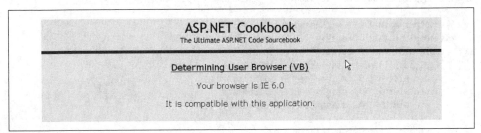

Figure 18-2. Determining the user's browser

Discussion

With the variety of different browsers in use today and the significant variation in their capabilities, it is not uncommon to need to determine the type of browser being used. Then, based on the browser, you may need to inform the user that the browser is incompatible with your application or output different HTML to support the specific browser.

Our example demonstrates the functionality provided in ASP.NET to determine the browser type and version, and then output this information along with a message indicating whether the user's browser is compatible with the application. The *.aspx* file contains two asp:Literal controls used to output messages to the user. The first outputs the browser version information, and the second informs the user whether his browser is compatible with the application.

In the Page_Load method of the code-behind, the Browser and Version properties of the Request.Browser object are used to create a message to inform the user of the detected browser version. The Browser property returns a string such as "IE", "Netscape", "Opera", etc. The Version property returns a string that represents the major and minor version of the browser. For Internet Explorer 6.0, for instance, the Browser property will return "IE" and the Version property will return "6.0".

Next, the browser type and major version number are compared to the minimum requirements for the application (IE and Version 5). If the browser is IE 5.0 or later, a message is displayed indicating the browser is compatible with the application. Otherwise, a message is displayed indicating the application requires IE 5.0 or later.

For your application, you might want to check the browser version on the home page. If the browser is compatible with your application, output the home page normally. Otherwise, redirect the user to a message page indicating the browser requirements.

The Request.Browser object contains many properties not used in this example but that may be useful in your application. Table 18-1 lists some of the commonly used properties. For a complete list of the available properties, refer to the documentation on the HttpBrowserCapabilities class in the MSDN Library.

Table 18-1. Commonly used browser object properties

Property	Description
Browser	Returns a string indicating the browser type (IE, Netscape, Opera, etc.)
Cookies	Returns a Boolean value indicating whether the browser supports cookies
JavaScript	Returns a Boolean value indicating whether the browser supports JavaScript
MajorVersion	Returns an integer value indicating the major version of the browser (integer portion of the browser version)
MinorVersion	Returns an double value indicating the minor version of the browser (decimal portion of the browser version)
Version	Returns a string representing the full browser version (integer and decimal portion)

> Properties that return Boolean values, such as Cookies and JavaScript, indicate what the browser is capable of supporting but not necessarily the current configuration. If the browser supports cookies but the user has configured the browser to disable cookies, the Cookies property will still return true.

See Also

HttpBrowserCapabilities documentation in the MSDN Library

Example 18-10. Determining the user browser type (.aspx)

```
<%@ Page Language="vb" AutoEventWireup="false"
        Codebehind="CH18DeterminingBrowserVB.aspx.vb"
        Inherits="ASPNetCookbook.VBExamples.CH18DeterminingBrowserVB" %>
<!DOCTYPE HTML PUBLIC "-//W3C//DTD HTML 4.0 Transitional//EN">
<html>
  <head>
    <title>Determining Browser</title>
    <link rel="stylesheet" href="css/ASPNetCookbook.css">
  </head>
  <body leftmargin="0" marginheight="0" marginwidth="0" topmargin="0">
    <form id="frmDetermineBrowser" method="post" runat="server" >
      <table width="100%" cellpadding="0" cellspacing="0" border="0">
        <tr>
          <td align="center">
            <img src="images/ASPNETCookbookHeading_blue.gif">
```

Example 18-10. Determining the user browser type (.aspx) (continued)

```
          </td>
        </tr>
        <tr>
          <td class="dividerLine">
            <img src="images/spacer.gif" height="6" border="0"></td>
        </tr>
      </table>
      <table width="90%" align="center" border="0">
        <tr>
          <td><img src="images/spacer.gif" height="10" border="0"></td>
        </tr>
        <tr>
          <td align="center" class="PageHeading">
            Determining User Browser (VB)
          </td>
        </tr>
        <tr>
          <td><img src="images/spacer.gif" height="10" border="0"></td>
        </tr>
        <tr>
          <td align="center" class="MenuItem">
            <asp:Literal ID="litBrowser" Runat="server" />
            <br /><br />
            <asp:Literal ID="litMessage" Runat="server" />
          </td>
        </tr>
      </table>
    </form>
  </body>
</html>
```

Example 18-11. Determining the user browser type code-behind (.vb)

```
Option Explicit On
Option Strict On
'-----------------------------------------------------------------------------
'
'   Module Name: CH18DeterminingBrowserVB.aspx.vb
'
'   Description: This module provides the code behind for the
'                CH18DeterminingBrowserVB.aspx page
'
'*****************************************************************************
Namespace ASPNetCookbook.VBExamples
  Public Class CH18DeterminingBrowserVB
    Inherits System.Web.UI.Page

    'controls on the form
    Protected litBrowser As System.Web.UI.WebControls.Literal
    Protected litMessage As System.Web.UI.WebControls.Literal
```

Example 18-11. Determining the user browser type code-behind (.vb) (continued)

```vb
'*************************************************************************
'
'    ROUTINE: Page_Load
'
'    DESCRIPTION: This routine provides the event handler for the page load
'                 event.  It is responsible for initializing the controls
'                 on the page.
'------------------------------------------------------------------------
Private Sub Page_Load(ByVal sender As System.Object, _
                      ByVal e As System.EventArgs) Handles MyBase.Load

    'output user browser
    litBrowser.Text = "Your browser is " & _
                      Request.Browser.Browser & " " & _
                      Request.Browser.Version

    'check to see if it is an acceptable version
    If ((Request.Browser.Browser = "IE") AndAlso _
       (Request.Browser.MajorVersion >= 5)) Then
       'output message indicating it is OK
       litMessage.Text = "It is compatible with this application."
    Else
       'output message indicating IE 5 or later must be used
       litMessage.Text = "This application requires IE 5.0 or later."
    End If
  End Sub  'Page_Load
End Class   'CH18DeterminingBrowserVB
End Namespace
```

Example 18-12. Determining the user browser type code-behind (.cs)

```csharp
//----------------------------------------------------------------------------
//
//   Module Name: CH18DeterminingBrowserCS.aspx.cs
//
//   Description: This module provides the code behind for the
//                CH18DeterminingBrowserCS.aspx page
//
using System;

namespace ASPNetCookbook.CSExamples
{
  public class CH18DeterminingBrowserCS : System.Web.UI.Page
  {
    // controls on the form
    protected System.Web.UI.WebControls.Literal litBrowser;
    protected System.Web.UI.WebControls.Literal litMessage;

    //*************************************************************************
    //
    //   ROUTINE: Page_Load
    //
```

```
//    DESCRIPTION: This routine provides the event handler for the page
//                 load event.  It is responsible for initializing the
//                 controls on the page.
//-------------------------------------------------------------------------
private void Page_Load(object sender, System.EventArgs e)
{
  // output user browser
  litBrowser.Text = "Your browser is " +
                    Request.Browser.Browser + " " +
                    Request.Browser.Version;

  // check to see if it is an acceptable version
  if ((Request.Browser.Browser == "IE") &
      (Request.Browser.MajorVersion >= 5))
  {
    // output message indicating it is OK
    litMessage.Text = "It is compatible with this application.";
  }
  else
  {
    // output message indicating IE 5 or later must be used
    litMessage.Text = "This application requires IE 5.0 or later.";
  }
} // Page_Load
} // CH18DeterminingBrowserCS
}
```

18.5   Dynamically Creating Browser-Specific Stylesheets

Problem

You need to vary the look and feel of your application pages depending on the platform (Mac or Windows) that is being used.

Solution

Place an asp:Literal control in the head section of the *.aspx* file, and then set the text property of the control to an HTML style element created programmatically in the code-behind. Use the properties of the Request.Browser object to determine the platform type and control the generation of the style element.

In the *.aspx* file, place an asp:Literal control in the head section.

In the code-behind class for the page, use the .NET language of your choice to:

1. Use the Platform property of the Request.Browser object to obtain the browser's platform.

2. Check the platform string for the presence of the substring, such as "mac", which indicates whether the browser is running on a Mac platform.

3. Based on the platform, programmatically create the HTML style element.

4. Set the Text property of the asp:Literal control in the head section of the *.aspx* file to the created HTML style elements.

The *.aspx* file used for this example is shown in Example 18-13. The code-behind is shown in Example 18-14 (VB) and Example 18-15 (C#).

Discussion

HTML is not always rendered the same. Different browsers and different platforms render the HTML in a variety of ways. This sometimes requires using a different stylesheet as a function of the browser or platform the browser is running on (Windows, Mac, etc.) to get the same visual effect. Refer to the Platform property of the HttpBrowserCapabilities class in the MSDN Library for a complete list of platforms detected.

For instance, the displayed size of a font of a given point size is larger on the Windows platform than on the Mac platform. This is caused by the difference in screen resolution. The Mac platform uses a display resolution of 72 dots/inch (DPI), resulting in 1 point being equivalent to 1 pixel. The Windows platform uses a display resolution of 96 DPI, resulting in 1 point being equivalent to $1^1/3$ pixels. To display a font the same size on both platforms, the point size must change as a function of the platform.

Our example programmatically generates a different stylesheet depending on whether the browser is running on a Windows or a Mac platform. It creates a stylesheet in the HTML that has four classes defined for a small, regular, large, and extra-large font. This technique is not new to ASP.NET, but the method of generating the stylesheet dynamically is much easier. Figure 18-3 shows the output of our example on a PC platform. Figure 18-4 shows the output on a Mac platform without generating a stylesheet specific to the Mac (the fonts are smaller than the ones in Figure 18-3). Figure 18-5 shows the output on a Mac platform using a specific stylesheet (the fonts are the same size as the ones in Figure 18-3).

Server controls can be placed almost anywhere in an *.aspx* file; they are not restricted to the body section of the page. In our example, an asp:Literal control is placed in the head section of the *.aspx* file to provide a mechanism to output a style sheet in the HTML sent to the browser:

```
<head>
    <title>Dynamically Generating Stylesheet</title>

    ...

    <asp:Literal id="litStylesheet" runat="server" />
</head>
```

ASP.NET Cookbook
The Ultimate ASP.NET Code Sourcebook

Dynamically Generating A Stylesheet (VB)

This is the small font.
This is the regular font.
This is the large font.

This is the extra large font.

Figure 18-3. Example program output for PC platform

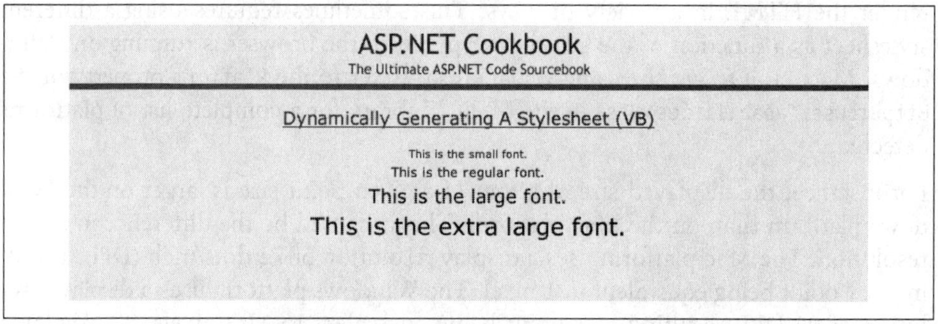

ASP.NET Cookbook
The Ultimate ASP.NET Code Sourcebook

Dynamically Generating A Stylesheet (VB)

This is the small font.
This is the regular font.
This is the large font.
This is the extra large font.

Figure 18-4. Example program output for Mac platform without specific stylesheet

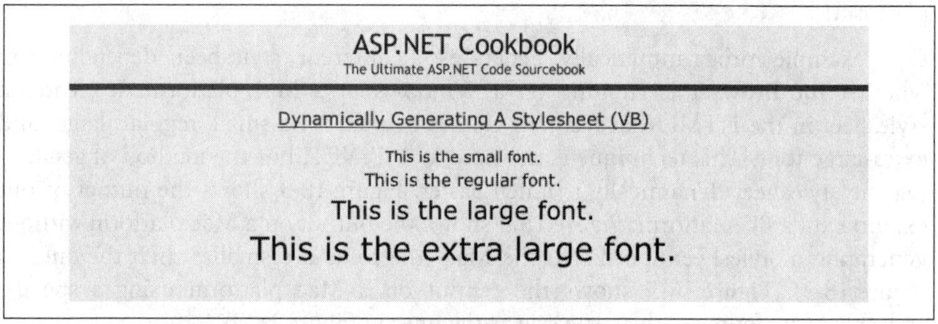

ASP.NET Cookbook
The Ultimate ASP.NET Code Sourcebook

Dynamically Generating A Stylesheet (VB)

This is the small font.
This is the regular font.
This is the large font.

This is the extra large font.

Figure 18-5. Example program output for Mac platform with specific stylesheet

> Any control that returns data when a form is submitted must be within the open and close form elements.

In the Page_Load method of the code-behind, the platform the browser is running on is obtained from the Platform property of the Request.Browser object. The platform name is converted to lowercase to simplify the check for the specific platform.

The platform string is then checked for the presence of the substring "mac", which indicates the browser is running on a Mac platform.

After determining the platform, four variables are set to indicate the point size to use for the small, regular, large, and extra-large fonts.

A StringBuilder is then used to create the HTML style element. The style element includes a class for smallFont, regFont, largeFont, and xLargeFont. Each class contains a font-family style along with a font-size style. The font size is set using the variables described earlier.

Finally, the Text property of the asp:Literal control placed in the head section of the *.aspx* file is set to the style element.

The resulting style element rendered in the HTML for the Windows platform is shown here:

```
<style type='text/css'>
  .smallFont
    {font-family: Verdana, Arial, Helvetica, sans-serif; font-size:8pt;}
  .regFont
    {font-family: Verdana, Arial, Helvetica, sans-serif; font-size:10pt;}
  .largeFont
    {font-family: Verdana, Arial, Helvetica, sans-serif; font-size:14pt;}
  .xLargeFont
    {font-family: Verdana, Arial, Helvetica, sans-serif; font-size:18pt;}
</style>
```

The resulting style element rendered in HTML for the Mac platform is shown here:

```
<style type='text/css'>
  .smallFont
    {font-family: Verdana, Arial, Helvetica, sans-serif; font-size:11pt;}
  .regFont
    {font-family: Verdana, Arial, Helvetica, sans-serif; font-size:13pt;}
  .largeFont
    {font-family: Verdana, Arial, Helvetica, sans-serif; font-size:19pt;}
  .xLargeFont
    {font-family: Verdana, Arial, Helvetica, sans-serif; font-size:24pt;}
</style>
```

The classes in the stylesheet can then be used like any other class that is hardcoded in the HTML or provided in a cascading style sheet (*css*).

```
<tr>
  <td align="center" class="smallFont">
    This is the small font.
  </td>
</tr>
<tr>
  <td align="center" class="regFont">
    This is the regular font.
  </td>
</tr>
<tr>
```

```
    <td align="center" class="largeFont">
       This is the large font.
    </td>
  </tr>
  <tr>
    <td align="center" class="xLargeFont">
       This is the extra large font.
    </td>
  </tr>
```

The solution provided in this recipe can be placed in a user control, giving you the ability to reuse the code in all pages of your application. Refer to Chapter 4 for examples of user controls.

An alternate solution to programmatically generating the stylesheet would be to place a link element in the head section and then set the href attribute to a different pre-built cascading stylesheet as a function of the browser and/or platform. This approach will yield better performance because the stylesheet would not be built for each page request.

To implement the alternate solution, place the following link element in the head section of the *.aspx* file. Be sure to add the / at the end to close the element or an exception will be thrown when ASP.NET parses the page.

```
<link id="linkCSS" runat="server" rel="stylesheet" />
```

Add the following protected reference to the linkCSS control in the code-behind. There is no "Link" server control, so it must be added as a generic HTML control.

VB
```
Protected linkCSS As System.Web.UI.HtmlControls.HtmlGenericControl
```

C#
```
protected System.Web.UI.HtmlControls.HtmlGenericControl linkCSS;
```

In the Page_Load method of the code-behind, add the href attribute to the linkCSS control setting the value to the required cascading stylesheet. The href attribute must be added using the Add method of the Attributes collection, because the generic HTML server control does not have an href property.

VB
```
'check the users platform
platform = Request.Browser.Platform.ToLower()

'set font sizes as a function of the platform
If (platform.IndexOf("mac") > -1) Then
   'platform is a Mac so add Mac CSS
   linkCSS.Attributes.Add("href", _
                          "css/Mac.css")
Else
   'since not a Mac, assume Windows and add Windows CSS
   '(production app may want to do additional checks if
   'required for styles)
   linkCSS.Attributes.Add("href", _
                          "css/Windows.css")
End If
```

```csharp
// check the users platform
platform = Request.Browser.Platform.ToLower();

// set font sizes as a function of the platform
if (platform.IndexOf("mac") > -1)
{
  // platform is a Mac so add Mac CSS
  linkCSS.Attributes.Add("href",
                         "css/Mac.css");
}
else
{
  // since not a Mac, assume Windows and add Windows CSS
  // (production app may want to do additional checks if
  // required for styles)
  linkCSS.Attributes.Add("href",
                         "css/Windows.css");
}
```

The resulting `link` element for the Windows platform is shown next. Note that an href attribute has been added to the rendered HTML, with the value set to the required cascading stylesheet:

```html
<link id="linkCSS" rel="stylesheet" href="Windows.css"></link>
```

The code for this alternate example can be placed in a user control to provide easy reuse in all of the pages in your application. Refer to Chapter 4 for examples of user controls.

See Also

Chapter 4 for user control examples; MSDN Library for more information on the `HttpBrowserCapabilities` class and `Platform` property values

Example 18-13. Dynamically generated stylesheet (.aspx)

```
<%@ Page Language="vb" AutoEventWireup="false"
 Codebehind="CH18DynamicallyGeneratingStyleSheetVB.aspx.vb"
 Inherits="ASPNetCookbook.VBExamples.CH18DynamicallyGeneratingStyleSheetVB" %>
<!DOCTYPE HTML PUBLIC "-//W3C//DTD HTML 4.0 Transitional//EN">
<html>
  <head>
    <title>Dynamically Generating Stylesheet</title>
    <link rel="stylesheet" href="css/ASPNetCookbook.css">
    <asp:Literal id="litStylesheet" runat="server" />
  </head>
  <body leftmargin="0" marginheight="0" marginwidth="0" topmargin="0">
    <form id="frmDynamicStylesheet" method="post" runat="server" >
      <table width="100%" cellpadding="0" cellspacing="0" border="0">
        <tr>
          <td align="center">
            <img src="images/ASPNETCookbookHeading_blue.gif">
          </td>
        </tr>
```

Example 18-13. Dynamically generated stylesheet (.aspx) (continued)

```
        <tr>
          <td class="dividerLine">
            <img src="images/spacer.gif" height="6" border="0"></td>
        </tr>
      </table>
      <table width="90%" align="center" border="0">
        <tr>
          <td><img src="images/spacer.gif" height="10" border="0"></td>
        </tr>
        <tr>
          <td align="center" class="PageHeading">
            Dynamically Generating A Stylesheet (VB)
          </td>
        </tr>
        <tr>
          <td><img src="images/spacer.gif" height="10" border="0"></td>
        </tr>
        <tr>
          <td align="center" class="smallFont">
            This is the small font.
          </td>
        </tr>
        <tr>
          <td align="center" class="regFont">
            This is the regular font.
          </td>
        </tr>
        <tr>
          <td align="center" class="largeFont">
            This is the large font.
          </td>
        </tr>
        <tr>
          <td align="center" class="xLargeFont">
            This is the extra large font.
          </td>
        </tr>
      </table>
    </form>
  </body>
</html>
```

Example 18-14. Dynamically generated stylesheet code-behind (.vb)

```
Option Explicit On
Option Strict On
'-----------------------------------------------------------------------------
'
'   Module Name: CH18DynamicallyGeneratingStyleSheetVB.aspx.vb
'
'   Description: This module provides the code behind for the
'                CH18DynamicallyGeneratingStyleSheetVB.aspx page
'
```

Example 18-14. Dynamically generated stylesheet code-behind (.vb) (continued)

```vb
'*****************************************************************************
Imports System
Imports System.Text

Namespace ASPNetCookbook.VBExamples
  Public Class CH18DynamicallyGeneratingStyleSheetVB
    Inherits System.Web.UI.Page

    'controls on the form
    Protected litStylesheet As System.Web.UI.WebControls.Literal

    '*****************************************************************************
    '
    '   ROUTINE: Page_Load
    '
    '   DESCRIPTION: This routine provides the event handler for the page load
    '                event.  It is responsible for initializing the controls
    '                on the page.
    '----------------------------------------------------------------------------
    Private Sub Page_Load(ByVal sender As System.Object, _
                          ByVal e As System.EventArgs) Handles MyBase.Load

      Const FONT_FAMILY As String = _
        "font-family: Verdana, Arial, Helvetica, sans-serif;"

      Dim platform As String
      Dim smFontSize As String
      Dim regFontSize As String
      Dim largeFontSize As String
      Dim xLargeFontSize As String
      Dim styleTag As StringBuilder

      'check the users platform
      platform = Request.Browser.Platform.ToLower()

      'set font sizes as a function of the platform
      If (platform.IndexOf("mac") > -1) Then
        'platform is a Mac
        smFontSize = "11"
        regFontSize = "13"
        largeFontSize = "19"
        xLargeFontSize = "24"
      Else
        'since not a Mac, assume Windows (production app may want to
        'do additional checks if required for styles)
        smFontSize = "8"
        regFontSize = "10"
        largeFontSize = "14"
        xLargeFontSize = "18"
      End If

      'create style tag
      styleTag = New StringBuilder("<style type='text/css'>" & _
```

Example 18-14. Dynamically generated stylesheet code-behind (.vb) (continued)

```vb
                        Environment.NewLine)

    'output the smallFont class
    styleTag.Append(".smallFont {" & FONT_FAMILY & _
                    " font-size:" & smFontSize & "pt;}" & _
                    Environment.NewLine)

    'output the regFont class
    styleTag.Append(".regFont {" & FONT_FAMILY & _
                    " font-size:" & regFontSize & "pt;}" & _
                    Environment.NewLine)

    'output the largeFont class
    styleTag.Append(".largeFont {" & FONT_FAMILY & _
                    " font-size:" & largeFontSize & "pt;}" & _
                    Environment.NewLine)

    'output the xLargeFont class
    styleTag.Append(".xLargeFont {" & FONT_FAMILY & _
                    " font-size:" & xLargeFontSize & "pt;}" & _
                    Environment.NewLine)

    'close the style tag
    styleTag.Append("</style>" & Environment.NewLine)

    'set literal in Head section to output style sheet
    litStylesheet.Text = styleTag.ToString()
  End Sub  'Page_Load
End Class  'CH18DynamicallyGeneratingStyleSheetVB
End Namespace
```

Example 18-15. Dynamically generated stylesheet code-behind (.cs)

```cs
//-----------------------------------------------------------------------------
//
//    Module Name: CH18DynamicallyGeneratingStyleSheetCS.aspx.cs
//
//    Description: This module provides the code behind for the
//                 CH18DynamicallyGeneratingStyleSheetCS.aspx page
//
//****************************************************************************
using System;
using System.Text;

namespace ASPNetCookbook.CSExamples
{
  public class CH18DynamicallyGeneratingStyleSheetCS : System.Web.UI.Page
  {
    // controls on the form
    protected System.Web.UI.WebControls.Literal litStylesheet;
```

Example 18-15. Dynamically generated stylesheet code-behind (.cs) (continued)

```
//*************************************************************************
//
//   ROUTINE: Page_Load
//
//   DESCRIPTION: This routine provides the event handler for the page
//                load event.  It is responsible for initializing the
//                controls on the page.
//-------------------------------------------------------------------------
private void Page_Load(object sender, System.EventArgs e)
{
  const string FONT_FAMILY =
    "font-family: Verdana, Arial, Helvetica, sans-serif;";

          string platform = null;
  string smFontSize = null;
  string regFontSize = null;
  string largeFontSize = null;
  string xLargeFontSize = null;
  StringBuilder styleTag = null;

  // check the users platform
  platform = Request.Browser.Platform.ToLower();

  // set font sizes as a function of the platform
  if (platform.IndexOf("mac") > -1)
  {
    // platform is a Mac
    smFontSize = "11";
    regFontSize = "13";
    largeFontSize = "19";
    xLargeFontSize = "24";
  }
  else
  {
    // since not a Mac, assume Windows (production app may want to
    // do additional checks if required for styles)
    smFontSize = "8";
    regFontSize = "10";
    largeFontSize = "14";
    xLargeFontSize = "18";
  }

  // create style tag
  styleTag = new StringBuilder("<style type='text/css'>" +
                                Environment.NewLine);

  // output the smallFont class
  styleTag.Append(".smallFont {" + FONT_FAMILY +
                  " font-size:" + smFontSize + "pt;}" +
                  Environment.NewLine);
```

```
    // output the regFont class
    styleTag.Append(".regFont {" + FONT_FAMILY +
                    " font-size:" + regFontSize + "pt;}" +
                    Environment.NewLine);

    // output the largeFont class
    styleTag.Append(".largeFont {" + FONT_FAMILY +
                    " font-size:" + largeFontSize + "pt;}" +
                    Environment.NewLine);

    // output the xLargeFont class
    styleTag.Append(".xLargeFont {" + FONT_FAMILY +
                    " font-size:" + xLargeFontSize + "pt;}" +
                    Environment.NewLine);

    // close the style tag
    styleTag.Append("</style>" + Environment.NewLine);

    // set literal in Head section to output style sheet
    litStylesheet.Text = styleTag.ToString( );
  } // Page_Load
 } // CH18DynamicallyGeneratingStyleSheetCS
}
```

18.6   Saving and Reusing HTML Output

Problem

To improve the performance of pages that rarely change, you want to capture the output of those pages and save it for reuse when the page is requested.

Solution

Create the page that contains the desired content just as you would any other page, including the server controls you need. At the end of the Page_Load method, use the RenderControl method of the Page control to generate the HTML and then save the HTML to a file.

In the code-behind class for the page, use the .NET language of your choice to:

1. Create an HtmlTextWriter to use for rendering the page.

2. Use the RenderControl method of the Page control to render the output of the page to the HtmlTextWriter.

3. Save the rendered output to a file and redirect to another page.

Examples 18-16 and 18-17 show the VB and C# code-behind files for our application that demonstrates this solution.

Discussion

Occasionally, it's beneficial to save the HTML output from a generated page. This is commonly done when using the saved HTML can significantly improve web site performance. If the content of a page is static, for example, there is no point in dynamically generating HTML each time the page is requested. Until the advent of ASP.NET, the only way to save the HTML was to use the "Save as Complete Web Page" feature of Internet Explorer or another browser. Although this method does save the HTML, it also copies all of the page images to the local machine and changes the image references to point to the local copies. If you are trying to improve performance by capturing a static copy of the page to use on your web server, this technique does not work very well.

With ASP.NET you can easily capture the HTML exactly as it would be sent to the browser. For our example that illustrates this solution, we have used the page from Recipe 18.3 and added code to the Page_Load method to save the rendered output.

The RenderControl method of the Page control provides the ability to render the output of the page to the HtmlTextWriter passed to the method. Unfortunately, the HtmlTextWriter does not provide any methods for reading the contents, so a little more work is required to access the rendered HTML.

By first creating a StringBuilder and then using it to create a StringWriter, which is then used to create the required HtmlTextWriter, the contents of the HtmlTextWriter are available by way of the original StringBuilder. This works because the underlying storage mechanism for the StringWriter is a StringBuilder; and because the StringWriter (a stream) is used to create the HtmlTextWriter, the RenderControl method is actually writing the rendered output to the StringBuilder. Our example code to accomplish this is shown here:

VB
```
renderedOutput = New StringBuilder( )
strWriter = New StringWriter(renderedOutput)
tWriter = New HtmlTextWriter(strWriter)
```

C#
```
renderedOutput = new StringBuilder( );
strWriter = new StringWriter(renderedOutput);
tWriter = new HtmlTextWriter(strWriter);
```

After creating the HtmlTextWriter, the RenderControl method of the Page is called to render the HTML for the page:

VB
```
Page.RenderControl(tWriter)
```

C#
```
Page.RenderControl(tWriter);
```

Now that the rendered HTML is available, it needs to be saved to a file on the server. This can be accomplished by creating the file with a FileStream and using a

StreamWriter to write the rendered output in the StringBuilder to the file, as shown here:

VB
```vb
filename = Server.MapPath(".") & "\" & OUTPUT_FILENAME
outputStream = New FileStream(filename, _
                              FileMode.Create)
sWriter = New StreamWriter(outputStream)
sWriter.Write(renderedOutput.ToString())
sWriter.Flush()
```

C#
```csharp
filename = Server.MapPath(".") + "\\" + OUTPUT_FILENAME;
outputStream = new FileStream(filename,
                              FileMode.Create);
sWriter = new StreamWriter(outputStream);
sWriter.Write(renderedOutput.ToString());
sWriter.Flush();
```

The last step is to redirect to another page. This is necessary because allowing the page to be displayed would result in an additional rendering and an exception being thrown indicating the page has more than one server-side form element. If you need the page to be displayable anyway, a parameter can be passed in the querystring and checked in the code to determine if the output should be rendered and written to a file or handled normally.

VB
```vb
Response.Redirect([next page])
```

C#
```csharp
Response.Redirect([next page]);
```

This technique can be used for individual controls in the same manner as for the entire page. For example, if you have a page that contains a DataGrid and you want the rendered HTML for just the DataGrid, you can call the RenderControl method of the DataGrid and then save the output as described earlier.

See Also

Recipe 18.3

Example 18-16. Capturing rendered output (.vb)

```vb
Private Sub Page_Load(ByVal sender As System.Object, _
                      ByVal e As System.EventArgs) Handles MyBase.Load

  Const OUTPUT_FILENAME As String = "CH18CaptureRenderedOutputVB.html"

  Dim renderedOutput As StringBuilder
  Dim strWriter As StringWriter
  Dim tWriter As HtmlTextWriter
  Dim outputStream As FileStream
  Dim sWriter As StreamWriter
  Dim filename As String
  Dim nextPage As String

  Try
```

Example 18-16. Capturing rendered output (.vb) (continued)

```vb
    'set the names of the XML and XSLT documents used in the
    'transformation
    xmlTransform.DocumentSource = "xml/books.xml"
    xmlTransform.TransformSource = "xml/books.xslt"

    'create a HtmlTextWriter to use for rendering the page
    renderedOutput = New StringBuilder
    strWriter = New StringWriter(renderedOutput)
    tWriter = New HtmlTextWriter(strWriter)

    'render the page output
    Page.RenderControl(tWriter)

    'save the rendered output to a file
    filename = Server.MapPath(".") & "\" & OUTPUT_FILENAME
    outputStream = New FileStream(filename, _
                                  FileMode.Create)
    sWriter = New StreamWriter(outputStream)
    sWriter.Write(renderedOutput.ToString())
    sWriter.Flush()

    'redirect to another page
    'NOTE: Continuing with the display of this page will result in the
    '      page being rendered a second time which will cause an exception
    '      to be thrown
    nextPage = DisplayMessage.PAGE_NAME & "?" & _
               DisplayMessage.QS_PAGE_HEADER & "=Information" & "&" & _
               DisplayMessage.QS_MESSAGE_LINE1 & "=HTML Output Saved To " & _
               OUTPUT_FILENAME
    Response.Redirect(nextPage)

  Finally
    'clean up
    If (Not IsNothing(outputStream)) Then
      outputStream.Close()
    End If

    If (Not IsNothing(tWriter)) Then
      tWriter.Close()
    End If

    If (Not IsNothing(strWriter)) Then
      strWriter.Close()
    End If
  End Try
End Sub  'Page_Load
```

Example 18-17. Capturing rendered output (.cs)

```csharp
private void Page_Load(object sender, System.EventArgs e)
{
  const string OUTPUT_FILENAME = "CaptureRenderedOutput_VB.html";
```

Example 18-17. Capturing rendered output (.cs) (continued)

```csharp
    StringBuilder renderedOutput = null;
    StringWriter strWriter = null;
    HtmlTextWriter tWriter = null;
    FileStream outputStream = null;
    StreamWriter sWriter = null;
    String filename = null;
    String nextPage = null;

    try
    {
      // set the names of the XML and XSLT documents used in the
      // transformation
      xmlTransform.DocumentSource = "xml//books.xml";
      xmlTransform.TransformSource = "xml//books.xslt";

      // create a HtmlTextWriter to use for rendering the page
      renderedOutput = new StringBuilder( );
      strWriter = new StringWriter(renderedOutput);
      tWriter = new HtmlTextWriter(strWriter);

      // render the page output
      Page.RenderControl(tWriter);

      // save the rendered output to a file
      filename = Server.MapPath(".") + "\\" + OUTPUT_FILENAME;
      outputStream = new FileStream(filename,
                                    FileMode.Create);
      sWriter = new StreamWriter(outputStream);
      sWriter.Write(renderedOutput.ToString( ));
      sWriter.Flush( );

      // redirect to another page
      // NOTE: Continuing with the display of this page will result in the
      //       page being rendered a second time which will cause an exception
      //       to be thrown
      nextPage = DisplayMessage.PAGE_NAME + "?" +
                 DisplayMessage.QS_PAGE_HEADER + "=Information" + "&" +
                 DisplayMessage.QS_MESSAGE_LINE1 + "=HTML Output Saved To " +
                 OUTPUT_FILENAME;
      Response.Redirect(nextPage);
    }

    finally
    {
      // clean up
      if (outputStream != null)
      {
        outputStream.Close( );
      }

      if (tWriter != null)
      {
```

Example 18-17. Capturing rendered output (.cs) (continued)

```
      tWriter.Close( );
    }

    if (strWriter != null)
    {
      strWriter.Close( );
    }
  }
} // Page_Load
```

18.7 Sending Mail

Problem

You want the user of your application to be able to send email.

Solution

Create a form to allow the user to enter the email information. When the user submits the form to the server, build a MailMessage object from the email information and then send the email using the SmtpMail class.

In the *.aspx* file:

1. Create a form to capture the sender's email address, the recipient's email address, the subject, and the message.
2. Add a Send button that initiates the sending of the email.

In the code-behind class for the page, use the .NET language of your choice to:

1. Create a MailMessage object, which is used as a container for the mail message.
2. Set the To, From, Subject, and Body properties to the data entered on the form.
3. Set the SmtpServer property of the SmtpMail class to the server that will send the email, and then call the Send method to perform the send operation.

Examples 18-18 through 18-20 show the *.aspx* file and the VB and C# code-behind files for an application we've written to demonstrate this solution. The output of the application is shown in Figure 18-6.

Discussion

Sending email is a common requirement in ASP.NET applications. In classic ASP, third-party controls are required to send email. In ASP.NET, all of the functionality required to send email is provided and is very easy to use.

To send email, you need the sender's email address, the recipient's email address, the subject, and the message. In our example that illustrates this solution, a simple form

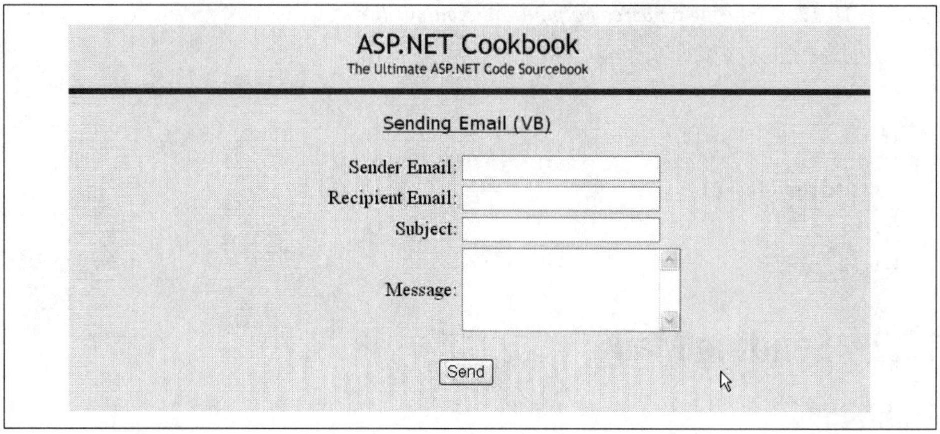

ASP.NET Cookbook
The Ultimate ASP.NET Code Sourcebook

Sending Email (VB)

Sender Email:
Recipient Email:
Subject:
Message:

Send

Figure 18-6. Send mail form output

is used to collect the information. The form includes a Send button that initiates the sending of the email.

When the Send button is clicked, the `btnSend_ServerClick` method in the code-behind is executed. This method is responsible for collecting the information from the form and sending the email. For simplicity, no validation is performed on the data in our example; however, you should provide validation of the data in your application. Refer to Chapter 2 for data validation examples.

The first step in sending an email is to create a `MailMessage` object. This object is used as a container for the mail message, as shown in our example.

After creating the `MailMessage` object, the `To`, `From`, `Subject`, and `Body` properties need to be set to the data entered on the form.

> The `To`, `From`, and `Subject` properties should always be set to valid values. Spam filters typically check these fields, and, if any are blank, the mail message may be branded as spam. In addition, some spam filters check the format of the From address, and the more thorough spam filters will verify whether the From address is valid.

After the `MailMessage` is initialized, the `SmtpServer` property of the `SmtpMail` class is set to the server that will send the email, and then the `Send` method is called to perform the send operation. The `SmtpServer` property and the `Send` method are shared (static); therefore, it is not necessary to instantiate a `SmtpMail` object.

Our example shows the very simple case of an email sent to a single recipient. To send the email to multiple recipients, set the `To` property to a semicolon-delimited string containing the email addresses of all of the required recipients.

Copies and blind copies can also be sent by setting the `Cc` property to the email address of copied recipients and the `Bcc` property to the email address of blind copy recipients. Like the To property, use a semicolon-delimited list for multiple recipients.

Attachments can be included with the email by adding MailAttachment objects to the Attachments collection, as shown here, where *[filename]* is the fully qualified path to the file that you need to attach to the mail message:

VB
```vb
mail.Attachments.Add(New MailAttachment([filename]))
```

C#
```csharp
mail.Attachments.Add(new MailAttachment([filename]));
```

See Also

Chapter 2 for data validation

Example 18-18. Sending email (.aspx)

```
<%@ Page Language="vb" AutoEventWireup="false"
        Codebehind="CH18SendingEmailVB.aspx.vb"
        Inherits="ASPNetCookbook.VBExamples.CH18SendingEmailVB" %>
<!DOCTYPE HTML PUBLIC "-//W3C//DTD HTML 4.0 Transitional//EN">
<html>
  <head>
    <title>Sending Email</title>
    <link rel="stylesheet" href="css/ASPNetCookbook.css">
  </head>
  <body leftmargin="0" marginheight="0" marginwidth="0" topmargin="0">
    <form id="frmSendEmail" method="post" runat="server" >
      <table width="100%" cellpadding="0" cellspacing="0" border="0">
        <tr>
          <td align="center">
            <img src="images/ASPNETCookbookHeading_blue.gif">
          </td>
        </tr>
        <tr>
          <td class="dividerLine">
            <img src="images/spacer.gif" height="6" border="0"></td>
        </tr>
      </table>
      <table width="90%" align="center" border="0">
        <tr>
          <td><img src="images/spacer.gif" height="10" border="0"></td>
        </tr>
        <tr>
          <td align="center" class="PageHeading">
            Sending Email (VB)
          </td>
        </tr>
        <tr>
          <td><img src="images/spacer.gif" height="10" border="0"></td>
        </tr>
        <tr>
          <td>
            <table width="60%" align="center" border="0">
```

Example 18-18. Sending email (.aspx) (continued)

```
            <tr>
              <td width="50%" align="right">Sender Email: </td>
              <td width="50%">
                <input id="txtSenderEmail" runat="server"></td>
            </tr>
            <tr>
              <td width="50%" align="right">Recipient Email: </td>
              <td width="50%">
                <input id="txtRecipientEmail" runat="server"></td>
            </tr>
            <tr>
              <td width="50%" align="right">Subject: </td>
              <td width="50%">
                <input id="txtSubject" runat="server"></td>
            </tr>
            <tr>
              <td width="50%" align="right">Message: </td>
              <td width="50%">
               <textarea id="txtMessage" runat="server" rows="4" ></textarea>
            </tr>
            <tr>
              <td colspan="2" align="center">
                <br />
                <input id="btnSend" runat="server"
                       type="button" value="Send" />
              </td>
            </tr>
          </table>
        </td>
      </tr>
    </table>
  </form>
  </body>
</html>
```

Example 18-19. Sending email code-behind (.vb)

```
Option Explicit On
Option Strict On
'-------------------------------------------------------------------------
'
'   Module Name: CH18SendingEmailVB.aspx.vb
'
'   Description: This module provides the code behind for the
'               CH18SendingEmailVB.aspx page
'
'*************************************************************************
Imports System
Imports System.Web.Mail


Namespace ASPNetCookbook.VBExamples
```

Example 18-19. Sending email code-behind (.vb) (continued)

```
Public Class CH18SendingEmailVB
  Inherits System.Web.UI.Page

  'controls on the form
  Protected txtSenderEmail As System.Web.UI.HtmlControls.HtmlInputText
  Protected txtRecipientEmail As System.Web.UI.HtmlControls.HtmlInputText
  Protected txtSubject As System.Web.UI.HtmlControls.HtmlInputText
  Protected txtMessage As System.Web.UI.HtmlControls.HtmlTextArea
  Protected WithEvents btnSend As System.Web.UI.HtmlControls.HtmlInputButton

  '*************************************************************************
  '
  '    ROUTINE: Page_Load
  '
  '    DESCRIPTION: This routine provides the event handler for the page load
  '                 event.  It is responsible for initializing the controls
  '                 on the page.
  '-------------------------------------------------------------------------
  Private Sub Page_Load(ByVal sender As System.Object, _
                        ByVal e As System.EventArgs) Handles MyBase.Load

  End Sub  'Page_Load

  '*************************************************************************
  '
  '    ROUTINE: btnSend_ServerClick
  '
  '    DESCRIPTION: This routine provides the event handler for the send
  '                 button click event.  It is responsible for sending an
  '                 email based on the data entered on the page.
  '-------------------------------------------------------------------------
  Private Sub btnSend_ServerClick(ByVal sender As Object, _
                                  ByVal e As System.EventArgs) _
            Handles btnSend.ServerClick
    Dim mail As MailMessage

    'create email object
    mail = New MailMessage
    mail.To = txtRecipientEmail.Value
    mail.From = txtSenderEmail.Value
    mail.Subject = txtSubject.Value
    mail.Body = txtMessage.Value

    'mail.Attachments.Add(New MailAttachment("D:\ASPNetBook\notes.txt"))

    'send the mail
    SmtpMail.SmtpServer = "mail.adelphia.net"
    SmtpMail.Send(mail)
  End Sub  'btnSend_ServerClick
End Class  'CH18SendingEmailVB
End Namespace
```

Example 18-20. Sending email code-behind (.cs)

```
//-----------------------------------------------------------------------------
//
//    Module Name: CH18SendingEmailCS.aspx.cs
//
//    Description: This module provides the code behind for the
//                 CH18SendingEmailCS.aspx page
//
//*****************************************************************************
using System;
using System.Web.Mail;

namespace ASPNetCookbook.CSExamples
{
  public class CH18SendingEmailCS : System.Web.UI.Page
  {
    // controls on the form
    protected System.Web.UI.HtmlControls.HtmlInputText txtSenderEmail;
    protected System.Web.UI.HtmlControls.HtmlInputText txtRecipientEmail;
    protected System.Web.UI.HtmlControls.HtmlInputText txtSubject;
    protected System.Web.UI.HtmlControls.HtmlTextArea txtMessage;
    protected System.Web.UI.HtmlControls.HtmlInputButton btnSend;

    //*************************************************************************
    //
    //    ROUTINE: Page_Load
    //
    //    DESCRIPTION: This routine provides the event handler for the page
    //                 load event.  It is responsible for initializing the
    //                 controls on the page.
    //-------------------------------------------------------------------------
    private void Page_Load(object sender, System.EventArgs e)
    {
      // wire the send button click event
      this.btnSend.ServerClick +=
        new EventHandler(this.btnSend_ServerClick);
    }

    //*************************************************************************
    //
    //    ROUTINE: btnSend_ServerClick
    //
    //    DESCRIPTION: This routine provides the event handler for the send
    //                 button click event.  It is responsible for sending an
    //                 email based on the data entered on the page.
    //-------------------------------------------------------------------------
    private void btnSend_ServerClick(Object sender,
                                     System.EventArgs e)
    {
      MailMessage mail = null;

      // create email object
      mail = new MailMessage();
      mail.To = txtRecipientEmail.Value;
```

Example 18-20. Sending email code-behind (.cs) (continued)

```
        mail.From = txtSenderEmail.Value;
        mail.Subject = txtSubject.Value;
        mail.Body = txtMessage.Value;

        // mail.Attachments.Add(new MailAttachment("D:\\ASPNetBook\\notes.txt"));

        // send the mail
        SmtpMail.SmtpServer = "mail.adelphia.net";
        SmtpMail.Send(mail);
    } //btnSend_ServerClick
  } // CH18SendingEmailCS
}
```

18.8   Creating and Using Page Templates

Problem

Your application uses a common page format for most of its pages, and you want to reuse and simplify the maintenance of the shared HTML.

Solution

Review the HTML to determine what is common on all of your pages, and then create a user control for each of the common sections. The HTML page used as the basis for our example is shown in Example 18-21. Our user control for the top of the page is shown in Examples 18-22 through 18-24 and for the bottom of the page in Examples 18-25 through 18-27.

Next, create a base page class that inherits from System.Web.UI.Page and loads the user controls you created at runtime. This base page class, along with the user controls containing the HTML for your pages, constitutes a "reusable HTML page template." Examples 18-28 and 18-29 show the VB and C# versions of our base page class that demonstrate this solution.

You can then create the pages for your application by inheriting from the base class you have created instead of System.Web.UI.Page and add only the HTML that is unique to each page. Examples 18-30 through 18-32 show the *.aspx* file and VB and C# code-behind file for an application that demonstrate the use of the base page class.

Discussion

Most applications use a common HTML design for the majority of their pages, and developers often find themselves cutting and pasting the common HTML in order to repeat the design on each page. Because of the replication, maintenance of the HTML is time consuming, expensive, and prone to mistakes. What is needed is the ability to code the HTML in one place and reuse it many times. This recipe describes how to implement a common design by reusing HTML.

The first step to creating reusable HTML is to analyze the HTML of your application pages to determine what elements are common across all of them. In our example that illustrates this solution, the two sections highlighted in Example 18-21 have been identified as being common across all pages. Figure 18-7 shows the output of the page in our example.

ASP.NET Cookbook
The Ultimate ASP.NET Code Sourcebook

Simple Example Of Using A Page Template

Title	ISBN	Publisher
Access Cookbook	0-596-00084-7	O'Reilly
Perl Cookbook	1-565-92243-3	O'Reilly
Java Cookbook	0-596-00170-3	O'Reilly
JavaScript Application Cookbook	1-565-92577-7	O'Reilly
VB .Net Language in a Nutshell	0-596-00092-8	O'Reilly
Programming Visual Basic .Net	0-596-00093-6	O'Reilly
Programming C#	0-596-00117-7	O'Reilly
.Net Framework Essentials	0-596-00165-7	O'Reilly
COM and .Net Component Services	0-596-00103-7	O'Reilly

Figure 18-7. Page template example output

For each common section, you need to create a user control. In our example, the first common section is placed in the CH18PageTopVB (VB) or CH18PageTopCS (C#) user control and the second common section is placed in the CH18PageBottomVB (VB) or CH18PageBottomCS (C#) user control, as shown in Examples 18-22 and 18-25. The title element and the table cell used to place a label at the top of a page in the CH18PageTopxx user control have been modified from the original HTML to provide the ability to change the values of the title and page heading in the code-behind.

 It may look a little odd to have HTML fragments in the user controls, but it is important to remember that the browser will only see the rendered page, which includes the HTML for each of the user controls, resulting in proper, well-formed HTML.

To provide the ability to change the values in the pages that use our example template, we have added the pageTitle and pageHeading properties to the code-behind of the CH18PageTopxx user control.

Our CH18PageBottomxx user control does not require any variation in the pages using the template; therefore, the code-behind for the user control does not require any additional code.

After creating the user controls containing the HTML to be reused, a new class must be created that will be used as the base class for all pages in your application. This class must inherit from the System.Web.UI.Page class to provide the base functionality needed for a page.

To provide the ability to change the properties in the pages that use our example template, the base page class must contain a property for each of the properties in the user controls. In our example, because a pageTitle and a pageHeading property were provided in the CH18PageTopxx user control, they must be added to the base page class.

 The check at the beginning of each of the properties is necessary to avoid an error message indicating an object reference is not set to an instance of an object when using Visual Studio .NET. The error is caused by the designer accessing the properties for display purposes, but the user controls are not created in the designer, resulting in mPageTop and mPageHeading being null.

The OnInit method in our example must be overridden from the Page class to load the CH18PageTopVB (or CH18PageTopCS) and CH18PageBottomVB (or CH18PageBottomCS) user controls when the CH18BaseClassVB (or CH18BasePageCS) object is created.

VB
```
Protected Overrides Sub OnInit(ByVal e As System.EventArgs)
    'load the user control containing the template for the top of the page
    'and add it as the first control in the page
    mPageTop = CType(LoadControl("CH18PageTopVB.ascx"), _
                                CH18PageTopVB)
    MyClass.Controls.AddAt(0, mPageTop)

    'take care of the base class initialization
    MyBase.OnInit(e)

    'load the user control containing the template for the bottom of the page
    'and add it at the end of the controls in the page
    mPageBottom = CType(LoadControl("CH18PageBottomVB.ascx"), _
                                   CH18PageBottomVB)
    MyClass.Controls.Add(mPageBottom)
End Sub   'OnInit
```

C#
```
protected override void OnInit(System.EventArgs e)
{
    // take care of the base class initialization
    base.OnInit(e);

    // load the user control containing the template for the top of the page
    // and add it as the first control in the page
    mPageTop = (CH18PageTopCS)(LoadControl("CH18PageTopCS.ascx"));
    base.Controls.AddAt(0, mPageTop);

    // load the user control containing the template for the bottom of the page
    // and add it at the end of the controls in the page
    mPageBottom = (CH18PageBottomCS)(LoadControl("CH18PageBottomCS.ascx"));
    base.Controls.Add(mPageBottom);
}  // OnInit
```

In our example, The CH18PageTopxx user control must be the first control on the page because it contains the HTML for the top of the page. In addition, the CH18PageBottomxx user control must be the last control on the form because it contains the HTML for the bottom of the page. Placing these controls at any other position in the controls collection will result in invalid HTML being rendered.

To use the page template, you need to create a web form as you normally would, but with two changes. First, the *.aspx* file should only include the HTML that is unique to the page being implemented, as shown in Example 18-30. In our example, the unique HTML is a simple table to provide the ability to format the content for the page.

The second modification is to change the inherited class for the code-behind class. This should be changed from the normal System.Web.UI.Page to the base class you created. In our example, the code-behind class inherits from CH18BasePageVB (or CH18BasePageCS for C#), which will result in the common HTML being output for the page.

In our example, two properties were included in the base page class to demonstrate how to reuse the HTML yet provide the ability to customize the output for each page. The properties must be set in the PageLoad method, as shown here:

`VB`
```
Private Sub Page_Load(ByVal sender As System.Object, _
                      ByVal e As System.EventArgs) Handles MyBase.Load
   If (Not Page.IsPostBack) Then
     'set the page title
     pageTitle = "Using the page template"

     'set the page heading
     pageHeading = "Simple Example Of Using A Page Template"

     ...

   End If  'If (Not Page.IsPostBack)
End Sub  'Page_Load
```

`C#`
```
private void Page_Load(object sender, System.EventArgs e)
{
   if (!Page.IsPostBack)
   {
     // set the page title
     pageTitle = "Using the page template";

     // set the page heading
     pageHeading = "Simple Example Of Using A Page Template";

     ...

   } // if (!Page.IsPostBack)
```

Our example uses fairly simple HTML to demonstrate the implementation of a reusable HTML page template, but the technique is not limited to simple implementations. In fact, the more complicated the HTML, the more important it is to apply reuse to reduce the maintenance cost of the presentation portion of your application.

See Also

Chapter 4 for user controls

Example 18-21. Original HTML page

```html
<!DOCTYPE HTML PUBLIC "-//W3C//DTD HTML 4.0 Transitional//EN">
<html>
  <head>
    <title>Original HTML Template</title>
    <link rel="stylesheet" href="css/ASPNetCookbook.css">
  </head>
  <body leftmargin="0" marginheight="0" marginwidth="0" topmargin="0">
    <table width="100%" cellpadding="0" cellspacing="0" border="0">
      <tr>
        <td align="center">
          <img src="images/ASPCookbookHeading_blue.gif">
        </td>
      </tr>
      <tr>
        <td bgcolor="#6B0808"><img src="images/spacer.gif" height="6"></td>
      </tr>
    </table>
    <table width="90%" align="center" border="0">
      <tr>
        <td><img src="images/spacer.gif" height="10" border="0"></td>
      </tr>
      <tr>
        <td align="center" class="PageHeading">
          <!-- Put page heading here -->
        </td>
      </tr>
      <tr>
        <td><img src="images/spacer.gif" height="10" border="0"></td>
      </tr>
      <tr>
        <td align="center">
          <form method="post">
            <!-- Put page content here -->
          </form>
        </td>
      </tr>
    </table>
  </body>
</html>
```

Example 18-22. User control for top of page (.ascx)

```
<%@ Control Language="vb" AutoEventWireup="false"
          Codebehind="CH18PageTopVB.ascx.vb"
          Inherits="ASPNetCookbook.VBExamples.CH18PageTopVB" %>
<!DOCTYPE HTML PUBLIC "-//W3C//DTD HTML 4.0 Transitional//EN">
<html>
  <head>
    <title id="mPageTitle" runat="server"></title>
    <link rel="stylesheet" href="css/ASPNetCookbook.css">
  </head>
  <body leftmargin="0" marginheight="0" marginwidth="0" topmargin="0">
    <table width="100%" cellpadding="0" cellspacing="0" border="0">
      <tr>
        <td align="center">
          <img src="images/ASPNETCookbookHeading_blue.gif">
        </td>
      </tr>
      <tr>
        <td class="dividerLine">
          <img src="images/spacer.gif" height="6" border="0"></td>
      </tr>
    </table>
    <table width="100%" align="center" border="0">
      <tr>
        <td><img src="images/spacer.gif" height="10" border="0"></td>
      </tr>
      <tr>
        <td id="mPageHeading" runat="server"
            align="center" class="PageHeading">
        </td>
      </tr>
      <tr>
        <td><img src="images/spacer.gif" height="10" border="0"></td>
      </tr>
      <tr>
        <td align="center">
```

Example 18-23. User control for top of page code-behind (.vb)

```
Option Explicit On
Option Strict On
'-----------------------------------------------------------------------------
'
'   Module Name: CH18PageTopVB.ascx.vb
'
'   Description: This class provides the code-behind for CH18PageTopVB.ascx
'
'*****************************************************************************

Namespace ASPNetCookbook.VBExamples
  Public Class CH18PageTopVB
    Inherits System.Web.UI.UserControl
```

Example 18-23. User control for top of page code-behind (.vb) (continued)

```vb
    'controls in the user control
    Protected mPageTitle As System.Web.UI.HtmlControls.HtmlGenericControl
    Protected mPageHeading As System.Web.UI.HtmlControls.HtmlTableCell

    '*************************************************************************
    '
    '    ROUTINE: pageTitle
    '
    '    DESCRIPTION: This routine provides the ability to get/set the
    '                 pageTitle property
    '-------------------------------------------------------------------------
    Public Property pageTitle() As String
      Get
        Return (mPageTitle.InnerText)
      End Get

      Set(ByVal Value As String)
        mPageTitle.InnerText = Value
      End Set
    End Property  'pageTitle

    '*************************************************************************
    '
    '    ROUTINE: pageHeading
    '
    '    DESCRIPTION: This routine provides the ability to get/set the
    '                 pageHeading property
    '-------------------------------------------------------------------------
    Public Property pageHeading() As String
      Get
        Return (mPageHeading.InnerText)
      End Get

      Set(ByVal Value As String)
        mPageHeading.InnerText = Value
      End Set
    End Property  'pageHeading

    '*************************************************************************
    '
    '    ROUTINE: Page_Load
    '
    '    DESCRIPTION: This routine provides the event handler for the page load
    '                 event.  It is responsible for initializing the controls
    '                 on the page.
    '-------------------------------------------------------------------------
    Private Sub Page_Load(ByVal sender As System.Object, _
                          ByVal e As System.EventArgs) Handles MyBase.Load
      'Put user code to initialize the page here
    End Sub  'Page_Load
  End Class  'CH18PageTopVB
End Namespace
```

Example 18-24. User control for top of page code-behind (.cs)

```
//-----------------------------------------------------------------------------
//
//   Module Name: CH18PageTopCS.ascx.cs
//
//   Description: This module provides the code behind for CH18PageTopCS.ascx
//
//*****************************************************************************
namespace ASPNetCookbook.CSExamples
{
  using System;

  public abstract class CH18PageTopCS : System.Web.UI.UserControl
  {
    // controls in the user control
    protected System.Web.UI.HtmlControls.HtmlGenericControl mPageTitle;
    protected System.Web.UI.HtmlControls.HtmlTableCell mPageHeading;

    //*************************************************************************
    //
    //   ROUTINE: pageTitle
    //
    //   DESCRIPTION: This routine provides the ability to get/set the
    //                pageTitle property
    //
    //-------------------------------------------------------------------------
    public String pageTitle
    {
      get
      {
        return(mPageTitle.InnerText);
      }
      set
      {
        mPageTitle.InnerText = value;
      }
    }  // pageTitle

    //*************************************************************************
    //
    //   ROUTINE: pageHeading
    //
    //   DESCRIPTION: This routine provides the ability to get/set the
    //                pageHeading property
    //
    //-------------------------------------------------------------------------
    public String pageHeading
    {
      get
      {
        return(mPageHeading.InnerText);
      }
      set
```

Example 18-24. User control for top of page code-behind (.cs) (continued)

```csharp
      {
         mPageHeading.InnerText = value;
      }
   }  // pageHeading

   //************************************************************************
   //
   //    ROUTINE: Page_Load
   //
   //    DESCRIPTION: This routine provides the event handler for the page
   //                 load event.  It is responsible for initializing the
   //                 controls on page.
   //
   //------------------------------------------------------------------------
   private void Page_Load(object sender, System.EventArgs e)
   {
      // Put user code to initialize the page here
   }  // Page_Load
}  // CH18PageTopCS
}
```

Example 18-25. User control for bottom of page (.ascx)

```
<%@ Control Language="vb" AutoEventWireup="false"
          Codebehind="CH18PageBottomVB.ascx.vb"
          Inherits="ASPNetCookbook.VBExamples.CH18PageBottomVB" %>
          </td>
        </tr>
      </table>
    </form>
  </body>
</html>
```

Example 18-26. User control for bottom of page code-behind (.vb)

```vb
Option Explicit On
Option Strict On
'------------------------------------------------------------------------
'
'   Module Name: CH18PageBottomVB.ascx.vb
'
'   Description: This class provides the code-behind for CH18PageBottomVB.ascx
'
'************************************************************************
Namespace ASPNetCookbook.VBExamples
  Public Class CH18PageBottomVB
    Inherits System.Web.UI.UserControl

    '************************************************************************
    '
    '   ROUTINE: Page_Load
    '
    '   DESCRIPTION: This routine provides the event handler for the page load
```

Example 18-26. User control for bottom of page code-behind (.vb) (continued)

```
'                    event.  It is responsible for initializing the controls
'                    on the page.
'-----------------------------------------------------------------------
   Private Sub Page_Load(ByVal sender As System.Object, _
                         ByVal e As System.EventArgs) Handles MyBase.Load
      'Put user code to initialize the page here
   End Sub  'Page_Load
 End Class   'CH18PageBottomVB
End Namespace
```

Example 18-27. User control for bottom of page code-behind (.cs)

```
//-----------------------------------------------------------------------
//
//   Module Name: CH18PageBottomCS.ascx.cs
//
//   Description: This module provides the code behind for
//                CH18PageBottomCS.ascx
//
//***********************************************************************
using System;

namespace ASPNetCookbook.CSExamples
{
  public abstract class CH18PageBottomCS : System.Web.UI.UserControl
  {
    //*********************************************************************
    //
    //   ROUTINE: Page_Load
    //
    //   DESCRIPTION: This routine provides the event handler for the page
    //                load event.  It is responsible for initializing the
    //                controls on the page.
    //-----------------------------------------------------------------------
    private void Page_Load(object sender, System.EventArgs e)
    {
      // Put user code to initialize the page here
    } // Page_Load
  } // CH18PageBottomCS
}
```

Example 18-28. Base page class (.vb)

```
Option Explicit On
Option Strict On
'-----------------------------------------------------------------------
'
'   Module Name: CH18BasePageVB.vb
'
'   Description: This class provides the class used as the base class from
'                which all ASPX pages in the application are derived.  It
'                provides the basic template for all of the common user
'                interface.
'
```

Example 18-28. Base page class (.vb) (continued)

```vb
'*****************************************************************************
Imports Microsoft.VisualBasic

Namespace ASPNetCookbook.VBExamples
  Public Class CH18BasePageVB
    Inherits System.Web.UI.Page

    'the following variables are used for references to the user controls
    'that contain the top and bottom sections of the page template
    Private mPageTop As CH18PageTopVB
    Private mPageBottom As CH18PageBottomVB

    '*****************************************************************************
    '
    '    ROUTINE: pageTitle
    '
    '    DESCRIPTION: This routine provides the ability to get/set the
    '                 pageTitle property
    '----------------------------------------------------------------------------
    Public Property pageTitle() As String
      Get
        Dim title As String = String.Empty
        If (Not IsNothing(mPageTop)) Then
          title = mPageTop.pageTitle
        End If

        Return (title)
      End Get
      Set(ByVal Value As String)
        If (Not IsNothing(mPageTop)) Then
          mPageTop.pageTitle = Value
        End If
      End Set
    End Property    'pageTitle

    '*****************************************************************************
    '
    '    ROUTINE: pageHeading
    '
    '    DESCRIPTION: This routine provides the ability to get/set the
    '                 pageHeading property
    '----------------------------------------------------------------------------
    Public Property pageHeading() As String
      Get
        Dim title As String = String.Empty
        If (Not IsNothing(mPageTop)) Then
          title = mPageTop.pageHeading
        End If

        Return (title)
      End Get
      Set(ByVal Value As String)
        If (Not IsNothing(mPageTop)) Then
```

Example 18-28. Base page class (.vb) (continued)

```
            mPageTop.pageHeading = Value
        End If
    End Set
End Property  'pageHeading

    '******************************************************************
    '
    '    ROUTINE: OnInit
    '
    '    DESCRIPTION: This routine provides the event handler for the OnInit
    '                 event.  It is responsible for loading the user controls
    '                 containing the page templates and adding them to the
    '                 page controls collection.
    '------------------------------------------------------------------

    Protected Overrides Sub OnInit(ByVal e As System.EventArgs)
        'load the user control containing the template for the top of the page
        'and add it as the first control in the page
        mPageTop = CType(LoadControl("CH18PageTopVB.ascx"), _
                                    CH18PageTopVB)
        MyClass.Controls.AddAt(0, mPageTop)

        'take care of the base class initialization
        MyBase.OnInit(e)

        'load the user control containing the template for the bottom of the page
        'and add it at the end of the controls in the page
        mPageBottom = CType(LoadControl("CH18PageBottomVB.ascx"), _
                                        CH18PageBottomVB)
        MyClass.Controls.Add(mPageBottom)
    End Sub  'OnInit
  End Class  'CH18BasePageVB
End Namespace
```

Example 18-29. Base page class (.cs)

```
//--------------------------------------------------------------------------
//
//    Module Name: CH18BasePageCS.cs
//
//    Description: This class provides the class used as the base class from
//                 which all ASPX pages in the application are derived.  It
//                 provides the basic template for all of the common user
//                 interface.
//
//**************************************************************************
using System;

namespace ASPNetCookbook.CSExamples
{
  public class CH18BasePageCS : System.Web.UI.Page
  {
```

Example 18-29. Base page class (.cs) (continued)

```csharp
// the following variables are used for references to the user controls
// that contain the top and bottom sections of the page template
private CH18PageTopCS mPageTop;
private CH18PageBottomCS mPageBottom;

//**********************************************************************
//
//    ROUTINE: pageTitle
//
//    DESCRIPTION: This routine provides the ability to get/set the
//                  pageTitle property
//----------------------------------------------------------------------
public String pageTitle
{
  get
  {
    String title  = String.Empty;
    if (mPageTop != null)
    {
      title = mPageTop.pageTitle;
    }
    return(title);
  }
  set
  {
    if (mPageTop != null)
    {
      mPageTop.pageTitle = value;
    }
  }
} // pageTitle

//**********************************************************************
//
//    ROUTINE: pageHeading
//
//    DESCRIPTION: This routine provides the ability to get/set the
//                  pageHeading property
//----------------------------------------------------------------------
public String pageHeading
{
  get
  {
    String title  = String.Empty;
    if (mPageTop != null)
    {
      title = mPageTop.pageHeading;
    }
    return(title);
  }
  set
  {
    if (mPageTop != null)
```

Example 18-29. Base page class (.cs) (continued)

```cs
        {
          mPageTop.pageHeading = value;
        }
      }
    }  // pageHeading

    // ***********************************************************************
    //
    //   ROUTINE: OnInit
    //
    //   DESCRIPTION: This routine provides the event handler for the OnInit
    //                event.  It is responsible for loading the user controls
    //                containing the page templates and adding them to the
    //                page controls collection.
    //-----------------------------------------------------------------------
    protected override void OnInit(System.EventArgs e)
    {
      // take care of the base class initialization
      base.OnInit(e);

      // load the user control containing the template for the top of the page
      // and add it as the first control in the page
      mPageTop = (CH18PageTopCS)(LoadControl("CH18PageTopCS.ascx"));
      base.Controls.AddAt(0, mPageTop);

      // load the user control containing the template for the bottom of the page
      // and add it at the end of the controls in the page
      mPageBottom = (CH18PageBottomCS)(LoadControl("CH18PageBottomCS.ascx"));
      base.Controls.Add(mPageBottom);
    }  // OnInit
  }  // CH18BasePageCS
}
```

Example 18-30. Using the base page class (.aspx)

```aspx
<%@ Page Language="vb" AutoEventWireup="false"
        Codebehind="CH18UsingThePageTemplateVB.aspx.vb"
        Inherits="ASPNetCookbook.VBExamples.CH18UsingThePageTemplateVB"%>
<form method="post" id="frmUsingPageTemplate" runat="server">
  <!-- Put page content here -->
  <table width="80%" border="0" align="center">
    <tr>
      <td>
        <asp:Xml ID="xmlTransform" Runat="server"/>
      </td>
    </tr>
  </table>
</form>
```

Example 18-31. Using the base page class code-behind (.vb)

```vb
Option Explicit On
Option Strict On
```

Example 18-31. Using the base page class code-behind (.vb) (continued)

```vb
'----------------------------------------------------------------------------
'
'   Module Name: CH18UsingThePageTemplateVB.aspx.vb
'
'   Description: This class provides the code-behind for
'               CH18UsingThePageTemplateVB.aspx
'
'****************************************************************************
Imports System

Namespace ASPNetCookbook.VBExamples
  Public Class CH18UsingThePageTemplateVB
    Inherits CH18BasePageVB

    'controls on the form
    Protected xmlTransform As System.Web.UI.WebControls.Xml

    '****************************************************************************
    '
    '   ROUTINE: Page_Load
    '
    '   DESCRIPTION: This routine provides the event handler for the page load
    '               event.  It is responsible for initializing the controls
    '               on the page.
    '----------------------------------------------------------------------------
    Private Sub Page_Load(ByVal sender As System.Object, _
                        ByVal e As System.EventArgs) Handles MyBase.Load
      If (Not Page.IsPostBack) Then
        'set the page title
        pageTitle = "Using the page template"

        'set the page heading
        pageHeading = "Simple Example Of Using A Page Template"

        'initialize controls on the specific page

        'set the names of the XML and XSLT documents used in the
        'transformation
        xmlTransform.DocumentSource = "xml/books.xml"
        xmlTransform.TransformSource = "xml/books.xslt"

      End If  'If (Not Page.IsPostBack)
    End Sub  'Page_Load
  End Class  'CH18UsingThePageTemplateVB
End Namespace
```

Example 18-32. Using the base page class code-behind (.cs)

```csharp
//----------------------------------------------------------------------------
//
//   Module Name: CH18UsingThePageTemplateCS.aspx.cs
//
//   Description: This module provides the code behind for the
```

Example 18-32. Using the base page class code-behind (.cs) (continued)

```csharp
//                    CH18UsingThePageTemplateCS.aspx page
//
//*************************************************************************
using System;

namespace ASPNetCookbook.CSExamples
{
  public class CH18UsingThePageTemplateCS : CH18BasePageCS
  {
    // controls on the form
    protected System.Web.UI.WebControls.Xml xmlTransform;

    //*********************************************************************
    //
    //   ROUTINE: Page_Load
    //
    //   DESCRIPTION: This routine provides the event handler for the page
    //                load event.  It is responsible for initializing the
    //                controls on the page.
    //---------------------------------------------------------------------
    private void Page_Load(object sender, System.EventArgs e)
    {
      if (!Page.IsPostBack)
      {
        // set the page title
        pageTitle = "Using the page template";

        // set the page heading
        pageHeading = "Simple Example Of Using A Page Template";

        // initialize controls on the specific page

        // set the names of the XML and XSLT documents used in the
        // transformation
        xmlTransform.DocumentSource = "xml//books.xml";
        xmlTransform.TransformSource = "xml//books.xslt";

      }  // if (!Page.IsPostBack)
    } // Page_Load
  }  // CH18UsingThePageTemplateCS
}
```

Index

A

accessing pages
  restricting by role, 459
  restricting selected, 455
ACT (Application Center Test), 520, 561
<allow> element, 446
AllowCustomPaging, DataGrid control, 61
AllowPaging attribute, DataGrid control, 61
AllowSorting attribute, DataGrid control, 76
application level error handling, 417, 427
Application object, 368
  data clearing, 370
  variables, hardcoding, 369
application state, maintenance, 366
application-level tracing, 526
  enabling, 526
applications
  components, tracing and, 534
  data caching, 656
  external, executing, 766
  stress testing, 561
Application_Start method, 367
arrays, displaying as checkboxes, 23
ascending sort, DataGrid and, 85
ASPStateTempApplications table, 498
ASPStateTempSessions table, 498
attributes
  custom controls, 329
  <forms> element, 445
  <trace> element, 527
authentication
  access restriction to selected pages, 455
  access to pages, restricting by role, 459
  cookies, Server.Transfer and, 447
  Forms authentication, 442
  FormsAuthenticationTicket, 461
  IAuthenticationModule interface, 442
  page access restriction, 443
  Passport authentication, 442
  principal object, 447
  tickets
    creating, 461
    parameters, 461
  user principal object, 447
  Windows, 474
  Windows authentication, 442
<authorization> element, 457

B

bar charts, creating on the fly, 618
bindData method, 64
breakpoints, conditional (debugging), 559
browsers
  caching and, 651
  user's type, determining, 775
browser-specific stylesheets, 780
button images
  drawing on the fly, 605
  makeButton method, 607

C

Cache object, application data and, 657
caching
  application data, 656
  latency and, 648

We'd like to hear your suggestions for improving our indexes. Send email to *index@oreilly.com*.

caching (*continued*)
   pages, 648
     browser type and, 651
     custom strings and, 653
     query string parameters and, 650
     version and, 651
   scalability and, 648
   user controls, 655
Catch block, page-level tracing and, 528
categories, trace log, 522
charts (see bar charts)
checkboxes, arrays displayed as, 23
CheckBoxList control, 23
checkForReturn function, keypress event
      and, 229
classes
   code-behind, reusing, 302
   custom configuration handlers, 506
   delegate classes, 305
   Hashtable, 28
   HTTP-specific information access, 763
   TraceContext, 521
   VBSiteConfigHandler, 507
   VBSiteConfiguration, 508
client validation, 179
CLR (Common Language Runtime)
   tracing and, 522
   web services and, 582
code-behind classes, reusing, 302
columnar data, DataGrid control, 121
components, dual-use, 542
concatenation, StringBuilder object and, 719
conditional breakpoints, debugging and, 559
configuration
   file hierarchy, 483
   state, maintaining across servers, 493
   (see also web.config)
<configuration> element, web.config, 483
configuration handlers, custom, 506
ConfigurationSettings.GetConfig, custom
      configuration, 510
confirmation pop up, row deletion,
      DataGrid, 141
consuming web services, 572
Control class
   custom controls and, 322
   WebControl class comparison, 323
controls
   CheckBoxList, 23
   custom, 322
     attributes, 329

     HTML controls and, 323
     state and, 337
   CustomValidator, 206
   DataGrid, 1
   DataList, 1
   focus, 269
     validation errors, 278
   RangeValidator, 188
   RegularExpressionValidator, 200
   Repeater, 1
   RequiredFieldValidator, 180, 195
   tabular, selecting, 1
   TextBox, numeric input, 358
   user controls
     caching, 655
     communication between, 303
     destination controls, 303
     dynamically adding, 314
     source controls, 303
   validation (see validators)
   xmlTransform, 769
cookieless atttribute, 498
CultureInfo object, currency format and, 675
currency, formatting override, 675
custom controls, 322
   attributes and, 329
   HTML controls and
     combining, 323
   properties, 330
   state and, 337
custom objects, web services and, 579
CustomValidator control, drop-down
      lists, 206

D

data
   applications, caching, 656
data entry
   database entry matching, 218
   input fields, matching, 195
   pattern matching, 200
   range requirements, 188
   requiring in field, 180
data types, serialized, custom objects, 579
DataAdapter method, performance and, 704
databases
   entry matching, data entry and, 218
   images stored, displaying, 625
   SQL Server, data access speed, 733
   uploaded file contents, 700
DataBinder.Eval method, 11

DataFormatString attribute, DataGrid
    control, 121
DataGrid control, 1
    AllowCustomPaging attribute, 61
    AllowPaging attribute, 61
    AllowSorting attribute, 76
    columnar data, formatting, 121
    date formatting, 121
    EditCommandColumn, 109
    editing data, 108
    first/last button, 42
    next/previous navigation, 33
    number formatting, 121
    paging, 61
        sorting and, 97
    ReadXml method, 16
    rows
        deletion confirmation, 141
        details pop up, 152
        selection within, 129
        totals row, 167
    SortExpression attribute, 76
    sorting
        ascending/descending, 85
        paging and, 97
    sorting data, 75
DataList control, 1
    Hashtable class and, 28
    navigation bar and, 290
DataReader method
    performance and, 704
    read-only data access, 725
DataSet class, ReadXml method, 16
datasets, XML files and, 17
date formatting, DataGrid, 121
debugging, 520
    breakpoints, 559
decimal places in number formats, 122
delegates, 305
deleting rows, confirming from DataGrid
    control, 141
<deny> element, 446
descending sort, DataGrid, 85
destination user controls, 303
direct page navigation, DataGrid control, 52
Directory class, downloading from web
    server, 678
display
    error messages, 434, 491
    tabular format, controls, 1
    XML file data, 16

DocumentSource property, 768
downloading files from web server, 677
downloads, file download handler
    creation, 754
drawing button images on the fly, 605
drop-down lists, requiring selection, 206
dual-use components, tracing and, 542
dynamic images, 605
    bar charts, creating on the fly, 618
    databases, displaying stored, 625
    thumbnails, displaying, 636

E

EditCommandColumn, DataGrid
    control, 109
editing DataGrid data, 108
email, sending messages, 795
Enter key for Submit button, 227
    validation and, 238
entering data
    database entry matching, 218
    input fields, matching, 195
    pattern matching, 200
    range requirements, 188
    requiring in field, 180
error handling, 416
    application level, 417, 427
    exceptions, 417
    method level, 416, 417
    page level, 416, 423
    recovery, 417
    Try...Catch blocks, 417
    Try...Catch...Finally block, 418
error messages
    custom, 491
    user-friendly, 434
    validators, 182
ErrorPage property, 423
errors
    parse errors, web.config, 484
    validation, focus on control, 278
event handlers, 36
    Page_Error event handler, 423
event log, trace data, 552
events
    keypress, Enter key, 227
    OnSend, 305
exception handlers
    HttpUnhandledException exception, 429
    implementation, 419
    trace output, enabling, 528

exceptions
    error handling and, 417
    NullReferenceException, 430
    page-level tracing and, 528
executionTimeout attribute, <httpRuntime>
        element, 486
external applications, executing, 766

F

fields, requiring data entry, 180
file download handlers, creating, 754
FileInfo class, downloading from web
        server, 678
files
    downloading from web server, 677
    uploading
        processing immediately, 692
        storing contents in database, 700
        to web server, 685
first/last button, DataGrid control, 42
focus controls, 269
formatting
    columnar data, DataGrid, 121
    currency, overriding, 675
    numbers, decimal places, 122
    tabular data
        controls, 1
        quick-and-dirty generation, 3
        templates and, 9
forms, 227
    multipage, simulating, 259
    Submit button, Enter key and, 227
    submitting to different page, 248
    validation, Submit button with Enter
        key, 238
Forms authentication, 442
<forms> element, attributes, 445
FormsAuthentication class, SetAuthCookie
        method, 446
FormsAuthenticationTicket object, 461
From First(s), Trace log, 522
From Last(s), Trace log, 522

G

GetFiles method, Directory class, 679
GetLastError method, 423
GetThumbnailImage method, 638
<globalization> element properties, 663
globalization (see internationalization)

H

hash tables, displays from, 28
Hashtable class, 28
headers, multiple pages, 281
HeaderStyle tag, 29
HeaderTemplate tag, 29
HTML
    controls, combining for custom
        controls, 323
    output, saving and reusing, 790
    Render method and, 324
    templates, 801
    transforming from XML, 768
HTTP handlers, 739
    built-in, overriding, 739
    file download handler, creating, 754
    IHttpHandler interface, 740
    image handlers, reusable, 740
    reusable, 741
HTTP runtime parameters, web.config, 485
HTTPContext.Current property, tracing
        and, 535
<httpHandlers> element, 739
HTTP-specific information, access from
        classes, 763
HttpUnhandledException, 429

I

IAuthenticationModule interface,
        authentication and, 442
IConfigurationSectionHandler interface, 506
IHttpHandler interface, 740
image handlers, reusable, 740
images
    button
        drawing on the fly, 605
        makeButton method, 607
    dynamic, 605
        bar charts, on the fly creation, 618
        displaying those stored in
            database, 625
        thumbnails, displaying, 636
information availability, 367
internationalization, 663
    currency format override, 675
    language support, 665
    request/response encoding, 663
IPostBackDataHandler interface, custom
        controls with state, 337
ItemStyle tag, 29
ItemTemplate tag, 29

J

JavaScript libraries, building, 270

K

keypress event, Enter key for Submit button, 227

L

language support, 665
latency, 648
libraries
   JavaScript, 270
   WebUIValidation, 239
localOnly attribute, <trace> element, 527
loginURL attribute, <forms> element, 445

M

MailMessage object, 795
makeButton method, 607
maxRequestLength attribute, <httpRuntime> element, 486
MessageEventArgs, 305
messages
   trace listeners, 542
   trace log, 522
method-level error handling, 416, 417
methods
   Application_Start, 367
   bindData, 64
   DataBinder.Eval, 11
   delegates, 305
   GetLastError, 423
   GetThumbnailImage, 638
   makeButton, 607
   OnPreRender, overriding, 359
   Page_Load, 16
   ProcessRequest, 740
   Render, HTML and, 324
   Response.Redirect, 431
   Server.Transfer, 249, 431
   SetAuthCookie, 446
   updatePage, 389
multipage forms, simulating, 259

N

name attribute, <forms> element, 445
navigation
   bar, creating customizable, 290

DataGrid control
   first/last button, 42
   next/previous button, 33
NullReferenceException, 430
number formatting
   DataGrid, 121
   decimal places, 122
numeric input, TextBox control, 358

O

objects
   Application, 368
   custom, web services and, 579
   information, page requests, 395
   MailMessage, 795
OnPreRender method, overriding, 359
OnSend event, 305
output, HTML, 790
@OutputCache directive, 649

P

page-level error handling, 416, 423
page state, maintenance, 367
Page_Error event handler, 423
page-level tracing, 528
   enabling, 521
Page_Load method, 16
pageOutput attribute, <trace> element, 527
PagerStyle-Mode, DataGrid control, 52
PagerStyle-PageButton attribute, DataGrid control, 52
pages
   access restriction, 443
      selected pages, 455
   caching, 648
      browser type and, 651
      custom strings and, 653
      query string parameters and, 650
      version and, 651
   controls, focus, 269
   forms, submitting, 248
   headers, multiple pages, 281
   size, ViewState and, 705
   templates, 801
paging, DataGrid control and, 61
   sorting and, 97
parameters, authentication ticket, 461
parse errors, web.config, 484
Passport authentication, 442
path attribute, <forms> element, 445

patterns, matching on data entry, 200
performance
    data access, SQL Server databases, 733
    DataAdapter method and, 704
    DataReader method and, 704
    read-only access speed, 724
    StringBuilder object, 704
        concatenation speed, 719
    <ViewState> element, 704
        page size and, 705
personalized information, users, 376
pop ups, DataGrid control
    row deletion confirmation, 141
    row details, 152
postbacks, state value and, 388
principal object, 447
processing files, uploaded, 692
ProcessRequest method, 740
properties
    custom controls, 330
    DocumentSource, 768
    ErrorPage, 423
protection attribute, <forms> element, 445

Q

query string parameters, caching and, 650

R

ranges, data entry, 188
RangeValidator control, 188
read-only access, increasing speed and, 724
ReadXml method (DataSet class), 16
references, methods, 305
RegisterHiddenField method, state
        information, postbacks and, 388
RegularExpressionValidator control, 200
Render method, HTML and, 324
Repeater control, 1
    bar chart creation, 618
    templates and, 9
    user controls and, adding
        dynamically, 314
requestEncoding property, <globalization>
        element, 663
requestLimit attribute, <trace> element, 527
request/response encoding, localizing, 663
RequiredFieldValidator control, 180, 195
Response object, drawing images on the
        fly, 607
Response.Redirect method, 431

reusable image handlers, creating, 740
reusing HTML output, 790
roles, page restrcition and, 459
rows, DataGrid control
    deletion confirmation, 141
    details pop up, 152
    selection within, 129
    totals row, 167

S

saving HTML output, 790
scalability, 648
script libraries, WebUIValidation, 239
security
    Forms authentication, 442
    Passport authentication, 442
    Windows authentication, 442, 474
sending email messages, 795
serialized data types, custom objects, 579
server validation, 179
Server.Transfer method, 431
    authentication cookies and, 447
    submit form to different page, 249
services
    stress testing, 561
    (see also web services)
Session object, user information, 376
session state maintenance, 366
sessionState element attributes, 498
SetAuthCookie method, 446
SortExpression attribute, DataGrid
        control, 76
sorting, DataGrid control
    ascending/descending order, 85
    DataGrid data, 75
    paging and, 97
source user controls, 303
SQL Servers, data access speed, 733
state
    application state maintenance, 366
    custom controls and, 337
    information availability and, 367
    maintenance, 366
    multiple servers, configuration, 493
    page state, maintenance, 367
    postbacks and, 388
    session state maintenance, 366
    updatePage method, 389
state server, 495
State Service, 494
stress testing, 520, 561

StringBuilder object
    concatenation speed, 719
    performance and, 704
strings
    custom, caching and, 653
    query parameters, caching and, 650
stylesheets, browser-specific, 780
Submit button, Enter key and, 227
submitting forms, different page, 248
System.Drawing classes, 605

T

tables (see hash tables, displays from)
tabular controls, selecting, 1
tabular format
    hash tables, 28
    quick-and-dirty generation, 3
    templates, 9
tags
    HeaderStyle, 29
    HeaderTemplate, 29
    ItemStyle, 29
    ItemTemplate, 29
templates
    pages, 801
    Repeater control and, 9
    tabular formats, 9
    XSLT, 770
testing, stress testing, 520, 561
TextBox server control, numeric input
    only, 358
thumbnail images, displaying, 636
tickets, authentication
    creating, 461
    parameters, 461
timeout attribute, 498
    <forms> element, 445
totals row, DataGrid control, 167
Trace attribute, settings, 521
<trace> element
    application-level tracing, 526
    attributes, 527
trace listeners
    creating, 542
    messages, 542
trace log
    categories, 522
    From First(s), 522
    From Last (s), 522
    messages, 522
    viewing, 527

trace output, enabling (exception
    handlers), 528
trace viewer, 527
TraceContext class, 521
TraceListener class, trace listener
    creation, 542
tracing, 520
    application components, 534
    application-level, 526
    CLR and, 522
    dual-use components, 542
    event log, trace data and, 552
    HTTPContext.Current property, 535
    page-level, 528
        enabling, 521
Try...Catch blocks, error handling and, 417
Try...Catch...Finally block
    error handling and, 418
    syntax, 418

U

updatePage method, 389
    state and, 389
uploading files to web server, 685
    processing immediately, 692
    storing contents in database, 700
URL of web services, setting at runtime, 601
useFullyQualifiedRedirectUrl attribute,
    <httpRuntime> element, 486
user controls
    caching, 655
    communication between, 303
    destination controls, 303
    dynamically adding, 314
    source controls, 303
user principal object, 447
users
    browser type, determining, 775
    email, sending, 795
    information, 376
        Session object, 376
    information availability, 367

V

validation
    client, 179
    data entry
        database entry matching, 218
        matching input fields, 195
        pattern matching, 200

validation (*continued*)
    drop-down lists, requiring selection, 206
    errors, focus of control, 278
    server, 179
    Submit button, Enter key and, 238
validators, 179
    ControlToValidate attribute, 181
    data entry, range requirement, 188
    EnableClientScript attribute, 182
    error messages, 182
variables, hardcoding, Application
        object, 369
VBSiteConfigHandler class, 507
VBSiteConfiguration class, 508
version, caching and, 651
<ViewState> element, 704
    performance, page size and, 705
ViewState property, Page object, 395
virtual pages, multipage forms, 259

W

Warn method, TraceContext class, 522
web references, adding to projects, 572
web server
    downloading files from, 677
    uploading files to, 685
        processing immediately, 692
        storing contents in database, 700
web services, 564
    behaviors and, 582
    consuming, 572
    creating, 564
    custom objects, 579
    URLs for, setting at runtime, 601

web.config
    applications, custom settings, 487
    authentication and, 443
    elements
        access, 498
        adding, 504
    error messages, custom, 491
    HTTP runtime parameters, default, 485
    modifications, 484
    parse errors, 484
    structure, 483
WebControl class
    Control class comparision, 323
    custom controls, 322
WebUIValidation.js, 239
Windows authentication, 442, 474
Write method
    trace data in event log, 552
    TraceContext class, 522
WriteLine method, trace data in event
        log, 552
WSDL (Web Services Description
        Language), 564

X

XML
    file data, displaying, 16
    transforming to HTML, 768
xmlTransform control, 769
XSL stylesheets, 770
XSLT, 770
    templates, 770

About the Author

Michael A. Kittel has nearly 30 years of experience in the software industry. He has been working with Microsoft technologies for more than 10 years and with ASP.NET since the alpha release of 1.0. He has been the system architect and has led the development of applications for Lexis-Nexis, Plow & Hearth, ReturnBuy, and many others. Michael has a Microsoft Certified Solutions Developer certification and is currently a senior consultant at Dominion Digital, Inc. (*http://www.dominiondigital.com*), a firm that specializes in helping companies envision and achieve maximum business value from investments in technology.

Geoffrey T. LeBlond is the coauthor of *Using 1-2-3* (Bantam), the first computer book that sold over 1 million copies. Geoff is the author of numerous computer books and was the developer of Oriel, an early scripting language for Microsoft Windows. More recently, Geoff has been focusing his attention on developing web applications using ASP and ASP.NET.

Colophon

Our look is the result of reader comments, our own experimentation, and feedback from distribution channels. Distinctive covers complement our distinctive approach to technical topics, breathing personality and life into potentially dry subjects.

The animal on the cover of *ASP.NET Cookbook* is a thorny woodcock (*Murex pecten*). This carnivorous marine snail is indigenous to the Indo-Pacific region of the world and is commonly found in the shallow waters off the coast of Japan's sandy beaches. Averaging 13 centimeters in length, the woodcock's elongated shell contains a stunning spine of thorns, and at first glance might be mistaken for the skeleton of a fish. While scientists are uncertain of the evolutionary advantages of this shell structure, some theorize that it serves to help ward off fish and other predators. They also believe the woodcock's needles may prevent the creature from being lodged in the soft sand and mud of its habitat.

The thorny woodcock has been immortalized in Western folklore, in which it is commonly referred to as the Venus comb or mermaid's comb. The animal's shell of needles is mythically purported to be the definitive fine-toothed comb, ideally suited for brushing even the delicate hair of a goddess.

Shell collectors are also drawn to the unique beauty of the thorny woodcock. Although its shell is not particularly rare, it is quite fragile, and a woodcock with a fully intact skeleton of thorns is a highly prized specimen for the distinguished conchologist.

Genevieve d'Entremont was the production editor and proofreader for *ASP.NET Cookbook*. Nancy Reinhardt was the copyeditor. Colleen Gorman and Claire Cloutier provided quality control. James Quill and Sanders Kleinfeld provided production assistance. Johnna VanHoose Dinse wrote the index.

Emma Colby designed the cover of this book, based on a series design by Edie Freedman. The cover image is a 19th-century engraving from *Animate Creation*. Clay Fernald produced the cover layout with QuarkXPress 4.1 using Adobe's ITC Garamond font.

Melanie Wang designed the interior layout, based on a series design by David Futato. This book was converted by Andrew Savikas and Julie Hawks to FrameMaker 5.5.6 with a format conversion tool created by Erik Ray, Jason McIntosh, Neil Walls, and Mike Sierra that uses Perl and XML technologies. The text font is Linotype Birka; the heading font is Adobe Myriad Condensed; and the code font is LucasFont's TheSans Mono Condensed. The illustrations that appear in the book were produced by Robert Romano and Jessamyn Read using Macromedia FreeHand 9 and Adobe Photoshop 6. The tip and warning icons were drawn by Christopher Bing. This colophon was written by Sanders Kleinfeld.

Related Titles Available from O'Reilly

.NET

.NET and XML

.NET Framework Essentials, *3rd Edition*

.NET Windows Forms in a Nutshell

ADO.NET in a Nutshell

ADO.NET Cookbook

C# Essentials, *2nd Edition*

C# Cookbook

C# Language Pocket Guide

Learning C#

Learning Visual Basic.NET

Mastering Visual Studio.NET

Object Oriented Programming with Visual Basic .NET

Programming .NET Components

Programming .NET Security

Programming .NET Web Services

Programming ASP.NET, *2nd Edition*

Programming C#, *3rd Edition*

Programming Visual Basic .NET, *2nd Edition*

VB.NET Core Classes in a Nutshell

VB.NET Language in a Nutshell, *2nd Edition*

VB.NET Language Pocket Reference

O'REILLY®

Our books are available at most retail and online bookstores.
To order direct: 1-800-998-9938 • *order@oreilly.com* • *www.oreilly.com*
Online editions of most O'Reilly titles are available by subscription at *safari.oreilly.com*

Keep in touch with O'Reilly

1. Download examples from our books

To find example files for a book, go to:

www.oreilly.com/catalog

select the book, and follow the "Examples" link.

2. Register your O'Reilly books

Register your book at *register.oreilly.com*

Why register your books?
Once you've registered your O'Reilly books you can:

- Win O'Reilly books, T-shirts or discount coupons in our monthly drawing.
- Get special offers available only to registered O'Reilly customers.
- Get catalogs announcing new books (US and UK only).
- Get email notification of new editions of the O'Reilly books you own.

3. Join our email lists

Sign up to get topic-specific email announcements of new books and conferences, special offers, and O'Reilly Network technology newsletters at:

elists.oreilly.com

It's easy to customize your free elists subscription so you'll get exactly the O'Reilly news you want.

4. Get the latest news, tips, and tools

www.oreilly.com

- "Top 100 Sites on the Web"—PC Magazine
- CIO Magazine's Web Business 50 Awards

Our web site contains a library of comprehensive product information (including book excerpts and tables of contents), downloadable software, background articles, interviews with technology leaders, links to relevant sites, book cover art, and more.

5. Work for O'Reilly

Check out our web site for current employment opportunities:

jobs.oreilly.com

6. Contact us

O'Reilly & Associates
1005 Gravenstein Hwy North
Sebastopol, CA 95472 USA

TEL: 707-827-7000 or 800-998-9938
　　　　(6am to 5pm PST)

FAX: 707-829-0104

order@oreilly.com
For answers to problems regarding your order or our products. To place a book order online, visit:

www.oreilly.com/order_new

catalog@oreilly.com
To request a copy of our latest catalog.

booktech@oreilly.com
For book content technical questions or corrections.

corporate@oreilly.com
For educational, library, government, and corporate sales.

proposals@oreilly.com
To submit new book proposals to our editors and product managers.

international@oreilly.com
For information about our international distributors or translation queries. For a list of our distributors outside of North America check out:

international.oreilly.com/distributors.html

adoption@oreilly.com
For information about academic use of O'Reilly books, visit:

academic.oreilly.com

O'REILLY®

Our books are available at most retail and online bookstores.
To order direct: 1-800-998-9938 • order@oreilly.com • www.oreilly.com
Online editions of most O'Reilly titles are available by subscription at *safari.oreilly.com*